SMG

SMG
A Biography of Sunil Manohar Gavaskar

Devendra Prabhudesai

Rupa & Co

Copyright © Devendra Prabhudesai 2009

Published 2009 by
Rupa & Co
7/16, Ansari Road, Daryaganj,
New Delhi 110 002

Sales Centres:
Allahabad Bangalooru Chandigarh Chennai
Hyderabad Jaipur Kathmandu
Kolkata Mumbai

All rights reserved.
No part of this publication may be reproduced, stored in a retrieval system, or transmitted, in any form or by any means, electronic, mechanical, photocopying, recording or otherwise, without the prior permission of the publishers.

The author asserts the moral right to be identified as the author of this work.

Photo Sources
BCCI Archives, Devendra Prabhudesai, *Mid-Day*, Milind Rege, Nandini Sardesai, PMG Archives, Patrick Eagar, Pradeep Mandhani, Prashant Bhoot, Rupa & Co. Archives, Srenik Sett, Sumedh Shah, Suru Nayak.

Typeset in
Mindways Design
1410 Chiranjiv Tower
43 Nehru Place
New Delhi 110 019

Printed in India by
Gopsons Papers Ltd.
A-14 Sector 60
Noida 201 301

*To my brother Chinu, my wife Anu,
and
my son Abhimanyu*

Contents

Acknowledgements	*ix*
Preface	*xi*

ADVENT — 1

1	The Game, the Land, the City	3
2	Climbing the Ladder	19
3	Bradmanesque Beginning	48
4	The Anglo-Australian Experience	69
5	A Lineage to Live Up to	87
6	From Manchester to London ... And a Lot in Between	103

ASCENT — 121

7	From Strength to Strength	123
8	Two Titans, Two Tests	138
9	Heir-Apparent	154
10	The Coronation and the Coup	175
11	Magnum Opus at the Oval	195
12	The Amitabh Bachchan of Indian Cricket	211

ACHIEVER — 233

13	Trans-Tasman Tribulations	235
14	In the Firing Line	258
15	'Imran'ed ... and Demoted	281
16	A Pipe Dream Comes True	301

17 'Don' to Dusk 322
18 A Seesaw Saga 344

APOGEE 371
19 Generalissimo 373
20 To Open or Not to Open ... 395
21 Five-figure Man 414
22 Swansongs 438

ALL-ROUNDER 457
23 Beyond the Boundary 459
24 The Legend and his Legacy 478

Sunil Gavaskar Fact File 499
Bibliography and References 517
Index 521

Acknowledgements

I extend my sincere and heartfelt thanks to the ones who have been of invaluable help in bringing this book to life. The BCCI, the Cricket Club of India, Ajay Madgaonkar, Ajit Wadekar, Allan Border, Anandji Dossa, Anshuman Gaekwad, Ashok Ambaye, late Ashok Mankad, Bapu Nadkarni, Chandrakant Pandit, Chandrashekhar Prabhudesai, Clayton Murzello, Clive Lloyd, David Gower, Dilip Vengsarkar, Dinar Gupte, Dr Vishwas Raut, Hemant Waingankar, John Wright, Karsan Ghavri, Madhav Mantri, Medha Prabhudesai, Nandini Sardesai, Shailaja Mudhale, Fredun De Vitre, Michael Holding, Mike Coward, Milind Rege, Mudassar Nazar, Navin Ambulkar, Piloo Reporter, Prakash Dahatonde, Prof Ratnakar Shetty, Rahul Dravid, Raj Singh Dungarpur, Raju Kulkarni, Raju Mehta, Sachin Tendulkar, Sandeep Patil, Sanjay Jaywant, Sudhir Vaidya, Sumedh Shah, Suru Nayak, the 1991 batch of IES's English Medium School (Dadar), the PMG team, V.S. Patil, V.V.S. Laxman, and Yajurvindra Singh.

Preface

Sunset at Bangalore

14 August 1948... When a roar followed the dismissal of Australian opener Sidney Barnes in the first innings of the final Test of the Ashes series, the bowler Eric Hollies, his skipper Norman Yardley, and their nine team-mates, were not fooled into believing that the capacity crowd at the Oval was celebrating the fall of the wicket. Seconds after Barnes had vanished into the dressing room, came the moment the spectators were waiting for. Much to their unbridled delight, the visiting team did not send in a nightwatchman in the closing stages of the day's play. The Australian captain, a bit of an achiever, came in himself. No sooner had he reached the wicket than he was surrounded by a cluster of opposition fieldsmen. But it was anything but a display of aggression by England, who trailed 0-3 in the series.

As the batsman surveyed the scene around him, Yardley took his cap off and beckoned his men to do the same. It led to one of the most unforgettable sights on a cricket field. A cricket team and an entire ground forgot twenty years of humiliation and subjugation to give three cheers to their greatest cricketing adversary. The action resumed shortly. The batsman negotiated the first ball he faced off the back foot. Hollies, a leg-spinner, then decided to dish out the ultimate shock delivery in his repertoire, the googly.

The ball dipped a bit as it descended, and the batsman lunged at it with his front foot and bat. But the cherry spun the other way, kissed the inside edge of the bat, and hit the stumps.

The Australian captain regained his balance, cast a cursory look at his fallen citadel and then looked heavenwards. He then thrust his bat under his left arm and commenced the long walk back to the pavilion with a wry smile on his face. The crowd, momentarily stunned, reverted to their deafening ways, and the fielders clapped till their hands ached, more for the departing batsman than the successful bowler.

England had been bowled out for only 52 in their first innings. Such was the batting form of Australia's 'invincibles' in that summer of 1948 that it was virtually certain that the visitors would not bat a second time in the match. The Australians duly amassed 389 when their turn came. They then bowled England out for 188, thus winning by an innings and 149 runs.

That made 14 August 1948 Donald Bradman's last batting day in Test cricket. A mere 4 runs in that outing would have given him not only a Test aggregate of 7,000, but a batting average of one hundred in Test cricket. But that was not to be.

∽

The conditions, circumstances and characters were totally different when another glorious Test career came to a close, thirty-eight years and seven months later.

Of high consequence was the irony. The spectators at the Oval in August 1948 had defied their country's traditional sober and silent ways while watching cricket matches, as they went ballistic to first welcome Bradman to the crease, and then to bid him farewell. On the other hand, the people seated in Bangalore's Chinnaswamy stadium on 17 March 1987 had lost their voice, a distinct departure from their boisterous ways. But it wasn't as if things were completely silent.

A small group of spectators, some of them females, was waving its country's flags and trying its best to provide back-up support to the eleven men who had become hysterical on the playing field. The three cheers of 1948 had given way to 'high-fives' in 1987, but these were definitely not directed towards the outgoing batsman, who had been dismissed for 96, only 4 short of what would have been his thirty-fifth Test hundred. More significant was the fact that he was the eighth batsman out, and his team was still 41 short of victory in a low-scoring game. This meant that the match was, for all practical purposes, in the opposition's pocket. Equally pertinent was the fact that for a period of 320 minutes, spread over 2 days of cricket and interrupted by a rest day, the batsman had, for the umpteenth time in his career, excelled when the chips were down. Not just that, but the strip of land he had batted on was as hostile as it could ever be, with the bowlers chipping away, supported by chirping and cursing fielders. Like Bradman in 1948, the batsman did not play another Test match.

The Indian cricket team had had more than its fill of international cricket by January 1987. They had lived in their cricket clothing for the better part of the previous fifteen months, in India and overseas. But the biggest assignment was still left: a five-Test series against their traditional rivals – Pakistan.

The series was keenly awaited, as all contests between the two nations generally are. Both sides had recently asserted their claim to the number two spot in world cricket, India with a successful tour of England, and Pakistan with an impressive show on home soil against the West Indies, the dominators of the era.

The on-field proceedings belied expectations. Not for the first time since the start of their cricketing rivalry in 1952-53, the Asian giants indulged in a listless sparring contest that extended for four Tests. But for a brief period in the first Test at Madras (now Chennai) during which Indian swashbuckler Krishnamachari Srikkanth went berserk, and another session in the second Test at Calcutta (now Kolkata) where seamer Roger Binny ripped through the Pakistani batting, the cricket was of the tedious type. Inevitably, both captains attacked each other for being unassertive, even as the fans got frustrated, and the authorities desperate.

One did not have to be a genius to figure out that the pitch at Bangalore's Chinnaswamy stadium, venue of the fifth Test, would not resemble the batting beauties of the earlier matches. Neither would it have hues of green. Spin bowling being India's much-touted strength, it was expected that this aspect of the game would be kept in mind by the groundstaff when it got down to preparing, or rather, underpreparing the pitch.

What the teams actually saw on the morning of the match exceeded their worst nightmares. They beheld a patch instead of a pitch, which would have deterred even a group of softball cricketers. Its character was downright suspicious and it was obvious that it would deteriorate rapidly once the match commenced. Imran Khan, the charismatic captain of the touring side, won the first round by calling correctly and opting to bat. Application was what was needed from the batsmen, but the Pakistanis did not display it. Left-arm spinner Maninder Singh took 7-27 to bowl the visitors out for 116.

Supporters of the home team were delighted. The catch was that they had not taken India's propensity to flatter to deceive against Pakistan into account. To their horror, the home team was packed off for only 145. Off-spinner Tauseef Ahmed and left-arm spinner Iqbal Qasim exploited the wicket splendidly, landing the ball on the right spots and letting the patch do the rest. Tauseef got 5 wickets, as did Qasim, who incidentally owed his presence in the XI to an eleventh-hour argument between Imran Khan and vice-captain Javed Miandad. Imran wanted to play the out-of-form leg-spinner Abdul Qadir, but was eventually convinced to pick Qasim by the canny Miandad, who sensed that the wicket would be more conducive to finger-spin than wrist-spin. With more than three days left and no rain in sight, a result was a certainty. The team that would hold its nerve would win.

Fired up as well as relieved after a pep talk by Imran, wherein he stressed that he did not mind losing as long as every member of the team fought to the finish, Pakistan scored 249 in their second innings. Kapil Dev Nikhanj, the Indian captain, did his best to rotate the spin trio of Maninder Singh, off-spinner Shivlal Yadav and left-armer Ravi Shastri from both ends by deploying them in short spells. The three men bowled well, but they invariably took an over or two to regain their rhythm after being reintroduced into the attack, and that was what the Pakistanis capitalised on.

India faced the onerous prospect of scoring 221 on a veritable minefield. They had all the time to do so, with two-and-a-half days left in the game, but Pakistan held all the aces. As the visitors saw it, they were only ten wickets short of a historic series win in India.

~

As they got ready to leave the pavilion, Sunil Manohar Gavaskar or SMG as he is known, expressed his desire to walk to his partner's right instead of the other way round as was usually the case. K. Srikkanth was surprised, but agreed when it was explained that the switch was for good luck. Given that they needed every ounce of it to succeed on that pitch, Srikkanth, as superstitious a cricketer as they come, agreed.

The Indian openers discovered that Imran had decided to do exactly what his Indian counterpart had done earlier. Roger Binny had not bowled in Pakistan's second innings, with Kapil Dev sharing the new ball with Maninder. Imran similarly held himself back and commanded Tauseef to bowl the second over after Wasim Akram had bowled the first one. The move was justified, for the wicket was such that a spinner could pose more problems to the batsmen than a paceman.

The score had reached 15 when Akram rapped Srikkanth on the pads and umpire V.K. Ramaswamy upheld the appeal by the bowler and fielders. SMG had a word with his partner as the latter passed him on the way to the pavilion. Was he sending a message to his team-mates? Was he appealing for a greater degree of application when their turn came?

Mohinder Amarnath knew all about application, but his stint in the middle was over even before he got his eye in. He nicked his first ball to the wicketkeeper Salim Yousuf. The score: 15-2. With the spinners expected to play havoc, Akram's double-dent was a bonus for his side. Dilip Vengsarkar, always a shaky starter, edged the hattrick ball, but it landed well short of second slip.

The twin strikes signalled the start of an absorbing duel. At one end was a quality bowling attack. At the other was a batsman intent on making optimal use of his hands, eyes, feet and grey-cells.

SMG took on Tauseef with his impeccable technique, immaculate footwork and monumental concentration. His stance was as always a connoisseur's delight, his head statuesque, and his backlift quick, creating an arc as it came down from second slip. With every ball bringing with it dust and particles of the pitch, SMG resorted to making contact as late as possible. It was a day on which every run-scoring opportunity had to be grabbed with both hands. When Tauseef overpitched, SMG essayed a majestic cover-drive for four. The off-spinner responded by holding the next one back. SMG bit the bait and went for another drive, but the ball hit the inner edge of his bat and missed the stumps and keeper on its way to the boundary. It was a near-miss.

The batsman used an Akram over to regain his equilibrium, despite the inadvertent attempts of some spectators seated above the sight screen to disturb his concentration.

Vengsarkar, India's top scorer in the first innings, was one batsman the Pakistanis wanted to dismiss. That explained the excitement of the fielders when Rameez Raja, standing at forward short-leg, claimed a catch. Umpire Ram Babu Gupta turned it down and encountered some strange sights: Salim Malik running in from mid-wicket, the bowler Tauseef kicking the air in disgust, and Miandad expressing himself in no uncertain terms. It was left to Imran to cool his players down.

As subsequent events proved, the fielders were only warming up.

A Vengsarkar single later, SMG faced Tauseef and got a vicious off-break that took off after hitting the pitch. He let it sail past him, and the cherry hit Yousuf on his left shoulder. In his next over, Tauseef conceded 4 byes when another delivery missed everything, including an attempted leg-glance. SMG had gone for the stroke with an angled bat and loose hands to eliminate the possibility of a catch to forward short-leg.

The 50 of the innings was posted without further damage, by which time Iqbal Qasim had replaced Akram. The left-arm spinner ambled in to bowl the dream ball of every member of his fraternity, one that drifted inwards, landed and then spun away from the right-hander. SMG picked it early and essayed a delectable drive against the turn. For most batsmen, essaying a stroke like that on such a diabolical wicket would have been disastrous. But this batsman was different. SMG got two runs to mid-wicket.

The Pakistanis, struggling as they were to tackle the opener, were thrilled to see the back of Vengsarkar, who played on to Tauseef. 64-3. They almost got another when Qasim tossed one up and SMG essayed an uppish straight drive. But the bowler could not get close to it and the ball sped to the boundary.

Tauseef, who was varying his line, length, turn and at times, even approach to the wicket (from over-the-wicket to around and back), was flummoxed to see SMG use his pace and turn to splendid effect. The batsman waited for the ball to turn from off to leg, and then rolled his wrists at the point of contact to dispatch it around the corner for the occasional single. Playing this stroke too early or too late would have been fatal. But SMG's timing was spot-on. Every delivery he doubted was played with loose hands, so as to keep it out of the reach of the five men around him—the keeper, two short-legs, one silly mid-off and one slip. One such stroke fell well short of forward short-leg and prompted Tauseef to lower his hands to his knees. This gesture of hopelessness wasn't expected from a bowler when just about everything was in his favour.

SMG's eyes lit up when Qasim served a rare full toss. He drove it past the umpire for 4, and followed it with a forward defensive stroke. When Qasim landed one just outside the line of off-stump, SMG let it pass, with the front pad as the first line of defence. When two deliveries by Tauseef reared off the minefield, SMG stepped across with a raised bat and took the ball on his body.

His batsmanship failed to inspire Kiran More, who surrendered his wicket to Tauseef with a horrendous sweep. 80-4. Kapil's attempt at doing an Imran by promoting a lower-order batsman had flopped. Mohammed Azharuddin, the new batsman, took a boundary off Qasim and watched a Tauseef delivery that landed on a length and took off vertically. SMG watched it all the way and let it fly past his left shoulder. Normally, it was the batsman who took evasive action against a bouncer. But here, it was the wicketkeeper who had to do so. Yousuf yanked his head away just in time, and the ball flew to the boundary. 'My God!' TV commentator M.L. Jaisimha's reaction said it all. The reference was as much to the batsman's judgement as it was to the deathtrap that the pitch was.

The score had crept closer to the three-figure mark, with the scheduled close of play only a few minutes away, when Imran got his spinners to change ends. Qasim bowled the final over of the day and SMG, on 49, drove to mid-off. A misfield gave him two runs, and the crowd cheered as Azharuddin walked down the pitch to congratulate his partner. Qasim then tossed up a big turner that Yousuf collected in front of slip. The next ball, the last of the day, was safely padded away. India were 99-4 at stumps on day three.

The teams and spectators had some breathing space in the form of a rest-day. It happened to be the day when Holi, the festival of colours, was being celebrated all over India. Rivalries were forgotten on the lawns of the Taj West End, where the teams were staying. Imran Khan, who had barricaded himself in his room, was dragged out by a group that comprised team-mates Javed Miandad and Manzoor Elahi, and opponent Ravi Shastri. The Pakistani players enjoyed themselves thoroughly, with the notable exceptions of Qasim and Tauseef. Their brief on the following day, as outlined by their skipper, was to get SMG. 'Yeh Baba Adam ne pareshaan kar rakha hai,'[1] they told an Indian journalist who had dropped in for a chat. How they were to get Baba Adam out, they did not know.

The Holi celebrations during the day were followed by a dinner, hosted by the man himself. The previous three seasons had witnessed intense speculation about his retirement plans, and most of the guests therefore presumed that the thirty-seven-year-old intended to make a formal announcement to that effect. It was not as if SMG was unaware of what his guests expected, but the announcement never came. Instead, the teams retired for the night, to resume hostilities the next day.

On the morning of 17 March 1987, the man discovered, much to his annoyance, that some spectators seated above the sight screen were persisting with their indifferent ways. After some order had been restored, he executed a couple of around-the-corner glances off Tauseef, who had been restored to his original end. Qasim was powerfully cut and then driven, but both shots were stopped by Elahi in the covers. Never had the Pakistanis been known for their fielding abilities, but this occasion was different. For all the batting talents of the Indian middle and lower-order, the visitors knew, as did the hosts, that a single individual stood between them and victory.

After sending down one that SMG played towards second slip, Qasim pushed one through a quicker delivery and hit the batsman on

---

[1] Prophet Adam has us worried.

his pad. A vociferous appeal followed, but Ramaswamy was convinced that the ball would have missed the leg-stump. Yousuf ran all the way from his wicketkeeping position to within handshaking distance of the umpire, and Malik sprinted in from mid-off like a man possessed. Ramaswamy promptly admonished him for doing so. Imran had to step in once again.

The desperation of the fielding side manifested itself again a few minutes later, and this time, it violated all norms of etiquette. SMG stretched himself to play Qasim off the front foot. The ball struck the knee-roll of his pad and ballooned into the air in the unmanned short-leg region. Rizwan-uz-Zaman, standing at silly point, flung himself across the pitch and claimed a catch. But Ramaswamy was sure that the ball had not made contact with the bat. He soon found himself surrounded by virtually the entire visiting team. The spectators could have been forgiven for thinking that it was a roadside brawl they were witnessing. At the forefront of this exhibition of over-the-top histrionics was the captain himself. Imran's patience had run out.

Ramaswamy's response was to put his hands on his ears. Qasim, who had backed off after seeing his team-mates take up the cudgels on his behalf, returned to the fray by tapping the umpire on his back. Things were getting increasingly deplorable and dangerously physical. Ramaswamy had a word with his colleague, who supported the decision, only to be confronted by a petulant Miandad. India needed a further 101 to win.

The worst thing that could have happened for India at that stage was a dismissal. Tragically for them, that was what happened, with Qasim diving full-length to his left to clasp a return catch offered by Azharuddin. 123-5. SMG carried on, twice driving Qasim against the turn for twos, then driving him straight for a boundary, taking deliveries with extra bounce on his thigh, and ignoring the big turners. When Imran deprived Tauseef of a slip, SMG steered him through the same region for two runs.

A rising delivery by Tauseef was treated like many of its predecessors—a loose top hand, and the withdrawal of the bottom hand at the moment of impact. In Qasim's next over, SMG produced a sizzling cover-drive that sped to the boundary. The left-armer retaliated with two deliveries that landed outside the off-stump and climbed awkwardly. SMG offered his front pad to the first. The second, he played at, and missed. The ball went past Yousuf for another two. The umpire did not make any signal, which meant that he had viewed it as a chance offered by the batsman. When Yousuf asked him whether he had nicked it, SMG replied in the negative.

It was the first time during his innings that he had displayed an awareness of the fact that there were human beings around him. For most of the time, he had blanked himself out from the world, the ball, an exception.

He kept out a terrific quicker ball from Qasim, and moved to 75 with another steer off Tauseef through the vacant slips. India were 147-5, the target another 74 runs away.

The singles kept coming with steers and tucks and glides in front of, and behind, the wicket. Like his bowling partner, Qasim was mixing his deliveries intelligently, but SMG's anticipation was uncanny. He countered the slightest error of judgement on his part by simply putting his head down to face the next delivery. It was pointless to reproach oneself on that pitch, lest it disturbed one's concentration. Every delivery had to be treated in isolation, as a separate event. The pundits had advocated this approach for many years, but very few batsmen had managed to implement it on a consistent basis. SMG was one such.

The least he expected and deserved was a semblance of stability at the other end, but Ravi Shastri and Kapil Dev were dismissed in quick succession by the strip and the spinners. 161-7.

His compatriots would have liked SMG to bat at both ends, but that wasn't possible. That he was conscious of his team-mates' impending mortality was evident from the manner in which he swooped on a Qasim delivery that was only just short of a length. He cracked it to the point boundary for a 4. It took him to 88 and India to 168-7.

Roger Binny's assured forward defensive strokes, as opposed to the half-cocked methods adopted by his team-mates, heartened SMG as much as it did the all-rounder's home crowd. All hope was not lost.

SMG then twirled his wrists to take 2 off a Qasim delivery that kept low. Predictably, the very next ball rose, and was allowed to proceed into Yousuf's gauntlets via the front pad. Qasim bowled a similar-looking delivery one ball later, but this time, Gavaskar advanced his bat and steered it dexterously between Rizwan and Elahi, the two slips, for a single.

It was epic batsmanship, exhilarating for the Indians and exasperating for the Pakistanis. It was almost as if there were two pitches on which the match was being played, one for SMG and the other for his teammates. A disconcerting delivery by either Tauseef or Qasim would then come about and shatter the mirage of a second pitch. But SMG would follow that moment of uncertainty with another spell of immaculate batting, thus resurrecting the mirage all over again.

SMG's admiration for Binny's precision was reflected in his encouraging words to the younger man after the latter survived an appeal for a catch at forward short-leg off Tauseef. Ramiz Raja, the concerned fielder, had clearly not satiated his urge to emote, as was evident from his protests to his captain. SMG took a single off Qasim in the next over, and stroked another single off Tauseef from the other end. He had now moved to 96. The target was only 41 runs away, and the man was only 4 short of his 35th Test hundred.

Ironically, he was done in by an umpiring error. In all fairness, V.K. Ramaswamy, one of India's best-ever umpires, was entitled to make the odd mistake, especially after he and his colleague had concentrated so hard for such a long time and battled the relentless pressure being applied by the fielding side.

SMG advanced onto the front foot for the first ball of a new over by Qasim. The ball hit the knee-roll of his pad and flew to Rizwan at first slip. Even as the fielders screamed, the umpire was misled by the non-existent gap between the batsman's bat and front pad. The absence of a 'breach' in SMG's technique had for once let him down. The index finger went up, and with it India's chances of victory. The only off-the-field cheers at the Chinnaswamy stadium came from the pavilion enclosure, where the wives and children of the Pakistani players were seated.

The record books state that India were eventually bowled out for 204, thus losing the Test, and with it the series. Pakistan annihilated its despondent opponent in the One Day Internationals that followed, and a red carpet welcome awaited them at home.

SMG subsequently expressed unstinting praise for the umpiring of Ramaswamy and Gupta in the Bangalore Test. The duo later confessed that they had aged by several years during the course of that game.

Imran Khan rated SMG's 96 as the best innings he had ever seen. He was seconded by several of his team-mates, most of whom had tried everything legitimate and illegitimate to fluster the man as he went about displaying his genius on a minefield-like pitch.

It turned out to be Sunil Manohar Gavaskar's last Test innings. But it was by no means his final demonstration of his extraordinary abilities as a batsman, and as an individual.

One
Advent

1

THE GAME, THE LAND, THE CITY

Calling cricket a sport in the Indian context would be a travesty. For a country plagued by the demons of corruption, poverty and unemployment, the exploits of Indian cricketers and to a lesser extent, Indian cricket teams, have served as antidotes. They have provided pleasant reminders that Indians are indeed capable of taking on the world, and winning. The nation's cricketing achievements were the precursor to its technological and corporate achievements in the late 1990s and the new millennium. It was not entirely coincidental that other sports started gaining popularity in the post-1991 liberalisation phase, when Indians started winning in spheres other than cricket too.

'Cricket is an Indian game accidentally invented by the English,' sociologist Ashis Nandy stated two decades ago.

Cricket writer Raju Mukherjee recently went several steps ahead, with his contention that cricket was actually invented in India and exported to Britain by merchants and traders in the Middle Ages!

Popular history tells us that the Indians started playing cricket in the nineteenth century with a conscious desire to imitate their colonial masters. The Parsi community was the first to take to the sport, and the Hindus and Muslims followed suit. Teams of Parsis toured England in 1886 and 1888. In January 1890, they took on Lord Vernon's touring side from Britain. The spectators could not believe it when the Parsis won a low-scoring thriller by 4 wickets. It was the Indian cricket team's first ever victory over a side from England. For many Indians who were still nursing the wounds inflicted during the War of Independence in 1857, the victory was a revelation. It was an indicator that the British were beatable, if not on the battlefield, then certainly in the sporting arena.

That historic match was played four years after the formation of the Indian National Congress, an institution established to further the interests of Indians as citizens of the British Empire.

The common factor between this victory and the birth of what went on to become India's biggest political outfit was Bombay, now known as Mumbai. Originally a cluster of seven islands separated from each other by creeks, a natural harbour on the eastern side prompted the British to make Bombay their premier port in India. The expansion of business activities in the city in the eighteenth and nineteenth centuries drew in people from all over the subcontinent.

The Parsis established their first cricket club in Bombay in 1848, and the Hindus and Muslims did likewise in later years. Cricket in the city got a fillip in the 1890s when Lord Harris, then the governor of Bombay province, allotted plots of land along the western sea front to the three cricket-playing communities. The Parsi, Hindu and Islam gymkhanas came into being as a result, and they became the hub of cricketing activity in the city. In 1892, a team of Englishmen based in Bombay took on the Parsis in the first annual Presidency match. Gradually this yearly event became a Triangular, Quadrangular and then Pentangular with the entry of the Hindus, Muslims and the Rest (Christians and Anglo-Indians) in 1907, 1912 and 1936 respectively. This competition came to be considered as the most prestigious in the subcontinent, with the spectators overlooking its communal overtones in favour of the game. The Pentangular was eventually abolished in 1945 at the behest of a staunch opponent of communalism – the Mahatma himself.

The establishment of the three Gymkhanas in Bombay was not the only significant cricketing event of the 1890s. In England, a certain K.S. Ranjitsinhji wowed the public with his batsmanship and initiated an affiliation between the sport and India's blue-blooded community. The eminence that he, the prince of the tiny state of Nawanagar in western India, gained in the eyes of the British due to his cricketing achievements, prompted his fellow princes to sit up and take notice. They then started pursuing and promoting the game, convinced that proficiency in cricket would earn them British praise.

In the twentieth century, cricket in India became a vehicle for social emancipation and national integration. The growth and development of the sport in India ran parallel to that of the country itself. The first prominent public figure from the ranks of the so-called untouchables, the lowest rung of the Hindu social hierarchy, was Baloo Palwankar, a left-arm spinner. His cricketing prowess enabled him to break the taboos of the time, and he became the spearhead of the Hindu bowling attack in the annual Triangular. He impressed all those who watched him on a tour of England by an All-India team in 1911. To Dr B.R. Ambedkar, the social reformer who made it his life's mission to fight the Hindu caste system, Palwankar was a teenage hero.

The performance of many Indian cricketers against a team sent by the MCC[1] in 1926-27 convinced Arthur Gilligan, the captain of the visiting side, that the land was ready for Test cricket. His support enabled the influential voices of the time to get together and eventually constitute the Board of Control for Cricket in India (BCCI) in 1928.

India was born as a Test-playing nation at Lord's in London in June 1932. The Maharajah of Porbandar was the captain of the touring side, and Prince Ghanshyamsinhji of Limbdi the vice-captain. Both men were blue-blooded all right, but they were modest cricketers. On the eve of the inaugural Test, they stood down in favour of Col C.K. Nayudu, who was for all practical purposes the country's first cricketing superstar. It was appropriate that he got the honour of being India's first Test captain. This was a time when the country was following the path prescribed by an individual not quite as well built as Col Nayudu, but no less charismatic. The British initially wrote him off, calling him a half-naked fakir, but they came around in later years to acknowledge the architect of the first successful non-violent struggle for independence in the history of mankind.

India's inaugural Test featured magnificent bowling by India's new-ball bowlers Mohammed Nissar and Amar Singh. However, England

---

[1]Marylebone Cricket Club.

won by 158 runs. India played their next Test at home, at the Bombay Gymkhana, in December 1933. Lala Amarnath became India's first Test centurion, but Douglas Jardine's visiting side won the game and the three-match series 2-0.

Those first two Tests at Lord's and the Bombay Gymkhana witnessed the birth of a tradition that lasted for decades. If the defeats were dark clouds, then their silver linings were the moments of individual brilliance. If Nissar and Amar Singh, India's new-ball bowlers, had excelled at Lord's, the young Amarnath had sparkled in Bombay.

This was very much an Indian phenomenon. The land had endured a plethora of foreign invasions for the past ten centuries. But every century had produced one or two extraordinary personalities who shone like beacons in the gloom.

Ranjitsinhji and Palwankar represented the two extremes of Indian cricket's social spectrum in the pre-independence phase. Between them were members of the groups that would eventually drive the country, as indeed, its cricket. These were the middle class and the working class. Prof D.B. Deodhar, Col Nayudu, Amarnath, Amar Singh and Mohammed Nissar were among the earliest representatives of these groups.

The joy of Independence in 1947 was offset by the trauma of Partition. A couple of months after Jawaharlal Nehru, India's first democratic 'monarch', hoisted the national flag atop Delhi's Red Fort, independent India's first cricket team departed to Australia for a full tour. At the helm was Lala Amarnath, who like Nehru had made it to the top on merit. His appointment marked the end of a bitter tussle between India's princes to control Indian cricket.

Although cricket was played all over the subcontinent, it was Bombay that got top billing. From the establishment of the Orient Cricket Club by the Parsis in 1848, to the popular Pentangulars, most of the significant cricketing events had occurred in the metropolis. Its eminence was underscored when the BCCI set up its headquarters there in 1928, and the Cricket Club of India did likewise in 1937. The city was home to the best cricketing infrastructure in the country, and deserved to be anointed India's cricket capital, tradition-wise as well as talent-wise. To say that the city has dominated Indian cricket is an understatement. At the time of writing, the metropolis has won the Ranji Trophy, India's premier domestic cricket competition, 38 times in 75 seasons, and produced a staggering 67 out of the 260 cricketers to have represented India from June 1932 to November 2008.

Mumbai's cosmopolitan nature is reflected in the diverse backgrounds of its cricketers. Most of them have hailed from the middle class. The approach of this socio-economic group towards the game in the early years mirrored its penchant for saving. Spending one's hard-earned income was almost a necessary evil, and saving synonymous with bliss, just as saving a cricket match was considered preferable to being bolder and thereby running the risk of defeat. Things have changed and attitudes transformed in the last two decades, with the opening up of the Indian economy and the advent of limited-overs cricket. Mumbai's middle-class citizen of today is not averse to living life to the fullest and taking risks.

Like his compatriots from across India, a middle-class Mumbaikar has traditionally enjoyed being part of an activity like cricket, which was performed by a group, but at the same time, gave its members ample scope to leave their individual imprints behind.

Bombay may have been renamed 'Mumbai' in the 1990s, but there are certain things that remain unchanged. Cricket still constitutes a significant component of the city's ethos.

A Mumbai boy was and is introduced to the sport in the open spaces in front of the apartment block where he lives. Here, he learns to play within limitations, for there aren't too many open spaces. His cricketing intelligence is also honed, as the paucity of space forces him and his friends to devise their own set of cricketing rules. When he grows taller and older, he and his friends start visiting the nearest playground to give vent to their cricketing instincts. This is where luck enters the picture. If the boy has talent, it is critical that a senior like an elder sibling, relative or neighbour, detects it at an early stage.

The boy is then guided to a cricket coach, who runs an academy of sorts on one of the city's maidans (playgrounds). Thus begins his relationship with official cricket, played with a proper cricket bat, ball and equipment. If the coach finds him impressive, the boy finds it easier to break into his school (and subsequently college) team. If he is relatively consistent, the coach recommends him to a cricket club. The boy, by now a teenager, goes on to cut his teeth in the annual Kanga League, the most competitive inter-club cricket tournament in the world. Here, he observes how his seniors tackle the vagaries of an unprepared pitch, cloudy conditions and slushy outfields full of unmown grass. Played during the Mumbai monsoon, the Kanga League is a batsman's ultimate nightmare. The history of the tournament is replete with tales of teams winning matches despite being bowled out for 40, only because they bowled their opponents out for an even lesser score. A knock of 20 on a dicey Kanga League pitch is equivalent to a double hundred on a featherbed in the official cricket season. The Kanga League has been cited as one of the major factors behind the remarkable records of Mumbai's batsmen against fast bowling at higher levels.

Success in the Kanga League in one's middle or late teens, if complemented by impressive performances in inter-school, collegiate or university cricket, puts into motion the famed Mumbai cricket grapevine. It gets its flavour from umpires, journalists, senior cricketers and even passers-by, onlookers and spectators. Anyone who is convinced that he has spotted a special talent on the maidans spreads the word around. The youngster becomes the topic of many animated discussions in the tents, Mumbai cricket's modest equivalent of a dressing room, or over a cup of tea in a stall or restaurant adjacent to a maidan. The outcome is that the men who select teams in junior or senior-level national tournaments put him in their shortlists, as do the recruiters representing commercial organisations that have a cricket team playing in the inter-office tournaments.

It was through this hierarchy that this writer, a Marathi Mumbaikar, wished to progress, but could not, for although the spirit was willing, the talent was weak.

It was through the same hierarchy that the subject of this book, also a Marathi Mumbaikar, graduated to the big league. A product of the middle class, his talent was never doubted by all those who saw him in his formative years. However, no one could have imagined the extent to which he would distinguish his chosen sport, his country and of course, his city.

'Your only inheritance is your brain, so make optimal use of it,' is a piece of advice every middle-class Mumbaikar father passes on to his children. The Marathi[2] is known for according top priority to academic proficiency, principles and perfection. Short cuts of any sort are anathema to him. He does not grant undue favours, and does not expect any in return. He knows that success that is achieved through a combination of penance, perseverance and patience, is easier to sustain in the long run. Add to the mix his forthrightness if and when provoked, and that makes him a tough cookie. Marathis constituted an integral part of the freedom movement, some of them subscribing to the non-violent methods prescribed by the Mahatma, and others preferring the violent approach advocated by the revolutionaries. After Independence, they carried out a successful agitation for a unified state of Maharashtra, with Bombay as the capital.

Ironically, the accent on values has made the Marathis slightly less worldly-wise than his counterparts from other states, who have made the city their home.

Enterprise is not an attribute the middle-class, working Marathi has traditionally been associated with. He has tended to eschew risks and has emphasised the security aspect. He is more at home as an employee than running a business, and prefers to be led rather than lead.

Of course, there have been, and there will be exceptions to this rule. Mumbai and Maharashtra have produced outstanding academicians, scientists, entrepreneurs, artistes, politicians and sports-personalities. Some of these luminaries had an inspirational effect on not only their co-Marathis, but also several others. This book spotlights one such.

Cricket apart, Mumbai happens to be the home of the Hindi film industry. The defining Hindi film, many people believe, is Ramesh Sippy's *Sholay*, which was released in 1975. Shekhar Kapur, who achieved international renown in the 1990s after directing films like *Bandit Queen* and *Elizabeth*, once stated that the history of Hindi cinema can be divided into *Sholay* BC and *Sholay* AD.

By the same token, the history of Indian cricket can be divided into Gavaskar BC and Gavaskar AD.

≈

---

[2]'Maharashtrians' is the favoured term to describe those whose mother tongue is Marathi, but technically, everybody who lives in the state of Maharashtra is a Maharashtrian, his mother tongue notwithstanding. Hence, I have tried to be specific, and used the word 'Marathi' to refer to those whose mother tongue is Marathi.

At first glance, nothing strikes you about the Bhagirathi buildings, located behind the Bhatia hospital in the area known as Chikalwadi, in southern Mumbai's Tardeo region. There are four structures in all, two on either side of an approximately fifty-metre long alley that extends from the main entrance of the compound to three garages. They provided the setting for the start of one of cricket's most glorious success stories.

It was in this four-building residential complex that Sunil Gavaskar spent his formative years. The Bhagirathi buildings were home to twenty-four middle-class families, most of them Marathi-speaking, with the odd Bengali family thrown in. Sunil was the first-born of Manohar and Meenal Gavaskar, a middle-class Marathi couple that resided on the second floor of the first building to the right of the main entrance.

> There wasn't anybody fabulously wealthy living there. Those years taught me the value of hard work. There were no lifts. You had to take the stairs. You looked around and felt that you needed to do the right things and get ahead in life. There was no room for shortcuts. You saw people who left for work at 8.30 am and returned at 7.00 pm. They would bring gifts and sweets for their kids. A sweet was a big thing in those days. I realised that hard work was mandatory. Had it not been for that experience, I probably wouldn't have become the cricketer I was to become. – Sunil Gavaskar, *The Boy from Chikalwadi* (PMG, 1999)

Sunil was born on 10 July 1949, close to two years after India had gained independence. He was thus a member of an independent nation's first generation. The mood of the people around him was vibrant and optimistic, even as they were in the process of coming to terms with freedom after centuries of foreign rule.

The events that followed Sunil's birth were straight out of a Manmohan Desai lost-and-found potboiler. Narayan Masurekar, a cousin of the child's mother, was among those who visited the hospital to see the newborn. He noticed what the others did not. The infant had a small hole in the left earlobe. When he returned the next day, he was shocked to discover that the left ear of the baby lying next to his sister did not have that hole. The hospital authorities were alerted, and his nephew was found next to a fisherwoman. The fishing industry's loss was cricket's gain.

His parents played the quintessential Indian middle-class family to perfection. They sought to inculcate the right values in their child by narrating bedtime stories of India's folk and mythical heroes. The *Ramayana* and *Mahabharata* figured prominently in these narrations, as did Aesop's fables. One of the stories was that of Lord Dhruva, the great sage, whose powers of concentration were phenomenal.

> The stories were all about how to be clever, how to overcome difficulties, to have a goal and an ambition. These things must have got into his bloodstream at an early age. It was ultimately up to him to develop them into assets that would help him in his career. – Manohar Gavaskar, *The Boy From Chikalwadi* (PMG, 1999)

Gavaskar senior was a wicketkeeper-batsman who represented Elphinstone, one of Mumbai's prominent colleges, and later played for Rajasthan Cricket Club and Forbes Campbell, the organisation he worked for. He was competent behind the wickets and attractive in front, and was a rarity among Bombay batsmen of the time, in that he favoured lofted shots. Slightly better than him in both departments was Madhav Mantri, his wife's brother, who captained Bombay for several years and represented India in four Tests in the early 1950s. Before becoming brothers-in-law, Gavaskar and Mantri were team-mates and friends at Elphinstone College.

> 'Sunil inherited his cricketing gifts from his father and uncle. Manohar Gavaskar was and is an astute reader of the game. Sunil also inherited his sense of humour from his father.' – Ashok Ambaye, Bhagirathi neighbour.

It was thus natural for the toddler to be gifted a toy bat and ball as soon as he learnt to walk. The first bowler in Sunil's life was his mother. They played in the balcony outside their second-floor home, with the closed door serving as the wicket. If Sunil missed and the ball hit the door, he would be out. If he were to take the aerial route and hit it out of the balcony, it would also entail a dismissal, and he would have to run downstairs to retrieve the ball. The boy did not take too long to work out that the key to survival was to play straight. So seriously did he resort to this tactic that at one point, a full-blooded straight drive hit his mother on the nose. It bled profusely, but she washed her face and resumed bowling. It was an incident that stayed with the youngster.

A gradual increase in Sunil's height and age led to his mother being replaced by boys of his height and age, and a wooden bat and tennis ball. Of all the boys whom Sunil befriended in that period, the one closest to him was Milind Rege. The duo spent their evenings and holidays duelling in the Bhagirathi alley, mostly with bat and ball, and occasionally with fists.

> 'Life was simple those days. One went to work in the morning, returned in the evening and assigned a lot of importance to the education of one's children. All twenty-four families were like one big joint family. Everybody knew and interacted freely with each other, unlike modern times wherein we don't see our neighbours for days together. The high point for us children was the Diwali festival. It was a four-day carnival. A stage would be erected in the compound and cultural events would be organised by the elders.' – Milind Rege

Their cricket ground was the Bhagirathi alley. Lofted strokes or placements on either side of the alley were an unviable proposition for the boys' parents. An airborne shot could smash a windowpane and the parents of the offender would have to compensate the victims. If it would not break the windowpane, it would strike the walls and rebound into the alley. The circumstances forced the boys to do what all Mumbai kids do when faced with a paucity of playing space – adapt. They decided that any shot that cleared the roofs of the ground floor flats would amount to a dismissal. Hence, the shot that was most productive was the straight drive. Having honed it during his batting sessions with his mother, Sunil was prepared for this particular adjustment.

> 'Sunil's father Manohar (Baba) had been brought up by his aunt Yamutai Pandit. His mother, whom we called Mami Aaji[3],

---

[3]Grandmother

> stayed close by at Forjett Hill. Baba[4] and his family shared the Bhagirathi flat with Yamutai and her sons, Pramod and Praful. It was Pramod, a metallurgical engineer, who initiated Sunil and me into cricket. He was a cricket fanatic. He was an avid reader of *Sports and Pastime*, the leading sports periodical of those days, and knew cricket statistics like the back of his hand. He was a big fan of the Australian team, and equally fascinated by the South African team of the time. Sunil and I used to play 'Test' matches against him in the balcony of their flat. He would 'represent' South Africa and we would pose as cricketers from any other team. A mat was our pitch. It was because of him that Sunil and I knew the names of all the international cricket teams and their leading players by the time we were five or six. He also introduced us to a cardboard cricket game.' – Milind Rege

Tennis-ball cricket did not take long to gain precedence over its cardboard equivalent. Like every cricket-loving boy who believes that he will grow up to become the world's best batsman and fastest bowler, Sunil was convinced early on that he was the solution to India's perennial fast-bowling woes. His first cricketing hero was the Australian paceman Ray Lindwall. He took great pleasure in terrorising his peers by hurling a bald tennis ball (with the hide worn off) at them with an action no less graceful than Lindwall's. But it was batting that enchanted him the most. When it came to countering his straight drives, his mates were not half as resilient as his mother.

> 'He was the youngest among us, and the only owner of a cricket bat and ball. I do not remember us getting him out. You could see his class even in under-arm cricket. He was impossible to dislodge. A part of the middle one of the three garage doors at the far end of the alley would serve as the stumps. A stage would be reached wherein we would shout 'Out!' the moment the ball would pass his bat and hit the door, regardless of whether the ball had struck the area that represented the stumps or not! He would then lose his cool, fight with us and go home. His exit

---

[4]Father

> would signal a premature end to the evening's play, for he would walk off with the bat and ball. Subsequently, he found a means to thwart our foul play by acquiring a set of stumps! He was short-tempered as a child, and would get angry whenever something did not happen as per his wish. But that did not come in the way of his being loved by the residents. One of our neighbours, Phanindranath Chachad, who must have been in his forties, would play with us on holidays. He would invariably captain one of the teams. As is the custom, the designated captains would toss and then take turns to pick their players. Whenever Chachad would win the toss he would immediately say, "I want the batkya (shorty)!" Sunil was always the first choice!' – Ashok Ambaye

The young Sunil was short-tempered, and his friends did not waste a single opportunity to try his patience. Matters came to a head one particular day, when they grabbed Sunil's bat, broke it into two and handed it back to him. A fight would be followed by a cold war, which would end even before the boys themselves realised it.

Fighting was something the young Sunil fancied, as it gave him an opportunity to imitate his wrestler-heroes. He loved being taken to the NSCI Ground, situated a couple of kilometres away, opposite the Haji Ali mosque, to watch the much-hyped wrestling bouts between outrageously-named fighters, a modest precursor to the WWF mania of modern times. Posters publicising wrestling bouts would be put up in the neighbourhood every Tuesday and Friday. Sunil and Milind would tear them from the walls and re-paste them in the former's house.

> 'I attribute my friendship with Sunil to pure destiny. My parents were a lot older than his. There were several boys of our age all around us, but how and why did Sunil and I become close friends? Destiny!' – Milind Rege

Destiny played its part in ensuring that both boys were admitted to the same school, St. Xavier's, which was situated in nearby Dhobi Talao. Of all the Marathi children who lived around them and played with them, Sunil and Milind were the only two to study in an English medium school. The Bhagirathi buildings and St. Xavier's school apart, the boys had a common family background. Milind's elder brother Surendra was a right-handed opening batsman who excelled for Siddharth, one of the city's best 'cricketing' colleges of the time. Test cricketers like Manohar Hardikar and Ramnath Kenny would frequently drop in at his house. When he finished his studies, Surendra was picked up by none other than Madhav Mantri, who led the Associated Cement Company (ACC) in inter-office tournaments. If this was not a case of it being a small world, then nothing was.

> 'Cricket wasn't Sunil's only love. I remember him going to the nearby Procter Road on Sunday mornings to play table tennis. Nobody forced him to play cricket.' – Madhav Mantri

Sunil and Milind went on to represent their school in table tennis.

> 'There was a TT table in the Bhagirathi compound. Both Milind and Sunil were good players. Marbles was the most popular sport during the rainy season. The Diwali celebrations would feature cricket matches, during which the seniors, like Sunil's father, would do commentary. There would be carrom competitions, and fun events like lemon-and-spoon races.' – Ashok Ambaye

When they were not playing either table tennis or cricket, the duo utilised their holidays to watch the ACC team in action, Sunil to watch Mantri, whom he called Nana mama (maternal uncle), and Milind to watch his elder brother. On school-days, they would pay a quick visit to the Azad maidan, situated a stone's throw away, during the mid-day lunch break if a significant game was in progress. They would also watch Sunil's father in action for his club Rajasthan and office Forbes Campbell.

> 'We fell in love with cricket because of our families. There was no cricketer in the surroundings besides my brother and Sunil's father. Hence, we did not face any opposition from our families when we evinced the desire to play competitive cricket. It was a natural progression of sorts. No other boy from the four buildings played inter-school cricket, as they were not encouraged by their parents to play cricket.' – Milind Rege

This natural progression led to their inclusion in the St. Xavier's cricket team at the age of twelve, when both were in the seventh standard. It was a foregone conclusion after their batting performances in the inter-class matches. Milind became an instant hit with his strokeplay, while Sunil was a revelation with his penchant for playing straight and not surrendering his wicket. His concentration, honed by batting for hours in the Bhagirathi alley, much to the consternation of his peers, was evident. The Bhagirathi boys added muscle and substance to what was an average cricket team.

St. Xavier's was one of Bombay's eminent Jesuit-run, boys schools. Although it placed a premium on the all-round development of its students, its attitude towards sports in general and cricket in particular was ambivalent.

> 'The cricketing environment at St. Xavier's School was non existent. We practised on a half-torn matting wicket. We had no coach, never had one. In fact, the only coach of sorts was Father Fritz, our sports-in-charge. His only advice was: Good ball, block. Bad ball, lagao[5]!' – Milind Rege

The non-existent cricketing environment manifested itself in the reluctance of the authorities to buy new balls. The only time the St. Xavier's cricketers saw a new ball was during an inter-school match! Father Fritz's concept of shine was radical, to say the least. He would give the boys balls polished with Cherry Blossom for the practice sessions. As a result, the boys' trousers would turn black or brown, depending on the colour of the shoe polish that had been applied to the ball! They practised at the Liberty ground opposite the school, which now houses the Home Guards Association. There was no pitch, only rolled mud. The bounce was unpredictable, but it helped to hone the boys' technique.

He may not have known much about cricket balls, but Father Fritz did have the knack of spotting a spark. A group of schoolboys two years senior to Sunil could not believe their ears when Father Fritz reprimanded them in the academic year of 1961-62. This was the season in which Sunil and Milind made their debut in inter-school cricket, and India beat England in a Test series for the first time. The group was conversing with Father Fritz, when one of them spotted the diminutive Sunil, batting on

---

[5]hit!

the school playground, wearing hopelessly oversized cricket gear, and burst out laughing. The others joined in, only to be silenced, when their sports-in-charge reprimanded them and predicted that the object of their derision would become a great cricketer. The boys were surprised, for Sunil at that stage had not revealed any remarkable cricketing qualities. Father Fritz's prediction stayed in the memory of atleast one member of that group – Mihir Bose, who went on to pen *A History of Indian Cricket* in 1990. The foreword to that book was written by none other than the boy he and his friends had mocked!

Sunil made his inter-school debut in the Under-14 Giles Shield tournament. He batted at number ten and scored an unbeaten 30. The mention of his name as 'G. Sunil' in the following day's newspaper did not please him. He had been looking forward to reading his name in print for the first time, a momentous event in any individual's life, and he was far too young to appreciate that scores in inter-school matches did not figure in the sub-editors' list of priorities.

Sunil's Lindwall impersonations stood him in good stead, with him opening the bowling for his school and affecting many a breakthrough. His consistency with the bat in the lower order resulted in a promotion, and tons of runs.

The Bhagirathi boys would massacre bowling attacks, only to be let down by their team-mates, who were not quite in the same league. The celebratory moment of the duo was a second-wicket partnership of 310 in a match against Maratha Schools, captained by a certain Eknath Solkar. They came together at 0-1 and scored hundreds. Milind was out for 120 and the team collapsed after his dismissal to be all out for 343. Sunil remained unbeaten with 147 runs.

> 'The St. Xavier's team apart, Sunil and Milind were the stars of our Bhagirathi team. We would participate in local tennis-ball tournaments. Sunil was our main batsman, and the only way the opponents could get him out was by running him out. These inter-locality games were very competitive. Up for grabs were the cups, purchased by the teams with every member making a contribution. These matches were played in open spaces in the locality. Milind, who used to wear spectacles, was nicknamed

Roy, after Pankaj Roy, the bespectacled Indian opener of the era. A victory would invariably be followed by a procession from the venue to the Bhagirathi buildings.' – Ashok Ambaye

Both were candidates for the St. Xavier's captaincy after two years of inter-school cricket. Milind was given the job because he was the more successful cricketer. And taller!

The new captain promptly asserted his authority. He was preparing to open the innings in a game against Anjuman-e-Islam, but panicked when confronted with a perennial allegation or fact in the history of Bombay inter-school cricket (depending upon whether you were an Anjuman supporter or opponent). Most of the Anjuman players were nearly twice as tall as their St. Xavier's rivals, and 'over-age' was a compound word that sprung to most people's lips, Milind's included. The St. Xavier's captain was, to say the least, apprehensive. He summoned his pal and ordered him to open instead. Sunil was not impressed, but had to obey his captain. He padded up and strode out to open for the first time in his cricketing career.

2

CLIMBING THE LADDER

'Milind and Sunil would often drop in at our *Times of India* (TOI) Shield matches at the Azad maidan, which was situated right next to their school. Sunil was always a good listener and sound observer. He possessed the ability to imbibe, which in the long run makes all the difference between success and failure. I remember a conversation with Kersi Meherhomji, one of India's keepers on the tour of England in 1936, and another former cricketer called Reshamwalla. They were watching a Bombay Schools game at the Bombay Gymkhana, and Reshamwalla remembered me when a batsman essayed a square-cut. Meherhomji then told him that the batsman who had played that stroke was none other than my nephew. But I had never coached Sunil, never did. He must have watched me play that stroke and internalised it.' – Madhav Mantri

Sunil's debut for his school was preceded by a seminal episode. Coincidentally, like the one in the hospital immediately after his birth, it starred a maternal uncle.

His batting, wicketkeeping and captaincy skills apart, Mantri was known for his no-nonsense approach. A stickler for discipline on and off the cricket field, he was respected, even feared, by cricketers across the city. His distinguished career had yielded a fair number of official caps, pullovers and autographed stumps, all of which the young Sunil loved to pull out of the cupboard whenever he visited Mantri's home in the locality of Dadar, a twenty-minute train-ride from Tardeo. One fine day, he convinced himself that Nana mama[6] would have no issues lending him a few items. The request, coming as it did from a boy who had just entered double-figures, would have been accepted by ninety-nine out of a hundred indulgent uncles. Nana mama just happened to be the hundredth. 'These things have to be earned, you shouldn't ask for them,' he replied.

When Sunil was subsequently picked in the St. Xavier's team and given an inscribed cap and pullover, he went straight to Dadar to show Nana mama his earnings. The uncle exhorted the nephew to treat it as only the beginning.

> 'My father (Sunil's maternal grandfather) never saw Sunil play, but he did follow his exploits in the papers. On his death bed, he predicted that Sunil would become a great cricketer. "The unfortunate thing is," he said, "I won't be around when that happens."' – Madhav Mantri

There was no dearth of outstanding schoolboy cricketers in Bombay in the 1960s. The schools in the metropolis were represented by run-hungry batsmen, nippy medium-pacers and canny spinners.

Sunil Gavaskar was one of the members of this elite community. A cascade of runs for St. Xavier's school in the Giles Shield inter-school tournament earned Milind Rege and him spots in the Bombay Schools side. Sunil did not do anything of note in his first few matches and was in fact left out for his poor fielding. Not for the last time in his career, he rectified his faults and returned.

> 'I kept Sunil in mind when I wrote a book in Marathi titled *How to play cricket?* around that time. The idea was to keep things as simple as possible, in view of the fact that I was writing for youngsters. I gave him a copy after it had been published. A few days later, I asked him whether he had read it. He told me

---

[6]Maternal uncle.

that he had read it at a stretch. I was surprised, for although the book was meant for youngsters, it contained certain unavoidable technical details. And mind you, it was in Marathi, and Sunil was an English-medium student.' – Madhav Mantri

The 1965-66 season belonged to Sunil. After a tepid start in the national inter-school tournament that yielded him 33 and 7 against Gujarat, he took 158 off the Gujarat bowlers. Then came an unbeaten 246 against Central Zone, during the course of which he added 421 for the first wicket with Anwar Qureshi. It was followed by 222 against East Zone and 85 and 9 in the final against North Zone. Four successive hundreds in Bombay's Under-16 Harris Shield competition earned him the J.C. Mukherjee Trophy for the Best Schoolboy Cricketer of the Year, and won him a place in a series between Indian Schoolboys and their London counterparts.

'It was the first time such a series was taking place. We had an outstanding All-India team. Eknath Solkar was captain and the Amarnath brothers were part of the side. Mohinder batted at no. 10. I was the most successful all-rounder in that series.'
– Milind Rege

Sunil warmed up for the Tests with an innings of 40 for West Zone against the visitors. He was looking good for many more when he was bowled by future cricket writer Mike Selvey. His opening partner in that game and the first three-day Test was Ramesh Nagdev, a destroyer of bowling attacks, who still holds the record for the highest individual score in the Harris Shield – 427 for Hindi Vidyabhavan against Amin High School. The duo opened for India in the first Test, and got their side off to a sound start.

'Gavaskar maintained his string of good scores, but his innings on Friday was a workman-like effort compared to his double century, century and near-century in the Schools tournament. He made only 19 in the first hour and though he relished the spinners to score 31 in the next, he gave a chance at 38 when he slashed at Moir and John Brooks, at slip, moved the wrong way. His 116 was the result of concentration, no doubt a virtue. He stayed for 250 minutes and hit seven fours. . . .' – *TOI*, 11 December 1965

> 'Gavaskar opened with Nagdev... they dominated the pre-lunch session, and made the visitors' pace attack look mediocre... Gavaskar, who excelled with firm cover drives, square-cuts and an occasional on-drive, was very sedate in the beginning. But he gained confidence and was on 50 to Nagdev's 71 in a total of 127 at lunch. He completed his hundred in 222 minutes....' – *Fress Press Journal*, 11 December 1965

The innings was a watershed of sorts. Sunil had barely got his eye in when he was struck on the thigh. Since he was not wearing a thigh-pad, it hurt, and he was hobbling and wincing when he overheard the fielding captain telling the bowler to do an encore. That intensified Sunil's desire to fight it out. The middle-class upbringing was showing.

The first Test was drawn, as were the next three. Sunil scored 55 and 15 in the second Test, and 35 and 57 in the third. He scored 6 in the fourth, and missed the last Test on account of the upcoming matriculation examinations. Milind, however, played and sculpted a win by scalping four batsmen on the last day. All-India won by 90 runs with only fifteen minutes left.

Sunil's consistency in the series was fuelled by his ability to shut himself from the rest of the world while going about his job.

> 'Two unique gifts which Sunil possessed from a very young age were a fierce determination to stay at the wicket and phenomenal powers of concentration. He was one of the first schoolboys to play with a Gray Nichols bat imported from the UK. Probably his uncle or father got it for him. He worked very hard on his batting technique. Unlike him, most of us were ignorant of the finer points. He wasn't very talkative, but approachable. At times, his focus on the game was so intense that he gave the impression that he was aloof and did not wish to be befriended. But it wasn't so.' – Ajay Madgaonkar, Bombay Schools team-mate

The Bhagirathi buddies were certainties for the Indian Juniors team that was to tour England in 1967, but Aai[7] put her foot down.

---

[7] Mother

By then, Mrs Meenal Gavaskar had taken charge of Milind. This was another Indian middle-class phenomenon. There was trust and an implicit understanding between neighbours, which made them treat each other's children like their own. This understanding is rapidly degenerating in an age characterised by monstrous high-rise apartments.

> 'Everything I achieved, from my school days to my graduation, was primarily because of Aai. She would make Sunil and me sit in separate rooms of their flat and subject us to tests. We were certainties for that 1967 trip, but she would have none of it. In fact, I might well have captained that side. However, had she not been so particular about our studies, I would not have been what I am today.' – Milind Rege

Sunil's parents understood their son's passion for the game, and allowed him to indulge it. When Bob Simpson's Australians stopped over on their way home from England to play three Tests in October 1964, Sunil sought his father's permission to skip school so that he could watch the first day's play in its entirety. His request was granted, and the fifteen-year-old lapped up everything that he saw, from the time the captains tossed, till the umpires drew the bails in the evening. The next morning, Gavaskar senior handed him a letter addressed to the vice-principal, wherein he cited a headache as the reason for Sunil's absence the day before. The vice-principal cast a cursory look at the letter and asked Sunil to narrate everything that happened at the match. That Sunil was cricket-mad was an open secret! Sunil provided the details, and his father paid the vice-principal a visit to apologise.

While one-off instances like this were fine, the Gavaskars offered a forward defensive stroke when it came to the broader picture. Nothing, not even cricket, was allowed to gain precedence over academics. It was a middle-class Marathi household after all. Gavaskar senior refused him permission to play the inter-school tournament after a dismal performance in the examinations, and it was only when Revd Serkis, the school principal intervened, that Gavaskar senior relented. Sunil proceeded to ensure that his parents were never again forced to object to his cricketing pursuits.

'The support of his family helped Sunil immensely. The Bombay Schools team would travel by train to other West Zone cities (Baroda, Rajkot, Ahmedabad, etc.) for matches. It was usually an overnight journey. There would invariably be a single family on the platform to see their son off – the Gavaskars!' – Ajay Madgaonkar

'His parents would often travel with the Bombay Schools and (later) University teams and stay in adjoining hotels. They treated us like their own children and ensured that we didn't miss our parents.' – Navin Ambulkar, team-mate, Bombay Schools, Bombay University

'Whenever he went on tour, his parents and sisters spent their holidays travelling to wherever he had gone and watching him play. Baba would occasionally treat the entire team for dinner.' – Dr Vishwas Raut, team-mate, Mumbai University

In the pre-TV age, budding cricketers had no alternative but to watch the stalwarts 'live' to learn. Sunil made it a point to visit the maidans whenever possible. He would take position next to the sight screen during the *Times of India* Shield matches, which would invariably feature several prominent cricketers of the time. The Bombay players apart, the companies also recruited stars from other states. Sunil's habit of crossing the western railway track that ran alongside the three gymkhanas on Marine Drive to save time, instead of climbing up and down the overbridge, backfired on one occasion. He was caught by a railway sentry, who demanded a fine. By the time a sobbing Sunil was let off after paying a fine, Ajit Wadekar and Hanumant Singh, who represented the State Bank of India team, had returned to the tent.

The Bhagirathi boys went on to join St. Xavier's College, located just behind their school. Milind was handpicked by Mantri to represent Dadar Union, one of the best clubs in the city, in the Kanga League and other inter-club tournaments.

Sunil too had improved hugely as a batsman since his school days, his basics having been honed by English guru Stan Worthington in a month-long coaching camp at Hyderabad after his final school examination. But Mantri still wasn't convinced that he was ready for the bigger league.

'I felt Sunil needed to hone his game further, and hence did not pick him in the Dadar Union side. It made more sense for him to continue playing for Rajasthan Cricket Club and fine-tune his skills. I had at the back of my mind the example of Madhav Apte, who started life as a leg-break bowler. He was in the middle of a golden run for his school when he was picked to play for Jolly Cricketers in a crucial game against Hindu Gymkhana, whom I was leading then. I requested Bhausaheb Apte, his father, not to play him, for we had an outstanding team. His time would come, I argued. But the boy played, and got hammered. He was so demoralised that he stopped bowling leg-spin altogether. Even in the nets, he would bowl only off-breaks. We lost out on a quality all-rounder as a result.' – Madhav Mantri

The assessment of those who followed junior cricket in Bombay in the mid-1960s was no different. Sunil was overshadowed in the St. Xavier's College side by the likes of Kailash Gattani, a promising new-ball bowler, the aggressive Ramesh Nagdev, Milind, and the captain Ashok Mankad, son of the legendary all-rounder Mulvantrai 'Vinoo' Mankad. A prolific batsman and off-break bowler who was three years Sunil's senior, Mankad was part of a Bombay University team that won the Cooch Behar Trophy, the premier national tournament for the Under-19s, for four consecutive seasons from 1963-64 to 1966-67.

Mankad appreciated Sunil's readiness to follow his family tradition and keep wicket in the inter-collegiate games, as that ensured a stronger batting line-up. This was because the specialist wicketkeeper in the St. Xavier's college team was a mediocre batsman. Sunil also tried to impress as a leg-spinner, apart from flaunting the quick bowling skills that he had displayed at school and the Bhagirathi alley.

'We would wonder why he was trying everything. We wanted an opener who could negotiate the new ball, and that he did splendidly. But there were times when he was hardly able to get the ball past the net! We could not figure out how he would get runs. But in retrospect, he was making his defence impenetrable and developing the ability to play the rising ball. Most batsmen at that age are greedy, but he wasn't. He had the patience to wear out a bowler and the shine of the ball. Once that happened, he ruled.' – Late Ashok Mankad

That some of his team-mates like Mankad, Gattani and Nagdev, had already been exposed to First-class cricket, might have resulted in Sunil feeling the pinch and wanting to make up for lost time by doing everything. His performances for his college were steady rather than outstanding.

The year 1966 was a turning point of sorts. Sunil made his First-class debut, albeit an academic one, in the 1966-67 season, as part of a Vazir Sultan Tobacco (VST) Colts side in the annual Moin-ud-Dowla trophy in Hyderabad. The Colts could not make much of an impact against their seasoned opponents, despite having a star skipper, the reigning captain of India, the Nawab of Pataudi. Sunil was also deemed good enough for Dadar Union, and he duly shifted from the Rajasthan Cricket Club.

Bombay cricket's epicentre had shifted northwards in the years after independence. While the traditional breeding grounds in the south like the Oval, Azad and Cross Maidans, and the three sea-front gymkhanas, continued to produce cricketers, they were having to contend with increasing competition from two maidans situated in the locality to which Dadar Union owed its name.

Dadar had come a long way since its outpost days of the early 1940s. Fears of a Japanese attack after their devastation of Pearl Harbour had resulted in an exodus from south Bombay to its outskirts, namely the area known as Dadar.

Dadar was where Bombay's lifelines, the Central Railway and the Western Railway, converged before charting independent routes into the Indian mainland. It was a thirty-minute train ride away from the city's business district. Apart from becoming the home of Bombay's industrious middle class in the immediate post-Independence phase, Dadar witnessed the evolution of two cricketing nurseries, the Shivaji Park in the west, along the sea front, and the Ruia-Podar ground in the east. The oval-shaped Shivaji Park, named after the man who had taken on the might of the Mughals and established a self-reliant kingdom in Maharashtra in the seventeenth century, came to be known as much for hosting political rallies and cultural events as for producing first-class cricketers. The rectangular Ruia-Podar ground was sandwiched between the Central railway lines and two educational institutions, the R.N. Ruia College for Arts and Science and the R.A. Podar College of Commerce and Economics.

The 1950s and '60s witnessed a series of titanic tussles between the Shivaji Park Gymkhana, based at the Shivaji Park, and Dadar Union, whose home ground was the Ruia-Podar maidan. The SPG-DU rivalry was even referred to as Bombay's equivalent of the 'War of the Roses', which is how games between the English counties of Yorkshire and Lancashire have been described. Both teams had supporters ranging from college peons to future Bombay University vice-chancellors.

There were inherent dissimilarities between the westerners from Shivaji Park and their eastern Ruia-Podar counterparts. The easterners were supposed to be more accomplished in terms of technique, a consequence of watching British officers play on the ground in Dadar's outpost days just before Independence. On the other hand, the westerners were more belligerent, and not averse to defying orthodoxy.

Both maidans housed ramshackle structures that were referred to, rather generously, as clubhouses. The Dadar Union clubhouse was (and is) the first clubhouse at the left end of the Ruia-Podar ground.

The playing area of both maidans was embellished with squares, each of which was home to three or four wickets. Like the Cross and Azad maidans, it was (and is) common for the Dadar maidans to stage many matches simultaneously. What tends to happen as a result is that the cover point fielder in one game runs the risk of being struck on the back by a full blooded cover-drive by a batsman playing in another. It was, and is tough, confusing, and even dangerous. But then, adapting comes naturally to a Mumbai cricketer. He has done it since childhood.

Dadar Union, in Sunil's own words, 'Had a tradition of excellent fielding, discipline, tenacity and the ability to fight back.' The Club had been served down the years by former India Test wicketkeepers Mantri and Naren Tamhane, and a former India batsman Ramnath Kenny. The stars of the side that Sunil joined were Vithal Patil, or Marshall as he was affectionately called, an outstanding medium-pacer, and Vasu Paranjape, an aggressive captain and brilliant fielder. Supporting them were left-arm seamer Urmikant Mody, who represented Saurashtra in the Ranji Trophy, and an aggressive batsman and off-spinner named Milind Rege.

These were real characters, all of whom hailed from the middle class and juggled their nine-to-five jobs with their passion for the game. To the triumvirate of Dedication, Discipline and Determination, the DU players had added a fourth D—Devotion.

> 'DU was completely responsible for the overall development of any young cricketer who had the privilege to represent it. Vasu has to be one of the greatest motivators in my book. He was a skilful captain who hated to lose. There was cricket everywhere, out on the field and amidst the discussions off the field. Everyone was dead serious about the sport. Juniors like Ramnath Parkar, Sunil and I would listen to the cricketing stories recounted by seniors like Naren Tamhane, Vasu and V.S. Patil.' – Milind Rege

> I remember Sunil coming with his father to watch our matches when Mantri was leading us. His father would ask us to bowl to him during the breaks. He wouldn't want to stop batting! His urge to excel was obvious even at that age. – Vasu Paranjape[8], *The Boy From Chikalwadi* (PMG, 1999)

His captaincy and fielding apart, Paranjape was a wonderful raconteur. One of his favourite stories concerned Hanif Mohammad, the 'little master' from Pakistan, and purveyor of one of the straightest bats in cricketing history. Paranjape was once late for the start of play in a Test against Pakistan being played at the CCI. He had just alighted from the train at the Churchgate station, situated five minutes from the ground, when he heard a 'thok' sound, which a cricket bat emanates when its middle makes contact with the ball. It made him draw a speedy conclusion—Hanif was on strike. He was right.

It was a story Sunil never forgot.

V.S. Patil was an astute bowler and teacher who spent his off-the-field hours fidgeting with a cricket ball and working on different grips. He loved to experiment and encouraged others to do likewise. It was he

---

[8] It was Paranjape who nicknamed Sunil 'Sunny'.

who encouraged Mody, a left-arm spinner, to switch to medium-pace. To enable its players to have quality practice in the afternoons, the club shelled out extra money to maintain a full cricket wicket, on which play was not permitted in the mornings.

> 'At Dadar Union, appearance was valued as much as discipline. We were expected to be immaculately dressed. We would make it a point to polish our shoes before every game. We had heard the story of Mantri dropping Kenny, a Test cricketer, because he was late for a game. For a game that was to start at 10.30 am, we were expected to reach the ground at 9.30 am, no questions asked.' – Sanjay Jaywant, former First-class cricketer

> 'Dadar Union was the best fielding unit in the city. When the season ended in May, we would assemble at the club every evening at 5.30 pm for fielding practice and physical training. That enabled us to be in perfect shape by the time the Kanga League got underway in July. Fielding was emphasised to the extent that given a choice between a class batsman or bowler who was a poor fielder, and a decent batsman or bowler who was a good fielder, we would pick the latter.' – Madhav Mantri

Sunil did not get to play alongside his uncle. But Dadar Union maintained its traditions and record under Vasu Paranjape. They were at their peak in the 1970s, winning the Kanga League from 1973 to 1977.

The Gavaskars shifted to eastern Dadar from Tardeo in the mid-'60s. Here, the family of five had a flat to themselves, after having shared the Bhagirathi home with Gavaskar senior's maternal cousins and their families. However, the bonds with Bhagirathi remained intact. They still do.

> 'Sunil was in college when they shifted to Dadar. But that did not prevent him from coming here every evening after his lectures. He would play here, and then catch the 8.30 pm train from Grant Road station to Dadar. I would escort him to the station and see him off. He maintained his daily dose of coffee and Parle Gluco biscuits.' – Ashok Ambaye

A lifelong fan of Parle Gluco biscuits (renamed Parle-G in the 1980s), Sunil in later years expressed his surprise that the biscuit manufacturers hadn't ever asked him to endorse their product, for he has been one of their most faithful consumers!

He even concocted a game of sorts, which according to him tested his precision. This game involved him placing four biscuits in a N-S-E-W pattern in a saucer. He would then pour the coffee gradually into the saucer, the objective being to fill it, but at the same time, to ensure that the outer crust of the biscuits remained dry. Once the saucer was relatively full, he would then tilt it to pour the coffee back into the cup. If any of the soggy biscuits was to fall into the cup in the process—an outcome of pouring too much coffee in the saucer in the first place, or tilting the saucer far too much to pour the coffee back into the cup—it would mean a defeat. If the biscuits were not to fall along with the coffee into the cup, it amounted to a victory.

The Dadar Union nets at the Ruia-Podar ground were a leisurely fifteen-minute walk away from his new house.

> 'One of the factors that helped Sunil improve his technique was the purposeful bowling he faced at the Dadar Union nets.' – V.S. Patil

> 'Patil was a master of swing and control ... He would use two-three new balls a day during his tireless stints at the nets to help young batsmen like Gavaskar.' – Sunder Rajan, *TOI*, 3 May 1971

The sessions apart, Sunil made it a point to buttonhole prominent cricketers and discuss facets of the sport whenever the opportunity presented itself. After shifting to Dadar, he established a rapport with Vijay Bhosle, a gifted Bombay batsman, who lived in the vicinity.

His First-class debut and acceptance into the DU fold apart, 1966-67 also witnessed Sunil's inter-university debut. Two hundreds in the West Zone league prompted the Bombay selectors to include him in the Ranji trophy squad, but he was omitted after serving as a reserve in just one match. An outsider might have been shocked to see a player being dumped without even getting a look-in, but Bombay's cricketing community was not. Many players had been in a similar situation, such was the abundance of talent in the metropolis. Sunil did not spend too much time brooding over his omission, knowing that his interests would be better served if he exploited every opportunity that came his way at the lower levels.

Like all teenagers, he had his heroes. Heading the list was Motganhalli Laxminarasu Jaisimha, whose elegant batsmanship inspired many boys in the 1960s. Sunil tried to walk like Jaisimha and bat like Conrad Hunte, the West Indies opening batsman. He was ecstatic when Hunte, in his capacity as chief guest at the Vizzy Trophy final between the West Zone and South Zone in the 1966-67 season, made a mention of him in his speech.

Sunil watched both men, plus Rohan Babulal Kanhai, another favourite, from a prized seat in the CCI pavilion during the Bombay Test of the 1966-67 series against the Windies. It was a risk, as the CCI rules did not permit minors to access the pavilion, but one worth taking. He was captivated by Hunte's backlift, and took it upon himself to replicate it.

Cricketing heroes apart, Sunil had reel-life heroes as well. Hollywood star Paul Newman was his favourite.

> 'Sunil believed that he looked like Newman. He would try to imitate the actor's lip-movements while talking. I used to call him Paul.' – Late Ashok Mankad

> 'Sharmila Tagore, who married Tiger Pataudi, a cricketer, was Sunil's favourite actress. We watched several English films together. I had studied in a Marathi medium school and hence wasn't familiar with the language. Sunil was my interpreter.'
> – Navin Ambulkar

The 1967-68 season began on an auspicious note, with the Bombay selectors picking Sunil in the squad for the Irani Cup fixture against the Rest of India at the start of the 1967-68 season. With most of Bombay's leading lights set to tour Australia and New Zealand with the Indian team, Sunil was eager to make a mark in the game, as that would establish him in the side for the entire season. But he failed, scoring 5 and 0. The Bombay selectors reacted by picking the veteran Madhav Apte, who hadn't played First-class cricket for a number of years, for the Ranji trophy, ahead of him. Sunil was disappointed for not getting another chance. He sought solace in his studies, even declining to tour with the Bombay University team that season.

It was thus a surprise when the Bombay University selectors appointed him captain for the 1968-69 season. The added responsibility brought out the best in him in the Inter-University Rohinton Baria tournament. Partisan umpiring denied Bombay a berth in the final, when they fell only two runs short of the target set by Indore in the second semi-final at Baroda. Bombay, needing 202 to win, found themselves playing thirteen opponents, with the local umpires joining the effort to keep the best team of the tournament away from the hosts, who had won the first semi-final. Valiant knocks by Bombay players Dilip Galvankar and Navin Ambulkar went in vain, although the latter's pockets were stuffed with money by an appreciative crowd.

> 'I shared a room with him on the University trips. He would pray before going to sleep. Sunil would visit the temple of Lord Hanuman every Saturday. If he was unable to go for some reason, his mother or sister would visit on his behalf. We were given a paltry weekly allowance of Rs 56 on those tours. Needless to say, the allowance did not last beyond three or four days. I used to be comparatively better-stocked, and so I became a "moneylender". The boys would reimburse me after receiving the next weekly instalment.' – Navin Ambulkar

The 1968-69 edition of the inter-zonal Vizzy Trophy was played in Delhi. Sunil shone with an unbeaten 247 against South Zone. He followed it with an undefeated 113 in the final against the North Zone. On home turf, he scored an impeccable 301 for Dadar Union against the Hindu Gymkhana in the final of the inter-club Purshottam Shield competition.

> 'I umpired that game. Every single person who watched that innings was convinced that this batsman was going to hit the headlines very soon.' – P.D. Reporter

The nephew was in no mood to disregard his uncle's admonishment after an inter-University game a few months previously. Sunil had added over 400 for the first wicket with Ramesh Nagdev and then had thrown his wicket away, only to be reminded by Mantri that the bowler ought to earn his wicket. Sunil put his uncle's advice into practice against the Hindu Gymkhana.

Vasu Paranjpe was shocked when Sunil ignored a delivery pitched in the corridor of uncertainty outside the off-stump immediately after completing his triple hundred. When Sunil returned to the dressing room, Vasu asked him why he had let that ball go. Sunil's response was prompt, 'Why should I gift the bowler my wicket?'

> It was Vasu who told me, 'Sunny, give the bowler the first hour, and the remaining five will be yours.' That made a lot of sense, as in the first hour, you don't know how the pitch is going to play, whether there will be movement, or what the bowlers would be trying to do. It is after you get your eye in that the feet start moving, and you get more confident.' – Sunil Gavaskar, *Boycs and Sunny Masterclass*, ESPN (2000)

What Mantri, Paranjape and the others preached was in relation to the traditional version of the game. Cricket then was a multi-day sport that demanded multitudes of application and commitment. Bombay had hosted a fifty-overs-a-side, one-innings-one-day tournament, played for the Padmakar Talim Shield[9], since 1956-57, but it was an exception. Young practitioners of the art of batsmanship were prescribed the virtue of patience, and any batsman who dispatched the ball at anything over six inches from the ground ran the risk of incurring the wrath of his seniors.

Sunil led a talented outfit in the 1969-70 edition of the inter-university tournament, which was played in Jabalpur.

> 'I remember one of my college mates, who had come to see me off at the railway station on our way to Jabalpur, being surprised at Sunil's height, or rather, the lack of it. I reminded him that even Napoleon was short-statured! What mattered was a killer instinct.' – Dr Vishwas Raut

---

[9]The world's first ever One-day cricket tournament.

That killer instinct ensured Bombay's conquest of the Rohinton Baria Trophy, by virtue of their victory in the All-India Inter-University final against Bangalore.

Sunil's inability to find a place in the Bombay squad notwithstanding, he was proving to be a better and quicker learner than most batsmen in his age group. However, he was not regarded as highly as Ramesh Nagdev. All those who had seen Nagdev thought the world of him.

> 'Nagdev was a gutsy and immensely talented bat, but he lacked patience. He probably wasn't as determined to stay on the wicket and play a long, deliberate innings as Sunil. I may be harsh on Nagdev, but then, that was his persona.' – Ajay Madgaonkar

Nagdev and Sunil caught the eye of the national selectors in a three-day game between a Combined Universities XI and the visiting New Zealanders in the 1969-70 season. Sunil scored only 25 and 10, but gave a splendid account of himself against the pace of Richard Collinge and Dayle Hadlee. While Nagdev[10] was rewarded with the twelfth man's post for the first Test of India's next series against Australia, Sunil was invited to watch the game from the dressing room.

Although he had led Bombay University excellently in the Rohinton Baria trophy, Sunil hadn't really got going with the bat. He returned to form in time for the final of the inter-collegiate Ibrahim Rahimtoola Cup. St. Xavier's had not beaten Siddharth College, their arch rivals, for seventeen years, and were the underdogs when the match got underway at the Hindu Gymkhana. Batting first, Siddharth were shot out for 170. The Bhagirathi boys then rubbed it in, adding 234 for the third wicket. Milind scored 119 and Sunil 228, and they took their side to a score of 522. Siddharth, thoroughly demoralised by this stage, was bowled out for 102, thus giving Xavier's an innings win.

> 'I first met him when Nana mama took me to his house in the mid-1960s, and introduced me as a promising cricketer. I had already heard about his cricketing exploits and seen him in action. I remember sensing back then that he was a special player.

---

[10]Nagdev might well have played for India had he not chosen to migrate to California. He passed away in January 2008.

> We became good friends thereafter. When we faced off in that Rahimtoola Cup final, I was in my first year at Siddharth College, and he in his final year at St. Xavier's. It was a literal face-off, as he was the opening batsman and I was a new-ball bowler. He scored 228 before I managed to bowl him. Till this day, he says that he doesn't know how he missed that ball. Every time he says that, I remind him that he had scored the small matter of 228 runs at that point!' – Hemant Waingankar

That performance won Sunil a Ranji recall, for the semi-final against Mysore (later known as Karnataka). Madhav Mantri was one of the selectors, and not surprisingly, there were allegations of nepotism.

> 'Mantri was the last person to push for anybody, least of all his nephew. He was too straightforward. In fact, he wouldn't talk about Sunil at selection committee meetings only because they were related. In a way, it was unfair to Sunil.' – Milind Rege

> 'Had Mantri pushed for him, Sunil would have played for Mumbai in his teens. He made it on merit.' – Navin Ambulkar

His detractors were jubilant when Sunil fell for a duck in the first innings of the semi-final. But one early wicket was never going to worry the champions, and Sunil's team-mates compensated with loads of runs and the crucial first-innings lead. An unbeaten 27 in the second innings and three catches helped Sunil retain his place for the final against Rajasthan.

> One who needs banking upon is Sunil Gavaskar, whom at least one high source reportedly considers the best Indian against the new ball. – Jayant Nene, *TOI*, 26 March 1970

The final was memorable for Bombay and its new recruit. Rajasthan were bowled out for 217, and the Bombay openers put on 279 before being separated. One of them was Sunil, who made the most of two lives to compile 114, his first Ranji hundred. Ashok Mankad, his partner, scored 171.

> The twenty-year-old Sunil Gavaskar, in the selection of balls to play and balls to leave alone, shows a maturity beyond his

years. True, Gavaskar was painfully slow to start with, but this was only because he has had to fight for a place in the Bombay team. Once he passed 50, Gavaskar matched Mankad stroke for stroke, using his feet delightfully to the spinners. This boy could just be the opener India is looking for, since he does not flinch from pace, as we saw when he faced Hadlee and Collinge for Universities v/s New Zealand early in the season. Even making allowance for the lack of sting in the Rajasthan bowling, it was a joy to watch Gavaskar step back to cut, lean into the drive and play the straight drive as we have not seen it played since Polly Umrigar. – Raju Bharatan, *Illustrated Weekly of India*, 26 April 1970

Bombay's victory by an innings and 59 runs was a perfect climax to what had been an unforgettable season for Sunil as batsman and captain, one in which he had proved to others and to himself that he was competent enough to succeed at the First-class level. Soon after the Ranji triumph, the Bhagirathi boys completed their graduation in Arts (Economics).

'His judgement was exemplary even at that age. If he was beaten by a particular delivery, he would want to know how far the ball had been outside the off-stump. He would ask me the same after crossing over to the bowler's end. His urge for perfection was obvious. He would want to know whether the ball had moved late. Coincidentally, Sachin Tendulkar was as inquisitive.'– P.D. Reporter

Sunil was appointed vice-captain of an Indian Universities side that toured Sri Lanka at the start of the domestic season of 1970-71. His best performance on what turned out to be a memorable tour was an unbeaten 203 against Sri Lanka University.

He returned home to discover that Sudhir Naik, another childhood friend-turned-Ranji player, had filled in for him successfully in the first Ranji Trophy game of the season against Baroda. There being little or no possibility of his figuring in the playing XI for the next game against Gujarat, Sunil arrived at the Brabourne stadium with his whites, but without his equipment. However, Ajit Wadekar was rendered unfit on the morning of the game, and Sunil was told that he had to fill in. He was forced to call his mother and tell her to rush to the ground with his gear.

Even as his mother complied, Sunil psyched himself to come to terms with the situation. It was an opportunity he simply had to make the most of. A failure could well have meant his relegation to the reserve-bench for the rest of the season. It was the Bombay cricket team after all.

His fortitude won the day, as did his mother's dash with his gear. He scored 104, and kept his place for the next game against traditional rivals Maharashtra.

Politically, Mumbai is Maharashtra's capital, but in cricketing terms, the city and the state have always been separate entities. Their rivalry is Indian cricket's equivalent of the Trans-Tasman tussle. Like the Kiwis, the Maharashtra players have often complained of being taken for granted and treated like younger siblings. Their resentment, coupled with Mumbai's eagerness to stand their ground, has made for some outstanding cricket. The metropolis has prevailed on most occasions. Mental resolve was, and is, as essential as technical ability in these encounters, and Sunil was not found wanting. He accumulated 176, his third consecutive Ranji hundred, but Maharashtra took the first-innings lead, and topped the West Zone points' tally.

What turned out to be a landmark season for Indian cricket featured two modifications which the BCCI discussed during its annual meeting in September 1970. The first was to extend the number of teams qualifying from each zone for the knockout stage of the Ranji Trophy from one to two. Had this not been done, Bombay, who finished the 1970-71 West Zone league at the second position, would not have made it to the knockout stage.

The second change concerned the National Selection Committee. It was decided to increase the number of selectors from four to five, with one individual representing each of the five zones.

The import of both modifications sunk in as the season progressed.

'I first saw Sunil in a game between Dadar Union and Shivaji Park Gymkhana. Ramakant Desai was making the ball talk on a fiery

Shivaji Park wicket, but Sunil handled him very well, and it was obvious that there was "something in him". He was then picked in the Bombay team. I remember a couple of instances wherein he was very disappointed after I got out playing an ordinary shot. I could see that he was upset, but he didn't articulate his feelings. After all, I was the captain and he a newcomer!' – Ajit Wadekar

It was late 1970, and India's tour of the West Indies in early 1971 was around the corner. Like their predecessors of the past thirty-eight years, the key concern of the national selectors was to bring together an effective 'Engine Room' at the top of the batting order.

India had been served by as many as forty-four different opening combinations in 116 Tests from 1932 to 1969-70. Opening batsmen were proving to be as elusive as new-ball bowlers. This was ironic, considering that India held the world record for the highest opening stand in Test cricket—413 between Vinoo Mankad and Pankaj Roy against New Zealand at Madras in 1955-56. But then, both batsmen were successful converts to the opening slot. Unlike them, several other middle-order batsmen and even wicketkeepers had been tried, tested and subsequently tossed away.

India had lost seventeen of their twenty-eight Test series from 1932 to 1969-70, with two being squared and four ending in a stalemate. Their overseas record was catastrophic, with only three Test wins from forty-seven appearances, all of them having been achieved in New Zealand in 1967-68. The absence of a quality opening combination made it easy for opposing pacemen to make inroads into the batting line-up. The opening woes were as evident on the supposedly benign tracks at home, as they were overseas. The team had reached triple figures for the loss of only one wicket just once in sixteen Test innings against the New Zealand and Australian visitors in 1969-70.

On the other hand, the reluctance of the Indian think-tank of the time to give a long rope to quick bowlers made it easy for opposition batsmen to play themselves in against batsmen who sent down a few desultory overs at the start of an innings. By the time India's greatest asset—the spinners—would come on, the batters would be well settled in the middle.

The need for quality opening batsmen prompted Dicky Rutnagur, the popular cricket writer and commentator, to come up with an out-of-the-box suggestion. He advised the selectors to pick John Jameson, an opening batsman who had scored 1,821 runs for Warwickshire in the 1970 County Championship in England. Jameson may have been an English citizen, but he was Bombay-born. 'Spurning a player of Jameson's merits under the circumstances would seem a narrow-minded policy,' Rutnagur wrote in the *TOI* on 5 December 1970. He referred to Jameson's Indian roots (his father had managed the Indian hockey team in the 1964 Tokyo Olympics) and the ICC's (International Cricket Conference) stipulation that a player was always eligible to represent the land of his birth, unless debarred by the Conference.[11]

Rutnagur's recommendation was overshadowed by the speculation that the National Selection Committee, headed by Vijay Merchant, India's best Test batsman of the pre-Independence era, would take some bold decisions. A successful convert to the opening position just like Mankad and Roy, Merchant was regarded the ultimate technician. Sunil had heard and read a lot about him. He had seen him bat as well.

This was in 1964, when Sunil was one of many schoolboys requisitioned to help filmmaker Zul Vellani make a documentary titled *The Spirit and Technique of Cricket*. Contemporary cricketers were invited to demonstrate different facets of the sport, but Merchant, who had played his last Test in 1951-52, was requested to execute his signature stroke – the late-cut. The maestro's countenance, as he arrived at the wicket in cream flannels and an India cap, made a deep impression on Sunil. The onlookers, Sunil included, were awestruck when he essayed the perfect late-cut to the very first ball he faced.

Six years later, the spotlight was once again on Merchant, who some Englishmen had wanted to paint white and take to Australia for the 1936-37 Ashes series. He had become the chairman of the Selection Committee in 1969-70, and hit the headlines for his 'experiments with youth'. Quite a few youngsters had made their Test debuts against New Zealand and Australia as a result, at the expense of some senior players.

---

[11]The International Cricket Conference was renamed the International Cricket Council in 1989.

However, the chairman of selectors was not on the same wavelength as the captain.

Mansoor Ali Khan, the erstwhile nawab of the principality of Pataudi, situated not very far from Delhi, had led India since the near-fatal injury to Nariman 'Nari' Contractor on India's previous tour of the Caribbean in 1961-62. 'Tiger' Pataudi's premier achievement as captain was India's first ever overseas series win in New Zealand in 1967-68. His approach to captaincy was a far cry from the conservative and caution-ridden days of the 1950s. Unlike many of his predecessors, he was not averse to taking a gamble if there was a possibility of achieving a win. Confronted with the prospect of leading a cricket team that had no paceman, leave alone pace duo, to speak of, Pataudi reacted by putting together the most lethal spin attack in the history of the sport. The quartet of off-spinner Erapalli Prasanna and Srinivas Venkataraghvan, left-arm spinner Bishan Bedi, and leg-spinner B.S. Chandrasekhar, was complemented by a group of competent catchers. An outstanding fielder himself, Pataudi inspired his players to uplift their fielding standards.

He led India to a series win against New Zealand at home in 1964-65, after levelling a series against a formidable Australian team. His tactical skills were on show in the second Test of the series against Australia at Bombay. India had lost the first Test at Madras, despite the skipper's 128, and needed to win to stay in the series. The visitors batted first and lost 5 wickets with only 146 on the board, but Peter Burge and keeper Barry Jarman then put together a fruitful partnership. The fifteen-year-old Sunil, who would carry the 'headache' letter to school the following day, would have been among those who were surprised to see Pataudi taking the new ball at the fag end of the day's play. It made little sense, for India's new-ball attack was pedestrian, to say the least. M.L. Jaisimha and Rusi Surti, the new-ball bowlers, were nowhere as effective as the spin trio of left-armers Salim Durani and Bapu Nadkarni, and leggie B.S. Chandrasekhar. Pataudi later asked Raj Singh Dungarpur, one of Indian cricket's most versatile personalities, what he thought of the move. Raj Singh's expression of disapproval prompted Pataudi to explain, 'When the captain of any other team takes the new ball, the batsmen become cautious. But when the captain of India takes the new ball, they relax!'

Sure enough, Surti dismissed Jarman. Pataudi brought the spinners back at the start of play on the second day, and Australia slid from 297-5 to 341 all out. India eventually snatched an exciting two-wicket win. The third and final Test was drawn, thus ensuring that the series ended with honours even.

The Indian team did not find glory in the series that followed. The West Indies toured in 1966-67 and won, and the trips to England and Australia in 1967-68 were disasters, with the team losing seven Tests in a row. As they had done in the past, the Indians sought solace in individual feats, notably Pataudi's batting and Erapalli Prasanna's off-spin bowling. Then came the tour of New Zealand, where everything clicked.

The victory over the Kiwis in 1967-68 was achieved a decade after Indian cricket had reached its nadir during the 1958-59 series against the West Indies. Four men had captained India at different stages in that five-Test series. There were two more captains on the subsequent tour of England, where India lost all five Tests. Gulabrai Ramchand (1959-60) and subsequently Nariman Contractor (1960-62) began the rebuilding operation, and Pataudi took things to the next level.

Like all successful men, he had luck on his side, in that the selectors gave him a certain degree of latitude to come to terms with the job, and in the process, the time to work on and with his players. Most of his predecessors, if not all, were not as fortunate.

But then, that stroke of luck was the least he deserved. An accident during his student days at Oxford had deprived him of his right eye. However, he had returned to the cricket field in a matter of months, after making some technical adjustments. Prior to the accident, he had been spoken of as a legend in the making; that he still turned out to be the batsman India's opponents in the 1960s feared the most, spoke volumes about his character.

An upshot of Pataudi's long reign was that Chandrakant Borde, a contemporary of his, who had impressed one and all with his captaincy of Maharashtra and West Zone, missed out on the ultimate honour. He served as Pataudi's deputy in a number of series, and led India in a solitary Test on the 1967-68 tour of Australia when Pataudi was injured.

The 1969-70 season was a forgettable one for the Indian team and its captain. A three-Test series against the Kiwis ended in a 1-1 stalemate.

In fact, the Kiwis would have probably won the decider at Nagpur, had there not been a downpour, and had the drainage facilities at the venue been better than what they were.

While Pataudi was not opposed to the chairman's policy, he did have reservations about favouring youth for the sake of youth. To him, it made little sense to do away with senior players who, although they were not in the best of form at the time, were good enough to spring back, and serve the country with distinction for a few more years. He was disturbed by the fact that Merchant, for all his preference for youngsters, had been reluctant to pick the most talented of the lot – Gundappa Viswanath – during the subsequent Test series against Australia. The captain had his way, and Viswanath scored 0 and 137 on his debut in the second Test at Kanpur. That game was drawn. Australia won the first Test at Bombay, and India drew level in the third at Delhi. The visitors took the lead in the fourth Test at Calcutta. The final fixture at Madras was an eventful affair. Australia started their second innings 95 runs ahead. The Indians then reduced them to 24-6, and spectators and radio-listeners all over the country sensed victory. But catches were dropped and chances missed, and Bill Lawry's side eventually won by 77 runs.

Pataudi's failure with the bat in both series generated gossip that his days were numbered. The cricketing community was divided in its opinion.

> Some Board officials, who appear to be riled by his (Pataudi's) complaint of a lack of empathy, have advanced the countercharge that Pat's aloofness and overbearing approach have cost India dear in many matches. – K.N. Prabhu, *TOI*, 1 November 1970

The uncertainty over Pataudi's future as national skipper prompted the South Zone selectors to take a shrewd call. For the inter-zonal Duleep Trophy, which was to precede the selection of the team for the Caribbean, they entrusted the reins to S. Venkataraghvan, the twenty-six-year-old off-spinning engineer from Madras. Their rationale was obvious. Venkataraghvan had years of international cricket, and possibly the India captaincy, ahead of him. This wasn't something that could be said about his popular predecessor M.L. Jaisimha, under whom Pataudi had played for Hyderabad in the Ranji Trophy and South Zone in the Duleep Trophy.

Pataudi is my choice (as captain for the West Indies tour) . . . We will not be able to field a side as good as the one I led (in 1962) . . . We don't have a good number two batsman . . . The closest I can think of is Gavaskar.' – Nari Contractor, *TOI*, 12 December 1970

The man Contractor rated highly was despondent to find his name missing from the West Zone side for the Duleep Trophy encounter against the South Zone, which was to be played just before the selection of the Indian team. As he saw it, his Ranji hundreds had been overlooked. But had he been left out because the national selectors were considering him for the West Indies tour? His near and dear ones certainly thought so.

'He was named captain of Bombay University for a tournament in Pune. The matches were to clash with the Duleep Trophy final, for which the West Zone squad was to be picked all over again. So there was a possibility of his being picked. But then, he would not have made it to the playing XI of the West Zone in any case. Hence, it was better that he went to Pune and played, rather than sit on the bench.' – Madhav Mantri

If Sunil was irritated with the zonal selectors, he certainly showed it in his contemptuous treatment of the opposition bowlers in the inter-university matches in Pune. He scored 226, 99 and 124 in the first, second and fourth matches respectively. In the third game against South Gujarat University, he batted for six hours to amass 327, inclusive of 54 fours and one six. It was the highest individual score and the fourth triple hundred in the inter-university tournament. K. Nagabhushan of Bangalore had scored 314 against Ceylon in 1965, and Amrik Singh of Punjab had got 300 against BITS, Pilani in 1968. The previous record-holder was Ajit Wadekar, for his 324 against Delhi in 1958.

Sunil's innings impacted several observers.

He plundered runs with such a wide array of strokes that there were times when the fielders stopped chasing the ball. But it was his drive that stood out. He timed it to a nicety and could seemingly direct it anywhere except past the wicketkeeper. – *TOI*, 5 January 1971

> 38 overnight, he raced from 132 at lunch to 258 by tea and reached his goal before close – 286 in a single day . . . He never asked for a glass of water out of turn. Nor did he ever gasp for breath or lean on his back to gain a respite . . . I felt the law of averages might work against him in the final against Pune, but he scored 124! – Sunder Rajan, *TOI*, 3 May 1971

> 'He was in the 220s when I went in. By the time I got to 20, he had moved to 327.' – Sanjay Jaywant

Like Sunil, the national selectors began 1971 with a bang. They announced that Farookh Engineer and Rusi Surti, who were based in England and Australia respectively, would not be considered for the Caribbean tour, as they hadn't played domestic cricket in India in 1970-71. Surti had proved his versatility on the twin tours of Australia and New Zealand in 1969-70, and the Indians were not alone in considering Engineer the best wicketkeeper-batsman in the world. He had, after all, represented a World XI captained by Garry Sobers in a Test series against England in mid-1970.

> Their decision will not only reduce the strength of the side, but also impair its spectator-appeal. – Dicky Rutnagur, *TOI*, 15 December 1970

The selectors took an even bolder decision on 8 January 1971, when they met to pick the captain of the team.

> Tiger knew that three of the selectors were in his favour. But he did not know that one of them, Dutta Ray, would not be attending. Suitably, a couple of days before, a technical objection had been raised to prevent the Bengal official from doing so'
> – Rajan Bala, *All the Beautiful Boys*, Rupa (1990)

In Ray's absence, two of the selectors plumped for Pataudi's retention as captain, while the other two favoured Wadekar, the captain of Ranji Trophy Superpower Bombay. Merchant broke the 2-2 deadlock by exercising the chairman's prerogative of a casting vote. He plumped for Wadekar.

The new captain was among the last to know about his appointment. He and his wife Rekha returned home that evening after purchasing curtains for the new flat allotted to him by his employers, State Bank of India, and found a large crowd waiting for them.

The industrialist in Merchant came to the fore as he explained the move in terms of a reaction to declining production. In such a situation, he explained, he had no option but to sack the works manager.

The works manager's supporters were livid. They went so far as to suggest that Merchant had avenged his humiliation of 1946. Back then, Merchant had been the frontrunner for the captaincy of the Indian team for the tour of England, only to be outvoted by a backdoor entrant, Iftikar Ali Khan Pataudi, who had represented England in the Bodyline series and famously refused to field in Douglas Jardine's infamous leg-trap. Merchant never got to lead India in an official Test, and those who loved the Pataudis were convinced that the chairman of selectors had a long memory.

The proceedings on 13 January, when the captain and selectors met in Bombay to select the team, yielded more surprises. Venkataraghvan was appointed vice-captain, thus elevating the decision of the South Zone selectors before the Duleep Trophy to the status of a masterstroke. Wadekar wanted some experience to boost the side technically and tactically in a region where they had been annihilated 0-5 on their previous visit. His demand ran against the chairman's stated youth policy. However, Merchant agreed! The long and short of it was that Wadekar got in 1970-71 what Pataudi was denied a year previously.

The inclusion of the left-handed Salim Durani was the most unexpected, his consistency in the 1970-71 season notwithstanding. He was thirty-six and had not played a Test since 1966-67. Had he harnessed his prodigious talent better, Durani could have been India's answer to Sobers. His career from the late 1950s to the mid-1960s mirrored the travails of Indian cricket in that era—the odd burst of glory interspersed between spells of mediocrity. Jaisimha, the deposed South Zone captain, booked his ticket to the Caribbean with knocks of 175 against Central Zone and 131 against East in the Duleep Trophy.

For Dilip Sardesai, Wadekar's insistence on picking him to bolster the middle order was a refreshing departure from a troubled past. Ironically, his sound technique had gone against him, with the selectors of the 1960s touting and then treating him as a solution to India's opening woes. Scores of 200 and 106 at the top of the order against the Kiwis in 1964-65 apart, he hadn't done much of note. He had played only one Test in 1969-70, that too as opener, before being discarded.

Among the youngsters who made it were three players who had made their debuts in 1969-70 – Ashok Mankad, Eknath Solkar and G.R. Viswanath. They were joined by three Hyderabadis; opener Kenia Jayantilal, wicketkeeper-batsman Pochiah Krishnamurthy and new-ball bowler K. Govindraj. Also in the party was a twenty-one-year-old opener from Bombay.

Sunil spent most of 13 January in the company of Saeed Ahmed Hattea, Bombay's new-ball bowler. The latter had had a good season, and had been tipped by some to make it to the Indian team. Sunil on the other hand was hoping that the assessment of his near and dear ones after his omission from the West Zone side was spot-on. Keen to keep themselves abreast of the deliberations of the selectors, the duo did the rounds of the Bombay Cricket Association, and then tried to while their time away in a cinema hall. The film turned out to be uninteresting, and they walked out midway and decided to go home. In the train that they boarded at Churchgate station, Hattea was recognised by co-passengers, who assured him that he would be selected. About Sunil, they were not so sure.

At home in Dadar, Sunil played with his cousin, all the time wishing that the phone rang. It did, after what seemed an eternity. Ashok Mankad was the caller. What he said was exactly what Sunil and his near and dear ones wanted to hear.

Sunil's First-class record at that stage was far from marvellous – 811 runs from twelve matches. However, his three successive Ranji hundreds and heroics at Pune had tilted the scales in his favour. Merchant was impressed with, and could relate to the youngster's application and run-hunger. The chairman convinced his colleagues that Sunil had all the makings of a successful batsman.

Sunil Gavaskar, I expect to be the success of the tour. You can't open the morning paper these days without (news of) Gavaskar scoring – like Merchant and Hazare in their salad days. Gavaskar in his approach provides an object-lesson in the choice of balls to play and balls to leave alone. He is also a fine placer of the ball and a good judge of a run . . . I have no doubt that he has it in him with his youth, aptitude and application. . . . – Raju Bharatan, *Illustrated Weekly of India,* January 1971

There was one attribute the junior members of the squad had in common. They had grown up in an independent country and considered themselves second to none.

3

BRADMANESQUE BEGINNING

> I helped Ajit (Wadekar) untie his leg-guards when he returned to the pavilion after scoring 323 in a Ranji game. I guess that helped. He probably thought it would be good to have someone to untie his leg guards if he scored 300 in the West Indies! – Sunil Gavaskar, *Summer of '71* (PMG)

Sunil was thrilled to be picked for the Indian team, but wise enough not to get carried away. It was, after all, a team of seventeen, and full of talented cricketers at that. On the eve of the team's departure, his mother saw him pen down the most likely Test XI. He picked Mankad and Jayantilal as the openers. His reasoning was that both players were in form. 'Do not get upset if I do not get to play in the Tests,' he told her.

> 'He gave me Rs 10 before leaving for the Caribbean. My brief was to visit the Hanuman temple every Saturday, garland the statue of the deity, and pray on his behalf.' – Ashok Ambaye

His diffidence concerning the composition of the Test XI was not reflected in the determined approach that he displayed in the practice sessions prior to the team's departure. To prepare himself for the West Indian fast bowlers, he practised on a concrete strip behind the East Stand of the Brabourne stadium, with the Bombay medium-pacers bowling to him from a distance of eighteen yards.

> 'I always took the nets very seriously, and expected others to do the same. Sunil seemed very keen to bat and confront the bowlers. He showed tremendous application. You could see the latent talent, the determination, the focus. He studied every bowler and batted accordingly.' – E.A.S. Prasanna

Sunil was forced to take a break from batting practice when he developed a whitlow on the middle finger of his left hand. He then threw himself headlong into bowling and physical training. What he did not do was pay attention to the finger, believing that it would take care of itself. He was only twenty-one, after all! His nail-biting habit did not help matters. Merchant's description of him as a big-innings player during an interaction with the team just prior to its departure, alleviated his discomfort, but not for very long. The pain got so unbearable after the team's departure from Bombay that Keki Tarapore, the manager, had to take him to a hospital in New York, where the team was to spend a night. The pus was removed, even as the medical staff complimented the duo for their timing. A delay by even a few hours would have made the wound gangrenous.

The worst had been averted, but Sunil was ruled out for the first two matches of the tour. He had company in the form of Jayantilal and Viswanath, who had problems with their thumb (broken) and knee (twisted) respectively. Viswanath's inability to play in the tour-opener against Jamaica gave Sardesai an opportunity to break into the first XI, and he grabbed it with an innings of 97.

Sunil's first game of the tour was a one-dayer against a President's XI before the first Test at Kingston. He scored 71, replete with lofted off-side drives and 9 boundaries. But it did not win him a place in the Test XI. Jayantilal, who had recovered by then, was earmarked to make his debut. Another debutant was the wicketkeeper Pochiah Krishnamurthy, whose inclusion at Engineer's expense had raised eyebrows. On the tour, he endeared himself to his team-mates by keeping well on the field, and inadvertently voicing his concerns about his receding hairline, off it. That was the cue for his team-mates to proffer tips on arresting the same, all of which were unprintable.

The first day was rained off, and Sobers won the toss and opted to bowl on a damp strip. Sunil, watching from the dressing room, had already fallen in love with the Caribbean.

> The sense of humour of the West Indian spectators, including the women, the sense of fun that is there, the music that is so much a part of watching the cricket makes it more like a rocking party than watching a game of cricket. Every ground has its own special people who invariably make a grand entry and are greeted with loud applause as they walk in to take their seats. – Sunil Gavaskar, *Ind-WI Special Feature* (PMG, 2006)

Jayantilal was the first to perish, caught brilliantly by Sobers off Grayson Shillingford. Abid Ali, the other opener, fell a little later, and he was followed by Wadekar, Durani and Jaisimha. At 75-5, it was up to Sardesai to guide India to the realms of respectability. His endeavour was made easier by the doughtiness of his new partner. Eknath Solkar, the son of a groundsman at Bombay's P.J. Hindu Gymkhana, was no stranger to adversity. A rearguard stand followed. Unlike his senior partner, whose bat only seemed to have a middle, Solkar played and missed quite a few times, but hung on. The partnership was going strong when the ball lost its shape. Seeing Sobers standing next to the officials as they perused the replacement balls, Sardesai commanded Solkar to join them and neutralise any possible impact that the Windies captain could have on the choice. When a ball was finally chosen, Solkar demanded to see it. Sobers was not impressed. 'What's the point? You will play and miss anyway,' he said. Solkar looked the ultimate cricketer squarely in the eye and replied, 'You play your game, we will play our game!'

Solkar, born in 1946, had grown up in independent India after all.

The association realised 137 runs, and was followed by another productive one between Sardesai and Prasanna that yielded 122. Sardesai scored 212, the first double hundred by an Indian against the West Indies, and the Indians were delighted with their final total of 387. The West Indies batsmen were then humbled by Prasanna, Venkataraghvan and Bedi. The last five wickets tumbled for 15 runs, and the innings ended at 217.

A little over a day's play was left, which ruled out any possibility of an outright win for India. But Wadekar wasn't going to miss out on a chance to win psychological points. In their twenty-fourth Test against the Windies, India found themselves in an unprecedented situation. Their first-innings lead of 170 was 20 more than the minimum difference necessary to enforce the follow-on in what had become a four-day game.

> Sobers wasn't aware of the elementary follow-on rule ... He was clearly taken aback ... Umpire Sang Hue confirmed that the decision was in order ... This apparently left its mark on the entire series ... It boosted our morale. ... – Ajit Wadekar, *My Cricketing Years*, Vikas, 1973

Bedi and Venkataraghvan dismissed the West Indian openers cheaply, but the Kanhai-Sobers combine ensured a comfortable draw. However, there was no doubt that the hosts were rattled. Never had they expected a follow-on in a Test against India.

The three-dayer against Leeward Islands at St. Kitts was Sunil's first major game of the tour. With India's opening problems persisting, the management wanted him to click. Click he did, with knocks of 82 and an unbeaten 32 that sealed a 10-wicket win with 15 balls to spare. The second-innings cameo featured five boundaries and an uncharacteristic straight six. In the next three-dayer against Trinidad at Guaracara Park, he scored 125, his first First-class hundred of the tour, and 63. His hundred in the first innings thrilled the spectators and his team-mates, who wanted to catch up on their sleep after reaching the venue in the wee hours of the morning. Sunil and Mankad were instructed to bat as long as possible, so that the others could doze off. They obliged with an opening stand of 155.

> Gavaskar played an innings as lambent as the flame that spurts from the refinery chimneys here. He cut and drove and his feet twinkled. ... – K.N. Prabhu, *TOI*, 3 March 1971

One of the bowlers Sunil encountered during the course of those two innings against Trinidad was Jack Noreiga, the thirty-five-year-old off-spinner, who had made his Test debut at Kingston on the strength of his successes for Trinidad in the inter-island competition. The pitch at the Queen's Park Oval in Port of Spain, the venue of the second Test, was expected to suit the local hero. But the Indians were not complaining.

For them, playing in Trinidad was almost like playing at home, thanks to the hospitality of the residents, whose forefathers had migrated to Trinidad and Guyana decades ago to work in the sugar plantations. When they saw the wicket, the visitors got the impression that the Queen's Park Oval groundstaff wanted to be as hospitable. The strip was reminiscent of the brown, slow and low wickets on which they had played all their lives. But the Indian captain was unsure of how it would behave in the initial stages. For once, he prayed that his legendary ill-luck with the toss continued.

The Indians were delighted when the West Indies selectors retained the 'manageable' Noreiga and ignored Lance Gibbs, then the most successful spinner in Test cricket. Gibbs, the Indians reckoned, would have been harder to handle on that strip. For Wadekar and his men, Noreiga's retention marked the successful culmination of a ploy to make heavy weather of his bowling in the three-day game, and thereby give the impression that they were having problems against him.

Sunil's 125 and 63 in the three-dayer won him several admirers and a trophy from the local cricket council. His place in the Test XI was also confirmed.

> When I was told by Ajit that I was playing, I was in the heavens. My real ambition has been to not only play for my country, but to play successfully. Only after I stepped on to the field for my Test debut did I wear the cap allotted to me for the tour. – Sunil Gavaskar, *The Record-breaking Sunil Gavaskar*, C.D. Clarke (1980, David and Charles)

His achievements, talent and the prayers of his near and dear ones had taken him as far as they could, from the Bhagirathi buildings on one side of the globe to the Queen's Park Oval on another. The ball, or rather, the bat, was now in the twenty-one-year-old's court.

Much to Wadekar's relief, Sobers won the toss and elected to bat. Contrary to popular perception, India's new-ball bowlers Abid Ali and Solkar were anything but the shine-removers they had been branded as.

Solkar's best moment as a new-ball bowler was yet to come, but Abid had already distinguished himself with a six-wicket haul on his Test debut against Australia at Adelaide in 1967-68.

Roy Fredericks, the West Indies opener, was mortified to receive a delivery that bounced and did not rise. The ball hit his toe, and then the stumps. One ball into the game, and the West Indies were 0-1. Abid reacted as he always did after taking a wicket. He returned to the top of his bowling mark, with ten team-mates in hot pursuit.

The second-wicket pair of Steve Camacho and Rohan Kanhai restored normalcy before the spinners struck. Another collapse followed, and the innings ended at a measly 214, Prasanna inflicting the maximum damage with four wickets. India's reply was commenced by the ex-St. Xavierites.

> My only aim was to not make a fool of myself. – Sunil Gavaskar,
> *A Tribute to 50 Glorious Years* (PMG, 1999)

Sunil was understandably nervous, and keen to get off the mark. The umpires may have been surprised when the debutant, after crossing over to Mankad's end, grounded his bat in his partner's guard, instead of taking a fresh one. One of the umpires stayed surprised long enough to overlook a deflection off the pads that gave Sunil his first Test runs. The tension had just started to dissipate when Vanburn Holder got a short ball to seam away after pitching. Sunil, who had committed himself to a back-foot drive, nicked it.

The only thing Garfield St. Auburn Sobers could not do on a cricket field was keep wicket to his own bowling. The low outside-edge offered by Sunil was one that he would have pouched with his eyes closed. But he spilt it! Unlike Jayantilal in the previous Test, Sunil had luck on his side. It was now up to him to capitalise on it.

The arrival of Sardesai at the crease after the dismissals of Mankad (44) and Durani (9) gave Sunil the option of dropping anchor. Sardesai dominated a stand of 96, which ended with Sunil pulling Noreiga to Clive Lloyd at square-leg. In his first Test innings, he had scored 65.

Sunil's euphoria at making a fine beginning to his Test career, as also the strong position the Indian team was in at stumps on the second day (247-4, Sardesai 83*[not out]), was evident at a dinner hosted by

Trinidad Prime Minister, Dr Eric Williams that evening. A steel band was performing, and it wasn't long before feet started moving.

> Sunil Gavaskar started conducting the band, although his timing was a little less perfect than what it was at the wicket. – Dicky Rutnagur, *The Indian Express*, 9 March 1971

Solkar essayed another effective innings, with Sardesai going on to score 112. The latter's insistence on staying in a hotel room whose digits totalled eight, his lucky number, was paying off. Salim Durani and he had stayed in room number fifty-three and room number 314 in Kingston and Port of Spain respectively.

India scored 352, thus taking a lead of 138. Noreiga took all the wickets but one, and his 9-95 is still the best performance by a West Indian bowler in Test cricket. He inspired a counterattack. Kanhai, who opened the batting, fell early, but Charlie Davis, promoted to number three, batted fluently along with Fredericks to secure a 12-run lead by the third day.

Neither side could have anticipated the events that unfolded on 10 March 1971[12], the scheduled fourth day of the game. It began with an incident that prompted Wadekar's critics to make him synonymous with the word 'lucky'. Fredericks essayed a full blooded drive in the nets, only to be mortified as the ball ricocheted off a pole to hit Davis, who was batting in the adjacent net, on the forehead. Davis had to be taken to hospital, and could not resume his innings. Fredericks' mood did not improve when he was run out after a misunderstanding with Lloyd. In came Sobers.

With two southpaws in the middle, the logical move for Wadekar was to recall Prasanna. But the offie was nursing a finger injury, sustained while attempting a return catch offered by Fredericks in the first innings, and hence was not available. It was then that Wadekar remembered the chat he had had that morning with Prasanna and Jaisimha, two of the four members of the Indian squad who had toured the Caribbean in 1961-62.

---

[12]10 March ought to be ranked alongside 25 June as a 'lucky day' for Indian cricket. It was on the same day in 1985 that India won the World Championship of Cricket in Australia.

On the night of 9 March 1971, Prasanna and Jaisimha, who were sharing a room, were visited by Salim Durani, who had also been on the 1961-62 tour, and was coincidentally rooming with Sardesai, the fourth member of the side to have been on that trip. Durani, one of the Indian spin-bowling heroes in the 1961-62 series against England, requested the duo to remind Wadekar that he was capable of being effective on the Queen's Park Oval wicket, which was by now infested with rough patches on and outside the left-handed batsman's off-stump.

Jaisimha and Prasanna passed on the message, and Wadekar was quick to spot the correlation between Durani's ability to hit the deck, and the rough patches. He threw the ball to Durani, and asked him to bowl his brand of left-arm spin.

Durani pitched one up to Sobers. The ball landed in the rough, rose sharply, turned viciously, evaded Sobers' bat and dislodged the bails. The ultimate cricketer had failed to open his account. Wadekar then stationed himself at short mid-wicket. As if on cue, Lloyd pulled Durani straight into the Indian captain's palms. Two of the most destructive batsmen of all time had fallen in quick succession, both to Durani. India scented victory.

Venkataraghvan completed what Durani had initiated. The vice-captain finished with figures of 5-95, and India needed only 124 to register their first ever win against the West Indies in the twenty-fifth Test between the two teams.

India's openers strode in, their intent being to finish it off on the fourth day itself. Seventy-four runs were scored before leg-spinner Arthur Barrett, who like Noreiga had made his debut in the preceding Test, dismissed Mankad and Durani. Sardesai's fall ten runs later prompted Wadekar to send in Abid Ali, with instructions to run quick singles and exasperate the opposition. In Sunil, Abid found a kindred soul. A flurry of singles and twos was complemented by a plethora of overthrows, and the hammering of the final nails in the West Indian coffin. A cover-drive off Holder and a hooked boundary off Shillingford were Sunil's best strokes of the innings. India were three runs short when he slapped Barrett to the mid-wicket boundary to complete a historic win. In the Indian dressing room, there was bedlam.

As many as eight Indians—Ranjitsinhji, Duleepsinhji and Pataudi Senior included—had scored a century on their Test debuts, but Sunil had outshone them all with his 65 and unbeaten 67 in a Test won by India on foreign soil!

In an age where corporate sponsorship of sport was not a universal phenomenon, fans back in India were pleasantly surprised to read in the papers that Wadekar had received 500 East Caribbean dollars (Rs 1,800) as the winning captain, and Sunil had received 250 East Caribbean dollars as Barclay's Incentive Award (Rs 900) for his performance.

The centuries scored by Jayantilal and Jaisimha in the four-dayer against Guyana, an encounter for which Sunil and Sardesai were rested, meant that Wadekar had an embarrassment of batting riches to choose from for the subsequent Tests. The enthusiasm of the players after the victory at Port of Spain was overwhelming enough for minor discomforts to be overlooked.

> 'The clothes that the BCCI had given us began to shrink after the first wash. So in the middle of the tour, I was wearing Salim Durani's trousers ... and Vishy was wearing mine!' – Sunil Gavaskar, *Summer of '71* (PMG)

If at all there was any possibility of recent successes going to Sunil's head, his new roomie, a man as old and tall as he, was determined to obliterate it. Gundappa Viswanath had finally recovered from his knee injury and was fit to play. Sunil, the junior among the two, did all the dirty work, like leaving his bed to open the door if the bell rang at an unearthly hour. He was mystified by his partner's daily request to room service for coffee at 7.00 am. The problem wasn't as much getting up to open the door and let the bearer in, as it was the fact that Viswanath would continue to sleep. He would consume it only an hour later. Sunil watched the charade for a few days, after which he protested and insisted that his partner order coffee at 8.00 am. However, Viswanath had the last word, 'I like cold coffee!'

Their joint visits to the hospital in the first half of the tour, and attempts to rag each other in the second, marked the beginning of a lifelong friendship. They also bonded with another talented youngster. The left-handed Alvin Kallicharran, a compatriot and disciple of Rohan Kanhai's, was inconsolable when he fell cheaply in the game between the Board President's XI and the Indians. He thought that he had blown his chances of playing for the West Indies. His spirits were restored by Viswanath, who at that stage had played four Tests, and by Sunil, who had played none. Speaking like seasoned campaigners, they exhorted him not to give up!

Sobers won the toss for the third time in the Test series at Georgetown, Guyana, and the Windies scored 363. India got off to another bright start. Sunil again had a reason to be grateful to Sobers, who dropped him in the slips off Holder. Mankad contributed 40 to a stand of 78 before being bowled by Noreiga. Sunil carried on in Wadekar's company till stumps on the second day.

Forty-eight overnight, he reached his third consecutive Test fifty with a glanced two off Gibbs, who had finally been picked. Wadekar fell early in the face of some hostile bowling, but Viswanath, who had replaced Prasanna in the XI, batted fluently. On a day marked by three interruptions due to rain, Sunil did not allow the frequent trips to and from the pavilion to affect his composure. In fact, he made watchers marvel at the manner in which he paced his innings. He dropped anchor in the morning session when the spinners were getting some purchase from the wicket, and went for his strokes when it turned placid in the afternoon.

He batted himself into the 90s, even as the darkened skies made another interruption imminent. Viswanath did his best to give him the strike for the best part of six overs, before the umpires called a halt. He was on 98 at the time. He had cocooned himself from the rest of the world, and wasn't thinking about factors that were beyond his control, like another life that had been granted to him by Sobers when he was on 94. This time, Sobers was at short square-leg when a Noreiga delivery rose higher than Sunil had imagined. Sobers moved to his left in anticipation of a chance, but the ball took the glove and landed in the region where the Windies captain had been standing originally.

The big moment came soon after the resumption. The Georgetown crowd, which like the one at Port of Spain, comprised several people of Indian origin, gave him a tumultuous ovation. As he raised his bat to acknowledge their cheers, as also those of his team-mates, Sunil remembered his parents, childhood and college friends, and of course, the Bhagirathi alley, where it had all begun. It was one of those special moments wherein his entire life flashed across his eyes.

He had reached 116 when Sobers induced him to nick in the slips. Carew all but dropped the catch before hanging on. India gained a slim lead of 13.

The West Indies crossed 100 for the loss of only one wicket, but local heroes Kanhai and Lloyd then fell within a few runs of each other. Sobers came in at 137-3 to a mixed reception. The ambivalence of the spectators was a consequence of his lackadaisical form in the series till that point, and his recent trip to Rhodesia[13], a land that at the time endorsed the 'whites-are-superior' perception of its neighbour South Africa. While Sobers' Barbadian compatriots were understandably guarded in their criticism, the Guyanese had gone hammer-and-tongs at him, with Forbes Burnham, the prime minister, even threatening to advise India, a champion of the anti-apartheid movement, not to send a team unless Sobers apologised.

Sobers put the matter to rest with a statement denouncing apartheid and emphasising that his team's interests were paramount. But the Guyanese, who had always been unhappy about Sobers being accorded more importance than their compatriot Kanhai, were still reluctant to forgive and forget.

With his team one-down in the series and ahead by only 124 runs, it was imperative for Sobers to deliver. He was aware of this, and had made it a point to touch Sunil, whom he had dropped thrice in the series, for good luck. However, Durani, for the second time, played spoilsport – almost. Sobers edged him onto his pads, and the ball flew to Sardesai at bat-pad. The Indians were ecstatic, but to their horror, the umpire made no signal.

> I have no problems with a batsman being reprieved by an umpire, for that is part of the game . . . However, it does bother me that the batsman in question continues to call himself a "walker".'
> – Late Dilip Sardesai, *A Memorable Tour* (PMG Special feature, May 2006)

Sobers went on to score a hundred, as did Davis. A declaration then gave India ninety minutes in which to score 295. They had no option but to

---

[13]Zimbabwe

play for a draw, and the St. Xavierites batted well to add an undefeated 123. Sunil's 64 meant that he had scored 312 runs in his first four Test innings.

> Gavaskar has become a household name in the West Indies. The lad takes his task seriously and yet, brings to it the fire, passion and adventure of youth. The drives in Shillingford's opening over were strokes of stunning power. It must certainly be a long time since any West Indian paceman suffered the mortification of being driven to the straight field. There can not be a more galling experience. – K.N. Prabhu, *TOI*, 24 March 1971 (filed)

> 'Opening with him was a great experience. He was so calm and collected that he made you stress-free. He was a brilliant judge of a run and keen to respond, especially for the first run. His defence was great. It was a pleasure watching him leave the ball. He played off his legs brilliantly. His concentration was so fierce that he was almost in a trance. He would look through me if I said something between overs. He would go into silent mode half an hour before the start and would not talk to anybody. He mastered the art of concentration and put it into practice.'
> – Late Ashok Mankad

The Georgetown Test was followed by a significant political event. It was on 25 March 1971, hours after the completion of the game, that the government of West Pakistan ordered its representatives in its Eastern wing, situated on the other side of the Indian peninsula, to act tough with the restless local populace. Sheikh Mujibur Rahman, an East Pakistani whose Awami League had won a majority in the 1970 general elections and hence ought to have been named prime minister of all Pakistan, was arrested, and his fellow East Pakistanis were subjected to a genocide that would have done Adolf Hitler proud. It resulted in an influx of thousands of East Pakistani refugees into India. In the months that followed, the Prime Minister of India made several unsuccessful attempts to draw the attention of the international community to the strain the migration was putting on India. Eventually, Mrs Indira Gandhi decided to take the bull by the horns.

Her disregard of the risks associated with a proactive stance, especially the possibility of the US and China throwing in their lot with Pakistan, wasn't quite in tune with India's conservative image.

Like her, the men representing India in cricket were eager to smash the subservient status imposed upon them by the rest of the cricketing world.

They encountered their first major hiccup of the Caribbean tour against Barbados, the best team in the Caribbean. A bowling attack that included the veteran Wesley Hall shot them out for 185 on a bouncy track. Sunil was run out for zero. Sobers then led from the front with 135, and despite some decent performances in the second innings, including 67 by Sunil, the hosts won by 9 wickets. The wicket for the Test match, the fourth of the series, was equally lively, and the Indians knew what they were up against.

On April Fools' Day, his thirtieth birthday, Wadekar won the toss and elected to field. It was more a defensive ploy than an attacking one, for the obvious idea was to deny the West Indian quickies first use of the wicket. It wasn't the best pitch on which to bowl spin, and the spinners struggled for the first time in the series. Sobers declared at 501-5, and India commenced their reply in fading light on the second evening. Sunil was livid when the umpire ignored his appeal against the light. His state of mind did not improve when Uton Dowe, who was bowling at the time, gave him a glare. What followed was an ungainly hook, which was accepted by Vanburn Holder at mid-wicket. Ironically, the umpire upheld another appeal made by Krishnamurthy, who came in as nightwatchman, moments later. It indicated that Sunil would have had his way had he been patient.

In a letter that he wrote to his parents that night, he swore not to let himself and his team down in such a fashion. 'Henceforth, I will only show my back to the bowler,' he wrote.

But Sunil's new found resolve did not quite rub off on his team-mates. They were reduced to 70-6 on the third morning, and it appeared that only 14 wickets stood between the West Indies and a series-levelling victory. But the hosts had to first dismiss Sardesai and Solkar.

In an encore of Kingston, the duo rescued India with a partnership of 186. The Indian players watched in amazement as Dilip Sardesai beat

Sobers in a battle of wits. When Inshan Ali came on to bowl his googlies, Sardesai pretended to not decipher the bowler, and instructed Solkar to do likewise. The longer Ali bowled, the better it was for them. They kept up the charade, and even the odd boundary failed to alert Sobers to the plot. The batsmen were also helped by the inability of the fast bowlers to make the second new ball count. Still, India were 17 short of avoiding the follow-on when the ninth wicket fell. But Bedi, the last man in, was missed twice. He added a record 62 with Sardesai, who was last out for a brilliant 150. The West Indies then went for broke in their second innings and set India a target of 335 to be achieved in five hours.

There was no way India would go for the target, and therein lay the danger of coming undone due to a defensive mindset. However, the visitors were inspired by Mankad's riposte to a Dowe bouncer that struck him on the left arm and broke it. He soldiered on, consuming invaluable time in the process. Wadekar and Viswanath fell soon after lunch, but Sunil was not ruffled. On a spiteful fifth-day wicket, against bowlers who were going flat out, he essayed a gem. India were 138-4 at tea, of which his share was 73. With Sardesai at the other end, the shutters had been put down for good. At stumps, Sunil returned undefeated on 117. He had proved his mettle on one of the fastest strips in the world.

> Sobers tried every trick in the book to unsettle Gavaskar. He tried every ruse and tactic, including the psychological one of using the heavy roller. – K.N. Prabhu, *TOI*, 6 April 1971 (filed)

The visitors were delighted to return to the Queen's Park Oval for the fifth Test. All they needed was a draw to win the series, but with Sobers having struck form, they could not relax.

Kenia Jayantilal fancied his chances of selection in the injured Mankad's place. The Hyderabad opener had scored 40, 76 and 65 in the previous two three-day games. However, the team management opted to persist with Jaisimha in the middle order, despite his lack of form. His strategic acumen, which Wadekar valued highly, might well have had something to do with it. Prasanna, who had not played since his finger injury in the second Test, was brought back, and Abid Ali asked to open.

At the end of a strenuous practice session, Sunil requested Mankad, who was performing the drinks-bearer's job, to pour a pitcher of chilled water straight down his parched throat. The outcome was that a small piece of ice got lodged in a tooth cavity.

He was destined to start and end his first Test tour in pain.

An individual who wanted to alter destiny was the Indian captain. Wadekar had been happy to lose the toss on the morning of the second Test at the same venue. But on the first morning of the fifth Test, he wanted to call correctly and bat first on a pitch that looked a lot healthier from a batsman's perspective than its second Test counterpart. In accordance with the prevalent custom, the game was to be a six-day affair, as it was the last Test and the series was still undecided. Wadekar chose to call tails instead of his regular heads, and won! Sobers wasn't very attentive, having presumed that his opposite number would call heads as always. It took him a while to realise what had happened.

His tooth was throbbing, but Sunil stopped thinking about it the moment he left the confines of the dressing room. Sobers dismissed Abid Ali early, but he could make no impact on the other opener.

Sunil warmed up with a hook off Dowe that flew past Noreiga at mid-wicket to the boundary. He then dispatched the same bowler past gully for another four. Sobers tried to entice him with a line just outside off-stump, but the youngster did not bite the bait. He preferred to wait, and was rewarded when Sobers overpitched. Sunil cover-drove him for four, and meted out the same treatment to a full toss a little later.

Sobers had not had much success against Sunil as bowler and fielder, but the latter's team-mates were not as lucky. The Windies captain dived to take a catch offered by Wadekar. The two skippers all but left the field together, as the ball got jammed between the turf and Sobers' diaphragm. The Windies captain was in pain, but pulled along till the lunch interval. Joey Carew deputised for him after the interval. Sardesai and Sunil added 122 for the third wicket. As Sunil neared his third hundred of the series, Carew tried rotating the bowlers to unsettle him, but to no avail. The crowds exploded when Sunil reached three figures for the third time in the series.

The West Indies hit back with three strikes in the space of nine runs, and India were in a tight spot at 247-6, with Sardesai and Solkar back in the pavilion. The second new ball was relatively new, and it was imperative that Sunil stayed in.

He took it upon himself to protect the tail, which commenced with his vice-captain.

Palmistry was one of Venkataraghvan's interests. He had read Sunil's palm earlier on the tour and predicted success. Therefore, it was not surprising that Sunil's respect for him had grown manifold by the time the fifth Test got underway!

Sunil assumed that he would be allowed to dominate the strike. But he had reckoned without his vice-captain's temper. Venkat, utterly unimpressed with his junior's refusal to run singles, let it rip, 'When I say run, RUN!'

As it turned out, Venkat outlasted Sunil. The opener fell for 124 and the vice-captain carried on and got 51. He then strode into the dressing room, towards Sunil and let fly, 'Do you think only you can bat?'

The verbal rocket did take Sunil's mind off his tooth ache, which by now had affected his eating and sleeping. Keki Tarapore, the manager of the team, had already refused to let him visit the dentist during the game, lest the extraction make him drowsy. In the circumstances, Sunil had two options. He could crib and lose his composure. Alternately, he could remember the story of Lord Dhruva and his powers of concentration. He chose the latter.

A combination of good batting, particularly by Sobers who scored his third hundred of the series, some generous umpiring, and ordinary fielding enabled the Windies to reach 526. The innings, having ended with about two hours left on the fourth day, the hosts were well-placed to level the series. India's priority was to bat as long as possible. Sobers dismissed Abid Ali with only 11 on the board, but his joy vanished once it became apparent that Wadekar had returned to form. And then, there was Sunil Gavaskar.

Sunil was helped along the way by Shepherd, who spilt him in the slips. The inevitable then happened, with Sobers failing to latch onto a streaky stroke off leg-spinner David Holford. Sunil reached his 50 in just over an hour, the strokes that stood out being a hook off Vanburn Holder and a drive off Dowe that went like a bullet between Maurice Foster at cover and Lloyd at mid-off. The Bombay duo batted into the fifth morning. When Wadekar fell for 54, India were only 7 runs behind.

Sunil entered the 80s and crept closer to the 90s with two hooks off Holford. It was appropriate that Sardesai, the man who had initiated India's golden run, was in the middle when Sunil completed his second hundred of the game. He had already become the fourth batsman after Patsy Hendren, Everton Weekes and Clyde Walcott to score 1,000 runs in a single cricket season in the Caribbean.

> He possessed the patience and run-hunger that he displayed in the West Indies since his school days. I remember him taking a fresh guard after completing a hundred in the West Indies. He was preparing himself to go for another hundred. – Dilip Sardesai, *The Boy From Chikalwadi* (PMG, 1999)

India were 28 ahead when Sardesai fell for 75. Viswanath then put on 99 with his room-mate before being bowled by Sobers. At stumps on day five, India were 324-4 with Sunil undefeated on 180. More than the imminent double hundred, he was excited at the prospect of visiting the dentist in less than twenty-four hours' time. The pain had taken a lot out of him, but only off the field.

Much like Sardesai's presence when he completed his hundred, the proximity of Jaisimha as Sunil crept closer to his double hundred was wonderfully appropriate. It was almost as if Sunil had willed his idol to be twenty-two yards away when he completed his double hundred, for Jaisimha led a charmed life. He gave three catches on the fifth morning, all of which were muffed. Sunil spent half an hour in the 190s and then took a boundary off Sobers to post the 50 of the partnership. A cover-driven boundary off Dowe brought him to the landmark and sparked off a spectator raid. Sunil was mobbed, swarmed with garlands and lifted off the ground.

> 'He was destined for greatness. He had a lot of time to play his strokes, and his patience was second to none.' – Clive Lloyd

> 'Sunil was fortunate to be dropped a few times, but he was good enough to capitalise and play some long innings. He fatigued the West Indian attack. Once he got set, the bowlers couldn't beat him. He made them feel hopeless. Sunil was instrumental in our saving the Test series, whereas Sardesai won it.' – Late Ashok Mankad

It was around 10 pm IST when Prof Chandgadkar, the BCCI secretary, conveyed the news to a speechless Manohar Gavaskar.

> Normally one would be nervous while making one's debut overseas. But he adapted like a senior pro. Some of us could have learnt from him. – M.L. Jaisimha, *A Tribute to 50 Glorious Years* (PMG, 1999)

Another hook off Holford stretched India's lead to 202. The next ball was magnificently straight-driven for another boundary. Clearly, Sunil's appetite was far from satiated, the five hundred minutes he had spent in the middle notwithstanding. But Shepherd produced the breakthrough, inducing him to play on.

Sunil returned to the pavilion with 774 runs from four Tests, inclusive of one double hundred, three hundreds and three fifties, at an average of 154.80. His sequence of scores read—65 and 67*, 116 and 64*, 1 and 117*, and 124 and 220. The last two scores made him the second batsman after Australian Doug Walters to score a century and a double century in the same Test. His aggregate of 774 was the highest by a batsman in his debut series, beating West Indian George Headley's 703 against England in 1929-30. His series average of 154.80 was second only to Bradman's 201.50 against South Africa in 1931-32. He finished the tour with 1,240 runs at an average of 95.38.

In the dressing room, Tarapore gave Sunil a hug. 'It was the best compliment I could have received from an individual who was more British than the British themselves, and known for keeping his emotions very much to himself,' Sunil would recall years later.

> He showed the purposeful, dedicated approach of a champion to sustain India's morale in the final Test. From Sardesai, Gavaskar learnt the most paying stroke—the dropping of the wrist to avoid the outgoing ball . . . when he lands in Bombay, there should be happy holidays for the faculty of economics at St. Xavier's, who could study the many runs he has accumulated in this series.
> – K.N. Prabhu, *TOI*, 21 April 1971

'He succeeded because he wasn't overawed by his opponents. He had immense confidence in his abilities. He handled pace very well despite hardly having played it in his formative years. Frankly, he knew how good he was even at that stage of his career.' – E.A.S. Prasanna

The West Indies were further frustrated by the lower order and a brief shower, which left them with 155 minutes in which to score 262. On a fifth-day wicket against India's spinners, it was an impossible task. But they went for it. Lloyd, promoted to number three, got things moving. Abid Ali then pegged them back by dismissing Kanhai and Sobers off successive deliveries. For Wadekar, Sobers' dismissal was a huge relief. He was convinced that his counterpart had begun his golden run only because he had touched Sunil at Georgetown.

> On the crucial last day of the last Test, Ajit locked me up in the toilet when Sir Garfield came over to make his customary greeting to the Indian team. And guess what! Sir Garfield was out first ball for a duck. – Sunil Gavaskar, *Mid-Day*, 25 February 2007

Foster assisted Lloyd in adding 51, but his run out, and Solkar's dismissal of Holford a few runs later, left the hosts with no option but to bat out time. Venkataraghvan snared two more batsmen, including Lloyd, but the hosts hung on. The score was 165-8 when the umpires called time for the last time in the series. Ajit Wadekar and his team had done it!

Sobers had started regarding Sunil as his lucky charm, although the latter was convinced that it was the other way round. The superman commented favourably on Sunil's proficiency at essaying the hook, one of cricket's riskiest strokes, and advised him to persist with it on the tour of England. His words of encouragement, as also Kanhai's, capped what had been one of the most outstanding debuts in Test history.

> Rohan Kanhai occasionally grunted his disapproval from first slip if I played a loose shot. It wasn't that these great cricketers did not want their team to win. It was just the fact that they had supreme confidence in their own ability and believed that helping an opponent only produced good cricket and was good for the game. – Sunil Gavaskar, Colin Cowdrey Spirit of Cricket Lecture (MCC, 2003)

It was a different era, that. The West Indian stalwarts were not alone in their attempts to encourage a talented youngster. His seniors had been a source of support, not only to him, but to all the junior members of the squad. Previous Indian squads had been notorious for the generation gap that existed between the green-horns and grey-heads, but this side was different.

Wadekar had declared at the start of the tour that the door of his room would always be open, should any member have anything to discuss. In Jamaica, Sardesai even took on a fan for making some disparaging remarks about Sunil. The rooms that Jaisimha and Prasanna shared witnessed many a discussion on the sport, and life. At least three junior players—Sunil, Viswanath and Solkar—made it their daily destination every evening.

Sunil was overwhelmed when Bishan Bedi announced that he had decided to christen his son (who was born during the final Test) 'Gavasinder Singh'.

> He had little or no practice against quick bowling at home, and yet he went to the West Indies and scored over 700 runs against fast bowlers! How did he manage this? I guess only he can tell us how he did so. I hope he does. – Kapil Dev at the BCCI's felicitation of the 1983 World Cup team, 22 June 2008

Fifteen thousand people congregated at the Bombay airport when the heroes landed early on 26 April 1971. Wadekar and Sunil were requested to stand on a table outside the customs enclosure, so that everyone could see them. The fireworks commenced after Sunil displayed the trophy presented to him by the Trinidad Cricket Council.

After the fireworks came the felicitations. The Bombay Cricket Association felicitated Sunil along with the Ranji Trophy side, which had won the title for the twelfth season in a row despite the absence of five stalwarts who were in the Caribbean. Sunil was named Bombay's Senior Cricketer of the Year and awarded the Justice Tendolkar trophy.

There were celebrations in the Bhagirathi buildings and in the Dadar apartment blocks where the Gavaskars resided.

'I went to meet Sunil after his return from the Caribbean. We spent the night discussing the tour. The phone rang in the morning and I answered it. It was from Mrs Gandhi's office. She spoke to him for about five minutes.' – Navin Ambulkar

His parents, friends, team-mates and new-found fans could only wish that the debut series was only the beginning of a long innings.

'Though it might sound outrageous, one cannot resist the temptation to say that there is a Bradman-like streak in this 21 year-old... He has picked up his way by watching others and reading books, through tips gathered from the regular postmortem on the game at Dadar Union, and above all, by processing all the data and available evidence through his analytical mind.' – Sunder Rajan, *TOI*, 2 May 1971

4
THE ANGLO-AUSTRALIAN EXPERIENCE

Sunil Gavaskar is a new star on the horizon and some sweaty days are predicted for bowlers . . . his virtues are age-old ones that have separated ordinary mortals from exceptional performers. He is perfectly balanced with no irritating mannerisms. No touching of pad and curling of bat. He looks down at his crease a couple of times whilst the bowler walks back and sets himself up comfortably with the minimum of fuss . . . his first inclination is to play back, but he is always in line (of the ball) with a still head and a straight back . . . he plays the ball very late and gives himself that vital extra yard to make up his mind. . . . – J.J. Warr, *Free Press Journal*, 8 August 1971 (filed)

Sunil had his first brush with controversy immediately after his return from the Caribbean. The *TOI* announced on 25 April 1971, a day before the team returned, that it was setting up a fund for him. The paper itself made a contribution of Rs 1,001 and invited readers to contribute a minimum of Rs 5. It had done something similar for the West Indian Everton Weekes after his prodigious run-scoring in India in 1948-49.

The response to the Gavaskar Fund was tremendous. But there were dissenters, one of them being Vijay Merchant himself. The chairman was of the view that if people desired a fund of this sort, then the entire team ought to have been the beneficiary, instead of just one person. He expressed himself in a letter that appeared in the *TOI* on 1 May 1971. 'Such a fund would have much more support from industrial houses, sportsmen who understand the game and teamwork, and from sporting institutions who may in the present case feel that Sardesai's magnificent performances are being forgotten.'

Merchant had a point, but so did those who did not agree with him. Two days before Merchant's letter appeared, the paper itself explained its stance: 'This team spirit business can be carried too far. For instance, if a player gets a lucrative contract, should he decline it until all the other members of the team are provided with equally good offers?'

Amidst the flurry of funds and felicitations, Sunil joined Associated Cement Companies as a junior executive. Among his colleagues was Madhav Mantri, and a left-handed all-rounder from Gujarat.

> 'We were in the same department – Industrial Relations. We had an excellent team at the ACC, which comprised stars like Polly Umrigar, Bapu Nadkarni and Dilip Sardesai. Sunil and I represented the ACC in local and outstation tournaments like the Moin-ud-Dowlah in Hyderabad and the Buchi Babu in Madras. Not only did we become good friends as time progressed, but we also teamed up in the interdepartmental table tennis tournaments. We fared quite well, reaching the semi-finals and final on a few occasions.' – Karsan Ghavri

With a tour of England on the anvil, Sunil resumed his sessions at Dadar Union. He may have scored 774 runs in his first four Tests, but as far as he was concerned, something was amiss.

> 'I first saw him after his return from the West Indies at the Dadar Union nets. I had just joined the club then. Everybody was convinced that he was God's gift to Indian cricket, but he didn't seem all that satisfied. Apparently, he had had problems facing away-going deliveries pitched on the off-stump in the Caribbean,

and was aiming to iron them out by batting against V.S. Patil, Urmikant Mody, Jitendra Bhuta and the other DU bowlers. I would not have known this had he not mentioned this to Patil. He looked extremely focused. As the days progressed, we got to know him better. The youngsters were in awe of him, although he went out of his way to interact with us. He would narrate anecdotes after practice was over. There used to be several onlookers around the DU nets those days, but he was never distracted. My first impression of him was that he was a genial individual. He had a sense of humour, and was a good mimic. His impersonations of his India team-mates were side-splitting.' – Suru Nayak

'The build-up in his discipline, the prowess of spending hours at the wicket, the concentration, the patience, and the ease with which he played pace and swing, and most importantly, the ability to leave the right ball, were all honed at Dadar Union.'
– Dr Vishwas Raut

The rave reviews continued to appear. Ray Robinson, the doyen of Australian cricket writers, did not conceal his compatriots' curiosity in the *Times Weekly* (23 May 1971): 'When will the Australians see Gavaskar? I hope the answer will not be as long as India, West Indies, South Africa, New Zealand and Pakistan had to wait to see Bradman bat. That would be another way to say 'never'.

It was one thing for Sunder Rajan, an Indian, to liken Sunil to the Don, and another for an Australian to do the same.

'If in Britain, he adds more lustre to his name,' Robinson wrote, 'I can picture the wireless office in Bombay almost choked with requests from other countries.'

Whether the Indian team would add lustre to its name in England, nobody knew. India had lost fifteen of the nineteen Tests on English soil, the last eight of those in succession – five in 1959 and three in 1967. Ironically, the players in 1932, 1936 and 1946 had performed far more creditably than their post-Independence successors in 1952, 1959 and 1967. A quarter of a century after vice-captaining what was considered the best ever Indian team to have toured England, Merchant joined his fellow selectors to try and pick an even better squad.

Jaisimha and Durani were axed for their poor form in the Caribbean, and Abbas Ali Baig, one of India's saving graces on the '59 tour, recalled. The selectors sensibly took Farookh Engineer's experience of English conditions into account. But there was a rider; Lancashire, his County, would release him only for the three Tests. That necessitated the selection of two keepers. Krishnamurthy kept his place, and he was joined by a Bangalorean named Syed Muijtaba Hussain Kirmani. The last spot in the team went to a player who like Engineer had missed the Caribbean tour. Bhagwat Chandrasekhar was happy to be picked, but unhappy to hear Merchant's description of him as a 'calculated gamble'.

Chandra was a true hero, a conqueror of adversity. Polio in early childhood had weakened his right arm and rendered it impossible for him to keep it raised for a prolonged period of time, but he was not going to allow that to deter his pursuit of cricket. He evolved a bowling action wherein his right arm completed a revolution at breakneck speed. Unlike conventional leg-spinners, Chandra used the leg-break as a shock option rather than a stock one, and relied on a combination of googlies and top-spinners, and an ability to extract bounce from the deadest of wickets. An integral part of the national side from 1963-64 onwards, things had gone downhill for him after he sustained an injury in Australia in 1967-68 and was sent back. A scooter accident in early 1970s had nearly decapitated him. But he had fought his way back.

Joining Wadekar and Venkataraghvan at the helm was Col Hemachandra Adhikari, who had represented India in the 1950s and captained in the last Test played by India before the 1959 tour of England. He ought to have led India on that tour, but such were the vagaries of Indian cricket in those days that he was omitted from the team altogether.

Adhikari's unremitting approach and military background made him the ideal guardian of a side, whose biggest potential enemy was complacency. His words to the players at the start of the tour left them nonplussed, 'I am not going to treat you like schoolboys. You know the responsibility of representing your country. So there will be no curfews... but I would like you to be back by 10 pm!'

The BCCI left no stone unturned to encourage the players. Prof Chandgadkar, then the honorary secretary, promised a red carpet welcome in the event of a victory, and the departure of the team from Bombay was delayed by two days on the advice of an astrologer. This individual had apparently predicted the victory in the Caribbean, so there was no way his diktat could be ignored.

The confidence they had gained in the Caribbean, coupled with the fact that they were touring in the relatively warmer and drier second half of the English summer, helped the Indian spinners get a grip on things, figuratively and literally. Fortunate they certainly were, but they were good enough to capitalise on that fortune, as four consecutive victories in the three-day games preceding the first Test indicated. Sunil was consistent, with a top score of 165 against Leicestershire. As was only to be expected after his debut series, a lot of people looked up to him for more.

> Inevitably he has been saddled, as were George Headley and Norman O'Neill, with the title of "Another Bradman". Granted that there is a variant – "The Little Bombay Bradman" is the tag his fans have stuck on him ... When the Indians arrived in London, their manager commented wisely, 'If he is going to be a name in cricket, as I am sure he will, it will be as Gavaskar, not Bradman.' And Gavaskar permitted himself the luxury of saying 'I hope we get some quick wickets in the Tests. I'd love to break Bradman's record.' – Murray Hedgcock, *Australian*, 22 June 1971

The Test series began at Lord's on 22 July. The victory in the Caribbean notwithstanding, the Indians were the underdogs against an opponent that had not lost a Test match since 1968. Earlier that year, Raymond Illingworth had become only the second English captain after Douglas Jardine to regain the Ashes in Australia. The team-sheet he gave Wadekar on the morning of the Test included the names of Geoffrey Boycott and John Snow, the two chief sculptors of that triumph.

Sunil's excitement at playing at the Mecca of Cricket had subsided well before the Test. He had opened in what was India's first game of the tour, against Middlesex County. The slope of the ground—from the left of the pavilion to the right—and the snootiness of the groundstaff had irritated him. Not for the last time, as it turned out.

> ... everything about this ground is over-hyped and overrated.
> – Sunil Gavaskar, *The Sportstar*, 17 August 2002

Illingworth won the toss and elected to bat. Bedi, Chandrasekhar and Venkataraghvan took charge after Abid and Solkar had sent down the first few overs. The scoreboard read a precarious 71-5 when wicketkeeper-batsman Alan Knott joined his skipper to salvage the innings. Snow chipped in with an effective hand, and the innings ended on the second day at 304.

Snow dismissed Mankad cheaply, and greeted the Indian skipper with a bouncer. Wadekar picked it early and hooked it for four. He could not have possibly made a more emphatic statement of intent. The message was loud and clear: he and his players were not going to be intimidated by pace.

Wadekar went on to score 85. Sunil got only 4, but Sardesai, Viswanath (68), Engineer and Solkar all chipped in. India gained a first-innings lead of 9 runs, only the second time they had done so on English soil.

It was a welcome change since 1959. At Lord's twelve years earlier, England were 100-7 in response to India's 168. But they recovered to reach 226, which turned out to be a match-winning score.

> It was just the tail that we had to get rid of. But catches were deliberately dropped off the bowling of Subhash Gupte. There were some senior members who were horrified that we could take the lead against England. They thought this was blasphemy. . . .'
> – V. Muddiah, former India off-spinner, as quoted in *Casting A Spell – The Story of Karnataka Cricket*, Vedam Jaishankar (UBSPD, 2004)

In July 1971, another off-spinner rocked the English, and this time, the catches were taken. Venkataraghvan bagged four scalps, including 3-10 on the fifth morning. England totalled 191 in the second innings. India had four hours and twenty minutes in which to score 183 to win. The catch was that rain, a frequent visitor during the match, was expected at around the halfway mark.

In the break between innings, commentator Brian Johnston, who had seen more than one Indian team flounder on English soil, asked

Adhikari whether his players had considered the possibility of losing the game. 'No!' was the manager's instant reply. The Indians had decided to go for it.

Mankad failed again, and he was soon joined on the balcony by Wadekar, who mistimed a pull off Price. As he walked past his fellow Bombayite, Wadekar muttered something about not losing confidence. Not that he needed to say that to someone who had scored 774 runs in his first four Tests.

The race against time prompted the think-tank to promote Engineer. The all-rounder was on his way with a couple of drives off John Price.

Sunil allowed his senior partner to take charge. The duo batted soundly and ran brilliantly. The score had moved to 45-2 when Engineer pushed Snow on the leg-side and called for a single. Sunil responded, but he found himself running alongside Snow, who was rushing towards the ball. The paceman's advance forced Sunil to adopt a more diagonal path. Snow may have possessed the better physique, but Sunil was younger and a much quicker runner. He had all but made it to the crease when Snow brought his right shoulder into play. A violent shove sent Sunil sprawling, his bat knocked out of his hands, but crucially, towards the crease. Sunil crawled to safety and rose, only for Snow to pick up his bat and toss it to him.

Not everybody was convinced that the bowler was in the wrong. Former England captain Ted Dexter defended Snow, arguing that the batsman had come in his way, but his fellow TV commentator Jim Laker, the first bowler to take ten wickets in a Test innings, disagreed. As did the men who ran English cricket.

Sunil was shaken, and stirred. Snow's gamesmanship convinced him that all was not well in the opposition camp. Having been so used to blowing Indian sides away, their erstwhile colony's charge for victory had taken them by surprise. Snow carried on with his distasteful ways when recalled for a new spell, taking his time to reshuffle the field and mark out his run-up. For India, time was of the essence, and Snow was determined to waste it. The score had moved to 70-2 from sixteen overs when Sunil brought the Indian supporters to their feet twice, by dancing down the wicket and driving Norman Gifford, the left-arm spinner, for fours.

The partnership ended when Engineer came down the wicket to left-arm spinner Norman Gifford, only to be stranded. He and Sunil had added 66 in fifty minutes. The latter batsmen tried to force the pace, but the English kept it tight. Sunil fell to Gifford for a magnificent 53 and India were 145-8, thirty-seven short, when the rain arrived. Both sides claimed a moral victory.

> India's performance in the first Test has undoubtedly shaken England. It has brought about a revaluation of standards . . . they are now accepted as equals, if not superiors, in certain aspects of the game. – K.N. Prabhu, *TOI*, 28 July 1971 (filed)

Two three-dayers later, the teams moved to Old Trafford, Manchester for the second Test on a greentop. Everything was in England's favour, Snow's absence apart. He had been suspended for one Test, for not knowing that tackles had no place in cricket.

Illingworth won the toss again, and his batsmen found themselves on the back foot yet again. This time, the cause was Abid Ali's deceptive seamers. Opener Brian Luckhurst battled along, and Knott and Illingworth clicked for the second time in the series. Peter Lever, who filled Snow's spot, got 88 to complement the skipper's hundred. England finished with 386 and the Indian openers took the team through to the close on the second day.

The third day's play began in bitter cold on a damp wicket. While Mankad was wearing a sweater, his partner wasn't. Sunil warmed up by straight-driving Lever for four. Mankad was batting well until he chased the same bowler to give Knott his hundredth Test dismissal. In the next over, Price bowled a bouncer that Sunil contemplated hooking, but did not. His decision not to essay the stroke did not come in the way of his positioning himself perfectly for the stroke before letting the ball sail over his head. The next delivery, he met with a dead, but straight bat, and the ball dropped dead at his feet. It was a backward defensive stroke as glorious as a cover-drive.

Sunil's stance was sound; the feet close to each other, the elbow of the front (left) hand facing the bowler, and a back-lift coming down from second slip. Most critically, his head was still, and his hand-eye coordination excellent. Price, in two consecutive overs, served him short-of-a-length deliveries just outside the off-stump. They were too close for him to ignore. The first, he played to Keith Fletcher in the slips. The second rose steeply, but Sunil's timing was spot-on. He stood on his toes and played it with a vertical bat and loose hands. The cherry hit the bat, then the turf, and went like a rocket to gully. Price in his following over was thwarted by another textbook backward defensive stroke. Price retaliated with one that took off, and Sunil fended it over slips' heads for a single. It was theoretically a life, but then, he deserved every ounce of luck, given the way he was shaping up on that wicket and in those conditions.

The score had moved to 32-1 when Hutton, son of the legendary Sir Leonard, was introduced into the attack. He paid the price for not loosening himself before taking the ball, for when he bowled a wide half-volley outside the off-stump, Sunil pounced on it and essayed a stinging square-drive that would have done his idol Rohan Kanhai proud. The bowler retaliated by having Wadekar caught behind by Knott, but he could make no headway against Sunil. Deliveries pitched on middle-and-leg were adroitly tucked off the legs for singles, and another wide ball outside the off-stump cut contemptuously for was a four. Price's return to the attack made no difference.

Sunil followed a succession of exquisite cuts, drives and deflections off either foot on either side of the wicket, with two cracking boundaries off Illingworth, one flying over the bowler's head and the other whizzing past the non-striker Sardesai. The second stroke gave Sunil his second consecutive 50 of the series and ninth 50+ score in 11 Test innings. He seemed composed and keen enough to score many more, but a group of pitch-invaders got too close for comfort after he completed his fifty. They were largely responsible for his losing his concentration. It was not long before he nicked an express delivery by Price to Knott. He was slow in getting his gloves out of the way of a rising delivery. But his innings of 57 impressed the sternest of English critics.

> Gavaskar is not producing anything like his West Indies output, but he is learning fast how to adapt his batting to prevailing conditions, and such are his natural attributes of eye and timing and his quiet dedication to the job that I believe he may almost

reach the topmost heights. Would we had a 22 year-old with similar gifts! – E.W. Swanton, *Daily Telegraph*

The wicket was green and it drizzled constantly. The outfield was wet and the ball wasn't travelling at all. To crown it all, Price was incredibly quick. It was the fastest spell I have ever faced. Getting runs was so difficult that I guess my 57 was worth a hundred and I do believe it was the best I have ever played. – Sunil Gavaskar, Article for Air India, *The Indian Express*, 2 December 1984

Solkar apart, none of the subsequent batters lasted for long. A score of 212 gave England an opportunity to pile on the pressure. The spinners bore the brunt of an onslaught spearheaded by Brian Luckhurst, who scored 101. With Solkar temporarily sidelined due to a finger injury, Sunil did a reasonable job with his seamers, conceding only 37 from twelve overs. Illingworth declared with his team 419 ahead, giving his team an entire day and a bit to bowl India out.

At stumps on the fourth day, India were 65-3 and sinking, with the openers and skipper back in the pavilion. But rain had the final say. Not a single ball was bowled on the final day.

There were two slots up for grabs in the Indian XI for the final Test at the Oval in south London. Mankad, who hadn't been among the runs in the Tests, kept his place with a timely fifty against Nottinghamshire. As for the third spinner's spot, Bedi and Venkat could not be touched on account of their consistency, and it came down to a choice between Chandra, who had played in the first two Tests, and Prasanna. On a bad day, Chandra could be pedestrian, but on his day, he could be lethal. Lethal is what he was on the final day of the three-dayer against Nottinghamshire, with figures of 6-34.

It meant that the man rated by the Australians as the world's best off-spinner missed out on a Test once again. Prasanna's cause was also not helped by the think-tank's belief that playing two flighters of the ball in him and Bedi was an unaffordable luxury against English batsmen on their own pitches.

Illingworth completed a hattrick of toss-wins at the Oval. England batted positively, but in the process, kept giving the Indian bowlers chances. The hosts lost all ten wickets for 355 on the first day. When he opened the Indian innings with Sunil on the third morning after a washed-out second day, Mankad wished the fast bowlers 'Good morning'. His attempt to appease the fast men appeared to have worked against Snow, who was back from his suspension, but not against Price, who breached his defence. At the other end, Sunil was given a torrid time by Snow and a dog. The animal, whose ilk Sunil abhorred, strayed onto the field and chose the opener of all players to approach and sniff. It then wandered away, but Sunil was upset. He was also flustered when the gold chain that he wore around his neck snapped as he evaded a Snow bouncer. He was then triply unfortunate to get a peach of a ball that took his middle stump.

Wadekar and Sardesai rallied the innings, scoring 48 and 54 respectively. After Viswanath's dismissal for a duck, Solkar and Engineer displayed caution and grit. Engineer was splendid, for it was not often that a batsman as belligerent as he scored as many as 59 runs without hitting a single boundary. The innings ended on the fourth morning at 284, and with nearly two days left, the hosts fancied their chances of going on the attack and setting a stiff target.

The England openers had increased their overall lead to 94 when a straight drive by Luckhurst ricocheted off Chandra's hand onto the stumps, with non-striker John Jameson out of his crease.

The run-out was not as dramatic as a similar dismissal effected by Dr W.G. Grace in a Test match at the same venue eighty-nine years previously. On 29 August 1882, Grace had hidden the red cherry and broken the wicket when Australian Sam Jones presumed the ball to be dead and left his crease to garden the pitch. The Australians were not very happy. Their resolve for revenge was reflected in the words of Frederick Spofforth, their pace-bowling spearhead, before they began their defence of a paltry 84; 'This thing can be done!'

He proved it by taking 7-44 to dismiss England seven short of the target. The next day's edition of the *Sporting Times* carried an obituary of English cricket, which was believed to have 'died' at the Oval. The piece further stated that the 'body' would be cremated and the 'ashes' taken to Australia. Months later, when the Hon Ivo Bligh took an English team to Australia for a Test series, he announced that his team's objective was to bring the ashes back. When England won the series, a group of ladies burnt a bail and put the ashes in an urn, which they gifted to Bligh. Thus was Test cricket's oldest prize instituted.

Words also played an equally vital role in transforming Indian cricket history on 23 August 1971.

'Chandra, Mill Reef!' was all that Dilip Sardesai, the man Merchant had described as being responsible for the renaissance of Indian cricket, said. The reference was to a swift horse that had impressed Sardesai and Chandrasekhar, both of whom were not averse to betting at the races. The hint was clear. Chandrasekhar took it and hurled a ripper that disturbed the timber before John Edrich could bring his bat down. Keith Fletcher, who came out to negotiate the last over before lunch, lunged tentatively at Chandrasekhar and got an inside-edge. It wasn't the best thing to do when surrounded by a cordon of outstanding catchers. Wadekar and Venkataraghvan were brilliant at slip, and Viswanath and Sunil were not very far behind.

> Sunil became a slip fielder and that was partly my doing . . . Wadekar became distracted by my habit of chatting to the slip fielders . . . Gavaskar took his place and we developed a good rapport, having a chuckle and a joke between balls and between overs. – Farookh Engineer, as quoted in *Farookh Engineer, From the Far Pavilion* (Tempus, 2004)

The fielders frequently interchanged positions around the bat, but there was one constant – Eknath Solkar at short-leg. He dived to take the half-chance offered by Fletcher, and England were 24-3.

Post-lunch, Venkat held back an off-break to D'Oliveira, and Jayantilal, who was substituting at mid-on, held the mishit. The arrival of Knott, as proficient a player of spin as D'Oliveira and one of England's most successful bats in the series, prompted Solkar to stand over the stumps in an attempt to prevent him from indulging in his favoured activity of touching the bails at the start of an innings.

Solkar was by no means in Sobers' class, but like the ultimate cricketer, there was little he could not do on a cricket field. Off the field, he could be as gullible as Clark Kent, inducing violent laughter among his team-mates when he expressed his surprise at the fact that children in England, unlike their Indian counterparts, spoke fluent English. But on the field, he was as enterprising as Superman himself. When Venkat bowled an off-break and Knott got a thin inside-edge, Solkar took a fraction of a second to convince himself that he was indeed Superman. He swooped headlong, and plucked the ball millimetres from the turf.

This Superman then metamorphosed into a singer, as he kept Chandrasekhar in a good mood by humming numbers rendered by Mukesh, the latter's favourite artiste. An inspired Chandrasekhar then blew away three batters in quick succession, two of them to low full-tosses, and one through a superb slip catch by Venkataraghvan. There were four men around the bat—Engineer included—when Chandrasekhar took his first wicket; by the time he bagged his fifth wicket, there were seven. Hutton and Derek Underwood added 24 before Wadekar replaced Chandrasekhar with Bedi.

The change worked, with Underwood slogging to Mankad at short fine-leg. Chandrasekhar was then brought back, and he had last man Price leg-before. The Indian fielders were mobbed as they returned to the pavilion. They had one-and-a-half days in which to score 173 and get a red carpet welcome in Mumbai.

They started poorly. Sunil was eager to complement the efforts of Chandrasekhar, who had roomed with him on the tour. But he padded up to a Snow delivery that had pitched outside leg-stump, and was adjudged leg-before for a duck, his first in Test cricket. Mankad wished the fast bowlers as always, and stayed in until he was caught at slip. Wadekar and Sardesai took the team through to the close, and India needed 97 more on the last day.

The players began the final day by requesting 'Shahji' Ram Prakash Mehra, their chain-smoking second official, not to accompany them to the ground. Mehra acquiesced, realising that his innate nervousness might rub off on the players. Even as the spectators settled into their seats, an Indian elephant was brought to the ground from the Chessington Zoo and paraded around the ground. It was 24 August 1971, and thousands of miles away, people in India were celebrating Ganesh Chaturthi, the day the elephant-headed deity visits his devotees' homes. Wadekar, his men and the Indian supporters at the Oval viewed the elephant's presence as a good omen.

However, they started disastrously. The captain was run out almost immediately. Sardesai carried on, and Viswanath was eager to compensate for his first-innings blob. The Indian players and supporters had just about started smiling when Sardesai and Solkar fell in quick succession to make it 134-5. In came Engineer, and as was the case in the first innings, he played dead straight.

As the Indians crept towards the target, the score was announced at the Bombay Racecourse. A punter there ignored the horses and offered the odds of 1000:1 on an English win! Viswanath fell when only four were required, and Abid Ali had the privilege of cutting Luckhurst for the winning boundary. Wadekar, who had dozed off on the masseur's table, was woken up and given the good news.

It was 19.15 IST. Cinema shows were interrupted to announce the news of the victory. There were traffic jams in Bombay, with fans taking to the streets to celebrate. It was pretty much the same story in the other major cities. The *Times of India* bestowed front-page honours on the win, hailing it as 'India's finest hour' (25 August 1971).

The team returned to a grand welcome. Their plane was diverted to Delhi, where Mrs Gandhi felicitated them. When they eventually reached their original destination Bombay, it was as if the entire city had lined up to receive them. Prof Chandgadkar had kept his word.

Indian sportspersons had done well at the international level before, but the country had never reacted in as extraordinary a manner. To have beaten England at their own sport on their own soil was viewed as the ultimate achievement.

Sunil missed out on the celebrations, as he had been invited to Bermuda for a double-wicket tournament. Like his team-mates, he was delighted at the victory, but was far from happy with his form.

> 'He bought a Fiat (nameplate: MRJ 3456) for Rs 22,000 after the Caribbean tour. He did not score too many runs in England, and after returning from there, he expressed his desire to drive to Shirdi to seek the blessings of Sai Baba. I accompanied him, along with his sister Kavita and Sudhakar Adhikari, the Mumbai opener of the 1960s.' – Ashok Ambaye

India are also conquerors of England, who trounced my own Australians. So India, once looked upon as the little league of cricket, are in the big league. And strong contenders for the best team in the world. . . . – Keith Miller, as quoted in *Indian Cricket: The Vital Phase*, Raju Bharatan (Vikas, 1977)

The twin triumphs fuelled speculation that Wadekar's side would be invited to tour Australia in 1971-72, after the proposed visit by South Africa fell through. India had just beaten the West Indies and England overseas, and boasted an array of attractive and productive batsmen and the world's best spinners and wicketkeeper-batsman. What they lacked was an effective pace-bowling combination. But there were quite a few talented youngsters in the wings, and there surely wasn't a better land for a paceman to be blooded into international cricket than Australia. The likes of Govindraj, who had toured both the Windies and England without getting a single Test, and Bombay new-ball bowler Saeed Ahmed Hattea, merited opportunities in helpful conditions. How else could their worth be determined?

But the Australian Cricket Board didn't quite endorse Miller's views. It chose to replace the South Africans with a World team comprising the best non-Australian cricketers of the world. In mid-1970, Engineer had been the lone Indian in a World squad that had played England in an unofficial Test series, after South Africa's tour of that country was cancelled. The World team that was to play a similar series against Australia in 1971-72 comprised three Indians – Engineer, Bedi and Gavaskar. This increase in the number of Indian representatives was a direct consequence of the twin triumphs.

Sunil's inclusion confirmed his eminent status in world cricket. Many Indian cricketers had gone through an entire career without touring cricket's three main powers, but he had now got the opportunity to visit all three, and in the process, enhance his cricketing education in his very first year at the international level.

However, not everything went according to plan. He allowed himself to get carried away by some flattering comments on his belligerent approach in the initial games against the state sides. He tried to bat in similar fashion in the unofficial Tests, and paid the price. It was not the first or last time that a batsman had struggled on his first tour of Australia. As had been the case in Trinidad, Sunil had two options. He could either indulge in self-pity, or return to the drawing board. He chose the latter, with team-mate Rohan Kanhai and skipper Garry Sobers happy to act as guides. The duo spent a lot of time with Sunil and Zaheer Abbas, another young Asian who had burst onto the international scene in 1971. But practical learning was a lot more effective than pep talks.

Sunil had the best view of Kanhai's 117 in the second Test on the world's fastest track, at the WACA (Western Australian Cricket Association) ground in Perth. Kanhai essayed that knock after a speedster called Dennis Lillee had annihilated the World XI for a mere 59, and Australian skipper Ian Chappell enforced the follow-on 290 runs ahead.

Kanhai arrived at the crease after Engineer, who opened with Sunil, fell to Lillee for the second time in a single session. Sunil's teenage idol had barely got his eye in when a Lillee flier hit him in the chest. He was dazed, but waved away all those who gathered around him. The next ball was another short delivery, and Kanhai smashed it to the mid-wicket boundary. Several years later, Sunil, who kept Kanhai company in a 67-run stand, rated it as the best innings he had ever seen—as spectator and student.

Those were extraordinary circumstances; even as Kanhai attacked, the World XI dressing room wore a pensive look, with the Indian and Pakistani players fiddling with their respective transistors to get updates on the war that had broken out between the two countries. To the credit of the players and team-mates, particularly Sobers, Kanhai, Clive Lloyd, Tony Greig and Richard Hutton, the tension did not affect their team-spirit. The camaraderie between the players remained fantastic. Sunil would later describe that tour as the happiest of his career.

Sobers' epic 254 in the third Test at Melbourne inspired his team to square the series. The next Test at Sydney was drawn, the highlight being a masterly exhibition of spin bowling by Bishan Bedi in front of his Australian wife's adoring home-crowd. His back-to-back dismissals of the Chappell brothers off consecutive deliveries brought the spectators to their feet. A team effort in the fifth International at Adelaide ensured a nine-wicket win for the World XI, and with it, the series.

The Best Fielder Award helped alleviate Sunil's disappointment at his batting failures, as did the opportunity to meet and converse with

Sir Donald Bradman, who in his capacity as Australian Cricket Board chairman, had been the driving force behind the series. Sunil's ten outings in the five Tests had yielded scores of 22, 7, 0, 21, 38, 27, 6, 68*, 18 and 50. Of the specialist batsmen in the team, his average of 28.55 was the worst. His most productive innings on the tour was a 95 against New South Wales.

But it was still a learning experience. He had been exposed to Kipling's twin impostors – success and failure – in his first year of international cricket. In many ways, the Australia tour was as critical as the Caribbean trip, as far as Sunil's technical and mental evolution as an international cricketer was concerned. The trip hardened and rounded his outlook, and his game.

Even as he battled a fiery Dennis Lillee on hostile wickets, his India team-mates continued to be feted and felicitated as they had been since their return from England.

> We have gone a bit too far in greeting our glorious cricketers. Cricket should not become a mercenary game. Ironic that thousands of rupees are being spent on [giving] receptions to cricketers, while lakhs are desperately asking for food, shelter and charity. – *Whither Cricket?* by R. Menon and others, *TOI*, 23 September 1971

Not many Indians, who had seen and heard their team suffer one humiliating loss after another, were inclined to agree. But what the entire country knew and recognised in the latter half of 1971 was the imminence of a face-off with Pakistan. During this period, talk of the twin triumphs and their architects were a source of encouragement and gratification.

The Australian Board's indifference had left the Indians with only domestic cricket to play in the 1971-72 season. The upside was that their compatriots could watch their heroes play in flesh and blood, but the flipside was that the players were bereft of a fresh challenge at a time when they were confident and raring to go.

Cricket took a backseat when war broke out in December 1971. India's victory changed the subcontinental map and sparked off fanciful comparisons between politics and cricket.

> It is for the political commentators to dwell on how we freed Bangladesh (formerly East Pakistan) from the shackles of tyranny. In cricket too, we got rid of all that had once bound us down. Our selectors, breaking away from parochial loyalties that had once fettered them, chose a team from the best talent available . . . The critics have already begun to denigrate him (Sunil) . . . but he is bound to have the last laugh . . . he still has miles and miles to go and promises to keep. . . . – K.N. Prabhu, *Cricket's Annus Mirabillis*, TOI, 26 December 1971

Sunil regained his touch after returning from Australia. Finally given the opportunity to represent West Zone in the Duleep Trophy, he responded with a century on debut. In the Ranji quarter-final against Bihar, he scored 282, his highest first-class score at that point. A hairline fracture of the thumb, which he sustained during the game, and a patchy performance in the semi-final against Mysore, made him consider skipping the final against Bengal. But the pain lessened on the eve of the game, and Wadekar urged him to play. He vindicated his captain's faith with a match-winning 157. One of Sunil's team-mates in that game was his Bhagirathi buddy.

> 'People ask me even today how Sunil overtook me despite my headstart. Sincerely, success for your school or college doesn't matter. What matters is how you fare at the next level. Most of us were simply happy to be a part of that strong Bombay team and win. But Sunil from the very beginning was a setter of those wins, alongside players like Wadekar, Sardesai and Mankad.'
> – Milind Rege

The Ranji final was preceded by a turning point. Members of the teams that had won in the Caribbean and England took on the 'Rest of India' at Delhi, in a game that was played in aid of the post-war National Defence Fund. Sunil wasn't among the runs in this game. In fact, he was to have missed the game altogether, and had only joined at the last minute. But the trip was well worth it. During the game, Dilip Doshi, the left-arm spinner from Bengal, introduced him to a girl from Kanpur. Her name was Marshneil Mehrotra.[14]

---

[14] Known to her near and dear ones an 'Pammi'

5

A LINEAGE TO LIVE UP TO

'The three assets of Mumbai batsmen were guts, determination and pedigree.' – Milind **Rege**

Sunil was fortunate to be a part of the city which had produced a whole lot of talented sportsmen, especially cricketers. But at the same time, he had the weight of the responsibility to keep up that image on his shoulders too. No doubt, he lived up to the expectations of many and made a special mark following the footsteps of prominent players like Vijay Merchant, Polly Umrigar, Madhav Apte, Manohar Hardikar, Ajit Wadekar and Dilip Sardesai. It was not as if other Indian centres had not produced quality batsmen, but no other region spawned them as consistently as Bombay.

'The Kanga experience may have had some role to play in enabling Bombay players to succeed at the highest level. You have to adapt to varying conditions in the tournament. You have to hang around on sticky wickets. I guess that made us tough. The experience of playing with senior players like Umrigar and Bapu Nadkarni (in my case) helped us to acquire that *khadoos*[15]

---

[15]unrelenting.

mentality that Bombay cricketers have become synonymous with. Cricket was in our blood, and our seniors helped circulate it effectively. What they did to us, we did to our juniors.' – Ajit Wadekar

'Pedigree' was the critical word. Sunil had grown up watching Wadekar, Manjrekar, Nadkarni and Sardesai, in much the same way as Wadekar himself had grown up watching Nadkarni and Umrigar. The inter-club and office matches played on the maidans in the 1950s and '60s were keenly contested and star-studded. The experience of rubbing shoulders with their heroes enabled the juniors to learn by simply observing, and then working out what best suited them. They were helped in this regard by their coaches, who followed an unstructured approach themselves and encouraged their wards to develop their own styles after mastering the basics. Sunil's father, uncle, and team-mates at various levels subscribed to the same philosophy.

'From Merchant's generation to Gavaskar's, youngsters in Mumbai were taught three things:
A. Come in line with the ball to play at it.
B. Don't take your eyes off the ball.
C. Play in the 'V' for the first hour.

When you play in the 'V', it means you essentially play straight. The youngsters followed these principles religiously. That explains why the city produced so many class batsmen. Attitudes started changing in the 1970s, when diversions like One Day cricket started gaining popularity.' – Bapu Nadkarni

Mumbai's cricketing ethos had ensured a staggering twenty-two Ranji Trophy wins out of thirty-eight attempts at the end of the 1971-72 season. The attitude of the average Mumbaikar towards the sport mirrored his approach to life. Every single opportunity was to be exploited, and every single moment utilised productively, for only the fittest survived. You were only as good as your last performance. Many a team had tried to break the city's stranglehold, but in vain.

The men who excelled for the city had done their best for the country as well. Given the propensity of success to beget enemies, it was not surprising that players from other parts of the country often complained of discrimination. This was more of an excuse to conceal their own shortcomings than anything else.

Bombay's domination notwithstanding, only three cricketers who represented the city in the Ranji Trophy had preceded Wadekar as India's Test captains – Mankad, Umrigar and Ramchand. The national selection committee had been headed at different times in the 1950s and '60s by Col C.K. Nayudu, Capt Vijay Hazare and Lala Amarnath, all three of them former India captains, astute readers of the game and non-Bombayites to boot. To accuse them, as well as the likes of Tiger Pataudi, of blindly favouring Bombayites, was ridiculous.

The 1970-71 Ranji Trophy final provided the most vivid illustration of the gap between Bombay and the others. A seasoned Maharashtra side, captained by Chandrakant Borde, veteran of several battles for India, took on a Bombay team led by the twenty-four-year-old Sudhir Naik. Five of Bombay's stars—Wadekar, Sardesai, Solkar, Mankad and Gavaskar—were on national duty in the Caribbean. Incredibly, Maharashtra lost!

It was in May 1972, a year after that win by Naik's team, that Sheshrao Wankhede, then the president of the Bombay Cricket Association, laid the foundation stone of a stadium on Lloyd's Reclamation, a vacant plot of land a few thousand yards away from the CCI. It marked the beginning of the end of an era.

Since 1937-38, the CCI and its showpiece, the Brabourne stadium, had been to Indian cricket what Lord's and the MCC were to world cricket. But for all its commitment to promoting cricket in the country, the CCI was essentially a private club. The patronising attitude of its elite members had more often than not infuriated representatives of the Bombay Cricket Association, the official representative of cricket in the city, and affiliated unit of the BCCI. Rarely did the BCA get what it demanded from the CCI whenever Test matches were staged at the venue. Virtually every Test was preceded by a face-off. The BCA would want a certain number of tickets for its constituent clubs and patrons, and the CCI would be reluctant to comply. The BCA on many occasions had to back down, for its hands were tied. It did not have a ground of its own.

Matters came to a head in the early 1970s, when the CCI challenged the BCA to build its own stadium. The CCI had convinced itself that the BCA would find the task impossible. However, Wankhede was a resourceful individual, and the finance minister in the then government of Maharashtra.

Even as the CCI continued to be in denial, the country looked forward to England's visit in the winter of 1972. However, the announcement of the touring party was a dampener. Ray Illingworth, under whose captaincy England had retained the Ashes in the English summer of 1972, declared himself unavailable, as did Boycott and Snow. At the helm was Tony Lewis, an elegant bat from Glamorgan who was yet to make his Test debut. The squad also included Derek Underwood, the unorthodox left-arm spinner, who had bowled England to victory in the Leeds Test of the Ashes series and Tony Greig, who turned down a well-paying contract offered by an Australian Club for the winter to come to India.

Sunil spent his evenings and weekends preparing himself for the contest. The mornings were reserved for ACC.

> 'He would board a train from Dadar station to go to ACC, which was situated bang opposite Churchgate station. But he had very little time for himself, with fellow commuters invariably disturbing him. Memories of 1971 were still fresh, after all. It was only then that he started driving his Fiat on a regular basis.'
> – Karsan Ghavri

Sunil had his first look at the English bowlers in Hyderabad, where he turned out for the Board President's XI and compiled 86.

> Gavaskar reminded me of Geoff Boycott—detached, insular, totally within himself and not given to banter with players, umpires or even his partner. He looked neat, five feet and four and three quarters inches tall, and strong in the legs and forearms. His kit was clean, his appearance smart. He scored slowly, but it was important for him and for India that he took as much practice as possible against the English bowlers before the Test series began. His concentration was absolute. – Tony Lewis, *Wisden Cricket Almanac*, 1989

WHERE IT ALL BEGAN

HIS FIRST 'PITCH' – *The balcony between the main door and the proper flat, where the young SMG broke his mother's nose with a fierce straight-drive.*

WHERE IT ALL BEGAN – *the flat with the red-coloured windows on the top floor, his house in the Bhagirathi Buildings, Tardeo, Mumbai.*

THE BHAGIRATHI ALLEY – *Scene of many a cricketing and 'physical' battle. The garage-door between the two cars would serve as the 'stumps'. The windows of the flat in which the Gavaskars lived are visible on the top right.*

ANOTHER EARLY 'PITCH' – *just outside the main door of the flat. He played here with Milind Rege and his uncle Pramod Pandit; the bowler would run up the stairs (not in picture) to deliver, and the ladder at the far end would serve as the stumps.*

THE WIDEST SET OF STUMPS IN THE WORLD – *when SMG was batting, that is. The ball had to hit the garage door anywhere, for his friends to shout, 'OUT!'*

A SIGN OF THINGS TO COME ... *the young Gavaskar takes strike.*

PARENTS: *The Gavaskar family, mid-1960s.*

M.L. Jaisimha, SMG's hero.

1970 – *'This boy could just be the opener India is looking for . . .'*
       –**Raju Bharatan (Senior Journalist)**

'THE LONG AND SHORT OF IT'– *Bhagirathi boys SMG (left) and Milind Rege during their match-winning partnership of 234 for St. Xavier's College against Siddharth College in the final of the Ibrahim Rahimtoola Cup in 1969-70.*

INDIA ALL SET TO WIN SERIES: GAVASKAR'S DOUBLE CENTURY

By K. N. PRABHU

PORT OF SPAIN, April 19.

INDIA are well within sight of winning their first ever series against the West Indies. Sunil Gavaskar saw to it that this dream was achieved when he hammered a masterly double century and helped his side total 427, today the final day of the fifth and last Test.

West Indies, who took a first innings lead of 166 runs, needed 262 runs for victory in the concluding period of the six-day match, but by the tea break they were 74 for four wickets. The chances of the home team drawing the series were dashed to the ground.

Twice in recent days the mornings have brought news of happy events. Yesterday, Bedi heard about the birth of his son and, today, Sobers was the recipient of similar news from Barbados. These were good omens as Gavaskar and Jaisimha set about their task of placing India in a safe position.

Gavaskar played Noreiga with a great deal of skill and assurance, but Jaisimha seemed to be unduly worried by the three shortlegs that were placed to him. The runs in the first half hour came mainly from strokes placed between gaps in the widespread field to Gavaskar who scored his first four of the morning when he steered Sobers past third man for four.

Jaisimha had scored 18 when he had a life. He pushed forward to Noreiga and snicked the ball to Shepherd who let the ball through at legslip. It is difficult to accept Jaisimha as one of our principal stroke-players when he is on the defensive. He is at his best when he uses his feet to attack the spinners.

As India moved ahead, the partnership was worth fifty in just under two hours. One felt that he should share part of the burden and leave Gavaskar, who was nearing his double century, free to bat as he would like to.

EXQUISITE STROKE

We need not have worried for, as Dove came on, Gavaskar produced an exquisite cover drive to reach his double century round about the time All India Radio would have been repeating the days headlines in the nine O'clock news bulletin. Thousands, of miles away, one could well visualise the calls to the night sports desk.

There were fantastic scenes out in the middle. Gavaskar was surrounded and chaired. He was crowned with marigold garlands and one presumed that his pockets were stuffed with currency notes and coins by his admirers. The police shepherded these volatile enthusiasts away and when order was restored the statisticians came up with the details.

Gavaskar's double century included 22 fours in a stay of 290 minutes. The only other batsman to have followed up a century with a double was Dough Walters who performed this feat curiously enough against West Indies last season.

One can well visualise the rousing reception that awaits Gavaskar. When he lands in Bombay there should be happy holidays for the faculty of economics at St. Xaviers who could study the many runs he has accumulated in this series.

After the rousing start, we were in the midst of a crisis as Shepherd came on to claim Jaisimha lbw for 23 after he had helped Gavaskar realise in a valuable fifth wicket stand of 81 runs.

TWO WICKETS

Three runs later, Gavaskar's long vigil came to an end. He played forward to Shepherd and the ball turned to take the edge of his bat and hit the base of his leg-stump. He had batted for just under nine hours to score 220 with 24 fours. He needed just six runs to surpass Weekes's total aggregate of 779 against India.

At Gavaskar's dismissal, half an hour from lunch, India were 211 runs ahead. Sobers rearranged his field, sensing a chance of a breakthrough. Venkatraghavan, however, relished Noreiga's offbreaks. He swept him twice for four to send India past four hundred, but, in the last over before lunch, Solkar was caught at slip by Sobers to make India seven down for 409.

On Sunday, Gavaskar achieved the distinction of scoring a century in each innings and, with an unbeaten 180 he brought his tally to 734 in the series. The records show that only Patsy Hendren among the great batsmen of the past had collected as much in the West Indies.

One has perforce to get rid of the statistics at first. For, one is still overcome by the emotion which this lad stirred in the most hardened among us and, judging by the reception he received in the vast, colourful assembly at Queen's Park Oval as he stood up to all that Sobers let loose at him, spin, seam and pace.

He faced them all without fuss and without worry as he pushed the score along from 94 for one overnight to 193 for two at lunch and then from 283 for three at tea to 324 for four at the close.

Gavaskar's vigil extended over seven and half hours. At every phase he had to deal with an attack which became the sharper as it thrived on success. In the period before lunch, he lost Wadekar, before tea it was Sardesai and immediately thereafter when Viswanath was removed, he had to contend with a cramp in his leg while also striving to shield Jaisimha from the pace bowlers.

It was an excruciating and intolerable burden that Gavaskar bore. He lost Wadekar when India were still seven behind and, when Sardesai fell to a casual shot in the second over after lunch to give Foster a tame return catch, Gavaskar lost the only batsman who could have shared the load and responsibility with him.

In the 45 minutes to lunch, Sardesai had started in his typically masterly fashion. Within a couple of deliveries, he had Sobers remove the short-legs Noreiga had posted to him. He defended and cut and stroked the ball with consummate ease but the interval was his undoing. He played a casual, indifferent stroke to one that did not come through as quickly as expected and Foster closed in gleefully on the catch. It was apparent from the reactions of the West Indies fielders that they had struck a mighty blow.

Viswanath played a subdued but useful innings of 38. He provided Gavaskar valuable support in a stand, which was worth 99 when Sobers, in a frenzy, came on after tea to york him.

USEFUL KNOCK

Viswanath, one felt, could have relieved Gavaskar of some of the pressure, but it was over. It took him over half an hour to show Sobers that he was not unduly perturbed by the close-in fields that were set to Holford and Noreiga. By the time he had dispersed them with the square-drive and flick to leg that he favours, he was confronted with the new ball.

Sobers has generally taken the new ball the moment it was due but, today, it was not till the 108th over, when India were at 260 half an hour from tea, that he claimed it. He apparently held it in reserve for the middle order batsmen.

Sobers returned after tea to bowl with great ferveour and zest. He removed Viswanath with a yorker and then harassed Jaisimha over a long spell, but Jaisimha came through this period of torment to help Gavaskar in his bid to give India a fighting chance of making a match of it on the final day.

Score-board

India (1st Innings): 360.
West Indies (1st Innings): 526.
India (2nd Innings): S. Abid Ali lbw Sobers 3; S. Gavaskar b Shepherd 220; A. L. Wadekar c Shepherd b Noreiga 54; D. N. Sardesai c and b Foster 21; G. Viswanath b Sobers 38; M. L. Jaisimha lbw Shepherd 23; E. D. Solkar c Sobers b Noreiga 14; S. Venkatraghavan batting 20; Extras 16. Total (for seven wickets) 409.
Fall of wickets: 1-11; 2-159; 3-194; 4-293; 5-374; 6-377; 7-409.
(Scores incomplete)

ઓલ્ડ થયો. ૩૭૭ ના જુમ્બે ૬ઠી નિકટ પડી. સુનીલ ૫૩૪ મીનીટ સુધી રમ્યો અને તેણે ૨૪ ચોગ ફટકાર્યાં હતા. તે બાદ રાઘનન સોલ્કર ૪૦ ઉપર જુમ્બો બંધ ગયા. ૪૨૦માં જુમ્બો ડાવ પૂરા થયો.

The Times of India *hails his double hundred at Port of Spain*

FIRST-EVER WIN OVER W. INDIES

By K. N. PRABHU

PORT OF SPAIN, March 10.

IT has been a long wait. But victory, when it came five minutes from the close here today, was all the sweeter for the hoping and the waiting. Now in the mellow twilight, with the tension drained out of us all, it is possible to look back on the tortuous course of this game and appreciate the men and the deeds that made this a memorable day for all Indians here and elsewhere.

It was but fitting that Sunil Gavaskar's winning stroke should also have marked India's first triumph against the West Indies. It was a thumping hit to the mid-wicket boundary and like the several other strokes that he played as he bore India today towards their target of 124. It proved that the lad has carved out a permanent niche for himself in Indian cricket.

The burden and the strain must have been unbearable as his seniors fell with the goal still a fair way off and the West Indies attacked to the very death. But Gavaskar was on his mettle. His sound defence backed up by imperious strokes carried the day for India.

As I type this dispatch with the mists settling over the "northern range" I can still see in my mind's eye his slashing cover-drive off Holder and a hook to a bumper from Shillingford. They were as clean as a cossacks sabre stroke.

No less vivid is the ball that bowled Sobers to swing the game in India's favour. It pitched on a length that pins the batsmen to his crease and draws the tentative stroke. It broke to clip the off bail. If ever a match was settled by tight bowling it was today when Durrani removed the pair of dreaded West Indies stalwarts.

It was Durrani's spell that really put India on the high road to victory. In the space of four overs in which West Indies were pulled down from 150 for one, to 152 for three, he had reduced the might of the West Indies batting.

At the end Wadekar, in an interview in the press box, acknowledged his debt to this veteran craftsman. Indeed Durrani bowled today the way he used to in the years when he was the spearhead of our attack. Venkataraghavan too played a major part as he finished what Durrani had begun, though he had to work hard for success in the teeth of a West Indies fightback. Everyone of his five wickets were richly deserved. He kept an intelligent line and held a tight length, pushing his quicker ones through to perplex the tailenders.

TORTURE AND SUSPENSE

There were however dreadful moments of torture and suspense before victory was assured. Though the captains and the kings have fallen the retainers stayed to give India no end of trouble. Sobers, Camacho, Lloyd and Kanhai contributed but 45 between them. But West Indies innings was alive and beating so long as Charlie Davis had the support he needed. Batting with stitches over his deeply gashed right eyebrow Charlie Davis played an innings that will rank amongst cricket's great deeds of grit, courage and determination. Davis as one has previously marked, has been at home against off-spin and though he was handicapped by the injury he had received during nets in the morning, he held on to produce the drive-in front of the wicket as good as any he had played earlier in his innings.

Davis was well supported by Barrett and Holder, who used the sweep with impunity against Venkatraghavan, who was unlucky in his appeals for leg before wicket. Indeed on a wicket which played easier as the day wore on, yielding turn only to a small degree the Indian bowlers and fielders had to work hard for their success. In the end it was smart fielding and catching and Venkat's unerring accuracy that turned the tide in India's favour. When West Indies were rounded up for 261 in the hour after lunch, Venkatraghavan had five for 95. Though handicapped by a strained groin, he had shouldered the burden of the attack over long spells, taking over the mantle of key bowler in the absence of Prasanna, who had injured his finger last evening in an attempt to hold a return by Fredericks.

Venkat has proved that he is just as much a force on these wickets. Whereas Prasanna depends on flight and break, Venkat has made his ploys with variations of line and length. His quicker ball certainly brushed the tailenders out of the way before they could prove troublesome.

It was a team victory with every man playing his part down to the reserves. In the field Jayantilal, who had helped India to a break through by throwing accurately from point to runout Fredericks, retrieved admirably all morning in the deep and the close in fielders lent an extra sharp edge to the bowling of the spinners. India's batsmen made good the advantage their bowlers had gained them. In the stand of 76 both Mankad and Gavaskar made certain that the game

over. Mankad brought an air of assurance to the start of the innings and Gavaskar, a sense of adventure. It was a happy union in the bid for victory. It was to West Indies's credit that they did not give up. Sobers bowled to the very end and kept his regulars on till the match had been decided. Barrett caused something of a flutter by claiming Mankad, Durrani and Sardesai.

India had to fight hard for the 40 odd runs that were needed, but with Abid flinging his bat about and Gavaskar responding to every run, the match was won with five minutes to spare. Fittingly the decisive stroke to the mid wicket boundary came from Gavaskar's bat. There should be many more of these in the future.

Score-board

West Indies (1st Innings) 214.
India (1st Innings) 352.
West Indies (2nd Innings): R. Fredricks run out 80, R. Kanhai c Venkatraghavan b Bedi 27, C. Davies not out 74, C. Lloyd c Wadekar b Durrani 15, G. Sobers b Durrani 0, S. Camacho b Venkatraghavan 3, A. Barrett b Venkatraghavan 19, M. Findlay c Solkar b Venkatraghavan 0, V. Holder b Venkatraghavan 14, G. Shillingford b Durrani b Venkatraghavan 1, J. Noriega c Solkar b Bedi 2. Extras (byes 18, leg-byes 7, noball 1) 26. Total 261.
Fall of wickets: 1-73, 2-150, 3-152, 4-169, 5-169, 6-218, 7-222, 8-254, 9-256.
Bowling: Abid Ali 5-2-3-0; Solkar 7-2-19-0; Prasanna 16-5-47-0; Bedi 29.5-11-50-2; Venkatraghavan 36-11-95-5; Durrani 17-8-21-2.
India (2nd Innings): A. V. Mankad c sub b Barrett 29, S. M. Gavaskar not out 67, S. A. Durrani b Barrett 0, D. N. Sardesai c Findlay b Barrett 3, S. Abid Ali not out 21. Extras (nb 2, lb 2, nb 1) 5. Total (for three wickets) 125.
Fall of wickets: 1-74, 2-74, 3-84.
Bowling: V. Holder 2-0-12-0; G. Shillingford 6-2-13-0; J. Noriega 18-4-36-0; G. Sobers 15-5-16-0; A. Barrett 8.4-0-43-3.

BATTING STATISTICS

Fredricks one six, 10 fours, 190 mins; Kanhai four fours, 104 mins; Davis seven fours, 272 mins; Camacho 28 mins; Lloyd two fours, 36 mins; Barrett two fours, 78 mins; Findlay nine mins; Holder two fours, 34 mins; Shillingford five mins; Noriega 10 mins. Innings lasted 375 mins, off 665. balls.

Mankad one four, 95 mins.; Gavaskar six four, 127 mins.; Durrani two mins.; Sardesai 13 mins.; Abid Ali 40 mins. Innings lasted 130 mins., off 298 balls.

A debut in a historic Test match . . . The Times of India *headline says it all.*

THE TWIN TRIUMPHS

With Dilip and Nandini Sardesai at the send-off accorded to the Indian team prior to its departure to the Caribbean.

The Indian team that toured the West Indies for what was SMG's debut series. Standing (from left): Kenia Jayantilal, Abid Ali, Ashok Mankad, Devraj Govindraj, Rusi Jeejeebhoy, Pochiah Krishnamurthy, Eknath Solkar, Sunil Gavaskar, Gundappa Viswanath. Sitting (from left): Salim Durani, E.A.S. Prasanna, M.L. Jaisimha, Ajit Wadekar (captain), S. Venkataraghvan (vice-captain), Dilip Sardesai, Bishan Bedi.

THE INDIAN TEAM TO ENGLAND, 1971 – Standing (from left): Sunil Gavaskar, Gundappa Viswanath, Ashok Mankad, Pochiah Krishnamurthy, Syed Kirmani, Bishan Bedi, Devraj Govindraj, Kenia Jayantilal, Eknath Solkar, Abid Ali. Sitting (from left): R.P. Mehra (treasurer), B. Chandrasekhar, Abbas Ali Baig, S. Venkataraghvan (vice-captain), Ajit Wadekar (captain), Dilip Sardesai, E.A.S. Prasanna, Col Hemachandra Adhikari (manager). Absent: Farookh Engineer.

Members of the team that toured England in 1971 during a radio programme for the BBC. Sitting (from left): Abbas Ali Baig, R.P. Mehra (assistant manager), SMG, Abid Ali, Ajit Wadekar, Dilip Sardesai and Col Adhikari (manager).

Members of the Indian team on the eve of the disastrous tour of England in 1974.

TWENTY YEARS LATER... Some of the men who created history in the West Indies and England in 1971 at the celebrations of the twentieth anniversary of the twin wins. Standing (from left): Rusi Jeejeebhoy, Eknath Solkar, SMG, Gundappa Viswanath, Syed Kirmani, Ashok Mankad. Sitting (from left): B.S. Chandrasekhar, Dilip Sardesai, Ajit Wadekar, Ravi Bhootalingam (managing director, VST), M.L. Jaisimha, Abbas Ali Baig, Bishan Bedi, Salim Durani.

HIS BEST TEST HUNDRED – *SMG on the offensive during his 101 against England at Manchester, 1974.*

MUMBAI MAESTROS

With Vijay Merchant.

WITH INDIA AND BOMBAY STALWARTS. *From left: Madhav Apte, Madhav Mantri and Naren Tamhane.*

THE THREE Ss OF BOMBAY – *Solkar, SMG and Sardesai with cine-artiste David.*

RANJI TROPHY CHAMPIONS IN 1976-77, *the first of SMG's three Ranji titles as Bombay captain. Standing (from left): Manek Edekar (masseur), Suru Nayak, Rakesh Tandon, Awadhoot Zarapkar, Sanjay Jaywant, Kiran Asher, Sandeep Patil, Karsan Ghavri, Rahul Mankad, Vijay Mohan Raj. Sitting (from left): Padmakar Shivalkar, S.V. Kadam (manager), Sunil Gavaskar (captain), Ashok Mankad, Eknath Solkar and Abdul Ismail.*

Passing on the baton to Sachin Tendulkar.

Mumbai's stars of yesterday and today at a recent reunion.

West Zone, winners of the Duleep Trophy under SMG's captaincy in 1976-77. From left: Naresh Parsana (back to the camera), Dilip Vengsarkar, SMG, Aunshuman Gaekwad, Rajendra Jadeja, Dhiraj Parsana, Uday Joshi, Ashok Mankad, Yajurvindra Singh and Jaswant Bakrania.

THE INDIAN TEAM THAT TOURED AUSTRALIA IN 1977-78 – Standing (from left): P.R. Umrigar (manager), Brijesh Patel, Karsan Ghavri, Dilip Vengsarkar, Aunshuman Gaekwad, Bharat Reddy, Madan Lal Sharma, Chetan Chauhan, S. Sriraman (second official). Sitting (from left): Gundappa Viswanath, Ashok Mankad, Erapalli Prasanna, Bishan Bedi (captain), Sunil Gavaskar (vice-captain), S. Venkataraghvan, B.S. Chandrasekhar. Sitting on the ground (from left): Mohinder Amarnath, Syed Kirmani, Surender Amarnath.

THE INDIAN TEAM THAT TOURED PAKISTAN IN 1977-78 – Standing (from left): Fatehsinghrao Gaekwad (manager), Syed Kirmani, Surender Amarnath, Yashpal Sharma, Kapil Dev, Aunshuman Gaekwad, Bharat Reddy, Karsan Ghavri, Chetan Chauhan, P.R. Mansingh (second official). Sitting (from left): Mohinder Amarnath, Erapalli Prasanna, Sunil Gavaskar (vice-captain), Bishan Bedi (captain), S. Venkataraghvan, Gundappa Viswanath, B.S. Chandrasekhar.

THE LATE 1970S – *Interacting with media personality Kishore Bhimani.*

At practice.

IN PAKISTAN, 1978-79 – SMG takes on Mushtaq Mohammed, the Pakistan captain, during the course of his 97 in the second Test at Lahore.

SMG cuts during the course of his 101 against England at Manchester in 1974.

For the first Test at Delhi, India made only one change in the XI from the one that had won at the Oval a year and a half ago. Ramnath Parkar, Sunil's opening partner for Dadar Union, Bombay and the West Zone, replaced Mankad on the strength of his consistency in the previous season and a terrific 195 in the Irani Trophy game at the start of the season. Every other component of the Oval XI had been retained. Viswanath was the only non-Bombayite in the top seven, followed by the versatile Abid Ali, and Prasanna sitting out. Col Adhikari was retained as manager, and Engineer picked as the wicketkeeper.

But a lot had changed mentally. The Indians were unable to summon the intensity of 1971, and ended up losing by six wickets. The selectors reacted by showing the door to Sardesai of all people. The man who had started it all for India in 1971 never played for the country again. In his place came Durani, his room-mate of the Caribbean tour.

Prasanna replaced Venkataraghvan in the XI for the second Test at Calcutta. There was very nearly another change. Wadekar had flu, but with his team 0-1 down, he decided to take a chance and play. The Test proved to be a humdinger, in which India scraped through by 28 runs. Although Wadekar batted well in the first innings, he stayed off the field for a sizeable period, leaving Engineer, the seniormost member of the team, in charge. Prasanna bowled well in his comeback game, but he was outshone by Bedi and Chandrasekhar. The leg-spinner was once again India's best bowler, claiming nine wickets to go with his nine at Delhi.

Lewis fancied his team's chances in the third Test, which was to be played in Madras, on what was then the bounciest wicket in India. But he was slightly worried by the return of Wadekar's predecessor.

A lot had changed in Tiger Pataudi's life since January 1971. He had unsuccessfully contested the general elections, and been stripped of his ceremonial title by the government a year later. When asked to join the independent Indian Union in 1947, the heads of India's 565 princely states were offered the carrot of an attractive monthly salary, called a 'privy-purse', and a promise that they could retain their princely designations. However, twenty-five years later, with the economy still grappling with the after-effects of three wars in a decade, Mrs Gandhi decided that enough was enough.

The Nawab of Pataudi thus became Mansoor Ali Khan Pataudi. He had watched the first two Tests as a columnist for the *Hindustan Standard*. Wadekar, jolted by his first Test defeat as captain, was convinced that Pataudi's inclusion would make a difference. It was at Wadekar's behest that the selectors spoke to Pataudi and recalled him for the next Test at Madras. Ironically, even as a swashbuckling batsman and brilliant fielder like Pataudi came into the XI, another superb fieldsman like Parkar went out. But the opener was not dropped altogether. With a slow mover like Durani in the fray, it was decided to utilise him as an 'active' twelfth man.

Pataudi survived a confident leg-before shout in a three-dayer between South Zone and the visitors, and proceeded to play himself into form before the Madras Test with a hundred.

Sunil did nothing of note in the first two Tests, with scores of 12, 8, 18 and 2. His most noteworthy contribution had been as Durani's runner at Calcutta, where the latter scored 53. Parkar had in fact outscored him, but when the XI for the Madras Test was named, it was Sunil who was retained. In Parkar's place came Chetan Pratapsingh Chauhan, the opener from Pune. Sunil had taken strike for the first time in his Test career in the first two Tests, but in Madras, it was Chauhan who did so. He was Sunil's senior, having made his Test debut in 1969-70.

It was the first Test between the two teams at the ground situated in the locality of Chepauk since the fifth Test of the 1951-52 series, in which India had opened their account in Test cricket. England had toured India twice thereafter and had played Tests at Madras' Corporation Stadium. Test cricket returned to 'Chepauk' after a ten-year gap in 1966-67, by which time the ground had been formally leased to the Tamil Nadu Cricket Association.

The 1951-52 Test had been dominated by Vinoo Mankad, who returned match figures of 12-120. The pitch for the 1972-73 game looked spin-friendly, and while the Indians were understandably delighted, they had at the back of their minds the presence of the deadly Derek Underwood in the England line-up. Like most Madras Tests the time, the game was being played in mid-January, during the Pongal festivities that commemorated the end of the traditional farming season. The Indians received a pleasant Pongal gift when they heard that Underwood was indisposed and hence not playing.

England struggled against the spinners after winning the toss and batting first. They scored 242. India began badly, with Chauhan falling for a duck and Sunil getting 20 and sustaining another hairline fracture of the thumb, courtesy a steep delivery by Chris Old. The middle order came to the rescue, with every batsman from number three Wadekar to number nine Prasanna entering double figures. Pataudi top-scored with 73, and a lead of 74 was more than enough for the spinners. Prasanna's 4-16 helped terminate England's second innings for 159, and India needed only 86 to win. The English, however, hit back hard, and they were helped by some insipid batting. Sunil, who did not open on account of his injured thumb, went in when the sixth wicket fell for 72. He defended long enough for Pataudi to knock off the required runs.

The thumb injury made Sunil a doubtful starter for Kanpur. The selectors retained him in the squad because of the two-week gap between the Madras and Kanpur Tests, but they wanted to be certain that he was fit before picking him in the playing XI. H.T. Dani, one of the selectors, subjected him to a gruelling test on the eve of the game, giving him around fifty catches, some of them at great speed from a distance of only five yards. When Sunil held most of the catches without difficulty, Dani gripped his hand hard to check if he was flinching. When Sunil didn't, Dani gave him the green signal.

India were in a spot of bother on the final day at Kanpur, being five down and only 35 ahead with an hour's play left. Viswanath bailed them out with an unbeaten 75, an innings that ensured a draw for his team, and enabled him to keep his place in the side. Interestingly, he had been as out of touch as Sunil, yet at no point was the latter's place in jeopardy on grounds of poor form. The fact that Sunil had provided an answer to India's opening woes not very long ago may have been the reason the selectors were reluctant to do away with him. He displayed a welcome return to form with 69 in the first innings, during which, he completed 1,000 Test runs. Playing in his eleventh Test, he was the fastest Indian to reach that figure.

The selectors surprisingly axed Chauhan for the fifth Test despite his having put on 85 with Sunil in the first innings at Kanpur. Engineer opened instead and scored a hundred, and Wadekar got 87. Viswanath batted magnificently to complete a century. None of the five men who had scored a century on Test debut for India before him had managed to score another Test hundred. Tony Greig, as adept at captivating the crowds with his extravagant gestures as at inciting the opposition with his colourful vocabulary, lifted the centurion and cradled him, even as the spectators cheered.

The England batsmen replied in kind. They scored 480 in reply to India's 448, and the game was headed for a draw when both teams attended a dinner at the CCI. Sunil was sought out by none other than India's greatest all-rounder and the father of his first opening partner in Test cricket. Vinoo Mankad told him that he was opening the face of his bat a bit too much and thereby giving the bowler a chance. The man, considered by many as India's greatest cricketer-coach, used a stick to illustrate his point. Sunil heard him out and put the legend's advice into practice in the second innings.

He scored a crisp 67, in the process adding 135 for the first wicket with Engineer, and was glad to end an unproductive series on a high note. An eventful series ended on a frustrating note, with Pataudi blocking everything in sight and Wadekar delaying the declaration.

> India pottered on and on, deaf to the crowd, who were urging Wadekar to declare. This was Indian cricket showing the remains of its inferiority complex. – Dicky Rutnagur, *TOI*, 12 Feb 1973

The proceedings ended with Tony Lewis' side, a popular one despite some theatrics over umpiring decisions, being cheered off the ground and the public rejoicing over the fact that Wadekar, unlike any of his predecessors, had a hattrick of series wins under his belt. The joys concealed some bitter truths. In times of strife, players who were not exactly long-term prospects—Engineer, Durani and Pataudi—had excelled, while the juniors had struggled.

One effective thing was the performance of the spinners. Chandrasekhar had established an Indian record for a series with thirty-five scalps, Bedi was hard to get away as always, and Prasanna had made an impressive comeback. But he could never relax with Venkataraghvan sitting on the reserves' bench. Why all four spinners were never picked in the XI after Pataudi had done so at Birmingham in 1967, is one of

Indian cricket's unanswered questions. The side did not comprise any fast bowler of quality in any case, and spin was the team's primary strength on turning tracks at home. So why weren't all four played on a more regular basis at home, if not overseas?

The 1972-73 edition of the Ranji Trophy ended in much the same way as the previous fourteen. Sunil scored 135 in the quarter-final against Madhya Pradesh, and 134 in the semi-final against Hyderabad. Bombay won both games by nine and eight wickets respectively, and flew to Madras to play Tamil Nadu in the final. In what was a bizarre game, Tamil Nadu skipper Venkataraghvan's instructions to prepare a square turner boomeranged on his side. Leg-spinner V.V. Kumar and he bowled Bombay out for 151 and 113 with some assistance from seamer Kalyansundaram. But Bombay responded by dismissing the hosts for 80 and 61. Twenty-seven wickets fell on the second day, and the match concluded on the first ball of the third day.

Bombay's achievement is unparalleled in cricketing history. The teams that came the closest were New South Wales, who won the Sheffield Shield nine years in a row, from 1953-54 to 1961-62, and Surrey, who won the English County Championship from 1952 to 1958.

Sunil did not do much in the Ranji final, but he finished the season as Bombay's highest scorer.

That distinction made him the first recipient of the S.V. Rajadhyaksha Trophy. He was happy, but he and his colleagues would have been happier had they played a top level international team in the subsequent season. Even a short series would have given the players, particularly the juniors, a chance to rectify their flaws before their next major assignment—a tour of England in mid-1974. All they got was a tour of Sri Lanka, which was then an Associate Member of the ICC.

The fact that the players were still being praised for their showing in 1971 was a curse in disguise. In May 1973, Ian Chappell, fresh from leading Australia to a series win in the Caribbean, declared that the 1974 series between England and India would decide the best team in the world. The raison d'être, according to him, was that both Australia and India had won series in the Caribbean since 1971, and the 1972 Ashes had ended in a 2-2 tie.

Three days after Chappell's views appeared in the Indian papers, the *TOI* carried an article by former Indian wicketkeeper Kersi Meherhomji, who had by then migrated to Australia and established himself as a cricket historian. He explained a ratings system that he had devised, which proved that India was the leading cricket nation in the world. He took into account all Tests played in the 1970s, and awarded every team three points for a win and one for a draw. According to this system, India, with four wins and eight draws out of thirteen Tests, finished with twenty points out of a possible maximum of thirty-nine, and a success percentage of 51.3 percent. Australia, with seven wins and eight draws in the same period, had a success percentage of 50.9 percent. Then came England, New Zealand and Pakistan with 42.7 percent, 29.2 percent and 27.8 percent respectively.

For a nation born and brought up on defeats, this was surreal stuff. Many people allowed themselves to get carried away, but Wadekar, to his credit, did not. With the Indians scheduled to tour England in the first half of the 1974 summer as opposed to the warmer and drier second half in 1971, he knew that his players in general and spinners in particular would find it tough to cope with the dampness and the cold. That his team had been successful in Sri Lanka in January 1974 was of no consequence.

His state of mind wasn't helped by a spate of reverses before and after the Sri Lanka series. At the start of the 1973-74 season, Bombay lost the Irani Trophy to the Rest of India, and the West Zone were then outplayed by eventual winners North in the Duleep Trophy semi-final. At the end of the season came the biggest reverse of all.

Bombay took on Karnataka in the semi-final of the Ranji Trophy at Bangalore's brand new cricket stadium. Karnataka, known as Mysore till the 1969-70 season, had borne the brunt of Mumbai's brilliance and belligerence every single time the two teams had met in the competition. But this was a different Karnataka outfit. Seniors like skipper Prasanna, strike bowler Chandrasekhar and artist Viswanath, had for company some determined young men. Prominent amongst them were Sudhakar Rao, a stylish middle-order bat, Brijesh Patel, a swashbuckling one, and Syed Kirmani, the best wicketkeeper-batsman in the country, considering that Engineer was now based in England.

A capacity crowd fell silent when Karnataka opener and makeshift new-ball bowler Vijay Kumar nicked the first ball of the match, bowled by Bombay's Abdul Ismail, to Sunil at second slip. Viswanath, the next man in, let the second delivery of the match go past him, and was struck on the pad, right in front, by the third. To even the most die-hard of Karnataka supporters, he looked plumb leg-before. However, the umpire gave him a reprieve. Viswanath proceeded to score 162. Patel got 112, and Karnataka finished with 385. Bombay's first priority was to take the first-innings lead, and Sunil put them on course for the same.

> 'Sunil was handling Chandrasekhar well. I told myself that I had to lift my bowling capabilities. I could bowl two floaters – one incoming, the other outgoing. I bowled him one that drifted in. He played for the turn, but became the victim of an optical illusion. The ball pitched and swerved past his bat, and dislodged the bails. It was what they call the "doosra" these days.' – E.A.S. Prasanna
>
> I can still see Gavaskar clapping his hand against his bat as he left the ground in acknowledgement of Prasanna's wizardry.
> – Ramachandra Guha, *The States of Indian Cricket* (Permanent Black, 2005)

Sunil's fall notwithstanding, Mankad and Wadekar batted well in tandem. They were going along smoothly when the former played Prasanna in the covers, and called his partner for a run. When he saw the fleet-footed Rao near it, Mankad changed his mind. Wadekar stopped in his tracks, slipped, and was run out.

Prasanna bowled, bowled and bowled, as did Chandrasekhar. By the time the final Bombay wicket fell for 307, the captain had bowled 63 overs and the leg-spinner 44. But crucially, Prasanna had taken five wickets and Chandra four, and only a little over a day's play was left. Karnataka won on the first-innings lead and thus ended Bombay's fifteen-year winning streak. Prasanna's men went on to beat Rajasthan in the final, and the off-spinner staked a claim for the post of Wadekar's deputy for the England tour.

> There are many candidates (for the vice-captain's post), but it would be embarrassing to choose someone who is not a certainty in the team, and it would undoubtedly be unwise to be guided

by parochial ties and resentment. My own choice would be Sunil Gavaskar; he has the ability to guide and encourage his teammates and he has the carriage, ability, dignity and sophistication that are needed for the job. It would be a wise departure from our narrow tradition after all, there have been precedents elsewhere of the captain and deputy belonging to the same state. – K.N. Prabhu, *TOI*, 27 March 1974

The Bombay selectors certainly concurred with Prabhu. Sunil had been made vice-captain earlier in the season, and had even led Bombay in a couple of games in Wadekar's absence. Sunil's style of leadership was typically Bombayesque; optimal utilisation of one's resources, taking calculated risks, and a hint of stubbornness.

'I remember the 1969-70 Purshottam Shield final against the State Bank of India. It was a one-and-a-half day game. Sunil won the toss and elected to bat. Bharat Narvekar, who led the SBI attack, told Sunil that he would get him out in two overs. Sunil laughed it off, but that is exactly what happened. Narvekar bowled him a tempting bouncer in his second over, which Sunil mishooked to fine leg. He was furious. As I was passing him, Sunil instructed me not to get out at any cost. I ended up batting till the next morning.' – Navin Ambulkar

Whatever frustration Ashok Mankad may have felt as a result of Sunil's elevation to the Bombay vice-captaincy ahead of him, he took it out on the Sri Lankan bowlers and booked his passage to England. Patel also made it, as did Kirmani, who had toured in 1971 as well. But these deserving selections apart, the national selectors, like the public, conveyed the impression of suffering from a 1971 hangover.

Prasanna and his fans could not believe it when Venkataraghvan was reappointed vice-captain. Sunil's candidature wasn't even considered. Madan Lal Sharma, a medium-paced all-rounder from Delhi who had done well in Sri Lanka, was picked, but his partner-in-arms on that tour who had done equally well, wasn't. Pandurang Salgaonkar, the new-ball bowler from Kolhapur in Maharashtra, was the fastest bowler in the land. Wadekar wanted him, but he was overruled by the selectors. Considering that as many as three members of the selection committee—Dattu Phadkar, Raj Singh and Dani—had been new-ball operators in their youth and hence expected to be aware of the dire need for some fire, especially on foreign soil, the decision to omit Salgaonkar was an odd one.

> Is this the way we encourage our young men to bowl fast? After this, what incentive can there be for a youngster to venture to bowl fast on our heartbreaking wickets? – Raju Bharatan, *Illustrated Weekly of India*

If the selectors erred, so did the BCCI, by accepting a playing condition that permitted only five fielders on the leg-side. It signified three things. Firstly, the Indian representative at the ICC was unaware that this experimental rule had been rejected by every other Test-playing nation. Secondly, off-spinners like Prasanna and Venkataraghvan would now have to modify the very essence of their strategy, which comprised a packed leg-side field. Lastly, it meant that the English batsmen had got a shot in the arm in their bid to unsettle India's main strength. It was an inauspicious start to the tour.

What also did not augur well for its prospects was that some senior players had misgivings about Wadekar's captaincy. These were essentially cricketers who had played a lot under Pataudi and were still upset about the casting vote that had cost him the job. The happenings of 1971 had given them little scope to express themselves. But subsequent events had changed the picture. Engineer's captaincy in the Calcutta Test, when Wadekar was off the field due to flu, had elicited several positive reviews. It had been perceived as enterprising, in sharp contrast to Wadekar's conservative approach.

Little has changed in Indian cricket, and this was one such instance, wherein people were falling over themselves to compare an acting captain's short-term tactics to the incumbent's long-term strategies. Wadekar, the incumbent, naturally had to take into account more factors, including the reality that 1971 had raised the bar as far as their supporters were concerned. Winning was everything, and defeat unpardonable.

Wadekar's critics continued to call him 'lucky', conveniently overlooking the fact that it takes a bit more than luck to win two consecutive Test series on foreign soil without raw pace. What the Indians achieved in 1971 has no parallels in cricketing history.

The tour of England commenced in mid-April with an altercation between Wadekar and Bedi after the end of the first day's play of the traditional opener against Derrick Robins' XI. Bedi, an excitable character, allegedly urged the captain to speak to the Board about increasing the players' remuneration. One thing led to another and Bedi was joined by Prasanna. The off-spinner wrote in his 1977 autobiography *One More Over* that Wadekar then accused the spinners of being 'Pataudi's' men. All hell broke loose thereafter, and the fact that it happened at an Indian expatriate's home where the team was having dinner made it worse. Sunil, who like Viswanath was neither a senior nor a rookie, feared that the incident would depress the juniors. He was not delighted to be proved right.

Wadekar and Bedi made up the following morning, but morale had already hit rock-bottom.

The team travelled to Worcester, which boasted one of the strongest County sides of the time. It comprised Ron Headley, son of the legendary George, whose exploits for the West Indies had earned him the sobriquet Black Bradman. His opening partner was the New Zealander Glenn Turner, who would go on to complete a century of First-class centuries. The middle order comprised Test batsmen like John Parker (New Zealand) and Basil D'Oliveira (England). Following them in the batting order were more Test stars like Englishman Norman Gifford and West Indian Vanburn Holder, both of whom Sunil had encountered in 1971.

The game looked to be heading for a draw until Gifford, the skipper, declared and challenged India to score 221 in 195 minutes. The Indians decided to go for it, and Mankad, who had been given the game off, positioned himself alongside the sight screen even as openers Sunil and Gopal Bose made their way to the middle.

> 'It was cold and damp, and Holder was deceptively quick. One of his deliveries rose, which Sunil tried to leave. But he got hit in the chest. He was wearing two sweaters, but no protection. The impact was sickening, but he carried on. Holder then bowled another lifter, which Sunil hooked for six. He went on to score 88. It was the best innings I have seen on a greentop. In terms of the quality of strokes, the extent of domination over the bowlers, and the impeccability of technique, it stands out.'
> – Late Ashok Mankad

When Sunil was run-out while attempting a second run, India needed 35 from 8 overs. They were handicapped by their lack of experience in limited-overs cricket. They finished 15 runs short of the target, but on a high. Wisden remarked favourably about the younger batsmen courageously getting behind the line and holding off first-class pace bowling in helpful circumstances.

The leg-side rule and weather were against the visitors, but the itinerary wasn't. There were as many as twelve three-dayers before the first Test, which gave them plenty of time to acclimatise. After ten draws, the Indians arrived at the Oval, a venue that brought back happy memories for Wadekar's men, for the three-dayer against Surrey. All the batsmen had struck form by then, with Sunil's best performance being an unbeaten 104 against Lancashire. Against Surrey, he scored 136, and Abid Ali bowled his cutters and seamers to take 6-23. India emerged winners by ten wickets, and proceeded to thrash Derbyshire by eight wickets in their last game before the first Test.

The back-to-back wins notwithstanding, the Indian camp was anything but gung-ho on the eve of the first Test at Manchester. Wadekar had broken his little finger and was unsure about playing. But he did, allegedly because some players were not enthused with the idea of playing under Venkataraghvan, who they believed should not have been vice-captain in the first place. However, the off-spinner was still picked on the premise that he would take over if Wadekar were to leave the field at some stage. It was a bizarre move, for Prasanna had been more successful than Venkataraghvan in the warm-up games. The management's decision meant that the Bangalorean had to warm the benches, with Bedi and Chandrasekhar being automatic selections.

Rain truncated play on the first two days. England batted first and scored 328-9, and their captain Mike Denness decided to let his seamers exploit the damp conditions in the last thirty minutes of the second day. The inconsistency of openers Gopal Bose and Sudhir Naik had forced the think-tank to promote Solkar to the opening slot. Solkar and Sunil had opened in the three-dayer against Lancashire and put on 187.

At the venue where he had essayed that priceless 57 three years previously, Sunil thrilled his team's supporters by hooking a Willis bouncer imperiously for a four. But Solkar fell early, nicking Mike

Hendrick to Willis in the slips. Venkataraghvan, who came in as nightwatchman, was bowled in the last over of the day. India were 26-2 at stumps.

Sunil had gone sixteen Test innings without getting a big one. That he had the technique to blunt the best of bowlers was never in doubt, but did he have the temperament? Did he possess the drive to prove that his success in the Caribbean was not a flash in the pan?

The country had waited for answers to these questions. It now wanted them.

6

FROM MANCHESTER TO LONDON...
AND A LOT IN BETWEEN

'When he was playing, I was far too young to understand what it took to be a great Test cricketer. At that age, I couldn't grasp the extent of the effort that I needed to put in to make it to the highest level. When you are young, you feel you can achieve anything... Honestly, I did not try to copy him. My coach firmly believed that I needed to develop my own style, rather than attempt something that may not suit me. However, we would discuss his concentration and his patience often.' – Sachin Tendulkar

When Wadekar fell to Chris Old moments after the umpires called Play on day three of the Manchester Test, it seemed as if there were threes everywhere. It was the third day of the Test, India were three down (for 32), England's three pacemen—Willis, Hendrick and Old—had taken a wicket each, and Viswanath arrived in the middle wearing three sweaters.

India's little duo dropped anchor. Sunil turned Hendrick to square-leg to bring up the 50 of the innings. He then steered the same bowler past the slips for four. At the other end, Viswanath warmed up with a regal square back-foot drive off Old. England's bowlers were good enough to capitalise on the conditions and get wickets, but that did not prevent them from trying non-cricketing tactics. When Underwood came on, the gigantic Greig stood barely three feet away from the batsmen, partly to latch onto any half chance that might come his way, and mainly to try and intimidate.

Sunil's first scoring stroke against Underwood was a straight drive that sped between the bowler and non-striker for four. Viswanath and he had added 73 through a combination of quality batting and smart running when Underwood served a vicious turner that took the former's off-stump. It was a big blow, for on that wicket and in those conditions, it was imperative that whoever got his eye in stayed in for a long time. With Viswanath gone, Sunil's presence in the middle was vital. He had by then discovered a hole in his trousers, on the inner part of the left thigh. But it wasn't impeding his movement, and he carried on, intending to change it at the next interval.

With the English bowlers providing little or no margin for error, every single lapse on their part had to be exploited. Sunil did just that when Underwood bowled one that was short and just outside the off-stump. A marvellous late-cut, executed when the ball had all but hit the stumps, gave him 3 runs and a 50. The least he deserved was a semblance of support, but Willis had Patel caught low down by Knott. Sunil was surprised to see Patel walk without confirming that the catch was clean. Engineer was welcomed warmly by his Lancashire home crowd, but Willis dampened their joy with a yorker that sent the middle stump for a walk.

At the tea interval, Sunil was persuaded to carry on in the same pair of trousers for superstitious reasons. The hole was not affecting his batting, and that apart, it made little sense to discard a pair that had yielded him so many runs in a perilous situation. England got off to a flying start in the post-tea session, literally. Hendrick uprooted Madan Lal's off and leg-stumps, but the middle stump remained standing. India were 143-7 and in the soup. It was just the situation a scrapper like Abid Ali relished.

He slapped Underwood through the covers for four and carried on in the same vein. Sunil tried to emulate his partner's ebullience by trying to pull an Underwood delivery that came onto him a little quicker than expected. The ball hit the splice and flew to Boycott at mid-on, but it turned out to be a no-ball. Sunil was relatively cautious thereafter. The sun, which had emerged from between the clouds during the tea interval, had disappeared by then, and the light had deteriorated. However, the batsmen were going along well and hence did not accept the umpires' offer to abandon play.

A fine-leg boundary off Willis took Sunil to 96. He then took a single, and Abid Ali struck Greig for two boundaries. Sunil was on strike to Underwood when he received one that was short and outside the off-stump. He lost the ball against the backdrop of the spectators who were seated below an unusually high sight screen. He sighted it when it had all but passed him, and sliced it through the covers. The ball did not make it to the boundary, but the batsmen completed an easy three. Sunil had barely completed the third run when he became the victim of a pitch raid. Denness did his best to extricate him from the raiders' clutches, in what was the second instance of unconventional assistance that Sunil had received during the course of his innings. He had earlier got his locks trimmed by umpire Harold Bird after the wind kept blowing them in front of his eyes.

Sunil was run out soon after. He returned to a magnificent ovation with his fifth Test hundred, his first in seventeen Test innings, and the best of his five, given the conditions. The English players joined the crowd in applauding him all the way back to the pavilion.

> Gavaskar's batting represents ascension of ability – he has worked on his technique, his bat is now straighter and closer to his pad in defence than it was at the start of the tour. – John Arlott, *TOI*, 8 June 1974

India finished with 248. England went on the offensive, but not before Eknath Solkar dismissed Boycott for the fourth time in six innings. John Edrich batted well to post an unbeaten hundred at stumps on the fourth day. Denness declared overnight, leaving the Indians 296 to win in six hours. It was a challenging declaration, for although it was an obtainable target, Underwood was expected to revel on the fifth-day pitch.

Willis started the final day with a succession of full tosses, and then bowled a short delivery that Solkar hooked for six. Sunil then steered the same bowler past the slips for four. Seeing that his new-ball bowlers were unable to penetrate, Denness brought on Underwood. He struck, dismissing Solkar to a one-handed catch by Hendrick at leg-slip. Wadekar, never completely at ease due to his finger, scored 14 before Knott pouched an attempted cut off Greig. In came Viswanath, who looked as assured as in the first innings. At the other end, his partner was all set to make a mark.

Sunil drove, cut, pulled, and indeed, defended with aplomb. He used his feet excellently and fed off the confidence gained in the first innings. A cut off Underwood gave him another fifty. The bowler then changed ends, but was subjected to similar treatment. India were 102-2 after the lunch interval, and the crowd fancied its chances of watching a memorable chase. But their smiles vanished the moment Old delivered one that jumped a bit more than Sunil had anticipated, and flew off his bat's shoulder to gully.

The match was still far from over, but not for the last time in Indian cricket history, the batsmen let their team down. The English bowlers kept striking at regular intervals and India sustained a 113-run loss with a little over thirty minutes' play left. A little more application would have ensured a draw.

Victories in three-day games against Oxford-Cambridge (Combined Universities) and Gloucestershire, livened the atmosphere in the Indian camp on the eve of the second Test. Wadekar, Solkar and Naik batted well, as did Sunil with 61 in the latter game, but these performances were overshadowed by those of the Oxbridge captain, who took four wickets and then scored 160 and 49. He had opted to finish his studies after making his Test debut for Pakistan in 1971. His name was Imran Khan Niazi.

What Wadekar needed at that stage was some luck. He did not get it on the first day of the second Test at Lord's, as Denness won the toss and elected to bat in bright sunshine. Amiss, Greig and Denness himself scored centuries, while Edrich missed his by 4 runs. Wadekar tried everything to stop the run-flow, but his cause wasn't helped by a finger injury to Chandrasekhar that forced him to leave the field. Bedi, always an attacking bowler, found it beyond him to adopt a more defensive line. Unlike their 1971 counterparts, Denness and his players were a lot more receptive to the idea of using their feet to counter the spinners. Bedi finished with six wickets, but at an astronomical cost of 226 runs. Prasanna, who was back in the side in place of Venkataraghvan, probably because Wadekar was now fully fit, bowled 51 overs for figures of 2-166.

With England amassing 629, India's best bet was to bat out the rest of the game. It was not an impossible task in the dry and sunny conditions. In his autobiography *Sunny Days*, published in 1976, Sunil used the word 'horrifying' to describe his partner Engineer's cavalier batsmanship in the final hour of play on the second day. Engineer drove, pulled and swung, occasionally across the line, with gusto, to take India to 51-0 at stumps.

The conditions continued to be tailormade for batting the following morning. Sunil took 2 off the first ball, bowled by Geoff Arnold. When the bowler dug one in short, Sunil took a sideways step and essayed a hook for six. Engineer drove Greig for 4 to bring up his fifty and then swept the same bowler to post the hundred of the innings. For the Indian supporters at the ground, there could not have been a better place to be at. The sun was out, the Lord's wicket had no demons in it, and the openers were flourishing. When Sunil pierced the two gullies placed to Hendrick's bowling to get a boundary, and then hooked the same bowler for another near-six, it seemed as if the person who had predicted a Gavaskar double hundred in the Test would be hailed as a seer.

But for the first time in his career since the Bridgetown Test of 1971, Sunil allowed his frustration to affect his concentration. Peeved at his partner's refusal to take a single thrice in the same over, Sunil chased a Chris Old delivery and guided it into Knott's waiting gloves.

Engineer fell for 86, Viswanath wowed watchers with a strokeful 52 and Solkar got 43. But the others slipped at the foothills of the mountainous English total and Denness enforced the follow-on after the innings ended at 302. Sunil and Engineer negotiated the last two overs of the third day, and the Indians spent Sunday, a rest day, trying to convince themselves that they could get out of jail. Monday was overcast and damp. The Indian supporters anticipated an uphill battle, but what they saw was a knockout.

As Sunil himself summed up the events that unfolded on 24 June 1974, the English bowlers delivered five quality deliveries, each of which was good enough to dismiss a frontline Indian batsman. The others then caved in. Solkar remained unbeaten with 18, as India were annihilated for 42 in 17 overs. Sunil was fifth out at 25, when he was caught in front by a seaming Arnold delivery that would have hit the leg-stump. The series was England's.

If the Indian cricketers felt that they had hit rock bottom, they were mistaken. The evening after the Test, they had to show up at a State Bank of India function and then attend a party hosted by B.K. Nehru, India's High Commissioner to the UK. However, the team's departure for the SBI function was delayed due to what seemed to be Adhikari's penchant for telephone calls. London's rush-hour traffic delayed them further, and the players reached the high commissioner's residence nearly an hour after they were supposed to. Wadekar and Adhikari apologised, only to be told by a fuming Nehru in full view of the other guests to 'get out'. The players returned to their bus and refused to heed Adhikari's pleas to return to the party. Eventually Venkataraghvan, the vice-captain, convinced them, and Nehru apologised. But it was pointless to expect the players to behave as if nothing had happened. Their reticence was misconstrued as arrogance.

> They not only play bad cricket, they also display bad manners.
> – Spokesman of the HC, as quoted in *TOI*, 27 June 1974

It was on the following day that the players learnt why their manager had seemingly fallen in love with the telephone and thereby caused the delay. An overzealous house detective at London's Marks and Spencer Departmental Store had apprehended Sudhir Naik on charges of shoplifting. It so happened that Naik had bought twenty pairs of socks for himself and his team-mates, who had given him money for the same. He had been asked to buy some other items as well, and was in the process of doing just that when two additional pairs of socks slipped below a pair of slacks into his bag. The shop authorities refused to believe him and summoned the police. That had forced Adhikari to make several phone calls to try and do his bit to avoid negative publicity.

In what was an extraordinary case of mismanagement, Naik was then convinced to plead guilty to get the matter over and done with. He did, and the press reacted with unbridled glee.

Not many people, some of his team-mates included, were initially prepared to believe Naik's version. But one man was. Sunil requested Adhikari to let him share a room with Naik. He intercepted abusive phone calls and psyched a despondent Naik to abandon thoughts of committing suicide.

Naik displayed his fighting qualities to score 73 and 68 in the three-dayer against Nottinghamshire, and was picked to make his debut in the third Test at Edgbaston, Birmingham. His 77 in the second innings was the highest individual score by an Indian in a Test that England completely dominated, winning by an innings and 78 runs. Sunil did not do much, falling on the first ball of the match in the first innings and scoring only 4 in the second. India's worst Test series since 1961-62 ended on 8 July 1974.

The deity of 1971 had become a demon. Wadekar was quoted in the 9 July issue of *TOI* as saying that he wished to play as long as he was fit. He also said that he hoped to remain the captain of the Indian team, but that amounted to being outrageously optimistic. It was unlikely that the selectors would defy public opinion, which had turned against the cricketers and their captain after their dreams of a third series win against England had come a cropper. In 1974, the genuine cricket-lovers—those who understood the nuances of the sport—were in a majority, and they were not particularly inclined to burn effigies and break under-construction houses after inviting the print and electronic media to capture their antics on camera. So no untoward incidents took place, barring the defacement of the twenty-foot Victory Bat that had been erected at Indore to celebrate the twin triumphs of 1971.

The players, pundits, press and public were unanimous in their view that Sunil was the silver lining of the series. He had excelled in adverse situations on and off the field, as the Naik affair demonstrated.

Favourable developments on the personal front had undoubtedly helped Sunil maintain his focus. He had fallen in love with the girl he had met during the National Defence Fund game in 1972, and spent a couple of years trying to elicit a favourable response from her. His patience and perseverance earned him a significant off-the-field victory. His marriage to Marshneil Mehrotra was solemnised on 23 September 1974. The newly-weds proceeded for their honeymoon, unaware of the weird turns Indian cricket was about to take.

∽

In a move that would have done an Australian selection panel of the new millennium proud, the West Zone selectors decided to discard Wadekar for the Duleep Trophy. His average of 35 in the First-class matches in England was not considered, nor his First-class record and standing as India's most successful captain. Wadekar was mortified enough to announce his retirement from First-class cricket.

Some historians have claimed that India would have attained independence way back in 1921-22 had the Mahatma not abruptly terminated the Non-Cooperation movement in the wake of the Chaurichaura massacre. Had India become independent then, it would have remained a single country, served by several outstanding talents – Jawaharlal Nehru, Subhash Chandra Bose, Vallabhbhai Patel, Maulana Azad – to name just four, all of them in the age group of thirty to forty five, in their prime, and raring to go. What India would have gone on to achieve had that happened, we will never know.

What Tiger Pataudi would have achieved had an accident not deprived him of one eye is Indian cricket's greatest 'what-might-have-been'. Alongside it is another—What if Sunil had been made captain of India in the autumn of 1974?

In 1974, world cricket was witnessing a change of guard. The stars of the 1960s were either in the process of retiring or had been eased out, and the greenhorns of the same phase had taken over. Less than a year later, England was to host the game's inaugural World Cup of limited overs matches, an exciting innovation.

The West Indies, who were scheduled to tour India for a full Test series in late 1974, were looking ahead. Sobers and Kanhai had quit, and the reins were entrusted to the thirty-year-old Clive Lloyd. It was a young and exciting team that he brought to India. It included Lawrence Rowe, who had scored a double hundred and hundred on his Test debut in 1972-73. Alvin Kallicharran had responded to the pep talk delivered by Sunil and Viswanath in 1971 with some convincing performances, and was being hailed as a left-handed Kanhai. Gordon Greenidge, a Barbados-born belligerent opener who believed in making his opponents pity the cricket ball, could have represented England, where he had resided for several years and represented Hampshire in County cricket. But he opted to represent his native land. The team also included two individuals from the tiny island-nation of Antigua. The first was a fast bowler who had it all—pace, bounce, variety and menace. His name was Andy Roberts, one of the fourteen children of a fisherman. Sunil, who very nearly grew up as the son of one, had reason to remember him. It was Roberts who had lent him the cassette of Lord Relator's calypso, composed in honour of the 1971 Indians, during the three-dayer between the fast bowler's county Hampshire and Wadekar's 1974 side. The calypso included a special tribute to Sunil, 'It was Gavaskar, just like a wall, the West Indies couldn't out him at all . . . you know the West Indies couldn't out him at all!'

Most of the West Indies players had contracts with County sides in England, including Roberts' fellow Antiguan, who like Greenidge, was yet to make his Test debut. Isaac Vivian Alexander Richards hadn't done anything of note for Somerset in the three-dayer against the 1974 Indians, but Brian Close, his County skipper, had told Sunil and the others to watch out for him in the years to come.

On the eve of the series, Sunil was twenty-five years old and supremely confident after his performances in England. It seemed easy to imagine him utilising the measured and methodical approach that had yielded him success with the bat, as a captain.

Surely, in a country where seniority was often valued a lot more than merit, Sunil's appointment would have ruffled some feathers. But by no means would it have been an unprecedented move. Vijay Merchant had been named captain at the age of twenty-six for a five Test series against Lord Tennyson's team in 1937-38. Then there was the decision to formally appoint the twenty-two-year-old Pataudi as captain at the start of the 1963-64 season. In both cases, the then selectors had detected a flair for leadership.

However, things were decidedly different in 1974. Public interest in the sport had grown manifold since the twin triumphs, and the nation was angry after the 1974 debacle. Given the circumstances, the Indian selectors opted to play safe. They pulled a tiger out of the hat.

'All five Tests or none,' was Pataudi's response when asked whether he was willing to accept the captaincy for the first two Tests of the five-match series. The erstwhile prince also made it clear that it was unwise to expect him to do wonders with the bat. But if it was a captain they were looking for, then he was very much available. The selectors accepted his terms, for they were convinced that he alone could alter the fortunes of a side that was clearly shellshocked. After all, most of the members of the side had made their debuts under him, and some of them still swore by him. It was a situation far too challenging for Pataudi to ignore.

Cricket lovers were desperate and willing to go with any move that could resuscitate the team. Sunil was not thinking about the India captaincy, but he was most certainly peeved to be sidelined for the Bombay captaincy. Ashok Mankad, who had not allowed his inconsistency in international cricket to affect his proficiency in domestic cricket, was assigned the job of winning back the Ranji Trophy.

Pataudi led the Rest of India in the Irani Cup encounter against Ranji champions Karnataka. After his side scored 359, Prasanna took it upon himself to prove that the Ranji win was no fluke. The Rest of India floundered after the openers had added 129. Pataudi scored only 1. The score was 193-8 when Bishan Bedi arrived at the crease. He went on to get 56. The innings eventually ended at 307 when Sunil ran out of partners. He had carried his bat for 156. It was an innings that Pataudi, watching from the dressing room, did not forget.

The selectors and he agreed on giving Sunil the vice-captaincy when they met to pick the team for the first Test against the West Indies. Sunil was informed accordingly, but strangely told not to tell anyone. He was even told not to stand next to Pataudi when the players were being introduced to a visiting dignitary on the first morning of the Test!

The Board had instructed the selectors not to consider Bedi for the first Test because he had appeared in a television programme in England without permission. In his place came Haryana's Rajinder Goel, who like Bombay's Shivalkar would have been a permanent part of any national side had he not been an Indian contemporary of Bedi's.

It was an eventful start to what turned out to be the most entertaining Test series on Indian soil till 2001. The West Indies dominated the first Test at Bangalore. They batted first and scored 289. Sunil began well, driving and hooking Roberts for fours before a perfectly timed stroke off Holder caught Richards, standing at short-leg, on the thigh. The ball popped up, and Richards dived to catch the rebound. India conceded a first-innings lead of 29, and hundreds by skipper Lloyd and debutant Greenidge took the Windies to an impregnable position.

The identity of the vice-captain was revealed to the nation when Pataudi left the field to tend to an injured finger. Venkataraghvan offered to step in, but Sunil asserted his number two status.

Sunil led till Lloyd declared and set India a target of 386. With Pataudi and Engineer unfit to bat, the writing was on the wall for the Indians, and they duly collapsed for 118.

Pataudi's dislocated finger ruled him out of the second Test at Delhi, and the selectors handed over the charge to the vice-captain. Sunil was thrilled. He had his task cut out. The team had now lost four Tests in succession, and needed to turn things around. To the Indian cricket lover, it seemed the ideal situation – a young achiever deputising for a veteran, thus gaining invaluable exposure to the top job, and eventually taking over from the latter.

What they proposed, Pandurang Salgaonkar disposed.

The two weeks between the Bangalore and Delhi Tests enabled the Indian players to turn out for their respective Ranji sides. Sunil travelled with the Bombay team to Nashik for the Trans-Harbour tussle against Maharashtra.

'I can never forget that game, as I got my first hundred against Bombay after going in to bat in the very first over. We played on a bouncy Nashik matting wicket. Sunil took the onus of playing Pandu as much as possible and I remember a ball rearing up steeply and hitting him on the gloves. We knew he had got hurt but he refused to show it and went on to remain not out till the end of play. He played with a broken finger (index finger of the right hand) that must have hurt a fair bit, but he still took all the strike to Salgaonkar, as he knew that if he retired hurt,

Bombay could lose a few wickets. The sad part of the incident was that Sunil had just been appointed the captain of India and could not lead India in the next Test. That incident amplifies the importance of the Maharashtra-Bombay clash and how the players perceived it.' – Yajurvindra Singh.

In an age wherein players were as concerned about their domestic teams as the national side, Sunil stayed on in Nashik until Bombay gained the crucial first-innings lead.

He wasn't the only player to be heartbroken at missing out on the opportunity to lead India. Engineer was given the impression by some people that he would captain the side at Delhi, only for Venkataraghvan to be formally appointed on the morning of the match. With Bedi back after his one-Test suspension and Venkataraghvan in charge, and the selectors still closed to the idea of playing all four spinners, it was inevitable that either Prasanna or Chandrasekhar would be left out of the XI. Strangely, the leg-spinner, who had taken six wickets at Bangalore, was axed, and Prasanna, who had got two, retained. A man most delighted at Chandrasekhar's omission was Viv Richards, who had fallen to him in both innings at Bangalore. So thrilled was he that he plundered 192, his maiden Test hundred, and played the lead role in a victory by an innings and 67 runs.

Sunil accompanied the squad to Calcutta, the venue of the third Test. But he decided to return to Bombay for treatment when he realised that the doctors there were more interested in watching the Test. His departure was followed by one of the most stirring comebacks in Test history.

Not for the last time, a south Indian batsman excelled at the Eden when the chips were down. Viswanath's 139 inspired Chandrasekhar, by now back in the XI, and Bedi, to bowl India to a win by 85 runs. A significant aspect of the triumph, India's first after five consecutive defeats, was the presence of a genuine new-ball pair for the first time since the early 1960s – Madan Lal Sharma and debutant Karsan Ghavri.

The Calcutta win revived the spirits of the nation and Sunil was keen to return to the fray in the fourth Test at Madras. The finger did not give him much trouble, until Ghavri struck it in the nets.

India without Gavaskar was bad enough. Without Gavaskar against the West Indies was worse. The onus was on Viswanath. – Rajan Bala, *All the Beautiful Boys* (Rupa, 1990)

Against the fiery Roberts, on a spiteful Chepauk wicket, Viswanath batted for his team, his friend and himself. His unbeaten 97 was rated by watchers as the best innings ever played on Indian soil. Prasanna, who had essayed a splendid supporting role to Bedi and Chandrasekhar at Calcutta, then got into the act. His nine wickets in the match ensured a hundred-run triumph.

Bombay's Wankhede stadium could not have asked for a better baptism—a series decider. Sunil had by then procured a special pair of gloves, with extra protection to the index finger and middle finger of his right hand. He had to wait for his turn to bat for the first time in nearly two months. On the plot of land that was previously called Lloyd's Reclamation, Clive Lloyd won the toss and blasted 242. His blitzkrieg was marred by the local police, when they roughed up Yogesh Barot, a twenty-year-old enthusiast who ran onto the field to congratulate the Windies captain when he completed his 200. That incensed the spectators, and a riot ensued. Play was called off after tea on the second day, but the game resumed on schedule the following morning.

Lloyd declared at 604-6. Engineer's fall without a run on the board brought in India's fifth number three of the series—Eknath Solkar. Wadekar's presence was being missed, both in the slips as well as that pivotal position in the batting order.

However, Solkar's handling of the situation was heartening. At the other end, Sunil looked anything but rusty. His feet were moving well, and the bat was coming down on the ball as smoothly as ever before. He struck fifteen boundaries and dominated a partnership of 168. Only five minutes were left for stumps when he was bowled for 86.

'After Sunil had got his manufacturer to insert the extra padding in the gloves, everyone started doing likewise. I remember him joking, "I wish I had patented this!"' – E.A.S. Prasanna

'I always thought that after his index finger injury, he was a slightly lesser player. He was forced to push his finger behind

his bat handle that bit more. It was not something he wanted to. "I lost my mid-wicket drive and extra-cover drive and I think there were changes in my life. . . . Both were not very straight."'
– Rajan Bala, *All The Beautiful Boys* (Rupa, 1990)

Solkar completed a hundred and Viswanath missed out on one for the second time in successive Tests, being bowled by Holder on 95. He brought the house down at the end of the day's play when the TV commentator asked him whether the fatal ball had been an inswinger or an outswinger. 'If I would have known,' he replied, 'I would still be batting!'

India reached 406, and the West Indians then beat the hell out of the leather to set India a target of 404. The hosts' back was broken when Roberts had Sunil caught for 8. It was Roberts' thirty-second and final wicket of the series. His colleagues then took over to bowl the Indians out for 202 and take the series 3-2.

The series was lost, but Pataudi was hailed for resurrecting Indian cricket. Youngsters like Aunshuman Gaekwad and Karsan Ghavri had impressed, and the triumvirate of Viswanath, Solkar and Sunil had restored stability to the batting line-up. The spinners had regained form. Pataudi's decision to make himself unavailable for international cricket after the series revived the captaincy conundrum all over again. The conundrum would have probably been resolved for good had Sunil led at Delhi, for he would then have been the obvious choice to succeed Pataudi.

India had a lot of cricket coming up, with a twin tour of New Zealand and the Caribbean in 1975-76, a home series against England the following year, and a full tour of Australia the year after that. It was important for the team to click in New Zealand and the West Indies, where they had created history on their previous visits in 1967-68 and 1970-71 respectively. The players were eager to avenge their loss in England in 1974, and were also aware that they needed to click in Australia, where they had lost eight out of nine previous Tests. To fulfil these objectives, it was essential to put together a vibrant cricket team, headed by a shrewd and seasoned think-tank.

In hindsight, Pataudi may well have regretted not leading India in the inaugural World Cup. His style of batsmanship was suited to the abbreviated version, and he had of course played a fair amount of it during his stint with Sussex in England in the 60s. But then, in 1975, this brand of cricket was not taken all that seriously. The Indians had little or no time for it, despite the introduction of the Deodhar Trophy in 1973-74.

Sunil ended the season with an obdurate 96 in the Ranji final against Karnataka. It was a resolute effort, compiled despite another blow on the same finger. It helped Bombay take a first-innings lead of 65. Splendid bowling by Ghavri, Solkar and Shivalkar, enabled Bombay to regain the title. Mankad, whose tactical nous had prompted many to tout him as a potential India captain, scored an unbeaten 48 in the fourth innings.

'From 9.30 am to 4.30 pm, the Bombay dressing room was a silent and serious place. Everybody was focussed on the game. But once it was over, everything changed. Ashok Mankad and Sunil would transform into star entertainers. Mankad had a great sense of humour and Sunil was a wonderful mimic. He was a big fan of cinestar Dev Anand, and would often enact his songs in the pavilion. His imitations of Vijay Merchant and Prof Chandgadkar were hilarious. Whatever the match-situation was, we would let our hair down in the evenings and have a ball.'
– Karsan Ghavri

'I was in the Bombay squad in the 1974-75 season, but I didn't get to play a single game. I did the scoring for the team. When we were in Hyderabad, I would have to walk to the opposite end of the Fateh Maidan, where the scoreboard was situated. I would return to the dressing room at lunch time, and then return to the scoreboard with the scorebook tucked under my arm. I remember Sunil telling me not to mind what I was doing, for every member of the playing XI had been in my shoes at some point in time. My time as a cricketer would come very soon, he told me.' – Dilip Vengsarkar

Venkataraghvan, one of the few Indians who was a regular on the County circuit and hence had some form of exposure to limited-overs cricket, was named captain for the World Cup. Sunil stayed on as vice-captain.

For the second consecutive year, a trip by an Indian cricket team to England was a disaster. The tour got off to a forgettable start, with only six of the fourteen selected players reporting for the five-day camp in Bombay. Three players turned up only on the last day, and five players, including Venkataraghvan, were already in England, honouring their respective County and League commitments. Sunil was chided by P.M. Rungta, the BCCI president, for not staying over at the stadium with the rest of the boys to foster team spirit. That he had been permitted by G.S. Ramchand, the manager, to go home, was something the president chose to overlook.

Nine June 1975 was a traumatic day for all those who made their way to Lord's to watch the inaugural game of the competition between England and India. England, one of the tournament favourites, batted first and scored 334-4 from the allotted sixty overs. There was no possibility of India overhauling that total, but the least a line-up comprising the likes of Engineer, Sunil, Viswanath and Solkar was expected to do was fight. Sunil and Solkar opened for India and the second ball of the first over, bowled by Geoff Arnold, landed short of a length outside the off-stump and rose. Sunil tried to use its pace and height to guide it over the slips' heads. But he missed, not completely though. The ball kissed his bat and flew to Alan Knott. Sunil was cross with himself, but it turned out that there was no appeal! He could have walked, but he chose not to. What followed made him regret that decision.

England bowled, and Sunil blocked. But for an ungainly lofted pull off Arnold that fetched him three, he defended and defended – till the end of the sixtieth over. India finished with 132-3, and Sunil with an unbeaten 36 off 174 balls. It was a display that infuriated even his staunchest admirers. Ironically, even as he went about compiling the worst innings of his career, his defence remained as impregnable as ever. The heckling from the stands did not help, nor did the English fielders, who dropped him thrice.

> To understand why India, and especially Gavaskar, batted as they did, it is probably necessary to remember what happened when they last played at Lord's. They were bowled out for 42. If they could not win on Saturday, as they had decided they could not after England's innings, then every effort had to be concentrated on averting another collapse. – John Woodcock, *The Times*

Ramchand, the manager, seemed satisfied with Sunil's explanation.

> I am satisfied. I have never seen a player who could force the pace, and England's attack was too professional to slog. – G.S. Ramchand, as quoted in *The Record-breaking Sunil Gavaskar*, C.D. Clarke, (David and Charles, 1980)

Those not satisfied with the explanation dished out (and continue to dish out) various 'conspiracy theories'. The thread common to most of them was (and is) Sunil's alleged 'unhappiness'. The reasons were varied: anger over Venkataraghvan's appointment as captain ahead of him, the fact that India had a seam-oriented attack as opposed to a traditional spin-oriented one, the 'paltry' allowances given to the players, etc.

Sunil displayed all his strokes in the next game against East Africa, and a ten-wicket win made India a strong contender for a spot in the semi-finals. But they were outplayed by New Zealand and knocked out.

His homecoming after a trip to Europe was not memorable, with Rungta demanding another explanation for his crawl at Lord's. Ramchand had apparently criticised Sunil in his tour report for his slow batting, and his inability to discharge his duties as vice-captain. Sunil was understandably upset.

> 'He told me what had happened during the England game. At the tea interval, he told the management – captain Venkataraghvan, manager Ramchand and selector Raj Singh – that he was struggling. He offered to throw his wicket away. But all three of them instructed him to stay at one end, and that is what he did. The Board subsequently decided to drop the matter. It was in any case unlikely that they would have taken action against him. You cannot censure a player for following instructions, can you?' – Madhav Mantri

Sunil, his team-mates and the Board moved on. But his detractors still haven't.

> Gavaskar was reportedly upset that the manager (Ramchand) did not undertake the responsibility of telling Rungta that he had granted permission to Gavaskar to return home. Was this the reason that Gavaskar occupied his crease for sixty overs to

teach manager Ramchand a lesson? – K.R. Wadhwaney, *Indian Cricket Controversies* (*Diamond Pocket Books*, 2000)

That episode brought to an end the most tumultuous twelve months of Sunil's career till then. The period from June 1974 to June 1975 brought him joy, elation, despair and humiliation at different times. On the personal front, he found a companion for life.

He ended the twelve-month period on a low. Subsequent events would prove that it was merely a case of darkness before the dawn—of a 'Sunny' era.

Two
ASCENT

7

FROM STRENGTH TO STRENGTH

Indian cricket and India the nation had pursued congruent paths in the first four years of Sunil's international career. The optimism of 1971 had given way to pessimism in 1975. Growing unemployment, poverty and inflation had beset the country and besieged Mrs Gandhi. Matters came to a head when her own election to Parliament in 1971 was declared null and void by the Allahabad High Court. She responded to the attacks on her government, party and reputation by imposing a state of Emergency in August 1975. After twenty-eight years of independence, India found itself shackled all over again, this time by its own people.

Indian cricket wasn't as badly hit as India the nation. But the wounds of 1974 had not healed, the comeback against the West Indies notwithstanding. The Indian cricket lover, who had hailed his team as a prospective world champion after 1971, was unsure of what to make of his team. The team itself was in a state of transition, just like the country.

The Indian government's bid to paint a picture of normalcy wasn't helped by the fact that independent India's first generation had progressed to young adulthood by 1975. The members of this generation were not as much concerned with the processes, as with the results. They did not hesitate to challenge conventional wisdom, especially the variety that in their opinion was ineffective. No longer were youngsters willing to run around in circles. They wanted action, and success.

That explained the younger generation's increasing expectations from its cricketers, who belonged to the same age group. That also explained a remarkable development in cinema, which had traditionally been one of three Cs – the Congress party and Cricket being the other two – that bound the nation.

Cinema screens in the Hindi-speaking regions of the country saw the advent of the 'angry young man', a protagonist who not only spoke strongly, but backed his words with action. He did not hesitate to take on the mightiest of the mighty in his bid to set things right. He also did not hesitate to push the envelope, if it meant that equity would be ensured. By mid-1975, Amitabh Bachchan had established himself as the numero uno of the Bombay film industry with standout performances in films like *Zanjeer, Namak Haraam,* and *Deewar*.

Not that he was an anger specialist. He unveiled the lighter side of his personality in films like *Chupke Chupke* and Indian cinema's biggest blockbuster *Sholay*. The son of Harivanshrai Bachchan, one of the nation's most venerated poets, Amitabh chucked a cushy job as an executive in Calcutta to join films at the relatively late age of twenty-seven. His first twelve films flopped, with the exception of *Anand*, in which his brooding introvert had been a perfect foil to the then superstar Rajesh Khanna's cheery extrovert. Many a pundit had advised him to stick to character roles. But fate willed otherwise. Scriptwriters Salim Khan and Javed Akhtar, supported by film makers like Prakash Mehra and Yash Chopra, created a protagonist whose primary aim was to shake the establishment out of its stupor and kick it in the backside, sometimes literally. When the masses saw Amitabh battle a gang of goons or use his rich baritone to express his frustration at the prevailing conditions, they felt as if it was their war he was waging. Some films in the 1950s and '60s apart, Indian cinema had not seen a proactive anti-hero of this type.

Neither had Indian cricket seen anybody like Sunil Gavaskar. His outstanding debut in 1971 had thrilled his contemporaries. His performances in England in 1974 delighted them even further. The prospect of a diminutive individual taking on the meanest of fast-bowling bullies, armed with a new ball and backed by ten team-mates, was appealing and endearing. India had always been served by talented middle-order batsmen, and Sunil's buddy Viswanath was among the best of the lot, but even a casual cricket follower knew that opening was by far the toughest job in the game. Similarly, none of Amitabh's distinguished predecessors could measure up to his popularity and professionalism.

The year 1975 signalled the start of a six-year period that Amitabh and Gavaskar made their own.

Sunil's fans, disappointed with his batting in the World Cup, expected him to bounce back with a bang. It happened sooner than anticipated.

When Bombay selectors Polly Umrigar, V.S. Patil, Madhav Mantri and Sharad Diwadkar met on the eve of the new season on 26 September 1975, not many people would have expected them to discuss the captaincy. After all, Mankad had won the Ranji Trophy the previous year. But they did.

> 'Ashok Mankad was a very good captain, no doubt about it. But we were unsure whether he would get to play for India. On the other hand, Sunil was a permanent member of the national team. He thus stood a greater chance of becoming captain of India. So we decided to make him the captain to enable him to enhance his experience as a leader. But I made the convener record our appreciation of Mankad as a captain. The Mankads, father and son, did not talk to me for a month.' – V.S. Patil

Ashok Mankad's supporters were shocked at what they believed was a Dadar Union conspiracy—Patil and Mantri were Sunil's mentors, and Umrigar was a close friend of the latter. But then, there was a precedent. Hadn't the South Zone selectors given the captaincy to Venkataraghvan for exactly the same reason in 1971?

It was a hard decision, one that was bound to hurt some people.

> 'I could well have gone on to become the India captain had I stayed on as Bombay captain. But the selectors thought of Sunil as a future India captain. In view of my place in the Indian team not being certain, they were right in the end. But back then, I thought it was a premature move. Sunil would have led India

anyway. My dream was shattered and my place in the national team became a confirmed uncertainty.' – Late Ashok Mankad

As had happened in his university days, the captaincy was a shot in the arm for Sunil. It provided a fillip to his efforts of forgetting all that had happened in the preceding few months.

He started the season with a hundred, his first in the Ranji Trophy since 1972-73, and a calculated declaration. Gujarat batted first in a Ranji game and scored 245. Sunil led the response with an innings of 112, and declared on the third morning, immediately after they had taken a first-innings lead. Abdul Ismail and Ghavri then bowled superbly to ensure an outright win. Sunil then led Bombay to victory in the Irani Trophy game by virtue of the first-innings lead. After the Rest of India had scored 210, the Nagpur spectators were treated to a breathtaking innings by a nineteen-year-old Dadar Unionite who had replaced the injured Solkar in the XI. Dilip Vengsarkar tore into the Rest bowling, Prasanna and Bedi included, scoring 110 off 80 balls. While he remembered the basics of batsmanship that he had imbibed at Dadar Union, Vengsarkar did not seem to believe in the Bombay dictum that carpet strokes were sacred and their lofted counterparts despicable. He was, in that sense, an exception to the rule, but that did not stop all of Bombay from celebrating the arrival of their newest batting star.

The young man was thrilled to be presented a Duncan Fearnley bat by his captain.

> 'The Bombay side that Sunil took charge of was outstanding. We were a complete side, in that we had run-hungry batsmen, effective new-ball bowlers, canny spinners and brilliant fielders. Sunil, Mankad, Solkar and Parkar were fantastic run-accumulators. Parkar and Solkar were electrifying fielders. Abdul Ismail was a prodigious swinger of the ball. He and I got quite a few breaks early on in the innings. Then there was Padmakar Shivalkar, the premier match-winner. Sunil did not have a lot to worry about.' – Karsan Ghavri

Sunil was unstoppable in the Ranji games that followed. He scored 190 against Maharashtra, 171 against Saurashtra, and aggregated 510 runs at the end of the league stage. These performances made him a frontrunner for the top job for the twin tours of New Zealand and the West Indies, but the selectors indicated their preference for Bishan Bedi by handing him the reins for an unofficial series against Sri Lanka.

Not many people had issues with the decision to elevate Bedi. The twenty-nine year-old was a proven achiever, and had impressed everyone with his captaincy of Delhi and the North Zone. Much like the Karnataka seniors of the late 1960s, Bedi had spent the first half of the 1970s building the Delhi Ranji trophy team. He was instrumental in convincing three youngsters, who like him had started their first-class careers for Punjab, to shift to the capital. Madan Lal had gone on to enter the national side. The other two, Surender and Mohinder Amarnath, sons of independent India's first Test captain Lala Amarnath, had been no less impressive.

Sunil scored 203 in the first Test against the Lankans and was then left out, with the selectors wanting to try out other players before the twin tours. India won the series against Sri Lanka easily, but Bedi found himself in hot water all over again, with the BCCI demanding an explanation for his alleged outburst over the boarding and lodging arrangements provided to the players at Nagpur during the Sri Lanka series. The matter was resolved when Bedi apologised to an inquiry committee that comprised Board President R.P. Mehra, Treasurer M.A. Chidambaram and Vice-President S.K. Wankhede. The national selectors took only five minutes to decide on Bedi as captain. The left-arm spinner was the third Indian skipper under whom Sunil was to serve as vice-captain.

The Indians began the New Zealand leg of their twin tour with three-dayers against the Central Districts and Northern Districts respectively. It was during the second of those games that Sunil took on a job he had done in quite a few Tests of his career—the shine-remover.

> 'Sunil opened the bowling and bowled me a couple of bouncers! I was shocked, for that was the last thing I had expected from him! I hung around until I was bowled by Chandrasekhar, who was a unique proposition.' – John Wright

Bedi suffered the same fate as Sunil did on the eve of what should have been his first Test as captain. A calf injury forced the left-armer to pull out, and his deputy took over. For Sunil, this was life at its most unpredictable. When he was appointed captain for the Delhi Test a year ago, Sunil had gone out of his way to prepare himself mentally. But injury had played spoilsport. A year later, the captaincy had come his way without his even thinking about it. While he was prepared for the possibility of taking over in case Bedi was indisposed, he hadn't expected such a situation to arise in the very first Test of a series.

It was a new-look India XI that took the field at Auckland's Eden Park after Glenn Turner, another debutant captain, won the toss and elected to bat. There were as many as six changes from the XI that played the West Indies at Bombay in January 1975. Bedi was sitting out, Pataudi and Engineer were not around, Solkar was part of the squad but not playing due to a finger injury, and Gaekwad was sitting on the reserves' bench. Ghavri, the sixth player, had been left behind in India.

Three of the six slots were filled by Venkataraghvan, Madan Lal and Mohinder Amarnath, the last two being the only new-ball bowlers in the seventeen-member touring party. At Auckland, Mohinder was picked to play the second Test of his career, and his first since the Madras Test against Australia in 1969-70. Alongside them were three debutants.

Vengsarkar's Irani blitz and Bombay pedigree had fast-tracked his foray into the national side. Ironically, he found himself being pushed into the same boat as his illustrious Bombay namesake. With the designated openers failing to impress in the three-dayers, the think-tank decided to take a chance with Vengsarkar, who had opened at the junior levels.

The second debutant was Syed Kirmani, who had come a long way since his childhood wicketkeeping stints in a park in his Bangalore neighbourhood, where a brick in each hand would serve as a modest substitute for gloves. His keeping and batting had played a critical role in Karnataka's rise to the Ranji forefront in the seventies. He had been Engineer's understudy in England in 1971 and 1974, and the selectors had decided to reward him for his perseverance. Technically, Pochiah Krishnamurthy, also a member of the side that went to England in 1971, was his senior, having kept in four Tests in the Caribbean in 1971, but Kirmani was better on both sides of the stumps. His biggest plus point was that he had kept wicket at the domestic level to Prasanna and Chandrasekhar for nearly a decade.

The troika of debutants was completed by Mohinder's elder brother Surender, a converted left-hander who had scored a mountain of runs in the 1975-76 season.

The loss of the toss was Sunil's solitary defeat during the course of his first Test as captain of India, as it turned out.

When he introduced the spinners, Sunil placed himself at Solkar's suicidal position. Most skippers would have almost certainly posted a youngster there. Solkar, watching from the pavilion, was delighted to see the acting skipper take a diving catch to dismiss his opposite number Glenn Turner off Chandrasekhar. New Zealand were 95-1 at lunch. Prasanna bowled superbly after the interval, frustrating the elegant Bevan Congdon into holing out in the deep, where Madan Lal held a good catch. Sunil then juggled his three spinners splendidly. Venkataraghvan, who had bowled a tight over to Hastings, the new batsman, was held back, and Chandrasekhar asked to have a go from his end. The leg-spinner responded by dismissing John Parker, another pillar of the Kiwi batting line-up. The wickets tumbled steadily until the tailenders offered obdurate resistance. Sunil then went on the defensive, with Venkataraghvan operating with a cover and extra-cover and two men in the leg-trap. The others were scattered in the outfield. The bowling was tight enough to force all-rounder Dayle Hadlee and keeper Ken Wadsworth to err. New Zealand slid from 187-5 at tea to 266 all out. India finished the day at 16-0.

Vengsarkar fell the following morning without adding to the overnight score. Sunil was contemplating a long stay at the crease, but it was not going to be easy. He had not been in the best of form on the tour, and the wicket had some juice in it.

Surender Amarnath took the weight off his captain's shoulders with a magnificent innings. Sunil was happy to play second fiddle, what with Surender stroking the ball beautifully. Richard Collinge, against whom Sunil had impressed for the Combined Universities many moons ago, gave the acting skipper a tough time, beating him time and again outside the off-stump. But Sunil summoned all his tenacity and hung on, providing glimpses of his repertoire of strokes every now and then. Collinge only had to make the slightest error in length, for Sunil to drive past him, or pull him to the mid-wicket boundary.

That the twenty-eight-year-old Surender was eager to make up for the lost years, was underscored by the manner in which he completed his hundred. As captain of the Indian Schoolboys team to England in 1967, he had found himself facing the penultimate ball of a game at Lord's with his side needing ten to win. He had gone on to hit two consecutive sixes to complete a stunner of a victory. At Auckland nine years later, he on-drove O'Sullivan for four to move from 88 to 92, and then deposited him over the long-on boundary to move from 93 to 99. A single made him the seventh Indian to score a century on Test debut. A continent away, his father, who was following the proceedings on radio on an icy Delhi morning, broke down.[1]

Amarnath fell for 124, during the course of which, he added 204 with his skipper. Viswanath was declared out caught behind when the ball carried to the keeper off his hip. Sunil top-edged Collinge for six and then cut the same bowler to complete his sixth Test hundred. His dismissal for 116 was followed by a slide, which the Delhi duo of Mohinder Amarnath and Madan Lal halted. Their stand of 93 enabled India to accumulate a lead of 148, and with close to two full days left and the track taking some turn, they fancied their chances of victory.

Congdon and Parker refused to see it that way. New Zealand were a healthy 161-2 at the end of the fourth day, and the Indians aggrieved at what they perceived as biased umpiring. They needed some magic on the final day, and it was provided by the man who had been their best bowler on the previous visit to New Zealand in 1967-68.

Prasanna began proceedings for his team on the fifth day. He had Parker caught at point off his second ball. In his second over, he bowled Hastings, and then carried on. He finished with figures of 6-16 in an eight-over spell, of which three were maidens, and overall innings figures of 8-76, his best in Test cricket. The innings ended at 215. Sunil scored 35 of the 68 runs India needed to complete a hattrick of Test wins in New Zealand. It was a belligerent cameo. He hit Collinge for four down the wicket, and then swung Hadlee over square-leg for six. Victory was achieved when he drove Howarth to the long-on boundary.

---

[1]Lala and Surender are the only father-son duo to have scored centuries on their respective Test debuts.

He was the first Indian captain after Polly Umrigar, who was coincidentally the manager of the touring side, to win his first Test as captain, and the second after Hazare to score a hundred on his debut as captain. The Indians celebrated the win with champagne and two distinctive Marathi delicacies, *chivda* and *sheera*. The players were also treated to the sight of the diminutive Sunil pulling the leg of the six-footer Umrigar for being tense during India's chase of the paltry target.

Sunil's post-match comments reflected the mood of the team. When reminded that the hosts were likely to retaliate with a green top in the second Test at Christchurch, Sunil said that a bowler like Chandrasekhar, who relied on bounce, would only be encouraged if that were to happen.

The greenish texture of the Christchurch pitch did not deter Bedi from electing to bat. The Dadar Unionites negotiated the first few overs well, but failed to consolidate. Viswanath essayed a masterly hand of 83 and India got 270 after the loss of more than a day's play to rain. New Zealand got 403 in response, with Turner getting a hundred. Syed Kirmani established an Indian record for the highest number of dismissals (six – five catches and one stumping). However, this achievement wasn't as significant from the Indian point of view as that of its faster bowlers. Nine of the ten wickets were taken by the new-ball duo of Amarnath and Madan Lal, making it the first such instance in Indian cricket history since the 1936 Lord's Test against England.

The Indians drew the game with comfort, thanks to its little stalwarts. Sunil thwarted the Kiwi bowlers to score 71, an innings replete with attractive strokes. Viswanath complemented him with a gritty 79.

The Indians expected another green top in the final Test at Wellington, and so it was. Bedi elected to bat once again. Sunil and Vengsarkar saw the opening overs through with ease, with the New Zealand pacemen unable to get the ball to rear off the track. The score was 40 when Dayle Hadlee's younger brother, who had got only one wicket in the previous Test and was a last-minute inclusion for this game, struck.

Richard Hadlee had Sunil caught behind off the first ball after the drinks interval. He then packed off Vengsarkar and Amarnath, in the process taking three wickets for five runs in fifteen balls. The others struggled, with the exception of Patel (81) and Kirmani (49). India got

220. The bowlers did their best to exploit the conditions as well as their Kiwi counterparts, but they were thwarted by a side determined to square the series. Turner and Congdon laid the foundation of their reply with 64 and 52 respectively, and their mates took it from there. The balance of power shifted on the third day, a disastrous one for India.

Bedi could not take the field due to fever, and then Sunil, stationed again at short-leg, could not get out of the way of a full-blooded sweep by Lance Cairns. He was hit on the cheek and stretchered off the ground. An examination revealed a slight fracture of the left cheekbone. The New Zealand innings ended at 334, and then Richard Hadlee blew India away with a series-levelling spell of 7-21. Sunil was unable to bat, and in an age wherein it was easier to trek to the South Pole than make a phone call to India from overseas, he was unable to communicate with his concerned family, particularly his wife, who was due to deliver their first-born any day.

For the second time in his career, Umrigar had on his hands the task of getting in touch with the concerned wife of an injured cricketer. As the seniormost member of the Indian team in the Caribbean in 1961-62, he had called Dolly Contractor about her husband's near-fatal injury in Bridgetown, Barbados. Of course, Sunil's injury was not as serious as Nariman Contractor's.

Sunil tried to make light of the situation when he was wheeled in for a minor manipulative surgery. When informed by the doctors that they were going to open him up, he asked whether they could make him look like Paul Newman!

His sense of humour vanished when the Board denied him permission to visit India to see his son, who was born on 22 February. The first Test in the West Indies was to start only on 10 March, and Sunil was not going to play for two weeks in any case. But the Board refused.

The New Zealand tour thus ended on a sour note for the Indians. Bedi, not one to take things lying down, lashed out at the Basin Reserve, and called it the lousiest cricket ground in the world. It was the kind of criticism Indian pitches tended to evoke from touring captains. Like their Indian counterparts in a similar situation, the New Zealanders labelled his outburst as a case of sour grapes.

Bedi's views did not alter those of two visitors to the Indian dressing room on the final day of the series. The Governor General and Prime Minister of New Zealand dropped in to compliment the team for its demeanour on and off the field. They went so far as to hail the Indian team as the best to tour New Zealand. That improved the mood of the players as they set out for the Caribbean.

'India had beaten us in 1971, but our fast-bowling attack of 1976 was far superior. We were waiting for them.' – Michael Holding

Eight of the players had been on Wadekar's trip six years previously, and knew the score out there. They reckoned that they had done their best in New Zealand, the green tops, Richard Hadlee and the umpiring notwithstanding, and had it in them to go one step further against a wounded West Indian outfit. Clive Lloyd's men had just been drubbed 1-5 in Australia in a series that had been tagged the unofficial World Championship of Test cricket.

Sunil joined his team-mates in Barbados after a flying visit to New York. He took the field for the three-dayer against the island nation a day later, leading in Bedi's absence. His first innings in three weeks yielded him 62 runs, inclusive of 8 boundaries and 1 six. However, the strongest team in the West Indies prevailed.

Prior to the first Test, the Indians requested the West Indies Cricket Board to replace Stanton Parris, one of the designated umpires. Their request was denied. Like its counterparts across the world, the WICB was perfectly entitled to back its officials.

In his sixth year of international cricket, Sunil was back where it had all begun. He had by this time evolved a distinct process of preparing for an innings. He would put on his gear and then cocoon himself from the rest of the world. Nobody was supposed to say anything to him once he would commence this process.

I did that when five minutes were left for us to go in, when the first bell for the umpires would ring. Basically, I would be thinking about what I was going to do. I would tell myself to play straight, as that is the best way to counter swing. But at the end, it's an instinctive game. If you see a wide half-volley, you should put it away for four. The whole point is to score runs. – Sunil Gavaskar, *Boycs and Sunny Masterclass* (ESPN, 2000)

Andy Roberts challenged Sunil's instincts more than once after Bedi won the toss and elected to bat. In his first over, he was no-balled thrice, and cut by Sunil for four. When he bounced, Sunil went onto the back foot once again, and hooked him for six.

Roberts then changed ends, but the runs kept coming. Sunil flicked him to the square-leg fence. A cut and drive took India to 50 off only 9 overs, of which Sunil had contributed 35. Holding then drew first blood when he dismissed Sunil's newest partner, Parthasarathy Sharma, for 6. That strike seemed to have restored Roberts' confidence. He avenged the earlier punishment by trapping Sunil leg-before. The dismissal broke the back of the Indian innings, and it was only a gallant stand between Madan Lal and Mohinder that helped the visitors reach 177.

The hosts piled on the runs. Vivian Richards, who had scored 101, 50 and 98 in the last three Tests against Australia, scored 142, helped along the way by the generosity of the Indian fielders and keeper. Kallicharran got 93 and skipper, Lloyd, 102. The Indians had a deficit of 311 to contend with. That figure would have seemed like '3110' when Sunil tried to hook a Roberts delivery in the first over, but could not clear Rafique Jumadeen, stationed at forward short-leg. The rest of the batting caved in, and the Windies won by an innings and 97 runs.

The Indians were disappointed, but not despondent. The next Test was to be played in Trinidad, their home away from home, after all.

The think-tank brainstormed on the composition of the side for the second Test. A stable top order was essential. Sharma, a specialist opener, had struggled, as had Vengsarkar, a converted one.

'We were at a party the night before the three-day game against Trinidad, when Bishan, Sunil and Polly kaka cornered me and asked me to open. Polly kaka (uncle) assured me that I would be able to do it as my technique was good. I had never opened before. In fact, I started my first-class career at number nine and worked my way up. I decided to give it a try. I opened against Trinidad and got a hundred. "There you are", the trio said to me that evening.' – Anshuman Gaekwad

The think-tank, however, decided to give Vengsarkar another chance as opener. The moisture in the wicket had prompted Bedi to elect to bowl after winning the toss, but it started pouring soon after, and the entire day's play was washed out. The teams arrived at the ground on the second day, to be confronted with a strip that was bone-dry. There was nothing Bedi or his team could do about the toss, and as it turned out, about Richards, who was once again on a roll. The Indians sought to compensate by targeting his partners. They were reasonably successful. The hosts were bowled out for 241 early on the third day, of which Richards' share was 130. Bedi bowled splendidly to take five wickets and Chandrasekhar got two. Venkataraghvan, who had replaced the indisposed Prasanna, went wicketless as a result of another lapse by Kirmani. Richards was 83 when the keeper missed a stumping.

The Indians had ample time in which to give their spinners runs to bowl within the second innings. But Vengsarkar fell in the first over. India then almost lost another wicket. Mohinder, their newest number three, took a fair bit of time to arrive at the crease. He had been lying on the masseur's table, probably after convincing himself that the openers would give the team a good start! Had Lloyd appealed, he would have been in trouble. Mohinder eventually rushed out, and batted well until he was caught at the wicket off Jumadeen. Viswanath and Surender got off to a good start and scored 21 each before getting out.

At the other end, Sunil was at his best. He had scored 52 and 57 in the three-dayer against Trinidad, and was at home on his favourite cricket ground.

Against Roberts and Holding, he preferred accumulation to acceleration. Roberts gave him a tough time in the first session, with a series of deliveries that skidded from a length, but Sunil handled them well, defending some and ignoring the others. He was 10 at lunch, 49 at tea and 90 at stumps. Patel provided him the support he so richly deserved. Sunil got more and more assertive as the innings progressed, and his fans at the Queen's Park Oval were treated to some fine strokeplay in the last session of the third day, and the first of the fourth day. He completed his hundred, his third in succession at the venue, with a single off Bernard Julien.

> In 1971, they composed a calypso to celebrate Gavaskar's tall scores. There should be another in the making... the innings was devoid of frills and flourishes. – K.N. Prabhu, *TOI*, 28 March 1976, (filed)

Sunil reached 156 before he was caught behind off Holding. Madan Lal filled his boots capably and Patel completed his maiden Test hundred before Bedi waved him in with India 161 ahead.

The Indian spinners did their best to force a win, but they were not helped by some gritty batsmanship, particularly by Lloyd, some questionable umpiring decisions, and most of all, their own ineptitude on the field. Lloyd got a miraculous life when Patel and substitute-fielder Solkar collided while attempting a catch. Richards, who was nursing a thigh injury, was incensed to be declared run out by umpire Ralph Gosein. The West Indian supporters at the ground took up his cause, and Gosein was flustered enough to play safe for the rest of the innings. The West Indies were 215-8 when a halt was called.

The disappointment of the Indians at missing out on a win at their Caribbean home ground was not assuaged by the rain that greeted them on their arrival in Guyana for the next three-dayer and Test. Boredom and homesickness were inevitable as the players remained cooped up in their hotel in Georgetown, with no option but to stare at the water falling from the loaded skies. After all, they had been away from home for nearly three months. The seniors did their bit to boost spirits by playing an April fools joke on Umrigar and the treasurer, Balu Alaganan. They orchestrated a phone call to Umrigar, with one of them claiming to be a representative of the Indian High Commission in Guyana. He told Umrigar that his Trinidad counterpart had received complaints about the Indian team's poor behaviour. Umrigar and Alaganan rushed to the High Commission, only to discover that they were chasing a wild goose.

Sunil was finding it hard to retain his focus. His newborn son was close to two months old, and Sunil had seen him only in photographs brought over to the West Indies by All India Radio commentators Suresh Saraiya and Ravi Chaturvedi. The father's keenness to see his son came to the fore when the players were asked to board a frail-looking aircraft for a trip to a military base. It was still raining heavily, and Sunil, along with four others, refused to board the plane. The quintet was apprehensive, but their team-mates returned in one piece.

Even as the rains refused to relent, came the news that the third Test had been shifted to Port of Spain.

To say that the Indians were overjoyed would be an understatement.

8

TWO TITANS, TWO TESTS

> Fear doesn't exist at the international level. It is never really an element. If it is there and you are worried about physical injury, then you shouldn't be out there. I believe it helps to be hit on the ribs, because you realise that although it is painful, it isn't going to kill you. It also makes you realise that you should use the bat more. – Sunil Gavaskar, *Boycs and Sunny Masterclass* (ESPN, 2000)

The West Indies were not too thrilled with the prospect of playing another Test on the slow and low Queen's Park Oval track. The selectors decided to rest Roberts for the last two Tests to keep him fresh for their forthcoming tour of England. Holding and Julien were assigned new-ball duties. The Windies XI comprised three spinners—Rafique Jumadeen (left-arm spin), and debutants Imtiaz Ali (leg-spin) and Albert Padmore (off-spin). The trio was nowhere close to India's trio in terms of class, but their seniors reckoned that they would be more effective on the Port of Spain wicket than fast bowlers. Needless to say, the Indians were not complaining.

The smiles on the faces of the Indians vanished when Richards feasted at their expense to score 177, his third hundred of the series in as many

Tests. The hosts reached 359, and 'Whispering Death' Michael Holding took six wickets. His first victim was Sunil, who was dismissed leg-before for 26, his lowest Test score at the Queen's Park Oval. India scored only 228. The Windies attacked in their second innings, with Kallicharran getting 103, but the Indian spinners by and large kept things tight. At 271-6, Lloyd declared, his team 402 runs ahead and by all means in the driver's seat. Around eight hours were left in the game, and in ninety-nine years of Test cricket, only Don Bradman's Invincibles of 1948 had scored more than 400 in the fourth innings of a Test to win it.

> Lloyd's declaration at 271-6 was not an act of charity. He wanted to win. Had we been in that position, we would have been happier, as Indian spinners have always enjoyed bowling fourth.
> – Bishan Bedi, *Great Moments of Indian Cricket* (1987)

Accompanying Sunil at the start of the Indian innings was Aunshuman Gaekwad, a new Test opener.

Mohinder replaced Gaekwad at 69 and demonstrated all the reasons that had prompted the management to elevate a 'new-ball bowler who could bat' to the number three slot, in place of his elder brother Surender, who had lost his way and place in the XI after the highs of Auckland. Mohinder had the best view of a batsman on a roll at his favourite venue.

In front of a capacity crowd, on a ground baked in sunshine, Sunil reached his sixth 50-plus score at Port of Spain in four Tests with a steer off Holding. The spinners failed to trouble him, and he ended the day with a sizzling cover-drive off Julien. He was on 86, inclusive of a dozen fours, and India were 134-1, well poised to save the match.

The final day commenced with the crowd roaring in anticipation of another Gavaskar hundred. Sunil wasn't able to recapture his fluency of the previous day. But there was no question of his throwing it away. He batted doggedly, keeping faith in the maxim he had followed all his life, 'Stay at the wicket, and the runs will come'. He completed his hundred, the eighth of his career and fourth in four Tests at Port of Spain, but was livid to miss a drive off Jumadeen and be stumped by the keeper Deryck Murray soon after. The scoreboard read 177-2. As he watched

Sunil leave, Lloyd permitted himself a smile. The danger man was gone, and he fancied his bowlers' chances of getting the remaining eight wickets on a deteriorating fifth-day wicket.

Mohinder and the new man Viswanath added twenty runs before the lunch interval.

One of the reasons the overseas media did not rate Viswanath as highly as Sunil was that the Karnataka batsman had played his best innings on Indian soil. However, it was always obvious to the discerning observer that while Sunil was a remarkable batsman, Viswanath was a genius. His hand-eye coordination, strong forearms, rubber-like wrists that could dispatch two similar deliveries anywhere from third-man on the off-side to fine-leg on the leg-side, and ability to essay the square-cut at will, were indicative of an approach to batsmanship that was spontaneous compared to Sunil's structured methods.

It wasn't that Viswanath abhorred tradition. His basics were solid.

It was just that he tended to improvise a lot more than Sunil. The nature of his job admittedly gave him the leeway to do so, for he batted in the middle order, as opposed to Sunil, whose brief was to open the innings for a team like India, and hence try to provide a safe start. If Sunil had one stroke to a delivery, Viswanath invariably had two or three, and one of the probable reasons he hadn't played as many long innings as his friend was a dilemma he often encountered while batting—Which of the three shots do I essay? He could have done better with Sunil's reserves of concentration although he possessed a god-given gift – the ability to pick the length of the ball a fraction of a second quicker than most batsmen, Sunil included.

Both men had adhered to a tried and tested principle of batsmanship in their formative years; the longer one stood still, the later one played the ball. His experiences against Snow and Lillee in his very first year of international cricket convinced Sunil that it was essential to be in the best conceivable position to play the ball just before meeting it. He had cultivated the habit of looking out for cues. For instance, several fast bowlers ran in quicker when they intended to bowl a bouncer.

Between 1971 . . . till the end of 1974, he was still evolving his technique. An injury to his right hand made him consciously push it a little more around the bat handle in his grip. – Rajan Bala, *Glances at Perfection, The Story of Indian Cricket Technique* (Dronequill, 2002)

By 1976, the batsman who never took guard in his first couple of series, opting to ground his bat in his partner's leg-stump guard, had perfected an initial back-and-across movement. He would ground his bat a wee bit outside the leg stump, and then move back and across just as the bowler was about to release the ball. That brought his eyes in line with the off-stump, and enabled him to judge the line of the delivery. When he moved, his body weight stayed equally distributed between both feet, thus enabling him to advance onto the front foot or move onto the back foot, depending upon the length of the delivery. As Dean Jones observed several years later, the final position of the batsmen who went back and across, wherein the toes of the front foot would point towards mid-off and the bat would be raised, wasn't too dissimilar to that of a boxer's before making a strike.

> In a BBC television interview, I asked him about that first move back and across. He replied, 'I just worked out the best method for my height. If I had gone looking to play forward, I would have been hit on the head all the time. Playing back gave me options to sway, duck and drop the wrists or hook if I was in [a] position to do so.' – Tony Lewis, *Wisden Cricketers Almanac*, 1989

A delivery that was headed well past his right, he would consider ignoring. Of course, it was risky to ignore deliveries pitched right in the corridor of uncertainty just outside the off-stump. But then, one had to be a really good bowler to maintain that line for long periods. Against accurate bowlers, patience was an essential attribute, and Sunil possessed loads of it. Anything that was in line or to the left of his head, he would either play or duck under, depending upon its length.

> 'I remember a club match at the P.J. Hindu Gymkhana years after Sunil became a Test cricketer. The dressing rooms there are parallel to the pitch. When Sunil made his way to the crease,

I asked the juniors to watch him closely, for everything about him – the stance, backlift, feet movement – was close to perfect.'
– V.S. Patil

Whatever technical differences there were between the two little masters, they worked for Indian cricket in the 1970s. This in itself was unprecedented, for rarely had Indian cricket seen two practitioners of diverse batting schools emerge and excel simultaneously for a prolonged period. Vijay Merchant, founder of the school of orthodox batsmanship of which Sunil was a member, had an illustrious and equally run-hungry contemporary in Vijay Hazare, but their approaches to batsmanship were similar. Tiger Pataudi followed the methods prescribed by the C.K. Nayudu school of belligerence. Unfortunately for Indian cricket, his rise coincided with the decline of Vijay Manjrekar, an accomplished technician and successor to his two namesakes.

The vicissitudes of fate and form had not helped either. Merchant formed a great opening partnership with Nayudu's disciple Syed Mushtaq Ali in 1936, but both batsmen were robbed of their best years by World War II. Indian cricket lovers of the 1960s had always wondered how the team would have performed had Tiger Pataudi struck form at the same time as Chandu Borde, an alumnus of the Merchant-Hazare school. Invariably, when one was going great guns, the other fired blanks.

But Sunil bonded and flourished in partnership with Gundappa Viswanath, a student of the K.S. Ranjitsinhji school, which imparted the virtues of wristwork and improvisation. Both had a lot in common with the pioneers of the schools they represented. Merchant was known to have prepared for the seaming wickets and swinging conditions in England by attempting to replicate the conditions in Bombay. He would practise against local quickies in Bombay very early in the mornings, when the wickets would have dew on them. There were times when he requested Amar Singh, his close friend and the celebrated half of India's first Test new-ball pair, to help him hone his technique by bowling to him in the nets. In England in 1936, Merchant, despite being in the middle of a golden run with the bat, requested Sir Jack Hobbs, the highest century-maker in first-class cricket, to observe him in the nets. Sunil's pursuit of perfection was no less intense than Merchant's, as was evident from his quality practice sessions at the Dadar Union nets, and regular requests to the likes of Mantri and Umrigar to watch him at the nets. Like Merchant, he had never been inclined to rest on his laurels.

> 'I was once invited to address a felicitation ceremony of Sunil's. There was a question and answer session at the end, and someone asked me to compare Merchant and Sunil as openers. I replied that a champion in one era would always be a champion in another, simply because they all possessed the same qualities.'
> – Madhav Mantri

Viswanath's batsmanship was no less enticing than that of his spiritual guru, K.S. Ranjitsinhji, the prince of Nawanagar. Both Ranji and he were adept at using the pace of the ball, utilising their wrists to dispatch the ball wherever they wanted to, and in the process, leaving watchers wonderstruck.

But it wasn't as if Sunil and Viswanath had nothing in common besides their heights. They shared a penchant for thriving in adversity.

On the afternoon of 12 April 1976, Viswanath and Amarnath added 26 runs in the first forty-five minutes after lunch. It was then that Lloyd realised that while his spinners were not conceding too many runs, they were not exactly troubling the batsmen. As a result, he called for the new ball, which was twenty-nine overs overdue. That turned the match.

> 'There was nothing in the track for the West Indian bowlers, least of all their spinners. The runs kept coming, but not in torrents as the ball had gone a little soft. Clive delayed taking the new ball that was due, preferring to continue with his spinners. By the time he asked for the new ball, Jimmy Amarnath and I were seeing it like a football.'– Gundappa Viswanath, *Ind-WI Special Feature* (PMG, 2006)

The West Indies team could only gape as Viswanath launched into Holding and Julien, the new ball notwithstanding. The runs and boundaries started flowing. The first 8 overs with the new ball yielded 39 runs, with Viswanath taking to the bowling and Mohinder abandoning his obduracy. India were 289-2 at tea. Holding did not accompany his team-mates after the resumption due to a stomach upset, and Lloyd took on bowling duties himself, with Julien operating from the other end. He set a deep off-side field for Viswanath, but the genius was in his element, as he had been at Madras against the same team a year previously. Holding's return to the attack made no difference. It was then that frenzied activity started in the press enclosure and the scorer's section. Just how many runs were India short of the target? Nobody had paid too much attention to it. It transpired that they had been 206 short at lunch, and were 114 short at tea. Viswanath's belligerence against the new ball whittled that number down rapidly.

India were only 67 short and the twenty mandatory overs were yet to begin, when the Bangalorean was run out for 112. It was his fourth Test hundred and his first overseas. He received a standing ovation, but he was still sceptical and superstitious.

He sat in an inner chamber of the dressing room, not wanting to watch the game, lest he brought his team bad luck. He thus missed out on Brijesh Patel's blitzkrieg. Only 11 runs were needed when Mohinder was run out for a monumental 85. Patel finished it off, and triggered off wild celebrations in the Indian dressing room. Some laughed, while others wept with joy. Mohinder tried to hide his tears until Bedi told him to feel free to display his emotions.

The Indian supporters gave the Queen's Park Oval a festive look. Congratulatory messages arrived from home, including one from the prime minister's office. That prompted a member of All India Radio's commentary team to ham outrageously. He attributed the win to the twenty-point programme that Mrs Gandhi had enforced during the ongoing Emergency!

> 'We were wrong to believe that our spinners would win it for us. The Indians batted very well.' – Clive Lloyd

Policemen had to escort Lloyd off the field. The West Indian supporters were furious.

> 'It is the greatest-ever victory. India had a deficit of 131 to handle, whereas the Australians were only 38 behind in 1948. The Indians were called the weakest batting team to tour the West Indies, while Bradman's team was the strongest of all time. In 1948, England did not have spinners to exploit the Leeds

wicket, whereas the West Indies had three.' – Madhav Mantri, *TOI*, 14 April 1976 (filed)

The Indians looked anything but homesick when they arrived in Kingston, Jamaica, for the decider. They could not be blamed for feeling that they could do an encore of 1971. After all, they had just achieved the improbable. The West Indies on the other hand, were upset, and their captain infuriated.

It wasn't the best of times for him and his side. The West Indies had won the inaugural World Cup in mid-1975, but the joy of that triumph had been nullified by their 1-5 annihilation in Australia. The primary reason for the World Championship of Test cricket being an anti-climax was Australia's pace-bowling resources. The West Indies had quality speedsters in Roberts, Holding and Wayne Daniel, but they were outbowled by Dennis Lillee, Jeffrey Thomson and Garry Gilmour.

That disaster had not endeared Lloyd to the Caribbean public. He had already been appointed captain for the tour of England in mid-1976, but that was only because there was no other candidate who had age, seniority and merit on his side. A draw, or worse, an Indian victory in the last Test, would have only encouraged his critics to sharpen their scalpels. The solution was simple—victory at all costs.

Two of the three spinners who had failed at Port of Spain were dumped, and replaced by fast bowlers Wayne Daniel and Vanburn Holder. It meant that the hosts would go into the decider with four pacemen.

Lloyd won the toss, and gave his quartet of quickies the first use of a bouncy strip. But Sunil and Gaekwad were unfazed. The fielding wasn't up to the mark, with a couple of chances being grassed. Holding did his best to make the batsmen hop off every delivery, without success. The openers played on merit. When Holding served a rare fuller delivery, Sunil drove it to the mid-wicket boundary. The bowler retaliated with a snorter that all but took Sunil's head along with it. The Indian vice-captain swayed away just in time. His cap fell, but fortunately not on the stumps.

A score of 60-0 at lunch implied that it had been a good toss to lose for the Indians. It also meant that the West Indian dressing room wasn't the best place to be in. Not many players would have sat next to Lloyd.

The hosts took the field after the interval, determined to go for the kill. If the Indian version of subsequent events was to be believed, their intention was literal rather than figurative.

As far as the Indians were concerned, what happened at Kingston in April 1976 was eerily similar to the events that unfolded at Adelaide in January 1933. Back then, Douglas Jardine, captain of the MCC[2] team that toured Australia for the Ashes, had evolved a strategy to nullify the threat posed by Don Bradman. The methods that Jardine preached were put into practice by a four-man pace attack headed by Harold Larwood, a miner from Nottingham. His sidekicks were the two Bills; Voce and Bowes. The latter's first-ball dismissal of Bradman in the second Test is still remembered.

Like Lloyd in 1976, Jardine wanted to win at any cost. There was nothing in the laws that prohibited him from adopting what he referred to as 'leg-theory', with the leg-side heavily populated with fielders. The bowlers were assigned the job of targeting the batsmen's bodies rather than the wickets. They responded magnificently, with Larwood leading the way.

Ironically, for all the acrimony that the Bodyline series generated, it witnessed only one serious injury. The casualty was Bert Oldfield, the Australian keeper-batsman, whose skull Larwood smashed at Adelaide. In the same innings, Larwood had hit William Woodfull, the Australian skipper, several times in the chest. More ironic was the fact that both Oldfield and Woodfull were hit when Larwood was bowling a conventional line, not 'leg-theory'. The acrimony that ensued resulted in an addition to the dictionary of cricket – Bodyline.

If Bradman had been England's main target in 1932, then Sunil Gavaskar, one of the architects of the win at Port of Spain, was West Indies' 'enemy number one' in April 1976. Gaekwad was doing fine, but Sunil's successes and stature made him the man the West Indians wanted the most. The first twelve overs after lunch produced 41 runs without any loss to the batting side, and Lloyd called for a change.

---

[2]Marylebone Cricket Club

Michael Holding, who was to Lloyd what Larwood was to Jardine, replaced Holder from the radio commentators' box end. What followed perplexed the batsmen. An umbrella field was set, with Fredericks and Julien stationed at leg-slip. Holding then informed the umpire that he intended to bowl round the wicket.

Sunil and Gaekwad braced themselves for a bouncer barrage. But Holding and Daniel, his comrade-in-intimidation, went several steps ahead. A volley of bouncers was interspersed with the beamer, a potential killer of a delivery at that pace. The attempts of the pacemen to claim that every beamer they propelled was accidental, failed to make the batsmen laugh.

Holding and Daniel had the support of not only their captain, but also the Jamaican spectators, whose behaviour convinced the Indian players and journalists that given a choice between watching opposition batsmen get out and get hurt, they would prefer the latter.

'The wicket was so hard that the spikes of our shoes were not going in. The West Indians kept bowling short, but couldn't get us out. There was no fielder in front of the wicket. For Daniel, I remember, Lloyd had placed four slips, two gullies, one deep fine leg, one short-leg and a point. Like Holding, he relied on the occasional beamer, and the yorker as a shock weapon. Sunil was upset with the three to four bouncers that were being delivered in every over, and he complained to one of the umpires at the drinks interval. The official's retort was a shocker. He laughed and said, "You are not used to this." It was then that Sunil lost his cool. When I tried to calm him down, he said to me that he wanted to see his son. He did not want to get killed.' – Anshuman Gaekwad

Sunil dug deep into his reserves of concentration. He wasn't averse to hooking, but it was one thing to attempt that stroke to the odd bouncer in an over, and another to do so when virtually every delivery coming at him was a bouncer. He had think of alternatives, and one such presented itself by accident.

One delivery from Holding badly crunched the fingers of my left hand against the bat handle. It became impossible to grip the bat with that hand. When playing a short-pitched delivery, the bottom hand invariably comes off the handle, because it is normally held loose. With my left hand unable to grip the bat firmly, when the next ball was also a bouncer, the bat handle could hardly be gripped as the bottom hand came off as a natural reaction to the bouncer. And when the ball hit the left glove, the bat got knocked to the ground, as there was no grip on the bat at all. However, what was surprising was that the ball just dropped at my feet, without lobbing in the air. When the same thing happened to the next ball, I was pleasantly surprised . . . Mind you, the bat had been knocked to the ground on both occasions . . . My analysis convinced me that because the ball, coming at great speed, had not met with any resistance, the ball did not loop up in the air, but fell at my feet. The next over from Holding was similar, and though by this time, the pain in the left hand was much less, I decided to experiment with keeping both hands loose on the handle, in case the ball bounced towards the shoulders. Once again, the result was the same, with the ball falling dead at my feet . . . In a little while, I got used to gripping the bat gingerly and not letting it get knocked out of the hands. – Sunil Gavaskar, *The Sportstar*, 13 August 1995

At one stage, fed up with the intimidatory barrage, he considered speaking to Ralph Gosein, one of the umpires. As he had expected, nothing came out of it, and he exhorted Gaekwad to carry on.

Sunil completed his fifty with a hook off Holder. The ball came on to him a little quicker than he had imagined, but he hit it off the middle, and the cherry flew over mid-on's head to the fence.

> The strain and tension seemed to show. He had borne the burden of the innings for seven Tests. His determination to stay and see things through drove the West Indies to sheer despair. – K.N. Prabhu, *TOI*, 22 April 1976 (filed)

Ironically, it was to a yorker that Sunil got out. He inside-edged Holding onto the stumps, and India had lost their first wicket for 136, a splendid performance in the circumstances. Only sixty-seven overs were bowled on the first day and India were 178-1 at stumps.

Gaekwad was defiant and Mohinder as assured as he had been in the fourth innings at Port of Spain. India had every reason to feel proud of their top three bats.

It was on 22 April, the second day of the Test, that everything fell apart. The score had moved to 199-1 when Lloyd took the second new ball. Holding then produced a missile that would have rammed into Mohinder's face, had he not fended it to Julien for an easy catch.

Viswanath was greeted with deliveries that had to be classified as dangerous. He was fortunate to survive, but Gaekwad wasn't. The man who had been pounded all over his body for more than a day, moved away to square-leg after taking yet another blow. Wicketkeeper Dereyck Murray and Viv Richards made their way to check whether he was all right, but he waved them away disdainfully. Gaekwad was furious, and driven to his wits' end by the onrush. When he looked up in Holding's direction, something snapped. He showed the bowler the finger.

Holding responded with a rocket that took off and hit the batsman behind his left ear. Gaekwad's spectacles flew and he collapsed with the blood spurting from the wound. He had scored a valiant 81.

> Every bouncer made the packed galleries buzz. – K.N. Prabhu, *TOI*

Gaekwad was carried off the field, only for the Indians to discover that the local cricket officials were as cold-blooded as the spectators. It was a while before they made arrangements to take him to the hospital. Umrigar, who had played under Gaekwad's father Dattajirao on the 1959 tour of England, accompanied him.

> I was about to get into the car to return to the ground when I got a call asking me to wait as 'another player was on the way.' Viswanath joined Anshu, and he was followed by Brijesh. It was unadulterated intimidatory bowling, and the umpires didn't seem to be inclined to do anything about the blatant violation of Law 46, which governs fair and unfair play. The opposition blamed the wicket, conveniently forgetting that we had reached a hundred without loss on the same strip. – Polly Umrigar, *Ind-WI Special Feature* (PMG, 2006)

The middle finger of Viswanath's right hand broke when it got jammed between another brutish delivery and the handle of his bat, as he tried to fend it away. To add insult to injury, the cherry flew to the slips, where it was caught. Another short delivery struck Brijesh Patel on the face, and the injury necessitated three stitches. Mohinder and Vengsarkar waged a heroic battle, adding 64. The score was 306-6 when Bedi declared. India took the field with substitutes filling in for their three injured batsmen.

'There was a ridge on the pitch. There had been a bit of rain as well, and what happened was that the ball started taking off. It wasn't the bowlers' fault. Let's not forget that runs were scored on the same pitch.' – Clive Lloyd

The 'ridge' theory was rejected by Bedi and Umrigar.

The hosts went on to score 391, with every member of the batting line-up save Lloyd (0) and Kallicharran (12) making a substantial score. Murray, Richards and Rowe, three players who had visited Gaekwad at the hospital and told him that there was nothing he could have done with that ball, contributed 71, 64 and 47 respectively. Chandrasekhar gave it everything, finishing with five wickets despite a broken thumb, and Bedi, another bowler with an injured finger, got two. Holding delighted his home crowd by scoring a half-ton.

There was no way Gaekwad could have batted in the second innings. The injury had damaged a nerve in his left ear. He heard a continuous whistling sound before undergoing an operation after his return to India. With Viswanath and Patel also indisposed, it meant that the three fit batsmen in the Indian line-up had to play the innings of their lives to save the match.

'I had batted at number five in the first innings. Being one of the three specialist batsmen who weren't injured, I opened with Sunil in the second innings. Before we went in, I insisted that I be allowed to take strike. Sunil refused, saying that it was the senior partner's duty to do so. And would you believe it? Holding's first ball took off, flew over Sunil's head, cleared the wicketkeeper, and reached the boundary. Had I faced that ball, it would have surely hit me. Sunil said as much at the end of the over.' – Dilip Vengsarkar

Sunil fell for only two. Vengsarkar impressed for the second time in the game with a gutsy 21, a display that convinced one and all that the selectors had been right in pitchforking him on the strength of that Irani Trophy innings. But he was overshadowed by Mohinder. His 60 comprised three sixes, including a hook off Daniel. It was a foretaste of things to come.

Holding hit Madan Lal on the head before bowling him. In fact, Mohinder, Madan Lal and Venkataraghvan fell at the same score to reduce India to 97-5. India at that stage were only twelve runs ahead. Watching Kirmani, the non-striker, returning to the pavilion with Venkataraghvan, watchers had all but christened Bedi's declaration as the most bizarre in the history of the game, only for the Indian captain to reveal that the innings had in fact ended at that point, as both he and Chandrasekhar were injured and hence unfit to bat.

The West Indies knocked off the thirteen runs they needed to win the series, but not before Sunil commanded Madan Lal to bowl a beamer and put up a finger-slipping performance in much the same way as Holding had earlier in the game.

On being questioned by this writer about their bowling in this Test, Holding simply said that he hadn't changed his view. On being pressed for an answer whether he thought that the Indian players and manager had overreacted all those years ago, he simply smiled in response. This was in contrast to a line from Rajan Bala's book, *The Covers are Off* (Rupa, 2004), wherein he has written about Holding admitting to him that he was 'ashamed' of that Test.

Lloyd decided to dispense with the spinners altogether. He knew pace had given him what he wanted. What went in his favour was the emergence of a glut of talented pacemen in the Caribbean islands in the mid-1970s. The Indians did not realise it then, but they had inadvertently altered cricketing history by winning at Port of Spain.

The lessons learnt by the West Indies in that game signalled the start of their domination of the sport, and the formal beginning of the pace age. What the Australian duo of Dennis Lillee and Jeff Thomson had initiated against England in 1974-75, West Indian pace quartets of the 1970s and '80s would patent and perfect.

Umrigar dwelt on the gains of the twin tour after the team's return. He told the media that India now had seven batsmen, as opposed to only two – Sunil and Viswanath – at the start of the twin tour. He praised the efforts of Gaekwad, Patel, Vengsarkar and Mohinder Amarnath, and opined that Surender needed to curb his impetuosity. The manager also clarified that neither he nor the captain had lodged an official protest against the intimidatory bowling.

> It was blatant Bodyline . . . Lloyd defended the tactic . . . he said it had been used against (Ian) Redpath in Australia . . . but Lloyd gave himself away by saying that the ball was bowled in line with Redpath's body . . . it could well be asked why he had tried his tactics only on day two after India had raised a score of 176-1. The answer would amount to a tacit admission of:
>
> a. Lloyd's failure in gambling with the toss
>
> b. The ability of Indian batsmen to withstand pace
>
> You had to see it to understand what it was all about. Four balls in an over were directed just short of a length at the batsmen's ribs. There was also the odd beamer. And it was bowled from round the wicket in line with the body. – K.N. Prabhu, *TOI*, 19 May 1976 (filed)

It wasn't only the 'Pace Age' that commenced with the Kingston Test. The remainder of 1976 belonged to Vivian Richards, who scored a record 1,730 runs in the calendar year, inclusive of three hundreds against India and 829 runs from four Tests in England in the middle of the year. His feats that year and in the future prompted pundits to liken him to Bradman. Outstanding and determined, he definitely was. But then, he never had to face the most potent attack of his time at the highest level.

Sunil Gavaskar, another batsman who scored over 1,000 runs in 1976, did face the best pace combination of his time, that too as an opener. Unlike Richards, he achieved four figures in a calendar year three more times in the years that followed. The records he would notch up consistently for the next decade and more, and the attitude he projected as he went about his job, gave the Indians who were born in the mid-1970s and grew up in the 1980s, an inspirational figure to look up to.

India's performance will rank in history among the most daring feats of batsmanship. And the performance at Kingston, for sheer grit, will take precedence above all else. It was a matter of pride to realise that a younger generation of batsmen was not inclined to tread on the toes of the square-leg umpire when facing pace – as some of our veterans are believed to have done in times past. – K.N. Prabhu, *TOI*

9

HEIR-APPARENT

'Technically he was supreme. His concentration was superb. He, like an Indian Ken Barrington, chose to limit the shots he would play to improve his chances of staying longer at the crease. Of the modern generation, the likes of Lara, Tendulkar and Ponting have all showed how it is possible to both play shots and play long innings. In that respect alone, he falls behind such players.' – David Gower

The 1976-77 season began with Bedi and Sunil walking out for the toss on the morning of the Irani Trophy encounter between Bombay and the Rest of India. The venue was Delhi's Ferozeshah Kotla. In Sunil's absence, Mankad had led Bombay to another Ranji win in the 1975-76 season.

Bedi won the toss and elected to bat, but the Rest were bowled out for 173. Bombay gained a lead of 154, and Shivalkar for the umpteenth time in his career demonstrated that he would have been an automatic selection in any other national side of the period, except India. His 6-88 demolished the Rest for 183, and Bombay won.

The injuries he had sustained and had watched the others sustain over the past two years had prompted Sunil to try and add another feather to his cap—in fact, a substitute to his cap.

'With the help of a local cap-maker, Gavaskar is working on a crash helmet-like cap, to be made of thin, but high-resistant fibreglass . . . Gavaskar has written to a sports manufacturing firm in India asking for a special pair of gloves . . . with extra protection to the right index and middle fingers. . . .' – Pradeep Vijayakar, *TOI*, 14 August 1976 (filed)

Sunil had first experimented with extra padding in the gloves in the Bombay Test against the West Indies in 1974-75, after missing three Tests due to his index finger injury. His strokeful 86 in the Test suggested that his fingers were not being impeded by the additional protection. He did not want to take chances with his fingers, and of course, his head. But nothing came out of the cap idea at that stage.

India were to host two teams that season, the first being the Kiwis, who knew that they would have to play on square turners, with the Indians keen to get even for their capitulation on the Wellington green top.

The first Test at Bombay was a significant one for Sunil. In his hometown, he scored 119, the ninth century of his Test career, but his first on Indian soil. He batted beautifully despite an attack of cramps. The best of his twenty boundaries, according to K.N. Prabhu, was a straight drive off the cheek-breaker Lance Cairns that took him past 50. Sunil appeared to have pushed at the ball, but even as the bowler bent to pick up the cherry, it sped past him to the sight screen. The hundred was a gift to a terminally-ill fan, who wanted to watch Sunil score one.

'There was that period, shortly before he went in to bat, during which no one was supposed to speak to him. I remember seeing him keep a glass of water in front of him at eye level, and concentrate on it for about five minutes, just before going in.'
– Dinar Gupte, cricket statistician

Sunil also had luck on his side as he went about scoring his first Test hundred in India.

'Clive Lloyd scored a brilliant 242 in the first ever Test played at the Wankhede stadium. In those days, there used to be a fair amount of fraternising between the two teams at the end of each day's play, and so one team would visit the other's dressing room alternately each evening. I had thus seen where Lloyd sat. As luck would have it, by the time the next first-class game was played at the Wankhede stadium, the Bombay Cricket Association had decided to switch the rooms for the home team and the visiting team... Clive Lloyd's seat was the one I picked and I used it for the rest of my career.' – Sunil Gavaskar, *The Sportstar* (8 February 1992)

It was the last seat along the left wall, if one entered the dressing room from the front.

'I occupied the seat next to his for ten years. There was a toilet right above the dressing room, and the ceiling had developed a leak. Sunil sat right below the leakage spot but he refused to leave his seat. I don't see the cricketers of today tolerating something like that. He also had to contend with my blabbering, but he managed.' – Sandeep Patil

India won at Bombay by 162 runs. New Zealand saved the second Test at Kanpur, but lost the third at Madras. The spinners had bowled well, all the batsmen had played at least one knock of consequence, and the mood was upbeat when England arrived for a five-Test series.

A full-strength England side represented the pleasant end of an unpleasant tradition. Despite that, India had the clear edge in terms of statistics, experience and confidence. It was up to England's captain, the South African-born Anthony William Greig, a streetsmart all-rounder and the first reigning England captain since Douglas Jardine in 1933-34 to bring a team to India, to show his side the way.

A few months earlier, Greig's use of the word 'grovel', an obsolete term that had been used in relation to the coloured slaves of yesteryear, had infuriated the touring West Indies and resulted in a crushing defeat for England. On his arrival in India, he was friendlier. His words at his team's first press conference were music to the ears of the Indian umpires, who had had everything from words to bails thrown at them by the Kiwis.

Scores of 119, 14, 66, 15, 2 and 43 against the Kiwis had taken Sunil's 1976 Test aggregate to 915. With the first Test against England scheduled to start in Delhi on 17 December, he had a maximum of two innings in which to become the first Indian member of a club that comprised eight others.

The Test was preceded by the launch of *Sunny Days*, Sunil's autobiography. While there were many who wondered about the wisdom of a cricketer who was only five years old in international cricket penning his memoirs, their doubts were squashed in emphatic fashion by his fans. His recollections of his highs and lows were lapped up, and the book strolled to bestseller status. Even as that happened, Sunil's seniors were exposed to the commercial viability of putting pen to paper. Not for the last time, the astute little man from Bombay had shown the others a way.

The sales of the book were not affected by some patchy performances. At Delhi, the spinners struck after Greig won the toss and elected to bat. But England's middle order clicked, and opener Dennis Amiss scored 179 to take his team to 381. In response, Sunil and Gaekwad put on 43 in twelve overs. Greig then complained to the umpires that the ball had lost its shape. It was a ploy often tried out by bowling captains in England when their side was struggling. At Delhi, the umpires chose to side with the visitors. That one move turned the match, and as it turned out, the series. The replacement ball swung viciously, and John Lever, who was making his debut, joined an unending list of left-handed pacemen who had destroyed an Indian batting line-up. India were reduced to 49-4 and eventually bowled out for 122.

Sunil put the shutters down after Greig's enforcement of the follow-on. He played Underwood, who as always was at the batsman, with caution, mindful of Greig's proximity at silly-point and his propensity to pressurise the umpires with overdramatic appeals. When Greig took the ball, Sunil swung him over mid-wicket for six. India were 82-1 at the close on day three, with Sunil batting on 40. England still held all the aces, but the public was excited. Their hero's 1976 Test tally was 993.

The Indian predilection for numbers and their penchant for seeking solace in individual glory amidst collective disasters have mystified many a westerner. While the love for numbers is a genetic phenomenon, the urge to celebrate individual excellence is an offshoot of centuries of political humiliation. It was quite appropriate that Delhi, a city that had been ransacked and razed to the ground on more than one occasion by a foreign power, the last such instance being as recent as 1857, witnessed a modern instance of Indians seeking solace in individual glory amidst a collective failure.

Sunil achieved the mark on the fourth morning with a single off Lever, and the spectators went ballistic. Some of them invaded the field to garland him. He went past fifty with a boundary off Greig, and kept reminding himself that his side needed many more. He had reached 71 when Underwood served an arm-ball. Sunil went for the leg-glance, but was unable to keep it down, and a fielder called Bob Woolmer took the catch at short square-leg. India were 133-3, and the nation now looked up to Viswanath for salvation. However, for all the strides that Indian cricket had made as a result of having two batsmen of contrasting styles as contemporaries, rarely had they done well in the same innings of a Test. Port of Spain had been a glorious exception. Viswanath fell for 18, and England triumphed by an innings and 25 runs.

England thus started the 1976-77 series on the same note as the one in 1972-73. Both series were following the same sequence of venues. As was the case in 1972-73, Delhi had hosted the first Test, and Kolkata, Chennai and Mumbai were to stage the second, third and fifth Tests. The one change in 1976-77 was Bangalore, which was to host the fourth Test. Kanpur had played host in 1972-73.

All of India expected their heroes to repeat their performance of 1972-73 and square the series. Greig, who had been on the 1972-73 tour, was mindful of the dangers of taking it easy after the victory at Delhi. He let his feelings be known with a verbal rocket to his team before the second Test.

The spectators who thronged Eden Gardens on New Year's Day in 1977 were thrilled when Bedi won the toss and elected to bat. They soon fell silent, as a clinical bowling display sent India packing for 155. Sunil fell in the first over for a duck.

The moment Gavaskar falls, the sun seems to set on the innings. For Vishy's batting glimmers brightly, like some star in a distant galaxy, only at rare intervals. – K.N. Prabhu, *TOI*, 1 January 1977 (filed)

England were 90-4 in response when in came Tony Greig, who had overcome fever the night before by wrapping himself in blankets and sweating it out. Seeing him, the stadium exploded.

It would be appropriate to say that Greig seduced the Indian crowds. His histrionics delighted the spectators. He would prolong and overdramatise his appeals while fielding and bowling, and collapse whenever a cracker went off in the stands while batting. His antics would have been frowned upon in most countries, but in India, he managed to get away. He regaled the crowd with his timely waves and flexing of his muscles. Indian crowds were used to individuals who played to the gallery, but this was probably the first time a cricketer from overseas had made a conscious effort to gain their affection. They reciprocated.

At Calcutta, Greig batted brilliantly without forgetting to bait the bowlers. There were times when he drove the spinners for boundaries and remained stationary in his follow-through for the next few seconds, almost as if to oblige the photographers. He was repeating the tactics he had employed against Lillee and Thomson at Brisbane two years previously. There, Greig had repeatedly signalled boundaries during the course of a hundred. Like the Australian speedsters, Bedi and his colleagues were furious, but unlike them, they had their limitations, for they didn't exactly pose a physical threat. Greig's 103 took England to 321, and the bowlers repeated in India's second innings what they had done in the first. That a full house watched India's subjugation for 183 on the final day was indicative of the visitors' popularity.

Could India do what Pataudi's side had done in 1974-75, and come back in the series after losing the first two Tests? England scored 262 in the third Test at Madras. India were 58-3 in response when umpire Judah Reuben picked up a gauze strip that had fallen off John Lever's forehead. It was found to have vaseline deposits on it, and Lever was subsequently accused of applying the same to the ball to aid its swing. The England management claimed that the bowler had worn the strip to prevent sweat from running into his eyes. But then, none of his bowler-colleagues had found it necessary to do likewise. The ball was sent to a laboratory for an examination, and the BCCI declared that they would write to the MCC if a foreign substance had indeed been used.

The 20 January issue of the *Times of India* reported that Ken Barrington, the manager of the touring side, had apologised to the BCCI for the use of a gauze strip daubed with vaseline by Lever. This implied that something had been detected in the laboratory. But the apology was made the day England won the Test by 200 runs and thus took the series. Bedi led his team's protests over the vaseline affair, but the three defeats gave his detractors another pretext to call him a bad loser.

Outplayed, the Indians certainly had been, but it did not make sense to blame Bedi alone. His batters had let him down. The bowlers did their bit at Madras by dismissing England for 262 and 185, neither of which could be called impressive scores. But India had made 164 and 83 in response. The knives were out for the losing captain. Among other things, Bedi was flayed for taking the field ten-fifteen minutes after the resumption of play. During these periods, Sunil would be in charge.

> I am of the view that Gavaskar should have captained . . . This is not meant to criticise Bedi, but I just think that a batsman-captain would have set better fields for the Indian spinners because as a batsman you know where you wouldn't want the fielders. – Tony Greig, *India-England Special Feature* (PMG, 2006)

There were three changes in the side for the Bangalore Test. Madan Lal made way for Ghavri. Surender Amarnath, who had begun the previous season's twin tour on a high, but finished it on a hospital bed in Kingston after undergoing an emergency appendicitis operation, was recalled. A right-handed batsman and close-in fielder from Maharashtra was picked to make his debut—Rajkumar Shri Yajurvindra Singh of Bilkha.

Eknath Solkar did not know it then, but the Calcutta Test was his last. It was an abrupt and tragic end to what had promised to be a fruitful career. Yet, the former Indian Schoolboys captain and one of the heroes of the twin triumphs of 1971 finished with a record that will in all likelihood stand the test of time. His fifty-three catches from twenty-seven Tests gave him a 'catch rate' of nearly two per Test, which is something no non-wicketkeeper has come close to achieving.

Amarnath's left-handedness provided a refreshing variation, with the English being forced to vary their approach while bowling for the first time in the series. His 63 in the first innings helped fill the breach caused by Sunil's early fall to a poor shot. He had tried to drive a shortish Willis delivery, but only managed to balloon the cherry into the mid-off region, for Underwood to take an easy catch.

Sunil was under pressure, professionally as well as personally. His concern about his inconsistency with the bat apart, he was worried about his father, who had suffered a heart attack during the course of the game. Sunil made a lightning trip to Bombay during the course of the Test, and returned after being assured that all was well. Despite the tension, he scored 39 and 24.

Another individual who was feeling the heat, albeit solely for professional reasons, was C.D. Gopinath, then chairman of the selection committee. With India 0-3 down, he was at the receiving end of criticism. He let his feelings be known at Bangalore.

India got 253. Chandrasekhar's 6-76 hastened England's demise for 195, but the star was Yajurvindra Singh, who proved to be a fitting successor to Solkar at the suicidal position. He took five catches in the first innings, and went on to take two more in the second, thus equalling Greg Chappell's world record for the highest number of catches by a non-wicketkeeper in a Test.

India needed to score quickly in the second innings, to give the spinners enough time to bowl England out in the fourth innings. Sunil compensated for his first-innings indiscretion with a round fifty. The highlight of his innings was his walk down the pitch after taking two boundaries off Old, one of the abusive characters in the England team, and clapping, almost as if he were demanding applause from the bowler!

When Viswanath scored 79, the result was a foregone conclusion. Bedi declared 318 runs ahead and India went on to win by 140 runs. However, the hosts lost the gamesmanship battle here as well. Greig, the losing captain, led his team on a lap of honour, and the spectators cheered!

The long and short of it was that Greig was a hit, on and off the field. Off it, he was swamped with opportunities to endorse products like two-wheelers and men's toiletries, and mobbed wherever he went. In an age wherein cricket was perceived as a sport played primarily by men and for men, Greig made several female admirers, a fair number of whom did not mind going the distance to display their affection for him.

The Indians wanted to win the final Test at Bombay to reduce England's victory-margin. Bedi won the toss and Sunil laid the foundation of a competitive score.

> His tenth century was mathematically precise in conception and ruthlessly efficient in execution. – *The Hindu*, 11 February 1977 (filed)

Patel's 83 played its part in ensuring a final score of 338. Sunil shared the new ball with Ghavri and sent down two shine-removing overs before Bedi took over. The skipper bowled and bowled, as did Prasanna and Chandrasekhar. India bowled 154 overs without changing the ball and dismissed England for 317. The hosts then scored 192 in the second innings, and with only four hours of play left on the last day and the pitch taking turn, Greig decided to play for a draw.

The innings got off to an unpleasant start. When Sunil began his first shine-removing over, he was accused by Amiss of scuffing the pitch on his follow-through. The England media took a self-righteous view.

Pat Gibson, writing for *The Daily Express,* also criticised Sunil for his 'display of bad sportsmanship', but he was kind enough to add that it could well have been a protest on his part against England's gamesmanship. In his *The History of Indian Cricket* (Rupa, 1990), Mihir Bose writes about Greig snatching the bat from Indian batsmen who played a false shot and demonstrating the right way to execute it, not to mention his flair for histrionics while bowling and fielding. As it turned out, Sunil bowled only one over in that innings.

> 'He barely bowled three overs in the match. There was a lot of sledging and verbal dialogue between the players. We needed to get the new ball rough as soon as possible and banging it short was one way to ensure that we did not give away runs and showcase our aggression. Sunil did not purposely rough up the pitch, but he did run up close to the batsmen after his short delivery to unsettle him and to proclaim that we also could bowl bouncers. The MCC side used it on him quite often

and it was frustrating as we did not have any pace bowlers to retaliate.' – Yajurvindra Singh

For Sunil, the question of allowing the opposition to run roughshod over him and his team, whether it was India or Bombay, did not arise. If the attempts of his opponents to stretch the rules irritated him, the subservient tendencies of some of his own compatriots incensed him.

'He led Bombay in a three-day game against the English tourists in Indore. I was part of the All India Radio team that covered the game. The Madhya Pradesh Cricket Association had organised a function on the second evening of the game. Both the teams were invited, and a member of the erstwhile royal family of Holkar was the special guest. Chairs had been arranged on the dais. When the English players arrived, they occupied all those chairs, without being asked to do so. Sunil was then asked by the organisers to join them on the dais. I was standing with the Bombay players some distance away from the stage. The function commenced with a couple of speeches. After a while, Sunil was asked to speak. What followed gave us an insight into his sense of timing. He stood up and said, "If the English players are guests of honour in Indore, then so are we. There was enough space on the dais for a few more chairs to have been arranged, so that my team could have sat here as well. Right now, the English team is sitting here, and my colleagues are standing in a corner. I would like to join them!" Having said that, he walked off and joined us! He hadn't protested at the start of the function, but done so when he had the mike in his hand, and every single ear at the function fixated onto every word of his. The protest was effective. The organisers admitted that they ought to have accommodated the Bombay team on the stage, after the English players had invaded it.' – Sudhir Vaidya

The Indian spinners made the initial inroads at the Wankhede, but the tension in the English dressing room dissipated with an injury to Chandrasekhar. Bedi then left the field as he had often done in the series, leaving Sunil in charge. One of the highlights of the vice-captain's short stints at the helm had been his positioning himself at an unconventional deep short-leg whenever Knott, one of the best sweepers in the game, was on strike. However, the tactic hadn't helped much, with Knott enjoying another productive series against the Indian spinners.

In Bombay, Sunil was more successful. He commanded the versatile Ghavri to bowl his brand of flattish left-arm spin. It worked. Ghavri took five wickets, including those of Greig and Knott, in a span of nine balls. But the English hung on for a draw.

> 'Bedi emerged from the pavilion even as we were returning. He "ordered" me never to bowl left-arm spin again, and stick to my medium-paced stuff. "But Paaji, I took five wickets bowling spin, didn't I?" I asked. He replied, "If you start taking wickets with your left-arm spin, then there will be nothing left for me to do." He was joking, of course.' – Karsan Ghavri

The defeat against England apart, it had been a season of highs for Sunil. He led West Zone to victory in the Duleep Trophy. His 120 in the Ranji semi-final against Venkataraghvan's Tamil Nadu set up a win for his side. He then completed a hat trick of sorts by leading Bombay to a 129-run win in the Ranji final. It was his first Ranji title as captain, and that it was achieved against Bedi's Delhi in Delhi made it even more satisfying.

> 'We batted first and gained a first-innings lead of 26. In the second innings, Sunil instructed the lower order bats to attack Bedi. "If you get out first ball, it doesn't matter, but go after him," he said. That was his way of upsetting Bedi, who he knew would not like to be tonked by lower-order batsmen. I was waiting to go in at number seven when Sunil handed me his Crown supershort bat. It was a good stick. As luck would have it, Bedi was bowling when I went in. I hit his first two balls out of the ground, and went on to score an unbeaten 70. The others also followed Sunil's orders to the letter, going after Bedi like men possessed. We gained a substantial lead and won easily.' – Karsan Ghavri

Sunil led the side intelligently, making the most of his side's strengths and the opposition's weaknesses. He used Ghavri shrewdly against the left-handed opener Venkat Sunderam even if it was for a single over, who he knew was a bit tentative against the Bombay left-hander's nippy short-pitched deliveries.

Another batsman who was tentative against Ghavri was the latter's rival Madan Lal. Ghavri was bowling spin with the old ball when Madan Lal came in to bat in the second innings. Sunil immediately ran in from slip and commanded Ghavri to revert to medium-pace. The change paid off, and Ghavri got Madan Lal for the second time in the match.

'Sunil was one of the best captains I have played under. He was a very clever thinker and had the ability to analyse the faults of his opponents. He hated to lose and was not an airy-fairy individual. For him there had to be a reason for any action and rarely believed in a gamble. That at times made him an individual who believed in systematic tactics, rather than the common attitude of "let's wait and watch and then decide what to do". His biggest drawback was that he could not absorb unprofessionalism. If he had worked out a tactic and the bowler or batsmen faltered in its execution, he would get totally ruffled and at times lose interest. He wanted a committed attitude from each player as he was a man who believed in perfection and he felt all players at the highest level should also be attaining the same. Unfortunately, it was because of this that players found him a hard taskmaster and a difficult captain at times.' – Yajurvindra Singh

The Ranji triumph ought to have been the perfect climax to the season, but the euphoria did not take long to evaporate. Sunil found himself embroiled in two controversies. It wasn't the last time that someone who set high standards for himself found it difficult to accept that others were not measuring up to them.

He slammed the umpiring after Dadar Union lost to a Mafatlals side captained by Ashok Mankad in the Police Shield final. The 24 April 1977 issue of the *TOI* reported him describing it as a 'hollow victory, for the umpiring decisions had constantly gone in Mafatlals' favour'. It aroused strong reactions, and he issued a clarification a couple of days later, saying that what he actually meant was that the opposition had been lucky with the umpiring decisions.

Barely had things settled down when there was another storm. Gopinath's outburst during the England series may well have been on Sunil's mind when he sat down to pen an article for the 1 May 1977 issue of *Sportsweek,* a popular weekly sports magazine. He went on to draw an association between the word selectors and the compound word 'court jesters'.

He was flayed from different quarters, the BCCI included. The Board asked him to report to a three-man committee comprising President M. Chinnaswamy, and Vice-Presidents B.C. Mohanty and Satish Malhotra, on 6 October 1977, in Bangalore. The *TOI* four days later claimed that Sunil had apologised. The paper carried a statement addressed to the committee, reportedly written by him: 'I assure you Sir, that in the future, I shall take due care to adhere to norms of conduct expected of a player of my standing. The inconvenience caused is regretted. It was most unfortunate and unintended.' A day later, Chinnaswamy told the same paper that Sunil hadn't apologised. Whatever was the case, the parties decided to forget and move on. There was far too much going on elsewhere in the cricketing world.

Nineteen seventy-seven was in fact a year of controversy. In March that year, England took on Australia in the Centenary Test at the Melbourne Cricket Ground. The game, played exactly a hundred years after the inaugural Test between the two countries at the same venue, was witnessed by 251 former Australian and English cricketers. The cricket itself was spectacular, with England falling only 45 short of a target of 463 on the final day. After the spectacle came the storm.

It had started brewing in 1976 when the Australian Cricket Board rejected an offer made by Kerry Baltimore Packer, owner of the Channel Nine TV network. He had offered a staggering 2.5 million Australian dollars for exclusive TV rights to all cricket played in Australia for a five-year period. But the board turned him down, for it had already signed a deal with the state-owned Australian Broadcasting Corporation (ABC) for roughly one-tenth that amount.

Packer, an astute media magnate who had sensed cricket's potential as a television sport, was determined to have his way.

He capitalised on the disharmonious relationship between the cricketers and their respective boards. Players all over the world were sick of earning peanuts despite pulling in capacity crowds and ensuring huge profits for their boards. Packer recruited fifty-five frontline cricketers from all over the world under a parallel association called World Series Cricket. The leading Australian and West Indian cricketers of the era signed up, as did cricketers from England, Pakistan and South Africa, to form a World squad. The brief of the signatories was to play a series comprising six one-dayers, six three-dayers and six supertests, all of which were to clash with Australia's official cricketing commitments in the 1977-78 season. Packer promised and paid the stars what they deserved, and his team of advisers conceived innovative tactics to package and market the sport and its stars.

The reactions were predictably emotional. The old-timers condemned the cricketers for tarnishing the game. Tony Greig, one of the first signatories, was stripped of the England captaincy, and the Australian cricketers were banned from representing their country and states.

The first season of World Series Cricket was to clash with India's tour of Australia, and even as they went through the rigours of a seventeen-day conditioning camp in Madras, the Indian players had mixed emotions. On the one hand, they were happy with the prospect of confronting a second-string Australian side; on the other, they felt jilted, for Packer had ignored Indian cricketers completely. Given that the best cricketers from across the world had been recruited, the rejection implied that in the eyes of Packer, the Indians were not good enough.

Bedi had under him a seasoned side, comprising the most consistent players of the previous two-three seasons, including two individuals who had made a comeback after an outstanding Ranji season in 1976-77—Chetan Chauhan and Ashok Mankad. Accompanying him for the toss in the first Test at Brisbane was the forty-two year-old Bob Simpson, who had been recalled to guide a team of youngsters. The presence of Jeffrey Thomson, who had pulled out of the parleys with Packer's agents, was a big boost to Australia.

India were still the favourites. For once, an Indian team lived up to this tag with victories in the four inter-state games that preceded the first Test. They began the Test series in the same vein, with Bedi and Chandrasekhar terminating Australia's first innings for 166 on the first morning. The stage was set for India's vice-captain and his colleagues to bat Australia out of the match. Sunil had scored only 3 when a delivery by debutant Wayne Clarke rose awkwardly, took the inside-edge, hit him in the chest and rebounded to the short-leg fielder. Hardly the start India wanted.

Sunil was as upset with himself as with the manager. Polly Umrigar, the then owner of virtually all Indian batting records, was a pragmatist who displayed a dogmatic streak from time to time. The 1977-78 team experienced his dogmatism when he insisted at the start of the tour that the batsmen wear a chest-guard. Of course, he had the players' well-being in mind. Sunil had missed a couple of the pre-Test games due to injury, and hence hadn't got used to wearing one while batting, by the time the first Test began. He therefore requested that he be allowed to bat without one. But Umrigar put his foot down.

Sunil believed that the ball had carried to the short-leg fielder only because it had bounced off the chest protector. The sight of his flinging the offending piece of equipment across the dressing room soon after his return convinced Umrigar to adopt a more flexible stance. He chided Sunil for reacting in that fashion, but bought his point. It was decided to let Sunil have his way.

Although he was uncomfortable with a chest-protector, Sunil had taken steps to protect himself from more serious injuries.

> '... what worried me most was the probable injury to the wrist and forearm. This to me was potentially the worst injury one would get, for the process of rehabilitation was long and invariably meant that the season was as good as over ... It was with this possibility in mind that I devised a forearm protector against Jeff Thomson in 1977-78. ... He had ruined the seasons of a couple of batsmen the previous year and I was not going to lose mine. Thus I took out the extra padding that I had designed for my right forefinger and with the help of a wrist-band, put the makeshift protector on the forearm. Thus, the discarded extra padding of a used and torn glove was the first forearm protector I used. ...' – Sunil Gavaskar, *The Sportstar*, 27 July 1991.

The Aussies batted a lot better in the second innings and set India 341 to win. What followed reminded every Indian cricket lover of the question asked by one of their statesmen, 'Why can't they play their second innings first?'

In the second innings, Sunil lost Vengsarkar, who was being tried out as an opener all over again, very early. Mohinder Amarnath and Viswanath both sparkled before falling to Thomson. Patel and Mankad also did not get going, and at 196-5, the Aussies sensed victory. Kirmani then lent his vice-captain the support he deserved. Sunil batted magnificently, driving and flicking the speedsters with élan, and confounding leg-spinners Simpson and Tony Mann with deft footwork. Not one bad ball, and there were plenty of those bowled by an inexperienced side, was left unpunished. He completed his first Test hundred on Australian soil with a cover drive.

'We played a few four-day games before that first Test. Sunil got out a few times to the cut shot, giving catches to gully or point. He was taking his time to adjust to the extra bounce in the wickets. During our meeting on the eve of the Test, he declared that he would cut only after crossing 100. Sure enough, he produced an electrifying cut soon after he had completed his century at Brisbane. He raised his bat towards the dressing room and told us later that that one stroke gave him a greater thrill than the hundred.' – Karsan Ghavri

Sunil looked headed for many more until Clarke produced the breakthrough, inducing him to nick one to keeper Steve Rixon. But India still went for it, with Bedi displaying his batting capabilities. Kirmani and he had all but seized the initiative with a 43-run stand when the keeper-batsman failed to clear the leg-side infield. That made it 318-9, and the last pair added six before Chandrasekhar fell to Thomson.

After today's pulsating finish, Mr Packer must regret that he set himself up in competition to a true, blue-blooded international sport. – Dicky Rutnagur, *The Indian Express*, 6 December 1977 (filed)

Sunil then led India against Western Australia (WA) before the second Test. India lost by 150 runs, but not before their stand-in captain lodged an unconventional protest against Western Australian Wayne Clarke, whose action, especially his bouncer, the Indians were not impressed with. Sunil made his point by chucking a bouncer at WA opener Graeme Wood. The Australians retorted by pointing a finger at Karsan Ghavri's bouncer.

It was the first time Sunil had taken on the Australians over a cricket-specific issue. It wasn't the last.

The Australians weren't alone in their disapproval of Sunil's behaviour. His achievements notwithstanding, several of his own compatriots were unsure of what to make of him. They were flustered by his inclination to wrap the tricolour around himself and demand parity with the masters of the cricketing world. For them, he was a novelty as well as an irony, in what was an 'old-mindsets-die-hard' situation. Thirty years had elapsed since India attained independence, but those three decades had been preceded by eight centuries of bondage.

The ambivalence of some of his compatriots resulted in a situation wherein there was no middle ground. One group swore *by* Sunil for his performances and achievements, and his impact on world cricket; the other swore *at* him for being insolent enough to take on the lords of the sporting ring and have the temerity to even think about beating them.

The quintessential Indian sports-lover of the era was more comfortable with players who sparkled in patches and posed a few problems to overseas giants without bothering them too much. The hockey team had been an exception of sorts in the pre- and immediate-post-Independence phase, but it hadn't been able to sustain its hold over the masses in non-Olympic years. It wasn't that India hadn't produced sporting greats before Sunil, but few had managed to convince their own people that they were as good, if not better, than the westerners. Cricketers Vijay Hazare, Vinoo Mankad and Subhash Gupte, hockey stalwarts Dhyan Chand, Balbir Singh and Shankar Laxman, billiards wizard Wilson Jones, 'flying Sikh' Milkha Singh, and tennis maestro Ramanathan Krishnan, constituted this elite community. However, they constituted the past. In 1977, Sunil had no peers. Ajitpal Singh, who had led India to victory in the Hockey World Cup in 1975, came the closest, but he was not a pan-Indian hero like Sunil.

The question marks over Clarke and Ghavri were wiped out by some unforgettable cricket in the Perth Test. Sunil's early dismissal in the first innings brought together Chetan Chauhan and Amarnath. They added 149 and laid the foundation for a final total of 402. India gained a slender first-innings lead of 8. Sunil then essayed a gem. Neither he nor Amarnath, who had scored 90 in the first innings, were fazed by the world's fastest bowler on the world's fastest pitch. Sunil's 127 comprised twenty boundaries, and gave him 3,000 runs in Test cricket.

> Gavaskar played his part as an Olivier[3] would play Hamlet. He knew the lines, of course, he knew the situations and he sensed the responses of the other characters in the drama . . . to make a hundred at the WACA must have been satisfying, for he had suffered a few indignities here as a very raw member of the World side. – Dicky Rutnagur, *The Indian Express*, 20 January 1978 (filed)

What his father hadn't done in five Tests in 1947-48 despite being in roaring form in the state games, Mohinder did in the second innings. He followed his first-innings 90 with a round ton in the second. The only worrying factor for his admirers was the forehead injury inflicted by paceman Sam Gannon in the first innings. Observers felt that he was not entirely comfortable while essaying the hook, and hence ran the risk of either mistiming it or missing it altogether and getting hit on the face.

The Test went down to the wire. The Indian bowlers gave nothing away, but they were thwarted by Tony Mann, who was sent in as nightwatchman and scored a hundred. Australia, set 342 to win, crept home by two wickets.

That they were 0-2 down against a second-string side was as difficult to swallow for the Indians as the fact that the scoreboard read 0-2 on the first morning of the third Test at Melbourne. They eventually finished with 256, and Chandrasekhar proceeded to dismiss the hosts for 213. In the second innings, Sunil and Viswanath added 98 without being unduly bothered by damp patches on a good length at both ends of the wicket.

The groundstaff's claim that seagulls had picked through the covers elicited laughter rather than abuse in the Indian dressing room. It was a

---

[3]Director actor Olivier's *Hamlet,* made in 1948, was one of the best made films based on Shakespeare's play.

happy place to be in on that tour. For Sunil, it brought back memories of the World XI series in 1971-72.

Bedi and he started the Sunday Club, a legacy of that World XI series. In funsters like Viswanath, Kirmani and Mankad, the team comprised enough antidotes to the homesickness that was bound to afflict the players on a three-month tour. Although the Sunday Club sessions in the team room at the hotel were meant for enjoyment, the players were supposed to take them very seriously. There were strict rules, especially those pertaining to the dress code. For one of the meetings, the code was a tie and an underwear, and nothing else. Not just that, but the players were expected to walk from their rooms to the venue of the meeting in that attire. Fines were levied on the violators, and it turned out that the players managed to undertake the journey, scurrying out of sight whenever they spotted people in the corridor, or sprinting past them before the latter overcame their shock.

The victory at Melbourne, which came about as a result of Chandrasekhar's match figures of 12-104, Viswanath's 59 and 54, and Sunil's third consecutive second-innings hundred of the series, gave the Sunday Club a huge impetus.

Sunil went on to introduce the Sunday Club to Bombay as well.

'Apart from watching and learning from the seniors in the Bombay team, my most memorable experience was the "Sunday Club". One evening would be kept aside for this Sunday Club during Ranji matches (it wasn't mandatory for it to be a Sunday!). The players would come together and anybody would be asked to do things not related to cricket. I was once told to don a bartender's costume, and on another occasion, the junior players were asked to imitate senior members of the team. I was once ordered to dress like a girl, with lipstick and all that. We would have a lot of fun at these sessions. The Sunday Club brought us together as a team, and the spirit generated during the sessions tended to extend itself to the field. In those days, someone would invariably bail us out whenever we were in a tight spot. We bonded well, and most importantly, we youngsters felt as if we were wanted.' – Suru Nayak

Bedi and Chandrasekhar, two pillars of the Indian team, dismissed the Australians for 131 on the first day of the fourth Test at Sydney. Sunil drove Thomson's first ball to the boundary, and carried on in the same vein, cutting anything that was short soundly and using his feet to the spinners. Chauhan cut and slashed hard at the other end, and it was after one such stroke that he remembered his team-mates ribbing him about his style of playing that particular stroke. The smile he flashed at Sunil as a result was misinterpreted by Thomson, who thought that the batsman was having a laugh at his expense.

He strode towards Chauhan, outlined a cross on his forehead, and let it be known that he fancied some target-practice. Chauhan was upset, and a heated argument ensued before Sunil intervened and led his partner away.

> My principle has always been: never enter into an argument with a fast bowler, because it only makes him bowl faster. Immediately after that exchange, Thomson bowled like greased lightning. We did our best to take singles and rotate the strike, because when a bowler is bowling fast, the best way to play him is from the non-striker's end. – Sunil Gavaskar, *SGP* (PMG, 1987)

The openers fell in quick succession after adding 97 for the first wicket, but Viswanath, and later Vengsarkar, who had by now been restored to the middle order, took it from there.

Bedi declared 265 runs ahead, and flagged off a superlative display of off-spin by the man who was known to his team-mates as the 'cunning old fox'. Erapalli Prasanna bagged four wickets. The Australians came close to making India bat again, before an outstanding outfield catch by substitute fielder Madan Lal accounted for their top-scorer Peter Toohey. India won by an innings and 2 runs.

Bedi was aware that he stood a chance of becoming only the second captain after Bradman in 1936-37 to win a five-match series after being 0-2 down. But the Australians hit back in the decider at the Adelaide Oval, accumulating 505. The Indian batters flopped for 269, but Simpson opted not to enforce the follow-on. His team amassed an overall lead of 492. Being the series decider, it was a six-day Test, and there were more than two days left. There was no way the Indians could have defended for that long. Their only option was to go for the runs.

Unfortunately for them, the man who had headed the chases at Port of Spain and Brisbane fell after a promising start. Sunil had scored 29 out of 40 when he succumbed to an attempted hook off Ian Callen, nicking it to the keeper. It wasn't the first time in the series that he had fallen to the stroke. The dismissal contributed to a conscious decision to eschew the stroke completely. His team couldn't afford it.

Chauhan's fall for 32 brought together Amarnath and Viswanath. They took India to 101-2 at stumps on day four. The fifth day witnessed some brilliant batting by them and Vengsarkar, but the Australians kept striking. India were 362-6 at the end of the fifth day, and in their mind, they still had a chance, with both Kirmani and Ghavri having got fifties earlier in the series. But the challenge proved to be a bit too stiff, and the tenth wicket fell at 445. India had lost 2-3.

They would have won, had the batsmen fared better in the first innings at Brisbane or Adelaide. There was nothing more the spinners could have done, and they did not have a fast bowler to exploit the bouncy Australian tracks. Madan Lal, who played the first two Tests, Ghavri, who figured in the last three, and Mohinder, who shared new-ball duties in all five games, were committed cricketers and great triers, but their bowling lacked the bite to make the opposition batsmen restless.

Ironically, by not winning the series, the Indians ensured that Packer's World Series Cricket did not get off to the flying start as envisaged by its promoters. Attempts by the likes of Ian Chappell to denigrate the series against India notwithstanding, the Australian public had thrown in its lot with cricket's official version. The words of Malcolm Fraser, the Australian prime minister, were a source of consolation, 'Their fighting cricket had captured the imagination of cricket followers everywhere, given hours of pleasure to millions of cricket lovers.'

Sunil ended the series with his reputation further enhanced and the memories of his lean trot in Australia in 1971-72 obliterated for good. He carried with him back to India, a compliment from Mr Fraser: 'After this series, there should be no doubt that Gavaskar is about the best of his kind in the game.'

10

THE CORONATION AND THE COUP

'He once asked me what field I would have set for him as a fielding captain. I told him that firstly, I would move third-man squarer. Being the master batsman that he was, he rarely edged the ball and almost always met the ball with the full face of the bat. It was therefore pointless to keep the fielder finer, behind the slips, for the ball would never go to him. A squarer third-man would take care of his square-cut, one of his most productive strokes. Secondly, I would ask mid-on to stand finer than usual. The idea would be to block his trademark straight-drives. This particular placement would force him to play across the line, which is exactly what I would want him to do. Thirdly, I would place a man to the right of the square-leg umpire. With a conventional field-setting, he would get four runs off the cut, four off the straight drive, and two off the glide in the square-leg region. However, my field-placing would only give him a single to third-man, and no runs off the other two strokes. Thus, he would be able to score only one run instead of the usual ten, and get frustrated as a result.' – Madhav Mantri

'His balance was exemplary. He only had to move his head by a fraction to avoid a bouncer.' – John Wright

Malcolm Fraser was not the only Australian celebrity to be impressed by Sunil's batsmanship. The Indian vice-captain's name figured prominently in a report filed in the *Times of India* on 10 October 1978, which said that seven Indians – Sunil, Bedi, Viswanath, Kirmani, Mohinder Amarnath, Vengsarkar and Chandrasekhar – were in the process of signing up with Packer.

The news appeared when the seven men were about to begin the most challenging assignment of their careers. They had all been to the West Indies in 1975-76, but Pakistan was an entirely different proposition.

The neighbours had fought wars in 1965 and 1971 since their last Test series in 1960-61. The efforts of both sides to revive sporting ties had borne fruit.

However, both sides were apprehensive of the consquences of a loss to the old enemy. Pakistan accordingly recalled their Packerites, after having kept them out of official international cricket for more than a year. Mushtaq Mohammad, one of Packer's recruits and the youngest of four brothers to have represented Pakistan in Test cricket, was reinstated as captain. He had debuted as a teenager in the 1960-61 series against India, and was thus the sole link between the two eras. He had also captained Bedi at Northamptonshire in England. The Indian captain's stint at the County had ended a year before, reportedly due to the vaseline controversy. It was alleged that the English authorities decided against renewing Bedi's contract because of his gall to cast aspersions on the integrity of the England players despite earning his bread and butter on their soil.

Pakistan's bowling attack was headed by two disparate characters. Imran Khan's looks and charisma made him cricket's answer to Sean Connery, an individual whom men wanted to be like, and women simply wanted. Sarfraz Nawaz, his new-ball partner, was for opposition batsmen, no less mean than the meanest of the baddies Connery had taken on as James Bond. Sarfraz possessed the ability to make the ball wobble almost at will, and a penchant for stretching the rules to their farthest limits. He displayed both attributes in successive Tests in Australia after the series against India. In the first of the two Tests, he bowled his team to a win with figures of 9-86, with the Aussies losing their last seven wickets for 5 runs. In the second, he appealed for 'handled the ball' when Andrew Hilditch, the non-striker, picked up the ball and handed it to him. The umpire had no option but to rule the good samaritan out, for Sarfraz was following the letter of the law, albeit not its spirit.

Sarfraz in later years would come to be synonymous with an extraordinarily fertile imagination, thanks to his proclivity to dredge out conspiracies from anywhere and everywhere.

Pakistan's batting line-up comprised the opening pair of Majid Khan and Mushtaq's brother Sadiq, Packerites Asif Iqbal and Zaheer Abbas, and a prodigy called Javed Miandad. The Indian squad was no less strong. A major attraction was the presence of the Amarnath brothers, sons of the man whose batting exploits in the pre-Partition phase continued to be remembered on the Pakistani side of the Punjab. The babies of the Indian team hailed from the border areas. Yashpal Sharma had mutilated scores of Ranji bowlers for his state, the Indian Punjab. He had for company, a quick bowler from the neighbouring state of Haryana. His name was Kapil Dev Nikhanj.

The latter possessed two attributes that most Indian cricketers of the era did not possess—the height of a matinee idol and the physique of an athlete. He owed his presence in the team to his performances in junior level and domestic cricket, and on a tour of East Africa with the Cricket Club of India team earlier that year. Pataudi was the captain on that tour, and Sunil, Viswanath, Solkar and Yajurvindra Singh were part of the squad, but Kapil outshone everybody else with his incisive bowling and spirited batting.

His ambition to become a fast bowler had been inadvertently fuelled by none other than Sunil's first India manager Keki Tarapore. It so happened that Kapil objected to the sparse food being served at an Under-22 camp in Bombay in the summer of 1975, and was taken to meet Tarapore, the chief administrator. When Kapil told him that he needed more food as he was a fast bowler, Tarapore started laughing. 'There are no fast bowlers in India,' the boy was informed. However, the food did get augmented.

Sunil had first seen Kapil in early 1978 in the Wills Trophy, a tournament that the BCCI had started to complement the Deodhar Trophy in its bid to help the players get used to limited-overs cricket. Sunil was representing Bombay and Kapil, the Wills XI.

I remember telling him, while I was at the non-striker's end, that he should bowl from closer to the stumps for his outswingers to be more effective . . . players from the Wills XI ran up to him to enquire if I was sledging him. One of them even told him to ignore my advice, when all I was trying to do was help a youngster.'
– Sunil Gavaskar, *The Sportstar*, 26 February 1994

Kapil chose to ignore his team-mates instead. The sprawling parks in his hometown Chandigarh bore testimony to his talent, as did those who had watched him being coached by the renowned Desh Prem Azad. His coach let nature take its course, but at no point did he forget to remind his ward that talent needed to be honed constantly. In taking cognisance of Sunil's tip, Kapil was only following his coach's advice.

The Board's decision to offer the manager's post to Fatehsinghrao Gaekwad, the erstwhile Maharaja of Baroda, was a masterstroke. They had lost their hereditary titles and kingdoms, but some rajas and maharajas of yore had retained their aura, Gaekwad being one of them. He had the Pakistani media and public eating out of his hands. He was a hit with his own players as well, as much for his encouraging words as well as the fact that all the spotlights were always trained on him. It took away some of the pressure they were under.

The first Test was preceded by two One-dayers. India came through in a cliffhanger in the first, and Pakistan won the second comprehensively. To beat a side comprising players who had loads of limited-overs experience was no mean feat, but the Indians did not take too much cognizance of their four-run win. For them, it amounted to nothing more than an uninteresting appetiser before the main course.

For owners of TV sets in India, the tour was a turning point, as it was the first time they were to receive live pictures of a series being played on foreign soil. However, the first day of live coverage from Faisalabad's Iqbal stadium didn't fill their hearts with joy.

Mushtaq won the toss on the morning of 16 October and elected to bat. What followed prompted some Indian fans to blame the strip, which had been rolled over and over again to blunt the Indian spinners. Others contended that the Pakistani batsmen were just too good. A third group reckoned that the spinners did not seem their usual self. The truth lay somewhere in between.

The Coronation and the Coup ☙ 179

Pakistan declared at 503-8 and the Indian openers found themselves at the receiving end of a bouncer-barrage. Imran and Sarfraz reckoned that the only way to achieve something with the ball on a placid wicket was by banging it in short. But Sunil and Chauhan were unperturbed. They put on 97, and Viswanath went on to become the first Indian to score a Test hundred against every contemporary Test-playing nation. His 145 and Sunil's 89 ensured an Indian response of 462-9. A draw was a foregone conclusion at the end of the fourth day's play. Still, there was no dearth of drama.

While standing at the non-striker's end, Sunil took note of the reluctance of the umpires to penalise the Pakistani bowlers for overstepping. When Shakoor Rana, one of the two officials, proceeded to reprimand Mohinder for transgressing onto the danger area on his follow-through in Pakistan's second innings, Sunil lost it. He took up cudgels on behalf of his team-mate. Rana and his colleague already had reason to be peeved with the Indian vice-captain, for what he had done earlier in the game. He had halted the game while batting and signalled to Bedi to come onto the field. Even as some people felt that he wanted to complain about the overdose of short-pitched bowling, it turned out that Sunil wanted to draw his skipper's attention to the fact that there was a difference of twenty minutes between the umpires' watches. Both officials were unsure of which watch to follow! The matter was sorted out, but the umpires were embarrassed to be caught on the wrong foot in a Test match. Sunil's outburst gave them an opportunity to get back at him.

Rana refused to take the field on the last day unless Sunil apologised. The official was quite adept at this brand of behaviour, as Mike Gatting was to discover nine years later. Bedi asked his deputy to apologise, but Sunil refused to lend credence to what was, in his view, an attempt to play to the gallery. Rana was eventually placated by Bedi, Gaekwad, and the umpire's younger brother Shafqat, who happened to be the liaison officer of the touring side. The match resumed fifteen minutes behind schedule.

Majid and Sadiq proceeded to bat without a care in the world until Kapil Dev Nikhanj, who had been hit for 71 runs from sixteen overs in the first innings, challenged Sadiq with a bouncer. The opener reacted by waving towards the dressing room. A helmet came out a little later. Even as Sadiq donned it, Kapil Dev's team-mates racked their brains to remember the last time they had seen a quick bowler from India induce fear in an opposition batsman. They did not spend too much time trying to recollect, for there wasn't any such incident, certainly not since Ramakant Desai had given Hanif Mohammad a tough time in the previous series between the traditional rivals.

Minutes after he had bowled that bouncer, Kapil induced Sadiq to nick an outswinger. The ball flew to Sunil at second slip, and his palms stung. But he hung on, thus giving the nineteen year-old his first Test wicket.

Zaheer Abbas, who had scored 176 in the first innings, was within striking distance of his second hundred in the match, when Bedi decided to rest his main bowlers and threw the ball to his deputy. Sunil decided to impersonate a bowler he had seen at the Hindu Gymkhana in Bombay. Zaheer had moved to 96 when Sunil reverted to his own action. Zaheer, who was clearly concentrating more on the outcome than the process, tried to hit him over the top, but failed to clear Chauhan at mid-on.

It was Sunil's first Test wicket. His victim had apparently anticipated the worst.

Zaheer turned to me and said, 'No Kiri, not this bowler at 96. I have a feeling I am going to get out to him.' – Syed Kirmani, *SGP* (PMG, 1987)

'That tour of Pakistan was my first outside India. All India Radio had told us to make our own transport and accommodation arrangements. When Sunil came to know that it was my first trip, he told me to get in touch with him if I had any problem. He said that I could share his room if need be. Whenever we met on that tour, he would ask me whether everything was all right. My sister-in-law, who is based in the US, wrote me a letter during the tour, asking me to get in touch with a Pakistani family she knew. She did not have my address, and hence wrote 'Sudhir Vaidya, c/o Indian cricket team,' on the envelope. The letter was delivered to Gaekwad in the dressing room during one of the matches. Sunil picked it up, and came up all the way from the dressing room to the commentary box to hand it to me. He expressed his concern at the fact that someone had written me a letter when I was on tour. He left only after I read the letter and reassured him that all was well.' – Sudhir Vaidya

The draw at Faisalabad was the thirteenth in a row between the neighbours. India had won the first and third Tests of the inaugural series in 1952-53, and Pakistan had triumphed in the second, but little had happened thereafter. The 1954-55 and 1960-61 tussles in Pakistan and India respectively had been stalemates, with each side waiting for the other to make the first move. The fear of failure was paramount.

The teams then moved to Lahore for the second Test, at a stadium named after Col Muammar Gaddafi, the Libyan dictator. What connection he had with cricket, nobody knew. But what Libya shared with Pakistan was the style of governance. Zulfiqar Ali Bhutto, who as prime minister of Pakistan had signed the Simla Accord with Indira Gandhi in 1972, had been overthrown in a military coup, and General Zia-ul-Haq was calling the shots.

Even as the teams got down to giving it everything on the field, something quite remarkable was happening in and around the Gaddafi stadium. Within the stadium and outside were several Indians, some of whom had been residents of Lahore before the 1947 vivisection. They had walked across the border at Wagah, thirty kilometres away from the city. They spent the mornings and afternoons at the ground and utilised the evenings to visit their ancestral homes and to renew relationships with childhood friends. The residents of Lahore went out of their way to make these explorers of their own lands feel at home.

It seemed that the Gaddafi groundstaff wanted to give their ground a respite from its traditional reputation as a graveyard for bowlers. What Imran and Sarfraz saw on the first morning of the game delighted them no end. The wicket was green, and Mushtaq did his men a good turn by ensuring that the coin did not fall the way Bedi wanted it to. When the Indian openers walked in, Mushtaq held Sarfraz back and opened with seamer Salim Altaf, whose brief was to bowl line-and-length into the corridor of uncertainty outside the off-stump. Altaf did his job to perfection, inducing Sunil to nibble at one, with keeper Wasim Bari doing the rest. When Imran bowled Chauhan, India were well and truly on the back foot at 19-2. The innings was provided respectability by Vengsarkar, who came in at 48-3 and scored 76. Viswanath contributed 20, as did Mohinder, who was hit on the head just before lunch by an Imran bouncer. He returned to the fray after repairs, only to dislodge his bails while trying to hook Sarfraz.

India finished with 199. They needed early wickets, but were undone by the paucity of fast-bowling resources. Kapil Dev was raw, and with Mohinder not taking the field initially, Sunil had to share the new ball. The wicket did not have anything in it for the spinners.

Bedi, Chandrasekhar and Prasanna were, in euphemistic terms, annihilated by Zaheer Abbas. His 235 ensured a lead of 340 for his team. With more than two days left and their pacemen raring to go, the Pakistanis were in command.

> 'Sunil was the epitome as far as technique was concerned. Chetan was not as correct, but he was gutsy, confident of his abilities, and possessed a big heart. He played some unorthodox shots and was always ready to take quick singles. They both complemented each other beautifully. Chetan was more adventurous while Sunil quietly accumulated runs. The one thing that the present lot of openers can learn from them is their penchant for taking singles and rotating the strike.' – Yajurvindra Singh

If Indian cricket lovers of the 1970s felt that their side had become stable, the Gavaskar-Chauhan axis at the top had a lot to do with it. They had bonded well in their very first Test as partners against England at Kanpur in 1972-73. But Chauhan was ignored by the selectors for four seasons thereafter. During that period, he shifted from Maharashtra to Delhi, where his batsmanship at the top played a pivotal role in the capital's advent as a cricketing powerhouse. Their stands in Australia in 1977-78, although not very productive, had convinced watchers that India had discovered their best opening pair since Vijay Merchant and Syed Mushtaq Ali. Coincidentally, both Sunil and Chauhan had been guided at some point in their formative years by the Pune-based Kamal Bhandarkar, one of India's most venerated cricket gurus.

> Sitting in the dressing room before going out to bat, Sunil and I decided that we must save the side from an innings defeat, and

we were determined to hang in there. Though we both were under immense pressure, the moment we looked at each other we found ourselves even more determined to succeed. – Chetan Chauhan, *Sunil Gavaskar Birthday Special, Rediff*, 10 July 1999

The openers took India to 92-0 at stumps on day three, and carried on the following morning. Their first century-stand could not have been better timed. On a difficult strip, and against bowlers who were using the short-pitched ball quite liberally and surrounded by fielders eager to display their repertoire of profanities, Chauhan was defiant, and Sunil resolute. The score was 192 when Pakistan drew first blood. The Indian view was that an umpire had done it, not a cricketer.

Chauhan was declared out caught behind off Miandad on 93, and Sunil followed him to the pavilion 10 runs later, having been given out to an alleged bat-pad chance off Mushtaq. Sunil expressed his displeasure by banging his bat on the turf repeatedly during his return to the pavilion. His gesture was interpreted as one of frustration of missing out on a hundred by only three runs. But then, it was not often that he knew his score.

I don't look at the scoreboard or the clock when I am batting, It surprises many people, but that's the absolute truth. It is not superstition, but because I feel under less tension and I am more relaxed like this than if I was aware I was close to a century . . . I have always believed that a century should be just a milestone in one's quest for more runs. – Sunil Gavaskar, *Runs n' Ruins* (Rupa, 1984).

Less than four sessions were left in the game when Sunil was declared out. Surender Amarnath, who was back at the number three slot, scored an adventurous 60. Viswanath, with whom he added 99, batted well, and when the scoreboard read 406-4 just before lunch on the final day, the Pakistanis themselves had all but put down the shutters. It was at this stage that Viswanath unveiled the most conspicuous chink in his armour—a penchant for losing his wicket against the run of play. He was on 83 when he attempted his favourite cut against Mudassar Nazar, and was bowled.

Like his father Nazar Mohammed, who had represented Pakistan in its inaugural Test series against India in 1952-53, Mudassar was an opening batsman. He was also a handy seamer, whose capabilities opposition batsmen were often guilty of underestimating.

That wicket gave the Pakistanis an opening they capitalised on, the stubbornness of Kirmani and Kapil Dev notwithstanding. The Indian innings ended at 465 and the hosts had less than two hours in which to get 126. Their experience of One Day cricket in their County stints in England came to the fore, as Zaheer (Gloucestershire) and Asif Iqbal (Kent) finished the game well in time. Bedi's instructions to Kapil Dev and Amarnath to bowl negatively down the leg-side came a cropper, although Majid Khan at one point got so irritated that he uprooted a stump and threatened to plant it on the return crease on the leg-side. His subsequent reprisal was more telling; he hooked Kapil Dev's next ball for six.

A public holiday was announced in Pakistan to commemorate its first Test win over the old enemy since Lucknow in 1952-53. India on the other hand, were left pondering over the abject state of their bowling attack.

In the prevailing circumstances, their performance in the third and final One-dayer at Sahiwal was stirring. Pakistan scored 205-7 and India batted exceedingly well in response. They were only two wickets down and needed less than 30 to win the match, and with it, the one day series, when Mushtaq instructed his quickies to bowl a series of moon-balls. These were beyond the reach of the tall Anshuman Gaekwad, leave alone Viswanath. When the umpires refused to intervene, Bedi called his batsmen in. The visitors stayed away from a function hosted by the local cricket body that evening.

'India were at a disadvantage in that series. After Faisalabad, we had a change of policy and both the pitches at Lahore and Karachi were as green as any I have ever seen in Pakistan. They were also hard, which made it difficult for the spinners to turn the ball. On top of this, India came across two of the best players of spin bowling in the shape of Zaheer and Miandad. The Indian spinners had also come to the end of their better days. They were completely overwhelmed.' – Mudassar Nazar

At the National stadium in Karachi, Bedi called correctly for the first time in the Test series. Sunil and Chauhan arrived in the middle to encounter an angry Imran Khan. His team management's decision to overlook the greener of the two strips that the groundstaff had prepared for the Test had cheesed him off. He could not understand why his seniors were content to sit on their 1-0 lead and not go for the kill.

For the first time since 1974-75, India entered a Test with two specialist new-ball bowlers in Kapil Dev and Ghavri, with a back up in Mohinder. More remarkable was the fact that for the first time in decades, they fielded only two spinners. Prasanna had been dropped after two traumatic Tests.

India began well, and leading the way was the vice-captain. Sunil completed the hundred that had eluded him twice in the series, and the Indians had reason to be satisfied with a score of 344. The bruised and battered Indian bowlers then hit back. They had Pakistan at 187-5 before they did what their predecessors and successors were known to do—take the foot off the accelerator when in charge. Every Pakistani batsman from number six to number eleven was allowed to enter double figures. Last man Sikander Bakht's contribution was the lowest – 22. Not for the last time, a batsman who answered to the name of Javed Miandad, thrived in a crisis, and guided and goaded a group of lower-order bats. His captain Mushtaq, no mean batsman, got 78. He declared at 481-9 on the fourth evening, thus giving his bowlers around eight hours in which to bowl the Indians out.

The visitors needed a combination of application and luck. They got the latter sooner than they had imagined. Imran got Sunil to edge one to Bari in the very first over. The Pakistanis went up in appeal, but the umpire's finger stayed in his pocket.

Unlike the 1975 World Cup game against England, this reprieve worked in Sunil's favour. He did not make a single mistake thereafter, even as his mates at the other end made several. Sarfraz was deceptive, while Imran with his open-chested action was making the ball rear even off the flat track. Chauhan was not as lucky as his partner, being snapped up by the keeper off Sarfraz for a duck. Mohinder, who came in one-down instead of his brother, was put down by Zaheer, and went on to score 53 before falling at 122. Kirmani, who came in as nightwatchman, did not last long, and he was followed to the pavilion by Viswanath and Vengsarkar. Surender played a couple of sparkling strokes, but he was declared run out when he appeared to have completed a two.

When Sunil displayed his deft footwork to cut Mushtaq for four, he became India's highest scorer in Tests, surpassing Polly Umrigar's aggregate of 3,631. India were 196-6 at lunch on the final day, with Sunil on 98. A three off the first ball after lunch made him the only Indian to score twin hundreds in a Test twice.

Even as the spectators applauded, Sunil's attention was drawn to Gaekwad, who had risen from his seat and was waving his wrist watch in his direction. Sunil had liked the watch, which showed the time in all the major cities of the world, and Gaekwad had promised to gift it to him if he scored two hundreds in the series. Nothing could deter the manager from demonstrating his intent to keep his promise when Sunil completed his second hundred, not even the fact that he was sitting next to the President of Pakistan.

'Sunil was par excellence throughout the series. He played a superb knock at Faisalabad, which prompted us to prepare a green track at Lahore. In fact, Salim Altaf was specially brought in the side to put pressure on Sunil early on his innings on the off stump. He obliged by dismissing him in the first innings. But in the second innings, it was back to normal, with us chasing the ball. It took a controversial decision to dislodge him. He took it to heart and punished us at Karachi by scoring hundreds in both innings. I had given him plenty of verbal sticks during the series, and in this game, he smashed me all over to put me in my place. Mind you, I wasn't the only one to suffer.' – Mudassar Nazar

Mudassar was taken off after only two overs that cost him thirteen runs. It took a clever move by Sarfraz to send the twin centurion to the pavilion. He adopted a round-the-wicket line and angled one across the right-hander. Sunil bit the bait. The ball flew off the outside-edge into Wasim Bari's gauntlets. His dismissal meant that India were 253-7 and Pakistan had regained the initiative. Kapil Dev then demonstrated that his strokeful 59 at Lahore was not a fluke, before being snapped up by Mushtaq in the slips. Ghavri, who had essayed a patient hand, fell to Imran, and Bedi and Chandrasekhar could not do much. India were all out for 300, leaving Pakistan with half an hour, plus the twenty mandatory overs, in which to score 164.

Majid Khan fell at 21 and Javed Miandad came in to join makeshift opener Asif Iqbal. The reshuffling of the batting order indicated that Pakistan were going for it. What followed was sensational, with runs being not so much stolen as hijacked from under the noses of the Indian fielders. Miandad and Iqbal, master improvisers and excellent runners, guided the ball into different parts of the outfield, and sprinted for broke. Ones were converted into twos, twos into threes, and singles conjured out of nowhere. The piece *de resistance* was delivered in a Kapil Dev over. Asif came down the wicket, swung, missed, and the ball went straight through to Kirmani. Seeing that the batsman was out of his crease, the keeper shied at the stumps, but hit them only after Asif had grounded his bat. The ball ricocheted off the stumps, and the batsmen scurried through for a bye before the Indians realised what was happening!

Their running earned them a few overthrows as well, and by the time the partnership ended with Kirmani catching Iqbal off Mohinder, the Indians wore a ragged look.

Imran came in, and a quiet period ensued until TV commentator Iftikar Ahmed said that the hosts needed a couple of sixes to regain the initiative. Imran seemed to have heard him, for he hit Bedi out of the ground twice almost immediately, and then cut him for four. They needed only 19 from the last four overs and got there in the penultimate over.

> 'Bedi erred in keeping himself going from one end and shuffling the bowlers at the other. In those days, overs were not a factor, minutes were. Kapil and I could have killed the game by taking time between deliveries. But Bedi bowled like wanting to buy wickets and Imran got after him.' – Karsan Ghavri

Bedi was one of the game's great optimists, but even he would have known at the end of the tour that he was in trouble. Ghulam Ahmed, former off-spin bowler and the Secretary of BCCI, met him at the Bombay airport on the team's arrival on 20 November 1978, one day after the conclusion of the Karachi Test, and handed him the pink slip.

On the same day, the national selection committee, headed by Umrigar, and comprising Dattu Phadkar, M.L. Jaisimha, Kishan Rungta and Vijay Mehra, summoned Sunil to the CCI. The press was then informed that the selectors had unanimously decided to entrust the leadership to Sunil.

What may well have happened in 1975, had happened three years later.

> There are reasons to believe that Gavaskar can lift India following the reverses in Pakistan. Gavaskar is one of those rare types in cricket. He is neither an intellectual like (Mike) Brearley, nor the rude, earthy types who have made cricket as rough a game as football. He stands somewhere in between... his handling of the bowling, his field-placing and above all, his ability to get the best out of every player (at Auckland) marked him out as a future captain. Bedi only had to slip for Gavaskar to displace him. And that is exactly what has happened now.' – K.N. Prabhu, *TOI*, 23 November 1978

Sunil's fans were delighted, as was the man himself. However, he was aware that his relationship with the media and the public, which had been harmonious till then, would now be tested.

The captaincy of the Indian team wasn't the only new challenge that Sunil took up in 1978. It was a period wherein organisations had very few outlets through which to publicise themselves and their operations. Many a corporate had attempted to latch onto cricket's popularity by putting together a competitive cricket team. The quality of talent on display in Bombay's *Times of India* Shield spoke for itself. Cricketers from Bombay apart, the competition featured recruits from other cities, who were on the payrolls of the Bombay-based organisations.

Virenchee Sagar, the managing director of Nirlons, an organisation that manufactured synthetic textiles, wanted to create a competitive cricket team. On Sunil's return from the tour of Australia, Sagar made him an attractive offer. Sunil accepted and quit ACC. His immediate brief at Nirlons was to build a team. Within three or four years, Nirlons established itself as a cricketing force to contend with. Sunil apart, the company had on its payroll the likes of Ravi Shastri, Sandeep Patil, Balwinder Singh Sandhu and Suru Nayak.

The period from 1978 to 1984 witnessed a fierce rivalry between Nirlons and Mafatlals, whose cricket team had dominated the TOI Shield, winning it in a row from 1971-72 to 1977-78. The Nirlon-Mafatlals rivalry was no less fierce and bitter than the India-Pakistan rivalry at the international level. Both sides gave it everything, as did their respective skippers. Mafatlals had as captain the canny Ashok Mankad, who knew Sunil's strengths and weaknesses inside out.

'Ashok Mankad would plan and ensure that something or someone would upset Sunil. The Mafatlal players would deliberately upset him, to the extent that he would lose his cool and in the process, the match. What I also remember is that the umpires tended to be thoroughly biased during these matches.' – Suru Nayak

International teams of the time probably bungled by not requisitioning Mankad's services as a consultant, to find out how he got under Sunil's skin! The experiences during the tussles against Mankad's side prompted Sunil to vow that he would never walk in matches against two teams—Pakistan and Mafatlals!

His first assignment as India's full-time skipper was a six-Test series against a Packer-stricken West Indies team. His old friend Alvin Kallicharran was the captain of the touring outfit. The West Indies outfit was short on experience, but potent in terms of pace. The bowling attack was headed by Sylvester Clarke, one of the fastest bowlers in the world. He had support in the form of the old warhorse Vanburn Holder, and two youngsters named Norbert Philip and Malcolm Marshall.

Sunil began on a bold note, playing five specialist bowlers in the first Test at Bombay, with Mohinder providing a sixth option. The factor that facilitated his decision was Kapil Dev Nikhanj. India were decidedly fortunate that the decline of their spinners had coincided with his rise. As a bowler, he was quick and versatile, endowed with a decent bouncer and a peach of an outswinger. As a batsman, he was breathtaking to watch, his free-flowing blade creating a lovely arc as it dispatched the ball towards the ropes and occasionally over them. As a fielder, he was brilliant at any position. Then, there was his build. He was the complete package.

There was unanimity on the view that he was the best thing to happen to Indian cricket for a long, long time. But the pundits were guilty of overreaction. They labelled him as India's first quick bowler since Ramakant Desai, conveniently forgetting the likes of Rajinder Pal, Ghulam Guard, Kailash Gattani, Subroto Guha and Pandurang Salgaonkar, to name just five, who came to the fore during the spin era. Contrary to popular perception, India was never ever confronted with a drought of quick bowlers. It was just that the captains, selectors and administrators of the 1960s and 1970s were for some reason reluctant to accommodate them in the team. Their ambivalence towards the pacemen was compounded by the presence of as many as four extraordinary spin bowlers. It would not be entirely out of place to contend that had Bedi, Chandrasekhar and Prasanna not been manhandled the way they were in Pakistan in 1978-79, Kapil Dev for all his talents may not have become an automatic choice in the first XI straightaway.

There was one change for the Bombay Test from the XI that had played at Karachi. Surender was replaced by Venkataraghvan. With Prasanna having been dropped after the thrashing in Pakistan, Venkataraghvan's backers were hoping that their man would now enjoy an uninterrupted stint. Bedi and Chandrasekhar were still there, but they could no longer take their places for granted.

The series got off to a damp and delayed start. Unseasonal rains in Bombay livened up the pitch and prompted Kallicharran to bowl after winning the toss. In the very first over, Sylvester Clarke fired a bouncer that came screaming at Sunil's face. Some onlookers, seated in the comfort of the stands, took their eyes off the ball, while others ducked. But Sunil rose on his toes and offered a straight bat. The ball dropped dead to his feet, and the city's club cricketers seated in the north stand, and the former international cricketers seated above the pavilion, clapped. That exhibition of assurance by Sunil set the tone for the rest of his innings. India were 57-2 at the close.

Sunil went on the offensive on the second morning. There was not one vertical or horizontal bat stroke that he did not essay. Even the hook made a fleeting appearance. He completed his fifty with an on-driven boundary off Clarke, and his hundred with a pull. The masses and classes lapped it up. By the end of the second day, India were sitting pretty at 351-5. Sunil had scored 205, his second double hundred in Tests and against the Windies. Those who saw it rated it as one of the best, if not the best innings they had ever seen.

That performance made a deep impression on a former Indian cricketer. He was moved enough to pen an open letter to Sunil, which appeared in the *TOI* the following morning.

'Words are not adequate to express my deep sense of admiration for your technique, your patience, your self-imposed restraint, your tremendous sense of responsibility, your adaptability, your superb timing, your excellent choice of the right ball to hit, your exquisite strokes and your unparalleled temperament of not being ruffled when beaten by any ball in the superlative innings . . . I admired and enjoyed every moment of it and felt proud that an Indian played it. I am quite sure that you will play equally well on any wicket. May next year's tour of England place the crown of glory on your grand cricket career. Indian cricket has produced no greater batsman.' – Vijay Merchant

The day the letter appeared, Merchant was taken to the Indian dressing room by Mantri, who was a senior functionary in the Bombay Cricket Association. The former chairman of selectors was taken aback when Sunil asked him about a fault he had committed while on 197. Sunil had essayed a hook, but the ball hadn't gone to the square-leg boundary, where all orthodox hooks were intended to go. Merchant was incredulous. He told Sunil that while he did remember the fault, it was only human for a batsman to make an error like that during the course of a double hundred. The senior man came away impressed by Sunil's pursuit of perfection.

India finished with 424 and the West Indies delivered a strong response of 493, with Kallicharran scoring 187. The game was drawn, as were the next two, played in Bangalore and Calcutta respectively. Sunil got a first-ball duck at Bangalore, but he compensated in style in the new year Test at the Eden Gardens. He scored 107 in the first innings, and an unbeaten 182 in the second, to become the first batsman to score twin hundreds in a Test thrice.

Sunil also passed 1,000 runs in the calendar year of 1978 during the course of that Test, making him only the second batsman after England's Ken Barrington to do so twice. In fact, he scored an astounding 1,014 runs at an average of 101.40, in seventy-eight days, from 16 October

1978 to 2 January 1979. In the process, he beat the world record held by England's Walter Hammond, who had scored over 1,000 Test runs in 124 days in the 1930s.

The second innings of the Calcutta Test featured an unfinished stand of 344 between the Dadar Unionites. Three years after his Test debut, and in his seventeenth Test, Dilip Vengsarkar finally went the distance.

> 'Sunil guided me as I approached my maiden Test hundred. He ensured that I did not lose my concentration, and coaxed me to carry on after I reached three figures.' – Dilip Vengsarkar

Vengsarkar was on 157 when Sunil declared at 361-1, with his team 334 ahead. He could have gone on to complete his double hundred, but he chose not to. India had a little over a day to bowl the Windies out, and they very nearly did so. In fact, they probably would have, had a pre-match agreement between the captains not resulted in their forfeiting the right to start play fifteen minutes early on the last day.

Ghavri and Venkataraghvan took four wickets each, even as the sun gradually slipped out of sight. The spectators did their bit to create light by torching their newspapers, in what was to become an abiding Eden tradition in years to come. But Marshall was put down by Viswanath in the slips, and he stayed on to consume invaluable deliveries. The darkness eventually won the battle and the umpires drew the bails with eleven balls left, and the Windies hanging on at 197-9. As far as Marshall was concerned, that was the least the umpires could have done.

> I will remain certain that I twice had Gavaskar out leg before. It may also smack of sour grapes when those same record books show how the Indian captain went on to score 107 and 182 not out . . . I rapidly formed the impression that in his home country, it is as easy to get an lbw decision against him as it is to steal the Taj Mahal. – Malcolm Marshall, *Marshall Arts* (Macdonald Queen Anne Press, 1987)

Marshall was on the same wavelength as his skipper, who had a confrontation with one of the umpires after the latter had turned down Marshall's second leg-before shout against Sunil.

In an era wherein every umpire was expected to be neutral in terms of adjudication rather than nationality, every country was home to a group of officials who tended to use their hearts instead of their heads. India was no exception. This is not to say that the official who reprieved Sunil at Calcutta belonged to that category, but there were undoubtedly some umpires who allowed patriotism to cloud their judgement. These people were in a minority, but invariably, it was they who gave the visiting teams and their media contingents a pretext to claim that two and two added up to twenty-two.

Sunil and Kallicharran had exchanged a hug after the toss at Bombay, but there was little bonhomie between the two sides by the time the fourth Test got underway in Madras. It happened to be the first Test since Bishan Bedi's debut in 1966-67 that the former skipper had missed on account of being dropped. He had missed Tests earlier on disciplinary grounds and also due to injury, but this was a different story.

The events at Madras left nobody in any doubt that a new era had begun in Indian cricket. The West Indies batted first on a spiteful strip and scored 228. India were 11-2 in response, when in came Viswanath to provide an encore of his 1974-75 heroics against the same team at the same ground. His 124 gave India a lead of 27.

Then, after years of ducking under and fending at short-pitched deliveries, the Indians decided that it was payback time. Kapil Dev, supported by Ghavri, subjected the Windies to a rigorous hop-duck-and-evade session. The bouncers he dished out to the visitors earned Kapil Dev the ire of Chetan Chauhan. As opener, Chauhan was at the receiving end of the retaliatory tactics of the West Indian speedsters, and wasn't very happy about it. He gave Kapil a piece of his mind, and it was left to Sunil to assure Kapil that there was nothing wrong in his methods.

Kapil Dev and Ghavri shared six wickets between them and ensured the West Indies' demise for 151. India needed 125 to win. The backlash from the West Indies pacemen duly came, and claimed the scalps of the Calcutta centurions Sunil and Vengsarkar. However, for the second time in the match, Viswanath flourished. The decisive innings was played by Kapil Dev, who came in at 84-6 despite a bout of fever. By the time he had moved to 26, India needed only 1 to win. Kirmani and he finished it off with a bye.

India dominated the next two Tests at Delhi and Kanpur, both of which were drawn, and thus registered their first ever series win against the West Indies at home. Sunil's 120 at Delhi was his fourth hundred of the series, and it gave him an aggregate of 732 for the series, which was second only to the 774 he had accumulated in the Caribbean in 1971.

Kapil Dev underscored his all-round utility with his maiden Test hundred at Delhi, reaching the landmark with a six of all strokes. His match-winning bowling at Madras had prompted Sunil to suggest to the BCCI that he be sent to Australia for a short fine-tuning stint. Pran, one of the Bombay film industry's icons and a sports fanatic, offered to bear the all-rounder's expenses for a stint at an Australian Academy headed by former England speedster Frank Tyson. However, the Board did not follow it up, probably because it had other issues to contend with.

'May next year's tour of England place the crown of glory on your grand cricket career,' Vijay Merchant had written in that open letter to Sunil. He was not alone in thinking along those lines. Sunil's admirers expected the world from the Indian team on its tour of England in mid-1979. They had a solid opening combination, a sound middle order and for the first time in decades, a varied bowling attack. Their captain was in his prime, and seemingly intent on conquering every batting peak.

Not everything went according to plan.

11

MAGNUM OPUS AT THE OVAL

'It is with a heavy heart that we will watch you go – a fallen idol in the eyes of those of us who would like to preserve the sanctity of cricket, as we know it . . . You brought honour not only to yourself, but to India . . . it is a sad thought that such a peerless artiste should now join the ranks of the hired gladiators. We can't bear to think of you, or for that matter any cricketer, playing in a strawberry-coloured suit . . . to men of our generation, cricket has been a game associated with sunshine . . . we can't understand your urge to prove that you are the greatest, for we have seen you at your best against Willis, Snow, Roberts, Holding . . . one cricket writer compared you to Alexander, looking for fresh worlds to conquer, and weeping because there was none. But when you desert us for Packer, it will be an act fit to make the angels weep.'

K.N. Prabhu's anguish was evident in his open letter to Sunil that appeared in the *TOI* on 23 February 1979. It was an upshot of cricket's greatest controversy of the era, which had come a long way since a tepid start in 1977-78.

Even as a third-string Australian side was being battered by England in the 1978-79 Ashes, Kerry Packer's brainchild was making waves on both sides of the great Australian desert.

His brand of cricket featured floodlights, white balls, black sight screens and coloured clothing. Playing it were cricketers, who the Packer machinery had packaged, marketed, and elevated to superstardom. A major achievement of the tycoon was the acquisition of a significant female audience. Channel Nine's TV coverage of the matches was unbelievably sleek, with more than ten cameras following the players' moves. On the screen, the image of a weeping duck would follow a batsman who hadn't troubled the scorers. A graphic of a ball hitting a set of stumps would indicate that a batsman had been bowled. Every dismissal, boundary or six would be followed by slow-motion replays of the moment from varied angles. Voluptuous models would accompany the drinks-trolley. As for the coloured clothing, the World XI wore light blue and the Australians yellow. The West Indians shifted from pink to maroon, after protesting that the former wasn't in tune with their macho image.

In other words, WSC was the antithesis of what K.N. Prabhu's generation had grown up playing, watching and loving.

The game had hardly changed since the legalisation of overarm bowling in 1864. Neither had the administrators, whose line of thinking had remained dogmatic down the decades. Cricketers the world over could not help but notice the innovations and the money that had crept into other sports. Had a visionary like Packer not arrived, the cricketers would have probably concocted one.

> Every single cricketer who wakes up tomorrow must thank Kerry Packer, and by extension, the fifty-five cricketers who signed up with him. – Late David Hookes, *The Chappell Era* (ABC, 2002)

It was on 18 November 1978 that the doubts over the viability of WSC were forgotten for good. The Australians took on the West Indians in what was the first ever 'day-night' One-dayer to be played at the Sydney Cricket Ground. It was the first time a traditional cricket venue was staging a Packer game, a consequence of the local council's decision to constitute a new SCG trust and permit the erection of light towers. More than 50,000 people turned up, and when the queues showed no signs of dwindling, Packer threw the gates open to let everybody in.

Of course, all the packaging and marketing would have amounted to nothing had the cricket itself not been of a high standard. The

Chappell brothers, Vivian Richards, Clive Lloyd and Barry Richards batted brilliantly, while the likes of Dennis Lillee, Andy Roberts, Mike Procter, Michael Holding and Imran Khan gave it their all with the ball. The batsmen felt the heat more than the bowlers, for most of the games were played on non-cricketing grounds, with pitches being created in greenhouses and dropped onto the playing arenas by giant cranes. They were usually of the hard and bouncy variety. A batsman who was out of form had nowhere to go, for Packer's recruits had been banned from participating in any form of official cricket in Australia. He had no option but to continue facing the Lillees, Holdings and Imrans.

The Indians may have felt aggrieved at not having been approached by Packer in the first two seasons, but the revolution affected them positively, as it did cricketers attached to the establishment all over the world. Like the Chappell brothers in the immediate pre-Packer era in Australia, Bedi and Sunil pressed for a hike in the match-fees. The BCCI's response was positive.

If the media was to be believed, it was for the third season of Packer's World Series Cricket that some prominent Indian cricketers were approached. Sunil was the biggest and the most obvious target.

Not everybody agreed with K.N. Prabhu. Behram Contractor, one of India's most popular columnists, made a pertinent point in his piece on 24 February 1979: 'If Vijay Amritraj can play professional tennis and also represent India in the Davis Cup, I don't see why Sunil Gavaskar can't do so. Especially as Gavaskar is much more useful to India than both the Amritraj brothers put together'.

The next day's *TOI* quoted Sunil as saying that while he was inclined to accept the WSC offer, he was still at the negotiating stage. He emphasised that the prime reason for the negotiations was his wanting to be available for India in Test cricket.

'Asif Iqbal and another representative of Packer's (Lynton Taylor) had met some of the Indian players in Pakistan and offered them contracts. I recall Sunil, Viswanath, Mohinder, Bedi and Kirmani being approached. But the deals did not materialise. The players were keen to continue playing for the country, and hence reluctant to sign. Playing for India was the first priority.'
– Karsan Ghavri

The BCCI reacted to the reports by asking the selectors to pick sixty-one probables for the 1979 World Cup and Test series against England, and revising the players' contracts. A bone of contention in the new contract was Clause 11, which forbade the signatories from playing for any individual or in any match not authorised by the BCCI in India or abroad for one year.

The clause was criticised by the Indian Players' Association, which had been revived after years of dormancy. The *TOI* on 2 April 1979 reported a meeting between M. Chinnaswamy, the Board President, and Sunil, Venkataraghvan and Viswanath, who were the Secretary, Treasurer and Executive Member of the Players' Association respectively, in Bangalore. The players' representatives demanded that the period of one year, as mentioned in Clause 11, be reduced to six months.

But by then, cracks had surfaced in the Association itself. Some of the peripheral players went ahead and signed the contract, sensing the possibility of being picked for the England tour in place of the seven alleged prospective Packerites.

Lynton Taylor, one of Packer's senior representatives, corroborated Sunil's statement of 24 February 1979, in the *TOI* on 11 April 1979. He said that no Indian had signed with them. He was on a visit to India, ostensibly to explore the possibility of staging WSC matches in the country.

Rajan Bala writes in *The Covers are Off* (Rupa, 2004) that Gaekwad's report of the Pakistan tour, wherein he had alluded to the approaches made by Packer's representatives to some of the Indian cricketers during the Test series, raised the hackles of the BCCI President M. Chinnaswamy, and the Secretary Ghulam Ahmed.

> I remember both of them reiterating to me, 'Both of us, and for that matter, everybody in Indian cricket, were so keen that Gavaskar led for a long time. All he had to do was to confide in us and we would have understood. He behaved as if we were out to get him. We were not. Our board was then with the ICC on the Packer issue ... We did not want international cricket to get disrupted in any way. We had already discussed higher payments to the players and other details that would benefit

them. We wanted Gavaskar to talk on their behalf.' – Rajan Bala, *The Covers are off* (Rupa, 2004)

The *TOI* on 9 April 1979 mentioned a possibility of Sunil retaining the captaincy. It mentioned him having informed Ghulam Ahmed that he had misplaced his copy of the contract. By then, sixty of the sixty-one probables had signed and submitted their individual copies. Sunil was the odd man out. The report also claimed that he had indicated his willingness to abide by the terms and conditions set by the BCCI.

But the selectors entrusted the reins to S. Venkataraghavan. It was reported that the Board President and Secretary had 'advised' them not to retain Sunil as captain for the England tour. Viswanath, who had by then become Sunil's brother-in-law, having tied the knot with Sunil's younger sister Kavita, was appointed vice-captain. C.D. Gopinath, who as the chairman of selectors had named Venkataraghvan skipper on the morning of the Delhi Test in 1974-75, was appointed manager. Bedi and Chandrasekhar were brought back after fruitful performances in the 1978-79 season. A surprise inclusion as first-choice keeper was Bharat Reddy, a resident of Madras like the new captain and manager. Sunil could be dropped as captain, but not as a player. Syed Kirmani, another player whose name had figured prominently in the Packer speculations, was made to pay a heavy price. He got the news of his omission in Bombay, and was so shocked that he jumped into a taxi and asked the cabbie to drive him wherever he liked.

> I still do not know the reasons why I was removed from the leadership, but I presume it had to do with the fact that I openly talked about the approach made to me by World Series Cricket. Kiri also was honest about it, while others who had been approached preferred to indicate otherwise. The real story – about the approaches, the responses and the reactions – is a juicy one, and will blow many a reputation to smithereens, and so it is best to preserve it for a book. . . . – Sunil Gavaskar, *The Sportstar*, 1 May 1993

Sunil's sacking and Kirmani's omission were ironic, given the developments in Packer's own country.

The Australian Cricket Board, stung by monumental losses in the 1978-79 season, had appealed for a compromise. The official word came out on 24 April 1979, two days after Sunil, in an interview with the *BBC*, expressed his surprise at losing the captaincy. The ACB accepted Packer's bid for exclusive TV rights to all international matches in Australia for a period of five years. In return, Packer disbanded WSC.

The Australian authorities, relieved that their stars had returned to the fold, crammed the 1979-80 season with three Tests each against England and the West Indies, and a triangular One-day series comprising fifteen preliminary games and best-of-five finals. The West Indies were scheduled to tour Australia that season, but England weren't, for they had toured Australia the previous year. However, it was a fact that they were a lot more marketable than the team that was originally supposed to tour – India.

The BCCI hit back at the annual ICC meet in June, threatening to cancel Australia's proposed tour in 1979-80 unless they were asked to visit in 1980-81. The threat was taken seriously.

Sunil had taken his deposal in his stride, or so it seemed when he was felicitated at the Wankhede stadium by the Government of Maharashtra on 27 April 1979. At the function, he brought a smile to many faces by saying that he owed Venkataraghvan a big score after the happenings of 1975.

The reference was to the World Cup, the second edition of which the Indians had to play before getting down to the serious business of the Test series. The Deodhar Trophy, Wills Trophy and one-dayers in Pakistan notwithstanding, the Indians continued to regard the abbreviated version of the game with contempt. India found themselves in the same group as the West Indies, New Zealand and Sri Lanka, and at no stage did the players and their fans expect a miracle. Their defeats against the West Indies, whose Packer players had returned to the fold, and New Zealand, were expected. But what wasn't anticipated was a loss to the associate member, Sri Lanka. That performance gave an impetus to the south Asian nation's bid for Test status.

The Indians then took to doing what they had been doing for several years, and drew vicarious pleasure from the exploits of the West Indies, who retained the title by trouncing England in the final. From the three

Ws—Weekes, Walcott and Worrell—to Vivian Richards, Indians had adored the men from the Caribbean, for their adherence to the three As – attitude, aggression and audacity. For the Indians, these attributes were a novelty, for not many of their own players possessed them.

But then, the Australians also possessed the same qualities. By 1978, the men from down under had opposed India in seven Test series, as opposed to the nine between India and the West Indies. So, in terms of series, there was nothing much to choose between Australia and the Windies. Unlike England and very much like the West Indians, the Australians had always sent their best teams to India. So what was it that made the Indians love the West Indies more than Australia? It was probably the fact that the Caribbean nations, like India, belonged to the category of 'developing' countries. Australia, despite its humble origins, was never considered a secondary nation, definitely not for most of the twentieth century, while India and the nations that constituted the West Indies certainly were. In the West Indians, the Indians found a group of kindred souls, who were far better equipped than them to beat the living daylights out of the erstwhile masters in the sporting arena.

The series against England got underway with the usual complement of First-class matches. There was a whiff of a controversy when Ghavri broke England captain Mike Brearley's nose and Wayne Larkins' finger in the three-day game against the MCC. The chucking allegations that had been levied on him in Australia in 1977-78 were resurrected by the British media, whose treatment of their own team vacillated from blind adulation to vengeful indictment. This time, they took up the cause of their hospital-bound skipper, and flayed Ghavri until Richie Benaud gave the latter a clean chit.

The first Test, played at Birmingham, brought no joy to the Indians. England batted first and amassed 633-5, with Geoffrey Boycott scoring 155, and the twenty-two-year-old David Gower carving out 200. The Indians weren't helped by Bedi's withdrawal from the game due to a stiff neck, and the consequent inclusion of a semi-fit Chandrasekhar. The senior batters in the Indian line-up clicked, with Sunil scoring 61 and 68, and Viswanath 78 and 51. But Chauhan apart, they had little support. England won by an innings and 83 runs.

Sunil felt more at ease during his second-innings 68 than in the first, thanks to a new bat, whose blade was an inch wider. He was perusing his team-mates' bats before the game, when he realised that Mohinder's bat, being an inch wider, enabled him to adopt a more upright stance. Sunil then sought out Duncan Fearnley, his bat-maker of the time, and acquired the new piece of willow.

It was around that time that Sunil provided a quotable quote in an interview with the London correspondent of a Bombay eveninger.

The period from July 1979 to April 1980 was the busiest in India's cricketing history. The four Tests in England were to be followed by two back-to-back six-Test series at home, against Australia and Pakistan respectively. They were to be followed by a one-off Test against England to celebrate the golden jubilee of the BCCI, and there was a full tour of the Caribbean thereafter.

'They will smash us to pulp,' Sunil replied when asked about India's prospects in the series against Pakistan. There was a reason for his pessimism. As he saw it, there was a distinct possibility of the cricketers being exhausted after the series against England and Australia. His detractors were quick to brand him a coward and a defeatist.

The controversy did not affect his batting. His 116 against Gloucestershire before the second Test made him the third Indian to score fifty first-class hundreds. He had now passed Umrigar's tally of 49, and ahead of him were Capt Vijay Hazare (57) and K.S. Duleepsinhji (52).

He carried on in the same vein on the first day of the second Test at Lord's. But his team-mates floundered. His 42 was the only noteworthy component of an appalling 96 all out. England replied with 419-9 and gave themselves almost two full days to take 10 Indian wickets. The visitors began on a much better note in the second innings, with Sunil sound and Chauhan solid, until the latter fell to the left-arm spinner Phil Edmonds. Sunil went on to complete his third fifty of the series and looked entrenched enough to achieve three figures at Lord's for the first time. His concentration was fuelled by his determination to not become the hundredth Test victim of a phenomenon called Ian Terence Botham. Just two years after his Test debut, the Somerset all-rounder was on the verge of becoming the fastest to complete the Test 'double' of 1,000 runs and 100 wickets.

THE JUBILEE TEST VS ENGLAND, 1979-80

Receiving the Commemorative Medal from Mr M. Chinnaswamy, the then President of the BCCI.

AN ENTIRELY UNEXPECTED START – SMG drives John Lever for six.

Garner and Gavaskar, team-mates and room-mates at Somerset in 1980.

On the attack for Somerset, 1980.

Carrying the hopes of an entire nation on his shoulders.

Offering a straight bat during the course of his marathon 172 against England at Bangalore in 1981-82. Keith Fletcher, his England counterpart, is in the background.

SMG ended the 1982 tour of England in pain. Ian Botham inspects and inscribes his broken ankle.

An experiment with tradition.

1982 – SMG's only tour of England as captain of India. Standing (from left): Ghulam Parkar, Shivlal Yadav, Suru Nayak, Dilip Doshi, Sandeep Patil, Ravi Shastri, Kapil Dev, Randhir Singh, Yashpal Sharma, Pranab Roy, Ashok Malhotra. Sitting (from left): Raj Singh Dungarpur (manager), Syed Kirmani, Gundappa Viswanath (vice-captain), Sunil Gavaskar (captain), Madan Lal Sharma, Dilip Vengsarkar, C. Nagaraj (assistant manager).

OPENING PARTNERS

With Chetan Chauhan.

With K. Srikkanth in a Veterans'
match in the mid-1990s.

Aunshuman Gaekwad (left) looks on as SMG hooks.

WORLD CHAMPIONS

THE INDIAN TEAM THAT CONQUERED THE WORLD ON 25 JUNE 1983. *Standing (from left): P.R. Mansingh (manager), Roger Binny, B.S. Sandhu, Sandeep Patil, Ravi Shastri, Sunil Valson, K. Srikkanth, Kirti Azad. Sitting (from left): Yashpal Sharma, Syed Kirmani, Mohinder Amarnath (vice-captain), Kapil Dev (captain), Sunil Gavaskar, Dilip Vengsarkar, Madan Lal Sharma.*

TWENTY-FIVE YEARS LATER . . . 22 JUNE 2008 – *The Indian team that won the World Cup poses for a photograph at the BCCI's Silver Jubilee celebrations of the triumph. The players and manager apart, the photograph also comprises Mr Sharad Pawar, the then BCCI President, and Mr M.S. Gill, Union Minister of Youth Affairs and Sports.*

ATTACK AND COUNTERATTACK

THE FIRST TEST, INDIA V/S WEST INDIES, SMG's bat is knocked out of his hands, the ball balloons into the air, and Winston Davis (not in picture) takes the catch.

SMG picks up the bat and leaves. The West Indies are ecstatic.

SMG equals Sir Don Bradman's tally of 29 Test hundreds, and Dilip Vengsarkar is the first to extend his hand.

A stunner of a straight-drive.

SMG's response to Marshall in the second Test at New Delhi. 'You bounce, I hook!'

India v/s West Indies, third Test, Ahmedabad - SMG acknowledges the cheers after completing his fifty.

Driving the Maruti presented to him at Madras in 1983-84, after he surpassed Sir Don Bradman's tally of 29 Test hundreds.

A TRIBUTE TO K.S. RANJITSINHJI, *essaying the leg-glance at Ahmedabad. He became the highest scorer in Test cricket during the course of this innings.*

The Brand Ambassador

Guzzling Thums Up with Imran Khan.

Take the world in your stride . . . DINESH!   *Flying Maharajah Class!*

India's two cricketing SGs of the 1980s.

THE START OF HIS LAST TEST SERIES AS CAPTAIN OF INDIA. *With England counterpart David Gower at the Wankhede Stadium, Bombay, in 1984-85. Both sides wore black armbands to mourn the deaths of Prime Minister Indira Gandhi and Britain's Deputy High Commissioner to India Percy Norris.*

Fooling around with a mask in Australia, 1980-81.

HIS LAST BOW

THE START OF SMG'S LAST STINT AS CAPTAIN OF INDIA. *The team that won the inaugural Asia Cup in Sharjah in 1984. Standing (from left): Ghulam Parkar, Manoj Prabhakar, Maninder Singh, Kirti Azad, Ravi Shastri, Raju Kulkarni, Surender Khanna, Chetan Sharma. Sitting (from left): Sandeep Patil, Syed Kirmani, Abbas Ali Baig (manager), Sunil Gavaskar (captain), Madan Lal Sharma (vice-captain), Dilip Vengsarkar, Roger Binny.*

The Indian team prior to its departure to Australia.

FRIENDS FOREVER - *The skipper with his deputy, at a time when their relationship was supposedly at its lowest ebb.*

An India-Pakistan cliffhanger in Sharjah - awaiting the new batsman's arrival.

The presentation ceremony.

Members of the Indian team with the World Championship of Cricket Trophy.

THE ACCEPTANCE SPEECH: '*I would like to thank the Manager and members of my team for giving me this wonderful present on my last day as captain of India. . . .*'

1986: With the memento presented to him by the BCCI to commemorate his 32 Test hundreds.

AS PROFICIENT AGAINST SPIN AS AGAINST PACE – *executing Vijay Merchant's trademark stroke, the late-cut.*

On the way to 92 against Pakistan in the Austral-Asia Cup final at Sharjah in April 1986. The knock was overshadowed by Javed Miandad's pyrotechnics.

With his Pakistani contemporary, Javed Miandad.

The bowler won an absorbing duel. Ball one of Botham's fateful over was short. Sunil gloved it away safely. The second was short and slow, and Sunil essayed the cut, but failed to beat Derek Randall at point. The third, a gem of an outswinger, was negotiated. The fourth was short and Sunil went for another cut, but it seamed inwards a bit more than he had anticipated. It kissed the bottom edge of his raised bat and Brearley held a superb catch in the slips. Even as England celebrated Botham's hundredth wicket, they could have been forgiven for thinking that they had things pretty much wrapped up.

But they were thwarted. Viswanath carried on from where his brother-in-law had left off. He had company in the form of Dilip Vengsarkar, Sunil's Dadar Union team-mate, who carried the confidence he had gained at Calcutta against the Windies, and his Bombay pedigree, into the Lord's Test. Unlike Vijay Manjrekar's 133 in 1952 and Sunil's 101 in 1974, Vengsarkar's 103 in 1979 was a match-saving effort. At the other end, Vishwanath compiled 113, with many scintillating drives and stinging square-cuts. The manner in which he executed the cut, his signature stroke, was remarkable. The upper half of his body would fall over in the opposite direction after the execution of the shot, in stark contrast to what the manuals recommended.

The third Test at Leeds was affected by rain, with two full days being lost. The highlights were Botham's 137 and Sunil's 78.

In the final Test at the Oval, England batted first and scored 305, and India replied meekly with 202. The hosts increased their overall lead to 437, aided by a Boycott hundred that spanned seven hours. With eight hours' play left, Brearley declared.

As the Indians made their way off the field, little did they realise that two of their all-time greats would not play another Test. Gower's scalp in the second innings of the final Test was Bedi's 266th and last wicket in Test cricket. Earlier, Chandrasekhar had been left out of the second Test after going wicketless in the first. He did not play again in the series. It was appropriate that the last Test of India's premier match-winner of the 1970s turned out to be the first in which Kapil Dev, the country's premier match-winner of the next decade, took his first 'five-for' in Tests.

The way they and their supporters saw it, the Indians needed to bat for eight hours to stave off defeat. Sunil and Chauhan were still there at stumps on the fourth day, the score having moved to 76-0.

> He (Sunil) came for a meal to my flat a few days before this Test. I asked him if there was anything he planned to do in London, before going home. I was thinking of shopping, or St. Paul's Cathedral. 'Yes,' he replied, 'there's one thing I came here for but haven't yet got. A century.' – Mike Brearley, *The Art of Captaincy* (Channel 4 Books, 2001)

Brearley expectedly went on the attack on the fifth morning. It was a glorious day for cricket, with bright sunshine and white clouds hovering above. Sunil came in bare-headed, while his partner donned a helmet, thus joining a club whose membership was growing by the day. The helmet had undergone quite a few modifications since Dennis Amiss donned a motorcyclist's headgear in the first WSC season. In cricket's pace age, the helmet was a godsend for the batsmen, especially those whose job it was to encounter the new ball. However, there were a few exceptions to the rule, like Viv Richards and Sunil Gavaskar. Cynics assailed them for their recklessness. However, the fact was that they trusted their respective reflexes and abilities a lot more than the others.

England had a quality bowling attack, headed by pacemen Willis, Botham and Hendrick, and supported by left-arm spinner Phil Edmonds and part-timers Peter Willey (off-spin) and Graham Gooch (medium pace). However, they could make no headway against a pair that had decided to bat as they would on the first day of a Test. Sunil and Chauhan played on merit. Good balls were respected and ordinary ones put away, like a loose ball from Edmonds that Sunil met in the middle of the wicket and cover-drove for four. It was the first boundary of the day, and it brought up Sunil's fifth fifty of the series. Sitting in the stands was C.D. Clarke, who had been working on a book on Sunil. He intended to wrap it up by the end of the England tour, and the best case scenario for him was a grand finale in the form of a Gavaskar hundred. Sunil had come close thrice in the series, only to fall short. At the Oval, he had promised to try his best.

Then came the hundred of the innings, after which Sunil pushed a Willis delivery through the vacant off-side for a four. When Chauhan completed his individual fifty, with a slashed boundary off Hendrick, Brearley contemplated dispensing with full-blown aggression. The batsmen made the most of Hendrick's withdrawal from the attack due to injury, and milked Gooch and Willey for runs. A clipped boundary and single off Gooch took India to 150. Sunil had moved to 96 when Willey dished out a long-hop. Sunil picked it early, came down the wicket and straight-drove it for four. Clarke was delighted, and Sunil's own team-mates relieved. It was his second Test hundred in England and twentieth overall. That it was scored in his fiftieth Test made the landmark all the more memorable.

The scoreboard read 192-0 at the lunch interval. Sunil was on 114 and Chauhan on 69. The match situation had transformed completely in two sessions of play. Could India better Port of Spain '76?

A single by Chauhan soon after lunch took India to 204-0. It meant that the openers had erased the previous record for the highest association by an Indian opening pair against England, which had stood in the name of Vijay Merchant and Syed Mushtaq Ali since 1936. When Sunil moved back-and-across and dispatched Botham to the long-off boundary soon after, the hosts appealed for divine intervention. Their plea was considered quickly enough. Willis twice induced Chauhan to edge, and Botham clasped the second. Chauhan had scored 80 and India were 213-1.

Vengsarkar, who had scored a duck in the first innings, was eager to avoid a pair. In Sunil, he had the perfect partner for such a situation. He only had to tap the ball and call, for his partner to respond. That single settled the butterflies in Vengsarkar's stomach.

Botham, whose uncanny ability to get wickets with seemingly mediocre deliveries was well known, then tried to surprise Sunil with a slower ball. But it ended up being a long-hop that begged to be hit, and Sunil obliged, thumping it to the cover boundary. It was his twelfth boundary, and watchers were convinced of his intent to pilot his team to a famous win.

Vengsarkar brought up the 250 of the innings, and Sunil his individual 150. Brearley then sought to protect Willey's off-breaks with four men in the infield on the leg-side. Backing them was a long-on and a deep square-leg. The mid-wicket boundary was left unmanned. What the England captain did not take into account was Sunil's occasional tendency to defy the carpet-stroke dictum that had been drilled into his head since his childhood. He accordingly came down the wicket and slammed the bowler to the mid-wicket fence. When Willey bowled short, Sunil transferred his weight onto the back foot and dispatched him through the covers for another boundary. A single off the same bowler gave Sunil 500 runs in the series. At tea, India were 304-1, and the mountain had become a hillock.

After the resumption, Brearley exercised the ultimate defensive ploy of an age wherein time mattered more than the overs. He slowed things down and ensured that only six overs were bowled in thirty minutes after tea. It wasn't in keeping with the spirit of the sport, but then, the record books had no column for the latter. The batsmen refused to get frustrated, and kept things moving.

The score had moved to 323-1 when Sunil drove Willis to mid-on to complete the third double hundred of his Test career. He soon discovered for the second time in his innings that the pitch-invaders were a lot more formidable than the English bowlers. He was in the process of regaining his breath after being manhandled by them when David Constant, the umpire at the bowler's end, walked up to him and said that he shouldn't have taken him so seriously. Apparently Sunil had been fielding next to Constant at square-leg the day before, and the latter had turned around to say that unless someone scored a double hundred, India had no chance of making a match of it!

> 'I was Sunil's room partner, and I recollect him telling me on the fourth night that the pitch was ideal for a double hundred. He was one of the few positive individuals in our side who felt that we could get the runs. As the day progressed, the injury to Hendrick made the side more confident. Most of the players had of course chased a big total in the West Indies in 1976. Sunil's innings was, in technical terms, one of the best I have seen. Apart from getting beaten by Willis twice after completing a hundred, he didn't play a single false stroke. It was a perfect innings, a masterpiece. Every ball was played on merit and the head and feet

movement and stroke-play were extraordinary. The drives, cuts and leg-side placements were executed with meticulous precision. Even in defence, the ball went precisely where it was intended to go.' – Yajurvindra Singh

Botham's intuitive skills were apparently sounder than Constant's. He spoke later about having had a premonition the previous day that the Bombay maestro would score a double hundred.

England's time-killing tactics notwithstanding, India were in control when the twenty mandatory overs commenced. They needed exactly 100 from nineteen overs when Vengsarkar tonked Willis over Constant's head for four. A further 20 runs were scored over the next five overs, during the course of which Sunil surpassed Tiger Pataudi's 203 at Delhi in 1963-64 to become India's highest individual scorer against England.

The singles and twos kept coming. The batsmen in the middle were aware of the need of interspersing them with the odd boundary. Seventy-nine were needed from fourteen overs when Vengsarkar completed his fifty by hoisting Willey to the mid-wicket boundary. He then played an ungainly slog, which was put down by Botham at long-on. Even as it seemed that luck was with the Indians, Vengsarkar gave a tame catch to the same fielder off Edmonds. The score was 366-2, the target 71 away, and the Indian supporters looked forward to the arrival of the other little master. But they were in for a surprise.

'The move to send Kapil was Venkat's. Somehow the idea of nearly achieving the target brought about a panic in his thinking, and at one time he had Kapil, Viswanath, Yashpal and me padded to go in next.' – Yajurvindra Singh

Kapil Dev went for an almighty hit as soon as he came in, and holed out to long-on. Venkataraghvan was subsequently criticised for the move, but his rationale was sound. As the captain and most experienced limited-overs cricketer in the squad, courtesy his stint for Derbyshire in the County championship, he was aware that his team-mates had little or no experience of handling the final, tense moments of a chase. He did not want to leave it till very late. It was his and India's bad luck that Kapil Dev gathered more height than distance[4]. 367-3.

But Venkataraghvan did follow Kapil Dev's exit with an error. Aggressive Yashpal Sharma certainly was, but the fall of two quick wickets, and the fact that Sunil wasn't exactly as fresh as a daisy, necessitated Vishwanath's reassuring presence in the middle. However, it was Sharma who came in.

A single off Phil Edmonds took Sunil to 221, his highest Test score. By then, Brearley had tossed the ball back to his trumpcard. Not for the last time, Botham justified his skipper's faith. Sunil tried to on-drive him on the up, but Gower came in the way. The catch was duly taken, and Sunil returned to a rousing ovation. He had batted for seven hours and eight minutes, and hit twenty fours. 389-4.

Vishwanath could be relied upon to pick up the baton. Unlike Port of Spain, he didn't even need to score a hundred. A cameo would do. He lofted Botham for four and reached 15 in next to no time, before attempting an inside-out drive off Willey. Spectators and TV viewers saw a cloud of dust rising from the ground when Viswanath hit the ball, and Brearley stooping at mid-off to catch it on what looked like the half-volley. Unfortunately for India, the umpire accepted the England captain's claim that he had caught it on the full. 410-5.

Yashpal Sharma was still there, and in Yajurvindra Singh, Ghavri, Reddy and the captain himself, there was a fair bit of batting to come. But that man Botham did it again. His leg-before shout against Singh was upheld. 411-6. Venkataraghvan promoted himself and played a couple of impressive drives, but he hesitated in responding to Sharma's call for a single and was declared run out. 419-7. Not one of the three consecutive dismissals had been straightforward, with the umpires having been involved in each of them. Botham then added insult to injury by winning a plumb leg-before shout against Sharma. 423-8.

The situation forced Ghavri and Reddy to put down the shutters. All four results were possible off the last two balls, with India needing

---

[4] A decade later, another Indian captain from Chennai, K. Srikkanth, promoted an all-rounder from Haryana, Chetan Sharma, to number four in an international game against England. The match in question was a league encounter in the Nehru Cup, which India hosted in 1989. On this occasion, the ploy worked, with Sharma scoring a match-winning hundred.

ten to win and England needing two wickets. Reddy stroked the ball to mid-off for a single, thus ensuring a draw. Delighted to be out of jail, the English players ran off the field without completing the over.

If only the Indian batsmen had a little more experience of limited-overs cricket, India might well have pulled off the most sensational victory in the history of the game.

> 'It was a very good pitch at the Oval, but nonetheless, the outstanding quality of his (Sunil) innings was the certainty of his judgement of each ball. To play an innings like that requires great concentration whatever the conditions, and it so nearly took India to victory.' – David Gower

Sunil's innings won him the Man of the Match award, and a stump from Botham. The all-rounder was the unanimous choice for the Man of the Series Award. Not only had he clicked when the going was good, but also when it was tough. It was he who had earned England a draw in the final Test, with three wickets, including that of Sunil, two catches and a run-out.

> We had a meeting last evening, wherein we decided to play it as it comes. The idea was to keep wickets intact till lunch and then accelerate slowly. I don't think we ever thought of defending or saving the match as such. The one thing that I stressed on yesterday was positive thinking, because miracles do happen.
> – Sunil Gavaskar, post-match TV interview (*BBC*, 1979)

> It would not surprise me even today if I learn from him that he produced that double century just to make a point. And the point? That he was the only cricketer in the country who could do the impossible. – Rajan Bala, *All The Beautiful Boys* (Rupa, 1990)

Sir Leonard Hutton compared Sunil's innings to Stan McCabe's 232 at Nottingham in 1938, which had moved Bradman to remark to his team-mates that they would never probably see another innings of that quality.

Curiously, there were people who disagreed. Even more curiously, they belonged to Sunil's own country. Twenty Test hundreds in only fifty Tests, accolades from every corner of the cricketing world, and a fourth-innings double hundred had failed to alter their perception.

They insinuated that Sunil had got out on purpose. He had done so, they alleged, because he did not want India to win under Venkataraghvan's captaincy. They might well have also claimed that it was Sunil who had ordered Brearley to slow the game down, forced Venkataraghvan to hold Viswanath back, and then scared the umpires into awarding marginal decisions in England's favour.

In a way, these charges were indicative of the fact that Sunil had attained legendary status. His enemies were growing by the day.

The selectors did not belong to this group. They reinstated him as captain for the 1979-80 season. The announcement had to be made as soon as possible, since there was only a week's gap between the final day of the Oval Test and the first day of the first Test against Australia at Bangalore. But their timing still went horribly awry. The Indian team heard the news just before they landed in Bombay.

> The announcement was made even as the plane was circling Bombay airport. The commander used the aircraft's internal communication system to inform all the passengers that Venkat had been deposed. So even as Venkat was picking up his bags and later conveying his impressions of the tour to the media, he knew he was no longer the captain. I really felt sorry for him. It was so crudely done. – Sunil Gavaskar, *Sportsweek*, 23 February 1983

A possible reason for the decision to revert to Sunil was Venkataraghvan's unimpressive bowling on the tour. Although Kapil Dev and Ghavri were doing fine with the new ball, the selectors were keen to bolster the spin department. After all, the next thirteen Tests were to be played at home on tracks that would suit spin more than pace. With three of the four spinning greats out of the reckoning, they figured that it was better to let Venkataraghvan concentrate on his bowling.

That having been said, Venkataraghvan was unfortunate to finish the England tour as the losing captain. As many a witness noted, even the most devout English supporters would not have minded an Indian victory at the Oval. The draw was just another entry in Indian cricket's list of what-might-have-beens. Would Venkataraghvan have kept the job had India squared the series? Probably yes.

12
'THE AMITABH BACHCHAN OF INDIAN CRICKET'

'What Dilip Kumar and Amitabh Bachchan are to Hindi Cinema, Sunil Gavaskar is to Indian cricket.' – Sandeep Patil

In the late 1970s, only one TV channel existed in India. Editors and readers of Indian newspapers and periodicals abhorred frivolous material. Cinema was the only form of entertainment, and there existed a certain mystique around India's heroes and heroines.

Sunil's fans were overjoyed to get an opportunity to peek into his private life through a feature that appeared in the *Bombay* magazine in October 1979. It was the kind of article normally reserved for film-personalities, not cricketers. But then, Sunil Gavaskar was as much a superstar, if not bigger, than those who called the shots in the film industry.

He began the feature, appropriately titled *A Day in the Life of Sunil Gavaskar*, with an admission that he started the day with a struggle to get out of bed. Breakfast constituted coffee and a slice of bread. He left for his workplace, the Nirlon Synthetic Fibres and Chemicals office, at around 9.15 am, which was a ten-minute drive from home.

He discharged his designated duties in the publicity and public relations wing till 1 pm. Then came a full meal, and he indirectly blamed his wife for slipping in an extra chapati or two in his lunch box and thus making him gain weight. According to him, his wife was a good cook, but his mother was better!

He returned to his desk at 2.00 pm and stayed there for the next two hours, at which point it was time to practise. Practice, with Nirlon's battery of Test and first-class cricketers, lasted for a good two-three hours during the cricket season. Once it ended, the gang let its hair down and discussed everything under the sun—politics, religion and girls.

He returned home by 7.00 pm and admitted to a habit of reading while eating. An avid reader, he preferred books that were no more than 250-300 pages long and printed in large type, so as to not strain his eyes. He was fond of music, although not of the classical variety. He regretted not being able to watch Marathi plays as frequently as he used to, because of his cricketing commitments. The remaining part of the day was spent playing with his three-year-old son, indulging in banter with his parents and sisters, and trying to take his eyes off the book he was reading whenever his wife wanted to make conversation with him.

He also waxed eloquent on his son's ball-sense, natural timing, and ability to hit the ball sweetly. 10.30 pm – 11.00 pm was when he retired for the night.

While all this made for interesting reading, the fact was that his routine wasn't anything like this when he gave that interview. He was to live out of a suitcase for the next five months.

Exactly a week after he had almost won the Oval Test off his own bat, Sunil accompanied Kimberley Hughes for the toss at the M.A. Chidambaram stadium in Madras, on what was the first morning of the series against Australia. The Packer affair had been sorted out, but the Australian selectors had decided to welcome the erstwhile rebels back to official cricket at home in November-December rather than overseas. Consequently, the Chappell brothers, Dennis Lillee and Rodney Marsh, stayed at home, and in their place came an inexperienced outfit headed by Hughes. He had with him Rodney Hogg, who had taken forty wickets in the 1978-79 Ashes series.

The makeshift side began positively. Australia's 390 in the first innings comprised 100 by Hughes and 162 by a left-hander from New South

Wales named Allan Border. India replied with 425, and the Australians achieved an honourable draw. India's biggest gain from the game was the discovery of a new spinning star.

Sunil had reason to be grateful to Dilip Rasiklal Doshi, for it was the left-arm spinner from Bengal who had introduced him to Marshneil during the National Defence Fund game in Delhi in 1972. Doshi and he had been team-mates on the Combined Universities trip to Sri Lanka in 1970. Sunil had gone on to represent India with distinction, while Doshi continued to play domestic cricket. The presence of the great quartet in general, and Bedi in particular, stood between him and a place in the national side. By 1979, Doshi had turned thirty-one, but he was younger when compared to Shivalkar and Goel, two other left-arm spinners, whose careers had coincided with Bedi's.

Rohan Kanhai was among those impressed by Doshi's performances for Nottinghamshire in the English County Championship. He conveyed the same to his devotee Sunil during India's tour of England in 1979. Bishan Bedi took more wickets than any other Indian on that tour, but the Indian selectors, team-management and administrators all felt that his best days were behind him.

The combined effect of all these factors was Doshi's inclusion in the Indian team for the first Test against Australia. He made it a debut to remember, with figures of 6-103 in his very first outing.

The second Test at Bangalore followed the script of the first, and the visitors once again drew comfortably. But not all of them emerged smiling. Rodney Hogg, a volatile character who had challenged his previous captain Graham Yallop to a fight in the midst of an Ashes Test, kicked the stumps after being no-balled several times by umpire K.B. Ramaswami. As at Madras, the receding south-west monsoon affected the proceedings.

It was in Kanpur, the venue of the third Test, that Australia had suffered their first ever Test defeat to India, on Christmas Eve in 1959. Their destroyer was Jasu Patel, an off-spinner from Ahmedabad, who took 14-146 in that game, inclusive of 9-69 in the first innings.

That Test had been played on a slow and low strip. The one that the Australians of 1979-80 saw was no different. Sunil's side comprised two members of Patel's breed; Venkataraghvan and the Hyderabadi Shivlal

Yadav. The latter had debuted along with Doshi at Bangalore and had taken seven wickets. Unlike Venkataraghvan, whose run-up and action were workmanlike and trajectory was on the flatter side, Yadav's action was modelled on Prasanna's. The off-spinners apart, there was Doshi, plus Kapil Dev and Ghavri.

Sunil won the toss, claimed first use of the pitch, and got off to a flying start, much to the delight of the spectators, who had come to watch a big innings from their 'son-in-law'. They were saddened by his dismissal for 76. His team-mates found it difficult to cope with the new-ball duo of Geoff Dymock and Hogg, who bagged five and four wickets respectively. India scored only 271, and the enormity of Sunil's contribution sunk in when the Australians batted enterprisingly to take a 33-run lead. But the wicket was steadily deteriorating, and India's top priority was to set a target in the region of 250. Chauhan (84) and Vishwanath (52) put them on course, and Syed Kirmani, who had been restored to his rightful place behind the stumps in the first Test, built on their efforts with 45. Kapil Dev and Yadav then bowled India to victory by 153 runs.

As crestfallen as the Australians was Venkataraghvan, whose inability to dominate the wickets-column had prompted the selectors to replace him with Narsimha Rao, the leg-spinning all-rounder from Hyderabad.

The next two Tests were high-scoring draws. Three Indians – Sunil, Viswanath and Sharma – scored hundreds at Delhi, and the hosts declared at 510-7. It was a typical Gavaskar innings, featuring some searing drives that left the bowlers and fielders gaping. The Australians were then bowled out for 298. Asked to follow-on, they got 413.

The visitors then suffered the ignominy of losing to East Zone, the weakest zonal side in the country. They came back strongly in the fifth Test at Calcutta, taking the first-innings lead. Hughes declared at 151-6 in the second innings, leaving India 247 to get in around seventy overs.

The hosts went for it, as was only to be expected from a side that had got within ten runs of 438 just two months previously. But Sunil fell for 25, and Vengsarkar and Viswanath failed to get going. Yashpal Sharma then drove and pulled vigorously. He had reached 85, and India were only 47 away from the target with less than fifteen minutes left, when the umpires concluded that the light was poor. Surprisingly, Sharma and Rao accepted the offer and came off. India were only four down at that stage, and there was no way they could have lost six wickets in three overs. The consensus was that they ought to have given it a shot, with Sharma in such scintillating form.

Most things went right for India in the final Test at Bombay. The hosts batted first and the openers put on 192. Sunil's 123 was his second hundred of the series and twenty-second in Test cricket. A healthy-looking 231-3 at stumps on the first day became 281-6 on the second morning, but Kirmani, who had come in as nightwatchman, scored his maiden Test hundred. Ghavri batted attractively to score 86.

What did not go right was Mohinder Amarnath's comeback. He hadn't played a lot since having his skull cracked by Richard Hadlee in India's three-day game against Nottinghamshire on the England tour. That blow was the worst of the many knocks he had taken on his head since 1975-76. Not only had the likes of Andy Roberts, Michael Holding, Sam Gannon and Imran Khan forced him to visit the hospital on different occasions, but they had also fostered a theory that he was susceptible to short-pitched bowling.

The spectators at the Wankhede stadium saw a batsman who looked like he had emerged from a time machine. Mohinder was wearing a solah hat, the favourite headgear of the cricketers of his father's era. It was sturdy, but nowhere as effective as a helmet. Why Mohinder wasn't wearing the real thing was anybody's guess, although it was claimed that his father had forbidden him from wearing one!

Even a dimwit could have predicted the future course of action. Hogg served a short ball. But Mohinder picked it early, and went for the hook. The ball came on quicker than he had anticipated, and caught between the two stools of attack and evasion, he fell in between. Even as he did, his feet touched the stumps and dislodged the bails.

Sunil declared at 458-8, and Kapil Dev, Doshi and Yadav then got into the act. A win by an innings and 100 runs sealed India's first ever series win against Australia. The cynics of course went blue in the face reminding people that it wasn't the frontline Australian team. It was pointless to draw their attention to the fact that Sunil and his teammates were not responsible for the Australian Board's decision to keep the erstwhile rebels out of the squad.

Sunil had now led India to two consecutive series wins. But a lot had happened in between the West Indies series in 1978-79 and the Australia series in 1979-80. The heady relationship he had shared with the Fourth Estate for several years was on the rocks.

> Gavaskar had nothing to say to the press after the win against Australia. It is hard to account for Gavaskar's grouse against the press. If anything, it has been on his side, when he has been in trouble. It was the press that chose to gloss over some unedifying incidents like the running on the pitch against England at Bombay and the slanging match with an umpire at Faisalabad. If the press took a dim view of his intentions to join Packer, this is the prerogative of the press, as also the right to comment on his captaincy, which to say the least, has been disappointing, unlike his batting, which is as 'super' as it ever was . . . Players tend to forget praise, only criticism rankles. One would have thought Gavaskar was above such petty considerations. How different it was, till only the other day, when he spoke of his plans for a get-together at the close of each day's play. It is hard to reconcile this with the man who met the correspondents with a stony silence after a singular achievement in Indian cricket. – K.N. Prabhu *TOI*, 8 November 1979

Sunil's reticence after the Bombay Test prompted Prabhu to christen him the 'Amitabh Bachchan of Indian cricket'. The reference was obviously to the megastar of the Hindi film industry, who had famously banned the press.

> I don't know why Prabhu called me that . . . I did avoid the press at the end of the Bombay Test. That's because I didn't have much to say . . . I am not against criticism. But I think, most of our sports writers get too technical, that too sitting far away in the press-box. – Sunil Gavaskar, *Super* (defunct periodical, December 1979)

He may have claimed that he wasn't unduly sensitive to criticism, but the fact was that he was, as any achiever would be. His 'ban' on the press at Bombay was a message of sorts that he wasn't very happy with the Fourth Estate's handling of certain matters, the Packer episode being one of them. In any case, simply refraining from talking seemed a polite option when compared to the means adopted by Ian Botham in 1981, when he waded through the British paparazzi with a towel wrapped around his mouth.

> Whatever I say is invariably blown into a big controversy. Just one sentence was picked out of context and used against me. I did say 'Pakistan would beat us to pulp', but in a certain context. I was referring to the strenuous series we were up against . . . In any case, my statement is not valid now, looking at the Pakistani side which is here . . . They will find it tough to get us out twice in a Test with just one match-winner—Imran. – Sunil Gavaskar, as quoted in *Super*, December 1979

Not many Indians were optimistic about their team's chances, given the way the Pakistanis had dominated the 1978-79 series. The wariness of the Indian public did not dispel despite the absence of Sarfraz Nawaz, the highest wicket-taker in the 1978-79 series, who wasn't picked because of his alleged differences with skipper Asif Iqbal.

From the time they set foot on Indian soil, the visitors were treated like royalty, with the Indians being as hospitable as the Pakistanis had been the previous year. The glamour quotient of the team was high, with Asif Iqbal and Imran Khan leading the way. The men and women who ruled Bombay's film industry welcomed the visitors with open arms, the men figuratively, and some of the women literally. The revelry got to a stage wherein the players had to be reminded that there was some cricket to be played. While the gossipmongers got down to doing their jobs, the Indian team's think-tank sat down to plot and plan.

> 'Sunil was a calculative captain. His philosophy was that we ought to either win the game or draw it. We discussed every Pakistani player at length and planned accordingly.' – Karsan Ghavri

Dominating the discussions were Zaheer Abbas and Javed Miandad. Zaheer was the bigger worry, given the manner in which he had taken the famed spinners apart, and priority was given to concocting a method to counter him. However, the way Zaheer started his innings after walking in at 5-1 in the first Test at Bangalore, seemed to indicate that the Indians had brainstormed for nothing. A series of drives and sweeps took him to 40, before Doshi bowled one down the leg-side. Zaheer went for the sweep, but the ball turned out to be a little too short for his liking. He had barely discovered that when he momentarily lost his balance and foothold. That was good enough for Kirmani, who collected the ball and whipped the bails off.

But Zaheer's team-mates filled in for him, and Asif declared at 431-9. India replied with 416, 46 of them being scored by the all-rounder Roger Binny, who in his hometown became India's first Anglo-Indian Test cricketer.

Imran had bowled well at Bangalore to take four wickets, and the Indians were slightly apprehensive of what he would do on a helpful track in the second Test at Delhi. Asif won his second toss of the series and Pakistan scored 273. That total began to look like 1,000 when Sikander Bakht, a wiry but nippy quickie, took 8-69 to dismiss India for 126. The hosts would have in fact struggled to reach 75 had Imran not been forced to leave the field with a ruptured rib-muscle after bowling only 7.3 overs. He was at his fieriest at the start of the innings, rapping Sunil on the knuckles so many times that the latter all but lost sensation in his fingers. In the second innings, Kapil Dev took four wickets to go along with his 5-58 in the first innings, and Pakistan were all out for 242. India needed 390 to win with more than a day left.

The hosts needed their numero uno to repeat his Oval performance, but as at Calcutta earlier in the season, he had one of his rare fourth-innings failures. At 37-1, India needed grit and guts, and Chauhan and Vengsarkar possessed both. By the time the umpires called time for the last time in the game, India were 364-6. Vengsarkar was undefeated on 146, and while he was censured in some quarters for not adopting a bolder posture in the closing stages, the fact was that the Indians had invariably lost wickets at the wrong time. They were coasting at 276-3 when Sharma fell to Bakht for 60. The Pakistanis then got Kapil Dev and Binny after both batsmen had essayed brisk knocks. Vengsarkar was justified in deciding that discretion was the better part of valour.

There was speculation that the wicket at Bombay, venue of the third Test, would aid the spinners as much as the Delhi wicket had the pacemen. Asif Iqbal could not have chosen a worse moment to call wrongly for the first time in the series. His problems intensified when Imran strained his injured muscle in his very first over. But the cricketer that he was, he carried on till the pain got unbearable, and even produced an early breakthrough. Sunil and Chauhan went quickly, and at 31-2, it was up to Vengsarkar to repeat his Delhi act all over again. He was complemented by Vishwanath, India's spiteful strip specialist. They added precious runs before left-arm spinner Iqbal Qasim accounted for both. Sharma and Binny came and went, and at 154-6, Pakistan had pushed India back into the hole. The situation demanded application from the Indian lower order.

Kapil Dev Nikhanj had a lot on his mind when he made his way to the middle.

> I had seen him get to 30 or 40 in no time and then chucking it all away, trying to play a shot that simply wasn't there. To me, it was a waste of talent and when all my efforts of trying to make him understand what wonderful ability he had as a batsman did not work, I wrote in a magazine that he would not score a 50 in a Test match. I had spoken to him in the dressing room, at dinners and at every other opportunity, but he would continue to play cameos that were enthralling, but which were all too brief not only for the crowd but also for the team. The day the article appeared, he scored 69 on a pitch where specialist batsmen were struggling to put bat to ball. But Kapil made it look as if he was batting on a featherbed. His was a vital innings and came at a time when India needed it and as he returned to the dressing room, he was all smiles. The first thing he said was, 'Captain, I got a 50,' and my reply was, 'Yes, that's what the team and I wanted, even if it meant you shoving my words down my throat. Well played.' – Sunil Gavaskar, *The Sportstar*, 17 November 2001

Very early in my career, I understood the psyche of the Indian sportsman, especially the Indian cricketer. What I learnt was that if you take the cricketer aside and tell him what was expected of him and how he should go about making the most of his ability, the chances are that you would get less than 50 percent results from him. But put down his shortcomings in print and he will try so hard to make you eat your words that the performance will not just be match-winning but electric. It is as if he wants to prove publicly that you are wrong. That is fine with me, for I have never been afraid to admit my faults if it is going to help the Indian team win, nor do I have an ego hassle about being proved wrong so long as the team benefits. – Sunil Gavaskar, *The Sportstar*, 1 July 1995

Kapil Dev was complemented by Kirmani (41), Ghavri (36) and Yadav (29). India finished with 334, a winning score on that wicket. Kapil Dev and Ghavri took the new ball as always, but Sunil surprised his opponents by introducing Binny at a very early stage. He responded with the scalps of Majid Khan, Zaheer and Miandad. The spinners then took over. Doshi, whom Sunil had spoken about before the game as a likely match-winner, bagged three, as did Yadav. They packed Pakistan off for 173.

With the ball turning at right angles, it was critical for at least two Indian batsmen to put their heads down. Sunil and Vengsarkar did just that. Their respective efforts of 48 and 45 took India to a lead of 331. Ghavri then did what Binny had done in Pakistan's first innings, and the spinners completed a win by 131 runs. It was India's first Test triumph over the old enemy since the ten-wicket win at the Brabourne stadium in the same city in 1952.

Even as the nation celebrated, the Pakistanis struggled to come to terms with the end of the honeymoon. Miandad, who had delayed the inevitable with a pugnacious 64, started batting in the nets without legguards, so paranoid was he about the Indian umpires raising their index finger everytime the ball hit them.

Imran's withdrawal from the fourth Test at Kanpur encouraged the authorities to prepare a greenish track. But the gambit backfired, with Pakistan reducing India to 69-8 on the first day. The lower order once again came to the rescue. Kapil Dev then had Pakistan on the back foot from the very beginning, but even he had no answer to Wasim Raja's left-handed brilliance. Raja, an ardent believer in the spirit of the game, scored an unbeaten 94 that took his team to 249. As he was returning to the pavilion, he was accosted by Binny, another player who would come to be known as a gentleman cricketer. The Bangalorean apologised to Raja for dismissing the number eleven batsman Ehteshamuddin, and leaving him stranded 6 short of a hundred!

It was an exemplary gesture in a game marred by some deplorable behaviour on and off the field. Bakht emulated Hogg's footballing tactics when a leg-before appeal was disallowed. Later, Asif spoke about aborting the tour.

India batted a lot better in the second essay, with the openers putting on 125. The Kanpur spectators were disappointed for the second time in the season when their son-in-law fell for 81. Chauhan carried on doggedly in the company of Vengsarkar, and India were 193-2 when rain had the final say.

The only way Pakistan could live up to their reputation was by winning the last two Tests. The two-week gap between the fourth and the fifth Test had given Imran enough time to creep close to complete fitness. Asif won the toss on a Madras strip that looked tailormade for batting. However, a combination of incisive bowling and indifferent batting ensured Pakistan's demise for 272. Imran threw himself headlong into the task of bowling his team back into the game. He would have, had it not been for a wall called Sunil Gavaskar.

Sunil opened India's innings early on the second day. By the close, India were 161-4 and he was on 92. How critical Sunil's innings had been could be gauged from the fact that the dismissed batsmen – Chauhan, Vengsarkar, Viswanath and the debutant Sandeep Patil – had scored only 53 runs between them.

The captain batted with caution and precision. If Iqbal Qasim, the lone specialist spinner, had any notions about troubling an opening batsman, they vanished when he was confronted with Sunil's straight bat, and his judgement of the turn and bounce. The only time Sunil let himself go was after tea when Mudassar came on to bowl his seamers. But his belligerence didn't last for long, and at a time when the post-tea session in Tests on the subcontinent was of ninety minutes' duration, the Indian captain pitched camp and played for the morning.

> ... There was one defensive drop off the back foot to one delivery, which rose unexpectedly from a length, which remains etched in my memory. That defensive stroke, the frozen blade,

the ball dropping right down, was a piece of cricketing action to be treasured. There was style, perfection, confidence and courage in that one run-less stroke. – Rajan Bala, *The Cricketer Asia*, January 1984

Sunil completed his twenty-third Test hundred the next day, and did not show the slightest inclination to get out. Imran apart, none of the Pakistani bowlers was world-class, and the temptation to go for it, especially after he had eschewed every risk for so long, would have been there. But it was overshadowed by his resolve to bat his opponents out of the game.

'His greatest strength was his concentration and mental toughness, and if you combine these with excellent technique, then you have a great player like Sunil in front of you. His reading of the game was remarkable. Once he had the initiative, he never relaxed his grip. The best example was the Madras Test, wherein he batted on and on till we were down on our knees. This is one of the reasons why I would have him in my team first even if I was offered players like Viv Richards and Sachin Tendulkar.'
– Mudassar Nazar

Yashpal Sharma and he took India to within seven runs of the Pakistani total when the former fell to Qasim. Imran then brought his team right back into the game by breaching Kirmani's defences. It was his hundredth Test wicket, and India were six down and only 7 ahead. Enter Kapil Dev. He added 60 with his captain before Sunil became Imran's 101st Test victim. Sunil had batted for seven minutes short of ten hours to score 166. He was livid, for Kapil Dev had refused his call for a comfortable single just prior to the dismissal, and at 339-7, the Pakistanis still had a chance of getting back. However, Kapil Dev carried on, and steered the score past 400 with Binny's help.

The Haryana all-rounder was upset to be adjudged leg-before when he was only 16 short of a hundred. In the dressing room, Sunil bawled him out for refusing that single.

Kapil Dev was obviously not very happy to be at the receiving end of his captain's outburst. He took it out on the opposition. Facing a deficit of 168, Pakistan lost their first five wickets for 58, four of them to Kapil

Dev. One of his victims was Zaheer, whose 1978-79 annihilation seemed to belong to another universe. The innings folded up for 233, and Sunil and Chauhan finished it off on the final afternoon.

'Looking back, I realise we thought the Indian bowling will be at the mercy of Zaheer, and Imran will bowl India out. It turned out to be the most difficult time in our careers. Sunil's contribution in this series was monumental. Not only did he lead from the front, but he had also worked out a different strategy for each of our batsmen. I thought his handling of Kapil was extremely astute. We had dominated the Indian spinners at home, but here we were, playing against the ever-improving Kapil on seaming pitches. We were being outplayed in every department, and finally at Madras, both of them knocked the stuffing out of us.'
– Mudassar Nazar

Kapil Dev Nikhanj's performances spoke for themselves; with the ball, nine wickets in a draw at Delhi, six in the only innings at Kanpur, and eleven at Madras, and match-winning knocks of 69 and 84 at Bombay and Madras respectively. No Indian all-rounder, not even Vinoo Mankad, had dominated an entire series as overwhelmingly.

No other Indian captain had been in as unassailable a position as Sunil was after the series win at Madras. The fact that India fielded the same XI in the first four Tests was as much a consequence of the players' consistency as it was of Sunil's faith in his men.

'Indian cricket can be strong or weak, pedestrian or joyous. It is never unpredictable', so wrote Mihir Bose in his *A History of Indian Cricket*. This statement was emphasised by what happened soon after the last ball had been bowled at Madras. The edifice of Indian cricket looked resplendent after the series win. But it retained its proclivity to throw up surprises.

It turned out that Asif Iqbal's threat to abort the tour wasn't the only notable off-the-field event to have occurred at Kanpur. The itinerary of India's two-month Caribbean tour had been announced a day after the Bombay Test. Like in 1975-76, India were scheduled to play four Tests. With the Jubilee Test against England scheduled to end on 19 February and the team scheduled to depart for the West Indies on 7 March, the weary players had only two weeks to recharge their batteries. That prompted Sunil to seek a meeting with M. Chinnaswamy, the Board President in Kanpur.

> I, as the captain, requested the president if the tour could be postponed by a week (mind you, only a week). Without even saying that he would try for a postponement, the president said that it would not be possible. I expressed reservations about the players' physical fitness and the demands being made of them, and added that if the scheduled programme was kept, then I would not be available to tour the West Indies. I valued my reputation, especially in the West Indies, and I prided myself on being able to give 100 percent. I knew it would have been useless to go to the West Indies in that mental and physical state. The president responded in the most dismissive tone possible. He said that if I was not available, there were 5,000 other cricketers who would be available. – Sunil Gavaskar, *The Sportstar* 26 October 1996

Sunil arrived in the press box of the M.A. Chidambaram stadium, even as the journalists were applying the finishing touches to their reports on the final day of the Test. He proceeded to announce his unavailability for the Caribbean tour. Needless to say, the press was shocked.

The president may have been dismissive of Sunil's request, but he did not direct the selectors to take what would have been a bold step. It seemed unwise to blood a new opener in the West Indies, given their fast-bowling reserves. But there were two Tests left in the Indian season – the sixth of the Pakistani series and then the Jubilee Test against England. Would it have been a good idea to try out one, if not two partners to Chauhan in these games, so as to give a newcomer a hang of Test cricket before the tour? That option was not exercised.

While Sunil's performances as captain and batsman in the 1979-80 season had forced most of his detractors to vanish into the woodwork, his withdrawal from the Windies tour invigorated them. By then, he was no stranger to slander, and countered all the criticism with silence. There seemed no point in responding to allegations that he was skipping the Caribbean tour because he was scared of the pacemen. His criticism in *Sunny Days* of the Kingston spectators for their behaviour during the

Bodyline Test of the 1975-76 series had apparently infuriated Michael Holding, a Jamaican. It was speculated that the man nicknamed 'Whispering Death' was waiting to give Sunil a welcome he would never forget. If anything, this theory advanced by Sunil's critics only endorsed the Indian view that the West Indians had violated the spirit of the game in that Test.

> 'There was a lot of talk that his refusal to tour the West Indies was because he was running scared of facing the West Indian quicks—Andy Roberts, Michael Holding, Malcolm Marshall. I was then in charge of Sports at Doordarshan and invited him over for a live interview. He agreed. It turned out to be a memorable one. I asked him: "How do you react to the suggestion that your refusal to tour is because you are running away from the West Indian quicks." I prefaced my question by saying "I am not saying so, this is not my view but some of your critics are saying so . . ." He was taken aback at the question. But he responded with words which in effect said: "My record is an answer to such a suggestion. Those who say such things need to have their heads examined!" There was no anger, in fact, if at all, a trace of amusement!' – Fredun De Vitre

Viswanath was assigned the captaincy for India's last two Tests of the season. His start, in the sixth Test against Pakistan at Calcutta, was bizarre, with some people claiming that the toss had been 'fixed' in India's favour.

Pakistan did everything they could to snatch a consolation win, but Doshi scuttled their chase of 265 from 70 overs on the final day, and the game was drawn. Asif Iqbal announced his retirement and his team returned home to a hostile reception.

By the time the Indian cricketers arrived in Bombay for the Jubilee Test against an England side that was on its way back home after suffering a 0-3 drubbing in Australia, news had come through that the Caribbean tour was in jeopardy, with Kapil Dev complaining about knee trouble. The WICB was sceptical of hosting a team that did not have two of its best players, and the tour was cancelled.

The Golden Jubilee celebrations of the BCCI began with a fireworks display at the CCI, and all living Indian Test cricketers were invited to watch the Test itself, to be played at the Wankhede stadium. Viswanath won the toss and elected to bat, and India got off to a thrilling, and entirely unexpected, start.

> 'We had an image of Sunil as the dour accumulator of runs in vast quantities, but he shattered that image with one blow; in the first over of the match, as I recall, he hit John Lever over long on for six. Whether that counted as a scolding for John's success in India previously I have no idea!' – David Gower

Watchers at the Wankhede were shocked beyond belief when Sunil took the aerial route at an early stage of the match. The ex-captain was merely responding to the conditions that were overwhelmingly in the opposition's favour. He was also making a statement.

There was no doubt that he had allowed the captaincy to affect his batting, in that he had curbed his belligerent instincts. He had initiated this process even before he entered the think-tank of the team.

> By 1974, Viswanath and I had become the senior batsmen in the team ... now the expectations were different ... they changed my game so much that I began to enjoy it less and less. I had to cut off many shots which I loved playing, because there was an element of risk in those shots. And taking a risk was not on because I was expected to score runs and the one way to ensure that I scored runs more often than not was to eliminate some of the shots ... the fun was beginning to go out of my batting, for tell me, which batsman does not like playing shots? – Sunil Gavaskar, *Sportstar*, 18 February 1992

Considering that the Indian team he led comprised Viswanath, Vengsarkar and Chauhan, all three of whom had bailed India out of many a hole after Sunil himself had failed, there was a view that he had gone overboard with his circumspection.

For some reason, his mindset seemed to be entirely different when he was not in charge. This in itself was strange, for there was absolutely no difference in the make-up of the Indian batting line-up that played

The Amitabh Bachchan of Indian Cricket ~ 227

Pakistan at Madras, where he scored 166 in ten hours, and the one that took on England at Bombay, where he hit a six in the initial stages. It was one of those mental phenomenas that could not be explained, like a specialist number three batsman saying that although he may have come in to face the second ball of a match many times, it still didn't mean that he was good enough to open the innings!

The Wankhede wicket for the Jubilee Test was a far cry from the ones on which India had beaten Australia and Pakistan earlier in the season. It was green, and England, whose fast-bowling resources outstripped those of the Indians, were delighted. India were restricted to 242 in the first innings. Kapil Dev and Ghavri retaliated by reducing England to 58-5. Botham hung on, and keeper Bob Taylor did his bit to give him the strike. They had barely restored some order when Kapil Dev and Kirmani won a caught-behind shout against Taylor. The batsman was unconvinced, and so was the fielding captain. Viswanath withdrew the appeal and asked Taylor to continue. The next wicket fell only after Taylor had helped Botham add 161.

England gained a 54-run lead. Botham scored 114, to go along with his figures of 6-58 in India's first innings, but he was far from satiated. India was bowled out for 149 in the second innings, with Botham returning figures of 7-49. It was the first instance of a cricketer scoring a hundred and taking ten or more wickets in the same Test match. England won by ten wickets.

While the visiting media hailed Viswanath for his magnanimity, many of their Indian counterparts castigated him. In a way, he was as unlucky as Venkataraghvan had been at the Oval in September 1979. Had Taylor been dismissed soon after the withdrawal of the appeal, Viswanath would have gained universal acclaim. But that was not to be. The Bangalorean was probably the only member of the Indian team who would have done what he did. Sunil, a product of Bombay's *khadoos* school, would certainly not have interfered with a call taken by an umpire. Both approaches were entirely legitimate.

'I made my debut for Bombay in 1979-80. Like the other youngsters, I was in awe of senior cricketers like Sunil and Ashok Mankad. Sunil was the hero of every cricket-crazy youngster of the time. I was eager to talk to him, and approached him for advice in the dressing room, when our game against Saurashtra was in progress. He said that I would learn a lot if I watched the match instead. That upset me, because I thought he was being indifferent. It was only later that I grasped the point he was trying to make. He was underlining the importance of observation. He believed that we were better off watching and imbibing. Both Mankad and he were reluctant to spoon-feed. That lesson helped me evolve as a cricketer. Today, I preach the same principle to my pupils.' – Chandrakant Pandit

Most things in the 1979-80 season had gone Sunil's way, with one odd exception. He was fond of Baroda's Motibaug cricket ground, which had been created, donated and maintained by the Gaekwads, the erstwhile rulers of the ex-principality. It is a picturesque venue, dotted by trees, with the palace of the Gaekwads keeping a close watch on the proceedings. It was Sunil's stated ambition to score a hundred at the venue, but he hadn't been able to throughout the 1970s. He was determined to do so when Bombay travelled to Baroda for a Ranji game.

'We used to rib him about the fact that he had scored only one hundred against us. He took it to heart and settled down at the crease. The way he was batting, we thought that a hundred was imminent. But he had a misunderstanding with Dilip Vengsarkar when he was on 86, and was run out. He was furious.' – Anshuman Gaekwad

'It was Vengsarkar's mistake. As he walked past him, Sunil stopped and told him to make it count. Dilip went on to score a double hundred.' – Dinar Gupte

The end of the season wasn't as memorable as its beginning and middle. Delhi hosted Bombay in the Ranji final in the third week of April. Leading Delhi was Bedi, who had not given up hope on an India recall. His resolve permeated to his players, and they gave Bombay the drubbing of a lifetime. Delhi batted first and gained a first-innings lead of 312, but Bedi opted not to enforce the follow-on, partly because his bowlers were tired in the April heat and partly because he wanted to shut his opponents out of the game. The hosts eventually set Bombay a target of 480. Sunil delayed the inevitable, batting at number five and scoring 93, but he had no support. It was sweet revenge for Bedi after the 1976-77 disaster.

The only positive that Bombay drew from the game was the performance of Ravishankar Shastri, an eighteen year-old left-arm spinner and lower order batsman, who returned figures of 6-61 in the second innings. His name hadn't figured among the thirty Bombay probables picked at the start of the season. But Sunil faced him in the nets, and liked what he saw. He then spoke to Sharad Diwadkar, the Bombay manager, and requested the selectors to do the needful. His bowling apart, Sunil was impressed with the teenager's confidence and cricketing intelligence.

> Sometimes there were occasions when Gavaskar contemplated a change in field-placing, and Shastri suggested it before the skipper could. . . .' – Pradeep Vijayakar, *TOI*, 1 June 1980

For Dilip Vengsarkar, the Ranji final marked the end of a prolonged season that had commenced with the tour of Pakistan back in October 1978. But his co-Dadar Unionite wasn't in the same boat. He was preparing for an extended stay in England.

A day before the Ranji final, the news came through that Sunil had signed a contract to represent Somerset County Cricket Club in the English summer of 1980. He was to fill in for their star-imports Vivian Richards and Joel Garner, who were touring England that season with the West Indies team.

At the end of a five-year period wherein he had smashed several records and created new ones, Sunil's decision to experience the rigours of County Cricket instead of putting his feet up for a few months, was indicative of his desire to further his cricketing education.

He ended up representing Somerset for the entire season, and came away with some memorable and not-so-memorable experiences on and off the field. Off the field, he struggled, for his favoured method of unwinding after a day's play was a quiet dinner and an early night, unlike his pub-thronging team-mates. Fortunately, they understood and did not brand him a snob, like the Lancashire team did Sourav Ganguly in 2000.

Ian Botham, Sunil's captain, did his best to make his opener feel at home with friendly gestures. These included parking a dog outside a public phone-booth that Sunil was using, thus ensuring that the latter stayed inside, a serpentine queue notwithstanding, until the canine was taken away. Botham also helped him acclimatise to the cold with kind gestures like stuffing ice-cubes in Sunil's socks if the latter were to take them off. When his wife and son were not with him, Sunil shared a flat with the gigantic Joel Garner, and gained insights into the Caribbean way of dining and partying.

On the field, his team-mates nicknamed him 'Swoop' for the way he covered his ground to field the ball while standing at mid-on or mid-off. But it was in the slips that he spent most of his fielding time. Batting-wise, it was ironic that Sunil was seen to be more comfortable in the shorter variety. His opening stand of 241 with Brian Rose in the inter-County Benson and Hedges limited-overs competition helped Somerset beat Kent. A few days later, Somerset took on Middlesex on home turf at Taunton to decide one of the quarter-finalists in the same tournament.

Middlesex batted first and scored a handsome 282-6 from their allotted fifty-five overs. Up against the new-ball combination of West Indian Wayne Daniel and South African Vincent Van Der Bijl, Sunil pulled out all the shots from his armoury.

> Gavaskar was known to be a Test batsman of the very highest class, one whose name was mentioned in the same breath as Bradman, Richards, Compton, Hutton . . . but when Somerset signed him, it was believed that although he would be a great asset in the County championship matches, he was unlikely to prove very effective in limited-over cricket, where the instant demands were out of character with his elegant, leisurely approach, bred in a country where time was not a vital factor . . . in his first home B and H game (Benson and Hedges, the tobacco company that sponsored cricket tournaments), he gave a further indication of his powers. He hit three sixes and twelve fours in an innings of great majesty. He batted for 165 minutes. It was superb stuff. . . .' David Lemmon, *Great One-day Cricket Matches* (Unwin, 1984)

He scored 123, but the subsequent batsmen couldn't sustain the momentum. Somerset lost by one run, but Sunil had done enough to stun many observers.

After nearly five years of careworn and cautious batsmanship, the aggressor within him seemed to want to break free. The six off John Lever was an early indicator of the same. Sunil was human after all and only thirty-one years old.

Hints of his reappointment as India's captain were dropped on the eve of the 1980-81 season. Would he revert to his abstemious ways if that were to happen? Or would he continue with what he had commenced in England?

It was a while before he resolved this dilemma, for confusion was around the corner.

THREE
ACHIEVER

13

TRANS-TASMAN TRIBULATIONS

> 'His patience amazes me. He was short-tempered in school and college, but he changed subsequently. Sometimes I wonder whether he is the same person I knew as a boy. Nothing angers him, except when he is driving and someone blows the horn from behind, or when a beam of light goes into his eyes. Otherwise, nothing seems to agitate him.' – Milind Rege

Sunil Gavaskar began the 1980s as Indian cricket's all time numero uno, on and off the field. His fans loved him, and his detractors detested him, for his achievements and assurance. The cricket-loving community hung on to every word he spoke in interviews, and every line he wrote in his newspaper columns. He received close to eighty letters from fans daily; his four-year-old son received five.

Gavaskar opened up entire new vistas of making money. He had noticed how cricketers once out of the limelight were actually shunned by the same people who had fussed over them . . . In Bombay only money seemed to matter, and there was more than one way to make it. Gavaskar found them all. Advertising, writing articles (on the same match but for different publications), taking a fee for organising matches, appearance-money and signing contracts with the manufacturers of sports equipment. He became the first Indian millionaire through cricket, rich enough to buy a flat in the centre of Bombay. In a capitalist cricketing country he would have been considered a financial genius. In India they began to call him a mercenary, and within the team he became the envy of some who felt that their contribution to Indian cricket was not being fully appreciated . . . Gavaskar had reached those dizzy heights to which no Indian cricketer in his right mind would even dream of aspiring . . . he was articulate where others were dumb, he was controversial where others dared not to be, he could even be witty, and this made him ideal material for the media and the advertisers. – Tiger Pataudi, *The Decline of Indian Cricket*, as quoted in *A Maidan View* by Mihir Bose (Penguin, 2006)

What was it that made Sunil the individual he was? It had a lot to do with his middle-class upbringing, wherein lessons of single-minded dedication to one's chosen field had been ingrained into his psyche at an early age. It also had a lot to do with the tenacity that his parents had cultivated within him, with a diet of stories that underscored the triumph of the human spirit. Then, there was the fact that he had grown up in Bombay, where silver and bronze medallists are looked upon with bemusement. Some of his contemporaries were more talented than him, and as technically skilled as he was, but Sunil had no peers as far as mental strength was concerned.

Although he had meant it in another sense, K.N. Prabhu's description of Sunil as the Amitabh Bachchan of Indian cricket was spot-on. He was the closest Indian cricket had to a superstar.

His 'larger than life' status wasn't confined to the cricketing world. His popularity prompted Madhumati, a prominent danseuse, to offer him a role in a Marathi film called *Saavli Premachi* (The Shadow of Love), soon after the 1975 World Cup. Sunil was cast in a romantic mould, and he did in the film what all romantic heroes in Indian films did. Marathis who loved their cinema as much as their cricket were amused to see him pluck a flower and gift it to his on-screen girlfriend, go down on his knees to profess his love for her, bat left-handed and allow himself to be bowled by her, hang onto a tree-trunk and sway his hips, all the while lip-synching a duet song that went, *Hey Dil, koonacha koonacha koonacha, hey dil majhya re manaachya preeti cha, veda zhaala ga, veda zhaala ga, tujhya saathi gaa, veda zhaala ga, I love you!* (Whose heart is this? It belongs to my mind . . . it has gone crazy . . . for you . . . I love you!) The film, a queer tear-jerker, featured heavyweights of the Marathi entertainment industry like Dr Shriram Lagoo and Vikram Gokhale.

The acting experiences he had gained by participating in plays in school and the annual cultural festivals at Bhagirathi building, may well have helped him muster the confidence to emote. He subsequently appeared in another Marathi film called *Zakhol*.

As far as the cricket and cinema-crazy Marathi populace was concerned, Sunil's dalliance with acting had more to do with novelty than histrionics. The curiosity factor prompted them to check him out on the silver screen. The conclusion drawn by the majority after watching him was that he was better off sticking to cricket. 'I am a better cricketer than he is an actor,' was the tongue-in-cheek response of noted actor-turned-director Amol Palekar, when asked about Sunil's flair (or the lack of it) for histrionics.

Film-based periodicals of the 1970s linked Sunil to Leena Chandavarkar, a popular Hindi film heroine of the time. That he had never met her was something the gossip mongers did not take cognisance of.

> I enjoy reading the one or two credible gossip columns, but I treat them as jokes. I have been told to take it all with a pinch of salt. And after my brush with gossip, I know how much of it is embroidered! . . . I'd sure like to act in Hindi films. If somebody asked me, I'd do it, but on the condition that cricket and films don't clash . . . can they finish shooting a film in ten-fifteen days? No? At least my portions? Otherwise it would be difficult. I can't really spare more than a fortnight at a time. And then the reflectors. They are bad for a batsman's eyes.' – Sunil Gavaskar, as quoted in *Super* (defunct periodical), December 1979

The novelty did not take too long to wear off. In September 1981, Sunil clarified to Makarand Waingankar (*The Indian Express*) that he had received no further offers from films. 'Even if I receive any, I will not accept them,' he said. His indifference to reel-life increased over the years, and resulted in a controversy of sorts in the mid-'80s. His comment that Hindi films were made by 'asses for masses', was indiscreet, to say the least.

> 'Here is a case of vindictiveness, and Sunny's remarks smack not only of frustration, but of malicious intentions he bore against the film-world that threw him out (sic). . . .' – Dev Anand, film actor, as quoted in *Sunil Gavaskar, India's Cricket God* (K.R. Wadhwaney)

Those who were at the forefront of the criticism cited his presence in two Marathi films and a number of advertisements. It was one of the rare occasions when Sunil got caught on the wrong foot.

He had another fling with the film world in the late 1980s, when he played himself in a Hindi film called *Maalamaal*. His appearance was restricted to a cricket match between Gavaskar XI and Dharavi XI, led by the film's protagonist and one of Indian cinema's most accomplished actor Naseeruddin Shah, who portrays a small-time cricketer who has been promised an inheritance of Rs 300 crores if he succeeds in spending one-tenth that amount in a month.

Sunil even tried his hand, or rather, throat, at singing. Padmakar Shivalkar, whose singing was a hit with his team-mates, was approached to cut a disc of Marathi songs by a music company. He requested Sunil to share the credits, as that would help give the venture publicity. Sunil was only too glad to help. The disc was released before the Bombay Test of the 1979-80 series against Pakistan.

One of the five songs rendered by Sunil emphasised the similarities between cricket and life. Shantaram Nandgaonkar, one of Maharashtra's eminent poets and lyricists, penned it. Its opening lines went: 'Life is like a game of cricket, with its ups and downs, and if you don't take the chances that come your way, you will be left behind'.

There was nothing new about Indian cricketers endorsing commercial products. Col Nayudu, Vinoo Mankad and Farookh Engineer had done their bit in their heyday. However, none of Sunil's predecessors or contemporaries had been sought after by so many brands simultaneously.

Stiff joints did not worry Sunil, for there was Iodex balm to put him back in action. The other advertisements were more creative: 'A close shave I don't like? A Chris Old outswinger.' 'A close shave I really like? Palmolive's moisturised lather!'

'Like Sunil at the crease, Televista TV will feast your eyes with its fascinating and scintillating performance. Innings after innings. . . .'

In subsequent years, he would exhort the masses to drink Thums Up, the most popular Indian soft drink of the time, skip feverishly after drinking Lipton tea because it made him feel *taaza* (fresh), and look smart enough in Dinesh Suitings to induce a female Egyptian Pharaoh queen to step out of her coffin, among others.

The Indian players of the 1970s were fortunate to be playing at a time when there was money in the game. They were entitled to pursue every legitimate course of action to secure their respective futures. Sunil was among those who reminded them at every stage that the additional income-earning avenues were the effect and not the cause. They would exist so long as they performed on the field.

In August 1980, when the annual Kanga League was getting off the blocks after its customary wet start in July, V.S. Patil received a message from Sunil, who was then with Somerset.

'He wanted to play a Kanga game on a certain date, as he was to return to Bombay the day before. He sent me a message to that effect from England. At around 8.00 am on the Sunday in question, I read in the newspaper that his plane was scheduled to land at around 2.00 am. Thus it was only five hours since he had reached home. I therefore felt that there was little chance of his playing, but decided to visit his house on my way to the ground all the same. And what do I see? He was getting ready for the game!' – V.S. Patil

The match in question was an away game for Dadar Union against Shivaji Park Gymkhana. Sunil batted in the final stages and hit two sixes over square-leg, continuing what he had done in the John Player League in England. He had been the leading six-hitter in that tournament before Glenn Turner, who was representing Worcestershire, overtook him. The news was greeted by his fans with surprise and disbelief. His performances since his decision to abstain from all-out attack had been so overwhelming that even they had forgotten that he possessed every single stroke in the book.

His stint at Somerset fetched him close to 1,300 runs in all types of matches, inclusive of three hundreds, two of them coming in the all-important County Championship, and the third in that thrilling B and H quarter-final. But his County Championship aggregate of 686 at an average of 34, which made him fifty-ninth in the list of the season's top scorers, fell well below the standards he set for himself.

> The (County) schedule is very demanding and leaves a player very tired at the end of the season. There is endless driving up and down the motorways to reach venues and sometimes the weekends are the worst. After playing a championship game on Saturday, a player has to drive hundreds of miles for a Sunday League game and then return to the championship game on Monday. The worst part, apart from the early season weather, is the absence of crowds on weekdays... the desire to perform goes down as the season progresses and the schedule begins to take its toll. – Sunil Gavaskar, *Sportstar*, 17 August 1991

Sunil had very little time to recharge his batteries after his return from England. The Indian team was to undertake a twin-tour of Australia and New Zealand. One of the novelties of the Australian leg was a triangular one-day series in coloured clothing against Australia and New Zealand, wherein each team was to play the other two five times in a round-robin league, with the top two sides qualifying for the best-of-five finals.

Sunil's reappointment as captain was confirmed when he was named skipper of the Rest of India team that took on Delhi in the Irani Trophy fixture. Viswanath, who was part of the Rest side, had been criticised for lacking tactical acumen. This was of course nonsense. Two Tests could hardly prove or disprove an individual's leadership capabilities. The Bangalorean was so popular among his team-mates that they would have given their right arm for him. As was his wont, he did not react to his demotion as vice-captain for the twin tours.

Neither did Yajurvindra Singh comment on the queerness of it all. He had been put in the hot seat for the Irani Trophy game of the 1979-

80 season, which was scheduled to be played after the Jubilee Test, as a selection trial for the Caribbean tour.

'With Sunil refusing to tour the West Indies and Viswanath not leading the side well, I was made the captain of the Rest of India team to play Delhi at Jalandhar. This put me in line for the Indian captaincy, which was indirectly conveyed to me through the BCCI grapevine. What favoured my appointment was that I had led Saurashtra to the Ranji semi-finals and had previously led Maharashtra for three years in the Ranji trophy. Rain played spoilsport and the match at Jalandhar was abandoned. The tour of the West Indies was cancelled. The first match of the next season was the Irani Trophy game, and Sunil was made captain, and leave alone not being in the side, I was not included in the thirty-two probables who were selected for the fitness camp. The mysteries of Indian cricket!' – Yajurvindra Singh

S.K. Wankhede, the new BCCI president, thanked Sunil for agreeing to lead India, at the team's official send-off. Some viewed it as a display of decorum. It was hardly unusual for the host of a function, in this case the Board president, to thank and compliment his guests for something they may have done, or had consented to do. Strangely, there were others who took a different view. Sunil's detractors contended that Wankhede's statement was akin to that of someone who had been granted a monumental favour by a benefactor. They called the Indian captain the most powerful man in Indian cricket, and it wasn't meant to be a compliment.

The spotlight was on the captain on the team's arrival in Australia. It had nothing to do with the fact that it was his first overseas assignment as skipper. Uppermost in the minds of the media was his record—twenty-three centuries from sixty-three Tests. The comparisons with Don amused him no end. He tried his best to squash them by drawing attention to Don's average of 99.94. However, the fact was that among his contemporaries, Sunil was the closest to Don's tally of twenty-nine centuries. It was even speculated that he would catch up with Sobers' tally of 26 hundreds during the three-Test series. Sunil himself was eager to encounter Dennis Lillee, who had dismissed him four times out of ten in the Rest of the World series in 1971-72.

Like in 1977-78, the Indians commenced their tour with First-class games against the state sides. The batsmen coped well with the bouncy wickets and the hostility of the hosts, which ranged from their approach to the game to their way with words. Sunil earmarked the game against Queensland to 'play himself in' before the Tests. He dropped down the order and asked Viswanath to lead. He scored 79 and 108, the first knock comprising ten boundaries and three sixes. Among the many people who were surprised with his aggression was Jeff Thomson. The paceman let his feelings be known, and Sunil replied in kind.

'Sunil and I shared a long partnership in that game. Thomson was trying to make a comeback to the Australian side. But we played him well. Sunil even picked an argument with him. That scared me. But Sunil then assured me that he would take care of Thomson. He did.' – Sandeep Patil

After the First-class games came the triangular series. Sunil and his team had no issues with the underdog status that was thrust upon them, what with Australia and New Zealand having a lot more One-day experience. What the captain did know was that India had a deep batting line-up, bowlers who could combine incision with precision, and youngsters who possessed the panaché and attitude to click in the shorter version. Besides highlighting his team's plus points on the eve of the series, Sunil said that he had been impressed with the Australian umpires that he had seen till that stage.

It was the first and the last time he felt that way.

India got off to a flying start in the tri-series, beating Australia in Melbourne by 66 runs. Sandeep Patil top-scored with 64, and Doshi got 3-32 from his allotted ten overs. Greg Chappell, the Australian skipper, was fuming at the end of the game, and the defeat wasn't the only reason.

I refused to criticise the Melbourne wicket after we beat them in the first one-dayer . . . Greg had been vocal in his criticism of the MCG (Melbourne Cricket Ground) wicket that season and was hoping that my joining him would strengthen his case to have Melbourne removed as the venue for the last Test against us. However, after our victory, I realised that Melbourne afforded us the best opportunity to win as the wicket suited our bowling strength and so I refused. – Sunil Gavaskar, *The Sportstar*, 26 October 1991

Their exchange after Australia won the next game, a day-nighter at Sydney, did nothing to improve their frosty relationship. Chappell was at the crease when his team won by nine wickets. When Sunil extended his hand to congratulate him, Chappell expressed his doubts about the legitimacy of Ghavri's bouncer, which had struck him on the head a little earlier. Sunil's response wasn't one that his counterpart expected. He told Chappell to look after Leonard Pascoe, the other half of Australia's new-ball attack, while he would look after Ghavri. The implication was obvious.

For Sunil, it was merely the start of an acrimonious assignment.

India went into 1981 and the New Year Test at Sydney on the strength of three wins from five one-dayers. Kapil Dev, Patil and Yashpal Sharma, three youngsters who had been expected to click in limited-overs cricket because of their aggressive approach, had delivered. It was time for the seniors to take over in the traditional format.

They did not. Sunil defied the experts by electing to bat in conditions that tended to favour fast bowlers in the first hour. He perished for no score, nicking one that Lillee had landed in the corridor of uncertainty and got to move fractionally away. Chauhan and Vengsarkar batted well until the Aussies broke through in the second hour. Vengsarkar was caught behind, Chauhan held at second slip, and Viswanath bowled at the stroke of lunch. Sandeep Patil then drove, cut and pulled with gusto to score 65 before Pascoe dealt him a sickening blow on the left ear. There was a fair amount of tension as Bapu Nadkarni, the assistant manager, ran onto the ground with the medics. Patil was taken to the hospital, and India finished with 201.

Kapil Dev, who had scored a belligerent 22, gave the Indians hope with two quick strikes before Chappell came in despite a bout of diarrhoea. The Australian captain scored a flowing 204, and a final score of 406 was good enough to shut the doors on India. An interesting feature of the Australian innings was the equal sharing of ten wickets between the new-ball bowlers Kapil Dev and Ghavri. This had never happened before in Indian cricket, and it in a way justified Sunil's pre-tour assertion that 'India would place more emphasis on seam than spin'.

> Our spinners are not getting any younger, and this is one department where we may find a big gap after the present crop of world-class spinners retires. – Sunil Gavaskar, *Sunny Days* (Rupa, 1976)

Sunil's words were prophetic. It wasn't that he devalued spin, but then, Doshi apart, the team of 1980-81 did not have a single bowler who was in the quartet's class. Shivlal Yadav and Kirti Azad, the off-spinners, were far from being the finished products.

India could not improve upon its first-innings batting performance. For the second time in the game, the visitors collapsed for 201, giving Australia victory by an innings and 4 runs. Sunil was criticised for sending in Sandeep Patil to bat in the second innings although the match had been lost by then.

> 'I had just returned to the hotel after spending a night in the hospital when I received a call from the ground. "Sunil wants you to bat," was all that was said. I accordingly went to the ground and got ready. The spectators gave me a standing ovation when I went in! Dennis Lillee displayed his Australianness by bowling a bouncer first up. I wasn't the epitome of confidence in any case, and fell a little later. And who do I see waiting for me at the gate? Sunil gave me a pat on the back and said "Well done!" He had reasoned that the very fact that I had returned to action only a couple of days after sustaining a head injury would give me a psychological boost. He was right.' – Sandeep Patil

Patil wore a helmet in the second innings, and in the days after the game, Sunil suggested that he get used to it by wearing it wherever he went, except to restaurants! The skipper may well have considered wearing one himself, if not against the fast bowlers, then to shield himself from the reactions to the defeat, his first as captain of India.

> Unless India's standards in the rest of the series are above those displayed in the first Test, this could be India's last tour of Australia for many years. Negotiations are no longer in the hands of well-meaning administrators ... rather, they are decisions taken by hard-nosed businessmen.' – Dicky Rutnagur, *The Indian Express*, 5 January 1981

The third-day finish at Sydney gave the Indians three full days to prepare for their last five preliminary games of the tri-series. Sunil dropped himself down the order in the first of those games, a One-dayer against Australia at the same venue. Had he hoped for some breathing space, he did not get it. He was out in the middle at 26-3, and back in the pavilion within moments. The Indians plummeted to 63 all out, with Greg Chappell of all bowlers taking five wickets. The slide only continued. India lost the next four matches as well, and thus failed to qualify for the best-of-five finals. Sunil opened and scored 80 against Australia at Melbourne in India's eighth match, but his contribution wasn't substantial enough to prevent another defeat. The Indian supporters blamed the gruelling itinerary. But then, what applied to the Indians also applied to the Australians and New Zealanders.

The Australian media put the Indians through the shredder.

> I have got a few harsh words for the Indian tourists—if you don't like the heat, move into the shade. In other words, if you are going to perform like second-raters, opt out of the big league. Go try your luck against Sri Lanka and Canada. I wonder if internal problems have contributed to India's lacklustre performance. Their manager (Wing Commander Durrani) had plenty to say to their players after their poor performance at Melbourne. Maybe this is irksome for some of the players. But why wasn't all this sorted out before the team left India? Personally, I think the captain should be left to do all the disciplining concerning the playing of the game ... After all, an appointed captain should know what is best for his team. If he doesn't, you have the wrong bloke in the first place ... There is no need to be a provider of gifts to every cricketing country that comes begging at our doorstep. – Ian Chappell, *TOI*, 25 January 1981

K.N. Prabhu retorted in the same publication:

> The Indians did not come begging to Australia. It was all arranged at the ICC. The Australian Cricket Board owed India a debt, for it was Bedi and his men who set Test cricket back on its feet after it had taken a body blow from the Packer outfit (in

1977-78) . . . If the Indians have not done themselves justice, it is because of the thoughtless manner in which the itinerary has been planned. I wonder what Chappell's reaction would have been had he been asked to play a match in Gauhati (India's eastern tip) one day and then at Porbandar (the western tip) the next and then made to shift from One-day cricket to the conventional mode . . . In defeat, as in victory, the Indians have carried themselves with dignity. . . .'

Prabhu made his point, but even he knew that only the cricketers were capable of putting together the best retort—by turning the tables on their opponents on the field.

Sunil elected to field after winning the toss in the second Test at Adelaide, home to the best batting wicket in Australia. It was a defensive ploy, as the Indians did not want to repeat their collapse on the first day at Sydney. The strip was expected to have something in it during the first couple of hours at least, and Sunil hoped that his new-ball duo would make it count. Kapil Dev almost did, inducing the left-handed Graeme Wood to nick the fifth ball of the game. But Kirmani muffed an easy catch.

The Indians spent the next day-and-a-half chasing hits in the outfield, mostly in vain. Kim Hughes celebrated the birth of twin sons with an innings of 213. Australia got to 528, thus effectively ruling out defeat. The Indian openers put on 77 before a ball from Pascoe hit Sunil on the left pad and then rolled along the ground to dislodge his off-bail. The skipper had scored 23. Chauhan played out time on the second evening and batted fluently the following morning, but he had insignificant support until Patil arrived at 130-4, wearing a helmet and a chest protector.

He began tentatively, as was only to be expected. However, he settled in pretty much quickly, and launched an audacious assault on the bowling. He went on to score 174, in what was one of the most stirring exhibitions of resilience at the international level. His stands with Chauhan and Yashpal Sharma helped India reach 419.

Australia's quest for quick runs on the fourth afternoon was quelled by Doshi, with figures of 33-11-49-3. His dismissals of Chappell and Border, two splendid players of spin, were a connoisseur's delight.

Chappell was lured down the crease, beaten in flight and stumped, and Border was bowled by one that turned and went right through him. When Chappell finally declared, India had seventy-five overs in which to score 331. A more realistic assessment was that the visitors had to bat for around five hours to draw the Test. But their captain disappointed once again, nicking Pascoe to Chappell at first slip.

> 'It was nothing more than a bad patch. Things just didn't go his way in the Tests. However, at no stage did his lack of form affect his captaincy. He was the best captain I ever managed.'
> – Bapu Nadkarni

What had gone wrong for Sunil in the international games? It was a combination of different factors—excellent bowling by the Australians and some technical faults that had crept into his batting at Somerset. Since the seaming and swinging conditions in England necessitated the predominance of the front foot, Sunil had made certain technical adjustments, and he was now finding it difficult to revert to his original self. The assured back-and-across movement had been replaced by a sideways shuffle, the manner of which suggested that he wasn't quite sure of where his off-stump was.

Sunil had barely taken his pads off when Chauhan, who had missed a hundred by only three runs in the first innings, was caught behind off Pascoe. Viswanath responded to the situation with three successive boundaries off Lillee, and the Indians had just about calmed down when Pascoe breached the vice-captain's defences. Patil fell soon after, but Vengsarkar and Sharma dropped anchor.

They were going along smoothly until a ball bowled by part-time left-arm spinner Border flew off Vengsarkar's left boot to Chappell at slip. There was an appeal, and the umpire ruled the batsman out caught! Even as an irate Vengsarkar knocked the bails down and stomped off in disgust, the Indian supporters got ready to leave the ground.

But the lower order gave it everything. They had an unexpected ally in the Australian captain himself. Chappell strangely opted to rely on his own leg-breaks and Bruce Yardley's off-breaks to finish the Indians off, instead of bringing his pacemen back. Sharma and Kirmani consumed a fair chunk of the twenty mandatory overs before falling to the spinners.

The ninth-wicket pair of Yadav and Ghavri resisted stubbornly, and only three overs were left when Chappell finally threw the ball to Lillee, and surrounded the batsmen with nine fielders. Yadav and Ghavri held on, and the Indians left Adelaide with the series still undecided.

Sunil elicited laughs on the eve of the Test by quipping at a party thrown by the Indo-Australian Society that he had had more X-rays taken than runs on the tour. The reference was to the stomach cramps that had troubled him before the game.

The third Test commenced at the Melbourne Cricket Ground, exactly six days after the Australian skipper instructed his younger brother Trevor to bowl underarm, when New Zealand needed six to tie the third of the best-of-five finals of the tri-series at the venue. That episode had made Chappell unpopular in his own country. His hatred for the MCG, and distrust of the wicket, was evident on the morning of the Test. He won the toss, but was so unsure of its behaviour that he asked Sunil to take first strike. The Indians, who had decided to bat if they won the toss, were delighted.

That feeling didn't last for long, thanks to Lillee and Pascoe. Chauhan popped a catch to short-leg, Vengsarkar was caught behind, and Sunil got one that reared off a good length, hit the splice of his bat and flew to Hughes in the slips. The score was 115-6 when Kirmani came in. At the other end was Gundappa Viswanath, who like his brother-in-law had failed in the first two Tests. The Karnataka duo added useful runs until Kirmani edged Lillee's leg-cutter. Ghavri stayed in for a while, and Yadav hung on despite a painful foot, the consequence of being struck by a Pascoe toe-crusher.

The obduracy of the lower order added to Viswanath's confidence. He essayed some superlative strokes, the best of the lot being a late-cut off a Lillee Yorker that took him to 99. The spectators rose when he completed a hundred with an off-drive off leg-spinner Jim Higgs. He fell soon after when umpire Rex Whitehead decided that the ball had made contact with his bat on its way to Chappell at slip, although the replays indicated that it had flicked the knee-roll of his left pad.

India were bowled out for 237, and securing a first-innings lead seemed an onerous task. Not only were they at least a hundred runs short, but their bowlers had problems too. Doshi had sustained a fracture after being hit on the foot while batting in the three-day game against Victoria. So eager was he to play the Test that he kept his injury a secret.

> 'I had a difficult decision in front of me. Either I conceal my injury from my team and do my best, or miss the Test. The latter was unthinkable as I had, quite frankly, dreamt of helping India win the final Test.' – Dilip Doshi, *Spin Punch* (Rupa, 1990)

Yadav's toe was found to have been fractured, but like Doshi, he braved the pain. India managed to get three Australian wickets for 81 runs before Chappell and Border came together. The Australian skipper had barely taken guard when Kapil Dev rapped him on the pads. The Australian captain looked plumb, but Whitehead didn't think so. Kapil Dev's frustration was compounded with a thigh injury that forced him off the field. Yadav carried on until he crossed the pain-barrier. He had Border bowled around his legs, only for Whitehead to ask his colleague at square-leg whether the ball had hit the stumps cleanly and not ricocheted off the keeper's pads. Kirmani wasn't thrilled with the aspersions cast on him, and told Sunil that he would have walked off had the umpires ruled in Border's favour.

Border's 124, Chappell's 78, Walters' 76 and Marsh's 45 enabled Australia to reach 419 on the third afternoon. With a deficit of 182 staring them in the face and the wicket deteriorating rapidly, the writing was on the wall for the Indians.

Lillee and Pascoe exploited the wearing wicket brilliantly, landing the ball on the right spots. Chauhan survived a confident leg-before shout when a delivery by Lillee kept low. At the other end, Sunil was nearly decapitated by a Pascoe thunderbolt that sprung off the pitch like a rocket and continued to rise, being stopped only by a leaping Marsh.

Both batsmen responded to the wicket and the situation by putting their heads down, forgetting about the deliveries gone by and concentrating on the upcoming one, an approach that would have delighted their guru Kamal Bhandarkar. Lillee's frustration at not breaking through was evident in a rare full-toss he dished out to Sunil shortly after the fifty of the innings had been posted. Sunil's eyes lit up, he plonked his front foot down the wicket and thumped the cherry past the bowler for four. That one stroke gave him a boost.

When Yardley tossed one up, Sunil lofted him over the infield for four. This was the Gavaskar of old, who had taken three hundreds off Jeff Thomson in 1977-78, the Gavaskar the Australians wanted to see, not the uncertain shuffler of the first two Tests. He was still moving a lot more within the crease than during his golden run from 1975 to 1980, but he seemed to be more aware of where his off-stump was for the first time in the Test series. A square-drive off Lillee gave him three runs and his first fifty of the series. At stumps on the third day, India were 108-0 and 74 short. Sunil's undefeated 59 hadn't been as dramatic as the 75 and 85 scored by an injured Tiger Pataudi at the same venue in 1967-68, but it was no less critical.

> 'It was one of his best innings. He had been struggling throughout that series, and the match situation could not have been more stressful. The way he countered the situation was amazing.'
> – Karsan Ghavri

The openers' immediate priority on day four was to reduce the deficit further, if not obliterate it completely. Dennis Lillee was the one paceman off whom Sunil hadn't got a hundred. India were unlikely to tour Australia for the next four years at least, and with both men in their thirties, Melbourne represented Sunil's final opportunity to add another distinction to his Curriculum Vitae.

He had got within 30 runs of the landmark, and his team within 17 runs of clearing the deficit, when Lillee delivered one that pitched on a length and kept low. Sunil brought his bat down, but failed to meet the ball with the meat. The ball hit his front pad, an appeal followed, and Whitehead raised his index finger.

Sunil was apoplectic. He raised his bat as soon as the ball struck his pad, but his contention that he had got an inside-edge before the ball hit the pad wasn't entertained. He continued to protest as he made his way past his partner and the umpire.

He had completed about one-fourth of the walk back to the pavilion when his ears were alerted to an association drawn by one of the Australians between him and a part of the female anatomy. It was then that Kirmani's walk-out threat of the previous day flashed across his mind. Something snapped.

He strode back to the pitch, ordered Chauhan to return to the pavilion with him, and actually pushed him towards the dressing room, even as the Melbourne spectators started booing the captain of an international team for the second time in a fortnight. No one quite knew what to make of the goings-on. But Durrani kept his wits about him, met Sunil at the gate, heard him out, and then motioned to Chauhan to wait, so that Vengsarkar, the next man in, could accompany him to the middle. Upstairs, Nadkarni got the players to vacate the dressing room, so that the skipper could 'ventilate' himself.

> 'Australians have always had a high regard for Sunil and it is well known that Sir Donald Bradman had a special regard for him and that the two would chat whenever Sunny was in Adelaide. Certainly there was an expectation that Sunny would score heavily each time he was here, the same expectation that befell Sachin Tendulkar in later years. So on that basis there was considerable disappointment when he was unproductive in 1980-81 because there was a genuine sense of excitement at again seeing a master batsman at work. The walk-out caused great disappointment, especially to his many admirers and the fact that he took Chetan with him stunned everyone. I think it is fair to say his action shocked the Australians.' – Mike Coward

At least one Australian – Richie Benaud – believed that Sunil had got an inside-edge.

The villain of the piece, as far as the Indians were concerned, was Rex Whitehead. His decisions to dispatch Vengsarkar and Viswanath at Adelaide and Melbourne respectively after Chappell had caught them at slip off their pads, the call to declare Ghavri run-out on the first day at Melbourne despite the bowler Higgs having elbowed the bails, and the first-ball reprieve granted to Chappell on the second day, were fresh in their minds.

Sunil's exasperation had as much to do with what he believed was another wrong decision for his team, as with the fact that he had displayed some form after his first barren patch in years. On a personal note, he was upset that he would probably never get another opportunity to score a Test hundred off Lillee. Yet, his behaviour could not be condoned.

> I have to admit that it was an absolutely inexcusable behaviour on my part, for whatever the provocation, I should have kept my cool as I was the captain of the team. – Sunil Gavaskar, *The Sportstar*, 20 February 1999

One individual to whom Sunil owed an apology was Chetan Chauhan. The hold-up broke Chauhan's concentration, and he could not regain it. He gave a tame catch in the covers off Lillee at 85, thus missing out once again on a Test hundred. That made Lillee Australia's greatest wicket-taker in Tests (249) ahead of Benaud.

The middle order failed to consolidate on the start. Vengsarkar scored 41, and Patil essayed a breathtaking cameo of 36. Kapil Dev, who came in with a runner, gifted Yardley his wicket when he went for an overambitious hoick and missed. Kirmani and Ghavri were involved in a mix-up that saw both stranded at the same end. With Yadav unfit to bat, India ended their second innings only 142 ahead.

The dismissals of Sharma and Doshi in the second innings had provided the visitors a glimmer of hope. Both batsmen had been bowled off shooters that hadn't risen at all after pitching. Could India bowl ten such deliveries on a wicket that had broken up completely? In Kapil Dev's absence, Patil shared the new ball with Ghavri.

Australia had reached 11 when Ghavri, bowling over the wicket, turned opener John Dyson around with one that pitched on leg and appeared to have tucked his thigh-pad on the way to Kirmani. But the bowler, keeper, and as it turned out, umpire, had heard two sounds. An appeal ensued and an incredulous Dyson was declared out. As they saw Chappell coming in, the Indians remembered their discussions on his shaky starts. Ghavri was told to bowl a bouncer. He agreed, all the while wondering how he would do it on a wicket that was on a ventilator.

He ran in hard and let the ball go, but the cherry did not take off. It skidded through at waist-height instead, beat Chappell's attempted flick down the leg-side, and crashed into the stumps. Australia were 11-2, match on.

Seven runs later, Doshi delivered one down the leg-side to Graeme Wood. The left-hander went for a front-foot drive, but missed and overbalanced momentarily. That was good enough for Kirmani, who collected the ball down the leg-side and whipped the bails off. The manner in which Sunil, positioned at silly point, punched the air in delight, underscored his side's resolve. Australia were 24-3 at stumps.

At the hotel that evening, Sunil sought out Kapil Dev. What he told him was not too different from what Douglas Jardine had told Eddie Paynter in the fourth Test of the Bodyline series. Paynter was in hospital, stricken by fever and tonsilitis. The match was in the balance, but Paynter was eager to do battle. Jardine did his bit to pep him up, reminding him of 'the fellows who marched to Kandahar' despite having fever. He then smuggled Paynter out of the hospital, and the latter played an Ashes-winning innings.

On the evening of 10 February 1981, the Indians found themselves in an unprecedented situation. Never before had they been so close to levelling a series against a full-strength Australian side in Australia. Kapil Dev, who was upset with his atrocious shot in the second innings, was as eager as Paynter to do battle. That night, he got into bed after setting the alarm to ring after two hours. When it rang, he woke up and took a pain-killing injection. He then reset the alarm to ring in two hours' time, and took another jab when it did. This sequence was repeated through the night.

> 'We were slightly nervous when we resumed the chase. The wickets the previous evening, especially Greg's, had induced some wobbles in the dressing room. We were surprised to see Kapil warming up. It was then that we realised that things may not be easy.' – Allan Border

For India, it was all or nothing. Kapil Dev and Doshi, the team's premier bowlers, were to operate unchanged. A couple of overs were all that the former needed to get a hang of things. He evolved the tactic of delivering the ball from a yard short of the popping crease. The idea was to ensure that it died after pitching, and did not rise above the batsmen's knees. The Australians, he reasoned, would go for their favourite cuts and pulls, and that would be their undoing on that wicket.

Hughes took two boundaries off Doshi before his impetuousness got the better of him. When Doshi served what looked like another long-hop, he went for a cut, but the ball whizzed through to make a mess of the stumps. The score of 40-4 would have become 40-5 had Whitehead not angered the Indians once again by disregarding a leg-before appeal against Border. Doshi, who like his captain wasn't known for displaying his emotions on the field, all but lost it, before Sunil stepped in and commanded him to return to his bowling mark. It was vital that India kept their nerve at that stage, as the likes of Border, Walters and Marsh were known to be excellent in pressure situations.

At the other end, Kapil Dev landed the ball exactly where he wanted to and spreadeagled nightwatchman Bruce Yardley's stumps. The pain he had endured for three days was forgotten, as he steamed in to seal the match in his team's favour. Border nicked him down the leg-side to Kirmani, Marsh played down the wrong line, and Lillee played all over. Vengsarkar's alertness at silly point accounted for Pascoe, and Higgs was trapped leg-before to give India victory by 59 runs. Rarely had a cricket team silenced its detractors as comprehensively as India did on the afternoon of 11 February 1981 at the Melbourne Cricket Ground. They had squared a Test series spanning thirteen playing days, after being under the pump for the first eleven!

In the dressing room, Sunil watched Kapil Dev, who had taken 5-28, sip his first ever glass of champagne. The captain was persuaded to interact with the All India Radio commentators, with bizarre results.

> When the match was won, there was an unseemly scramble... Indian cricket's finest hour was ruined for the enthusiast by the commentators' bid to push each other out... There were times when the commentators asked him questions and supplied the answers as well. – Bystander, *Mid-Day*, 16 February 1981

Another discordant note was struck by an Australian journalist, who could not come to terms with what had happened.

> I was asked. . . ., 'Now that you have failed in the Tests would you call yourself a great batsman?' Taken aback by the query, because I had never ever bothered to grade myself, I did manage

to ask him why he asked that question. His reply was, 'Since you didn't score on hard, bouncy pitches you cannot be called a great batsman!' 'Fair enough,' I said, though I did not care to inform him that on my previous tour to Australia I had three centuries against Jeff Thomson and Co. on the same pitches. But I did tell him that if the criterion for a great batsman was to score on hard, bouncy pitches, then by the same token, the criterion for a fast bowler to be called great should be him capturing wickets on slow pitches. He agreed with that, but when I queried whether we should then call Dennis Lillee a great fast bowler because he had taken just a couple of wickets on the slow pitches of Pakistan, he said, 'No, Dennis is an all-time great fast bowler. That was just a bad series for him.' Of course, there were the other usual excuses like food, conditions and umpires thrown in as well.
– Sunil Gavaskar, *The Sportstar*, 9 February 2002

The Indians flew to New Zealand on a high. Sunil made a bright speech on behalf of his team at a reception hosted by the Carbine Club of New Zealand, before their first tour game. 'If I have been received like a film star, it is because I have tried my hand at being one,' he informed the gathering. He made a mention of all his players, including Doshi, who was not available for the first Test at Wellington due to his broken toe. 'He used to complain about pain in his foot during the (Melbourne) Test, and we thought it was a pain in the you-know-where,' Sunil quipped, much to the amusement of the other guests.

The Indians were in for a disappointment. New Zealand won the first Test at Wellington and drew the last two, thus handing Sunil his first series defeat as captain of India. The story could well have been different had he continued from where he had left off at Melbourne. He could not get going, his best effort being 53 in the second Test at Christchurch. Even that innings was owed to an umpiring error. He appeared to have nicked Richard Hadlee to the wicketkeeper when he was on 14, but the umpire turned the appeal down. In the third Test at Auckland, he hit five boundaries in a score of 33, but gave a catch to mid-wicket while attempting to attack John Bracewell's accurate off-spin.

'New Zealand has never been an easy place to adjust to. The wickets in 1980-81 were spicy, and we had a bloke called Richard

Hadlee, who targeted the corridor of uncertainty just outside the off-stump. Hadlee bowled very, very well in that series. Openers generally found it difficult to deal with him. Interestingly, quite a few big names have struggled in New Zealand, Viv Richards among them.' – John Wright

India's only gain from the series was Ravishankar Shastri. Doshi's withdrawal from the first Test prompted the think-tank to ask the board for a left-arm spinner. Bedi was still playing for Delhi, but neither he nor Rajinder Goel were considered. Sunil plumped for Shastri instead. The nineteen-year-old left a Ranji game midway to catch a flight to New Zealand, and went on to take fifteen wickets in the three-Test series.

It wasn't only Shastri's bowling capabilities that Sunil was impressed with. Batting at number ten in the first two Tests, the left-arm spinner scored 3, 19 and 12. Although the scores did not exactly make for jawdropping reading, he displayed application. In the third Test at Auckland, he was promoted to number seven, above Test centurions like Kirmani and Kapil Dev. It wasn't a case of Sunil throwing the boy at the deep end; the boy was keen to jump and show that he could swim.

Shastri's success did not prevent Sunil's bashers from levying charges of parochialism. They alleged that his players were petrified of him, and that no one went out of his way to contradict anything he might have said. What the detractors did not talk about was the manner in which Sunil had drawn the best out of the youngsters. Among them was Shivlal Yadav. He had thrown his wicket away in one of the early state games in Australia, playing like a typical tail-ender. Rebuked by Sunil for his lack of professionalism, his response was one that would have done a specialist batsman proud. At Adelaide, he batted for nearly two hours to save the game and keep the series alive. At Melbourne, he bowled thirty-two overs in the first innings with a broken toe, and dismissed Hughes and Border.

The New Zealand series ended on 18 March 1981, thus bringing to an end the most momentous decade in the history of Indian cricket upto that point. It was on 10 March 1971 that India had achieved its first ever Test victory in the Caribbean. The likes of Wadekar, Sardesai and the spin quartet had laid the foundations of a team that did not blink in adverse situations, and considered itself capable of beating anybody and everybody. Sunil Gavaskar and Gundappa Viswanath had been able successors to the seniors of 1971. In later years, they had done their bit to encourage the likes of Kapil Dev, Vengsarkar and Patil, all three of whom seemed set to guide Indian cricket in the 1980s. The 1981 Melbourne Test, where a twenty-two-year-old all-rounder defied injury to help his team achieve a famous victory, was as significant as the 1971 Port of Spain Test, wherein a twenty-one-year-old debutant steered India to victory with knocks of 65 and 67.

14

IN THE FIRING LINE

Gavaskar is a superstar all right... He has used the press to his own advantage.... this he has done in two ways. One is to talk to young, impressionable freelancers who will swoon over him, unlike hard-boiled cricket correspondents who will critically examine whatever he says... the other method is to write himself. Here, he can not only give free vent to his spleen, but also earn a small fortune in the process. He utilises this opportunity not only to question the knowledge of cricket writers and ridicule them, but also to train his guns on whoever may be weighing on his mind at a particular moment, be they officials, fellow players, umpires or even hapless spectators. – Sunder Rajan, *Why Gavaskar Throws Super-tantrums, TOI* 11 October 1981.

Three months before Sunder Rajan wrote this, Sunil found himself at the receiving end of a diatribe that is usually attributed to an all-time great. In an interview to *Sportsworld*, a magazine edited by Tiger Pataudi, which appeared in its issue dated 22 July 1981, Bishan Bedi was quoted as saying that Sunil had been instrumental in getting him dropped from the Indian team. It came as a surprise to all those who knew Bedi as someone who called a spade a shovel. Sunil rubbished the piece, contending that had Bedi indeed felt that way, he would have told Sunil the same on his face.

The topmost priority in Sunil's mind, as the new season approached, was to play himself back into form, after his ordinary showing in Australia and New Zealand.

> The summer in County cricket (1980) may have something to do with his failures ... he played on different pitches everyday ... consequently, he found himself committed to the forward stroke ... not playing far too many deliveries and not getting the bat away in time from the moving ball. ... – K.N. Prabhu, *TOI*, 16 March 1981

Sunil's bashers had another opportunity to go hammer and tongs at him in September 1981. He and three other West Zone cricketers – Shastri, Patil and Ghavri – expressed their inability to play in the inter-zonal Deodhar Trophy in Chandigarh, as the tournament clashed with the Moin-ud-Dowla tournament in Hyderabad. Nirlons had won the latter tournament with its full-strength side the previous year, and they were keen to retain the title. The quartet was panned for putting its office ahead of a national tournament, although Umrigar, the chairman of selectors, sided with the cricketers.

> After all, it is a matter of bread and butter for them, and one should not forget the handsome salaries they are paid by their offices to represent them. – Polly Umrigar, *The Indian Express*, 12 September 1981

A compromise was worked out, with P.R. Mansingh, the convener of the Moin-ud-Dowla tournament, being convinced to postpone the start of the key matches from 21 September to 22 September, so that the four cricketers could fly to Hyderabad after representing West Zone in the Deodhar Final (if they qualified) in Chandigarh on 20 September. As it turned out, Sunil had to pull out of the Deodhar Trophy due to an injury sustained in a charity game in Bhavnagar, Gujarat, a couple of days prior to West Zone's scheduled semi-final against South Zone. Shastri, Patil and Ghavri travelled to Chandigarh for the game, which South Zone won by three wickets. Shastri was West Zone's best bowler, with figures of 3-30 from his allotted eight overs. The defeat was just that—a defeat. It gave the three cricketers an extra day to prepare for the Moin-ud-Dowla tournament in Hyderabad, and Sunil an extra day to recover. The matter should have ended there and then, but a few people were keen on laying the blame for the semi-final loss at the door of someone who hadn't even played the game.

> When the dates were adjusted for him, he complained of injury. When a very senior man contacted him, Gavaskar made no mention of the injury nor declared his intentions. The point is that at no stage had Gavaskar shown an eagerness to participate in the Deodhar Trophy... why has he become so abrasive, inscrutable and prone to starry moods? The cares of captaincy, the controversies in which he seems to revel, as well as the need to live up to his expectations as a master batsman have begun to tell on him, and his failures with the bat have in turn begun to affect the team. He must now be freed from this vicious cycle. Like Boycott, he must be left alone to concentrate on his batting, which is his chief asset. – Sunder Rajan, *Why Gavaskar Throws Super-tantrums*, TOI, 11 October 1981

It was absurd to accuse Sunil of crying off from an official game, but the deed had been done.

Sunil was retained as skipper for the six-Test series against England, who were coming off a 3-1 triumph over Australia in one of the most memorable Ashes tussles of all time. Ian Botham, the hero of the series, was expected to continue in India from where he had left off in the Jubilee Test in February 1980. He had alongside him several distinguished names. The party comprised Derek Underwood, probably the only English frontline cricketer of the period who deigned to tour India thrice. Geoffrey Boycott, who had cried off from earlier visits to the country, was part of the party. The fact that he was close to surpassing Sir Garry Sobers' Test aggregate of 8,032 and thereby becoming the highest scorer in the format, would have been on his mind when he agreed to board the plane.

The visiting side's weakest link was at the top. Keith Fletcher, who hadn't played a Test since March 1977, was made captain on account of his successful leadership of Essex in the County championship. It was the quintessential English style of bestowing leadership. Every other international cricket side of the period followed the dictum of first picking the team on merit, and then giving the captaincy to one of the prominent members. The English did things differently. Leading Essex in the English County Championship was one thing, and skippering at the international level another. What made it an odd appointment, especially from an Indian perspective, was that English cricket was thriving at the time. They had won the Ashes, for god's sake!

The Indian selectors dropped two bombshells on the eve of the first Test. The decision to axe Chetan Chauhan was as bizarre as it could be. He had batted excellently in Australia and New Zealand, and had in fact outscored Sunil. Supporters of the move contended that India needed a younger and more aggressive player at the top to complement Sunil, instead of Chauhan, who was well over thirty, and whose conventional approach was similar to Sunil's. Be that as it may, it seemed daft to drop a player who had succeeded against Lillee, Pascoe and Hadlee on their pitches.

> To me personally, Chetan was of great assistance as an opening partner. If I played a stroke wrong or lost concentration, after every over, every ball, he would walk up to me and correct me. The younger players who open with me are perhaps too overawed by the fact that I am senior and a captain. – Sunil Gavaskar, interview with Fredun De Vitre, *Mid-day*, 14 September 1982

Even if the selectors had made up their minds to break Indian cricket's most successful opening combination, there were other ways of doing it. Chauhan ought to have been the first choice after his performances in Australia and New Zealand. Sunil, who wasn't in good form at the time, could have considered shifting to the middle order till he regained his form and assurance. As it turned out, it wasn't very long before he himself started thinking in terms of batting down the order.

Subsequent events indicate that the dissolution of the Gavaskar-Chauhan axis did not benefit Indian cricket. The duo first opened together in two Tests in 1972-73. Their partnership was restored after the Brisbane Test in December 1977, and they went on to open in thirty-four of India's next thirty-six Tests. Chauhan batted in the middle order in one game and missed another. In these thirty-six Tests, Sunil scored 3,326 runs at an average of 57.3, which was more than six points above his final career average of 51.12. Chauhan and he were involved in nine century stands and one double-century stand. In the fifty-six Tests that Sunil played after Chauhan's omission, he averaged 48, and was involved in only six century stands and one double-century stand, with a succession of partners.

What India achieved in One-day cricket in the 1980s is well-known and documented. What the team would have achieved in Test cricket during the same period with a stable and successful opening pair, we never will know.

Chauhan's replacement was a fidgety character who loved to explore the area between the popping crease and square-leg between deliveries. Unlike his predecessor, Krishnamachari Srikkanth was a man in a hurry. As far as he was concerned, it wasn't merely appropriate, but mandatory to dispatch every ball to the boundary, or if possible, beyond it. He had been reproached for his aggression during his formative years, but was wise enough to continue playing to his strengths. While Chauhan and Gavaskar played the odd aggressive shot at the start of the innings, Srikkanth's defensive strokes were few, far in between, and almost forced.

Madan Lal, who had not played a Test since 1978, was recalled at the expense of his old rival Ghavri. It meant that one half of India's most successful opening and new-ball combinations had been discarded simultaneously. Ghavri had had a difficult time in New Zealand, but what was bizarre was that his replacement, like him, had just turned thirty. A section of the cricket-loving public felt Ghavri's replacement should have been a much younger player.

Of course, Madan Lal would have the last laugh, as would Srikkanth in due course.

The selection was preceded by dramatic developments. The Indian government had objected to the presence of the two Geoffreys, Boycott and Cook, in the England squad, both of whom had cricketing links with South Africa. The series itself was in jeopardy at one point, and it was only after both players had issued statements denouncing apartheid that the Indian government gave the green signal.

The Ashes winners got down to business straightaway, winning their first two three-day games and then putting it across India at Ahmedabad, in what was the first One Day International on Indian soil.

The first day of the first Test was no different. On a wicket that did not look too different from the one on which England had played in February 1980, India batted first and were dismissed for 179, with Botham taking 4-72. Sunil was the top scorer with 55, but the discerning observers were far from satisfied.

> For a large part of his three-hour innings, Gavaskar reminded me of a myopic man who stumbles along a dimly-lit corridor. One lost count of the number of times he played and missed and was beaten outside the off-stump by Botham. – K.N. Prabhu, *TOI*, 28 November 1981

England lost Graham Gooch early, and Boycott and Chris Tavare then added a laborious 92 from thirty-five overs, before Kirti Azad, the off-spinning all-rounder from Delhi, had Boycott caught by Srikkanth at short-leg. Doshi then took over, and bowled splendidly to take 5-39. The English were convinced that he had enjoyed umpiring support. India gained an unlikely lead of thirteen.

When India were reduced to 90-5 in their second innings, it became obvious that the Wankhede wicket was on its way to becoming India's equivalent of the MCG pitch. The previous three Tests played on the strip had all ended in less than four days, and the 1981-82 Test was headed the same way.

England would have fancied their chances with the Indians only 103 ahead and the top five batters back in the pavilion. But they were thwarted by Azad and Shastri. The Bombay left-armer, who had batted at number ten in the first innings, was sent in at number six in the second, once again ahead of Kapil Dev and Kirmani. As had been the case in New Zealand, he did not let his captain down. His two-and-a-half hour long 33 took the wind out of England's sails. Kapil Dev then banged 46, and the English were thoroughly dispirited by the time they began their pursuit of a target of 241. The Indian spinners were expected to finish it off, but the new-ball pair of Kapil Dev and his teenage hero Madan Lal did the job instead. They took five wickets each to bowl England out for 102.

The English cricketers, thoroughly dispirited by the defeat, found themselves ducking for cover as firecracker after firecracker exploded in the stands.

Strangely for a side that was trailing 0-1, the visitors decided to play for draws in the next two Tests at Bangalore and Delhi, and wait for the fourth and fifth Tests at Calcutta and Madras to hit back. Rarely has this sort of approach succeeded in cricket, and the 1981-82 series was no exception. The visitors' resolve to play safe manifested itself in some insipid batting, which saw them score 181-4 and 190-1 on the first days at Bangalore and Delhi respectively. They made little or no effort to come hard at the Indian bowlers, who were disciplined enough not to concede easy runs, but happy to consume minutes.

The failure of the Indian and England cricket boards to decide on a minimum number of overs per day, led to a situation wherein England's pace-oriented attack was found to be bowling less than thirteen overs an hour. Sunil was quick to work out that the Indians would end up bowling a lot more, given that theirs was a spin oriented attack. He was not going to be generous.

Sunil instructed Doshi, his number one stock bowler, to take his own time between deliveries. Given that the left-armer had nothing more than a two-step run-up, it seemed a tall order. But the captain's commands had to be followed. Sunil did his bit to help Doshi out by ambling up to the bowler between deliveries and indulging in small talk.

'It was this series that must finally have convinced the world's authorities that something must be done to regulate over-rates. They were appalling. Gavaskar's cynical approach to over-rates was entirely legal and the umpires were powerless to do anything meaningful about it. I remember endless discussions over field placings with Dilip Doshi, seemingly taking place after every ball, with little or no change after each discussion. It gave us little chance to gain any advantage and so Keith Fletcher opted to go the same way if India at any stage held the upper hand.'
– David Gower

Bob Willis' claim that Sunil had at one stage walked up to Doshi and asked him what he had had for breakfast, was lapped up by the media.

> Gavaskar had told me that if I failed to follow the code, he would simply take me off and put Shastri on to bowl. My attacking instincts were further curbed by such defensive instructions. . . . When I was being singled out for my slow over-rates, I feel strongly that Sunil Gavaskar should have defended me publicly. After all I was carrying out his orders. His only defence appears to have been to counter by saying that the opposition was also bowling slow over-rates. His silence on this sensitive issue showed he was selective in his responsibility as a captain.
> – Dilip Doshi, *Spin Punch* (Rupa, 1990)

Sunil and Doshi had been good friends for a long time. However, Doshi, a high-strung individual who was the butt of many a practical joke played by his team-mates, was no longer on amicable terms with his captain. He had earlier been upset with what he had perceived as Sunil's indifference to his toe injury in the Melbourne Test. Sunil was to respond to this charge in later years, stating that he had had no clue about the injury as Doshi had kept it a secret.

Their relationship worsened with Sunil's orders to go slow during the England series.

India held on to the lead they had gained in Bombay, with the tactics of both teams condemning every other Test to unfinished status. However, not everything was listless. After an indifferent time in the first two Tests, Viswanath returned to form with a brilliant 107 at Delhi. At Madras, he scored 222 to become India's highest individual scorer against England, bettering Sunil's 221 at the Oval. Kapil Dev's 116 in the final Test at Kanpur was a rousing rejoinder to Botham's 142 in the same game. Botham's team-mates had their moments with the bat. Boycott scored 105 at Delhi, in the process surpassing Garry Sobers' aggregate of 8,032 to become the highest scorer in Test cricket. The Yorkshireman was enjoying himself at a function held that evening to celebrate the achievement, when Sunil was asked to speak. The Indian captain told the man with whom he had been compared the most, to enjoy the record for two years.

Not for the last time was Sunil, a member of independent India's first generation, making a statement. He had already made one on the field, in the second Test at Bangalore.

> He is bound to make some bowlers suffer, and that too very soon. A batsman of Sunil's class cannot remain out of form and out of luck for such a long time ... Gavaskar nowadays tries to reach for the ball instead of allowing the ball to come to him, with the result that he edges it or misses the line of the ball more often. As there is no thinker in the present team, Gavaskar has not been able to sort out this defect. – Tiger Pataudi's statement at the *Rotary Club (Midtown)* meeting, as reported in the *TOI*, 25 February 1981

However, Sunil did struggle in the games that preceded the arrival of the English team. His sluggishness at the crease worried his fans, including those who had played the game competitively, and therefore understood his nuances.

One such fan attempted to do something about it, and that led to the start of an association that was professional as well as personal.

> 'I had been Sunil's fan right from the time I saw him score 176 against Maharashtra in the Ranji Trophy in 1970-71. Several years later, I wrote a letter to the editor of an Australian cricket magazine, explaining how Lever and Co. actually used vaseline in the 1976-77 series against India. SMG read that letter and presented me with an autographed copy of *Sunny Days*. I next met him when I was representing Baroda in the Ranji Trophy. The game in the 1979-80 season wherein he was run out for 86 was my last for Baroda. I was in awe of him as a cricketer and had heard about his infamous temper from friends like Aunshuman Gaekwad and Yajurvindra Singh. Sunil struggled in Australia in 1980-81, and his poor run continued even after his return. I will never forget that evening in late 1981. Milind Gunjal, who was representing Tatas in the Times Shield in Bombay at the time, dropped in at my Pune hotel for a chat. We discussed Sunil's form, and both of us came to the conclusion that things could improve

if Mr Kamal Bhandarkar, our coach, had a close look at him. Just as we were talking, a car pulled up at the hotel door, and a voice asked if a room was available. It was Sunil! Pammi was with him. Since he was staying overnight, I mustered the courage to ask him if he would like to have a net with Bhandarkar Sir watching. He agreed, but told me that I would have to organise the net, bowlers and kit. I was able to do that. Sir watched him for about forty-five minutes and pointed out what the fault was.'
– Jairaj (Raju) Mehta

At Bangalore, Sunil batted for eleven hours and forty-eight minutes to score 172, and squashed all the talk of his decline. It was the longest innings played by an Indian. Sunil in fact broke his own record, which he had set at Madras in January 1980.

Beautiful Bangalore burst the black bubble; it shattered the ugly bauble that had been sought to be flung around Gavaskar's mane. Truly did Gavaskar's marathon innings of 172 and the mahayogic control he exercised during its entirety prove to be the Bangalore Test's only decisive result . . . Sunil Gavaskar is still the supremo of batting skills, the titan of his technique. – Arvind Lavakare, *Sunday Observer*, 20 December 1981

Sunil Gavaskar was an absolute hero. I used to be involved in big arguments at home about who was the greatest batsman. I even used to keep track about his bat brands—Duncan Fearnley in 1974-1979 with Symonds for a brief period in 1976-77. Then Grey Nicholls, SG, Morrant, Slazenger (in England 1986), and back again SG. His hundred at Bangalore in 1981-82 came after a long gap. I remember skipping my Hindi and Marathi tuitions and watching the innings with a crowd outside a television store near Portuguese Church in Dadar. The shop was just a minute away from my teacher's home. But I put myself in jeopardy and ensured I watched him reach his hundred and then headed home, only to report ill the next day.' – Clayton Murzello, sports editor, *Mid-Day*.

Sunil was slow, but steady and most importantly, sound. The Bangalore spectators, born and brought up on Viswanath's cultured unorthodoxy, were transfixed by Sunil's demonstration of the art of defensive batsmanship. On the third day, he was 28 at lunch, 60 at tea and 71 at stumps. He had moved to 99 on the fourth morning when a section of the spectators misconstrued a bye and invaded the field. Sunil could have done without the premature mobbing and garlanding. Botham, who could always be counted upon to exploit a chink in an opponent's armoury—technical or mental—then served him four consecutive outswingers, each of which came within inches of inducing an edge. But it was Sunil's day. He got a single with a drive in the mid-off region after twenty scoreless minutes, and the spectators erupted for the second time.

Sunil's next three outings yielded scores of 46 (Delhi), 42 and an unbeaten 83 (Calcutta). The last of the lot was another of his fourth-innings masterpieces. Fletcher's declaration on the fourth evening left India to get 306 in a day and thirty minutes. The visitors fancied their chances, having dismissed India for only 208 in the first innings, but they were undone by the Calcutta smog. The Indian batsmen were offered the light on the fifth afternoon, as their English counterparts had been the previous morning. Like them, the Indians accepted it and made for the pavilion.

England's only chance of victory after the resumption was the dismissal of the Indian captain. That did not happen, and the match ended with the spectators being upset because Sunil had preferred putting down the shutters to getting a hundred. A knock of 52 at Kanpur gave him 500 runs from the series and the winners' trophy.

> Having seen the little genius dismissed for 46 and 42 in successive Tests, I can understand the headlines of the 30s; 'Bradman fails, out for 70!' For Sunil Gavaskar started his innings of 42 (Delhi) with a brilliance of touch that only he, of current Test openers, can achieve. Every remotely overpitched ball was dispatched with a minimum of movement to the appropriate boundary – if the ball was on leg-stump, wide of mid-on; if on middle, back past the bowler; if outside the off-stump, to either side at mid-off.
> – Mike Brearley, *Sunday Times*

Brearley's compatriots were not as effusive. They were offended when Sunil drew the attention of the umpires during the Kolkata Test to his opposite number Keith Fletcher's constant tapping of the wicket on the good-length spot to loosen the soil, and then flicking the turf that came out as a result with his shoes. Sunil's contention was that Fletcher was doing that to ensure that the ball misbehaved when India batted. He wasn't going to take things lying down.

A major surprise was India's 2-1 win in the One Day series. They put up a splendid show in the second one-dayer at Jalandhar, overhauling a target of 162 in 36 overs with three deliveries to spare. In the third game at Cuttack, India chased 231 in 46 overs, getting home with four overs left. The victories underscored the strides made by the side in the shorter version since the tour of Australia in 1980-81. Sunil did not have much to do at Jalandhar, as he limped off the field with a strained hamstring during England's innings, leaving Kirmani in charge. With Dilip Vengsarkar scoring a majestic 88, he wasn't even required to bat. At Cuttack, Sunil set up the chase with a solid 71. Vengsarkar apart, the junior members of the side carried on from where they had left off in Australia; Patil scored 64 at Cuttack, and Yashpal Sharma played a part in both wins with undefeated knocks of 28 and 34. Kapil Dev failed with the bat, but he gave nothing away with the ball. These performances indicated that India's future as a limited-overs side was anything but bleak.

England dished out the usual excuses of poor umpiring and even poorer wickets. While making the first excuse, they overlooked the fact that the umpiring had been as good or bad as in other cricket-playing countries. While putting forth the second, they ignored the scorebook, which indicated that most of the Tests had been high-scoring affairs. Most amusing was their contention that Kanpur should not have hosted the sixth Test because the last three Tests played there had been affected by rain.

'It's funny that the Englishmen should ask for bouncier wickets. We do not find too many bouncy wickets in England normally... the wickets lasted all the five days... If a Test should not be held at a centre because there is a likelihood of its being ruined by rain, then there should not be any Test cricket in England at all. . . . – Sunil Gavaskar, *Sportsweek*, 8 February 1982

Not for the first or the last time in his career, Sunil was not hesitant to draw people's attention to what was overwhelmingly obvious. He had justified his eminent status in world cricket with the manner in which he had returned to his run-scoring ways.

However, his detractors continued to be uncomfortable. It had been a decade since his international debut, but they still did not know what to make of him. What was he? A phenomenon who was bent on demonstrating to the cricketing world that the Indians were as good as anybody else, if not better? Or was he an upstart who had the cheek to take on the establishment (which at the time, constituted the likes of Australia and England), and hence needed to be brought down to earth?

> 'I umpired a TOI Shield game between Nirlons and Tatas that season. Sunil ensured a draw with a hundred in the second innings, but Tatas won on the basis of the first-innings lead. Nirlons were in trouble on the last day, with half their side out for less than hundred. Sunil was at the non-striker's end when Dilip Vengsarkar, who was representing Tatas, pouched the ball in the slips, and Padmakar Shivalkar, the bowler, went up in appeal. I agreed and declared Rahul Mankad, the batsman, out. Sunil was shocked. "Out! How?" he asked. "Caught!," I replied. But I suspected that something was amiss, for he wasn't the type who reacted like this on the field. There was a break a little later. I sought him out in the Nirlons room and asked him whether there was anything wrong with the decision. He then told me that the ball had gone off Mankad's pad and not his bat! The bat had been behind the front foot at the moment of impact, and I hadn't noticed it. "It means that I have made a mistake," I said. But he put me at ease by saying that there was no need to feel guilty, as everybody made mistakes. It was nice of him to have said so, especially when that decision had taken his team one step closer to exiting from the tournament.' – P.D. Reporter

His critics kept swooping upon him at the slightest opportunity. Their obsession to nail him by hook or by crook led to some peculiar situations. One such was witnessed in March 1982, during the Ranji semi-final between Bombay and Karnataka in Bangalore. The game was played after Sunil had scored 340, his highest First-class score, in an earlier game against Bengal, during the course of which he added 421 for the first wicket with Ghulam Parkar.

Karnataka ended up having the better of an acrimonious affair. Bombay batted first and could muster only 271. The hosts replied with 470, in a display that was marked by some peculiar player and crowd behaviour. Viswanath of all people wasn't too thrilled with the bat-pad decision awarded against him, and the spectators reacted violently. Bombay's bane in the game was the left-arm spin of Raghuram Bhat. They needed 39 to avoid the ignominy of an innings defeat when Sunil came in at number eight. The fate of the game was long sealed, but the least he could do was to deny his opponents an outright win.

Against Bhat, who was making the ball swerve away from a rough spot outside the right-hander's leg-stump, Sunil adopted a remarkable ploy. He decided to bat left-handed! With this approach, he thwarted the Karnataka bowlers for sixty balls, playing forward with the pad as the first line of defence, until Viswanath brought on an off-spinner. Sunil then reverted to batting right-handed, and Bombay achieved a draw.

In any other cricketing land, Sunil's stratagem might well have fetched him accolades, but not in his own country.

> Some blokes just have no sense of humour. Look at how they reacted to your great show on the last day. One indignant soul stood up and chanted, Left, right, left. For a moment, I imagined that it was a military command coming from the nearby MEG Parade Ground . . . Great show, skipper. You have proved a point. No one would have guessed that India had an ambidextrous captain . . . I am sure it will be another record in your already bulging copybook . . . I presume that your behaviour that day could vaguely be called gamesmanship. I also suppose that, to quote your own words, on the question of gamesmanship, you believe "the best way [is] to try and take it as part of the entertainment so long as it is not destructive, so long as it is

not personal and so long [as] it does not offend public taste". I wonder how many of your team-mates who were witnesses believe that your pranks were not destructive, not personal and did not offend public taste. – Late Ashok Kamath (Open letter to Gavaskar), as quoted in *Gavaskar – India's Cricket God* by K.R. Wadhwaney

Mr Kamath was not alone in his criticism. Cricket writers and lovers from different parts of the country took potshots at Sunil for his ambidextrous display. Simply put, the reactions were childish. It did not matter to the bashers that people who were involved in the thick of the action thought otherwise.

The ball was beating the bat and the only way to play on that day was to play left-hand and play forward and offer pad. That's how Gavaskar played and he really played well and saved the game for Mumbai. It was a great thing to bowl to him and the guts he showed in batting left-handed, for some twelve to thirteen overs, was amazing . . . I won't consider it as negative batting, he was trying to save the game and that was his duty than to get embarrassed by losing outright. His footwork on the day was something to be seen to be believed. If I had recorded that game on video I would have shown that to young cricketers as an example. Sunny was middling the ball, no edges, no tension.
– Raghuram Bhat, *Cricinfo*, 10 January 2007

Although he seemed to have regained his touch, there were signs that Sunil wasn't enjoying the game as much as he wanted to. The expectations of millions of people, and the responsibilities of captaincy, were taking a lot out of him. He was only human, after all.

'He had his hands full with the captaincy of the Indian team, and the job of opening the innings. These dual challenges left him too exhausted to captain Bombay and Nirlons. Once, he arrived at the Wankhede Stadium for a Ranji match and announced in the dressing room that Ashok Mankad would lead. That was indicative of his mental fatigue.' – Suru Nayak

Nayak's inclusion in the Indian team that was to tour England in mid-1982 gave Sunil's detractors more ammunition. Ghulam Parkar was another Bombay player who made it. Nayak happened to be Sunil's colleague at Nirlons.

> Suru Nayak is an all-rounder who bats left-handed, bowls seamers, is a brilliant fielder and can occasionally bowl leg-spinners. He is a utility cricketer. He has been playing in England in the Leagues, and is therefore experienced in the playing conditions prevailing there. And Ghulam Parkar, his performances in the Ranji Trophy over the last two years have been outstanding . . . Parkar, I said, was a thirty-plus like me. The selection committee members raised their eyebrows . . . I hastily added that I meant that as far as Ghulam was concerned, it was runs saved in the field, and in my case, it was my age! – Sunil Gavaskar, *Sportsweek*, 11 April 1982

The insinuations that Nayak and Parkar made it on parochial grounds irritated Sunil. In his second book *Idols*, released a year later, he was at his sarcastic best in a few lines in the chapter on Syed Kirmani. While recalling the keeper's omission for the tour of England in 1979, Sunil wrote:

> If Sunil Gavaskar was captain of that Indian team, he would have been accused of regional considerations in dropping Kirmani. But in this particular instance, the captain[1] and manager[2] came from the same state[3], and the wicketkeeper[4] to be the beneficiary from the dropping of Kirmani was also from the same state. At that stage, these facts didn't enter anybody's mind. And why should they? For Sunil Gavaskar is the only captain who is thought capable of such regional considerations, and none else in Indian cricket is capable of similar considerations when he is picking a side! – Sunil Gavaskar, *Idols* (Rupa, 1983)

Nayak had acquitted himself well in domestic cricket in the season gone by, as had Parkar, who had scored mountains of runs at the top of the

---

[1]Venkataraghvan
[2]C.D. Gopinath
[3]Tamil Nadu
[4]Bharat Reddy

order. But not many people outside Bombay were remotely interested in the facts.

What infuriated them even more was the decision, admittedly a peculiar one, to ignore Mohinder Amarnath. The right-hander, who hadn't played for India since the 'Solah topee' fiasco at Bombay in 1979, had impressed in the 1981-82 season as batsman and captain. He ended the season by leading Delhi to a victory over Karnataka in a remarkable Ranji final. Karnataka batted first in what was a six-day game, and amassed 705. Delhi sensationally overhauled the score, with their skipper scoring 185.

However, the selectors were wary, as they had been with the older Amarnath in 1980-81. Back then, Surender Amarnath's 235 in the Irani Cup game against what was, for all practical purposes India's bowling attack – Kapil Dev, Ghavri, Doshi, Yadav and Binny – had failed to win him a place for the tour of Australia. Now, it was his brother's turn to be overlooked.

> 'It was a stressful period for me and my family. The campaign against me was started by the media from the north. A number of ex-players from that region could not see eye-to-eye with Sunil as he was a successful cricketer. They did not have the guts to say anything to him directly, and tried to settle old scores by targeting him through me.' – Suru Nayak

The *Time of India* on 17 April 1982 reported the possibility of a split in the BCCI, following protests by a few state associations, including Delhi and Punjab. Nothing untoward happened, and S.K. Wankhede reminded one and all that it was irrational to expect the composition of a cricket team to be acclaimed universally.

> I have very little to say about Mohinder Amarnath. What could he have been taken in for? For bowling? How many Test wickets has he taken? Twenty maybe? He could not be included as a batsman. There are any number of players better than him, and preference should be given to youngsters. I cannot see him as an all-rounder in my team. – Sunil Gavaskar, as quoted by Kuldip Lal in *Mohinder Amarnath – Grit and Grace* (Vakils, Feffer and Simons Ltd. 1996)

Sunil's observations in the above paragraph may be interpreted as insensitive and cruel, but then, this is what he had to say about the same player and Dilip Vengsarkar, back in 1976:

'Mohinder and Dilip are still very young, and in the years to come, they will be the mainstays of India's batting.'[5]

While Vengsarkar had established himself in the side since, Amarnath had struggled to do so. In all fairness, injuries and the indifference of the selectors hadn't helped his cause. Sunil's Bombay upbringing may have influenced his 1982 perception of Amarnath as 'a very fine player who had not somehow produced a performance befitting his potential at the Test level.[6]' Not many cricketers from Bombay were known to have got a second chance to prove themselves, given the preponderance of talent in the city. Many people felt that Amarnath, who was now thirty-two, had had his opportunities, and it was time to try out younger cricketers who had proved themselves in domestic cricket. In any case, the decision to keep Amarnath out of the squad had been made by the selectors.

Whether right or wrong, the decision had been taken, and it had to be accepted and the next step taken, just as it was up to Mohinder Amarnath to make the selectors regret it.

The tediousness of the previous series prompted the TCCB (Test and County Cricket Board) to become the first cricket board to advocate a minimum over-rate in Test cricket. The English and Indian boards agreed on an over-rate of sixteen per hour.

Although Sunil declared on arrival in England that his team had come to play cricket, not politics, the visitors had already made it clear that they would not play against any side containing a 'rebel'. This word, which had entered the cricketing lexicon after the outbreak of the Packer revolution in 1977, was now being used to refer to the English cricketers who had undertaken a tour of South Africa soon after the series in India. That party comprised some of the best cricketers in the land, like opener Graham Gooch, off-spinner John Emburey, and veterans Boycott, Underwood, and Knott. There were many Indians who viewed the rebel tour in general and Boycott's role in organising it in particular, as a stab in the back.

---

[5]*Sunny Days.*
[6]*Idols.*

It was Boycott's condemnation of apartheid in October 1981 that had influenced the Indian government to give a green signal to England's tour of India. The revelations that most of the planning and recruitment for the South Africa tour took place during England's tour of India, was adding insult to injury.

Of course, the rebels cared a damn for what a developing country like India thought. They earned pots of money for making the trip to South Africa, and it was all that mattered. A backlash was only to be expected, considering the prevalent international stance on apartheid. The self-righteous behaviour of some of the rebels after they were handed out three-year bans from international cricket was amusing to say the least.

The English selectors sprung a surprise at the start of the season by appointing Robert 'Bob' Willis as captain. The tour of India and Sri Lanka had not gone off very well for Fletcher. He had struggled to get going with the bat, and that had only made his job of leading players who were far more successful Test cricketers than him tougher. There had also been some unsavoury incidents, like the one concerning the pitch in Calcutta, and another at Bangalore wherein he dislodged the bails with his bat after getting a dodgy caught-behind decision. He subsequently apologised, but the authorities, English as well as Indian, were reluctant to forgive the captain of a visiting team. This was of course ironic, considering Tony Greig's gamesmanship on the previous tour. But then, he had led England to victory. What ultimately went against Fletcher was his failure to win. Willis became England's fourth captain within a twelve month period, after Botham, Brearley and Fletcher.

The new captain started on a winning note, leading England to victories in the two One Day Internationals prior to the Tests.

The first Test of the series marked India's Golden Jubilee as a Test-playing nation. India had commenced its inaugural Test against England at Lord's on 25 June 1932. Another Test between the two teams commenced at the same venue on 10 June 1982.

There turned out to be some similarities between the two games. Like in 1932, one of the two skippers in 1982 was Bombay-born. India's commercial capital had been as much Douglas Jardine's hometown, at least during his childhood, as it was Sunil Gavaskar's. The 1932 Test was made memorable by India's new-ball pair of Mohammed Nissar and Amar Singh; the 1982 game witnessed a magnificent display from an Indian bowler who combined the roles of the duo. Like Mohammed Nissar in 1932, he bowled splendidly on the first day. Like Amar Singh in 1932, he batted spectacularly in the second innings. Like Vinoo Mankad at Lord's in 1952, he was outstanding in both departments of the game. And as had been the case in 1932 and 1952, his team lost.

Kapil Dev had England in some strife at 96-4 on the first day, before Botham and Derek Randall engineered a recovery and ensured that they reached 433. The seamer trio of Botham, skipper Willis and debutant Derek Pringle then reduced India to 92-5 at stumps on the second day. India were all out for 128 on the third morning, of which Kapil Dev's share was an enterprising 41. Sunil hung around for 48 before being bowled by Botham. Willis then enforced the follow-on. If ever his team needed Sunil to click on one of his least favourite grounds, it was now. But Sunil fell for 24, giving a catch to Cook off Willis, shortly after Parkar was bowled by Willis.

Viswanath failed for the second time in the game, but Yashpal Sharma played a good hand of 37. He lent invaluable support to Dilip Vengsarkar, who was at his imperial best. He drove, pulled and cut superbly to complete his second Test hundred at headquarters in as many games, eventually getting 157. Kapil Dev's 'death-or-glory' pyrotechnics, during the course of which he essayed some stunning strokes, yielded him 89 from 55 balls. India totalled 369, but England needed only 65 with more than a day to spare. Both sides went through the motions, with one notable exception. Kapil Dev bagged three more wickets and finished with match figures of 8-168. That, coupled with his 89, won him the Man of the Match award despite being on the losing side. Frederick Trueman, Test cricket's first 300-wicket man, hailed him as a 'giant among present-day all-rounders'. It was no insignificant compliment, given that the English team comprised Ian Botham, who scored 67 in the first innings and bagged 6-149 in the game.

Not for the first or the last time, an Indian cricketer, in this case Kapil Dev, went on to complete the transition from 'good' to 'great' in a Test series in England. His failures with the bat on the 1979 tour had been at the back of his mind, and he was determined to showcase his all-round abilities on this trip. He followed up the 89 with 65 in the second Test and 97 in the third. Botham scored 128 and 208 in the same games. Both Tests were drawn, with India's ineptitude on the second day at Lord's giving England the series.

All those who had hoped for a repeat of Sunil's 1979 run-fest were disappointed, as his three outings yielded scores of 48, 24 and 2. In the final Test at the Oval, he was fielding at silly-point on the first day when he came in the way of a searing Botham drive off Shastri. His left ankle bore the impact and broke. Sunil was escorted off the field, and took no further part in the match.

Botham then brutalised the bowling to complete his first double hundred in Tests. That was not the only reason he was beaming when he met Sunil on the latter's birthday on 10 July, the third day of the game.

> Botham came to my room with a bottle of champagne which he said was partly for my birthday and partly for a double hundred which he claimed he had won on a bet against me . . . during the rest day of the Lord's Test, we had gone to one of the indoor schools . . . I was having a bowl all by myself and trying my legspinners when Ian said he could play my legspinners left-handed. To which I retorted that he could not. So he bet me a fiver that I would not get him out . . . And I did get him out . . . Then, in the second Test . . . he smashed us all over the place (he scored 128) . . . I told him that he had thrown it away by getting out when he was in sight of a double hundred. He said he would do it in the next Test. I replied that his temperament was just not suited for a double hundred . . . Again, he decided to have a bet . . . he said that if he got a double hundred, it would be double or quits. His first reaction after scoring the double hundred was to come up to me and say, 'Well, that makes us quits.' – Sunil Gavaskar, *Sportsweek*, 29 September 1982

In 1979, Botham had had a premonition about Sunil scoring a double hundred at the Oval. Three years later, he appeared to have had a similar premonition about himself! India was one of his favourite opponents, as the runs and wickets he had taken off them indicated. He would describe his experience of touring India in 1979-80 and 1981-82 as 'absolutely wonderful' in his 1995 autobiography. Little did he know then that it would be nearly a decade before he played another international game against India. The gap notwithstanding, his love for the Indians endured, as he proved by winning the Man of the Match award against Mohammad Azharuddin's team in a round-robin match of the 1992 World Cup.

Like Botham, Sunil's team-mates opted to scribble birthday wishes on the plaster instead of giving him cards.

It had been a series wherein Sunil the captain had outshone Sunil the batsman. The repeated failures of openers Parkar and Pranab Roy prompted him to ask Ravi Shastri to accompany him to the middle in the second Test at Manchester. The all-rounder's failure to trouble the scorers did not bother the skipper. Sunil assigned him the same task at the Oval. There, in Sunil's absence, Shastri scored 66. Obviously, Sunil had seen something that others hadn't.

Sandeep Patil's was another success story. Personal problems had bogged him down in the 1981-82 season and the first half of the England tour. Matters came to a head shortly after the Lord's Test, when Patil informed Sunil that he wished to retire. The youngster's mood improved substantially when he received a letter written by Ashok Mankad. Sunil then did his bit by including him in the XI for the second Test! Patil, who hadn't done anything of note on the tour till then, went on to score a 129, moving from 80 to 104 with six boundaries in one Willis over. It was the second time in two years that he had displayed the temperament and never-say-die spirit that exemplified cricketers from Bombay.

However, as far as some people were concerned, the Bombay factor was precisely the problem.

> In the team selections and also in the way he has handled his bowlers, Gavaskar . . . has left himself open to the charge that he is looking after his own [people]. – Henry Blofeld, *The Guardian*, 9 July 1982

> During an official TCCB dinner at Lord's, I met the late Sir Len Hutton . . . he was shocked that I was bowling from the pavilion end at such a crucial stage of the game. He added that in his

playing days, left-arm spinners always bowled from the nursery end. I had a choice then. I could have exposed the frail side of Gavaskar's personality that affected his captaincy, or take it as a part of the game. Naturally, I chose the latter, even if Sunil did not agree. – Dilip Doshi, *Spin Punch* (Rupa, 1990)

The implication was that India could have been in a better position at Lord's had Doshi, the most experienced spinner in the side, been brought on from the nursery end to turn the ball down the slope, when the hosts were 37-3 on the first day. Shastri was brought on ahead of his more seasoned partner. Doshi bowled more overs in the game than any other Indian bowler save Kapil Dev, but not all of them were delivered from the nursery end.

Sunil has never given his version of the story. His rationale could well have been that the Bengal left-armer was experienced and proficient enough to bowl from any end, unlike Shastri, who needed the extraneous assistance of the slope. That England recovered and got 433 indicates that Sunil had made a mistake.

Ironically, in imploring the cricketing establishment and cricket loving public to decry Sunil, his decisions and his methods, his detractors were only deifying him. For his fans, Sunil was an extraordinary cricketer, who was prone to making the odd mistake. But for his detractors, he was God incarnate; who had no right to err.

15

'IMRAN'ED ... AND DEMOTED

'One thing about him as a batsman has always stayed with me. When facing a bouncer, most of us had barely enough time to get out of the way. But he would always either duck underneath the ball or sway out of the way. He then still had enough time to look around and watch the ball till it thudded into the keeper's gloves. I have never seen anyone else do that since.' – Mudassar Nazar

The ankle injury forced Sunil to use crutches for a couple of months. He accompanied eight colleagues – Viswanath, Patil, Nayak, Parkar, Roy, Shastri, Madan Lal and Kirmani – on a cricket promotion trip to the United States. There, he attended a dinner in Washington hosted by K.R. Narayanan, India's then ambassador, in honour of Mrs Gandhi, who was on an official visit to the country. He then returned to London for treatment of his injured foot.

Another marathon season was on the anvil. India were to play a one-off Test and three One Day Internationals against Sri Lanka, after which they were to tour Pakistan for a six-Test series. On its heels was a full tour of the Caribbean, and thereafter the World Cup.

Sunil's recovery was monitored after his return to Bombay by Dr Vishwas Raut and Dr Deepak Kachalia. The solitary Test against Sri

Lanka at Madras was identified as the comeback game. His withdrawal from the two One Day Internationals that preceded the Test prompted the selectors to take a singular decision. Kapil Dev was appointed skipper. It meant that they had decided to make him Sunil's deputy for the series in Pakistan, and wanted to groom him as a future leader. The appointment made sense, for Kapil Dev had become the most valuable member of the team, and unlike Viswanath, had age on his side. However, there were many who feared that the cares of captaincy would affect him adversely the way they had Ian Botham in 1980-81. India simply could not afford an off-key Kapil Dev.

He got off to a rollicking start as captain. India avenged the defeat in the 1979 World Cup by winning both One-dayers comprehensively. At the forefront was K. Srikkanth, who blasted 57 in the first game and 95 in the second. The second knock enabled India to overhaul a formidable target of 278 with nearly ten overs to spare. The wins, coming as they did after India's 2-1 win in the One-day series against England the year before, and decent performances in the tri-series in Australia in 1980-81, indicated that the side had finally decoded limited-overs cricket.

The Madras spectators gave Sunil a warm ovation when he accompanied his opposite number Bandula Warnapura for the toss on the first day of the one-off Test. Warnapura won the toss and elected to bat, but he fell cheaply, as did his partner Goonatillake. The innings was revived by Roy Dias and Duleep Mendis. It was appropriate that two batsmen who had incorporated bits of Viswanath—Dias his elegance and Mendis his build and panaché—in their batting styles, excelled at the Chidambaram stadium, which had witnessed some extraordinary performances by the little genius.

India's response to Sri Lanka's 346 was commenced by Sunil and Arunlal, a debutant from Delhi. The Indian captain, playing his first game in two months, showed no signs of fatigue, despite having fielded for a day-and-a-half. The openers put on 156. Sunil went on to complete his twenty-fifth Test hundred, and batted on, crossing 150 with a six off leg-spinner Somachandra De Silva. He eventually fell for 155, making it a momentous return. 'Ask Sunil to do a lap of the ground and he will not be able to do it, but ask him to stay at the wicket the whole day and he will do that easily,' S. Venkataraghvan said on television during the course of the innings.

Vengsarkar's 90 and Patil's unbeaten 114 took India to 566. However, Dias and Mendis batted brilliantly once again, and ensured that India had only fifty-three minutes and twenty mandatory overs in which to get 175. It was a tall order, but the Indians went for it. A stiff neck forced Sunil to drop down the order, and Vengsarkar accompanied Arunlal in his place. The openers fell early, but Patil and Kapil Dev added a quick 62 before the former was run out. That sparked off a collapse of sorts, and the Indians put down the shutters. But they kept losing wickets, until Sunil came in at number nine and played out the last five overs in the company of Yashpal Sharma.

Although India came back strongly in the final One Day International, with Sunil once again missing out, they were unable to avoid the brickbats that were hurled at them for coming precariously close to losing a Test against the babes of international cricket.

The players then immersed themselves in the Duleep and Irani Trophy games to bolster their chances of selection for the Pakistan tour. Sunil and Kapil Dev were rival captains in the Duleep final between the West and the North. India's new vice-captain won the bout by eight wickets. For the West, Aunshuman Gaekwad, who hadn't played a Test since 1979, reminded the selectors of his existence with a knock of 104 in the second innings, and Shastri returned match figures of 9-142. For the North, Madan Lal excelled with 11-122. However, the show was stolen by another player who hadn't played a Test since 1979.

Mohinder Amarnath followed up on his 207 in the semi-final against East Zone with scores of 80 and 67 not out. He then led Ranji champions Delhi against Sunil's Rest of India in the Irani Trophy fixture. In what turned out to be a humdinger, Sunil and his team had a day in which to score 421 to win. Remarkably, they took up the challenge.

Sunil, who had batted at number four in the first innings, held Arunlal back and opened with Srikkanth. He did not have much to do, with Srikkanth smashing 110. Arunlal came in at number three and scored 82. Ashok Malhotra's 116 and Patil's 41 sealed a five-wicket win in the eighty-fourth over of the innings.

Srikkanth and Arunlal were picked for the Pakistan trip, as was Sunil's Delhi counterpart. With knocks of 207, 80 and 67 in the Duleep Trophy, and 127 and 52 in the Irani game, Mohinder Amarnath had made it impossible for the selectors to ignore him.

Fatehsinghrao Gaekwad was drafted in once again for another diplomatic assignment. Sunil and he were in charge of a side whose batting, at least on paper, seemed devoid of weaknesses. The bowling department wasn't as redoubtable, although Doshi and Kapil Dev were there. There were two queer selections.

Why a selection committee that comprised Bishan Bedi had picked not one, but two teenaged spin bowlers for a tour of Pakistan, no one knew. Rather, not many people wished to know, as hailing the advent of the eighteen-year-old Maninder Singh was a far more convenient option. He was a Sikh, and a left-arm spinner, and it followed that he was touted as Bedi's successor. He had for company Laxman Sivaramakrishnan, a seventeen-year-old leg-spinner from Tamil Nadu. They had made their First-class debuts in the same game, the 1981-82 Ranji semi-final between Delhi and Tamil Nadu, and taken nine wickets apiece. On the eve of the Pakistan tour, Maninder returned figures of 9-114 for North Zone in the Duleep semi-final against Central Zone. He had gone on to take 6-66 for Delhi in the first innings of the Irani Trophy game. On the flipside, his two wickets in the second innings had cost him 180 runs, with Srikkanth and the others running amok. Sivaramakrishnan had taken four wickets for the Rest in the second innings, but he had also conceded 127 of the 258 runs that Delhi had scored. The decision to blood them in Pakistan seemed as daft as the one taken by a panel comprising three former seamers to leave Pandurang Salgaonkar out of the team that toured England in 1974. The selectors seemed to be unmindful of the presence of Zaheer Abbas and Javed Miandad, who had annihilated Prasanna, Chandrasekhar and Bedi himself in 1978-79.

India's first notable game of the tour was a One-Day International at Gujranwala, which they lost by 14 runs. Sunil scored only 1 before falling to his opposite number – Imran Khan.

It was only four months ago that Imran Khan Niazi had been appointed captain of Pakistan, after the senior players in the squad rebelled against Javed Miandad. His first assignment in the hot seat was the tour of England in mid-1982. His exploits with bat and ball in the three Tests, coming as they did soon after the show by Kapil Dev earlier in the summer, made it the second consecutive English season to be dominated by all-rounders. While Botham, the hero of 1981, had given Kapil Dev a run for his money in the first half of the summer, he was completely overshadowed by Imran in the second. The captain of Pakistan scored 212 runs at 53, took 21 wickets, and led Pakistan to their second Test win on English soil. Although England won the series 2-1, it was Imran who dominated the proceedings and headlines. He finished the series with the Player of the Series award and the appellation 'The Lion of Pakistan'.

The lion proceeded to lead his pride to a 3-0 sweep against the visiting Australians in September-October 1983. A leg-spinner by the name of Abdul Qadir was Pakistan's best bowler in the series, but he wasn't expected to be a force against the spin-bred Indians. To avenge the loss of 1979-80, it was imperative that the lion himself led the charge.

Zaheer Abbas atoned for his 1979-80 failures with a double hundred in the first Test at Lahore. On a greenish strip, India strangely went in with two left-arm spinners in Doshi and Shastri, and only two specialist seamers in Kapil Dev and Madan Lal, with Amarnath providing a third option. Pakistan on the other hand, played four quick men. The hosts scored 485, with Zaheer becoming the first Asian to complete a century of first-class hundreds. Doshi returned figures of 5-91.

The Indians began well, watched by an appreciative TV audience back at home. Colour TV had only recently come to India, during the ninth Asian Games in Delhi, shortly before the Pakistan tour. The fact that Pakistan TV had gone colour several years ago, and had a multi-camera set-up to cover cricket matches, was not lost on the Indians. At the time, Pakistan TV's Indian counterpart, Doordarshan, believed in interpreting its name literally. It accordingly offered a view from afar.

Not for the first or the last time, with Sunil's defensive strokes and leaves came in as much praise as the shots that fetched him runs. Sarfraz Nawaz surprised him with a short ball, but Sunil's response was exemplary. He watched it all the way, took his head and left shoulder out of the way, and let it go. He then left an Imran bouncer with aplomb, and killed another short ball with a straight bat and loose hands. Imran's riposte was a brute of an indipper that pitched just short of a length, and whizzed through the tiniest of gaps between Sunil's pad and bat, which he had raised to execute a backward defensive shot. It didn't miss the stumps by much, and the cameras caught a mystified Sunil. He soon had something else to think about. Imran dug in one short, and the cherry rose and hit Sunil on the left arm as he aimed to play it down defensively. A few inches higher, and it would have struck him on the temple. Sunil was wearing his trademark floppy sun hat, a forearm protector, and padding on the ribs in addition to a thigh-pad and box, but the commentators were concerned. Former Pakistani captain Javed Burki and Sunil's 1971 team-mate Abbas Ali Baig both felt that it was time he added a helmet to his list of accessories.

There was another observation Burki made, with reference to the Pakistani pace bowlers: 'They think they can gain more movement with a semi-new ball. Imran is a firm believer in this. They don't fancy their chances with a new ball. They get more movement with a semi-new one, keeping one side rough and the other shining.'

For the listeners, this was a revelation. Weren't fast bowlers known to prefer a brand new cherry? So what was Burki implying?

Although Imran and Sarfraz appeared to be flouting convention, they were in reality flaunting what would come to be accepted as Pakistan's premier cricketing tradition.

This tradition had its genesis at the First-class and junior levels in the country, where most of the matches would be played on grounds with coarse outfields. The red ball would not take too long to lose its shine, and the batsmen would make merry. The bowlers had no option but to adapt. It was one Dr Farrukh Ahmed, who represented Lahore in nine First-class matches in the sixties, who hit upon a solution. He realised that if one side of the ball was to be kept relatively new, even as the other got older and rougher, it was possible to get the ball to swing late, and that too prodigiously, if delivered at a decent pace. A ball cultivated in this manner could even swing inwards, late and viciously, despite being gripped and released like a conventional outswinger, and vice versa. Dr Ahmed tutored Sarfraz Nawaz in this art in the late sixties, and he passed it on to Imran Khan in the mid-seventies.

At Lahore, Arunlal brought up his own fifty and second consecutive century stand with his skipper. By then, intermittent rain had pushed the game into the fourth day, so there was no possibility of a result. But Indian viewers did become nervous when Arunlal and Vengsarkar fell in quick succession. The score was 114-2 when Imran bowled one that landed on a length and hit Sunil on the box. The fielders congregated around him, but the Indian captain waved them away, taking a few extra seconds to regain his composure. Baig's assessment was that Sunil realised that the ball would have passed over the stumps, and had therefore let it hit him. Imran followed up with a beauty that moved away after pitching, and just missed the outside edge. Not that Sunil thought too much about the hit and the near-miss, for he was one of those who believed that the previous delivery was history, and only the imminent one important. A single off Imran made him only the fifth batsman in Test history after Hammond, Cowdrey, Boycott and Sobers, to complete 7,000 runs. It was his eighty-third Test. He completed his fifty with an off-driven boundary off the seamer Jalal-ud-din.

Viswanath, who replaced Vengsarkar in the middle, was unlucky to receive an Imran special that moved away after pitching, and Bari did the rest. In came Mohinder Amarnath for his first Test innings in three years. The last time he had batted in a Test, he had worn a Solah hat; this time, he was wearing its younger and more contemporary sibling – a helmet. It being his first Test innings in three years, he was understandably tentative, but well aware of what lay in store. Imran subjected him to a series of short deliveries, once hitting him on the shoulder and head in the same over. But the batsman was unflustered. When he bowled another short delivery, Amarnath quickly moved into position and hooked the cherry to the boundary. He proceeded to bat magnificently.

> Although I had an open stance, when I met the ball, I was absolutely side-on. This helped me because earlier I used to go across too much. It was okay to play the outgoing delivery, but I was struggling against the incoming ones, since my left shoulder was moving towards the off-side. With a square-on stance, I was able to tackle these deliveries better. – Mohinder Amarnath, *Sportstar*, 1 May 1993

Whether it was his unconventional open stance that was responsible for the way he played, or the urge to make up for all the lost years, or a combination of both, the fact was that Amarnath flourished. Sunil, who had done his bit to encourage his partner, got to 83 before nicking Sarfraz to Bari. Amarnath carried on. The spectators rose when he completed a hundred in his comeback game. The proudest man at the Gaddafi stadium was the seniormost member of the TV commentary team. For Lala Amarnath, who was still revered by the locals of Lahore, it was a day to cherish.

The Lahore Test ended in a draw, with Mohsin Khan completing a hundred in Pakistan's facile second innings. The second Test at Karachi was preceded by a high-scoring one-dayer at Multan, which Pakistan won by 37 runs. Patil spearheaded India's attempt to achieve a target of 264 in only forty overs with a knock of 84, but the hundreds scored by Mohsin Khan and Zaheer Abbas earlier in the day made the difference. The Indians then played a three-day game against the Punjab Governor's XI in the same city. Stodgy batting enabled the home team to escape with a draw, after it appeared at one stage that India would win. Maninder Singh bowled himself into the second Test with a match haul of 10-84.

The square at Karachi's National Stadium, the venue of the second Test, had been relaid recently and was a bit of an unknown quantity. Imran read it well by asking India to bat after winning the toss. When Sunil took strike to the first ball, it was only the third instance of the rival captains opposing each other at the start of a Test.

This particular instance featured a suicide. Sunil tapped Imran on the leg-side, and in what can only be explained as a rush of blood, went for a single. But Arunlal, who was a lot closer to the ball, sent his captain back. Imran stopped in his follow-through, darted across the pitch, picked up the ball and hurled it to break the wickets before his counterpart could get back. Vengsarkar was caught in the slips off the very next ball to reduce India to 10-2. Viswanath then counterattacked with four consecutive boundaries before he was declared out, caught behind off Qadir. The fall of Amarnath and Patil to the Imran-Qadir combination reduced India to 70-5. Kapil Dev then batted as only he could to score 73 before giving Sarfraz a return catch. He helped India reach 169, as did Arunlal, whose gritty 35 impressed several watchers.

Three strikes by Madan Lal had Pakistan reeling at 18-3, before Miandad and Zaheer initiated a recovery. Zaheer went on to get 186, and Mudassar, who had dropped down the order, scored 119. The hosts finished with 452, thus leaving the Indians with no option but to play for a draw.

Doshi was particularly unhappy. His skipper and team-mates had celebrated his thirty-third birthday on 22 December, the day before the game. However, the strain in the relationship with his captain persisted. The left-armer had already been deeply hurt by what he had perceived as a deliberate attempt by the skipper to devalue his five-wicket haul at Lahore. According to him, Sunil had hinted that his five victims had thrown their wickets away in the dash for a declaration, and hence, it wasn't appropriate for Doshi to take the credit for them.

Sunil copped flak for allowing the opposition to escape from 18-3. His decision to introduce the spinners as late as eighty five minutes after the start of the innings was particularly frowned upon.

> Any captain in his right senses would have bowled his wicket-taking bowlers at this juncture to drive the advantage home. But instead, he got bogged down in personal likes and dislikes . . . So delayed was my call to bowling that Asif Iqbal on Pakistan TV was prompted to say that it had to be something personal to Gavaskar. I was becoming quite disgusted with Gavaskar's shameless performance as a captain and head of the team. It was becoming increasingly clear that he wanted to show the world that I had failed, before he could justifiably drop me. – Dilip Doshi, *Spin Punch* (Rupa, 1990)

That was of course, one way of looking at it. However, the fact was that the Pakistanis were acclaimed murderers of spin. With Madan Lal, a seamer, having made those early inroads, Sunil may well have decided to give his seamers the best possible chance of coming good on a helpful wicket. As it turned out, Kapil Dev and Madan Lal took eight wickets between them, although they were far too expensive.

So quickly had the Pakistani batsmen got their runs that their bowlers had more than two days in which to take ten Indian wickets for the second time in the game. Arunlal fell early at 28, but his skipper looked untroubled, as did Vengsarkar. Imran gave Sunil a tough time, beating him on at least two occasions. The first delivery swung away late, and the second rose sharply after pitching. However, Sunil soldiered on. The Dadar Union pair took their side through to the tea interval, and continued to display a cool and collected countenance after it. Imran, who had bowled five overs in the second session, reintroduced himself after tea with the intention of bowling another short spell.

He contemplated taking himself off after his fourth post-tea over. But the late afternoon breeze floating across the National Stadium prompted him to give himself another one. There was another reason: the ball was semi-new. In other words, it had assumed the age that Imran and his co-pacemen liked. India were 102-1, and the shadows were lengthening.

Sunil, as always, placed his bat in his guard and his left foot parallel to the popping crease, then put his right foot next to the toe of the bat, and settled into his stance. He then shifted his gaze to his counterpart, who was at the top of his run-up. As Imran bounded in, Sunil shifted into a tunnel-vision mode, focusing on Imran's wrist and whatever little the bowler was allowing him to see of the ball. The Pakistani captain passed the umpire, and then launched into the pre-delivery jump that had endeared him to an entire generation of cricket lovers.

He had started his career with an open, slingshot action, similar to Jeff Thomson's. However, the experience of World Series Cricket, and the realisation that bowlers like Dennis Lillee and Andy Roberts, who were slower than him in terms of raw pace, were taking more wickets, had made Imran return to the drawing board. He had adopted a more conventional side-on style and worked hard on his variations. The outcome was one of the best bowling actions of all time.

Up against him was one of the best techniques in the business. Sunil went back-and-across, and brought the toes of his right foot in line with the off-stump even as Imran released the ball. He saw the ball land just short of a length outside the off-stump, and detected the in-swing. He accordingly transferred his body-weight onto the back foot, and raised his bat so that it was perpendicular to the ground.

So astute was Sunil's judgement that on most occasions, the ball would have made contact with the bat and dropped dead at his feet.

That did not happen. The cherry did a lot more than what he or for that matter, everybody else expected. It swung inwards in the air, pitched, and continued its inward journey past the inside-edge of Sunil's bat, and whizzed between the bat and pad to hit the wickets. Some people called it a brute of an inswinger; others called it a vicious in-dipper. Whatever it was, it was a wicket to cherish, for it wasn't every time that a bowler managed to breach the defences of Sunil Gavaskar.

Facing Imran in his next over was Gundappa Viswanath. The Pakistani captain delivered another ball that landed short of a length outside the off-stump. The batsman reasoned that the ball would sail past the off-stump, and accordingly raised his bat to let it go. To his horror, the ball moved inwards viciously, and shattered the stumps. It was Imran's two hundreth Test wicket. As the spectators cheered, Imran banished all thoughts of taking a break.

Luck was on his side. He delivered a ball from the edge of the popping crease, which seemed certain to pass the leg-stump, when Amarnath's fully-stretched front foot came in the way. The umpire responded to the Pakistani captain's appeal in the affirmative, and in the commentary box, Lala Amarnath did everything he could to prevent himself from uttering unparliamentary language. Two in-dippers accounted for Patil and Kapil Dev. Patil was bowled all ends up, and Kapil played on. By the time stumps were drawn, India were 118-7.

In a display that was as outstanding as it was astounding, Imran Khan had turned the game on its head by scalping five Indian batsmen in the space of twenty-five balls at a cost of 3 runs. Hanging on at the close in Madan Lal's company was Vengsarkar, who had had the best, albeit not very pleasant, view of an exhibition of what was eventually christened 'reverse swing'.

> I have never seen Imran Khan bowl so fast . . . he gathered pace off the pitch after the ball deviated a great deal in the air. – Sunil Gavaskar, *The Indian Express*, 27 December 1982

Vengsarkar and Madan Lal delayed the inevitable with an 83-run stand on the fourth morning before Imran hammered the final nails in the

Indian coffin. He had Vengsarkar caught behind, Maninder leg-before and Doshi bowled. Pakistan won by an innings and 86 runs, with Imran taking 8 wickets in the innings and 11 in the match.

The Indians presented Imran with a cake for taking two hundred Test wickets. That they were good losers did not hide the fact that they were shellshocked.

The win in the truncated third One Day International, which preceded the next Test, restored some of their self-belief. Hundreds by Zaheer and Miandad took Pakistan to 252-3 in the allotted thirty-three overs. K. Srikkanth struck Imran for two consecutive sixes, and contributed 39 to an opening stand of 57. Patil maintained the attack, and Sunil was no less aggressive. The duo added 115 in only eighty deliveries in fading light. But both fell in quick succession, as did Kapil Dev, and the score was 192-4 when Amarnath and Sharma appealed against the light. The rejection of their plea prompted Sunil to run onto the field for a discussion with the officials, one of whom was his old friend Shakoor Rana. It was eventually decided to declare the match closed, and as per the prevalent limited-overs rules, India were declared winners on account of their having a superior run-rate at the time of the termination. While Pakistan's rate had been 6.48 at the end of the twenty-seventh over of their innings, India's was 7.14.

Put into bat in the third Test at Faisalabad, the visitors were 22-3 when Viswanath and Amarnath initiated a recovery. Patil then scored 84, and 372 was a fighting total on which to finish. Kapil Dev then dismissed Mohsin, Mudassar and Mansoor Akhtar with only 79 on the board. But India were thwarted once again by Zaheer (168) and Miandad (126). Worse was to follow. Imran and Salim Malik scored 117 and 107 respectively, and ensured a final total of 652. Kapil Dev finished with seven wickets, but they cost him 220 runs. India needed to bat for a day-and-a-half to save the match.

They were 48-3 when Sunil was joined by Amarnath.

Amarnath was a year junior to his skipper in terms of age, but he had made his Test debut before the latter. However, Sunil had left him far behind in terms of international cricket experience. While the path the captain had taken was marked by a trail of milestones, Amarnath's featured a plethora of potholes. The way he had batted since his return to the team in Pakistan, he seemed determined to divert his route and bring it in line with that of his skipper's.

Sunil was given a torrid time by his Pakistani counterpart. At one point, he edged three consecutive deliveries bowled by Imran through the slips, getting four, four and two in the process. But he hung on. Amarnath's defiance at the other end helped him maintain his focus. At stumps on the fourth day, India were 181-3, with both batters in their seventies. Another two hours of defiance would have ensured a draw, but Imran had another stroke of luck. As had happened in the second innings at Karachi, he struck Amarnath on his fully stretched left foot, and the umpire agreed with the leg-before shout. The Pakistani captain proceeded to order an upset Amarnath off the pitch.

That wicket broke the back of the innings. The next six batters produced scores of 6, 16, 6, 10, 2 and 4. Even as the ship sank, its captain did his best to plug the leaks. But he simply could not do it on his own.

> 'I don't think Sunil Gavaskar will be able to save this match even if he bats at both [the] ends.' – Lala Amarnath on Pak TV

Sunil was solid and stubborn, but quick to pounce on the slightest lapse. However, an innings defeat looked imminent until Maninder Singh dropped anchor. He helped his skipper ensure that the Pakistanis batted again. By then, Sunil had completed his hundred, his twenty-sixth in Test cricket. He did his best to farm the strike, but there was too much time left for the Pakistanis. When the final wicket fell, India were only nine runs ahead.

> It was a gutsy knock from a very gutsy man. – Imran Khan, *Mid-Day*, 9 January 1983

> The man sat with his head in his hands, staring pensively at the ground. He had just returned from the field with an unbeaten 127 against his name, a record of sorts . . . But there was no pleasure on his face. In a voice which he made sound as cool as he could, but still failing to conceal his dejection, he said, 'I don't know what has gone wrong with the Indian team . . .' – Ayaz Memon, *Cricketer Asia*, January 1984

Sunil was devastated by the defeat. He could not quite comprehend how a batting line-up as proficient as the one under him had floundered on a pitch that was flat, familiar, and friendly. That he had become the first Indian to carry his bat through a completed Test innings and drawn level with Sobers' tally of Test hundreds was hardly a consolation. Neither was Imran's comment that he would have traded his eleven wickets in the game for his counterpart's scalp in the second innings.

> There was nothing in the wicket, and what we required was application . . . I am too stunned to think of remedial measures. We might think of something over the next few days. – Sunil Gavaskar, *Mid-Day*, 9 January 1983

Sunil recovered his poise to make the point that the team needed to steer clear of a 'sour grapes' mentality, their issues with the umpiring notwithstanding. He accordingly issued a statement to the effect that the Tests were being played in magnificent spirit. It was a rejoinder to the criticism of the Pakistan umpiring by the Indian media, to which Imran had responded by inviting Indian umpires to stand in the remaining three Tests and see how Pakistan won again.

The Pakistan captain had not forgotten the abuse and ridicule that was heaped on him after the loss to India in 1979-80. He had been expected to pulverise the Indians then, but illness and then injury had come in his way. That hadn't prevented his compatriots from accusing him of ignoring cricket for nocturnal pursuits. Three years later, he was determined to obliterate those memories. His bowling figures of 11-180 and innings of 117 made him only the second all-rounder after Botham to score a hundred and take ten wickets in the same Test. In both the instances, the team at the receiving end was India.

The Indians went into the fourth Test at Hyderabad (Sind) after a four-wicket win against the North West Frontier Province Governor's XI. Srikkanth, who had led the chase on the final day, was inducted into the Test XI at Arunlal's expense, and Balwinder Sandhu, the Bombay seamer, was picked to make his debut. He replaced Madan Lal, whose heel injury had compounded India's bowling concerns. Pakistan were 60-0 when Sunil gave Kapil Dev a break after an eight-over spell from the northern end of the ground, and brought on Sandhu.

The debutant responded by dismissing Mohsin and Haroon Rashid off consecutive deliveries. The next wicket fell at 511. Mudassar Nazar and Javed Miandad's 451-run stand was the highest for any wicket in a Test, putting them on an even keel with the Australian duo of Bradman and Ponsford, who had added the same number against England at the Oval in 1934. The declaration was made early on the third day when the score was 581-3 and Miandad 85 short of the highest individual score in Tests, which was Sir Garry Sobers' 365. He was upset, but Imran would have none of it. There was a match and series to be won.

> Sunil Gavaskar seemed a beaten and battered general... He failed to inspire his army of men, who bowled mechanically and fielded lethargically... Pakistan has been the Waterloo for many Indians. It may well be the case with Gavaskar, who has shown little or no involvement with the team, except for achieving his personal ambition of toppling Bradman's record of 29 centuries.... – K.R. Wadhwaney, *The Indian Express*, 15 January 1983

The skipper's handling of Doshi was especially panned, as it had been during the previous Test.

> Doshi did not enjoy the confidence of his skipper, who almost humiliated him by the manner in which he handled him... Gavaskar also did not give the impression of being involved in the game whenever India was on the field... Doshi did not get the field he wanted... he was almost a mental wreck and thoroughly demoralised.' – R. Sriman, *TOI*, 23 January 1983.

A look at the scorecard of the Hyderabad Test indicates that Maninder bowled nine overs more than Doshi. But it also tells you that the junior left-arm spinner conceded less than 3 runs per over, while Doshi went for more than 3 per over. Against batting of that quality and on the deadest of wickets, did Sunil have any option, other than to go on the defensive?

Victory was out of the question, but India possessed the batting wherewithal to draw the game on what was essentially a flat track.

Srikkanth fell to Sarfraz with only eight on the board. In came Amarnath, who had been promoted to number three for obvious reasons. Sunil and he looked untroubled until Imran extracted late outswing from one that pitched on a length just outside the off-stump. It being in the corridor of uncertainty, Sunil had to play at it. The ball kissed his outside-edge and flew to Bari. Not for the first time, the floodgates opened after his dismissal.

In what was probably Imran's best spell of the series, considering that there was nothing in the track for him, he took six wickets at a cost of 35 runs with an assortment of in-swingers, in-dippers and the odd bouncer. The visitors would have struggled to reach 189 had Amarnath and debutant Sandhu not scored 61 and 71 respectively. Following on, Sunil (60) and Amarnath (64) added 125, but it wasn't enough. Viswanath (37) and Vengsarkar (58) only delayed the inevitable. The victory margin of an innings and 119 runs made it Pakistan's biggest win over India.

The series lost, the dispirited Indians would have liked to go home, but there were two more Tests to be played. In the rain-affected fifth Test at Lahore, the visitors could take heart from Kapil Dev's 8-85 in Pakistan's only innings, and Amarnath's second century of the series. Mudassar Nazar carried his bat for 152 after being dropped twice by Sunil in the slips. The game was attended by Gen Zia-ul-Haq, who presented Sunil and Vishwanath Rs 25,000 each for completing 7,000 Test runs and playing eighty-six consecutive Tests respectively. Viswanath had overtaken Sobers' world-record tally of eighty-five consecutive Tests at Hyderabad.

For the final Test at Karachi, Sunil made another attempt to fix the problem of opening by doing what he had done in England six months previously. He assigned the job to Ravi Shastri, despite the fact that the latter hadn't played a single game after injuring his bowling arm before the second Test. Shastri was told to take the three stitches between his left thumb and index finger off and get ready. All he needed to get into the groove technically, was a session in the nets against Madan Lal's replacement T.A. Sekhar. Temperamentally, he was always ready. He exceeded his captain's expectations by scoring a hundred, his first in Test cricket.

After I scored a hundred, Sunil said, 'When people who have played a lot more than you tell you something, you better listen to them.' – Ravi Shastri, *Mid-Day*, 14 March 1987

India batted for nearly two days to score 393 and Pakistan replied with 420-6, with Mudassar Nazar scoring his fourth hundred of the series. The final day of the series was an eventful one, with Imran taking two wickets to complete a record forty for the series, Amarnath completing yet another hundred, and the spectators raiding the arena when Sunil reached his fifty. It was not the first invasion in the game: members of a political outfit had raided the field the day before, ostensibly protesting against Pakistan's dictatorial regime. The players were not harmed, but the demonstrators and some spectators were, when the police brought their batons and teargas shells into operation.

There was more than one tensed face in the Indian dressing room when Sunil was mobbed. When the crowd showed no signs of dispersing, Imran took matters into his own hands, literally. He uprooted a stump and shooed the spectators away!

Sunil reached 67 before Imran breached his defences for the second time in the series. It was an ironic mode of dismissal, in that India's slide in the series had started when Sunil first fell to his counterpart in that fashion at the same venue a few weeks previously. An interesting feature of Sunil's final innings of the series was his employment of a stroke that not many people had seen him play for a long time. He hooked Sarfraz twice. Sunil had in fact exercised the stroke in the first innings off seamer Tahir Naqqash, but had only got a top-edge that was held by Bari. However, there was nothing wrong with his hooking in the second innings.

Pakistan's 3-0 win concealed the fact that without Imran, the Pakistani bowlers would have struggled as much as their Indian counterparts. Kapil Dev had taken 24 wickets, but this particular duel between two all-rounders had ended with a comprehensive win for Pakistan.

'By the time India came to Pakistan, we had had a reasonably good tour of England, and shortly prior to the Indian team's arrival, we had beaten Australia 3-0 at home. All the batsmen were in top nick, and Imran was in his prime. He was at his best in this series. India, I thought, came with just plan A, and when things did not go well, they did not change gears. For instance, in my case, Kapil had dismissed me frequently on the leg-side in the 1979-80 series, and despite not being able to disturb me, they persisted with the same tactics. I felt that Kapil with his natural late outswinger, would have been better off had he attacked me on my off-stump.' – Mudassar Nazar

The only Indian skipper who impressed me was Sunil Gavaskar, mainly because of his extensive knowledge of the game. People talk about Mike Brearley as the outstanding cricket brain, but I think that Gavaskar lost nothing by comparison. He was a very sound captain, and had to cope with the knowledge that often his only hope was to draw matches, because India's bowling attack was not good enough to bowl the other side out twice. – Imran Khan, *All Round View* (Chatto and Windus, 1988)

Sunil had done his best as skipper, on and off the field. At one of the many official dinners that the team attended, Gaekwad introduced the captain to an eminent Pakistani lady. Her reaction was standoffish. 'I only know Imran Khan,' she said. Gaekwad, a little flustered, then introduced the lady to his skipper. 'She is Mallika-e-Tarannum[7] Noor Jehan,' he said. Sunil's response was prompt: 'I only know Lata Mangeshkar!'

Although he went out of his way to attribute the loss to purely cricketing factors, the fact was that he was being diplomatic. On the field, he had drawn the attention of the umpires to Sarfraz's blatant overstepping of the popping crease at Faisalabad, and had even spoken to Imran about it. Sandhu had done likewise while batting at Hyderabad. Some members of the Indian team were convinced that there had been some foul play.

It is no secret that the Pakistani bowlers have always been under a cloud when it comes to tampering with the ball. Sarfraz Nawaz, reportedly, was a master in this subject. During India's tour of Pakistan in 1982-83, we found that the Pakistani pacemen were

---

[7]Empress of Melody

achieving prodigious swing after forty or fifty overs. The amount of movement they were able to get was abnormal. We were told later that bottle-tops were being brought into the ground during the drinks break, and that some of the Pakistani bowlers even kept them in their pockets for later use! – K. Srikkanth, *The Hindu*, 24 May 2003

Imran's revelation a decade later that he had once used a bottle-top to rough up the ball during a County game for Sussex, only added fuel to the fire.

There has been talk about naming the (India-Pakistan) series after Kapil Dev and Imran. But to me, personally, Kapil will always be the greater cricketer of the two. Simply because he never tampered with the ball; he always played fair. – B.S. Sandhu, *Rediff.com*, 10 March 2004

Back in 1982-83, the Indian team did not go out of its way to protest. Had it done so, the series would have degenerated into one of squabbles and ugly on-field confrontations. The captain kept his cool despite the defeats and resultant pressure, and got his players to do the same. The conduct of the skipper and his players left no one in any doubt that they saw themselves as 'sporting ambassadors' of their nation. It was Sunil who ensured that the Indian team did not do in 1982-83 what the Pakistanis did at Bangalore four years later.

'I remember the respect he commanded within the team as well as the Pakistani players and the people of Pakistan, including President Zia-ul-Haq, who was genuinely fond of him.' – Dr Vishwas Raut

The likes of Sandeep Patil did their bit to revitalise the spirits of their team-mates in a country where there weren't many entertainment options. When Yashpal Sharma went to the Lahore airport to receive his newly-wedded wife, Patil decided to play a prank on the couple. He got his team-mates to take turns to pay courtesy visits to Sharma's room, the idea being to deny the couple the privacy desired! Sharma himself was no hapless victim. The team's only source of entertainment in most of the hotels was a TV-Video room. Sharma seized control of the VCR early on the tour, and insisted on playing *Kranti*, a Hindi potboiler, over and over again. Fed up with the repeated screenings, Shastri and Patil then connived to steal the cassette.

Relations between the players of both sides were excellent. There were quite a few occasions when the Indian batsmen found themselves in splits, either due to the never-ending conversation between close-in fielders Miandad and Mudassar, or because of the constant bickering between members of the opposing side. It was one of those rare instances wherein a fielding team, comprising as it did three former captains, the same number of vice-captains and the odd wannabe captain, sledged itself and not the opposition. Only a forceful character like Imran could have kept such a team united in its quest for victory.

With the tour of the Caribbean only a few days away, the Indian players were eager to reach home and get as much rest as they possibly could. Those from the north had accordingly decided to fly to Lahore from Karachi and cross the Wagah Border by road.

> I knew I was not going to be the captain for the West Indies tour on the rest day of the Karachi Test . . . That was the day I learnt that Kapil Dev had cancelled his plans of returning to India by the Wagah Border and instead decided to come to Bombay with the team. – Sunil Gavaskar, *Sportsweek*, 23 February 1983

What happened to Bedi in 1978-79, and what would have happened to Asif Iqbal in 1979-80 had he not pre-empted the move and retired, happened to Sunil in January 1983. His conduct on the tour, and reluctance to offer excuses for the defeat, could not, in the eyes of the selectors and the public, overshadow the fact that he had committed the cardinal sin—losing to the old enemy.

16

A PIPE DREAM COMES TRUE

Although he did not say as much, Sunil was hurt at being sacked after just one poor series. His record as captain, eight wins, six defeats and twenty-six draws was, by Indian standards, outstanding. But memories of Indian cricket lovers being notoriously short, all they could see was the defeat in Pakistan. They ignored the fact that he had scored more runs in the series (434) than any other Indian save Amarnath. They also overlooked Imran Khan's bowling.

The Pakistani skipper's elation at achieving his objective had been dampened by a painful left shin. There was later found to be a crack in the shin-bone, which very nearly ended his international career.

Kapil Dev was Sunil's obvious successor. Not many dissenting voices were heard against the decision to blood a captain against the most formidable opponents in the world, that too on their own pitches. Not only had Kapil Dev replaced Sunil as skipper, but he had also taken over his mantle as the blue-eyed boy of the media and the masses.

The desire to win matches for their team and country apart, there was little the two individuals had in common. While Sunil's approach to cricket was calculative, Kapil Dev's was instinctive. The media would subsequently anoint the duo as defensive and aggressive respectively, despite there being conclusive proof that Sunil could be as attacking in his methods as anybody else. Melbourne in 1980-81 was a case in point.

Mohinder Amarnath's 584 runs in Pakistan at an average of 73 made him the new bulwark of the Indian middle order. The man who held that title for nearly fifteen years wasn't forgiven for letting that Imran in-dipper hit his stumps on Christmas day in Karachi. Gundappa Viswanath, India's premier match-winner of the 1970s, was axed. The fact that he had suffered from some questionable umpiring decisions was not considered.

However, not too many tears were shed, for his fans believed that he would return after a break, which they reckoned he needed after the horrors of the Pakistan tour. Sandeep Patil took the Caribbean tour off to tend to his shoulder. Another conspicuous absentee was Doshi. He had been left out of the last two Tests in Pakistan on account of poor form, and in a way, expected the sack. The man who he believed hadn't supported him in Pakistan, was part of the team of course, as an ordinary player.

Sunil's presence in the squad confounded those who had tried hard to convince the world that he was a coward. *The Indian Express* on 14 December 1982 had reported an announcement by Mr Kanmadikar, the BCCI Secretary, that Sunil was available for the West Indian tour. A line that was not attributed to the secretary, and was the paper's own, was that NKP Salve, then president of the Board, had had a pep-talk with Sunil and convinced him to tour. For the person in question, however, touring the West Indies was never an issue.

> I started my career there twelve years ago and so I have fond memories of the place. I think all the doubting Thomases must be disappointed that I am actually going to the West Indies. All their preconceived ideas have come to nought. – Sunil Gavaskar, *Sportsweek*, 23 February 1983

However, not many people were falling over each other to back him. Criticising Sunil was in vogue, a far cry from the highs of the mid-and late-1970s. No one bothered to appreciate the situation he found himself in, and his attempts to come to terms with it. It could not have been easy to be demoted for just one major failure as skipper and then asked to play under someone who was ten years junior, however meritorious he may have been.

> There were some people who bucked the trend.
>
> He played in Pakistan (first Test) with a bad cold and sore throat . . . and yet, they sneer at him . . . They thought Gavaskar was too keen to maintain his record, which may be demolished by Lloyd's men. He had declined to tour two years ago, for he had played more than he could. And yet, we call him a coward and a traitor. No one in Australia ever used these adjectives about Greg Chappell, who has not been touring abroad for some seasons, and Australia has been drubbed both in England and Pakistan . . . Did not Botham say last year that he was surprised when Gavaskar returned undefeated in Calcutta and was not given a standing ovation! Botham believed it was a match-saving innings, and we thought that Gavaskar was downright negative and robbed India of an exciting victory . . . We want our heroes to walk six inches above the turf. If they don't, we want to see them buried beneath it. They appreciate Gavaskar's value in Pakistan. In India, we suspect he may still not be going to the West Indies. Do you deserve us, Sunil? – Prakash Joshi, *The Indian Express*, 16 February 1983

The Board accepted Sunil's request to join the team in the Caribbean a week after its departure, as he had to sign some business-related documents in Bombay and Pune. He had by this time started using a pair of lightweight boots and leg-guards, both of which enabled him to be quick on his feet. He would unveil another unique accessory in the second half of 1983, a seminal year for Indian cricket.

> 'The Indian team played a practice game against a Bombay side before its departure to the Caribbean. SMG opened the batting for India. In fact, I made my debut for Bombay that season. I had bowled to him in the nets earlier, and he had christened me "Veda[8] Thomson". I was going through the paces in this practice match, when Ashok Mankad, who was leading Bombay, walked up and told me to let it rip. I was surprised, because it was a practice game after all. But I then went at full-tilt and bowled

---

[8]Mad.

a few bouncers, all of which SMG negotiated with ease. Most importantly, he did not reproach me for bowling short stuff on the eve of the tour. He even acknowledged some of the deliveries.'
– Raju Kulkarni

His fans hoped that Sunil would forget the events of the recent past and start afresh on the arenas where it had all begun in 1971. The team's first port of call was Kingston, Jamaica, whose residents Sunil had panned in *Sunny Days*.

Both sides matched each other wicket for wicket in the first innings. The quadrangular pace battery laid the Indians low for 251, but the Indian bowlers hit back to concede a slim 3-run lead. Most interesting were the happenings that preceded the dismissal of the West Indian skipper Clive Lloyd. Soon after he had arrived at the crease, India's debutant captain was accosted by the seniormost member of his team. The thirty-eight-year-old Venkataraghvan, a surprise selection for the trip, expressed his desire to bowl to Lloyd. But Kapil Dev wasn't all that keen. It was the cricketing equivalent of waving a red rag at a bull.

Venkataraghvan's disposition hadn't changed much since he had given Sunil a dressing down for trying to shield him in the Caribbean in 1970-71. He was as respected for his craft and physical fitness as he was feared for his temper. On Venkataraghvan's tour of England in 1979, Kapil Dev, then a gangling twenty-year-old, had been so petrified of the skipper that he dared not request him for a break, even from a side game. It was only when Bedi spoke to the captain on his behalf that the 'boy' got a break. Four years subsequently, Kapil Dev was in charge, and while he held Venkataraghvan in high esteem, he did not see any reason to bring him on just because the latter felt like bowling to a particular batsman.

Finally, the expected happened. Venkat waited and watched till he ran out of patience. He strode towards his skipper and all but snatched the ball from him, reiterating all the while that Lloyd was his man. Kapil relented, and sure enough, the veteran bowled Lloyd with a gem of a delivery!

A draw seemed imminent when India were 167-6 in the second innings at tea on the final day. But Andy Roberts took the last four wickets after the interval in next to no time, and left his batsmen 172 to win in thirty minutes and twenty mandatory overs. They made it off the first ball of the last over, thanks to a breathtaking 61 by Viv Richards. Kapil Dev was panned for introducing Amarnath into the attack at a critical stage of the chase, after Venkataraghvan had done a decent containing job.

India's cause wasn't helped by the failure of its most experienced batsman. Sunil made 20 and 0.

The visitors then flew to Trinidad, where a warm welcome awaited them. His devotees expected the world from Sunil, but they were in for a disappointment. In the three-day game against the island nation, Sunil was criticised for asking the umpires to adjudicate on a caught-behind call. The officials ruled in his favour, only for him to lose his wicket to an injudicious shot.

> I can well see the need for a batsman, who has so often carried the burden of a side, to let himself go, especially in a match where there is not much at stake, as it was in the game against Trinidad . . . But the facts are that India's superstar is in need of repairing the rather distorted image that he now presents to followers of the game, here and abroad. – K.N. Prabhu, *Cricketer Asia*, May 1983

When asked by a journalist to comment on Sunil's dismissal, Kapil Dev said that his predecessor had let his fans down.

That one statement laid the foundation for one of Indian cricket's deepest rifts, or the ultimate media myth, depending on the version one chooses to believe. Reports were sent back to India to the effect that Sunil had been severely ticked off by his successor for throwing away his wicket.

Sunil's fans hoped for the best in the Test, but to their mortification, he scored only one in the first innings. One of his fans was unfazed. He laid a bet with a fellow spectator that the entire West Indies top order would not outscore his idol.

His optimism was not misplaced. Shortly after the Indians had been bowled out for 175, Sandhu dismissed Greenidge and Haynes, and Kapil Dev sent back Richards, with only 1 run on the board! The left-handers Lloyd and Gomes then added 237, and the lower-order batsmen made useful contributions. The outcome was a hefty lead of 219. Sunil fared much better in the second innings with a knock of 32. Hundreds by Amarnath and Kapil Dev ensured a draw.

It all came together for Sunil when the Indians flew to Guyana. By this time, the married members of the team had been joined by their better-halves. Sunil's resolve to reverse his poor run resulted in his taking a key decision.

On 29 March 1983, the teams boarded helicopters to travel to the Albion Sports Complex in Berbice for the second of the three One Day Internationals. The Windies had won the first.

Batting first, India were given a sound beginning by the mentor and protégé. Sunil got going with a flicked boundary off Holding in the second over. He was determined not to let the bowlers dictate terms. The method he adopted to achieve this end was entirely unexpected. When Roberts tested him with a bouncer, Sunil brought the hook shot out of cold storage, like he had done at Karachi, and dispatched him to the fence. Malcolm Marshall, who had come a long way since his debut in 1978-79, was subjected to the same treatment a little later.

Sunil's confidence rubbed off on his partner Shastri, and excited the spectators. They could not get enough of a short-arm pull off Marshall that went like a rocket to the fence.

A significant component of the 93-run opening stand with Shastri was the electric running between the wickets. Shastri was caught behind off Marshall for 39, and in came Amarnath, who along with Sunil, milked the slow men Richards and Gomes. The batsmen rotated the strike superbly, and did a lot to confound backers of sledgehammer batsmanship in limited-overs cricket. The thirty-plus duo batted on merit, and proved that adherence to the basics could be as effective in limited-overs cricket as in its traditional counterpart.

Amarnath contributed 30 to a stand of 59 before being stumped off Richards. A score of 152-2 with more than twenty overs left was just the platform the skipper needed. Kapil Dev promoted himself to number four and went for his shots. Sunil was happy to play second fiddle and watch the carnage from a distance of twenty-two yards. The score had reached 224-2, and Sunil was ten short of a hundred, when he called his captain for a leg-bye. Going by the manner in which he had run throughout his innings, it should have been a cakewalk. But Jeffrey Dujon, the West Indian keeper, was quicker on this occasion. His underarm flick dislodged the bails before Sunil could make his ground.

Sunil left the ground to a rapturous ovation, with a couple of fans escorting him into the pavilion. There was more entertainment in store for the spectators. Kapil Dev's 72 off thirty-eight balls enabled India to finish with 282-5. The visitors then bowled superbly and fielded splendidly to do the unthinkable, winning by 27 runs.

Sunil carried his form into the Test, which like all Georgetown games, was plagued by rain. The fate of the match was sealed when there was no play on the second and the fourth day. The West Indies batted first and scored 470.

Aunshuman Gaekwad, recalled as Sunil's opening partner for the Tests, scored 8 before edging Holding to Dujon. Amarnath looked good until he was devoured in the slips by Richards off Marshall. At the other end, Sunil was outstanding. Glides, deflections, rock-solid defence and of course, flowing drives—there was not one component of his repertoire that he did not display. Even the hook was on show. The relative slowness of the track may well have played a part in prompting him to essay that stroke, but whatever was the reason, he showed at Georgetown, as he had at Berbice, that he was open to modifying his approach if the situation demanded it. The West Indian bowlers were not giving him or his team-mates too many deliveries to drive in any case. Their stock delivery was short-pitched, and one could either keep ducking or evading them. To get runs, it was imperative to take them on.

Marshall was the one bowler who had troubled the Indians the most in the series, with his propensity to go around the wicket and dig it in short, angling it across the right-handers. Lloyd had left a gap on the off-side, inviting the batsmen to cut. The slanting deliveries apart, Marshall owned a delivery that tended to climb onto the batsman. It was a lethal variation, as Yashpal Sharma had discovered at Port of Spain. He had been hit on the head and concussed.

Sunil had moved to 44 when Marshall induced him to nick one to Gordon Greenidge in the slips. But the catch was spilt. Marshall's reaction was to bowl a fuller delivery, which Sunil drove straight for four. It was too much for the paceman to take.

The first ball of his next over was short and swift. It pitched in line with Sunil's body, rose and flew. Sunil's initial reaction was to watch the ball all the way, but this one was too quick for him. It hit him on the left side of his head. Since he was wearing only a hat, his brain wobbled at the impact. The West Indian fielders rushed towards him. What they and the crowd saw was a batsman who was dazed, but was not showing it.

Veteran journalist Dicky Rutnagur, who was part of the radio commentary team, did not hide his shock. 'I have seen him since 1971 and I cannot remember him getting hit on the head,' he said.

Meanwhile, Sunil held his head with both hands, then adjusted his hat, wiped the sweat off his forehead, and, as the fielders dispersed, practised a forward defensive stroke. All this, he did without removing his hat. A flick to mid-wicket in the same over gave him his first fifty of the series, and he then settled all doubts about his well-being with the shot of the innings—a square-cut that went past gully for 4.

Sanjay Karhade, who compiled an anthology of writings on the Little Master in the early 1990s, recounted the queer situation that Kiran More, the reserve wicketkeeper of that Indian team, found himself in shortly after Sunil had been struck on the head. He quotes More as follows:

> Being the junior-most in the team, I was thrust with an ice bucket and ordered to go onto the ground. I didn't have a choice, in fact I was happy! For I had got an opportunity to serve my idol. Without wasting any time, I strode onto the field and all of a sudden I heard a few choicest of Marathi abuses. I was surprised, looked here and there and wondered as to who is it in the West Indies with that perfect pronunciation and slang. Not before long, I discovered that it was no one else, but, Gavaskar, my idol, who was trying to get me out of the ground. Caught halfway between the tent and the icon, I didn't know where to go. Ultimately, another one came from Sunil and I decided to be loyal to him! I went back. Ten minutes later, it was lunch time. Sunil caught me by my arm and pulled me before the entire team and started shouting, 'Who the hell asked this boy to come onto the ground with ice? I had not asked for help. I am toiling hard

out there, wanting to show them that we are not soft guys, we won't give in easily and that we take a lot of pride in representing the country, and you are sending unsolicited help? Whoever it may be, he should take the first flight back to India if he can't take a blow or two for his country . . .' By then, my arm, in the clutches of Sunil, was in pain. Sunil went on and on for the entire lunch break without removing any of his gear and without having lunch. Obviously, no one else dared to [have] lunch too!'- Kiran More, as quoted in 'The Day Gavaskar Was Hit On the Head' Sanjay Karhade, Cricketnext.com, 11 July 2003

Sunil began the post-lunch session with a straight-drive that sped past Roberts on his follow-through for four. As magnificent as his scoring strokes was a stab to keep a Holding bouncer down. He loosened his grip and withdrew his bottom hand from the handle at the moment of impact, and the ball dropped down dead. He reached three figures with a cut off the off-spinner Larry Gomes. It was his twenty-seventh Test hundred, which meant that he had crossed Sobers' tally of twenty-six, and was only two behind the Don himself. He had moved to 147 by the time a halt was called.

The innings was a shot in the arm for him and his team-mates before the next Test, which was to be played on a spiteful strip at the Kensington Oval in Bridgetown, Barbados.

The Test duly followed the script that had been penned by the staff that shaped the strip. The West Indies won by ten wickets and took the series, but not before India's comeback man scripted a saga of grit and resilience.

'The Eye of the Tiger', the signature tune of Sylvester Stallone's *Rocky*, had been Mohinder Amarnath's companion during his years in the wilderness. In the 1982-83 season, he was in the process of sculpting a comeback that was no less spectacular than the one made by *Rocky Balboa* in the third instalment of the series, which had been released a few months before the Pakistan tour. Amarnath had made a habit of listening to the tune over and over again as he trained and psyched himself before the season started.

At the Kensington Oval, he put together a stunner of a performance.

His 91 in the first innings helped India reach 209. The West Indians then benefited from some pedestrian bowling and catching to reach 486. Against Holding, Roberts, Garner and Marshall, an Indian surrender seemed only a few overs away.

When he arrived at the wicket after the openers had put on 61, Amarnath repeated the mantra he had concocted for himself: 'If the line of the ball is over my left shoulder, I will hook. If it is over my right, I will leave. Left, hook. Right, leave. . . .'

Pundits claimed that his open stance had put him in the ideal position to essay horizontal-bat strokes like the hook and cut. Whatever the reason, the strokes in question still had to be essayed against bowling of that pace and quality. Not for the first time on the tour, Amarnath did just that. He was going great guns until Marshall unleashed a flier. The ball rammed him in the face, brought out lakes of blood, and a couple of teeth. Amarnath had to retire hurt.

The first thing he did after undergoing repairs was to wash his blood-stained shirt. He wanted to wear it when he resumed battle the next day. When Shastri fell the following morning, Amarnath returned to take guard against the man who had injured him on the previous day. Sympathy was never one of Malcolm Marshall's attributes on a cricket field. He steamed in and banged the ball in short. Amarnath saw it early, went onto the back foot, and hooked it off his eyebrows for four. A delay of even a fraction of a second, and he would have sustained another serious injury. It was stirring stuff.

Amarnath's 80 saved India from an innings defeat, but the West Indies needed only one to win. Kirmani discarded his leg-guards and gauntlets to do a Michael Holding. He did his best to impersonate the paceman's smooth run, but overstepped the crease. The umpire signalled a no-ball and the Windies won.

The final Test at St. John's, Antigua, ended in a high-scoring draw. Gordon Greenidge retired after scoring 154 to rush home to be with his daughter Rea, who passed away a few days later. Haynes scored 136, and Dujon and Lloyd also got hundreds. On the Indian side, Vengsarkar got 94 and Shastri 102 in the first innings. Amarnath scored 116 in the second innings to finish the series with 598 runs at an average of 66.44. It meant that he had scored 1,182 runs from eleven Tests in 1982-83. The West Indians' endorsement of Imran Khan's pronouncement that he was the world's best batsman against pace said it all.

A 0-2 loss in a five-Test series against the West Indies wasn't exactly a disaster, considering the horrors Australia and England underwent on tours of the Caribbean in the mid-1980s. In his tour report, Manager Hanumant Singh mentioned the manner in which the players had bonded with each other and also how even under immense pressure had played like a team.

However, not everything was hunky-dory. A junior member of the team did not endear himself to his team-mates by displaying an aversion for taking the field even in the island games. This individual made a habit of avoiding the captain's gaze whenever the XI was chosen. As far as he was concerned, it was better to be a king in the Ranji Trophy than run the risk of getting hit by the West Indian fast bowlers.

The highs of Guyana apart, it had been a forgettable tour for Sunil. Scores of 20, 0, 1 and 32 before the Georgetown Test, and 2, 19, 18 and 1 after it, did him no credit.

Was he unable to rise to the heights of 1970-71 and 1975-76 because he was still hurt over the captaincy affair, despite having made all the right noises in public? Or was it that his reflexes were no longer as sharp as they were back then? Was it that the West Indies fast bowlers were on song, and therefore adept at capitalising on the slightest lapse, technical or mental? Or was it that he was going through a bad patch? The actual reason was a combination of all the four factors.

Sunil was now thirty-three. It made little sense to expect his concentration and reflexes to be what they were in his twenties. There was also the fact that the events of the preceding few years, starting from the 1980-81 tour of Australia, had taken a lot out of him. He wasn't enjoying the game as much as he had earlier. After battling the torchbearers of cricket's pace age for years, he was finally feeling the strain.

The pacemen had also made it a point to be at his throat throughout the series. It was in line with their stated policy of targeting the premier player in the opposition ranks. That, however, did not prevent Sunil from displaying an almost forgotten aspect of his batsmanship. A notable aspect of his knocks at Berbice and Guyana was the number of attacking strokes he essayed, especially those played with a horizontal bat.

Considering the proclivity of the Indian public to kick a man when he was down, it was hardly surprising that there was talk of his being dropped when three former Test captains and two former Test cricketers met to pick the fourteen-man squad for the third edition of the World Cup.

Messrs Chandrakant Borde (chairman), Chandrakant Sarwate, Bishan Bedi, Pankaj Roy and Hanumant Singh, members of the Selection Committee, fairly excelled themselves. The batting line-up they chose was a mix of strokemakers, grafters and adapters. Srikkanth and Patil were recalled, and Vengsarkar and Sharma kept their places. Sunil was retained to lend solidity to the top order, and Amarnath rewarded with the vice-captaincy. There were two spinners, both of whom could bat—Kirti Azad and Ravi Shastri. In fact, the side had a cluster of all-rounders; Roger Binny, Madan Lal, Kirmani, Sandhu, Shastri, Azad and Amarnath. Towering over them was the captain.

Nobody, not even their own compatriots, expected anything from the Indians. Kimberley Hughes, the captain of Australia, was an exception, in that he described Kapil Dev's side as the dark horse of the tournament. The players were only too happy not to be under any sort of pressure. It helped that the men who constituted the core of the side had been playing, travelling and staying together for the last six months and more. Every player knew what made his team-mates tick. The wives of the married members of the side were also there, giving the team the look of a harmonious Indian joint family.

At least three members of the side—Kapil Dev, Amarnath and Shastri—were hopeful of making it to the semi-finals. It wasn't going to be easy, given that they were in the same Group as Australia and the West Indies.

The team commenced its World Cup campaign with a meeting in their bus, en route from London to Manchester, the venue of their opening clash against the defending champions.

Yashpal Sharma's 89 helped India reach 262-8 from the allotted sixty overs. The players then took the field, reminding themselves of Berbice, and the fact that the West Indies were not invincible. Incisive bowling and smart fielding ensured the decline of Lloyd's team at 157-9. The Indian supporters had all but begun the celebrations when the last pair of Roberts and Garner staged a momentous recovery. They went for their shots and got their team back into the match. With 35 required from 36 balls, Sunil suggested to Kapil Dev that Shastri, who had earlier been punished by the tail enders, be brought back. The skipper agreed, and the left-armer had Garner stumped off his first ball.

It was the West Indies' first defeat in a World Cup game.

A six-wicket win over Zimbabwe took India to the top of its group. The players were confidence personified on the eve of the clash against Australia. The proceedings were anti climactic, with Australia winning by 162 runs. Two days later, India lost to the West Indies at the Oval by 66 runs. It was the 1980-81 tri-series in Australia all over again, in that the Indians were running out of steam after gaining a headstart.

A notable feature of both defeats was the absence of the ex-captain. Sunil had done little of note in the wins over the West Indies and Zimbabwe. His fitness concerns on the eve of the Australia game gave the think-tank the opportunity to play Shastri as an opener. They stuck to the same combination against the Windies as well.

'....From all available evidence, there does exist in the upper echelons of Indian cricket, a mafia, which has issued a contract to spell finish to the cricketing career of Sunil Gavaskar ... The conspirators, having succeeded in removing Gavaskar from the captaincy, have now sworn that they will not rest until the illustrious batsman is sent packing ... The writing is on the wall. Gavaskar had better watch out. He was dropped under instructions from back home ... The saner elements in the cricket control board must immediately unite to frustrate the despicable designs of the game's Rasputins.' – Khalid Ansari, *Mid-Day*, 19 June 1983

With two defeats after two wins, the Indians were back to square one. Their fifth game, against Zimbabwe at the Nevill Ground in Tunbridge Wells in the county of Kent, was a must-win affair.

Sunil was knocking up on the outfield when Kapil Dev decided to pick him in the XI ahead of Vengsarkar, who had been hit on the mouth by Marshall at the Oval. Kapil Dev told P.R. Mansingh, the Administrative Manager of the team, that he would inform Sunil about his inclusion. However, he forgot, probably because of his keenness to win the toss. The Indians had studied the run-rates before the game and concluded that a score of 300-plus would enhance their chances of a semi-final berth. What they did not take into account in the bargain was that the strip had a lot of juice in it.

It was only after the toss had been completed and Kapil Dev won it that he informed his predecessor. It did not quite fit in with Sunil's methods of preparation for a game. He did not hide his displeasure. P. R. Mansingh then entered the fray and placated him in the dressing room.

Sunil opened with Srikkanth, and fell to Peter Rawson, Zimbabwe's spearhead, for a duck off the last ball of the first over. He was soon joined by Srikkanth, Amarnath, Patil and Sharma. When the fifth wicket fell with only seventeen on the board, it seemed certain that it was raining troubles for India. Kapil Dev dropped anchor and took the team through to the mid-innings lunch interval. India at that point were 106-7 and the captain was batting on 50.

What happened after the interval is part of cricketing folklore.

It wasn't as if Kapil Dev waged a lone battle to score an unbeaten 175, inclusive of sixteen boundaries and six sixes. He was aided by the likes of Binny, Madan Lal and finally Kirmani, who dropped anchor at one end, and had the best view of the greatest limited-overs innings ever. The others also did their bit, by remaining glued to the positions they were in when he began his innings! Sunil was leaning against the bar counter, Sharma was sitting with folded feet, and Bob, the bus driver, was standing with a leg on a chair. The wives' brigade did their bit, skipping lunch to bring the team luck.

India finished with 266-9 and ended up winning by 31 runs. Their next game against Australia was a veritable quarter-final. After every player except number-one Sunil and number-eleven Sandhu had entered double figures and ensured a score of 247, Binny and Madan Lal displayed their love for the English conditions by making the ball swing and swerve. They weren't express bowlers by any stretch of the imagination, but they did know how to exploit damp strips and overcast

BREAKING THE ULTIMATE BARRIER

7 MARCH 1987, AHMEDABAD – SMG late-cuts Ijaz Faqih (not in picture) and sets off for his 10,000th run in Test cricket.

The spectators take over.

With Hemant Waingankar. Alongside them is Kenia Jayantilal, former India Test cricketer.

Sunil Gavaskar with his wife Marshneil in the mid-1980s.

WITH THE LEGENDS

Sir Garry Sobers, the ultimate cricketer.

Sir Vivian Richards, the Master Blaster.

MISCELLANIOUS

Testing his percussion skills in the company of former Pakistani captain Ramiz Raja.

Doing a Pele at a charity event.

Leading India in a Veterans' tournament at Sharjah in 1995-96.

With Lala Amarnath.

With Rahul Dravid during his stint as 'Batting Consultant' of the Indian team at the start of the 2004-05 season.

The second father-son combination to represent India in One-Day International.

GENERATION-NEXT

SMG welcomes Sachin Tendulkar to the '34 Test hundreds' club in Dhaka, 2004-05.

Queen's Park Oval at Port of Spain in Trinidad happens to be the home ground of the individual on the left, and the favourite venue of the individual on the right.

...AND COLLEAGUES

The TV commentary team for the 1996 World Cup. (from left) Ian Chappell, Ravi Shastri, Tony Greig, Richie Benaud, Michael Holding, Mark Mascarenhas and SMG.

The Caribbean and Karnataka – (from left) Sir Vivian Richards, Roger Binny, B.S. Chandrasekhar, Gundappa Viswanath, SMG and Erapalli Prasanna.

Opponents, Contemporaries...

With Clive Lloyd, his successor as chairman of the ICC's Cricket Committee.

Team-mates in 1971-72, opponents in 1972-73, 1974 and 1976-77, and fellow commentators several years later . . . with Tony Greig.

With Geoffrey Boycott, whose record he broke to become the highest scorer in Test cricket.

Four skippers – (from left) Ajit Wadekar, Asif Iqbal, SMG and Clive Lloyd.

The shoot of 'Beyond the Boundary' – 'Host' SMG with badminton great Prakash Padukone, billiards ace Geet Sethi and cricketing contemporary Mohinder Amarnath.

Being sworn in as Sheriff of Mumbai by His Excellency P.C. Alexander, then Governor of Maharashtra.

PMG, Sunny Sports & Sheriff

The 'Sunny Sports' and 'PMG' think-tank at SMG's fiftieth birthday celebrations. From left: Shubhangi Kulkarni, Arti Mehta, Raju Mehta, SMG, Marshneil Gavaskar, Sumedh Shah and Meera Shah.

With Sumedh Shah on the sets of 'Sunil Gavaskar Presents . . .'

Presenting the Filmfare Lifetime Achievement Award to Amitabh Bachchan in 1991.

KINDRED SOULS – *With Sir Don Bradman in 1986.*

With Ian Chappell, opponent-turned-colleague.

The two legends pose with Test cricket's premier prize of the modern era- the Border-Gavaskar Trophy.

India's Cricketer – Emeritus.

With Indian cine-star Hrithik Roshan.

After his felicitation at the BCCI's celebrations of the Golden Jubilee of India's independence.

conditions. They shared eight wickets, thus sealing Australia's demise for 129 and confirming India's first ever semi-final foray in a World Cup.

The delighted Indians were slightly chastened when a communication-gap between the captain and his predecessor came to the fore in a team meeting prior to the semi-final. Kapil Dev at one point exhorted Sunil to put his head down and get his game together. From the captain's point of view, what he had said was nothing but an attempt to boost the confidence of a team-mate. But Sunil was upset. He proceeded to tell P. R. Mansingh that the management was welcome to drop him if they felt that he was not trying. Kapil Dev felt that he had been misunderstood because of his inability to communicate in fluent English.

> If a senior player wants to be difficult, he can make life very hard for the team. . . . A world-class player can make things even more difficult . . . I did not wish to be upset by anything that happened. In fact, I told Sunny: 'I am prepared to apologise to you in front of the whole team if you have misunderstood me or if I have caused you hurt.' I have always been willing to do anything in order to help the team cause. – Kapil Dev, *Cricket My Style* (Allied Publishers, 1987)

The matter was forgotten as the Indians readied for the most important One Day International of their lives.

England, the hosts and 1979 World Cup runners-up, won the toss, batted, and looked in control until Binny dismissed the openers. Then followed some canny strategising by Kapil Dev. He asked Amarnath and Azad, both of whom were fifth bowling options, to operate in tandem 'till they got hit'. They ended up bowling 24 overs between them, in which they conceded only 55 runs, took three wickets, exclusive of a run-out, and turned the tide in their team's favour.

With only 213 on the board, England went flat out for an early breakthrough, only to be thwarted by the Indian openers. Srikkanth went after the bowling and Sunil put his head down to compile his most substantial innings of the competition. They put on 46 before Sunil nicked seamer Paul Allott to the keeper. Four runs later, Srikkanth fell to an impetuous stroke off Botham. But a score of 50-2 was just the platform the in-form duo of Amarnath and Sharma needed. What they started, Sandeep Patil completed with an audacious 51.

Thousands of miles away, millions of Indians were incredulous. Was it really their team that was within one step of the summit? For the first time since their arrival in England, the players felt some pressure, as they arrived in London to try and prevent Clive Lloyd's men from completing a treble of World Cup triumphs at the Mecca of the sport – Lord's. Some of the tension was dispelled by the announcement of N.K.P. Salve, the BCCI president, that every player would receive a cash prize of Rs 25,000, regardless of the outcome.

History, it appeared, was on India's side. The final was to be played on 25 June, on what was the fifty-first anniversary of India's inaugural Test match at the same venue.

Lloyd won the toss and elected to bowl on a lively pitch. The Indians started disastrously. Sunil edged Roberts to Dujon with only two runs on the board. Srikkanth and Amarnath had just about stabilised the innings when both fell one after the other. Sharma and Kapil Dev holed out to Gomes, and when the scoreboard read 111-6, the British media cursed its team for losing the semi-finals and thereby making the final a one-sided affair. Madan Lal, Kirmani and Sandhu then exhibited some enterprise, and ensured that the Windies would have to score at slightly over three an over to win.

The Indian dressing room wore a desolate look moments before they went out. They had to be reminded by their captain that they had absolutely nothing to lose. 'We have done it twice, we can do it again. *Chalo Jawaanon, ladenge* (c'mon soldiers, let's fight!),' Kapil Dev proclaimed. His words had the desired effect. The Indian players took the field with smiles on their faces, and absolutely no pressure on their shoulders. They had nothing to lose, and the universe to gain.

His experience of bowling to Greenidge in the Caribbean had convinced Sandhu that the former was a shade tentative against swing bowling early on in an innings. And sure enough, after being crashed through the covers by Haynes for four, Sandhu produced a banana inswinger that swung inwards late and dislodged the bails as Greenidge watched, his bat lifted, intent on letting the ball pass to the keeper. In came Richards, who set about the bowling as if he had a train to catch.

He put Kapil Dev and Sandhu away for boundaries and then took three fours off a Madan Lal over. Kapil Dev would have been tempted to take the bowler off, but he held on. Madan Lal responded with the wicket of Haynes, caught off an uppish drive when the score was 50.

A lot of people were surprised to see Lloyd come in at number four, ahead of Gomes, who had manned that position with distinction throughout the tournament. Why had an exception been made for the final? Was it because the defending champions wanted to give their skipper every possible opportunity of being in the middle when the target was achieved, so that he could bow out with a hattrick of World Cup wins? Was it that the holders were thinking only about the outcome and not the process? As it happened, Lloyd tore his right thigh-muscle as he went for his first run, and Haynes reappeared as his runner.

The fall of Haynes made no difference to Richards, nor did it affect the spirits of the West Indian supporters. In the outfield, Sunil, who was stationed at deep point, made an attempt to lighten the situation. He requested Patil, who was standing at third-man, to tell his wife to meet him at the St. John Wood's station in an hour. The way Richards was batting, the match and presentation ceremony were likely to conclude by then!

Kapil Dev was in no mood for humour. The way Richards was going about his job, the Indian captain sensed that a chance was just around the corner. The score was 56-2 when the master blaster sighted a short delivery by Madan Lal and went for a pull. But the ball rose a little higher than he had anticipated, and he got a top-edge. The cherry went miles in the air, and looked like it would land in no man's land near the mid-wicket boundary. 'Good shot,' was Richie Benaud's first reaction in the commentary box. 'Not so good,' he said a few seconds later.

Kapil Dev had forced Benaud to contradict himself. The Indian captain sprinted from the infield, first judging the ascent of the ball, and then its descent, to perfection. He completed a catch in front of the mid-wicket boundary. Richards had indeed given a chance, and the captain of India had grabbed it with both hands, literally.

By this time, Sunil had returned to the slips. He clasped a thick outside-edge by Larry Gomes. The score was now 66-4, and Madan Lal had taken his third wicket. Kapil Dev's belief in the Delhi all-rounder had paid off. It was up to Lloyd to take the initiative, but his thigh was distracting him. Binny played his part to perfection, pitching it up to force Lloyd to play off his injured foot. The skipper drove hard, but uppishly, and Kapil Dev did not have to move from his mid-off position to hold on. 66-5.

'He is gone!' Benaud all but screamed into the mike. It was that kind of situation, wherein a man known for his understated approach to commentary could not help but do a Tony Greig. As Lloyd left, the Indian players, supporters and their compatriots back in India, who were watching the game on TV or listening on radio, confronted the enormity of what they had achieved, and what they would accomplish if they were to take five more wickets.

Faoud Bacchus fell soon after the tea interval to a stupendous catch by Kirmani. The score was now 76-6. Dujon and Marshall fought back, raising the hundred. They had all but put the chase back on track when Kapil Dev tossed the ball to his 'knight in shining armour.'

Amarnath's first ball was as innocuous as innocuous could be, but Dujon somehow contrived to inside-edge it onto the wickets. 119-7. Marshall fell 5 runs later, nicking the same bowler to Sunil at slip, and Kapil Dev pounded in to dismiss Roberts leg-before. Garner and Holding pushed and prodded until Amarnath rapped the latter on his pads with the target 44 runs away. The bowler was halfway into his appeal when umpire Harold Bird, one of the game's premier 'not-outers', ruled that the batsman was plumb in front.

It was the greatest upset in cricketing history.

Back in India, millions took to the streets of Bombay, Calcutta, Delhi and other cities, towns and villages to celebrate their side's conquest. Dilip Vengsarkar, who had missed the last four games, appeared on the Lord's balcony, grinning from ear to ear. Behind him were Mansingh, Salve, and a dozen other gatecrashers. Some of the players managed to snatch stumps and bails as souvenirs during the course of their escape from the raiders of the field. Sunil was especially fortunate, for the ball had come straight to him off Holding's pads.

For Mohinder Amarnath, the recipient of the Man of the Match award for his innings of 26 and three wickets, the win marked the culmination of a remarkable comeback, during the course of which he had scored 1,182 runs from eleven Tests, earned encomiums from the world's most formidable opponents, and won the individual award in a World Cup final of all matches. There was nothing more he could have achieved in such a short span of time.

The champagne corks popped in the Indian dressing room, as each and every occupant savoured the moment. The laughs and screams were interspersed with the odd tear. When the spectators demanded the players to appear on the balcony, Sunil was reluctant to do so for he felt that he hadn't contributed anything to the victory. But he ultimately acquiesced, and delighted the fans and cameramen by holding Kapil Dev's hand and raising it skywards. It was a wonderful gesture by the man who was the sole link between the 1983 World Cup win and Indian cricket's previous mega-feat – the twin triumphs of 1971.

Sunil then remembered his and Bedi's tussles with the Board over payments to players in the late 1970s. He took it upon himself to obtain a congruent commitment from the Board president. There was no greater achievement than winning a World Cup, after all.

> 'I will never forget what the players did to me on the balcony. Sunil Gavaskar was leading them, and Kapil Dev instigating from behind. "How much will we get for this, Sir?" Sunil asked me. "Rs 2 lakhs," I said. "Sir, we don't want a tip," he responded. I then quoted Rs 3 lakhs. But he wasn't happy. "Sir, what is the difference between Rs 2 lakhs and Rs 3 lakhs?" he asked. Well . . . the difference is Rs 1 lakh, you know . . . I then quoted Rs 5 lakhs and then Rs 7 lakhs, but the players wouldn't listen. The BCCI didn't have the kind of money back then as it has now. . . .' – N.K.P. Salve at the 1983 World Cup Silver Jubilee Celebrations of the BCCI (Delhi, 22 June 2008)

The World Cup was handed over by Sir Anthony Tuke, the president of the MCC, to Kapil Dev, amidst delirious scenes. The champions danced through the night in London, and returned to Bombay a couple of days later to a ticker-tape welcome. Around 10,000 fans greeted them at the airport, and the residents of India's cricket capital lined the streets from the airport to the Wankhede stadium.

The felicitation of the players by the government of Maharashtra at the Wankhede was the first of a series. The high points were the meeting with Prime Minister Indira Gandhi, and a tea party hosted by President Giani Zail Singh, in Delhi. Salve, who had promised an astronomical Rs 1 lakh per player, was advised by his BCCI colleague I.S. Bindra to seek help to raise the requisite money from Lata Mangeshkar. The nightingale, a cricket fanatic and one of the witnesses of the triumph, was only too happy to oblige. A Lata Mangeshkar Nite was organised in Delhi, the highlight of which was the rendition of *Bharat Vishwa Vijeta* (India is the world-beater), a song that had been specially written and composed to commemorate the World Cup win. Mangeshkar was the lead singer of course, and she was supported by the players, each of whom rendered a line.

The euphoria of the World Cup win was all-pervasive, but it did not prevent some people from alluding to Sunil's poor form. They were of the view that like Viswanath, his time had come.

> SUNNY DAYS ARE OVER: ... Gavaskar plays jittery cricket these days. Once hailed as the epitome of technical excellence, concentration and stamina, he plays now in a slap dash fashion that generates anxiety. He has an air of insecurity throughout his stay at the crease. He often plays a series of rash shots in a bid to prove that his game has not changed ... What a great bat he was then (in the 1970s)! And what a great pity that he has spoilt his record in such a short span. – Prakash Parayath, *The Indian Express*, June 1983

Sunil was aware that he could have done a lot better in the World Cup. However, there was another side to the story. The deliveries that had accounted for him in the semi-final and final, delivered by Paul Allott and Andy Roberts respectively, weren't exactly long-hops. Both had pitched on a good-length and moved a wee bit away after pitching. An ordinary batsman would have most certainly missed them, but Sunil was good enough to get his bat close to them.

'I believe that Sunil's lack of form in the tournament had a lot to do with my being his roommate (till his wife joined him)! How could he have been at peace when I was around? I did, however, try to behave well, by tiptoeing when he was asleep. After all, the country wouldn't sleep if he didn't! I asked him the silliest of questions. On the eve of our first encounter against the West Indies, I asked him whether I would be able to see the ball after it was released. He reminded me that I had played the likes of Dennis Lillee and Imran Khan.' – Sandeep Patil

The selectors concurred. The way they saw it, Sunil was only one good innings away from regaining his run-hunger. Form was in any case a fickle concept, as another Indian player was to discover.

17

'DON' TO DUSK

> I realise that my reflexes are definitely not the same. I know that I don't play the new ball as confidently as I did when I started. I know I am not as certain about the off-stump as I was when I started. The chinks in the armour are more exposed now. – Sunil Gavaskar, *Doordarshan* interview, 29 October 1983

Malcolm Denzil Marshall reached the top of his run-up, turned and hitched his trousers. For Sunil, who was on strike, the implication of that act was obvious. It signified that a bouncer was on the cards.

There was an added spring in Marshall's sprint as he passed the umpire, and his hands converged briefly over his head before he let the ball go. As Sunil had anticipated, the ball landed well short of a length, and rose. Sunil took a backward step, opened himself up, and brought his bat down horizontally, closing its face at the point of impact. The ball made for the fine-leg boundary.

It was 29 October 1983, the first day of the second Test of the 1983-84 series between India and the West Indies. Kapil Dev had earlier won the toss and given his batsmen first use of what was known in Indian cricketing parlance as a 'Sitaram special'. Sitaram, the curator at Delhi's Ferozeshah Kotla, enjoyed a reputation as a batsman's best friend.

Sunil hooked again in Marshall's next over, albeit not as convincingly. A bumper took the top-edge of his bat and flew over Dujon's outstretched gloves, giving the batsman 4 more runs. The next bouncer, Sunil hooked resoundingly over long-leg for six.

So transfixed were the spectators at the ground and TV viewers across the country by this belligerent display that the dismissal of Aunshuman Gaekwad, and a confident start by the new batsman Dilip Vengsarkar, did not register.

When Holding attempted to test his patience with a fuller line and length, Sunil steered him past gully for four. An on-drive gave him three runs.

Clive Lloyd shuffled his bowlers around. Winston Davis was brought on from Marshall's end, only to bear the brunt of two stupendous strokes. An extra-cover drive set the stands alight, and a square-cut left the point fielder high and dry. An imperious hook off Davis gave Sunil his first fifty of the series, and he celebrated it with an on-driven 4. At lunch, India were 99-1, Sunil's share being 62.

The fireworks continued in the afternoon. Holding over-pitched and was subjected to a 'Bhagirathi' stroke – a straight drive that sped past him like a bullet. It was followed by two hooks off Marshall, the second of which neatly bisected the two men posted on the long-leg boundary for just that shot.

Sunil then produced the stroke of his innings, a cut off Marshall, which he essayed by going down on one knee. When he on-drove Marshall for another boundary, his Dadar Union team-mate accosted him in the middle of the pitch and offered his hand. Sunil was perplexed, and it was left to Vengsarkar to inform him that he had equalled Sir Donald Bradman's tally of twenty-nine Test hundreds. Sunil, never one to look at the scoreboard, had no clue of what he had achieved.

> 'I remember watching that innings on the TV. In fact, that was the first time I saw him bat. I was nine at the time. There was something endearing about an Indian mastering all those big guys running in to bowl to him.' – V.V.S. Laxman

The spectators exploded, as did Anupam Gulati, the TV commentator. A group of Indian players emerged from the dressing room to applaud the achievement from the edge of the boundary line. Lloyd, Dujon and Richards went over to extend their congratulations, and Sunil raised his bat and left hand to acknowledge the cheers. The hundred had taken him only ninety-four balls to achieve, which made it the fastest of his career.

> In a lot of ways, Gavaskar must be considered the best batsman in the world... his footwork is almost an art form... it is never faulted. The stillness of his head should be matched by every schoolboy. No wonder he needs no helmet. The Don may remain the only begetter of records, but they were logged with a diet of long-hops from leg-spinners like dear old Peebles and half volleys from the Fleetwood-Smiths, military medium-pacers who had not many points to prove, or so it seems to us, years later... Richards has his scything hook through mid-wicket, Boycott makes room for himself for his famous force backward of point, Zaheer has that velvet cover-drive... Sunil does nothing flamboyant, but just gets his feet in position, his head out of the way, and makes runs. – Frank Keating, *Guardian*, 1 November 1983

Sunil drew level with the Don during a phase wherein Kipling's twin impostors of success and failure kept him intermittent company.

The 1983-84 season began with the new limited-overs world champions taking on a Pakistani side captained by Zaheer Abbas. Imran Khan, who had played in the World Cup as a specialist batsman, had taken the tour off to tend to his shin. Also missing was Sarfraz Nawaz, who kept the tabloids busy by alleging that he had pulled out after refusing to be part of a plan to play for three draws.

The series was the outcome of a joint decision by the Indain and Pakistani boards to make up for all the lost years by playing each other annually. However noble the thought may have been, it was fundamentally flawed. Firstly, there was the danger of an overkill destroying the novelty factor that characterised tussles between the traditional rivals. Secondly, with both teams having a packed calendar for the rest of the cricket season, the series had been scheduled for September, a month when the Indian monsoon was very much active.

It was in the visiting side's first game; a One-Day international at Hyderabad, that Sunil unveiled another custom-made accessory. Unlike his lightweight leg-guards and boots, this one was visible only when he took his sun hat off. It was a skullcap made of fibreglass. He had got it made during his stint with Somerset, after seeing Mike Brearley wear it. The skullcap maker, who was based in Nottingham, had made the headgear in accordance with Sunil's instructions, one of which was that the top be left open, so that he could wear the sun hat over it.

His tendency to have stiff necks, a consequence of his habit of reading in bed, had prompted him to eschew the helmet, the weight of which, he reckoned, would accentuate the chances of his straining his neck while taking evasive action against short deliveries.

He had waited three full years after acquiring the skullcap to actually wear it.

> I wanted to stop jabbing the ball from my face, and give it the treatment instead. – Sunil Gavaskar, *Runs n' Ruins* (Rupa, 1984)

Simply put, he wanted to play his strokes after years of restraint.

He scored 33 at Hyderabad, but for the umpteenth time in less than a year, he and his team-mates were overshadowed by Amarnath, whose 60 took India to a six-wicket win.

The players were not as effervescent as their compatriots thought they would be when they congregated in Bangalore for the first Test. They were not very happy with the reluctance of Kapil Dev and Amarnath to share the prize money they had won in the form of the Man of the Series awards in the previous season. Kapil Dev had won the award for the England tour in 1982 and Mohinder for the Caribbean tour.

Among the many perks the world champions had earned after conquering the cricketing world, was the status of newspaper columnists. However, the BCCI wasn't too keen on the players expressing themselves in print. The matter was temporarily resolved, with Salve permitting them to write during the Pakistan series. However, by no means was it a harmonious start to the season.

In whatever play that was possible in Bangalore when the rains took a breather, India scored 275 and Pakistan replied with 288. Sunil was far from fluent in the first innings, but he brought all his experience into play and hung around. He had reached 42 when he was declared out leg-before off seamer Tahir Naqqash. Roger Binny and Madan Lal batted well to rescue India from 75-6, and Javed Miandad batted beautifully later to score 99. There was nothing left in the match when India's second innings began just before lunch on the last day.

Sunil was the dominant partner. At the back of his mind was a prediction made by Jitu Patel, an astrologer whom he had met at the start of the season. He had told Sunil that he was destined to score a hundred on 19 September, the last day of the Bangalore Test.

> Gavaskar shed his defensive nature. When in the mood, he can play every stroke in the book. Today was such a day. He batted without inhibition. At the same time, he seldom chanced his arm. He displayed remarkable judgement of the ball and control over his shots as he repeatedly pierced the field with the cut and the pull, the drive and the sweep. – Sunder Rajan, *TOI*, 19 September 1983

Sunil was batting on one at lunch. By the tea interval, he had reached 37. It was in the final session that he and his partner Anshuman Gaekwad pulled out the shots. Sunil reached his fifty just before the start of the mandatory overs. He stroked his way past the 60s and 70s, and into the 80s, even as the sprinkling of spectators realised that there was something to look forward to. Sunil was on 86, and six mandatory overs were left, when Zaheer Abbas took his team off the field, on the grounds that the daily target of at least 77 overs, which the boards had agreed upon, had been completed. Twenty-seven minutes were lost as the umpires attempted to draw the Pakistan captain's attention to the fact that the stipulation did not apply to the final day, on which it was mandatory to bowl twenty overs in the last hour.

The Pakistanis had no option but to return. Sunil moved to 99 by the time the final over, bowled by Mudassar Nazar, commenced. He steered the first ball to the third-man fence to complete his hundred, his twenty-eighth in Tests. Five deliveries were left, but Zaheer walked off again. This time, the umpires did not stop him!

The episode gave Sunil's detractors an opportunity to flay the umpires. Why was it that they had not insisted on the final over being completed? But of course, Sunil and his fans weren't complaining. He was happy to play himself into form with a Test hundred.

> Gavaskar now appears to have come to terms with himself. The skull-cap he presently dons also seems to have boosted his morale. Not that he was ever intimidated by the bouncer. He is getting along in years, and at thirty-four, has to be more careful in guarding against injury than in the past. What is heartening is that he continues to bat with all the application, concentration and technique of old. Such a man simply cannot fail. – Sunder Rajan, *TOI*, 25 September 1983

The teams then flew to Delhi for an unofficial day-night One-dayer, which Kirti Azad won for India single-handedly. Rain was expected to reign at Jalandhar, the venue of the second Test, and so it did, with only two innings being completed. Wasim Raja scored a hundred for Pakistan, and Gaekwad responded with the slowest ever double hundred in Test history.

Sunil made amends for his Jalandhar failure with two half centuries in the third Test at Nagpur. Pakistan's off-spinner Mohammad Nazir bowled excellently on a turning track in the second innings to give his team an outside chance of victory. India were 207-8, and only 130 ahead, on the final afternoon, but the obduracy of Kirmani and Madan Lal saved the day. Their cause was further boosted by what many people perceived as the Pakistani skipper's defensive captaincy.

It had been an odd series. While Indian fans were upset with the 0-0 scoreline, Sunil was mystified with the think-tank's reluctance to strategise before the matches.

There had been some strange omissions. Vengsarkar and Shastri, who had scored 94 and 102 respectively in the final Test in the Caribbean, were dropped for the Bangalore Test. Binny was left out at Nagpur despite scores of 83 and 54 in the earlier two Tests. Given that he hadn't been effective in his primary role as a bowler, it was a fair call. But what did not make sense was the management's decision to fly Sandeep Patil from Bombay on the morning of the Test when Amarnath fell ill, despite Binny's presence in Nagpur.

Fortunately for Patil, who was permitted by the chief minister of Maharashtra to travel in a state-owned aircraft that was flying to Nagpur anyway, Kapil Dev won the toss and elected to bat. Had Pakistan batted first, India would have had to field with ten men, for Patil reached the ground only at the end of the truncated first day's play. He was welcomed to the wicket by the spectators the following day, but scores of 6 in the first innings and 26 in the second did him no credit.

Three days after the Nagpur Test, the Indian players found themselves in picturesque Srinagar, for the first of five One Day Internationals against the dethroned world champions. The mindset of Clive Lloyd's players on their arrival in India to play six Tests and six One Day Internationals was encapsulated in a statement credited to Wes Hall, their manager: 'The worst thing India could have done was beat the West Indies (in the World Cup final). We intend to make them pay.'

The West Indians had noted the plaudits and gifts heaped upon the Indian cricketers for the World Cup win with disbelief, and more with a hint of anger. They had subsequently tried to recall the rewards they had received for winning the first two World Cups, and failed. The reason was simple – they hadn't got anything!

Lloyd wanted to retire after the World Cup, but was persuaded to stay back. That they were to play the team that had ruined his dream of completing a hattrick was a key incentive for him to carry on.

The visitors commenced 'Operation Vengeance' with a victory on superior run-rate at Srinagar.

They then took on the North Zone in a three-dayer at Amritsar. The game featured a hundred by Navjot Singh Sidhu, an opening batsman endowed with a fine technique. Another performer was Chetan Sharma, a pupil of Kapil Dev's guru D.P. Azad, who surprised the likes of Greenidge and Richards with his pace and nip. Although the match was drawn, North Zone were in charge for most of it despite Kapil Dev's absence.

If the Indian captain was over the moon at the showing of his juniors, one look at the pitch at Kanpur's Green Park, which was to stage the first Test, brought him down to earth. It was home to a smattering of grass, and seemed to have been made to order for the Caribbean speedsters.

Malcolm Marshall was handed the new ball by his captain on the second afternoon of the game, shortly after he had contributed 92 to his team's first innings total of 454. Andy Roberts was not part of the XI, and Garner had opted out of the tour due to injury. Holding himself was to bowl off a shorter run-up. It left Marshall as the fastest member of the XI, a fact that Holding reminded Lloyd of.

The Barbadian paceman was determined to obliterate the memories of what had been a baptism by fire in India in 1978-79. The responsibility of opening the bowling only boosted his confidence.

He marked out his run-up and sprinted in, unveiling the open-chested whirlwind action that gave his opponents little or no time to focus on the incoming cherry. Sunil played the first ball to Haynes at short-leg. The second delivery was full and slightly wide. Sunil attempted to drive, but only got an edge, and Dujon snapped up a comfortable catch. Amarnath came in and went out, trapped leg-before by the same bowler. India were 0-2.

A snorter took Gaekwad by surprise, and Dujon took his second catch of the innings. The wicket of Vengsarkar, bowled neck-and-crop, was Marshall's fourth in five overs. India, 18-4 at that stage, ended the second day at 34-5. The slide continued on the third day, before Binny and Madan Lal added 117. The innings folded up for 207. Marshall had figures of 15-7-19-4, and he was well supported by fellow pacers Holding, Winston Davis and Eldine Baptiste.

Lloyd's enforcement of the follow-on didn't hit the Indians as hard as the manner of Sunil's second-innings dismissal. He had scored 7, when a Marshall delivery pitched short of a length and reared. Sunil followed his time-tested technique of loosening his grip to lessen the impact on his fingers if the ball were to hit them. But the ball kept just a shade lower than he had anticipated, and hit the shoulder of the bat. That made the bat slip out of his loose hands, and the ball ballooned into the air. Davis took a good catch at backward short-leg. Sunil picked up his bat and began the walk to the pavilion, even as the Windies players went wild.

While Sunil's fans were mortified, others brought their crystal-balls out of the closet.

The more I watch Gavaskar bat, the more I am convinced that it will be difficult for him to get even one century against Marshall

and the other seamers in the current series. – K.R. Wadhwaney,
The Indian Express, 23 October 1983

Vengsarkar and Shastri, both of whom had returned to the Test side by then, were the only batters to offer resistance, as the innings ended at 164 to give the Windies a stunner of a win by an innings and 83 runs. Marshall, with match figures of 8-86, was the undisputed player of the match. The defeat punctured Indian pride and prompted Kapil Dev to call for net-practice on the scheduled last day of the Test.

India's woes were compounded by the failure of Mohinder Amarnath, their player of the previous season. He had bagged a pair and shown little indication of having recovered from the illness that had forced him to miss the Nagpur Test against Pakistan.

Nothing had changed for him on the morning of the second Test at Delhi, which began four days after the end of the Kanpur game. He was far from fit, but was surprisingly included in the XI. When Kapil Dev won the toss and elected to bat, Amarnath asked to be dropped down the order. It turned out that he wasn't the only member of the side who was thinking along those lines.

I have batted down the order for Bombay, but would prefer to open for India than 'fidget around' till my turn came to bat.
– Sunil Gavaskar, as quoted by K.N. Prabhu, *TOI*, 16 March 1981

More than two-and-a-half years after he made that statement, Sunil had started thinking differently. He was considering a move down the batting order.

It wasn't quite a case of an individual shirking a challenge. For Sunil, the move was a practical course of action after twelve years of international cricket. Although he was still physically fit, it was the mental aspect that was getting to him. He had started finding it difficult to rush through with the change of clothes and donning of protective gear in the ten-minute changeover period, especially whenever India bowled first. He had come to the conclusion that it was better that a younger man opened.

Dilip Sardesai, who managed the Indian team during the Delhi Test, told the *TOI* in an interview that appeared on 31 January 1984, that

Sunil had evinced a desire to bat lower down the order, only for Kapil Dev to ask for the request to be given to him in writing.

The skipper's reaction may have been officious, but in all fairness to him, Sunil as captain would have been similarly bewildered had Kapil asked to be allowed to bowl off-spin instead of taking the new ball. Sunil's 'declining reflexes' notwithstanding, there was no one in the Indian team better equipped than he, technically and mentally, to handle the West Indian speedsters.

Ironically, Sunil proceeded to provide the biggest argument in favour of his retention as opener, with a 94-ball hundred. If his twenty-eighth hundred had followed a prediction by an astrologer, his twenty-ninth delighted a bevy of female fans, who had exhorted him on the eve of the game to score the fastest hundred of his career!

> And this one is for Sunil Gavaskar, cricketer and man. Written-off, discarded from captaincy, criticised, and advised by men who had never held a cricket bat in their hands. What a way to enter the book of records! As batsman number one, on the opening day of a Test match, against the most dreaded pace attack, immediately after the Kanpur debacle, at a time when the Indian team was most demoralised. The stamp of authority all over again: ability, guts, determination . . . the master-craftsman back at his job . . . the same man who set the cricket world alight thirteen years ago, returning to neatly round-off his career. The intervening years had been hard and not always fruitful. Opening innings after innings facing the great fast bowlers of the world, always fresh and ready at the dawn of a new Test, knowing that 60 percent of his team's total (sometimes more) depended on how many runs he scored and how long he stayed. And the added burdens of captaincy. A captain who not only led his team in the field, but fought for it in the boardrooms of cricket in order that his players got the money they deserved . . . And the ingratitude of it all. To be talked about as a has-been . . . to be unsure of a place in the World Cup team. I think, finally, the man triumphed over the cricketer. The man with guts, determination, the will to score runs. . . . Sunil Gavaskar, we are all beholden to you.
> – Behram Contractor, *Mid-Day,* 30 October 1983

As though such a great milestone cannot be reached without the aura and sanctity it deserved, Gavaskar made it an occasion to remember by spraying vintage strokes in a manner that would have won the approval of the incomparable Australian [Sir Don Bradman]. – R. Sriman, *TOI*, 29 October 1983

The twenty-ninth hundred out of the way, Sunil refused to delude himself.

I have never really considered it a record. It is purely an achievement. Sir Don Bradman scored twenty-nine centuries in only fifty-two Tests. The record will only be broken if someone scores more than twenty-nine hundreds in less than fifty-two Tests. – Sunil on *Doordarshan*, 29 October 1983

There was another point he made in the same interview:

I don't think I have played as many shots before, mainly because the responsibility of getting a good start was on my shoulders. It weighed me down considerably. Over the last one year, I have decided to enjoy cricket, play my shots, and if I have to get out, I would rather get out playing an attacking shot than a defensive shot.

He probably did not realise it then, but the declaration of his intent to enjoy his cricket delighted his detractors as much as his fans. For them, it was now a question of waiting for an opportune moment to strike.

The Delhi Test was drawn. Sunil's 121 apart, the highlights were Vengsarkar's 159, Lloyd's 103, and a nasty spell by Marshall in the second innings that gave his team an outside chance of victory. But Binny and Madan Lal were defiant once again. Their first-innings score of 464 gave the Indians plenty of heart as they dispersed for a few days. Among those who received Sunil at the Bombay airport was his mother, who presented him twenty-nine crimson-red roses.

The *TOI* on 7 November 1983 reported the planning of an interesting tribute to Sunil. Arun Kukreja and Faisal Alkazi, directors affiliated to the Delhi-based Ruchika Theatre Group, spoke about their desire to present Sunil in programmes in Delhi, Bombay, Calcutta, Madras and Bangalore, the idea being to let him narrate his life and experiences like an actor in a play. Dr Narottam Puri, the radio and TV commentator, was to compere the programmes. Sunil had welcomed the idea to stage these programmes in March 1984. However, things did not work out.

Another off-the-field venture during the series was a huge success. The World Cup win induced Thums Up, India's leading soft drink brand, to launch a cricket souvenirs contest during the Windies series. Cricket lovers were promised attractive gifts in return for collecting caricatures of the Indian and West Indian players, which were affixed to the insides of Thums Up bottle-tops. Contestants who collected an entire team bagged a miniature Thums Up fun-bottle. The submission of these bottles at a Thums Up outlet yielded gifts of different valuations. The most prestigious gift was a miniature bat, autographed by the Indian and West Indian teams. Next in line was a miniature ball signed by Kapil Dev, and then, a bottle opener. But the gift, or rather, gifts most sought after, were those at the bottom of the hierarchy. These were action-flickers of Sunil, Kapil Dev, Patil, Lloyd and Richards, which two fun-bottles could fetch. Flicking the pages in one direction provided the visual of a player essaying an aggressive stroke, and in Kapil Dev's case, running in to bowl. Flicking them in the opposite direction enabled cricket lovers to watch the same player guzzle Thums Up. Sunil was appropriately captured essaying the straight drive.

For a generation that had not heard the word computer, leave alone CD-ROMs and Playstations, ownership of these souvenirs was the ultimate dream. For kids who were born in the 1970s and grew up in the 1980s, the caricatures in the bottle-tops introduced them to the barter system long before they were taught the origins of currency in school. Quite often, a fan would unearth a caricature he/she already possessed, thus necessitating an exchange with a friend.

The cricket souvenirs contest was gaining momentum by the time the second One Day International was played at Baroda. The West Indies won by four wickets, thus taking a 2-0 lead in the one-day series. If they were ruthless, the Indians were seemingly clueless, judging from the manner in which they were outplayed in every department.

The pitch at the brand new Sardar Patel stadium in Ahmedabad, the venue of the third Test, was an unknown quantity, in that it was yet to stage a First-class match. For once, Kapil Dev was hoping to lose the toss. However, he won it, and asked to be given some time to take a call. The wicket seemed firmer than what it had been on the previous evening, which prompted the majority to advocate bowling first and thus deny the Windies pacemen the opportunity to exploit whatever juice there may have been in the track.

When the Windies batted, it became obvious that the wicket would deteriorate rapidly. India's only hope of making a match of it was to bat just once, and bat big, in response to the visitors' 281.

The Indian openers had six minutes to negotiate before lunch on the second day. In the late 1970s, Sunil may well have offered a dead bat to every delivery in such a situation. However, this was November 1983, and only a few days had elapsed since he had talked about enjoying his cricket. He got going with an emphatic back foot cover-drive off the very first ball. The boundary took him past Sir Garry Sobers' tally of 8,032, making him the second-highest scorer in Test cricket. He then flicked Marshall to the square-leg fence for another boundary. It was followed by an extraordinary stroke. Holding dug one in short outside the off-stump. Sunil met the ball with the meat of the bat and opened the face at the point of impact. The ball flew over gully for four. It was a stroke that his brother-in-law had essayed to perfection several times over, and one that another diminutive batsman from Bombay would patent in the new millennium.

Sunil continued his orthodox assault on Marshall and Holding after lunch, flicking and driving with aplomb. He was certainly enjoying his cricket, but in a manner that was carefree, not careless. The spectators went ballistic when he reached fifty with a single off Holding. Wayne Daniel, who had come in for Baptiste, was first off-driven for four and then hit straight down the ground.

Holding drew first blood after tea, sending Gaekwad's off-stump for a walk. The openers had put on 127, of which Gaekwad's share was 39. That brought in the debutant Navjot Sidhu. Like all newcomers, he was nervous, and Sunil knew it. Sidhu only had to tap the ball in the covers and scream for a single, for Sunil to respond.

Sunil's response to the debutant's call ought to have silenced all those who persisted in drawing comparisons between him and Geoffrey Boycott, who had a propensity to run his colleagues out and put self before team, if the autobiographies of some of his contemporaries are anything to go by.

Boycott figured prominently in the thoughts of all those who were following the proceedings at Ahmedabad. Sunil was on 82 when Davis bowled one on middle-and-leg. Sunil glanced him to fine-leg for a single, to take his Test aggregate to 8,115, one run more than Boycott's. He had now become the greatest run-scorer in Test cricket.

For Sunil, it was the ultimate achievement. As the news spread across the cricketing world, Boycott would have remembered the Delhi Test of 1981-82, wherein he had surpassed Sobers' tally to claim the record, and Sunil's subsequent quip that he could enjoy the record for two years. Sunil had kept his word.

The spectators now braced themselves for another feat – a record-breaking thirtieth Test hundred. For Sunil, the drinks interval, which was taken when he was ten short, and fresh off another cover-driven boundary off Marshall, was an irritant, to say the least. He had never relished breaks in situations wherein he was on top of the bowling.

His frustration was compounded by one of the drinks-bearers, who kept appearing in front of the sight screen. Umpire Hanumantha Rao had to step in and ensure that the attendant vanished from view, but the damage had been done. Sunil's focus had gone. Holding had started running in for his fourth ball of the over when there was another movement, this time over the screen. Sunil considered moving away, as he was entitled to do, but, like many people caught in similar situations, he froze. The walker was directly above Holding's bowling arm at the point of delivery. The ball pitched on a length, moved slightly away, and found the outside-edge of the bat. Lloyd made no mistake at first slip.

Sunil was angry, and he made no attempt to conceal it. He cooled down after spending some time in the dressing room. The TV replay of his dismissal convinced him that the ball would have been fatal even if there had been no disturbance. It was a beauty, pitching as it did on a length just outside the off-stump, and moving away. Sunil, being well-set, would have got his bat to it, regardless of the loitering spectator.

'Don of a Sunny Era', was the tagline adopted by one of India's leading butter manufacturers on their hoardings, soon after Sunil drew level with Bradman. His dismissal for 90 at Ahmedabad prompted them to add a footnote of sorts to their billboards, which went, 'Easy Sunil. We can't change our designs so fast!'

The 'Gavaskar effect' had gripped one and all, from his fans to his detractors, from children to copywriters! No one was willing to give him the benefit of doubt. As far as everybody was concerned, it was mandatory for him to score a century every single time he made his way to the crease. Anything less than a three-figure mark was unacceptable. His failures earlier in the year seemed to belong to another world. The twenty-ninth hundred had changed everything.

The remainder of the West Indies series would emphasise Sunil's propensity to elicit extreme reactions from the classes and the masses.

The demons in the Ahmedabad wicket asserted themselves on the third morning of the Test. India, 173-2 at stumps on day two, were bowled out for 241. Kapil Dev then threw himself headlong into the task of bringing his team back into the game. He bowled through the innings to take 9-83 from 30.3 overs, and if only his co-bowlers—Sandhu and the spinners Shastri, Maninder and Kirti Azad—had complemented him, the West Indies would have struggled to get half of the 201 they ended up with. An injury to Binny, which prevented him from bowling, did not help India's cause. For the hosts, a target of 242 was a gigantic order.

The wickets tumbled like ninepins, and the score was 63-9 when Kirmani and Maninder came together to take it to triple digits. Sunil, who had earlier taken a sensational diving catch at mid-wicket to dismiss Lloyd, was leg-before for 1. The West Indies were now 2-0 ahead in both series, and memories of the World Cup win were fast fading from the minds of the Indian public.

The defeat marked the beginning of the end of Kapil Dev's honeymoon with the media. Till then, he had been given the benefit of the doubt, by virtue of his being the World Cup winning captain, and a young leader to boot. That was forgotten, as the media castigated him for electing to bowl. Not for the first time, the fourth estate chose to ignore the fact that the entire team, Kirti Azad excepted, had been party to the decision. What they also ignored was Lloyd's criticism of the umpires in his mid-match newspaper column.

At a very vital phase of the Ahmedabad Test, Lloyd was able to put extra pressure on the umpires. West Indies did not win because of these tactics, but as an Indian, I felt somewhat humiliated at the different kind of treatment that was being meted out to the home team and the visiting team's captains. – Kapil Dev, *Cricket My Style* (Allied Publishers, 1987)

The Indian captain was angry with the ban issued by the Board on newspaper columns by Indian cricketers during the West Indies series. Some players believed that they ought to have been allowed to counter the charges being made by their opponents in the same medium.

The fourth Test in Bombay was preceded by a three-dayer between the visitors and the West Zone, which Sunil skipped to honour the invitation extended to him by the visiting Queen Elizabeth II, through the ambassador of Great Britain.

He met the Queen and Prince Philip in Delhi, and returned to Bombay thinking how wonderful it would be if he were to overtake Bradman's tally in his hometown. However, Marshall got the better of him in both innings. He was leg-before for 12 in the first, and caught at mid-off for 3 in the second.

At the Wankhede stadium, India brought back Shivlal Yadav on a pitch expected to take turn. While he justified his recall with five wickets, his team-mates let themselves down with some dreadful fielding and catching. Their lapses enabled the West Indies to reach 393 in response to India's 463, and achieve a draw with ease. Viv Richards scored 120 in the first innings, but he was outshone by Vengsarkar, whose second hundred of the series featured some delectable strokes, each one of them embarrassing the selectors who had dropped him at the start of the season.

The Indian team's departure to Indore, the venue of the must-win third One-Day international, was preceded by a bizarre episode. Sunil deposited his baggage in the team bus at Bombay's Taj Mahal Hotel, and drove to the apartment block in the central Bombay region of Worli where he resided, to deposit his car there. He instructed the bus driver to pick him up from a spot close to his house en route to the airport, but the latter did not turn up. Sunil ultimately took a taxi to the airport, and reached with minutes to spare for the flight. The end of Kapil Dev's honeymoon with the media was reflected in the allegations of the latter that it was he who had ordered the coach-driver not to take a detour for Sunil.

There is reason to believe that the relationship between Kapil Dev and his predecessor wasn't exactly harmonious during this period, their denials notwithstanding. Earlier in the series, Kapil Dev had given the impression of not being too thrilled with his predecessor's belligerence at the top of the order. On the other hand, Sunil was finding it hard to comprehend his successor's methods, particularly the reluctance to strategise that had bothered him during the Pakistan series. While Sunil understood and acknowledged Kapil Dev's preference for action over discussion, he was of the view that every piece of action needed to be backed by sound planning.

It was probably inevitable that two fiercely proud individuals, whose respective cricketing backgrounds were as disparate as one could imagine, would not see eye-to-eye on certain issues. The end of the Bombay Test signalled the start of a period wherein their relationship was stretched to its farthest limits.

India lost both the One-dayers that preceded the fifth Test at Calcutta, thus conceding the shorter series to the ex-World Champions. At Indore's Nehru stadium, India scored 240-7 in forty-seven overs. Amarnath showed a welcome return to form, scoring 55, but the smiles on the faces of Indians vanished when Gordon Greenidge got going.

In the fourth game at Jamshedpur, Greenidge got the hundred that he had missed at Indore by only 4 runs. However, he was, not for the first or the last time, outshone by Viv Richards. A brutal assault saw the West Indies amass 333-8 in forty-five overs. India were never in the game, although Sunil scored 83 and added 105 with Ashok Malhotra.

The fifth Test at Calcutta represented a break in tradition, for it was played in the second week of December and not the last week of the year, like most of the earlier Eden Tests. The game got underway on 10 December 1983, and by the time it ended four days later, every Indian cricket lover wore a shattered look.

The beginning itself was disastrous. Sunil got a glove to the first ball of the match and Dujon did the rest. The middle order caved in, and it was left to the captain to bail his team out. Kapil Dev's 69 ensured a recovery from 63-6. Binny and Kirmani did their bit, scoring 44 and

49 respectively, and India totalled 241.

They fought back with the ball. The spectators were ecstatic when the eighth Windies wicket fell at 215. Lloyd was still there, but he could not bat from both the ends. The hosts had an opportunity to gain a slim lead and then build on it. But not for the last time, an Indian cricket team failed to deliver the knockout blow.

The tail, represented by Andy Roberts, who was playing his first Test of the series, did not merely wag; it punched, kicked and eventually prevailed. Lloyd completed his second hundred of the series, and batted on. India's agony ended after what seemed an eternity, when Roberts was caught in the deep for 68. Last man Davis fell soon after, and the innings ended at 377.

It was well past tea time on the third day when the Indian openers made their way to the middle, having spent nearly three hours mentally psyching themselves to pad up. The Calcutta spectators were as fed up. It was in Sunil's batsmanship that they sought smiles.

Sunil sensed their mood from the reception he got after he flicked, straight-drove and then cover-drove Marshall to the fence. Gaekwad fell, bowled by Holding. Sunil's response was a searing square-drive off the same bowler. Holding in his next over pitched one outside the off-stump, and Sunil went for another square-drive. However, the ball wasn't as full or as close as he had anticipated. By the time he realised this, it was too late. The cherry rose off the turf, made contact with the outside-edge of the bat, and flew to Dujon, who clasped a comfortable catch. The West Indians celebrated as much for the dismissal, as for the fact that they could suddenly hear each other. The colloseum had gone silent. Sunil dragged himself off the pitch and into the pavilion.

At the end of the day's play, India were 50-6, and hurtling towards another defeat, their third of the series. The shock of the spectators had long given way to fury, and Sunil, who pleaded guilty to the charge of playing an atrocious shot, found himself being barracked like never before.

The rot really started with Gavaskar's dismissal. There are several here who believe that Gavaskar was discouraged by the inability of the bowlers to bring the West Indies innings to a swift end and

that the ultimate pressure would be on him. But certainly, there can be no rational explanation for the manner in which he threw his wicket away. Perhaps, one can put this aberration down to the tensions of modern cricket, which make batsmen of great stature do the strangest things at the most critical moments.
– K.N. Prabhu, *TOI*, 13 December 1983

He could not come to terms with the shot that had cost him his wicket. He took his time to take his gear off, mentally replaying the shot. Back at the hotel, he shut himself in his room and stared at the ceiling. The following morning, he departed from his practice of not reading the newspapers during a match, and discovered that he had been crowned the villain of the piece. The bowlers who had allowed the West Indies tail to punch and prevail had got away.

It happened to be the rest-day of the game. His detractors hit the roof when the news of his attending a signing session of copies of his book *Idols* during the day did the rounds. They flayed him for his selfishness and shamelessness for attending such a ceremony after costing his team the match. Some even alleged that his differences with Kapil Dev had prompted him to throw his wicket away.

The bashers had a trumpcard – the lack of objectivity of most Indian cricket lovers. In that frame of mind, it was unlikely that the public would take cognizance of the fact that the signing sessions had been organised on the rest-days of *all* the Test matches. A commitment had been made, and he had to fulfil it.

The Test match ended within an hour of the start of the fourth day's play, with India being bowled out for 90, thus losing by an innings and 46 runs. The West Indies had won the Test series in addition to the One Day series, and how!

The losers were a wary lot when they boarded their bus. They could not have donned helmets a moment too soon, for a volley of stones hit the glass windows even as the vehicle revved up. The players hit the deck, but not all managed to escape unhurt. Malhotra and Abbas Ali Baig, the Manager, sustained minor injuries. Ironically, the front seat at that point was occupied by the two men who had stood hand-in-hand on the Lord's balcony six months previously. While Sunil lowered himself like his team-mates, Kapil Dev retained his posture as the stones kept crashing into the vehicle, unmindful of the risks he was exposing himself to. Indian cricket had come crashing down the summit in as inglorious a manner as one could imagine, in less than six months.

Sunil wasn't the only Gavaskar to be targeted by the hooligans.

> What got me hopping mad, and something I will never forgive, is the crowd throwing fruit and rubbish at my wife ... Here were people who talk about culture and respecting women, throwing fruits at the wife of a player who has played for thirteen years. And for one bad shot? When everybody else had also failed? Why her? It was not her fault. – Sunil Gavaskar, *Runs n' Ruins* (Rupa, 1984)

By 2007, Sunil had forgiven and forgotten.

> There is a misconception that I was upset because of such an incident. I asked her but she said there was nothing thrown at her. Maybe nobody had a strong or accurate throw! – Sunil Gavaskar quoted in *War of the Willows* (souvenir brought out by the Cricket Association of Bengal on the eve of the 2007 Test against Pakistan)

While Sunil received scores of apologies for the spectators' conduct, not much sympathy was shown for another individual. Mohinder Amarnath's decline had been as extraordinary as his resurgence a year previously. The most astute of experts were hardpressed to explain how a player who had scored 1,182 runs in eleven Tests and pocketed Man of the Match awards in the World Cup semi-final and final, had got two pairs and eventually finished with only 1 run in six innings.

> It was one of those burn-out syndromes actually. When you reach the peak in a very short time you are bound to go down. I had achieved everything I wanted to in twelve months' time. I was a nobody before going to Pakistan, and I was the best after the World Cup ... So in a way, I had it coming. I was also not keeping too well at the time. I was down with a virus, but still kept playing.
> – Mohinder Amarnath, *The Sportstar*, 1 May 1993

Kapil Dev subsequently blamed himself for forcing Amarnath to play the earlier Tests despite his illness. Rajan Bala offered a technical explanation for Amarnath's slide. He identified Roberts as the bowler who had identified a chink in Amarnath's armour.

> The shrewd fast bowler felt that an attack near the blockhole on a consistent off-stump line would expose Jimmy and his open stance. – Rajan Bala, *All The Beautiful Boys* (Rupa, 1990)

The media was obviously not going to keep mum. *Mid-Day* on 15 December 1983, the scheduled last day of the game, carried a quote by one P. Karunakaran Kutty of the State Bank of India. Taking into account the match fee of Rs 15,000 that the Indian cricketers got, he said, Amarnath had got Rs 45,000 to score 1 run! The title of the piece said it all – 'The Costliest Run in History!'

Rajan Bala's pessimism came through in the same issue: 'No logic, even stretched to an extreme, could explain his (Sunil's) attitude, and if his captain feels that the man he has depended upon is not keen, it is going to be very difficult for Indian cricket. It is sad, but there is more than meets the eye in his attitude.'

Kapil Dev unburdened himself in an interview with Pradeep Magazine, a young journalist working for the Chandigarh edition of *The Indian Express*. The reporter was elated to get a scoop – a declaration by the captain of India that his players were more interested in 'making money than playing the game'.

The captain's reported statement was merely a part of what was the most unpleasant fallout of the series defeat. What people had been dismissive about in 1979-80—the toss episode at Calcutta—they were inclined to take things a little more seriously in 1983. The World Cup win had resulted in the gradual transformation of a sport into a veritable industry. The stakes were higher than ever before, and the expectations of the public almost unreal. Having won the limited-overs World Cup, the Indian cricketers had been expected to steamroll the West Indies in the Tests. While there was no way the three defeats could be condoned, what the masses missed considering were the fundamental differences between One Day cricket and five-day cricket. While they certainly were a quality limited-overs team, the Indians of 1983 were a long way away from being considered a perfect Test side. The middle order was inconsistent, and the bowling line-up devoid of another bowler as capable of winning Test matches as Kapil Dev.

In his article titled 'What 'Price' Cricket?' that appeared in *The Indian Express* on 29 November 1983, Pradeep Shinde wrote that a former India batsman and captain had made a killing when Sunil fell for 90 in the Ahmedabad Test. He also referred to reports that Sunil's dismissal ten short of a hundred had broken the backs of several gamblers and bookies.

The detractors lived up to their reputation and took the next step, which was to question Sunil's integrity. The only thing they did not do was accuse him directly of taking money to gift his wicket away.

As was only to be expected, they sought support in Kapil Dev's statement, which was flashed across the country. Sunil was aghast to read his captain's quote. He called the Board president to express his unhappiness, and offered to pull out of the final Test if Kapil Dev indeed felt that way.

Salve summoned the duo to his home in Delhi. A discussion ensued, wherein Kapil Dev claimed that he had been misquoted. A statement to that effect was released to the media, and the issue resolved. Sunil's desire to drop down the order was also discussed. The brittleness of the middle order during the series, and Amarnath's inexplicable eclipse, may well have been in Kapil Dev's mind, when he acquiesced.

Sunil was not all that enthused with Kapil Dev's denial, but happy to be allowed to bat in the middle order. A lot more delighted was Marshall, who believed that his bowling had forced Sunil to withdraw.

Destiny would have the last laugh.

18

A SEESAW SAGA

> I can't see myself going beyond another year at the most, and I am tired of travelling, of the constant pressure to do well and the tension of being a Test player. My talent has been drying up for the last four years. I think the country's attention should be easing up. I have had enough of the country's attention. I have reached a stage where success or failure does not stir me as it used to. – Sunil Gavaskar, *Sunday,* 25 December 1983

The ploy to bat two down was part of an effort to ease up the country's attention. After the West Indies had batted first and scored 313, Sidhu accompanied Gaekwad to the middle to begin India's reply. Marshall had Gaekwad caught at fourth slip off his first ball. Off his next, he dismissed Vengsarkar in identical fashion. India were 0-2, and its greatest opening batsman-turned-middle-order-bat came in to open the innings for all practical purposes.

Richards ribbed him about it at the end of the first over. Not that Sunil thought too much about having to rush in. As far as he was concerned, the extra five minutes he had got to spend in the dressing room were worth their weight in gold.

Sidhu and he had just about got the innings off the blocks when Davis was struck on his right collar bone by a missile from the stands. Lloyd led his team off the field, and it took a while for the officials to placate him. Sidhu fell immediately after the resumption, and Malhotra followed him. India, 69-4 at stumps, would have been in deeper trouble on the following morning, had umpire Swaroop Kishen agreed that Sunil had gloved Marshall to Harper in the slips. However, the umpire had seen it strike Sunil's forearm protector.

The first day's play having been washed out, the match was already into the fourth day. There was nothing India could do, other than prevent a fourth defeat. Sunil had another escape when he inside-edged Marshall, and the ball sped past Dujon to the boundary. Holding maintained a teasing line and did his best to induce him to nibble at one outside the off-stump, but Sunil was not tempted. A pulled four off Marshall gave him his third fifty-plus score of the series. Yadav, who had come in as nightwatchman, was fifth out at the stroke of lunch. The score was 92-5. Ravi Shastri came in and saw his mentor square-cut Marshall for four.

The square-cut was more the exception than the rule. Sunil's innings at Madras marked his return to his conventional style.

> Gavaskar dropped down the order, but in effect, he was back to his usual position. Back too, with the responsibility of blunting the pace attack and building the innings. And he was equal to the task. There were no extravagant flourishes. He cut out the risks for the percentage strokes. – K.N. Prabhu, *TOI*, 27 December 1983

When Marshall and Roberts set traps for him and bounced, he preferred ducking to hooking. He milked the bowling, and let himself go only against rank bad deliveries. He moved into the 90s with a square-drive off Davis, and took a fresh guard a little later – at 94. A misfield by Marshall gave him four more, and an 'around-the-corner' single off Harper took him to 99. He turned the first ball of a fresh over by Davis to square-leg. Shastri responded, the spectators roared, and Sunil raised his bat to acknowledge the cheers for his thirtieth Test hundred. The record that had belonged to the Don for five decades was now his.

> His brashness and impetuousity had betrayed him and India in Calcutta and enraged critics had thirsted for his blood. Some of them went so far as to suggest that if the selectors had any self-respect, they should drop Gavaskar for this Test. Gavaskar was circumspect and cautious, now that his wish to bat at number four had been granted. He was cool, calculated, controlled. He batted with a fine sense of discipline and responsibility. He did not take an undue risk, play a rash forcing shot or an intemperate stroke. He was sedate, composed, dignified. . . . – Ron Hendricks, *The Indian Express*, 28 December 1983

He carried on despite an attack of cramps, and gifted his bat to Dujon at the tea interval. The Windies wicketkeeper had won several admirers for his elegant batsmanship during the series, Sunil being one of them. Dujon had in turn become a fan of Sunil's bat. Dujon was delighted to receive the bat, but Mrs Gavaskar wasn't when she discovered that her husband had gifted away yet another of his century bats.

Lloyd continued to attack in the final session, with three slips in place, but all they could do was stand and watch when Sunil essayed an exquisite late-cut off Holding. He then wowed the connoisseurs by dropping his arms and letting two 'perfume' balls by Davis fly past his nose. Crossing over to the other end, he square-drove Roberts for another boundary. Shastri fell for 72 minutes before the close, and Sunil came in, unbeaten on 149.

He was completely drained, but found the energy to repudiate the statements attributed to him in *Sunday* in a TV interview.

> Dr Narottam Puri: 'There has been a lot of talk going on that once you get your thirtieth hundred, there will be no more cricket.'
>
> Sunil: 'Well, I am very tired at the moment. I have certainly not taken any decision. I will be ready for the next season, which is ten months away!'

With one innings, Sunil had won back the hearts of all those whom he had angered at Calcutta. It was unfortunate that a player of his standing had to essay a marathon innings to 'prove' to a section of the masses that he wasn't as irresponsible as they had made him out to be.

> The Little Master is now the master of them all. With a library of records to his credit, Gavaskar left Bradman behind in the record books here today... he could not have chosen a better ground than Chepauk or a timelier occasion than this. They talk of the witching hour of midnight. For over 40,000 at the Chidambaram stadium and countless others gathered around TV sets and radios in the far corners of the land, it was the second hour past high noon which was the memorable, magical moment when Gavaskar made history for himself and those who shared in this noble litany. – K.N. Prabhu, *TOI,* 28 December 1983

The imminence of a draw did not prevent the spectators from thronging the Chidambaram stadium on the fifth morning to watch their idol. He completed his 150 with a push to mid-wicket off Marshall. Holding was glanced to the long-leg fence for his first four of the day. Doordarshan at this stage produced a wagonwheel, which indicated that he had got most of his runs behind square on both sides of the wicket. It implied that he had used the pace of the bowlers effectively.

The connoisseurs continued to get their money's worth. Sunil was on 159 when a delivery from Marshall leapt at him. Sunil met it with a straight bat, and the ball dropped at his feet.

Kapil Dev scored 26 before giving Marshall a return catch, and thereby providing the spectators with an opportunity to applaud another record. It was Marshall's thirty-third wicket of the series, taking him one ahead of Roberts' tally of 32 in 1974-75. The claps were soon overshadowed by the cheers when Sunil took a two to give India the first-innings lead.

The man whose record Marshall had broken had a lot to play for. Andy Roberts had missed the first four Tests due to a combination of injury and poor form, and it was clear that his place in the XI was no longer a certainty. When Lloyd brought him on from the pavilion end, he had everything to bowl for.

He bowled Sunil a bouncer that died after pitching, and was taken by a kneeling Dujon. A couple of short deliveries were followed by a fuller one. It wasn't the ideal ball to bowl to a batsman on song, and Sunil drove it through the covers for four. The boundary took him to 181. He had added 7 runs to his score when Roberts dug one in with all his might. The ball climbed and for once, Sunil, who had refrained from playing the hook, went for one. But the ball was a lot quicker than anticipated. He gloved it, but Dujon made a mess of the catch, giving Sunil an unintended, but welcome boundary. An upset Roberts retaliated by a scorcher of a bouncer that all but took Sunil's head off. The batsman's timely jerk away from the firing line was enough to convince everybody that the decline of his reflexes was grossly exaggerated.

A single off Roberts took him to his fourth double hundred. At the other end, Kirmani had got into a rhythm on what was his birthday, and India were 443-8 at tea. Kapil Dev, eager to bowl a second time in the game to give himself a chance of winning the Man of the Series award ahead of Marshall, declared at the end of the first over of the post-tea session, after Sunil became India's highest individual scorer in a Test. The record stood in the name of Vinoo Mankad, who had scored 231 against New Zealand, coincidentally in Madras, but at a different venue – the Corporation stadium. However, the Indian captain's quest to beat Marshall in the facile second innings was unsuccessful.

> The main attribute which Gavaskar has in common with Bradman is the ability to concentrate for hours on end. A wonderfully quick eye and a steely temperament have obviously helped Gavaskar, as they did the great Australian, but as with Jack Nicklaus or Bjorn Borg, it is the power to concentrate, which has accounted for their prodigious success. – John Woodcock, *London Times* (As carried in *Mid-Day* on 1 January 1984)

Clive Lloyd's 'Operation Vengeance' had been successful, but there was a catch. For the Windies, the series ended in much the same way as it had begun. At its start, they had been bewildered by the gifts received by the Indian cricketers after winning the World Cup. At its end, they felt the same way, as Sunil, the Man of the Match, was inundated with trophies, cash awards and even a Maruti car, which had just been launched in India, during the presentation ceremony. He drove the car through a cluster of officials and flashbulbs, and did a lap of the ground, thrilling the spectators and overshadowing the series winners!

Sunil then shifted his gaze to the Ranji Trophy, which had eluded Bombay since 1980-81. The success of the Ghulam Parkar-Lalchand Rajput opening combination gave him the liberty of batting in the middle order. His 87 in the semi-final against Haryana helped Bombay take the crucial first-innings lead. Delhi beat Baroda in the other semi-final by 440 runs, setting up a clash at the Wankhede between Indian cricket's bitterest rivals of the era.

As they walked out to toss, Sunil and Mohinder Amarnath would have wondered about the extraordinary events of the previous few months. What India would have achieved in Test cricket had Sunil complemented Amarnath's efforts in the Caribbean, and Amarnath complemented his at home, nobody will ever know.

Amarnath had displayed some form in the Ranji games, but his mind was as cluttered as it had been earlier in the season. Nothing else could have explained his decision to ask Bombay to bat after winning the toss. The hosts amassed a modest 625, of which Sunil's share was 206. Delhi were bowled out for 333 in response, but Sunil did not enforce the follow-on. He effectively killed the contest by doing so, but it was entirely in accordance with the way Bombayites played their cricket. The match was drawn, and Sunil received the Ranji Trophy for the second time since 1976-77.

'Each of us had a designated seat in the Wankhede dressing room. Mine was bang opposite Sunil's, next to the door that led to the washroom. I remember him taking it session-by-session during that innings. He would come in at an interval, wrap himself in a towel, and immerse himself in a book. One of the reserves would alert him when the resumption was ten minutes away. He would then put the book aside, and begin his preparations. I got to observe him closely during this game, and what I saw was that his face would change the moment he would fold his trousers before padding up. It is hard to describe the expression on his face – 'illuminated' is probably the apt word. I went on to share Bombay and India dressing rooms with him for the next few years and thus got to observe him on other occasions as well. That expression on his face, I will never forget.' – Raju Kulkarni

A couple of weeks after the Ranji final, Sunil received another trophy, this time in the oasis that was the Sharjah Cricket Ground in the

United Arab Emirates. India clinched the inaugural edition of the Asia Cup, beating Sri Lanka and Pakistan in round-robin encounters. The triangular tournament was the first official competition to be staged in Sharjah, where India and Pakistan had played some exhibition games in the early 1980s.

The Asia Cup win was a significant achievement, coming as it did after the debacle against the Windies, and despite the absence of the team's most valuable player.

Kapil Dev's dodgy right knee, which had been operated upon in 1980, had given way all over again. With India's next Test series scheduled for October 1984, he went in for an arthroscopic surgery at the end of the West Indies series, as there was ample time to recover. It meant that he was unavailable for the inaugural edition of the Asia Cup.

There was no question of the captaincy being passed onto someone who was around his age, or even younger. Shastri, who impressed as captain of a Young India side that toured Zimbabwe after the Windies series, was only twenty-two, and the selectors were as closed to the idea of assigning responsibility to the experienced Dilip Vengsarkar as they were to the thought of blooding pace bowlers in the pre-Kapil Dev era. Syed Kirmani was very much around, but with Delhi's keeper-batsman Surender Khanna all set to open the batting in Sharjah after a fabulous domestic season, there was a possibility of the senior man not figuring in the XI.

That left only one man in the fray. Sunil had under him a young side, with as many as five men who were part of the World Cup winning squad—Kapil Dev apart—missing.

Sporting a splendid moustache, Sunil began his fourth stint as captain of India with a ten-wicket thrashing of Sri Lanka. He backed youth, holding back veterans Madan Lal and Binny, and handing the new ball to Chetan Sharma and the Delhi all-rounder Manoj Prabhakar. The move paid off. Early wickets fell, and Shastri and Madan Lal applied the finishing touches. Ninety-seven was all that India needed to score, and the opening combination of Khanna and Ghulam Parkar finished it off in the twenty-second over.

> 'He had confidence in the abilities of the youngsters. He would go out of his way to make me feel comfortable in the team meetings. He was very supportive if I bowled a poor over.'
> – Chetan Sharma

Pakistan had lost to Sri Lanka in the opening encounter, and with the competition comprising only three round-robin games and no final, they needed to win comprehensively against India to bring the run-rate factor into the picture. India batted first and scored 188-4, effectively pocketing the tournament even if Pakistan were to win by ten wickets. Sunil went on the offensive in a stand of 78 with Patil, during the course of which the duo added 57 in eight overs.

Another splendid bowling performance followed, and Zaheer Abbas' team was bowled out for 134. India thus ended what had been a traumatic season on a high. They had begun it as World Champions, and ended it as Asian Champions. Among those who participated in the celebrations in the dressing room was the World Cup winning captain. Kapil Dev flew to Sharjah and for all practical purposes became a non-playing member of the squad.

A momentous event occurred on 19 July 1984. The ICC approved the joint bid put forth by India and Pakistan to host the 1987 World Cup. This meant that the premier quadrennial event would leave English shores for the first time. Would the Asian giants have been emboldened to go ahead with the bid, leave alone winning it, had 'Kapil's Devils' not triumphed on 25 June 1983?

A fully fit Kapil Dev began the 1984-85 season by leading the Rest of India to victory over Sunil's Bombay in the Irani Cup.

The World Cup winning skipper's next assignment was a private one; an all-rounders championship in England. He was about to board the plane when he heard the news of Sunil's appointment as captain for the forthcoming annual tour of Pakistan and series against England.

The Indian Express reported on 12 September 1984 on that the selection committee, headed by Ghulam Ahmed, took 'less than fifteen minutes to decide' on Sunil's candidature. It was conveyed to the media that the decision to reinstate Sunil was 'unanimous'.

It was a peculiar call. There was no doubt that the selectors had erred by deposing Sunil after the defeat in Pakistan. But by the same logic, it was equally wrong to remove Kapil Dev for losing one series.

Ironically, as it invariably happens in cricket, both mistakes worked to India's advantage.

The first international engagement of the new season was a five-match One Day series against Australia, organised to commemorate the Golden Jubilee of the Ranji Trophy. The series kicked off with a bash at the Taj in Bombay, which was attended by the past and the present of Indian cricket.

The festivities failed to obscure the fact that the mistake of staging international matches in September and early October, when the monsoon was active, had been repeated. The 1983 World Cup champions continued to flounder in the shorter variety, losing three of the five matches, with two others being abandoned due to rain. The third game of the series, which was played at Jamshedpur, gave the Australian and English cricket communities, both of whom hadn't been able to digest the development of 19 July 1984, the perfect excuse to lash out at the organisational capabilities of the BCCI.

With only a day separating the abandoned second encounter at Trivandrum and the third at Jamshedpur, the teams travelled to Madras, from where they flew to Calcutta to spend the night before the match. On their arrival, the Indian players discovered that no official was present to receive them. They had to walk to a nearby hotel and arrange their accommodation. Both teams were to fly to Jamshedpur the next morning in the same plane, a tiny Fokker Friendship aircraft. When the players were about to board along with their kits, the authorities realised that the aircraft would not be able to take the weight. It was then decided to transport the kits by road. The scheduled start to the match was only a couple of hours away.

The players reached the venue and began their wait for the equipment. To placate the capacity crowd that was starting to get restless, the umpires were told to make pitch and ground inspections at regular intervals. Fortunately for the organisers, there had been some rain on the eve of the game, and so the charade looked authentic. What did puzzle the spectators was the sight of some Indian and Australian players emerging from their dressing rooms in casuals! By this time, more than an hour had elapsed since the scheduled start of play, and a message reached the ground that the van carrying the kits was stuck in heavy traffic. A convoy of vehicles was immediately despatched to the trouble spot. After the bags finally arrived, the authorities decided to play an official twenty-four-over encounter. India were 21-2 in the sixth over when the rains came and did not go away.

Sunil was criticised for the 0-3 defeat and his reluctance to open. What the media conveniently forgot was that the Khanna-Parkar combination had done well in the Asia Cup and therefore deserved to be persisted with for at least three games. Unfortunately, they did not click, and Shastri and Binny did the job in the fourth game and put on 104. Parkar accompanied Shastri in the fifth, with Binny dropping down to number three.

Sunil attributed the defeat to poor cricket, and the suspect fitness-levels of some of his players.

> I want our cricketers to understand that they carry the hopes and the best wishes of the Indian people. What was disappointing in the One-Day series was that I was never sure which player was fit. Whatever the qualities of a cricketer, he must possess the integrity to state that he is not fit when he is not. And more importantly, work on his fitness. – Sunil Gavaskar, *The Indian Express*, 8 October 1984

Strong words, but they hold true even today.

The efforts of the players to get their act together moved him to declare on 10 October 1984 that the team he was taking to Pakistan for yet another annual series was one of the fittest he had ever seen.

> Skipper Sunil Gavaskar's hand in the selection of the Indian team to Pakistan can be seen ... Knowing his thinking, he will do his best not to lose and to win if he possibly can ... The selectors have clearly seen eye-to-eye with his views because this (Pakistan) is no place to blood youngsters. – Rajan Bala, *The Indian Express*, 19 September 1984

The Indians started the Pakistan tour miserably, losing the first One-Day international at Quetta by 46 runs, and prompting watchers to suggest that they be packed off to the nearby Mianwali Jail.

They regained their confidence with a win in an exhibition One-dayer at Rawalpindi just before the first Test at Lahore. There was excitement in the air, for the Indian captain was about to become only the fourth cricketer, after Englishmen Colin Cowdrey and Geoffrey Boycott, and West Indian Clive Lloyd, to play a hundred Tests. Sunil's stature as a cricketer was underscored when Gen Zia-ul-Haq took time off from his state commitments to visit the Gaddafi stadium and felicitate the first Asian to complete a century of Test appearances.

On the eve of the game, Sunil expressed his determination to break the voodoo that had plagued the last two Indian sides to visit Pakistan. His side was to face a bowling attack that did not include Imran Khan, who had recovered from his shin injury, but had opted to test his fitness by turning out for New South Wales in Australia's domestic circuit.

> I may have to open. . . . Can't say right now. It will depend on many factors. Honestly, I have gone off opening. . . . But if the situation arises wherein I have to do so in the interests of the side, do I have a choice? – Sunil Gavaskar, quoted in *The Indian Express,* 10 October 1984

Sunil had batted in the middle order in the One-dayers against Australia, the Asia Cup, and of course, his team's last Test against the West Indies at Madras. The squad for Pakistan comprised six other players who had opened in First-class cricket – Gaekwad, Shastri, Khanna, Parkar, Binny and Vengsarkar. But the psychological factor won hands down, considering that it was a series against the old enemy. Sunil decided to revert to the top of the order.

His hundredth Test was an absorbing affair. Batting first, Pakistan had an early hiccup when debutant Chetan Sharma uprooted Mohsin Khan's off-stump in his first over in Test cricket. He went on to dismiss Mudassar and Miandad before they could settle down. Pakistan were 110-4 and looking vulnerable, at which point Zaheer Abbas dropped anchor. Salim Malik and Ashraf Ali assisted him in a recovery operation, which saw Pakistan totalling 428-9 by stumps on the second day. Although Zaheer scored 168, his was by no means a flowing innings like his earlier hundreds against India.

Pakistan declared overnight. Gaekwad fell with only seven on the board, but Sunil and Vengsarkar got stuck into the bowling. They added 87, before Sunil flicked left-arm paceman Azeem Hafiz to Salim Malik at square-leg when he was two short of his fifty. That triggered off a sensational collapse. In 1984, there was no Imran, but Hafiz proved to be a competent substitute.

As was the case in 1982-83, the Pakistani bowlers extracted prodigious swing, and were aided by what the Indians perceived as ordinary umpiring. Kapil Dev was so livid at being adjudged leg-before that he first let his feelings be known on the field, and then attacked a kitbag in the dressing room with his bat. Sandeep Patil was anything but amused, for it was his kitbag that had been singled out for this special attention. The last nine wickets fell for 62 runs, and India were asked to follow-on, 272 runs behind, early on the fourth day. Hafiz apart, the star of the third day was stand-in captain Javed Miandad. Zaheer, the incumbent, could not take the field due to a wrist injury, but Miandad ensured that he wasn't missed.

The start of play on the fourth day was preceded by an episode that was straight out of the 1978-79 series. The umpires, Khizer Hayat and Sunil's old pal Shakoor Rana, threatened not to take the field on the fourth day unless Kapil Dev tendered an apology for his reaction on the previous day. The issue was sorted out when Raj Singh Dungarpur, the Indian manager, reminded the concerned people that the west was looking for opportunities to argue that India and Pakistan were incapable of working together.

In the second innings, Sunil put on 85 with Gaekwad before seamer Jalal-ud-Din hit him on the front pad well outside the off-stump. An appeal ensued, and the umpire promptly raised his index finger. Sunil was far from happy, for the ball had hit his bat before hitting the pad. Vengsarkar fell at 114, and in came Mohinder Amarnath.

Not even his most fanatical supporters would have expected Amarnath to return after his flop show in 1983-84. On the eve of the Pakistan tour, he had dropped in at the Ferozeshah Kotla, where his erstwhile team-mates were engaged in a trial game. He caught up with the reinstated captain, and got a shock. Sunil asked him to borrow equipment and play! Gaekwad gladly lent him his gear. Amarnath played, and did well.

A bigger surprise was in store. At the selection committee meeting, Sunil made no bones of his preference for experience over youth. The selectors agreed, and recalled Amarnath.

On his arrival at the crease in the second innings, Amarnath, who had scored 36 in the first, would have definitely experienced a feeling of déjà vu. The similarities to the start of the 1982-83 series were striking; the Gaddafi stadium at Lahore, the first Test of a series, a big score by Zaheer Abbas earlier in the game, and for the umpteenth time, his own career at stake. There were, however, two key differences. There was no Imran in the Pakistani bowling line-up. And more crucially, Amarnath had adopted a new batting stance; the conventional side-on stance, in contrast to the open one that had fetched him all those runs in 1982-83 and then all but ended his career in 1983-84. He had realised during a post-season introspection that his stance and backlift were to blame for his shocking decline. From the commencement of the 1982-83 tour to Pakistan till the end of the World Cup, his backlift had been relatively straight. However, in 1983-84, it had become angular, and was leaving a gaping hole in the 'gate' – the area between bat and pad at the time of playing the ball.

At the Gaddafi stadium in October 1984, Amarnath was the epitome of orthodox batsmanship. 'Use your bat, and only your bat,' he kept telling himself, apprehensive of how the fielders and umpires would react if the ball were to hit his pads.

Gaekwad had moved to 60 when a Tauseef delivery seemed to have ricocheted off his front pad to Malik in the close-in cordon. The umpire, however, agreed with the appeal of the bowling side, and sent the batsman on his way.

The score was 164-4 when Shastri came in. The duo stayed on for the remainder of the fourth day and most of the fifth, before Shastri became the victim of another inexplicable leg-before verdict for 71. Amarnath and he had added 126 for the fifth wicket. Binny then met with a similar fate, when Hayat raised his index finger the moment Wasim Raja struck the batsman on the left boot, without even waiting for a proper appeal. Binny made his way back, and was asked by a furious Raj Singh why he had walked off so promptly when he was so obviously not out. 'But didn't you tell us that no kind of dissent against umpiring decisions would be tolerated?' Binny posed a counter-question. The manager had no answer.

This exchange notwithstanding, the Indian dressing room was in a relatively good mood at that stage, for the match had been saved by then. Kapil essayed an entertaining cameo, keeping Amarnath company as the latter completed a hundred, his eighth in Test cricket, and by far his best, given the circumstances.

His team's fightback prompted Sunil to launch an offensive, which was not too dissimilar to Lloyd's at Ahmedabad:

> I think it (the draw) is a miracle, achieved despite the best efforts of the umpires. I had, before I came here, expected some close decisions, but what happened in the Test is beyond belief. – Sunil Gavaskar, as quoted in *The Indian Express*, 22 October 1984

Injuries and illnesses hit the visitors hard in the second Test at Faisalabad. They batted first on a featherbed of a track and scored 500, with Patil and Shastri getting hundreds. Kapil Dev tore a muscle in his lower back and left the field after the fifth delivery of his fifth over. That put paid to any outside chance the Indians may have had of making a match of it. The Pakistanis proceeded to play for records, with Mudassar scoring 199, and Qasim Omar 210. Sunil was stricken by influenza and did not come to the ground on the fourth day, and a throat infection laid Patil low. Shastri ran into the fence while chasing a hit and gashed his right forearm. The young veteran impressed many watchers by declining to go to the hospital to get the wound stitched, as that would have left Amarnath, the stand-in skipper, with hardly any bowling options. Pakistan eventually got to 674-6 on the final day, before a halt was called.

> 'It was a memorable tour for me. I made my debut at Lahore and took a wicket in my very first over. I was ecstatic, but brought down to earth fairly quickly when we batted. I went in at number ten, when we were struggling to avoid the follow-on. The instructions were to stay there, and let Mohinder Amarnath do the scoring. When I faced Azeem Hafiz, who had done all the damage, something came over me, and I hit him for four. I was thrilled with the stroke, and became overconfident. An awful stroke followed, and I was bowled. Even as I returned to the pavilion, I was under the impression that I would be appreciated for hitting that boundary. But that didn't quite happen. Nobody said anything to me, and after a while, Sunil broke the silence: "Young man, if you play a shot like that again, I can assure you

> that you will never play for India," he said. I got the message. In the next Test at Faisalabad, he promoted me to number eight. I batted for nearly one-and-a-half hours, determined not to play a bad shot. Abdul Qadir struck me in the chest on a few occasions, but I refused to attack. I realised that it was wrong to gift your wicket, when as a bowler, you knew how difficult it was to take wickets. Thanks to SMG, I started taking my batting a lot more seriously, and eventually finished with an international hundred.'
> – Chetan Sharma

Amarnath stayed in charge for the one-dayer at Sialkot, with both Sunil and Kapil Dev out of action. The Indians batted first and scored 210-3 from the allotted forty overs, with Patil and Vengsarkar batting superbly. They were oblivious of the happenings in and around the dressing room.

> 'The Indian innings was on when Jasdev Singh, who was part of our AIR (All India Road) team, received a call. He was told that Mrs Gandhi had been assassinated. "We have to cut short our trip," Jasdev said. He asked me to convey the news to the Indian team. I went to the dressing room and informed Raj Singh and Sunil. I remember tears rolling down Sunil's cheeks. The others were informed at the lunch interval. Every Indian present at the ground—there were fifty-five of us, the players included—was told to gather in the dressing room. A decision was taken to abandon the rest of the tour, which included a One-dayer at Peshawar and a Test at Karachi.' – Sudhir Vaidya

The Indian contingent flew to Karachi, and then returned to India in two groups, one going to Delhi and the other to Bombay. By the time the players had returned, David Gower's England team was already in India, to play a series of five Tests and five One Day Internationals. The entire country having come to a standstill following the assassination, the English team flew to Sri Lanka to get some much-needed practice. They returned to face a slightly revised itinerary after normalcy was restored.

Sunil's immediate priority was to end an embarrassing drought. It was three years since India had won a Test. The last win had been achieved against England at Bombay in November 1981. On the eve of the first Test of the 1984-85 series against the same team at the same venue, he sensed an opportunity to break the thirty-one-Test deadlock, in the form of the leg-spinner Laxman Sivaramakrishnan.

'Siva' was only eighteen. He had made his Test debut in the Caribbean in 1982-83, and done reasonably well in domestic cricket since. He was inducted into the squad for the first Test after a match-winning performance against the visitors for the Ravi Shastri-led India Under-25s. The England batsmen had found it difficult, if not impossible, to figure him out, and Shastri, as astute a judge of temperament as his mentor, was convinced that the boy was ready for the big league. There were two other members of that under-25 side whom he strongly recommended to Sunil: a slim and wristy batsman from Hyderabad named Mohammad Azharuddin, and a wicketkeeper-batsman from Bangalore named Sadanand Vishwanath. Azhar, who had impressed one and all with his unbeaten 51 for the Rest of India in the Irani game, was drafted into the fourteen for the first Test.

Siva lived up to his promise with figures of 12-181, with India completing an eight-wicket win on the fifth morning. He spun England out for 195 in the first innings. Shastri (142) and Kirmani (102) led India's response of 465. The fact that the middle order wore a settled look, with Vengsarkar, Amarnath and Patil among the runs, left Sunil with no option but to open. He began well, but was caught behind off Norman Cowans for 27.

England were as upset with the umpiring as the Indians were with the Pakistani umpiring at Lahore.

> So what to do? Sunil Gavaskar again offers the conclusion that came to recently, that an international panel of umpires be set up. Then the finger of bias cannot be pointed. – Scyld Berry, *Mid-Day*, 4 December 1984

These were prophetic words uttered by the captain of India.

The Indians were not amused with Allan Lamb's reaction after being declared out, stumped off Siva in the second innings. The batsman had apparently looked towards where his compatriots were seated in the press box, and shrugged his shoulders. He would have been embarrassed to check out a photograph in a leading newspaper the following day, which showed his right toe dangling in the air, and the bails off.

England batted a lot better in the second innings, scoring 317, but the hosts needed only 51 to win. The openers fell, but Vengsarkar and Amarnath knocked off the required runs with ease. As the firecrackers exploded across the Wankhede to end India's thirty-one-Test drought, Sunil emphasised the need to not get carried away to the media, and gifted Siva a box of chocolates named Black Magic. The media in turn highlighted the woes of his counterpart David Gower, who had now suffered his seventh defeat in his tenth Test as captain.

> 'It would be appropriate to say that we bowlers would vie for Sunil's praise. It was not often that he paid compliments to a bowler. There were times when I took quite a few wickets, and he said nothing. On the other hand, there were instances wherein he expressed his satisfaction, although I had gone wicketless. Most of us would have preferred the latter option any day. If he praised you, your day was made.' – Raju Kulkarni

Kapil Dev had reason to be delighted, for Allan Lamb's wicket in the first innings had made him only the second Indian after Bedi to take 250 Test wickets. However, he wasn't very happy.

Stories of his being unhappy with the handling of a single-wicket tournament in Varanasi did the rounds during the Test. On 1 December 1984, the third day of the Test, *Mid-Day* reported that Kapil Dev got Rs 7,000, Amarnath, Vengsarkar, Patil and Chetan Chauhan Rs 4,000 each, Yashpal Sharma Rs 3,500, and Sandhu and Ghavri Rs 3,000 each, for participating in the said event.

The all-rounder's alleged contention was that Sunil, who had played a lead role in organising the tournament, was paid Rs 75,000 instead of Rs 50,000, as had been originally decided. What was also reported was that while Kapil Dev agreed that Sunil, being the organiser, was entitled to be paid more than the others, the other cricketers ought to have been paid equal amounts. The same *Mid-Day* issue carried a response of sorts by Sunil: 'If I tell you that I will give you Re 1 and I give it to you, then there is no reason for you to crib.'

Rajan Bala, in a piece that appeared in *The Indian Express* on 19 December 1984, wrote about an 'annoyed Sunil looking up at the press box during the Bombay Test, calling out to the correspondent of a local eveninger (might well have been the *Mid-Day* representative) and asking him who had named him in the report in question.' Bala also wrote about asking Sunil at lunch on the fourth day of the Bombay Test, what the affair was all about. 'Charges have been levelled by him. So you ask him,' is what he reported Sunil as having replied. Who the 'him' was, one can only guess.

Sandeep Patil, in a piece for *Shatkar*, the Marathi sports weekly he edited, accused Kapil Dev of leaking the news to the media himself. Patil alleged that Kapil Dev, after learning that Sunil was getting Rs 25,000 more, provoked the other players to demand higher amounts. 'Kapil had first agreed to play for the amount given to him, and hence his subsequent act is like stabbing Gavaskar in the back,' Patil wrote. The latter responded by reminding Patil in the 18 December 1984 issue of *The Indian Express* that prize money was always shared equally.

The stage was set for a series of events that was to make the happenings at Calcutta in December 1983 look like a bed of roses.

England won the first One-dayer at Pune, and then had the better of the first three days of the second Test at Delhi. Trailing by 111 in the first innings, India were 15-2 in the second, when Amarnath joined the captain for a fruitful stand. The comeback man batted beautifully, warming up with a hook for six off paceman Norman Cowans. Sunil was initially tentative, but gained in fluency as the innings progressed. The six he hit off off-spinner Pat Pocock was cheered lustily by the spectators. His 51 at the close comprised five boundaries and that six. India were 128-2 and a draw was imminent.

At close, Sunil expressed his satisfaction with the bowling of Siva, who had bagged great wickets in the first innings. He told the media that his and Amarnath's aim would be to go for quick runs on the last day.

Amarnath fell early on the fifth day, but Sunil batted on until he tried to cut off-spinner Pat Pocock's stock delivery, missed, and was bowled for 65. Patil reached 41 before chancing his arm against left-arm spinner Phil Edmonds. The ball gathered more height than distance, and Lamb held a catch in the deep. Kapil Dev hit Pocock for a six over long-on, and then went for another, only to be caught at extra cover. This was the cue for the spectators to begin scratching their heads, unable as they were to comprehend what was happening. Their hands remained on their heads, and then slid in front of their eyes, as four more wickets fell for next to nothing. From 207-4, India slid to 235 all out, and England found themselves needing only 125 to level the series. They had more than a session in which to do so, and cruised home with eight wickets in hand. It was as stunning a turnaround as India's victory in the World Cup final.

> 'India began as favourites and became even hotter favourites having won the first Test. The triumph in Delhi that got us back into the series, hinged on getting Kapil out in the final session. I suspected that at lunch on that day, we had almost lost our chance, but gave the team a talk to rouse them into one final effort, and when Kapil played one big shot too many, it opened the door for us. Had he played properly for another half hour, we could not have won. Rumour had it that there had been a falling out between Kapil and Sunny. How true that was, I do not know.' – David Gower

Sunil was incensed with the defeat, as were the selectors when he joined them. In what turned out to be one of the most dramatic meetings in the history of Indian cricket, the selectors decided to drop Kapil Dev from the next One-dayer and Test for batting irresponsibly. One of the selectors went so far as to recommend that the all-rounder be docked his match fees. Obviously, the matter was debated, and the pro-Kapil Dev section placated by a suggestion to omit Patil for the same reason.

With all due respect to the selectors, it was a knee-jerk reaction. The selectors had chosen to ignore the fact that Kapil Dev, for all his qualities, was human. As he wrote in his autobiography later, the shot that had cost him his wicket was no different from the one he had perished to in the 1983 World Cup final. It was a poor piece of cricket, but to axe him for one mistake was ridiculous. That he had top-scored with 60 in the first innings, when many of his colleagues had lost their wickets to careless shots, was overlooked.

Sunil, who like his predecessors and successors did not have a vote during selection meetings, knew what was coming. The news broke, and all hell broke loose.

> 'I don't want Kapil Dev, Gavaskar was supposed to have told the selectors...' – K.R. Wadhwaney, *The Indian Express*, 18 December 1984

There was no question of Sunil denying what he had never said. There was no point doing so, for a section of the media had decided to nail him by hook or by crook. It did not cross the minds of his detractors that Messrs Chandu Borde (chairman), Hanumant Singh, Ambar Roy, Kripal Singh and Bishan Bedi, who constituted the selection committee, had minds of their own, and did not need anybody else to think on their behalf. What ought to have opened the eyes and heads of the detractors was the panel's refusal to reconsider its decision despite a directive issued by the BCCI President Salve himself.

> Did it mean that all my sacrifices I had made had been forgotten suddenly because someone said I hadn't followed instructions? Should any batsman who loses his wicket, and thereby acts against a captain's instructions to stay there, be dropped?... Were they implying that Kapil Dev was not trying? If I am a non-trier, there is no trier in Indian cricket. – Kapil Dev, *Cricket My Style* (Allied, 1987)

Back in December 1984, the stories flew thick and fast. Sunil was said to be unhappy with Kapil Dev for skipping the Pune One-dayer due to a damaged finger, and upset with him for rearranging the field for other bowlers at Delhi. The muck got too much for the BCCI president to ignore, and Salve summoned the duo for the second time in a year. The duo, along with Patil, attended the BCCI Tours Committee meeting in Nagpur on 22 December 1984. Sunil and Kapil then had two rounds of talks with Salve, during which they told the president that they bore no rancour towards each other.

The third Test at Calcutta, which commenced on the last day of 1984, was drawn, unlike the game of the previous season, but it was as controversial. Sunil won the toss and elected to bat. India's first innings was interspersed with several interruptions due to bad light. A draw was a foregone conclusion after only four overs were bowled on the second day. Sunil's decision to prolong the innings till the fourth day earned him the ire of the spectators for the second year in succession, and they let their feelings be known. The fusillade of stones and fruits put Sunil off the Eden for the rest of his career.

> He argued that he didn't declare because he had set a target of 450 ... the wicket had rolled out well and no miracles were expected on the last two days ... 'Why should I expose our regular bowlers for long unnecessarily?' – *Mid-Day*, 5 January 1985

> The India skipper, who commands a substantial fee for each Test appearance, should learn to spare a thought for the cash customers instead of adopting postures that can kill the goose that lays the golden eggs of cricket. – Ron Hendricks, *The Indian Express*, 4 January 1985 (filed)

It was claimed that the police had to force Sunil to declare, for fear of a violent reaction from the crowd. Sunil denied this charge. He closed the innings when India were 437-7.

> 'In Calcutta, I felt Sunny could have been more positive in his attempts to force a win. I said so to the local press in [a] conference and earned myself the title of preacher from Sunny in return – he felt I should have kept my thoughts to myself. I was happy to have drawn the game and happy to put the pressure onto my opposite number, knowing that he was not a great fan of Calcutta!' – David Gower

Not everything about that match was forgettable. Sunil wanted to drop down the order to accommodate Srikkanth, who had scored 99 in the second one-dayer at Cuttack. However, Borde, the chairman of the Selection Committee, pushed for Azharuddin, who had scored two hundreds in a Ranji game prior to the Test. Had Sunil been the Hitler-like figure that sections of the media were claiming he was, he would have refused to abide by the chairman's instructions. But he did not. Azharuddin was picked, and he went on to become the seventh Indian to score a century on debut. Shastri's 111 was his third hundred in four Tests, a superlative performance by a player who had batted at number ten on his debut.

Azharuddin and Shastri notwithstanding, there was more action in the newspapers than on the field in the first week of 1985. A fair bit of it would have done the scriptwriter of a Bollywood melodrama proud.

In an interview that appeared in Patil's *Shatkar*, Kapil Dev was quoted as saying that 'he would be happy if a meeting was convened between him and Sunil with G.R. Viswanath as the moderator.'

> I am ready to forget my differences with Sunil in the interests of the country. But I do not know if he will forget. I will be happy if the meeting between Sunil and me, along with Vishy, is held as soon as possible. . . . Give my regards and convey my best to Sunil for the Calcutta Test. He may be against me, but I am not against him. Whenever he needs my help, he may call me and I will be there. The only thing I did not like was the way I was removed. – Kapil Dev, as quoted in *Mid-Day*, 2 January 1985

Two days later, *The Indian Express* carried Sunil's response to Kapil Dev's offer: 'Kapil knows that I have a phone. He also knows the telephone number. It's as simple as that.'

> 'There was never any war between Sunil and Kapil Dev. They would always laugh at the attempts of the media to create a conflict.' – Bapu Nadkarni

If one went with Mr Nadkarni's interpretation, and indeed, those advanced by the antagonists themselves in subsequent years, one gets the impression that the conflict between Sunil Gavaskar and Kapil Dev was nothing but a myth created and propounded by the media, but admittedly cultivated by the so-called foes themselves!

> It somehow must have been destined that we should be set on a collision course on various issues. There are incidents when I feel I have been badly done in, and I too may have hurt Gavaskar's feelings on other occasions. But our differences are never so distressing that we couldn't make up as men and

forget everything except the job on hand when we step into the field. – Kapil Dev, *Straight From the Heart, An Autobiography* (Macmillan, 2004)

Shastri, who was in the batting form of his life, followed up on his Calcutta hundred by blasting the Baroda bowlers for 200 off 123 balls in a Ranji game at the Wankhede. It was the fastest double hundred in First-class cricket. Baroda's Tilak Raj underwent the gruesome experience of being hit for six sixes in an over.

That performance, and Kapil Dev's return to the team after his one-Test suspension, may well have been on the minds of the Indian batsmen on the first day of the Pongal Test at Madras. They were in a spot of bother at 45-3, with Sunil, Srikkanth and Vengsarkar back in the pavilion, but Amarnath (78) and Azharuddin (48) set out to prove that attack was the best form of defence. Kapil Dev (53) and Kirmani (30) were as assertive later in the innings, but too many wickets were lost in the quest for strokes, and the innings ended at 272 with a bit of the first day's play still left.

Sivaramakrishnan had taken eighteen wickets in the first three innings of the series, but had done little of note thereafter. Gower was out of touch, but his deputy was very much on song. Mike Gatting had shown his team-mates the way by using his bat and feet against Siva during his 136 in the second innings at Bombay. At Delhi, opener Tim Robinson took a leaf out of his vice-captain's book and scored 160.

At Madras, Graeme Fowler, the other opener, stood up to be counted. He put on 178 with Robinson, and stayed on to add another 241 with Gatting. The vice-captain scored 207 and Fowler 201. England totalled a modest 652.

Neil Foster, who had figures of 6-104 in the first innings, then tightened his team's grip on the game by scalping Sunil, Srikkanth and Vengsarkar with only 22 on the board. Amarnath and Azharuddin counterattacked again, but the deficit was far too much. While Amarnath fell five short of a hundred, Azharuddin reached the magic figure. It was his second hundred in his second Test. As long as Shastri and he were in the middle on the last morning, India had an outside chance of saving the game, but both fell pretty early. England needed only 35 runs to go 2-1 up in the series.

Going by the pre-series projections and relative-known strengths and weaknesses of both sides, India were one Test away from suffering their worst-ever series defeat at home. England had been in disarray after being blackwashed 0-5 by the West Indies in the summer of 1984. Lamb apart, the batting looked fragile, and Botham had taken the tour off. The fast-bowling department, consisting of Norman Cowans, Richard Ellison and Neil Foster, was inexperienced. Edmonds and Pocock, the spinners, were seasoned campaigners, but they were not in the class of Derek Underwood. Yet, these men had made the Indian batsmen struggle by simply doing the basics right.

For once, Sunil found himself in a hopeless position. There was nothing he could have said or done to his players, for his own performances were poor. His sequence of scores at the end of the Calcutta Test read 27, 5, 1, 65, 13, 17 and 3. He studied himself on video and realised that his backlift had been coming down from third-man instead of the slips. Its angle was making him play across the line of the ball.

It was his second bad patch in less than two years, after the Caribbean tour in early 1983. The issues he had, vis-à-vis opening the innings, had done nothing to mitigate the state of affairs.

He had wanted to drop down the order since 1983-84, and had done so at Madras against the West Indies. The absence of a competent replacement had forced him to return to the opening slot in the 1984-85 season. In the wake of Srikkanth's success in the One-dayers, Sunil had re-thought about dropping down for the Calcutta Test, but Borde had come up with the inspired suggestion to play Azharuddin. Any thoughts that Sunil might have had about batting in the middle order in the Madras Test against England were thwarted by the selectors, who omitted Gaekwad from the squad. Sunil had no option but to open with Srikkanth.

Although Shastri was very much around, and had in fact put on a record 188 for the first wicket with Srikkanth in the second One-Day International at Cuttack, his success in the middle order in Test cricket probably prevented Sunil from pushing him upwards.

Ironically, Sunil accompanied Srikkanth to the middle in the third one-dayer at Bangalore. The move did not make sense, given the world record established by Shastri and Srikkanth in the previous game.

It certainly did not appeal to the spectators, who booed the Indian captain.

Sunil thrived in the face of hostility, scoring 40 before being dismissed by his former Somerset colleague Vic Marks. India finished with 205-6. It was a defendable total, but the bowlers were not supported by the fielders, much to the annoyance of the spectators. They reacted by doing what their counterparts in Pune and Calcutta had done earlier in the series, and Sunil took his team off the field after some players stationed in the outfield were struck by missiles. England eventually completed a three-wicket win with one over to spare, thus winning the One Day series.

Playing for pride in the fourth game at Nagpur, India overhauled a competitive target of 240. The highlight of the innings was a stand of 76 in sixty-six balls by the superstars. Kapil Dev scored 54, and Sunil, this time batting at number five, made 52.

Not surprisingly, anti-Gavaskar banners greeted the Indian team on its arrival in Chandigarh, Kapil Dev's hometown, for the final game of the One Day series. Overnight rain reduced the game to a fifteen-overs-a-side encounter. England scored 121-6 and restricted India to 114-5.

India needed to win the final Test at Kanpur to square the Test series. The rival captains had indicated their preference for an underprepared pitch, but unfortunately from the Indian viewpoint, a batting beauty was dished out. When Sunil won the toss and elected to bat, his team's only chance of victory was to amass a big total and then get England out twice. Given the situation, the decision to play an extra batsman and get Amarnath to share the new ball with Kapil Dev was peculiar.

Mohammad Azharuddin, whose form had earned him a promotion to his favourite number three position, created history on the second morning when he became the first batsman to score a hundred in each of his first three Tests. Vengsarkar scored 137 and Sunil declared at 553-8. England were 286-6 in response, when Gower, who like his counterpart had had an ordinary series, added 100 with Edmonds and effectively got both hands around the winners' trophy. There was no possibility of a result when India began their second innings on the final day, only 136 ahead. Sunil, with nothing more to lose, held himself back and instructed Shastri and Srikkanth to attack.

Shastri fell early, but Azharuddin got stuck into the bowling. Srikkanth, assurance personified after his 84 in the first innings, complemented him perfectly. The score was 97-1 when Sunil declared.

England batted out time to take the series 2-1, and Gower found himself on his team-mates' shoulders shortly after he had taken possession of the trophy.

> 'Did England win the series? Or did India lose it? A bit of both. We could not have won in Delhi without Kapil's help and that disagreement in the Indian dressing room. Maybe they could have put more pressure on us in Calcutta? However, we won fair and square in Madras with the sort of cricket that makes a captain's task easy. With two men getting double hundreds and Neil Foster bowling beautifully on a pitch with some unexpected pace, it made for a superlative performance.' – David Gower

Where had India gone wrong after the first Test? They had batted well in the odd-numbered Tests, and poorly in the even-numbered games. However, their bowling had been patchy throughout. Kapil Dev and Siva, the two strike bowlers, had been ineffective after the first Test, and the likes of Chetan Sharma and Shivlal Yadav inconsistent. They hadn't helped their chances of levelling the series by playing only four specialist bowlers at Kanpur. Most critically, their premier batsman had failed.

> 'Sunil was a studious and streetsmart captain. His management, knowledge of the game and assessment of the opposition was immaculate. However, when he would not score as a batsman, he would be disappointed, and that probably affected his ability to lead. This happens with all performance-oriented captains. So intensely do they channelise their energies into performing that they tend to find it difficult to devote them to others. He deserved the honour to be captain of India. But he ought to have been utilised as the number one player thereafter. The media created unnecessary controversies during his tenure, and those pressures may well have got to him whenever he underwent a bad patch. If you look at his career, it makes no difference whether he was the captain or not. For an average player, the captaincy can be a highlight. In Sunil's case, his performances as a batsman were the highlight.' – Late Ashok Mankad

While the Indians licked their wounds at Kanpur, their compatriots in the press box readied themselves to give the losing captain another bollocking.

> He went into his shell. He withdrew completely, avoiding meeting and guiding his colleagues, some of them extremely green, not realising that he was the captain of a team, which looked up to him for uplifting drooping spirits in difficult times. Gavaskar's defeatist approach and thinking played a pivotal role in India's loss. – *The Indian Express*, 15 February 1985

The *Hindu* had already accused Sunil of not coming out of the dressing room to applaud when Azharuddin completed a hattrick of hundreds. The others went hammer-and-tongs at the Indian captain on the final day, for declaring at 97-1 when there was absolutely no chance of a result. Azharuddin, who was batting on 54 when the innings was declared, could have gone on to score a fourth hundred, they believed.

> IS GAVASKAR JEALOUS OF AZHARUDDIN? . . . Cricket lovers all over the country are already lining up behind Azhar. Is Gavaskar missing his status as a messiah? . . . Has he deliberately tried to place obstacles in the young superstar's (sic) way? . . . What kept Gavaskar away during Azhar's moment of glory may never be revealed. Was it pique that a man far younger and far more inexperienced had stolen his thunder (first innings)? . . . Did Gavaskar honestly expect to dismiss a side, which had batted for over two days and scored over 400 runs, in just over two hours (second innings)? Or was it just another gesture of empty defiance, crafty enough to prevent Azhar . . . from getting another hundred. . . .' – *Sunday*

This was speculative journalism in all its glory. While Azharuddin was bewildered, Sunil, whose height had come in the way of his being noticed amongst his team-mates after Azharuddin's hattrick, was amused.

However, he was in complete agreement with one line in the piece, albeit in a different context: 'Perhaps the limited-overs matches in Australia next month will provide the answer.'

Four
APOGEE

19

GENERALISSIMO

'... Gavaskar is finding it increasingly difficult to psyche himself sufficiently for the big challenges. Even his most loyal supporters have not failed to notice a marked indifference over happenings on the field of play. He gives the impression that he just couldn't care less... But Gavaskar will once again captain India in limited-overs cricket, for which he is, by common consent, not quite equipped...' – *Mid-Day*, 1 February 1985

He scaled the wall that surrounded Chandigarh's Hotel Mountview, and slithered down the other side.

It would have reminded him of the thrillers he loved to read, and of his childhood in Chikalwadi. It would have made him realise that his limbs were still flexible. But the one emotion that overrode every other was anger.

There wasn't too much time to dwell on it, though. A few hours after the final One Day International against England had ended on the evening of 27 January 1985, a message was delivered to Sunil at the hotel where the Indian team was staying. The instructions issued to him were to climb the wall, so as to 'escape' the media that had congregated at the main entrance, cross the road, and jump into a car in which Ranbir Singh Mahendra, the Joint Secretary of the BCCI, was waiting for him.

Sunil was driven to another hotel, where the selectors had just finished a marathon meeting to pick the captain and the team that was to participate in a limited-overs tournament in Australia, which had been organised to celebrate the 150th anniversary of the founding of Victoria state.

The reactions were predictable. The selectors were slammed, and Sunil's capabilities as limited-overs batsman and captain questioned. The fact that India under Sunil had a lost a One-Day series to England 1-4, and was on the verge of losing the Test series as well, was expectedly highlighted and hurled at A.W. Kanmadikar, the BCCI Secretary, when he faced the media.

> 'I had been appointed the manager of that team two months before it was selected. What probably went in my favour was the fact that I had convinced the players to walk from the Calcutta airport to the hotel when no one came to receive us during the One-Day series against Australia earlier in the season. I was a co-opted member of the selection committee when the meeting took place in Chandigarh. It can be said that I had some sort of role to play in persuading the selectors to retain Sunil, as all of them were not in favour of it. I felt he deserved the job. As for Kapil Dev, I was his first ever roommate, way back in 1978-79. I spoke to both regarding the so-called problems between them, and that was that.' – E.A.S. Prasanna

Kapil Dev's appointment as vice-captain shocked all those who were convinced that the relationship between him and Sunil was beyond repair. Another decision that raised the hackles of the pundits was the one to pick L. Sivaramakrishnan. He hadn't played in any of the One Day Internationals against England, and had been ineffective in the last three Tests. Given the prevalent theory that spinners had little to do in limited-overs cricket, his inclusion was interpreted as another instance of the selectors' insanity.

Shastri, who had been considered for the captaincy, picked himself, as did Azharuddin, Srikkanth and Vengsarkar. Amarnath, who hadn't played in the One-dayers against England, but had been discussed as another candidate for the captaincy, was included. Binny and Madan

Lal were recalled after outstanding domestic seasons. Chetan Sharma and Manoj Prabhakar were selected as back-up bowlers, and Ashok Malhotra as the back-up batsman. Sadanand Vishwanath's performance behind the stumps in the last three One-dayers against England, and his showing for Karnataka in Kirmani's absence, earned him the nod ahead of the latter.

Although Sunil was happy with the squad assigned to him, he was none too thrilled with the Spiderman episode. To him, it did not make sense for the captain of India to be told to scale walls. On the eve of the team's departure, he informed Borde and Salve of his decision to stand down from the captaincy on the eve of the team's departure to Australia. He had had enough of the pressures, tensions and hassles.

It was one of the two decisions he took. The second was to leave on a high note.

In retrospect, it could be said that the selectors had done everything they could to complement his desire to bow out with a flourish. If there was one word that characterised the squad, it was serendipity. Each of the selected players had something to prove. The captain and vice-captain wanted to forget the England series and show that their team's success mattered more to them than anything else. Azharuddin and Srikkanth were eager to build on their performances against England, and Shastri was keen to display his all-round prowess in the game's premier land. Vengsarkar, whom everyone had been taking for granted, wanted to make his presence felt. Binny, Madan Lal, Amarnath and Siva, all of whom had missed the One-dayers against England, were keen to show what the team had missed.

The mindset of the Indian players on their arrival in Australia was akin to that of a group of students who had finally been allowed to pursue a stream of their choice, after being forced to mug up dreary books for months. The euphoria of the World Cup win had faded away after the losses at home, and in a foreign land, there was little or no pressure on them. They were looking forward to being themselves.

The World Championship of Cricket was the first cricket tournament other than the World Cup to involve all seven Test-playing teams of the time. All the matches were to be played in coloured clothing, some of them under lights. The event began with an Olympic style opening ceremony in the capital of Victoria. The Melbourne Cricket Ground was refurbished for the competition and embellished with floodlights. India and Pakistan were slotted in the same Group as the Ashes rivals. The West Indies, New Zealand and Sri Lanka constituted the other.

An indicator of Sunil's cluttered mind during the One-dayers against England had been his inability to allot a fixed position for himself. He had opened twice and batted in the middle order thrice. In Australia, he eliminated the ambiguity and declared that Ravi Shastri would open with Srikkanth. There was also no ambiguity on the role that Sivaramakrishnan was supposed to play.

The land of Grimmett, O'Reilly and Benaud had made no bones of its appreciation of the teenaged practitioner of one of the game's most specialised, and at the time, dying arts. All of Australia was delighted when India included Siva in the XI for their first game against Pakistan at the MCG, one day after Australia beat England in the inaugural encounter at the same venue. 'The good news is that India are playing the leg-spinner,' Ian Chappell said in his pre-match analysis on TV, 'and the bad news is that we have to pronounce his name!'

With Siva, a first-class centurion, slated to bat at number eleven, it meant that the Indians, like in the World Cup, had no tail.

Sunil won the toss and adhered to his team's preferred ploy of bowling first. India had batted first in the first three one-dayers against England, and lost every game. They then batted second in the fourth game at Nagpur, and won.

The bowlers and fielders excelled themselves to restrict Pakistan to 183. Every bowler bar Madan Lal had something to show in the wickets column, with Binny taking four. Siva, who was brought in after the fielding restrictions in the first fifteen overs had been lifted, took some stick from half-centurion Qasim Omar, but he then switched to a round-the-wicket line and held two return catches. The fielding was a revelation, with the players throwing themselves all over the lush green MCG outfield, and judging the mis-hits of the Pakistanis to perfection. Kapil Dev was accurate with the ball and sensational in the field, his flat throw from third-man getting rid of Mudassar.

The score of 184 was by no means an intimidating target, but there was Imran Khan to contend with. He had done well for New

South Wales, and was ready to return to the international stage. In his comeback series, he was just another member of the squad, with Miandad, the man he had replaced as captain in 1982, in charge.

It was déjà vu time for both camps as Imran dismissed Shastri, Srikkanth and Vengsarkar, the last two off consecutive deliveries, to reduce India to 27-3. All three batsmen gave catches in the slip-and-gully cordon off deliveries that pitched on a length and reared awkwardly.

As he walked in, Sunil may well have remembered Imran's spell at Karachi in December 1982. Back then, the slide had started when Imran pierced his defences: in March 1985, it was up to him to halt it. Sunil was also aware that he needed to get off the mark. The match was being played on Rohan's birthday, and the son had requested his out-of-form father not to score a duck!

Sunil did what his son wanted him to do. At the other end, Mohammad Azharuddin displayed steely nerves within elastic wrists. Being a predominantly leg-side batsman, he found Imran, whose stock delivery was the in-swinger, manageable. The score moved at a snail's pace, but India could afford that. Sunil brought up the fifty of the innings in the fifteenth over with 3 runs off seamer Rashid Khan. The bowler, who had an unusual tangled action, then got one to kick off a length. The TV cameras showed the ball passing within kissing distance of the outside-edge. Anil Dalpat, the keeper, claimed a catch, as did the bowler. But the umpire thought otherwise and Sunil stayed his ground. He had in fact got a thin edge, but there was no way he was going to walk out against Pakistan!

He continued to milk the bowling, and Azharuddin carried on whipping the ball off his pads elegantly, driving impeccably, and running superbly. With Azhar in such glorious nick, Sunil opted to play second fiddle.

The score had moved to 159 when Sunil was given a leg-before decision off a Mudassar delivery for a fine 54. The match as a contest had ended by then. Azhar was on 93 when Amarnath scored the winning run.

They had practised intensively since their arrival in Australia, but the Indians needed a win more than anything else to shed the baggage of the loss to England. The six-wicket triumph over Pakistan put them in the right frame of mind to take on their erstwhile tormentors in the second game, also a day-nighter, at Sydney.

Srikkanth got going with some audacious strokes after Gower won the toss and elected to bowl. Shastri anchored a stand of 67 before flicking Ellison to Fowler at mid-wicket. Srikkanth had made 57 out of a score of 74, when he was run out. That set the innings back a bit, although Azhar and Vengsarkar batted well. Kapil Dev, sent in at number five to get a move on, essayed a blazing cameo, which included a huge six off Vic Marks. Sunil, who came in at the fall of the fourth wicket, surprised many a watcher with a lofted straight boundary off Cowans.

India at one stage looked like reaching 250, but England struck back by dismissing Kapil Dev, Amarnath, Binny and Madan Lal in quick succession in the slog overs. Vishwanath gave his captain good support, but England had reason to be pleased with only 236 to get.

The England openers Fowler and Martyn Moxon were in no hurry in the initial overs. The score was 39-0 in the twelfth over, when Fowler attempted to flick Binny, only to get a top-edge, which was well-judged by Vishwanath. Gower then displayed the form and fluency that had eluded him in India till the Kanpur Test. The runs came at a steady clip, and when Sunil missed a chance offered by Moxon off Siva at mid-wicket, and the leggie himself spilt a return catch given by the same batsman, the Indians appeared to have blown it.

Luck smiled on them when Gower hit a rank full-toss by Siva down Vengsarkar's throat at mid-wicket. At the halfway mark, England were 99-2.

England then gained another life when Vishwanath missed an opportunity to stump Moxon off Siva in the same over. However, the fact that Siva had turned the ball right across the batsman from around-the-wicket gave the Indians hope.

What followed was a watershed in the history of limited-overs cricket.

The score was 113-2 when Moxon gave Siva another catch. This time, the bowler held on. Thirteen runs were added over the next four overs, before Lamb made a mess of Siva's googly. He went for the sweep, missed, and heard the death rattle.

At the other end, Shastri struck gold when Gatting tried to cut, only to nick the ball into the keeper's gloves. England were now 126-5, the cream of their batting back in the pavilion. Marks attempted to assert himself against Shastri, but the ball spun past his bat, and Vishwanath had the bails off in a flash. After Downton hit Kapil Dev straight to Shastri at gully, Edmonds attempted to drive the left-arm spinner, missed, and fell over. The ball turned a mile, and Vishwanath did not have to appeal after dislodging the bails.

It wasn't that spinners hadn't won One Day Internationals before. But never before had a pair combined so well to prove that the slow men could be as potent in the limited-overs variety as their faster counterparts.

> 'I was asked in an interview what I believed our chances were, considering that we had thought it prudent to include two spinners in the XI. My response was to wait and see. India's strength has always been spin, and we had to play to our strengths. Being a bowler myself, I knew that we had to think in terms of taking ten wickets, as opposed to containing.' – E.A.S. Prasanna

India's spin duo was backed by Vishwanath, whose consistency behind the stumps and belligerence with his mouth, were fast making him as popular as his under-25 team-mates Azhar and Siva. For those who were accustomed to Indian cricketers who preferred to let their actions speak for them, and reacted only when provoked, Vishwanath was a novelty. Not only did he have no issues with taking on opponents, but he also did not hesitate to turn the heat on his team-mates, if he got the impression that they were displaying diffidence or lethargy. In the modern era, Sadanand Vishwanath would have been an advertiser's dream.

With four victims under his belt, he volunteered to stand up to Madan Lal, who despite his age—thirty-four—wasn't exactly the slowest bowler in the world. In an age wherein not all batsmen used helmets all the time, and no wicketkeeper even considered wearing one, it was a move fraught with danger. But everybody else was more nervous than him, or so it seemed, as he held an edge by Ellison with ease. Foster holed out to Srikkanth at long-on, and England, 99-1 at one stage, were all out for 146. The Indians had every reason to be ecstatic.

England crashed out of the tournament with a 67-run loss to Pakistan at Melbourne in their final round-robin game. Pakistan had beaten Australia earlier, which meant that they completed their complement of three games with two wins and one defeat.

India's third encounter was a day affair against Australia, who had won one game and lost one. India, on the other hand, had two wins from two. Thus, Australia's only hope of qualifying for the semi-finals was to beat India comprehensively, so as to draw level with the Asian countries and get run rates into the equation.

The Australian dressing room resonated with the punching of calculator keys after Sunil won the toss and elected to bowl. How much did they have to score to feel safe enough?

All those discussions were rendered pointless by India's new-ball bowlers. Opener Robbie Kerr misread Kapil Dev's line in the third over, shouldered arms, and was bowled. In the next over, Binny uprooted Graeme Wood's off-stump. Allan Border, the captain, hung around for a few deliveries before playing across to Binny. He missed, and the off-stump took a walk once again. As had been the case in the World Cup, the Karnataka all-rounder was enjoying himself against the southpaws, disconcerting them with late swing. Kapil Dev then undid Kepler Wessels, another left-hander, with a delivery that climbed into him. A mis-hook landed in Madan Lal's palms at fine-leg, and Kapil Dev's animated celebrations suggested that his plan of catching Wessels, primarily a front-foot player, on the wrong 'back' foot literally, had worked. Australia at that stage were 18-4.

The Indians for once did not loosen their grip. The fifth wicket fell at 37, the sixth at 75 and the seventh at 85. Madan Lal, Amarnath, Shastri and Sivaramakrishnan bowled as well as their new-ball counterparts, and the fielding was outstanding.

Orchestrating the proceedings was the Indian captain. Gone was the forlorn countenance that had characterised him in the series against England. In fact, no one mirrored the transformation of the Indian side better than its skipper. Wearing a navy blue floppy hat, chewing gum *a la* Viv Richards and flailing his arms around while issuing instructions to his lieutenants, the Little Master resembled a general: astute, assured, aggressive, and supremely confident of his side's abilities. In many ways, this was a Sunil Gavaskar the cricketing world had never seen before. For once, he seemed to be enjoying the top job both on and off the field. With many of his Indian 'friends' in the media not around, he was relaxed and communicative during the post-match press briefings. He had earlier stated that his favourite place to play cricket, India apart, was Australia. He was now showing that he was relishing captaining there as well. Of course, his transformation owed itself entirely to the manner in which his team-mates responded to him. They seemed to revel in their leader's new incarnation, and were as determined as him to prove to the cricketing world that the 1983 World Cup win was not the fluke that some sections of the media had made it out to be.

Australia reached 163, courtesy a rearguard stand between Philips and Rodney Hogg. It was the third consecutive time the Indian bowlers had bowled the opposition out in the tournament.

Geoffrey Lawson and Rodney Hogg did not give Shastri and Srikkanth any loose deliveries, but conceded quite a few extras. The openers got going after the tenth over, with Srikkanth hitting over the top, and Shastri pushing and gliding away, executing from time to time his bread-and-butter 'chapati' shot, a combination of a leg glance and a flick.

Rod McCurdy, who along with Terry Alderman, replaced the new-ball bowlers, got Srikkanth to play an ungainly cross-batted swipe early on in his spell, but the catch was put down by Simon O'Donnell.

The Indian openers first raised the 50, and then the 100. Shastri edged O'Donnell to Phillips after putting on 124 with his partner. He had scored 51. Azharuddin fell first ball, lbw to Alderman, but Vengsarkar was ice-cool. A despondent Australian team and a flock of seagulls watched as Srikkanth banged McCurdy over the bowler's head to take his individual score to 93, and his team into the semi-finals.

Also watching were millions of Indians, who had something to cheer about while having lunch on the afternoon of Sunday, 3 March 1985. Never before had the nation watched a cricket match being played in Australia 'live'. The fans lapped up Channel Nine's coverage, as much as it did the performance of their team. That Indian TV had recently gone colour from black and white was the icing on the cake. The coloured clothing and white ball, the slow motion replays from different angles, the stump-microphones that picked the sound of the bat making contact with the ball, and the image of a sobbing duck accompanying a batsman who had failed to trouble the scorers, made a deep impression on the Indian audience. The love affair between the Indian masses and One-

Day cricket, which had commenced during the 1983 World Cup, was consummated during the 1985 World Championship of Cricket.

The Indians had only a day's break before taking on New Zealand in the first semi-final at Sydney. They were understandably peeved, but then, the schedule had been decided well in advance, and there was no point complaining about it.

Sunil won the toss and opted to bowl on a slow track. The bowlers once again flourished. Kapil Dev had John Wright caught behind off his third ball, and the others maintained the pressure, striking fairly regularly. The fielding was as splendid as it had been in the earlier matches. Azhar, Siva and Srikkanth led the way, supported by the likes of Binny, Amarnath, Shastri and of course Kapil Dev, who pulled off another superb throw to send Geoffrey Howarth, the Kiwi skipper, on his way.

The seventh wicket fell at 151, and in strode the big-hitting Lance Cairns, with his trademark bat which was sawn at the shoulders. He studied the field, and flayed. His counterattack appeared to have taken the Indians by surprise, as was evident when Kapil Dev of all bowlers strayed down the leg-side in the penultimate over. The 200 was posted in the final over, bowled by Madan Lal. Cairns went for an almighty hit off the third delivery and sent the ball miles into the air in the mid-wicket region. Srikkanth failed to hold on, and New Zealand gained two runs in the process. The next ball was skied in the same direction. Vengsarkar gave pursuit from the infield, but Srikkanth, who was chastened after the spill off the previous delivery, did not go for it. As the ball crossed the rope, one of the Channel Nine cameramen turned his gaze on the Indian captain.

Sunil was livid. Not only had Srikkanth not gone for the catch, but his indifference had cost the team at least two runs. The skipper clapped his hands, called for a better effort, and got Srikkanth to swap spots with Kapil Dev, who was stationed at deep square-leg. What happened off the next delivery could have happened only to the restless Tamil Nadu swashbuckler, who was known for being fidgety and funny, intentionally and unintentionally. Cairns went for another big one and swung towards deep square-leg, and Srikkanth this time hung on, much to the amusement of his team-mates.

Martin Snedden was caught by Azharuddin off the next ball, which meant that India had taken ten opposition wickets for the fourth successive time in the tournament. India needed 207 to win.

The immediate priority of Shastri and Srikkanth was to negotiate the new-ball threat posed by Hadlee. They did not surrender their wickets, but found it arduous to rotate the strike. Hadlee was relentless, and Cairns, accurate. Srikkanth pushed and plodded until he lost his patience and fell to a pull off Ewen Chatfield. India were 28-1 in the ninth over. Azharuddin came in to confront four men in the infield on the leg-side, and a fifth at deep square-leg. The Kiwis had done their homework.

So well did Chatfield and Snedden bowl that the runs dried up. India were a shoddy 46-1 at the end of the twentieth over, and under pressure for the first time since the game against Pakistan. Shastri and Azhar broke the shackles with a boundary apiece off Jeremy Coney, the weakest link in New Zealand's bowling line-up, in the twenty-second over. Azhar came down the wicket to drive Chatfield for another four in the next over. However, just as the tension in the Indian dressing room was beginning to dissipate, he went for a big hit off Chatfield, and was well caught by Coney at deep mid-on. The twenty-fifth over was in progress, and India were 73-2.

Shastri and Vengsarkar brought up the hundred in the thirty-first over, shortly after the opener had completed his fifty. Howarth then brought Hadlee back and demanded a wicket. Hadlee obliged with his first ball, inducing Shastri to hit straight to Paul McEwan at gully. India now needed 105 from 113 balls with seven wickets in hand. The team that would hold its nerve would win the game.

> 'Things were getting tight in the semi-final, when Sunil asked me what I thought we should do. We decided to push Kapil, for he was one player who could swing the game our way in no time.'
> – E.A.S. Prasanna

The New Zealand supporters were more vocal than their Indian counterparts when one great all-rounder arrived in the middle to face another. There was a healthy rivalry between them. Kapil Dev demonstrated it after slicing a good-length delivery to the boundary. He patted Hadlee on the back, and the latter returned the compliment. The game went on unhindered, because none of Hadlee's team-mates thought the way Andrew Symonds did at the same venue in January 2008.

That Hadlee over yielded nine runs, and the score had moved to 118-9 when he commenced the thirty-fourth over of the innings. Kapil Dev smashed the first ball for four. The second, he dispatched past point's left for another boundary. The Indian supporters found their voice, but Kapil Dev's own team-mates in the dressing room were slightly sceptical. They knew what was coming. Hadlee's riposte was a beauty of a slower ball. Kapil Dev misread it completely, and much to the chagrin of his team-mates, hit it straight to John Reid at mid-off. But the fielder dropped it!

'That could be the match,' Richie Benaud quipped, and Kapil Dev seemed to have heard him, as he drilled Hadlee's next ball past a diving Reid for another boundary. A single brought Vengsarkar on strike, and he cut Hadlee to third-man for four. That made it 17 runs from the over.

Twenty-six runs from twelve Hadlee deliveries had transformed the game completely. Kapil Dev and Vengsarkar then did pretty much what they pleased and overhauled the target with thirty-nine balls to spare. Kapil Dev finished with 50 from 30 balls, a sensational performance in the circumstances.

> My assessment of Kapil was that if we were in a situation in which runs were needed, he would get them. – Sunil Gavaskar, *Madras Magic* (ABC, 2006)

> 'Pakistan were to play the West Indies in the second semi-final. One of the broadcasters asked Sunil if he wanted the West Indies team to reach the final, but he replied he would rather face our brothers from Pakistan. He made our day and won the hearts of Pakistanis all over the world.' – Mudassar Nazar

The pundits and public predicted a repeat of the 1983 World Cup final, but Pakistan played spoilsport with a seven-wicket win over Lloyd's team. The stage was thus set for a summit clash that none could have anticipated prior to the tournament.

On the eve of the final, Sunil remembered having visualised himself holding the trophy a month previously. He was only one step away from making it a reality. He and his players prepared for the big game in much the same way as they had the earlier games, practising and planning.

They were pleased when Miandad won the toss on the afternoon of 10 March 1985 and elected to bat, as they would have opted to bowl first in any case.

Binny was down with flu, and hence not playing. But Chetan Sharma rose to the occasion with a nippy spell. Kapil Dev broke through when Mohsin Khan flicked him to Azhar at square-leg. That brought in Wasim Raja's younger brother Ramiz, who had scored 60 against the Windies. Mudassar and he had just started to fuse together a stand when the opener chased a wide delivery from Kapil Dev. The result was an edge, and a tumbling catch by Vishwanath. Qasim Omar, who had scored an unbeaten 42 against the Windies, came in, and was unlucky to receive a ripper of a Yorker first-up. He missed it completely, and walked off without even bothering to look at his fallen citadel. There were only 30,000 odd spectators in the colloseum that was the MCG, but the cheers of the Indian supporters were deafening enough to reach Sydney.

Although Miandad prevented the hattrick and drove the next ball for four, Pakistan were under the pump.

The pressure intensified when Srikkanth knelt at square-leg to catch Raja off Sharma. At 33-4, Pakistan's last hope was a long association between Miandad and Imran. Sharma, who was charged up after Raja's dismissal, produced a short ball that beat Imran's attempted hook, and appeared to have kissed a glove on the way to Vishwanath. But Ray Isherwood, the umpire, disagreed.

The Pakistani seniors then put their heads down. Amarnath and Madan Lal carried on the good work done by the new-ball bowlers, not giving the batsmen the liberty and latitude to bat freely. Vishwanath, who carried on encouraging and goading his team-mates, achieved the unthinkable by earning Miandad's ire. The Pakistani skipper, who never ever hesitated to display his colourful vocabulary on the field, actually complained to his counterpart. Simply put, Sunil was amused.

So well did Madan Lal and Amarnath bowl that Siva was introduced only in the thirty-fourth over. It was a critical stage of the game. Although the score had only just crossed 100, both Miandad and Imran had got their eye in, and with Salim Malik and Wasim Raja still to come, there was a possibility of an onslaught.

That possibility was nipped in the bud when Imran placed Siva to point and called Miandad for a non-existent run. The Indian captain, who was manning that position, moved swiftly to his left, picked the ball and hurled at the one visible stump. He hit bull's eye with Imran short out of his ground.

Miandad and Malik added a frantic 30 in the next six overs, before Siva tempted the latter to launch into one that was tossed up. The mishit was excellently judged and held by Sharma in the long-off region. What followed was sensational.

Siva served a leg-break, which drew Miandad, an excellent player of spin, out of his crease. As the Pakistani captain shaped to drive, the ball dipped, pitched, and spun past the outside-edge. Vishwanath collected and whipped off the bails. There was no need to appeal, as Miandad had overbalanced, and was well out of the crease. If there was one moment that underscored the talent of Sivaramakrishnan and Vishwanath, this was it.

Tahir Naqqash hit the hattrick ball for four, but perished when he nicked Shastri into Vishwanath's gloves. Anil Dalpat hit a Siva googly to Shastri at cover, and Pakistan were 145-9. The leggie had bowled splendidly to take three wickets.

Sunil kept him going in the end overs, thus defying another convention of limited-overs cricket. The skipper also endeared himself to his opening batsmen with a deft display of gamesmanship. He ensured that the Pakistani innings lasted beyond 5.30 pm, thus preventing the possibility of his openers having to negotiate a few testing overs before the supper break at 6.00 pm. The ninth wicket having fallen at 5.28 pm, Sunil killed time by asking Shastri to take a break and summoning Sharma from the outfield. By the time Sharma had taken possession of the ball, the cut-off point had passed, and Sunil promptly passed the ball back to Shastri! There was nothing umpire Tony Crafter could do, other than offering a knowing smile!

Wasim Raja guided Azeem Hafiz into making the most of the remaining deliveries, and Pakistan finished with 176-9.

The score of 177 wasn't the only target on Ravi Shastri's mind when he accompanied K. Srikkanth to the middle. At the start of the tournament, he, like many of the participants, had succumbed to the charms of the Audi 100, which was to be presented to the Player of the Tournament. His all-round consistency, not to mention Man of the Match awards in the games against Australia and New Zealand, had made him a frontrunner for the title, along with the likes of Kapil Dev and Mudassar.

Imran gave it everything he had in the early overs, but Shastri and Srikkanth were content to see him off. Hafiz kept it steady at the other end until the tenth over, when Srikkanth drove him on the rise for six. That took the score to 20-0, and Srikkanth took charge.

Shastri allowed his partner to hog the limelight, pulling out his chapati shot whenever the bowlers strayed on the leg-side. By the time Wasim Raja was brought on to bowl leg-breaks in the eighteenth over, Srikkanth was on song. In Raja's third over, the opener came down the wicket and deposited him over the long-off fence. Ramiz, giving chase, ran into the iron fence, whereupon he clutched his chest and collapsed. There was tension all around, and there was relief when Ramiz walked off to tend to what was nothing more than a bruise.

Srikkanth completed his 50 a little later and then went for another big hit, but the ball did not gather as much distance as the previous one. Malik, who was fielding at Ramiz's position, got his hands to the ball, but scooped it onto the fence. The opener then rubbed salt on the leg-spinner's wounds by late-cutting and sweeping him for fours in his next over. The hundred of the innings was posted in the twenty-eighth over.

Imran had Srikkanth caught by Wasim Raja in the very next over. The opener had scored 67, and India were 103-1.

Although the run rate dropped thereafter, there was never any doubt as to the outcome of the game. Azhar essayed a cameo of 25, which included a booming straight-drive off Malik and a magnificent hook off Naqqash that was exclusively his own: he met the ball with a horizontal bat, as was the norm, and thereafter his wrists took over, closing the face of the bat at the point of impact.

The target was only 35 away when Naqqash breached Azhar's defences, and Vengsarkar came in. Shastri's circumspect approach had earned him many admirers, but with only a few runs left, he found himself being subjected to a slow hand clap by the Indian supporters, who wanted a quick end. He was cheered when he reached his fifty, as much for the achievement, as for the fact that the spectators felt they would now witness some action. They got it when he hoisted Mudassar over mid-on for four.

The scores were levelled off the last ball of the forty-seventh over, and the TV cameras caught Vishwanath brandishing a bottle of champagne in the Indian dressing room. Fittingly, two men who had watched their team's World Cup win from the balcony, were in the middle when the 'mini-World Cup' was won. Vengsarkar placed Raja on the leg-side for a single, and with seventeen deliveries to spare, the World Championship of Cricket was India's.

For the second time in a year-and-a-half, India had conquered the world.

Champagne corks flew all over the Indian dressing room, and firecrackers dotted the Melbourne skyline. The 35,216 spectators, who had established a record for a neutral game at the MCG, stayed on to watch Srikkanth receive the Player of the Final award, and the captain of India receive the trophy.

> Ladies and gentlemen, first of all, I would like to thank the manager, and the members of my team, for having given me this wonderful present on my last day as captain of India. I don't think I could have asked for a better gift than this superb trophy . . .' – Sunil Gavaskar (acceptance speech, WCC final, 10 March 1985)

The biggest cheers were reserved for Shastri, who was crowned the Champion of Champions, and presented the keys to the Audi 100. Then followed a lap of honour that remains etched in the memory of every Indian who witnessed it; Shastri himself at the wheel, Sunil seated next to him, holding the trophy aloft, a champagne-guzzling Amarnath on the bonnet, Kapil Dev on the boot, Vishwanath on the top, and Siva and Sharma hanging from the sides.

> 'No one expected us to win, but everything clicked. Ravi Shastri, Sadanand Vishwanath, Siva and Azharuddin were at their best. I got to play the final after Roger went down with flu. SMG informed me in the meeting before the game that I was playing. He told us at the start of the tournament that he believed in each

and every player, regardless of whether he was part of the first-choice eleven or not. We had a great time in Australia. We were encouraged to enjoy ourselves on the field, for it was a game we were playing after all. The slogan youngsters like me had adopted was: "Enjoy the game, don't put undue pressure on yourself, get money for nothing, and 'chicks' for free!"' – Chetan Sharma

Sunil's abdication had been made unforgettable by some terrific cricket. If he and his captaincy were to be blamed for the loss to England, then it was only fair that he got the lion's share of the credit for the turnaround in Australia.

He had got off to a splendid start as captain of India, with a Test win in Auckland in 1976. However, he had attracted more brickbats than bouquets in later years. His critics branded him as defensive, even negative. They relished comparing him to attacking captains like Clive Lloyd and Ian Chappell, conveniently ignoring the batting and bowling arsenals that both men had at their disposal. For the better part of his tenure, or tenures, Sunil had no one apart from Kapil Dev Nikhanj, and to an extent Dilip Doshi, to turn to, in order to get twenty wickets in Tests on a regular basis. That the Indian bowling attack of the early 1980s was among the weakest in the game, and the batting over-reliant on its captain, were factors that were not highlighted as much as they should have been.

> I would like to acknowledge Sunil Gavaskar... when he was captain, his team was not good enough to win (Tests) regularly... therefore, he decided that his job was not to lose... during that period, a draw was [as] good as a win, because he did not have a team....' – Kapil Dev at the 1983 World Cup Silver Jubilee Celebrations, organised by the BCCI, 22 June 2008

Although the West Indies remained the dominant force in Test cricket, there was no doubt that India was the new numero uno in the shorter version of the sport. The 1983 World Cup winners had lived up to the challenge of staying on the summit. Given that five matches were won out of five, the opposition was bowled out four times, and only three catches were dropped, the World Championship of Cricket win remains India's most comprehensive, and yet, unsung triumph.

> Home are our heroes! Fling wide the gates, Hang out the flags, Blare the trumpets, Crash the cymbals... Home, from their derring-do in Melbourne and Sydney, are our intrepid, doughty champs of champs... Beat a tattoo. Fire a salute. Home are our gallant soldiers, undisputed champions of one-day cricket not once, but twice over.... Pull out the stopper... Let's have a whopper. For home are our pride and joy after their ecstasy-inducing performances....' – Khalid Ansari, *Mid-Day*, 16 March 1985

And yet, the cynical voices persisted. One of them ventured to ask Sunil during the team's stopover in Singapore whether India would have won had the West Indies made it to the final. Sunil's response mirrored the mindset of his team: '... I do not know if our batsmen would have scored as freely as they would have liked. But I am certain we would have won because our bowlers would have torn them apart.'

Sunil was asked about a bandage on a middle finger and a tape on his forehead on the team's arrival in Bombay. His explanation brought the house down: 'I had a fight with Kapil Dev!'

Kapil Dev's reinstatement as captain of India marked the end of a bizarre period.

> Consider this sequence and you will realise why I say the events after the Delhi Test represented the most illogical phase: 1. I was dropped from the team for the Calcutta Test... 2. I played no cricket between the Delhi and Madras Tests. 3. I was reinstated in the team for the Madras Test. 4. Soon after the series, I was made the vice-captain of the team. 5. Soon after the WCC in Australia, I was made captain. – Kapil Dev, *Cricket My Style* (Allied, 1987)

Joining him in the think-tank was India's Cricketer of the Year. Ravi Shastri, the new vice-captain, accompanied Sunil to Delhi before the team's departure to Sharjah for a four-nation tournament, to meet the new prime minister.

There was a lot that Ravi Shastri had in common with Rajiv Gandhi. It was just two months since the forty-year-old had led his party, the Congress-I, to a landslide victory in the general elections, winning 414 of the 533 seats. A spirit of optimism pervaded the country, which seemed destined to enter the new millennium in due course with its young prime minister at its head.

A similar spirit pervaded Indian cricket. Never since the inaugural Test in 1932 had the future of Indian cricket looked as promising as it did in March 1985. The future seemed secure in the hands of the twenty-two year-old Rajiv Gandhi of Indian cricket. He was thrilled to be informed by the prime minister that the Customs department had been directed to waive duty on the Audi 100, which was on its way to the country by ship.

His elevation to the vice-captaincy meant that Shastri was only one step away from doing what he had been groomed for since the early 1980s. He had already led India at the under-19, under-22 and under-25 levels, and his leadership capabilities and tactical acumen been appreciated. With players like Azharuddin, Siva, Srikkanth and Sivaramakrishnan in top form, cricket lovers in the country were an excited lot on the eve of the clash against Pakistan in Sharjah, twelve days after the WCC victory.

It took one hell of a spell by Imran Khan to abate that excitement. After Miandad had won the toss and put India in, the all-rounder trapped Shastri leg-before off his first ball, got Srikkanth to mishook to square-leg, had Vengsarkar, Sunil and Madan Lal caught behind, and Amarnath bowled. He finished with figures of 6-14, and left the Indians contemplating the prospect of defending a paltry 125 after a ninety-minute Friday lunch interval.

The Indians worked out that it made little sense to mope around. The entire team dozed off, the animated chatter emanating from the Pakistani dressing room next door notwithstanding. They awoke in time for the resumption, and left the dressing room after Kapil Dev repeated his words of 25 June 1983.

Mohsin and Mudassar seemed untroubled by their opponents' resolve to fight, until the former took on Amarnath's throwing arm. The run-out brought Ramiz Raja to the crease. He took his time to play himself in, for there was a lot of time, and his partner was batting beautifully. Mudassar dispatched Binny to the boundary twice in succession, and the score was 35-1, when he got an outside-edge. The batsman looked back to see Sunil throw himself to his right and take a sensational one-handed catch. Just as the commentators had begun to convince themselves that Sunil had never taken a better slip catch in his entire career, he made them do a rethink with another dive and one-handed steal, when Miandad nicked Shastri.

Kapil Dev, aware of the turn that off-spinner Tauseef Ahmed had extracted earlier in the day, introduced the spinners fairly quickly. Siva tossed one up to keeper-batsman Ashraf Ali, who had surprisingly been promoted in the batting order. Ali, completely clueless, gloved it into no-man's land, but Vengsarkar swooped upon it from his position at silly point. Imran, the new batsman, then gave Siva the charge, missed, and Vishwanath did the rest. Pakistan, in a matter of moments, had slipped from 35-1 to 41-5.

Ramiz and Salim Malik dampened the exuberance of the Indians with a 33-run association, which ended when the latter nicked Shastri and gave Sunil his third catch of the innings. The hope of the Indians turned to conviction when Ramiz edged Kapil Dev and Sunil held his fourth catch. Manzoor Elahi gave a tame return catch to Madan Lal, and Naqqash was caught behind. Kapil Dev bowled Tauseef with the fifth ball of his seventh over, to complete an incredible victory. Pakistan had made only 87. Even as the Indians went bananas celebrating one of the greatest limited-overs wins of all time, the Pakistani players were put under virtual dressing room arrest by their distraught supporters.

> 'Sunil had a very safe pair of hands. His greatest strength was his temperament and balance. He rarely dived for the ball, but like his batting he also moved quickly to be behind the ball and made some difficult catches look relatively easy. He was a very good close-in fielder and his height gave him the advantage to snap some very low catches. His greatest feat would be the catches that he took during the World Cup final in 1983. Each one was taken very comfortably. That showed his temperament, as a catch during such a crucial period is in the midst of intense nervous tension, and for one to remain calm is a feat in itself.'
> – Yajurvindra Singh

The final against Australia was a low-scoring affair on a low and slow pitch. The Aussies batted first and were bowled out for 139. They had the Indians in some trouble at 37-3, but the seemingly inexhaustible batting resources of the world champions came to the fore, and victory was achieved with three wickets in hand. Those who continued to insist that Sunil had no role to play in limited-overs cricket were embarrassed when he was declared the Player of the Series for his five catches in the tournament and knock of 20 in the final. The win gave India the Rothmans Cup, their fourth limited-overs title of note in a year-and-a-half.

Within a couple of hours of landing in Bombay, Sunil and Madan Lal tossed the coin for the Ranji Trophy final between Bombay and Delhi. Sunil won the toss and contributed 106 to his side's first-innings total of 333. It was his twentieth Ranji hundred. Raju Kulkarni's pace gave Delhi grief at the start of their response, but the middle order staged a recovery and they finished with 398. Bombay's only hope was an outright win.

A partnership of 115 between Sunil and Shastri in the second innings emboldened the skipper to declare at 364-7, leaving Delhi 300 to get on a wearing wicket.

Delhi fancied their chances. Their confidence was boosted when openers Surender Khanna and Chetan Chauhan negotiated the new ball, and proceeded to handle the spinners with ease.

> 'Sunil was unwell, and he did not take the field on the last two days. In fact, I don't think he came to the ground. The Delhi openers put on 95, and their side was well placed on the fourth evening. Khanna and Kirti Azad rubbed it in by discussing within earshot of Ravi (Shastri) that Bombay ought to polish the trophy and keep it ready for the Delhites to take away. Sandeep (Patil), who was leading us in Sunil's absence, conveyed a message from Sunil. It was essentially a reminder that we were playing for Bombay. We proceeded to bowl them out for 209, with Ravi taking eight wickets. Sunil invited us home that evening to celebrate.' – Raju Kulkarni

It was Bombay's thirtieth Ranji win in fifty-one seasons, and Patil, who had supervised the city's progress to the final in the absence of Sunil,

Vengsarkar and Shastri, accepted the trophy on behalf of the victors.

Sunil proceeded to make it clear that it wasn't just the India captaincy that he had relinquished. At thirty-five, he was in the twilight zone of his career. He reckoned he still had a lot to offer to Indian cricket, but was entitled to a certain amount of latitude. He had contributed in no small measure to the evolution of the Indian team, and felt that he deserved to be given the freedom to fall back from the forefront, literally and figuratively. After all, never before in his international career had the batting line-up seemed as solid as it did, in terms of potential as well as performance, at the end of the 1984-85 season. The bowling line-up had also acquired more teeth and variety.

He was looking forward to play the kind of role that Bob Simpson had essayed against India in 1977-78. In that series, Simpson, an accomplished opener himself in his heyday, had opted to entrust the responsibility of taking the initiative to his younger colleagues. He had preferred to keep things going in the middle after a start had been provided, and/or stabilise the innings whenever the opposition looked like getting on top.

20

TO OPEN OR NOT TO OPEN...

Q – Will you open the innings in Sri Lanka?
A – I think you are asking this question from the wrong person... as far as I am concerned, I will open doors, windows, shops, seminars, and of course, bottles.

Q – Won't you like to retire as an opening batsman?
A – I have also batted in the middle order. So there is no harm if I continue batting in the middle order till I quit. In fact, my highest score has come in that position. - Sunil Gavaskar, Interview (*Sportsweek*, 28 August 1985)

Has Sunil said that he would not open?... If he feels that he is more suited to the middle order it is all right, but a decision to this effect can only be taken on the tour. – Kapil Dev in the same issue.

Prior to the tour of Sri Lanka in August 1985, Sunil wrote a letter to Chandrakant Borde, informing him of his reluctance to open the innings.

Kapil Dev's response in the *Sportsweek* issue suggested that he hadn't been kept in the loop. It wasn't the only time there appeared to be a communication gap between the superstars in the new season.

Theoretically, the Indians could not have chosen a better opponent or setting to start the 1985-86 season against. Sri Lanka were the newest entrants to international cricket, and while they had given a good account of themselves at Madras in 1982-83, the Indian team had come a long way since then.

The limited-overs world champions were expected to dominate the three Tests and three One Day Internationals. That did not happen, as for the umpteenth time, Indian cricketers choked when the 'favourites' lanyard was put around their necks.

The first One-Day International went right down to the wire, with the Indians winning only in the final over.

India would not have reached 218 in the first innings of the first Test at Colombo's Sinhalese Sports Club, had Sunil, batting at number five, not dropped anchor to score 51. His occupation of the crease for 342 minutes made it the slowest Test fifty of all time. The Lankans replied with 347. Lalchand Rajput, who opened with Srikkanth, scored 61 in the second innings, but he fell at the wrong time, as did most of his team-mates. India were 153-4 at stumps on the fourth day, only 24 ahead. The first two hours of the last day were rained off, but seamer Rumesh Ratnayake took his team within sniffing distance of victory with three wickets in three overs. Last man Maninder Singh then assisted Vengsarkar in an obdurate stand. Vengsarkar was eventually left stranded two short of what would have been a heroic ton.

Sri Lanka needed an unlikely 123 from eleven overs. Duleep Mendis, the hero of the Madras Test of 1982-83 and now the captain, opened with Aravinda D'Silva. The latter hooked Kapil Dev's first ball for six. They were going for it!

However, it was too tall an order, and the hosts pulled the shutters down after losing four wickets. Not surprisingly, their frame of mind was a lot more positive than that of the visitors when the second Test got underway at the P. Saravanamutthu stadium in the same city. Kapil Dev's concerns about his team were compounded by his worries about the umpiring, which had tended to favour the home team at crucial junctures.

However, there was no way the umpiring could have been blamed for the Indian bowlers allowing Sri Lanka to post 385 in the first innings. India slid to 88-5 in response before Sunil and Amarnath put their heads down to score fifties. Two hundred and forty-four was what India finished with, and Mendis reshuffled his batting order once again. His men did not let him down, and he declared at 206-3 in the second innings, leaving India 348 to win in six-and-a-half hours, plus twenty mandatory overs. It was a canny declaration, for although the Indians were capable of getting the runs, they were anything but confident. Mendis expected them to play for a draw, always a dangerous course to adopt on a fifth-day strip.

New-ball bowlers Asantha De Mel and Ratnayake began working their way through the Indian batting on the fifth morning, watched by an expectant crowd. Srikkanth and Vengsarkar, two of India's most successful batsmen against the island nation, were unlucky to be declared out leg-before and caught behind respectively, but their teammates created their own misfortune. The scoreboard read 98-7 when Sivaramakrishnan joined Kapil Dev in a defiant stand. But once Siva fell, the outcome was a foregone conclusion. India were 198-9 when Kapil Dev gave Ratnayake a return catch. It was Sri Lanka's first-ever Test win.

In any other situation, the sight of P.W. Vidanagamage, one of the umpires, grabbing a stump as a souvenir, would have amused the Indians. But this situation was different. As far as they were concerned, the umpire's behaviour said it all. The official had already antagonised them by lashing out at Maninder Singh earlier in the game for picking up the ball (that the umpires themselves had strangely left on the pitch) during a drinks interval. Kapil Dev panned the umpiring after the game, but also admitted that his team could have batted and bowled a lot better.

The teams then took off to Kandy for the third Test. Here, India dictated the course of the game for the first four days, and Kapil Dev set the Lankans 377 to win. With the hosts tottering at 34-3, the Indians were rampant, until their tormentors of the Madras Test did an encore.

Mendis and Roy Dias took up most of the first two sessions of the last day in a partnership of 216. Both fell on either side of tea, but they inspired the lower order to bat out the remaining overs and give their side a historic series win.

Sri Lanka won the One-Day International that followed, and India were in a dominant position in the third when the umpires ruled that the light was poor. Kapil Dev's parting gift to Sri Lanka was a prediction that they would never win a Test abroad unless they improved their umpiring standards.

How had the limited-overs world champions lost a Test series to the world's lowest-ranked team? There were reasons aplenty. For starters, the balance of the team had gone for a toss. In his 1987 autobiography, Kapil Dev referred to Shastri's reluctance to open in the Tests. That resulted in the inclusion of Lalchand Rajput, who had done well for Mumbai in the previous two seasons. He scored 32 and 61 in his debut game, but failed in the second Test, getting 12 and 0. It was then that Kapil Dev had to prevail upon Shastri, and get him to open, in the third Test. Srikkanth, who opened in all three Tests, underwent a torrid time. That he and Vengsarkar, India's two most successful batsmen against Sri Lanka, had several decisions going against them, had not gone unnoticed. Mohinder Amarnath, whose consistency in the Test series against England had been bettered by only Azharuddin, did not play the first Test. He returned for the second and became India's lone centurion of the Test series in the third.

Azharuddin, the star of the previous season, struggled to get going, in what was an instance of 'second-season blues'. The same applied to Sivaramakrishnan, who looked a far cry from the tweaker who had left Javed Miandad stranded at the MCG six months previously. The Sri Lankan Colts had thrashed him in a three-dayer at the start of the tour, and he had been taken for 38 runs from five overs in the first One Day International. Left out of the first Test, he was brought back for the second. Thirty-eight wicketless overs resulted in his being relegated to the reserve bench for the third Test. His fellow spinners – Shastri, Maninder and 'offie' Gopal Sharma – were dealt with as harshly. Kapil Dev and Chetan Sharma took eleven and fourteen wickets respectively, but the spinners failed to complement them.

Roger Binny, one of the heroes of the WCC triumph, was strangely left out of the squad altogether, and then flown in for the third Test at the captain's request. A player who missed out as a result was Rajinder Singh Ghai, who had been picked as the third seamer in the original squad.

... Many of the difficulties were due to the problem over the opening of the innings. – Kapil Dev, *Cricket My Style* (Allied, 1987).

Sunil hadn't done badly as a middle-order batsman, scoring 186 runs at an average of 37, inclusive of two fifties and a 49. However, Kapil Dev was not alone in thinking that the story of the series could have been different had Sunil done what he had for the first thirteen years of his international career.

There was another reason for the flop show: the Indians hadn't put the euphoria of the limited-overs wins behind them. Also, they were guilty of underestimating their opponents.

Kapil Dev, still searching for a win after seventeen Tests at the helm, had a lot on his mind when he accompanied his former captain-turned-manager S. Venkataraghvan to attend the deliberations of the selectors on the team that was to tour Sharjah and Australia in the winter of 1985.

The meeting was convened after two eventful matches. Shastri's West Zone beat Srikkanth's South Zone in the final of the Duleep Trophy at Bangalore. A highlight of the game was Sunil's treatment of Sivaramakrishnan. Even as he went about decimating the leg-spinner in an innings of 119, Sunil, who batted at number three, must have wondered what had gone wrong with the discoveries of the previous season. Azharuddin flopped once again, scoring 6 and 1, and Sadanand Vishwanath could not even find a place in the South Zone side. Behind the wickets, and back in the reckoning, was Syed Kirmani.

His mother's demise before the tour of Sri Lanka had left Vishwanath, an emotional character who wore his heart on his sleeve, rudderless. He had done his best in the island nation, but the pressures of being the only stumper in the squad had taken their toll.

What Vishwanath, as also Sivaramakrishnan, probably needed at that stage, was a hand on the shoulder, and some counselling. They had experienced the dizzying heights of success, and then the trauma of landing on Ground Zero with a thud. It will be fair to say that the story of Indian cricket would have been very different had the duo received the support that Ricky Ponting did in Australia in the late 1990s.

> Things went brilliantly for two years, then all of a sudden, they changed. I realised I was doing something wrong, but couldn't figure out what. The people around me, instead of looking at what was going wrong technically, questioned my ability to handle pressure, and whether I had let success go to my head . . . The lack of guidance and support was key. There were people to tell me the basics – toss the ball up more, attack the bat, things like that. But I was not balanced in my delivery stride, and no one could tell me that. – L. Sivaramakrishnan, *Wisden Asia Cricket*, August 2003.

Both Siva and Sadanand were given opportunities to prove themselves in the Irani Cup game that followed, as was Azharuddin. While the stylist regained his touch with knocks of 100 and 49, Vishwanath had a so-so game. Siva, completely out of sorts, bowled sixteen overs without success, and was caned for 92 runs by the Bombay tailenders. He was a little more successful in the second innings, getting 3-132 from thirty overs, even as Shastri preferred batting practice to an outright win after Bombay gained the first-innings lead. Fortunately for Siva, the selectors kept his WCC showing in mind and retained him in the national squad. Vishwanath wasn't as lucky, losing out on even the second keeper's slot to Baroda's Kiran More.

Bombay was delighted at the inclusion of Raju Kulkarni, but disappointed at Sandeep Patil's exclusion.

> The astonishing element was the statement of Chairman Borde that Sunil Gavaskar had been chosen for the tour only as opener . . . But is it worthwhile to make anybody a reluctant opener? . . . Should Gavaskar not be willing, are the selectors willing to drop him from the side? . . . It is likely though that the selectors have spoken to Gavaskar during the Duleep Trophy final and have impressed on the little master the need for him to open . . . It is obvious though that Kapil Dev's insistence has paid off. – Ayaz Memon, *Sportsweek*, 6 November 1985

Asked for his opinion on where his senior statesman ought to bat, Kapil Dev had expressed himself in no uncertain terms, and got what he wanted. The squad for Sharjah and Australia comprised only two specialist openers in Srikkanth and Sunil, not counting Shastri and Binny, thus making it a *fait accompli* of sorts for the former captain. Borde assured the media that Sunil had the best interests of Indian cricket at heart, and would therefore open. But when questioned whether Sunil would be overlooked for selection if he did not agree to open, Borde offered a dead bat.

Some reports suggested that Sunil was upset with the selectors for not consulting him before making the announcement. Others said that he had acceded to the request.

While the majority, Kapil Dev obviously included, was delighted, there were some who thought otherwise:

UNFAIR TO FORCE GAVASKAR TO OPEN – His record as opener against England was unimpressive . . . On the bouncy Australian tracks, he would face more formidable opposition. . . .
– Sunder Rajan, *TOI*, 5 November 1985.

Rajan further mentioned his stonewalling in Sri Lanka, and his scores in the middle-order in the Duleep Trophy. 'Perhaps the best solution would be to ask him to continue in this (middle-order) position,' he wrote.

The limited-overs world champions flopped in the tri-series in Sharjah that preceded their departure to Australia. Pakistan beat them by 48 runs, thus ending a sequence of three consecutive limited-overs losses to the old enemy. The Indian bowlers did well to restrict Pakistan to 203, but the batsmen mucked it up. The Pakistanis were delirious, and their new captain relieved. Imran Khan was back at the helm, with Miandad, not for the last time, deciding to concentrate on his batting.

In their next game, India were subjected to an eight-wicket thrashing by the West Indies, thus finishing at the bottom of the table. The losers attracted the sort of criticism that is invariably heaped on a losing side.

To anybody who even casually meets the players off the field, it is as clear as daylight that the zone-wise rift among certain prima-donnas of the side is once again rearing its ugly head. – Khalid Ansari, *Sportsweek*, 27 November 1985

The fact that the same set of players had won two limited-overs tournaments just six months previously was ignored.

There was one redeeming feature for the Indians. The opener-turned-middle-order batsman-turned opener had batted magnificently.

Sunil scored 63 against Pakistan and 76 against the Windies. With some support, he would have taken India to victory in at least one game, if not both.

The two knocks underscored his attitude. It was hardly a secret that he was far from happy to open. However, once he had made up his mind, he re-occupied the opening slot with an assurance that suggested that he had never ever considered abandoning it.

He did not make his presence felt in the encounter against Pakistan, his first as opener in almost a year, with his batting alone. At a time when everybody on the field, neutral umpires Harold Bird and David Shepherd included, had forgotten about the playing condition that restricted the number of leg-side fielders to five, it was Sunil who pointed out the lapse by the Pakistanis. A discussion ensued between the umpires, captains and tournament coordinator Asif Iqbal, who conceded that his erstwhile rival was spot-on.

Trust Sunil Gavaskar to be thorough with the rules, even local ones . . .' – *Sportstar*, 30 November 1985

The players had a brief stopover in India before boarding the plane to the land where they had won the mini-World Cup the previous season.

Australia were 'under the pump'. The holes created by the simultaneous retirements of Greg Chappell, Dennis Lillee and Rodney Marsh in 1983-84 were proving to be too large to fill, and a rebel tour of South Africa had further robbed the country of several seasoned figures. Allan Border was in charge of an inexperienced outfit, which was beaten in the Ashes in the English summer of 1985, and subsequently stung by Richard Hadlee at home. He took thirty-three wickets in the three-Test series and took his team to a 2-1 win over the big brother. More than the Ashes, the loss to New Zealand was a blow to Australian pride.

Kapil Dev was determined to prolong Australia's agony. His innings of 88 in the four-day encounter against South Australia set up a four-wicket win. The next four-dayer against Victoria was hit by rain.

The Test series commenced at the Adelaide Oval. Border won the toss, and Australia were put on course for a big score by the stocky duo of David Boon and Greg Ritchie. Boon, a middle-order batsman-turned-opener, batted superbly to score 123, and Ritchie got 128. At 318-4, a score in the region of 500 looked a possibility, before Kapil Dev came up with an inspired burst. His 8-106 ensured the end of the innings for 381, with around two hours of the second day's play left.

Sunil accompanied Srikkanth to the middle and took strike as a Test opener for the first time since January that year. Craig McDermott, one of the few Australians to emerge with any credit from the Ashes series, slipped after his pre-delivery leap early on in the innings. He followed it up with a brutish delivery that reared off the pitch, struck Sunil on the left arm, and flew towards the square-leg region for a leg-bye. Sunil appeared to have been taken by surprise. Even as the Indian media contingent wondered whether Sunder Rajan had had a point, the Little Master warmed up with a bundary apiece off McDermott and his new-ball partner Merv Hughes. Both were imperious square-drives, the bat coming down from the slips and dispatching the ball along the carpet. India were 97-1 at stumps on day two, with Srikkanth having fallen for a kamikaze 51 and nightwatchman Chetan Sharma giving Sunil company at the other end.

His throbbing arm, a consequence of the previous day's blow, prevented Sunil from resuming his innings on the third morning. Sharma frustrated the Australians with a half-century, and Amarnath scored 37. When the latter was fifth out at 247, Sunil returned to the middle. McDermott welcomed him with another snorter, but this time, Sunil offered the deadest of bats and kept it down.

Mini-stands with Shastri and Kapil Dev ensued. The cloudy conditions prompted Sunil to discard his hat and exhibit his skull-cap to the world. He cut McDermott hard and over the gully area for four, and nicked Bruce Reid through the slips for another. It took him 111 balls and 148 minutes to complete his third fifty in four consecutive Tests, and his first as Test opener since the Delhi Test in December 1984.

Shastri scored 48 before Reid bowled him through the gate. Hughes greeted Kapil Dev with a bouncer and an unsuccessful appeal for hit-wicket. The umpire rightly ruled that the wind had blown the bails off. An upset Hughes retorted with another bouncer, to which Kapil Dev essayed his unique Nataraja[1] pull. The ball struck a seagull before striking the fence.

Sunil had a close shave when Boon missed a run-out opportunity. The connoisseurs at the ground warmly applauded a classy late-cut off Ray Bright that went for four. It followed a splendid cut off Hughes that produced the same result.

Kapil Dev was bowled by Bright when he missed a sweep, but his disappointment could not have been as acute as his sense of vindication. His predecessor had put together a beauty after returning to the opener's slot, though ironically, he had scored most of his runs after returning to the crease in the middle order!

Just when it seemed that only a run-out could dismiss Sunil, he had a lapse in concentration, only for David Hookes to drop him in the slips. Binny and he secured the lead, and at the close on the third day, India were 391-7 with Sunil on 94.

The score had moved to 393-7, and Sunil to 96, when McDermott fed him a half-volley on middle-and-leg. The cherry was greeted with a flick that dispatched the ball to the mid-wicket fence. As the spectators and his team-mates rose, the man with the biggest grin in the Indian dressing room was Kapil Dev Nikhanj.

Sunil's first act, after acknowledging the cheers for his first Test hundred in two years and thirty-first overall, was indicative of the mindset that had seen him get the previous thirty; he practised a drive, and then raised his palms to his face to create a corridor of sorts in front of his eyes. It was a gesture those who had followed him for years were familiar with: he was psyching himself to strike better, concentrate harder, and to go on.

> The lapses of concentration still keep coming. I have not got over that. I feel I am playing the same way for the last two years or so. It is just that in these two years, my first mistake became my

---

[1] Kapil Dev's signature posture while executing a pull shot—the outstretched left leg creating a right angle with the ramrod straight right leg—was not too dissimilar to the posture most sculptors and statue-makers have portrayed Nataraja—the Indian God of Dance—in.

last. I used to stick around and look for the big innings all the time, but I do believe luck was against me. It happened again when I chased that wide half-volley and offered a chance that Hookes let through. I need not have played that ball at all. So the lapses do keep occurring. It is just a question of which is your lucky day . . . I have got to sit and think why I have not been able to sway away or beyond the line of the ball cutting into the body. Maybe, it has something to do with the shuffle. I feel I might be getting just a little flat-footed on the shuffle. I am not on my toes like I used to be. – Sunil Gavaskar, *Sportstar*, 28 December 1985

The fall of the ninth wicket at 426 brought in Shivlal Yadav, whose stubbornness had saved India at the same venue five seasons previously. The Test was already into the fifth day by then, thanks to the rain that had robbed the third and fourth days of several overs, but the Australians could have done without the Indian number eleven's grit. A three off Reid took Sunil to 129, his highest Test score on Australian soil. The hosts tried attacking Yadav, only to be confronted by drives and slashes that went to the boundary. When Greg Matthews, the off-spinner, was brought on, Sunil walloped him high and hard into the mid-wicket fence. It wasn't something he had been known to do.

> The upbringing I had was not to hit the ball above the ground . . . If you hit it six inches above the turf, your coach made you run an extra lap as a punishment. – Sunil Gavaskar, *The Men Who Changed The Game* (Sky Sports, 2006)

The cover-drive in the same over that left cover and point gaping and took him to 149, was more like the Sunil Gavaskar the world knew. He completed his 150 with a single off Matthews, and another boundary brought up India's 500. A single off Bright made Sunil the first batsman to score 9,000 runs in Test cricket.

Australia's agony ended when Yadav pulled relief bowler Hookes and was well-caught by Hughes at deep square-leg. India's last pair had added 94, and although the Test ended in a draw, the visitors had won more points than their opponents. The man who had earned those points for India left the field to a warm ovation.

Kapil Dev called correctly and elected to bowl on the first morning of the Boxing Day Test at Melbourne. The Indians were of the view that the wicket wasn't conducive to strokeplay. They were right. A thoroughly professional display then restricted the hosts to 262. Siva, brought back at Sharma's expense, went for 51 runs from thirteen overs, but he got the key wickets of skipper Border (off a full toss), and the debutant Stephen Rodger Waugh.

Sunil failed, but his partner was in blistering form. Srikkanth top-scored with 86, and numbers three to seven scored 45, 75, 37, 49 and 55 respectively. Kirmani, who like Sunil had resumed duties behind the stumps as if he had never been away, got 35. India finished with a lead of 183, and sensed victory.

Allan Border, not for the first or the last time, produced a classic in a crisis. However, his team-mates showed little inclination of fighting it out. With Australia only 45 ahead at stumps on the fourth day and eight wickets down, not even Border, it seemed, could come between Kapil Dev and his first Test win as captain.

Reid fell early on the fifth morning, and the Indians surrounded David Gilbert, the number eleven. He hung on, even as Kapil Dev persisted with the tried and tested method of crowding the tail ender with fielders, and pushing them back whenever the specialist batsman, Border, was on strike. The Australian skipper had by then completed a fine hundred. The Indians, on a roll after getting nine wickets, gave it everything, but Border and Gilbert refused to budge. The visitors finally broke through, or so it seemed, when Border tried to sweep Shastri, and the ball flew to Sunil at first slip instead. But Ray Isherwood, the man who had pronounced Imran Khan not out off Sharma in the WCC final at the same venue, thought otherwise.

Gilbert got more and more confident, and stodgier as the overs passed. He got through to lunch. For Australia, it was almost like victory. India's agony ended soon after the resumption, when Border was stumped off Yadav for a valiant 163.

The hosts were not out of jail by any means, for India had almost four hours in which to get 126. The forecast of a thunderstorm at around tea time led to speculation that Kapil Dev would reshuffle the batting order. However, that did not happen.

'Inexplicable' is the word that sums up the approach of the Indians in the post-lunch session. At tea, they were 59-2, after having batted for twenty-five overs! Srikkanth, who alone showed some urgency in scoring 38 (Sunil fell for 8), subsequently recalled sipping tea in the dressing room with visions of a win, when he and his team-mates heard a roar from the Australian dressing room. It had started pouring cats and dogs! The match ended in a draw.

India's ineptitude on the final day, first with the ball and then the bat, took the sting out of Kapil Dev's acerbic remarks on the umpiring. So scathing was the Indian captain's outburst that it provoked even the usually restrained Richie Benaud. 'Lay off the umpires,' Benaud retorted, and added that Kapil Dev ought to have considered attacking Border earlier in the day, by bringing the field in and challenging him to hit over the top.

Really, people in glass houses should not throw stones. – Allan Border, *TOI*, 31 December 1985

The Indian fans who reckoned that there was no way their team would repeat their fifth-day display at Melbourne, were in for a shock on the second day of the New Year Test in Sydney.

It commenced with India holding all the aces, kings, queens and jacks. India were 334-1 at stumps on day one. Srikkanth had scored his maiden Test hundred, and Sunil his thirty-second. Amarnath, who had come in at the fall of Srikkanth's wicket, was unbeaten on 72.

Srikkanth considered retiring for repairs when he was hit on the toe by a Gilbert Yorker early on the first day, but Sunil convinced him to continue. The Tamil Nadu opener stayed in to brutalise the bowlers, with Siva doing a fine job in as his runner. Sunil, missed at 3 and 27, survived a testing opening spell by Reid, defending impeccably and leaving astutely.

The leg-spinner Robert Holland, hero of the previous year's New Year Test against the Windies, could make no headway against batters born and bred on spin.

Sunil took his time to get going after lunch. Gilbert once hit him on the thigh, and then got him to inside-edge a delivery one onto his pads. But the bowler wasn't consistent enough, and conceded his ground with a rank full-toss that was straight-driven for four. Sloppy fielding did not make things any better for the hosts.

The bowlers, flustered as they were with Srikkanth's belligerence, were frustrated by the straightness of Sunil's bat. The bowlers only had to make the slightest error in line and length, for the willow to become a rapier.

> 'Our coaches and guides would advise us to watch him. They would tell us to observe the straightness of his elbow, and his classical side-on stance. We used to stand like him, and try to play with as straight a bat.' – V.V.S. Laxman

Sunil slammed Matthews over long-on for four to bring up his second hundred of the series. The Australians did not quite like what followed, with Sunil looking down the pitch and creating the corridor around his eyes; they had had enough of him! With Amarnath going strong, Bill Lawry was prompted to liken the Indian batting to the Barry Richards–Graeme Pollock hammering his team had got at Durban in 1969-70.

Considering all that had happened on the first day, the Australians could not have been blamed for feeling like lambs being led to an abattoir when play got underway on the second morning. However, by the time the umpires had called 'lunch', the hosts were feeling like lambs whose slaughter had suddenly been outlawed.

The long and short of it is that Sunil and Amarnath managed only 64 runs in the first session. Even as they went about playing themselves in for an extended period of time, the spectators got restive, followed by the commentators. 'Sedate' and 'strange' had become the in-vogue terms at the SCG by the time the duo came in for lunch, Sunil having scored 36 off eighty balls and Amarnath 18 off ninety-one.

Amarnath, unbeaten on 72 overnight, was intent to complete his hundred. At the other end, Sunil allowed himself to get bogged down, the way Rahul Dravid did quite a few times in the mid-2000s. Whatever the reason was, the Indians inadvertently gave themselves lesser time in which to bowl their opponents out twice. Their best bet had been to reach a total of about 600 as quickly as possible, and then let loose their three spinners—Yadav, Shastri and Siva—on the spin-friendly SCG track.

Kapil Dev promoted himself to number four. He came in soon after lunch, when Sunil missed a sweep off Holland and was bowled for 172. The first ball the captain received, he thumped to the extra-cover boundary. He scored a rapid-fire 42. Amarnath went for his strokes after reaching three figures, and Vengsarkar and Azharuddin went for broke. The declaration was eventually made at 600-4, at least twenty overs behind schedule.

The Australians were provided a sound start by their new opening pair of David Boon and Geoffrey Marsh. They batted through the third day, of which 75 minutes were lost to rain, and took the score to 217, before Kapil Dev got Boon to play on for 131. With the total having moved up to 347-4 by the end of the fourth day, the Australians were a buoyed lot.

Yadav and Shastri, who had bowled without luck for nearly two days, set about spinning their team back into the game on the final morning. Aided by some reckless batting, they terminated the Australian innings for 396, and Kapil Dev enforced the follow-on. With the pitch turning square by then, the spinners had the Aussies on the hop again, but they ran out of time. The hosts were 119-6 at close, and the Indians could only wonder what might have been, had there been some communication between the veterans in the dressing room on the second morning.

The series ended in a stalemate, but the Indians took away two-thirds of the prize money for being the dominant team. That was hardly a consolation for missing out on an opportunity to win a Test series in Australia. Kapil Dev finished with eighteen wickets, but he lost out in the table to Yadav, whose tally of nineteen underscored Australia's traditional weakness against off-spin.

The subsequent tri-series featured cricket that was largely exhilarating and occasionally incomprehensible. As it turned out, Sunil figured prominently at both ends of the spectrum. His blitzkrieg in India's first encounter against the Kiwis left watchers incredulous. He drove high and handsomely, and slashed hard in a cameo of 27 off seventeen balls, at the start of India's pursuit of a target of 260. At one point, the Channel Nine cameras captured a bemused and smiling Srikkanth. His senior partner had for once, outscored and out-stroked him. India won that game by five wickets, but lost to Australia the very next day at the same venue.

Kapil Dev and the rest of them then settled scores by beating the Aussies by eight wickets at Melbourne. Bowled out for a mere 161, the hosts went flat out for early wickets, only to be thwarted by Sunil's 59. In the next game against Australia, he scored an unbeaten 92, but the reactions he elicited were anything but positive. Some people went so far as to draw comparisons with his unbeaten 36 in the 1975 World Cup.

Australia batted first and amassed 292-6. Sunil and Srikkanth began the Indian reply at more than a run per ball, the latter looking in tremendous nick until he was superbly caught by Border at short mid-wicket. The innings nosedived from this point onwards. Sunil kept it going, but his partners kept faltering. Kapil Dev came in at number 5 and added 65 with his predecessor, but when he fell at 158, the innings was hovering around the forty-over mark. The match virtually lost, Azharuddin and Sunil played out their time, and when the final ball was bowled, India were a hundred runs behind.

> WHAT HAS GONE WRONG WITH INDIA? Despite their vehement denials of a split and their public pleas, it is clear that Kapil Dev and Gavaskar are not pulling together. Else, why should the skipper publicly criticise Gavaskar after the game against Australia? Besides, reports indicate that Gavaskar was spoken to by manager Venkataraghvan and told that his batting was not in the team's interest. – Sunder Rajan, *TOI*, 25 January 1986

That Sunil missed the next two matches, both of which were played against New Zealand, due to back trouble, wasn't considered entirely coincidental. He returned to the fray against Australia at Adelaide on Australia Day and India's Republic Day. It was a special occasion, as Sunil received a salver from the man whose record for the highest number of Test hundreds he had surpassed. 'It pains me that I did not get the opportunity to play alongside Sunil, but then, I had retired from Test cricket before he was born,' the Don said during the course of his speech.

The world is aware of Sir Don Bradman's pronouncement that Sachin Tendulkar reminded him of himself, as he batted like him.

But what very few people know is that he said the same thing to Sunil as well! – Hemant Waingankar

The match wasn't special for Sunil's team. Set to score 263 to win after another impressive Australian batting performance, Sunil scored 77, but Shastri and Kapil Dev apart, no other batsman put up a fight. In the subsequent game, also against Australia, Sunil got 72, and this time, found himself on the winning side, as India overhauled a target of 236 with six wickets in hand. The fifteenth and last game of the round-robin stage was a veritable semi-final between India, who had eight points, and New Zealand, who had seven. Australia had already qualified with thirteen points. India started badly, being reduced to 127-7 at one stage, but a stand of 53 between Sharma and Binny took them to 202. Binny then took over with the ball, and along with Kapil Dev ensured a 34-run win.

Australia's success notwithstanding, the reigning world champions were the favourites when the first of the best-of-three finals commenced. Australia were restricted to 170-8, but an insipid batting display saw India tumble to 52-4, and eventually die for 159. Sunil could not open due to a bruised finger. This may have made a difference to the outcome, for he was the batsman in form, and could well have given his team a sound start. The hosts dominated the second final, achieving a target of 188 with seven wickets in hand. Fittingly, it was Border, the man who had denied India victory in the Test series, who stroked the winning runs.

Once again, an Indian cricket team returned from a tour asking itself the same thing – what might have been.

For Sunil, the trip had been a personal success. He scored two hundreds in the Tests and topped the averages in the tri-series. His performances had delighted his fans, and left pundits in no doubt that he had acquired a second or probably third wind. The end wasn't far away, and he knew it better than anybody else, but he was determined to go out in a blaze of glory. Not that he had any intention of doing the same in the near future.

'I retire only to bed,' he quipped when quizzed about his retirement plans at a felicitation ceremony organised by the P.J. Hindu Gymkhana in Bombay. 'After my retirement, I would campaign for One-Day Internationals, so that they would wipe out Test cricket, and as a result, my records would remain intact,' he joked.

An integral part of his desire to bow out with a flourish was the 'enjoyment' factor. His belligerence in the One-Day Internationals, and new-found chemistry with K. Srikkanth, indicated that he was having the time of his life. His aggressive approach in the shorter variety had proved to be overwhelmingly effective.

The connoisseurs had loved him all along for obvious reasons, but his relationship with the masses hadn't quite been the same. While they respected him for his achievements, technique, concentration, sage-like dedication and contribution to the sport, they had never got down to loving him as they did his brother-in-law Viswanath and Kapil Dev, whose approaches to the game were comparatively easier to unravel and relate to.

Sunil's batting in the limited-overs variety in 1985-86, ironically after he had been made to return to the opening slot, made the general public warm up to him like never before.

The proliferation of television sets across India in the mid-eighties was critical in this regard. Those who had listened to Sunil's exploits on their transistors in the years gone by and had come to consider him to be an epitome of perfection, whose name, or rather, surname, was to be taken in hushed tones, now *saw* him demonstrate a hitherto unknown facet of his personality. The methods he utilised to attack bowlers like the cavaliers of yesteryear—C.K. Nayudu, Mushtaq Ali and Salim Durani—were hailed. It was like a celebrated exponent of Hindustani classical music recording a pop album to reach out to the younger generation. Of course, it was easy for Sunil to perform the cricketing equivalent of a pop album, for like the greatest of classical singers, his foundations, and understanding of the fundamentals, were strong.

He was eager to enjoy himself in the inaugural Austral-Asia Cup, a limited-overs tournament in Sharjah that featured Australia and New Zealand, in addition to the three Asian nations. After falling for no score in the first game against New Zealand, which India almost made a hash of, but won eventually by three wickets, Sunil scored 71 in the semi-final against Sri Lanka, matching Srikkanth stroke-for-stroke in a stand of 93. He maintained the momentum after Srikkanth's dismissal, at one stage hitting left-arm spinner Don Anurasiri off the back foot for an uncharacteristic six. Needing 206 to win, India were a comfortable 165-1, when Sunil was caught behind off De Mel. The middle order then caved in, and the Indians were made to huff and puff to reach the target.

The final between the Asian giants, played at the Sharjah Cricket Ground on Friday, 18 April 1986, will live forever in the memories of those who watched it. 'India did not lose this match, Javed Miandad won it,' Raj Singh Dungarpur, India's manager, told the media at the end of the game. The universe corroborated his statement.

A closer look at the scorecard suggests otherwise. India, who batted first, were 167-1 at the end of the thirty-fifth over, and 225-3 at the end of the forty-fifth. From that position, they ought to have strolled to a total of around 275. But 245 was what they finished with, after Sunil and Srikkanth had pulverised Imran, Wasim Akram, Abdul Qadir and the others in a partnership of 177.

Sunil was fourth out when he was bowled off his right pad by Imran for 92. Srikkanth scored 75 and Vengsarkar 50. However, the middle order proved to be as ineffective as it had against the Kiwis and Lankans. Had even one of the batsmen made an individual contribution of around 25, Miandad's six off the last ball would have amounted to nothing.

Not many people were aware that Sunil had not been keeping well on the eve of the final.

> 'He told me that he was unwell and was considering skipping the game. I asked him to step outside the dressing room, and pointed to a cluster of Pakistani supporters. They were carrying flags and were making a lot of noise, out-shouting the Indian supporters. You could see the expression on Sunil's face change. "I am playing," he said.' – Raj Singh Dungarpur

Sunil won the Man of the Series Award for his knocks in the semi-final and final, but Miandad grabbed all the headlines. His six, which fetched Pakistan their first ever limited-overs trophy, affected cricketers and cricket-lovers on the subcontinent in more ways than they could have possibly imagined.

21

FIVE-FIGURE MAN

'Sunil Gavaskar has never given me the same kind of support playing under me that I gave him when I was playing under him. I remember saying to him at a team meeting when I was captain: "I also expect runs from you." To which his reply was: "If you don't think I am good enough, then you can drop me." This was an arrogant attitude. Grossly unfair . . . I have always felt [that] he has played under my captaincy on sufferance. All I can say is that: "Sunny, you can't have your cake and eat it too." He doesn't have the responsibility of captaincy but he shouldn't forget the responsibility he has to his team and to his country.'

Thus went the first paragraph of the penultimate chapter of *By God's Decree, the Autobiography of Kapil Dev,* the release of which coincided with India's tour of England, one month after Miandad's match.

It was damning stuff, and for the tabloids, a godsend. They claimed that Sunil wanted a retraction and apology. The captain in turn argued that his remarks were distorted, and announced that he was initiating legal proceedings against his co-author for adding three chapters without his approval.

That Kapil Dev had a point was proved when he came out with another autobiography—this one credited to his wife—a year later.

India were originally slated to tour England in the second half of the summer of 1986, having played in the first in 1982. However, the Board had opted for the first, the idea being to give the cricketers some time to breathe before a backbreaking home season, which was to commence in September 1986.

This book controversy notwithstanding, the Indians began the England tour well, with most of the frontline players striking form. Sunil scored 81 in a One-dayer against Surrey at the Oval, and starred in a three-dayer against Kent in unconventional fashion. These games generally featured a give-and-take in the form of declarations, but Kent had ideas of their own. The Indians were infuriated by the home team's reluctance to declare even after batting for two whole days. Sunil, who wasn't playing, walked around the boundary line and distributed newspapers to his team-mates fielding in the deep. Not that the English had any right to complain, for Edmonds had done something similar when the Indian innings had gone on and on at Calcutta in January 1985.

The Indians bowled superbly in the first One-Day International at the Oval to bowl England out for 162. Srikkanth fell first ball to Graham Dilley, who was making a comeback to international cricket after a long lay-off due to injury. Sunil looked distracted. A wild waft outside the off-stump when he had barely got his eye in did not thrill the Indian supporters. 'Looks as though he is out to enjoy himself,' one of the BBC commentators quipped.

He then drove Dilley far too soon, and gave the bowler a sitter of a return catch. But Dilley spilt it. That life changed everything.

Sunil settled down to drive and flick the England bowlers with aplomb. At the other end, Mohammad Azharuddin unveiled his wristy wizardry. As the partnership gained in magnitude, the England fielders wilted. Azhar beat his senior partner to the fifty, and when Sunil completed his with a single off Dilley, he repeated the gesture he had made in the Austral-Asia Cup final. He first acknowledged the cheers with his bat, and then raised his right hand and drew a T. It was a reminder to the selector who in the previous season had advocated that the 'thirty-plus' members of the side—Sunil, Amarnath and Madan

Lal—be put to pasture. The message Sunil intended to convey was straightforward, 'Thirty-plus, not out!'

Sunil's 65 and Azhar's 83 ensured a nine-wicket win. England won the second game, but only just, and Kapil Dev took possession of the Texaco Trophy by virtue of a faster scoring rate.

The Indians shifted to the Test mode with a stirring performance in a three-dayer against Northamptonshire. Amarnath and Azharuddin scored hundreds, and Kapil Dev bowled splendidly, at one stage taking four wickets in eight balls without conceding a run. He and his fellow seamers rekindled memories of India's seam-and-swing show in the 1983 World Cup. Off the field, Raj Singh convened a press conference in the Indian team bus to address the 'book' issue. Sunil denied that he had demanded an apology, Kapil Dev brought up the distortion factor, and everybody decided to move on. The first Test was only a couple of days away.

India went into the Test with a debutant wicketkeeper in Kiran More, who had kept wicket in most of the one-dayers in Australia after Kirmani sustained a groin injury. Chandrakant Pandit, the highest scorer in the Ranji season of 1985-86, had kept wicket in Sharjah and the two One-dayers in England, and was part of the squad in England. But the think-tank picked More for the Test, on the grounds that he was the better keeper of the two. The presence of More and Pandit in the Indian outfit put paid to the prospects of the Karnataka duo; while Kirmani's career was virtually over, it appeared that Vishwanath would have to do something spectacular to supersede not one, but two contemporaries.

England went into the Test with their captain on trial. David Gower, who had endeared himself to his country by winning the Ashes the previous summer, was feeling the heat after his side's 0-5 annihilation in the Caribbean earlier that year. He had been appointed captain for only the two One-dayers and the first Test.

In a way, Sunil too was on trial. His feelings for Lord's in what was his fifth Test there were ambivalent as always, but he had at the back of his mind a fact consistently brought up by his detractors; he was yet to score a hundred at Headquarters. He took up the challenge.

The dampness in the pitch prompted Kapil Dev to bowl after winning the toss. Openers Graham Gooch and Tim Robinson negotiated the initial overs, putting on 66 before Robinson was caught at silly-point off Maninder Singh. The left-arm spinner had been recalled to the side after an outstanding domestic season, as had Patil. Even as Maninder came in, Sivaramakrishnan went out. The selectors had run out of patience.

An incisive bowling performance by Chetan Sharma, and three late strikes by Roger Binny, restricted England to 294, Gooch top-scoring with 114. Srikkanth and Sunil batted positively until the Tamilian was caught at fourth slip. Amarnath came in, and then began a circumspect phase that brought back memories of the Sydney Test earlier that year. However, unlike that game, the England bowlers tested the veterans. The veterans played and missed at deliveries that could be classified as unplayable, but hung on. India were 83-1 at stumps, with Sunil on 30.

> GAVASKAR HOLDS THE KEY: If he can use his vast experience to score a big hundred and help India take a useful lead . . . on a pitch which will take spin increasingly, it could give India victory in this first Test. – Henry Blofeld, *Mid-Day*, 7 June 1986

He began the third day with an imperial extra cover drive off Richard Ellison. But Dilley had the last laugh. He produced one that kicked off a length, and moved just a wee bit away. Sunil had committed to play at it, and he did. Third slip took an easy catch.

He was replaced in the middle by a man who only had to step onto the Lord's Cricket Ground, bat in hand, to feel as if he was wearing a red cape and blue jersey with 'S' emblazoned on it. Two of Dilip Vengsarkar's previous four Test innings at Headquarters had yielded him scores of 103 and 157. He was intent on continuing in the same vein.

Amarnath and Azharuddin got out just when they seemed to have entrenched themselves in the middle. A mini-collapse ensued, but Vengsarkar was in a league of his own. He was beaten by the odd delivery, but nothing could beat his self-belief. His state of mind was underscored in a Dilley over. The bowler delivered a beauty that moved away and just missed the outside-edge. His next ball, Vengsarkar drilled past point by going down on one knee, to complete his fifty.

The wickets continued to go down as he batted his way into the 80s. India were 267-8, and in danger of conceding the first-innings lead, when debutant More came in and proceeded to bat gutsily. India led by nine when he fell, and last-man Maninder arrived in the middle. He offered a straight bat to everything and watched Vengsarkar, batting on 95, driving Dilley for four. Gower brought the field in, but his fielders could only watch as Vengsarkar tapped the ball into a gap and called for a quick single. Maninder responded, and the Bombay batsman became only the sixth batsman, and first non-Englishman, to score three Test hundreds at Lord's.

Maninder stayed on, helping Vengsarkar to take the score to 341. The last two wickets had added 75.

The stage was set for India's captain and crunch specialist to deliver. Kapil Dev scalped Robinson, Gooch and Gower to reduce England to 35-3. Although Lamb and Gatting resuscitated the innings, the bowlers kept pegging away. The last wicket fell at 180, and India had the whole of the final day in which to get 134 to register their first ever Test win at the venue where they had made their debut in 1932.

It was their eleventh Test at Lord's, and while that may not have been at the back of the batsmen's minds, their heads were far from uncluttered. Their ineptitude in Test cricket in the 1980s was to blame. Since March 1981, the Indian team had won only two Tests, both against England at Bombay; a paradox, given their successes in the limited-overs format in the same period. They and indeed, their fans, weren't quite used to the situation they had played themselves into. Of the XI who figured in the game, only four players—Sunil, Amarnath, Vengsarkar and Kapil Dev—knew how it felt to win a Test overseas.

Srikkanth fell early, and Amarnath ducked into a Dilley delivery and got hit on the head. Fortunately, he was wearing a helmet. Sunil, who had got going with a straight drive off Ellison, reached 22 before chasing Dilley outside the off-stump. Downton held a good catch, and Sunil took his time to leave the crease. He would end his Test career without a Test hundred at the hallowed ground, after all.

The Indians got slightly jittery when Amarnath and Vengsarkar fell after taking the score past the halfway mark. Shastri and Azharuddin allayed their fears with some fluent strokes. The score had moved to 110 when the pair bungled up on the calling and found each other at the same end. Azharuddin departed, and was replaced by his captain.

Kapil Dev got the blood circulating by backing away to leg and cutting Edmonds for four. He then repeated the shot, before directing his gaze on the leg-side. A sweep off Edmonds yielded 4 more, and the target was a mere 4 runs away when he went down on his right knee and deposited the left-arm spinner over the mid-wicket boundary. India had won, and Kapil Dev had opened his account as captain in his twenty-first Test at the helm. The icing on the cake for him was the Man of the Match award, which he won ahead of Vengsarkar for his spell on the fourth day, and cameo on the fifth.

The sight of P.C. Alexander, India's then High Commissioner to the UK in 1986, standing next to Kapil Dev on the balcony when a bottle of champagne was uncorked, was an unforgettable one for those who remembered the humiliation of the 1974 side by his predecessor B.K. Nehru.

As he looked around, Alexander was taken aback to see Sunil crying. He sought an explanation, and was left speechless: 'We have won a Test at Lord's! LORD'S!'

His personal views on Lord's notwithstanding, Sunil had been a student of Cricket history all his life. He therefore understood the significance of what his team had accomplished. True, India had won the World Cup there in 1983, but then, this was a Test match. The battering the team had taken on previous visits to the HQ was forgotten for good.

The victors were determined not to surrender the initiative, regardless of the problems that engulfed them before the second Test. Chetan Sharma, who was involved in a scuffle with spectators during the three-dayer against Leicestershire, strained his back, as did Amarnath, and both dropped out of the second Test at Leeds. It was a double blow, considering Sharma's six wickets and Amarnath's 69 in first innings at Lord's. The think-tank reacted boldly. Patil, the hero of the previous tour, was the obvious replacement for Amarnath, but he had been struggling for runs. Pandit, who had batted a lot better than his Bombay senior, was drafted in as a specialist batsman.

The choice of Sharma's replacement was startling. Manoj Prabhakar was part of the team, but his captain did not consider him to be the finished product that they wanted. He plumped for one of the architects of the 1983 triumph, who was playing in the Central Lancashire league. With the blessings of Sriraman, the BCCI president, Madan Lal was inducted into the squad.

Accompanying Kapil Dev for the toss at Leeds was Mike Gatting. The England selectors had sacked Gower after his sixth consecutive Test defeat, and the tabloids had got into the act, hailing Gatting as some kind of messiah.

Kapil Dev called correctly again, and this time, chose to bat. He and his team-mates then sat on the balcony to watch Sunil compile a gem of what unfortunately turned out to be a cameo. He began by clipping Dilley off his toes for a boundary, and then essayed a scintillating cover-drive off his old adversary John Lever, who had been recalled for the Test. India were up and running when Srikkanth gave a tame catch to mid-on. Derek Pringle, the successful bowler, struck again when Sunil fished outside the off-stump and was caught behind for 35. It was yet another instance of the lapses in his concentration that he had referred to earlier in the year.

The highlight of India's 272 was a flawless 61 by Vengsarkar. His contribution acquired astronomical proportions when England, to put it simply, caved in. It was 1983 all over again, as the ball was made to talk by Binny and the man condescendingly referred to by many Englishmen as 'dear old' Madan Lal. This 'dear old' man started the slide with two early strikes, and Binny took up the baton. Kapil Dev chipped in with the wicket of Gooch, and England were all out for 102. A spectator who could not believe his eyes was Fred Trueman, India's nemesis in the 1952 series.

The bowlers continued to dominate the proceedings. Sunil, Srikkanth and Shastri at number three fell in the second innings with only 29 on the board. Azhar failed to come to terms with the 'Mexican wave' that was doing the rounds of the ground, and was fourth out at 35. Pandit was dismissed just before the close of the second day. With three days left, India were 70-5 and 240 ahead. Vengsarkar was batting on 33. His consistency notwithstanding, he had been looked at as a nearly man of sorts since his international debut a decade previously. His fans rued the fact that he had been taken for granted and not given his due. Sunil and Kapil Dev apart, the likes of Viswanath, Amarnath, Patil, and later

Azharuddin, had been accorded higher billing than Vengsarkar. Shastri's ascent in the mid-1980s had pushed him further into the background. Only an extraordinary effort, it seemed, would enable him to emerge from the shadows.

In England in 1986, he did just that.

The ball wasn't coming onto the bat, and the bowlers were making it wobble, but Vengsarkar was unflustered. He batted brilliantly, ensuring that his bat and front pad moved in unison, and the ball played as late as possible. Kapil Dev threw his bat purposefully to get 31, and the lower order handled the pressure magnificently. More scored 16, Madan Lal his second 20 of the game, and Binny 26, the highlight of which was a hook off Dilley that sailed out of the ground. Vengsarkar was one short of the three-figure mark when the ninth wicket fell. A single took him to the magic figure, and his team-mates and the spectators rose to applaud a gem. He had scored 61 in the first innings and an unbeaten 102 in the second; the second-highest individual score in the match turned out to be More's 36 in the first innings. That said it all.

England needed 408 to win, a tall order in those conditions. Kapil Dev and Binny took two wickets each, and Maninder four, to hasten their demise for 128. Madan Lal capped a memorable game by running last-man Dilley out with a direct hit from third man. The series was India's. 'This time, I didn't give him a chance,' Vengsarkar, the undisputed Man of the Match, said when asked how he felt when Kapil Dev won the individual award ahead of him at Lord's.

England missed Ian Botham, who was serving a two-month suspension for admitting to smoking pot, but that did not justify their abject failure.

The third and final Test of the series at Edgbaston, Birmingham, was Sunil's 115th. It made him the most-capped Test cricketer of all time, leaving behind Colin Cowdrey, who had played 114.

Way back in 1986, Colin was the one with the record for the most appearances in Tests, when yours truly went past him. On the first morning of that game, I was pleasantly surprised to see Colin being ushered into the Indian dressing room by Raj Singh Dungarpur, the team manager. He had come all the way from his home just to congratulate me and wish me luck. He was most effusive in his congratulations and wished that I would celebrate the occasion with a century. – Sunil Gavaskar, MCC Spirit of Cricket Speech, 2003

Sunil went into the game on the back of a 136 against his old county, Somerset. In a commanding display, he hit fourteen fours and four sixes, two of them in succession off Vic Marks. Both shots landed in the Tone river that ran alongside the County ground at Taunton.

He hadn't scored a hundred in his hundredth Test, and his fans were hopeful that he would do so in what was most certainly his final Test in England.

A captain's hand of 183 by Mike Gatting helped England reach 390. India responded with the same total. The top nine Indian batsmen entered double figures, with number six Ravi Shastri's 18 being the lowest score of the lot. Leading the way were Amarnath (79), Azharuddin (64), More (48) and Binny (40). The Indians went on to be as professional with the ball, bowling England out for 235 in the second innings, and giving themselves the opportunity to make a clean sweep. Chetan Sharma, the enemy number one for many an Indian after the Austral-Asia Cup final, completed a memorable Test series, with sixteen wickets from two games. His 10-188 in the third Test was inclusive of a haul of 6-58 in the second innings.

Sunil added another feather to his cap when he caught Gower off Sharma in the second innings. It was his hundredth catch in Test cricket. He was the first Indian, and seventh non-wicketkeeper overall, to reach the milestone, after Englishmen Walter Hammond and Colin Cowdrey, Australians Bob Simpson and the Chappell brothers, and West Indian Sir Garry Sobers.

Srikkanth and he then put together their third fifty-plus stand of the Test series. At 101-1 and a lot of time left in the game, India were well placed, but Edmonds brought his team back into the game by dismissing Amarnath, Vengsarkar and Shastri in quick succession. Sunil, who had completed his first fifty of the series, was on 54 when he nicked Foster to the keeper. At 105-5, the game had opened up. More, whose batting in the series had overshadowed his admittedly impressive wicketkeeping, came in to add 69 with Azharuddin before the skies opened. The game was drawn.

The series win convinced cricket lovers in India that their team was the frontrunner for the title of the second-best in the world, after the Windies. The last time they had thought this way about their side was in 1971, the year Sunil had made his Test debut.

The team had evolved since Wadekar's twin triumphs. There were the victories in the World Cup and World Championship of Cricket, not to mention the triumphs in Sharjah. As for Test cricket, the team had progressed by leaps and bounds in the 1970s, with Sunil leading the way, but had tapered off in the early 1980s. This was largely due to the paucity of a consistent opening pair with the bat and new ball. It wasn't entirely coincidental that India's Test-drought, which stretched to thirty-one games, commenced in November 1981, soon after Sunil and Kapil Dev had had their most successful partners taken away from them. The batting had flowered only in fits and starts, with a purple patch of one player clashing with a bad patch of another. The bowlers had by and large struggled. India had taken nine Tests after the end of the Test-drought in 1984-85 to register another Test win, at Lord's in June 1986.

It was this phase, in the first half of the 1980s, which triggered off a remark attributed to Sunil. When asked which team had the toughest attack in world cricket, he was supposed to have said, 'What I know is that the team with the weakest attack is India! Play out Kapil Dev's first five overs, and a century is yours!'

A comparison of the scorecards of the Tests of the 1970s and those from the drought period, reveal that the pressures of performing eventually got to the superstars. Sunil scored his twentieth Test hundred in his fiftieth Test in 1979, but his next twelve hundreds took him another sixty-two Tests to make. While Kapil Dev's statistics do not show as glaring a discrepancy, he was to experience a dip in his bowling productivity after the 1986 England tour.

It was a pointer to the evolution of the team that the series in England had been won despite it being played in the hostile first half of the summer and despite a sizeable contribution by Sunil.

There were other pointers as well. The superstars had waged a lone battle for most of the 1980s, but things seemed to be changing. In Srikkanth, Sunil had discovered an opening partner who was relatively consistent and complemented him perfectly. The middle-order wore a settled look, with Amarnath and Azharuddin cementing their places and Vengsarkar in the form of his life. Shastri had already metamorphosed into a quality all-rounder. On the bowling front, Binny and Sharma had forced the batsmen to change their habit of growing in confidence whenever Kapil Dev wasn't bowling. Maninder Singh was high on confidence, and there was hope that Sivaramakrishnan would return. The wicketkeeping was in safe hands, with Kiran More having done a fine job, and Pandit and Vishwanath keeping him on his toes. There was every reason to regard the loss to Sri Lanka in mid-1985 as an aberration, for it had been followed by an impressive showing in Australia, and of course, victory in England.

Confidence-wise, India could not have hoped to be better placed at the start of the 1986-87 season, wherein they were to host as many as three series, against Australia, Sri Lanka and Pakistan respectively. The calender year of 1979-80 had featured as many teams and thirteen Tests, as opposed to eleven in 1986-87, but the additional dimension in the latter season was sixteen One Day internationals – six each against Australia and Pakistan, and five against Sri Lanka. These assignments apart, the team was to play two tournaments in Sharjah.

The members of the national selection committee were as optimistic as the masses, when they met to pick the squad for the first two One-Day Internationals against Border's Australians. They had three things in mind when they commenced their deliberations:
1. The sixteen One-dayers (not counting the games at Sharjah).
2. The fact that Sunil wasn't getting any younger.
3. The need to try out a youngster or two in the lead-up to the 1987 World Cup.

They ended up taking an experimental decision.

'We didn't want to drop Gavaskar. We only wanted to rest him ... It just happened that the player in question was Gavaskar, and a hue and cry was raised ... We had in mind the tight schedule ahead. Hence, the decision to rest each one for a game or two....' – Chandu Borde, *Sportsweek WOC*, November 1986.

Borde and Co had not taken into account the likely repercussions of their 'experimental' decision. 'Kapil takes his revenge,' *Mid-Day* claimed on 1 September 1986, the obvious reference being to his omission two years previously. The *TOI* three days later quoted Sunil expressing his shock at the decision. Fans turned the heat on Borde, bombarding him with threats and abusive phone calls.

There were some who believed that the selectors had left Sunil out for his alleged violation of the England tour contract. The *TOI* on 23 August 1986 had reported that Sunil had incurred the wrath of the establishment by sporting the logo of an international sports goods manufacturer on his bat, when the contract had forbidden the players to do so. However, Raj Singh had made no mention of this in his tour report.

The BCCI president then continued what had almost become an annual tradition in the 1980s, as far as issues pertaining to Sunil were concerned. Sriraman requested the selectors to reconsider their decision, and Sunil was reinstated.

The three-dayer between the Australians and Bombay at Gwalior just before the first two One-dayers featured some attractive batting by both sides. At the end of the game, the spotlight was on Sandeep Patil, who scored 64 in Bombay's only innings and announced his retirement.

It was a huge loss to Indian cricket. One thousand five hundred and eighty-eight runs from twenty-nine Tests, and 1,005 runs from forty-five One-dayers, were figures that hardly did the man any justice. He possessed god-given talent, as Sunil himself had noted in his foreword to the player's 1984 autobiography, *Sandy Storm*. But he had failed to exploit it to the optimum. His good looks and aggressive approach to the game had made him one of the most popular Indian cricketers of the 1980s. An individual with diverse interests, Patil emulated Sunil by acting as the leading man in a film titled *Kabhi Ajnabi The* and appearing in a host of TV commercials. He edited a weekly sports magazine, and even dabbled in singing, among other things.

There were unsubstantiated stories of Sunil calling Patil's parents and entreating them to ensure that their son did not skip his practice sessions. The senior man did everything he could to ensure that his Nirlons, Bombay and India team-mate continued to focus on the top priority – cricket.

Spells of ill-luck had played their part in bogging Patil down. He could have gone from strength to strength after his heroics in Australia in 1980-81, but personal problems came to the fore, and made him desperate enough to contemplate retirement during the tour of England in 1982. Sunil's riposte to his retirement-talk was to draft him into the Test XI even thought the latter's form did not warrant it. Patil went on to score 129, a knock that underscored his temperament as much as it did his talent.

There was another setback in 1984-85. He was omitted after the Delhi Test in 1984-85, just two games after scoring a hundred at Faisalabad, as the selectors attempted to show that Kapil Dev was not being singled out for his poor stroke.

Patil made a comeback when he was picked for the tour of England in 1986, but, he could not get going. His indifferent fielding was also held against him. That did not prevent him from being the character that he was off the field. He seized control of the VCR in the bus that transported the team all over the country, and subjected his team-mates to a film titled *Andheri Raat Mein Diya Tere Haath Mein* for the entire duration of the tour. This particular film belonged to the double-entendre genre, replete with suggestive jokes and bizarre situations. The players watched the film so many times that they ended up learning the dialogues by heart.

Patil was subsequently persuaded to reverse his decision by the erstwhile ruler of the city where he had called it a day. The late Madhavrao Scindia, a prominent member of Rajiv Gandhi's cabinet and a future president of the BCCI, convinced him to not just lead, but virtually construct Madhya Pradesh's Ranji Trophy team, in the late 1980s. Patil played his part to perfection.

The One-Day series against Allan Border's Australians kicked off in Jaipur. Australia batted first and scored 262. Boon and Marsh continued their love affair with the Indian bowling, putting on a record 212 for the first wicket. Both got hundreds, but they were overshadowed by Srikkanth, who did likewise and set up a seven-wicket win. The Australians drew level in the second encounter, played in picturesque Srinagar. Sunil scored 26 in the first game and 52 in the second. The visitors then played a three-dayer against India's under-25s at Chandigarh before flying to Madras for the first of the three Tests.

SWANSONG

IMPERIOUS – during his 188 for the World XI against the MCC in the Bicentenary Test at Lords in August 1987. He announced his retirement from First-class cricket during the game.

The Complete Batsman

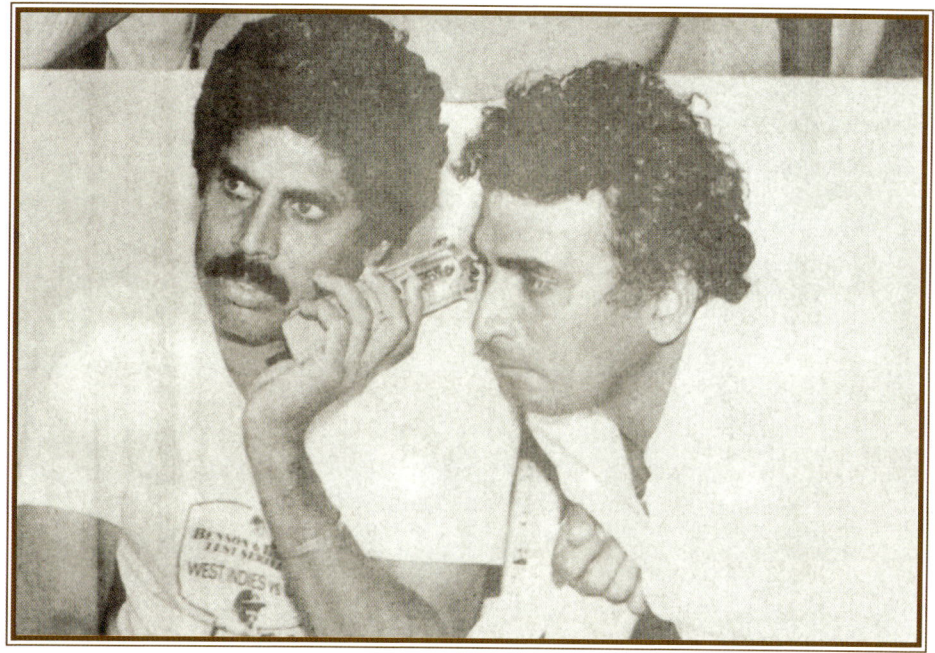

With his successor, predecessor, and successor as captain of India.

India's 'new-ball' bowler in quite a few Tests in the 1970s tries his hand at spin bowling.

Battling the premier purveyors of cricket's pace age ... without a helmet!

WRITER EXTRAORDINAIRE

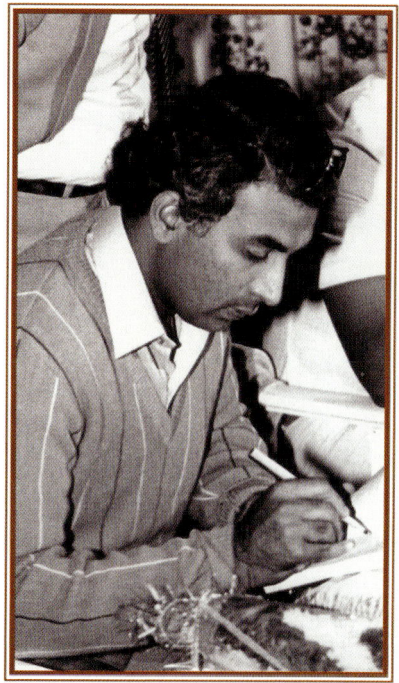
Sunil giving autographs.

Idols, SMG's 1983 bestseller

Queue at Madras for Sunil's autograph.

At the launch of *Sunny Days*, with Bishan Bedi.

Kapil Dev releases *Idols* with Clive Lloyd on 28 October 1983, a day before Gavaskar equalled Don Bradman's record of 29 Test centuries.

People wishing Sunny on 28 October 1983 for his 29th Test hundred.

The match was preceded by a presentation. Sunil received a silver salver for becoming the first cricketer to complete a century of consecutive Test appearances. He had figured in every Test played by India since the Bombay Test of the 1974-75 series against the Windies. As was his wont, he downplayed the achievement. He was lucky, he said, because there had been long gaps between Tests whenever he had sustained serious injuries, thus giving him ample time to recover. The reference was to his broken cheekbone in New Zealand in 1975-76 and the fractured shin in England in 1982. Another reason for his longevity, he jokingly contended years later, was his minimal accent on fitness. In his view, he wasn't as susceptible to strains and niggles as those who subjected their body to rigorous workouts!

'In those days, fitness was considered important, but it wasn't as professionally managed as it is today. The amount of cricket was also far less than what it is today. As far as Sunil was concerned, he was mentally very, very strong, and that easily compensated for the physical injuries he sustained over the years.'
– Dr Vishwas Raut

Kapil Dev, who incidentally hadn't missed a single Test since his debut due to injury or illness, stepped aside to let Sunil lead the team out on the field, after Border won the toss and elected to bat.

Australia batted for two full days and a bit of the third to score 574-7. The highlight of the innings was an innings of 210 by Dean Jones, during the course of which, he lost fluids, weight, control over his bodily functions, and finally, his consciousness, as the Madras humidity took its toll. Boon scored his third Test hundred in four innings against India on the first day, and Border the nineteenth of his Test career. The Indians faltered in their response after a typical start by Srikkanth. Sunil was caught and bowled by Matthews for eight, Amarnath run out, and then Srikkanth himself caught at point.

At stumps on day three, the hosts were precariously poised at 270-7, and found themselves at the receiving end of a verbal lashing by their skipper. Kapil Dev let his feelings be known, as he castigated his players for their propensity to take the aerial route.

His team-mates could not believe their eyes the following morning, when their captain warmed up with three lofted boundaries off Steve Waugh. Kapil Dev Nikhanj clearly did not believe in walking the talk.

What he did do is drive the Australians to despair with a blazing innings. Chetan Sharma and Shivlal Yadav kept him company, and the stadium exploded when Kapil Dev hooked Craig McDermott to complete his fourth Test hundred. There was another roar a little later, when he took a single to avoid the follow-on.

The Australians, 177 ahead, went for their shots, and were 170-5 at stumps on the fourth evening. Border wanted to bat on, but Bob Simpson, the Cricket Manager of the Australian side, convinced him to declare overnight. As he viewed it, they had eighty-seven overs in which to bowl the Indians out on an ageing pitch. What the Australians did not know is that their desire to take ten wickets matched that of the home team to score the 348 runs that were needed for a win. The Indians hadn't even considered victory when confronted by a similar target at Colombo a year previously, but their success in Australia and England had changed their mindsets.

Srikkanth got off to another flier. It was against the run of play that he lofted Matthews and saw Steve Waugh take a superb catch on the long-on boundary. The score at that stage was 55-1, of which his share was 39. Their main threat had gone, or so the Australians thought. Border exhorted his bowlers, particularly the spin duo of Matthews and Bright, to attack Sunil and the new man Amarnath.

It did not take very long for the TV and radio commentators to start using the word 'attack' to describe the Indian approach rather than the Australian. While Amarnath kept it ticking, Sunil changed gears.

He came down the wicket to deposit Matthews over the mid-wicket boundary. With Amarnath at home against the spinners, Border reintroduced pace at one end, and persisted with Matthews, who had taken five wickets in the first innings, at the other.

Bruce Reid was given the ball, but banished to the outfield after Sunil timed a defensive push so well that the ball sped away for four. He was replaced by Waugh. Sunil followed a straight-drive with a cut, after which the bowler was replaced by McDermott. Sunil greeted him with two cover-drives that hit the advertising hoardings. The strokes, both essayed by going down on the right knee, brought the spectators to their feet and the Australians down on their knees.

'I have this innings among the great hands I have witnessed, and as long as I live, I will never forget the two cover drives he played from one knee against Craig McDermott. Pure genius. It was thrilling, unforgettable.' – Mike Coward

'I had seen him score a lot of runs since I first saw him in 1977-78, but never had I seen him go down on one knee to cover-drive a fast bowler.' – Allan Border

The chase was on, powered by the man who had spearheaded three of India's many 300-plus chases of the previous decade. In the three encounters in question, India had beaten the West Indies at Port of Spain in 1976, lost to Australia by 16 runs at Brisbane in 1977-78, and come within 9 runs of victory against England at the Oval in 1979. Sunil's fourth-innings contributions in these games had been 102, 113 and 221 respectively. At Madras in 1986, he seemed intent on adding a fourth Test to the list. Amarnath's dismissal did not affect him, as a cut and straight-drive off Matthews just before the tea-interval suggested. At the break, India were 193-2, needing 155 in the final session, the twenty mandatory overs included, and Border was a worried man. He pondered on the absurdity of it all: his side had scored 574 in the first innings and declared twice, and yet, was in danger of losing!

If I could hang in there till tea time, we would have a good platform for the likes of Kapil, with their extraordinary stroke-making ability. – Sunil Gavaskar, *Madras Magic* (ABC, 2006)

The Australians fought back after the interval. Sunil was ten short of a hundred when he drove Bright uppishly and was held by Jones in the covers.

'It was one of the best I had seen him play. We had set a daunting target, but Sunil's display of controlled aggression was stupendous. He put us on the back foot, and gave India the momentum. He set it up for his team.' – Allan Border

What ensued was an epic battle under intense pressure. It featured remarkable bowling, most of all by the indefatigable Matthews, batting that was a combination of the brilliant and the reckless, and some appalling behaviour by members of both sides. The umpires weren't mere bystanders, as it turned out, with Border letting off steam when told to speed up the over-rate. Amidst the tantrums and face-offs, Ravi Shastri managed to retain his sanity. After Kapil Dev's early exit, the vice-captain marshalled the chase in a manner that would have done Javed Miandad proud. The Australians targeted the other end, and succeeded.

With 17 needed from four overs with four wickets in hand, the Indians were breathing easy, but Bright dismissed Sharma and More in quick succession. In came Shivlal Yadav, and in the following over, he deposited Matthews over the long-on boundary. That one stroke made the spectators rediscover their voice. Three balls into Bright's next over, India had whittled the equation down to four runs from eight balls with two wickets in hand. Nothing, it seemed, could come in their way now, but Yadav got overambitious, went for an almighty sweep, missed, and was bowled. Maninder Singh survived the final two balls, and Shastri took strike to Matthews in the last over. He negotiated the first delivery and got two off the second, thanks to a misfield by Waugh in the deep. The third, he tapped to Border at mid-wicket, and ran a single to level the scores. The vice-captain had ensured that India could not lose.

'Try and score off the fourth or fifth ball if you can. Last ball, just go for it, you have nothing to lose,' Maninder was told by his vice-captain. The number eleven blocked the fourth ball, and appeared to have inside-edged the fifth onto his pads. As he bent to collect the ball from his new position at silly-point, Border heard an appeal being made. He picked up the ball and looked up, to see umpire Vikram Raju's index finger pointing towards the heavens, and Matthews and the other Australians running towards the dressing room like men possessed. It was only the second tie in the history of Test cricket. While the Australians were ecstatic, the Indians felt cheated; not by the weather for a change, but by one of their own. Raju obviously defended the decision, as did his colleague Dara Dotiwala, but they did not have much support in the Indian, and as it turned out, Australian ranks. Border confessed later that 'there might have been a hint of an inside-edge'.

The next Test at Delhi was washed out by rain, with only one day's play being possible. This wasn't entirely unexpected, given the timing of the tour. The Australians as always had refused to tour during the regular Indian cricket season, which clashed with their own. Sunil and Amarnath put the enforced break to good use, by paying a visit to the capital's Tihar prison and playing cricket with the inmates.

Australia batted first and scored 345 in the third Test at Bombay. India got 517-5, with the local trinity scoring a hundred apiece. Vengsarkar, who had missed the Madras Test, scored an unbeaten 164, Shastri an unbeaten 121, and the seniormost man from Bombay, 103.

Sunil batted beautifully. The highlight of his innings was the three boundaries he took from a Matthews over. He began by coming down the wicket and hitting over cover. He then advanced again, and this time targeted the long-on boundary. He completed his fifty with a straight hit over the bowler's head. An on-drive off Bright took him to three figures, and left the BCCI office-bearers in a dilemma.

On the eve of the game, they had awarded him a memento embellished with thirty-two diamonds, each of which represented a Test hundred of his, only to watch him score his thirty-third! It was his fifth at his home-ground, and first after his 123 against the same team in 1979-80.

> This hundred is dedicated to Sriraman and other board members, also to the fans at the Wankhede. There must have been many who have grown up with me, seen me play from my schooldays. I wanted to get a hundred for them. – Sunil Gavaskar, *TOI*, 21 December 1986

His fans could not help but marvel at the manner in which he had practically reinvented himself as a batsman. For years, he had eschewed the riskier strokes in his repertoire, but in the evening of his career, he seemed to have regained his boyish enthusiasm for the game. The Sunil Gavaskar of the late 1970s would have thought a hundred times before playing lofted strokes in a Test.

Sunil's statement after his Wankhede hundred indicated that he would never play a Test at his home-ground again. There had been some speculation earlier in the year that he would call it quits after the Bombay Test, but he wasn't thinking along those lines. Imran Khan, who was considering retirement himself, had spoken to him about having a final bash against each other, and Sunil had agreed. Hence, there was reason to believe that the series against Pakistan would be his last.

The Test series against Australia ended in a stalemate, with the Indian spinners failing to exploit the deteriorating wicket on the last day. The One-Day series, which saw some fine batting by the Delhi opener Raman Lamba, ended in a 3-2 win for the hosts.

The first of the two four-nation tournaments in Sharjah was a disappointment for India. They beat Sri Lanka, but went down against West Indies and Pakistan. The loss to the old enemy was particularly galling. Chasing 145, Pakistan were 65-6, but the Indians failed to deliver the knockout punch, and all-rounder Manzoor Elahi took his team through. Sunil had an average tournament, his best effort being 63 against the West Indies.

Sri Lanka made a good start to their tour of India. They scored 420 in the first Test on a featherbed at Kanpur, and left the hosts with little time in which to go for a win. India played for landmarks instead, and scored 676-7, their highest in Test cricket at that point. Kapil Dev slammed a seventy-four-ball hundred, the fastest by an Indian, and went on to score 163. Azharuddin got his first hundred after his three in a row in 1984-85, and fell on 199. The third centurion of the innings was Sunil, who scored 176, his thirty-fourth Test hundred, but his first in his wife's hometown.

The first One Day International, played at the same venue, was a disaster for India, who were bowled out for 78 in response to Sri Lanka's 195. Stung by the loss, the Indians came back with a vengeance in the second and the third Test. Vengsarkar scored 153 in the second Test at Nagpur, and 166 in the third at Cuttack on a poor strip. His knocks ensured that India did not have to bat a second time in both the games, and the spinners then took over. The Nagpur spectators, who had seen Sunil compile 50 and 64 against Pakistan three years previously, were disappointed when he did not open the innings due to fever. However, he came in at number five and facilitated a declaration with 74 off seventy-nine balls.

Kapil Dev's sole wicket in the second innings at Cuttack was his 300th in Test cricket. It made him only the second all-rounder to complete the double of 3,000 runs and 300 wickets after Botham. The 2-0 triumph over Sri Lanka was his second as captain in six months, and India's first Test series win at home since 1981-82.

The Indians maintained the momentum in the four One-dayers that were left, winning every game. However, they had a scare in the final encounter at Bombay. Batting first, India amassed 299-4 from only forty overs. Sunil and Srikkanth were at their belligerent best early on. The fun they were having at the expense of the bowlers manifested itself in an exchange of headgear, with Sunil borrowing Srikkanth's cap and the latter wearing the skullcap. Azharuddin later scored his maiden one-day hundred, and Vengsarkar and Lamba blazed away towards the end. The Lankans, with nothing to lose, went for the target, and finished only ten runs short. Sunil won the Man of the Series award for his 70 in the second game at Guwahati, 36 in the third at Delhi, 69 in the fourth at Baroda, and 25 at Bombay.

The Indians had no time to recharge their batteries. The final bash between Sunil and Imran commenced with a Test at Madras. Pakistan totalled 487-9, with Imran getting 135. The Indian openers delivered a stunning response.

Srikkanth marked Imran out for special treatment, hooking him for a boundary and a six off consecutive deliveries. The Pakistani captain wasn't all that impressed, and waited at the end of his run-up to vent his spleen on the batsman. But Srikkanth outfoxed him, albeit inadvertently, by undertaking his trademark walk to square-leg. 'Can't even swear at the . . ., he is too far away,' Imran muttered under his breath, even as he retraced his steps past a smiling Sunil. The smile stayed on Sunil's face as he went on to beat his partner to the fifty-mark. It was the first time Sunil had done so in a Test, and given the kind of player Srikkanth was, it was no ordinary feat.

They put on 200, and while Srikkanth completed his second Test hundred, Sunil surprisingly hit a Qadir full-toss to Tauseef Ahmed at mid-wicket when he was nine short of his thirty-fifth. It was the second time he had fallen in the nineties that season. Amarnath and Vengsarkar also batted superbly, and the match was drawn, with Sunil doing a fair impression of Qadir's mangled-and-tangled bowling action in the facile second innings.

If the events of 1983-84 and 1984-85 were anything to go by, then a Test at Calcutta was synonymous with turmoil. A trilogy of sorts was completed when the second Test against the Pakistanis got underway at the Eden, with the spotlight being very much on Sunil. He had decided to skip the game for personal reasons.

It was entirely in keeping with tradition that he evoked extreme reactions. Some hailed him, and others denounced him. That he was deeply disturbed by the events at the Eden in 1983-84 and 1984-85 was widely known, but no one had expected him to take the stand he did in 1987. The outcry in newspapers and the state of West Bengal forced Sriraman and the BCCI Secretary Ranbir Singh to try to placate him. They discovered that his resolve was as impenetrable as his defence.

The response of his detractors was entirely expected. They burnt his effigies and submitted a memorandum demanding penal action by leaving him out of the team for the subsequent Tests as well. The memo was delivered to Hanumant Singh, then chairman of selectors, and copies were marked to the presidents of the BCCI and Cricket Association of Bengal, the union minister of sports, and West Bengal's sports minister.

> This is specially for my fans in Calcutta . . . Can there be no other reason behind my decision? Reasons that I wish to keep private? Why do people presume it is because of the booing? Is it because of a guilty conscience? Eden Gardens does not need a certificate of behaviour from anybody. Today, with television, one can see for oneself. . . . – Sunil Gavaskar, *Mid-Day*, 11 February 1987

He had his share of supporters.

> Being a highly educated and sensitive individual, he has every right to take occasion to register his strong disapproval of the way not only he, but any national player, is treated when failing to live up to the expectations of a mob. – A.F.S. Talyarkhan, *Mid-Day*, 9 February 1987

Arunlal, his replacement for the Calcutta Test, made an impressive return to the Indian team, with scores of 52 and 70. India were in command when the Pakistanis conceded a first-innings lead of 174, but the hosts let things meander along in the second innings, and the game ended in a draw. Sunil also missed the One-dayer at the same venue, in which Srikkanth's 123 in the first half was forgotten when Salim Malik took Pakistan to victory with an unbeaten 72 off thirty-five balls.

Sunil was reinstated for the third Test at Jaipur, ironically at Arunlal's expense. It was an anti-climax of a comeback, with Imran having him caught in the slips off the very first ball of the match. The game was a dreary affair, with only two innings being completed. Unseasonal showers prompted the umpires and groundstaff to sprinkle sawdust on the pitch to quicken the drying operations. However, the visitors contended that the nature of the surface had changed, and play was abandoned on the third day. General Zia-ul-Haq had a shot at cricket diplomacy during the game. He paid a flying visit, in what was viewed as an attempt to dispel the tension that had been building up on both sides of the border.

Sunil, who was on a pair, avoided it with a first-ball square-cut off Wasim Akram for four in the second innings. He moved to 24 before being caught at short leg off Tauseef, shortly after surviving an appeal for a similar dismissal. His knock was the cue for the nation to forget Kolkata and start thinking about the next Test at Ahmedabad. His Test tally now stood at 9,942, which meant that he was 58 short of the ultimate barrier. The residents of Ahmedabad were ecstatic. It was in their city that he had become the highest scorer in Test cricket in November 1983. Three years later, they had been granted the opportunity of watching him achieve another milestone.

For those who made their way into the Gujarat stadium on the morning of 7 March 1987, the third day of the Test, the imminence of a fourth consecutive draw hardly mattered. The tenth Pakistani wicket fell at 395, and a roar went up as the Indian openers emerged from the pavilion.

The spectators watched Sunil enter double figures, and then the 20s and 30s. Srikkanth and Amarnath fell in quick succession, but Vengsarkar dropped anchor. That encouraged Sunil to open out. As he neared his fifty, even the TV commentators got excited. They could not be blamed, for the unprecedented was about to happen.

The spectators warmed up for the big moment when Sunil on-drove Iqbal Qasim for four to reach his fifty. Some spectators managed to breach the security cordon and engulf him, probably because the men entrusted with the security arrangements were as interested in the on-field proceedings as the people they were supposed to control.

The boundary took him to 53, and his tally to 9,995. As a nation watched, viewed and listened, Sunil came down the wicket to Iqbal Qasim in a bid to give the crowd a six. He connected well, but the cherry landed just short of the rope, and four was what he got. The imminence of the landmark had induced the man 'who never looked at the scoreboard' to depart from his stand. He was now on 57, his Test tally 9,999. Ijaz Faqih, an off-spinning all-rounder who had scored 105 earlier in the game, then began a fresh over to Vengsarkar. India's number four did what everybody wanted him to do. He took a single.

The cheers commenced, and did not cease, as Sunil settled into his stance, his eyes fixated on the bowler's wrist. It was an off-break, pitched just short of a length outside the off–stump. Sunil watched it land and turn towards him. He then pulled out his predecessor Vijay Merchant's signature stroke – the late cut. As the ball travelled off the bat, past the vacant slips and into the third-man region, Sunil flashed a huge grin, raised his bat, and began the twenty-two yard journey that stood between him and the barrier. He completed it, and returned for a second run. The mind boggles at the thought of all the thoughts that would have crossed his mind as he ran those forty-four yards—the Bhagirathi buildings, his father's bedtime tales, breaking his mother's nose, his maternal uncle's reminder, the inter-school and inter-university tournaments, the debut series in 1971, the contests against the torch-bearers of cricket's 'pace-age', the wins in 1983 and 1985, his near and dear ones. . . .

In any other set of circumstances, he would have been infuriated to be mobbed, but for once, he didn't care, for he was in a world of his own. Barring Melbourne in 1980-81, he had always kept his emotions to himself while batting. But this was different. He had gone where no cricketer had gone before.

'I roomed with him during the series against Sri Lanka and Pakistan. Although he was the type who never looked at the

scoreboard while batting, and was known to switch off once he was off the field, the fact is that he was edgy as he approached the 10,000-mark. That was the only time I have seen him tense.'
– Raju Kulkarni

Even as the nation celebrated, there was one institution that betrayed its ignorance.

'Anupam Gulati and I were the English commentators, and Ashok Mankad was the [guest] expert. At the end of the day, the station director of Ahmedabad Doordarshan asked me to get down to the pitch for an interview with Sunil. Raj Bhargava, the Hindi commentator, was asked to take over the mike with Ashok. I chatted with Sunil, but found it very strange that Ashok was not called down to the field for the interview, as he had been Sunil's first opening partner in Tests, in the West Indies in 1971. Most broadcasting networks would have flown him down. Here, he was contracted to DD at Ahmedabad, but they would not involve him with the interview. I mentioned this to the station director, only to be rebuffed, and told to get on with it. When I got back to the box, Ashok was understandably miffed. He couldn't fathom why he had been kept out.' – Fredun De Vitre

22

SWANSONGS

'I was relatively young when SMG played, and television in India was very much primitive then. My generation therefore missed out on some of his best innings. We made up by listening to the radio commentaries, reading about the game, collecting photographs of our favourites, maintaining scrapbooks, etc. These pursuits made me realise that he was a model of technical brilliance. But when you are young, you don't understand technique. All you see at that age is the achievements. GRV (Gundappa Rangnath Viswanath) and he were the heroes of every cricket-loving Indian boy who grew up in the 1980s. Whenever we played the game in any form, be it in the backyard, every batsman imagined that he was either Gavaskar or Viswanath. Even when we played book cricket, 'Sunil Gavaskar' would always score a hundred!'
– Rahul Dravid

Had he not undergone bad patches in Australia and New Zealand in 1980-81 and against England in 1984-85, Sunil would have broken the 10,000-barrier long before Ahmedabad. But cricket lovers on the subcontinent were not complaining about the timing of the feat.

It gave them the opportunity to hail one of their own, and in the process, take their minds off what was turning out to be a painful Test series.

The 1986-87 edition of Asia's Ashes had been as tedious as those of 1954-55, 1960-61, 1983-84 and 1984-85. The first four Tests had provided conclusive proof that neither Kapil Dev nor Imran Khan, two of the game's aggressive characters, were immune to the fear of failure that had afflicted most of their predecessors. The Indian captain was hesitant, and his Pakistani counterpart diffident, as could be gauged from the replacements he requisitioned well after the series had got underway. Younis Ahmed, a left-handed batsman, was requisitioned after the first Test, and left-arm spinner Iqbal Qasim and off-spinner Ijaz Faqih after the second. The BCCI was understandably not impressed, and indicated its unwillingness to bear the expenses of the surplus players. The Pakistan Cricket Board then got three members of the original squad to return home.

Younis Ahmed's inclusion was the most bizarre. He was thirty-nine years old, and had played his previous two Tests way back in 1969-70! It was with him that Sunil had an altercation at Ahmedabad, after the former had survived a confident appeal for a close-in catch. 'Will you stop complaining now?' Sunil was reported to have asked Younis. The batsman did not take it too well, and an ugly exchange ensued. In the previous Test, Ahmed had flung the ball down in disgust after the umpire had negatived an appeal for a catch against Sunil.

The visitors had generally been petulant whenever decisions had gone against them. Their behaviour in such situations had been condemned by the media and spectators alike.

The surfaces on which the Tests had been played were as lifeless as lifeless could be. There was nothing in them for the bowlers.

The groundstaff at Bangalore's Chinnaswamy stadium, the venue of the final Test, responded to the outcry against dead wickets by deciding that it was payback time for the batsmen.

The sight of Sunil accompanying Imran for the toss on the first morning of the final Test was interpreted by most people as a giveaway of sorts. Although Sunil requested the fourth estate not to jump to conclusions, not many people were in any doubt that the Test would be his last.

Their view was corroborated by Kumar Krishnan's write-up that appeared in the *Mid-Day*, a day after the Ahmedabad Test.

> I AM RETIRING WHEN ON TOP: In the 1984-85 season, when I was having a lean patch, people asked me why I wasn't retiring. Now they are asking me, "Why are you retiring?" . . . I will make an official announcement on the eve of the Bangalore Test. – Sunil Gavaskar, *Mid-Day*, 10 March 1987

However, no official announcement was made. Sunil was quoted in the *TOI* dated 12 March 1987 as saying that he would 'consider retirement only after the last ball of the 1987 World Cup'.

The media then predicted that Sunil would make the announcement at a dinner that he was to host for both teams in the middle of the game. The dinner came and went, but Sunil stayed silent! He had never shied from playing practical jokes, and it appeared that he was playing one on the media, his fans, and on the cricketing world.

Maninder Singh shot the Pakistanis out for 116 on the opening day, and then saw his team-mates come apart against off-spinner Tauseef Ahmed and Iqbal Qasim. India led by only 29 runs, with a lot of time left in the game, and it boiled down to a battle of wits between the captains.

Imran reacted to the situation by sending in Miandad to open with Ramiz Raja. Aware that all his specialist batsmen, like India's, were right-handers, he promoted Iqbal Qasim to number five, with instructions to utilise his left-handedness to attack and thereby rattle the Indian spinners. The Pakistani skipper also attempted to take the pressure off his team-mates by telling them that he wouldn't mind losing if they gave it everything. Kapil Dev rotated his three spinners, with Maninder getting the highest number of overs, although it was apparent that he wasn't bowling as effectively as in the first innings. Pakistan totalled 249. India needed 221 to win.

On a dustbowl, Sunil essayed a masterpiece.

> What a marvellous exhibition Gavaskar provided! Unmindful of all the setbacks, he carried on like a one-man army and all but won the battle. In the afternoon, he seemed determined to get all the requisite runs on his own, as with Binny for company, he

farmed the strike and tried to bat at both ends. – Sunder Rajan, *TOI*, 17 March 1987

'The 96 at Bangalore typified Sunil. On a pitch not fit to stage a cricket match, where the ball was bouncing off a length and the spinners were turning it by miles, he repeatedly hit Iqbal Qasim against the spin through mid-wicket and mid-on! On a pitch where everyone struggled, he batted like he was batting on a cement pitch. It was an apt batting lesson for all of us and generations of batsmen to come.' – Mudassar Nazar

India lost the Test by sixteen runs, and with it, the Test series. The Pakistanis proceeded to win three of the remaining four One-dayers. For Imran, it was the first of what he intended to be a farewell trilogy. He wanted to beat India in India, then beat England on their soil in mid-1987, and follow it up with the ultimate—the World Cup. Like Sunil, he wanted to quit after the quadrennial event, preferably on a high.

Sunil batted fluently in the One-dayers against Pakistan and the end-of-season tournament at Sharjah. Knocks of 70 and 69 against Pakistan, and an unbeaten 78 against Australia at Sharjah, fuelled the contention of his fans that he had it in him to carry on for another season, if not more.

Sunil himself could not agree more. But then that was precisely why he wanted to quit. 'Better to quit when people ask why rather than why not' was the operative thought. He was looking forward to help his team defend the title it had clinched at Lord's in 1983.

But before that, there was another challenge on the anvil.

The highlight of the MCC's Bi-Centenary celebrations in August 1987 was a five-day First-class match between the world's eminent cricketers. They were divided into two sides—the MCC, and the Rest of the World.

Sunil's inclusion in the World squad made him the only link between the 1987 World XI and the one of 1971-72, which was the last time a World XI had been drawn up for a First-class series. Clive Lloyd, one of his 1971-72 team-mates, was the manager of the World squad. Kapil Dev, Vengsarkar and Maninder were the other Indians who made it. Ravi Shastri was picked in the MCC side.

'I dropped Sunil at the airport on his way to England. On our way, we talked about local cricket. I expressed my shock that the fourteen year-old Sachin Tendulkar had not received the annual Best Junior Cricketer Award given by the Mumbai Cricket Association. By this time, we had reached the airport. Sunil had heard of the boy earlier. He pulled out his letterhead, placed it on the bonnet of the vehicle, and penned a letter, exhorting Sachin to carry on in the same vein, and not neglect his studies. He also wrote: "Don't be disappointed at not getting the Best Junior Cricketer Award from the MCA. If you look at the names of the award-winners, you will find one name missing, and that person has not done badly in Test cricket!" I handed over the letter to Sachin's elder brother Ajit.' – Hemant Waingankar

'I had scored twice as many runs as the others in the 1986-87 season, and was deeply disappointed not to get the award. But I forgot all about it when I received the letter. That was a huge moment in my life.' – Sachin Tendulkar

Had the cricket administrators of 1987 been as amenable to extend the boundaries of traditional Test cricket as their 2005 counterparts, the Bi-Centenary Test would have been granted Test status. That did not happen, but the participants, who constituted the world's cricketing elite, were expected to treat the game like one.

There were three conspicuous absentees. Ian Botham and Martin Crowe, both of whom were to represent the MCC, pulled out due to injuries. Viv Richards chose to honour the contract that he had signed for Rishton, a club in the Lancashire league. There were those who believed that he was aggrieved at losing out on the captaincy of the World XI to Allan Border. If this was true, then Richards certainly had a point: the West Indies were the supremos of world cricket, and Border was yet to win a Test series since his appointment as Australia's captain three years previously.

Both sides played a few games against the Counties to familiarise the players with each other. Those waiting to see Sunil bat one last time at Headquarters were worried when Caribbean paceman Patrick Patterson struck him on the foot in a One-dayer against Lancashire, five days prior to the big game. Sunil hobbled off the field and had an X-Ray taken; thankfully, there was no serious damage.

The dream start and nightmarish climax of the Bi-Centenary Test were entirely in keeping with the vagaries of the sport it sought to commemorate. The game commenced in glorious sunshine, and concluded abruptly under weeping clouds. Some excellent cricket was played in between.

MCC's innings of 455-5 and then declared, featured hundreds by Gatting and Gooch, a 52 by Gordon Greenidge, and an unbeaten 59 by the South African all-rounder Clive Rice, for whom it would be the closest he had ever come to playing Test cricket. As spectacular as the quality of batsmanship were the reflexes of Roger Harper. Gooch came down the track in an over of his, but hit the ball straight back at the bowler. Harper in turn hurled it back and broke the stumps even before Gooch could think about regaining his balance.

The purists were thrilled with the exhibition of cricketing skills and the pre-Packer muted reactions to wickets. There weren't many screams of delight or high-fives doing the rounds. This was only to be expected, for the players, for all their travels over the previous couple of weeks, were not used to sharing their on-field joys with each other. Not only did they behave like their predecessors of a bygone era, but they also played to the gallery like the stars of yore. Miandad, brought on to bowl his brand of leg-spin after Qadir left the field, was flicked by Rice through square-leg umpire Harold Bird's feet. Kapil Dev, who was fielding in the deep, then made an unusual underarm return, his objective being to dispatch the ball through Bird's legs once again. As the ball began its journey, the capacity crowd roared. Bird realised what was happening and thwarted Kapil Dev's designs with smart footwork.

Sunil opened for the World XI with Desmond Haynes, and took strike to his old adversary Malcolm Marshall. The bowler started with a no-ball. He then let one go that pitched on off and nipped back. It came onto Sunil quicker than he expected, and hit him on the pads. It seemed so plumb even on TV that Marshall could have been pardoned a celebratory dance even before the umpire raised his finger. However, 'Dickie' Bird didn't.

'Marshall would later joke that the only reason Dickie negatived the appeal was because he hadn't warmed up when the appeal was made. It was very early in the innings, after all.' – Dilip Vengsarkar

Marshall eventually did get the breakthrough, having Haynes brilliantly caught by Rice at first slip. At a time when Nelson Mandela was still behind bars and apartheid thriving in South Africa, it was a moment that stood out—a black West Indian and white South African combining to dismiss a black West Indian. Sports, for once, had triumphed over politics, albeit only momentarily, for at that stage, the likelihood of South Africa returning to the mainstream was remote.

Dilip Vengsarkar came in next, and Marshall immediately switched to around-the-wicket to attack the man he loved to hate. Nearly a decade had elapsed since his debut in 1978-79, but Marshall continued to hold Vengsarkar responsible for his failures with the bat in that series. So incensed had Marshall been with what he perceived as Vengsarkar's umpire-bullying tactics that he swore revenge. The outcome was a series of compelling duels between the duo in the 1980s, which ended in a draw. Marshall dismissed Vengsarkar on quite a few occasions, but the latter also scored lots of runs and hundreds against him.

Vengsarkar was in the mood for another big one on his favourite ground, but Marshall had other ideas. He got one to kick off a length, and Vengsarkar, who had hit four fours in a knock of 22, fended it into gully's hands.

The two wickets could not obviate the flowering of the innings. Sunil's first authoritative stroke was an on-drive off Richard Hadlee. He then sent the connoisseurs into raptures with a push off Rice that beat a sliding Shastri at mid-on and sped to the boundary.

He brought up the hundred of the innings with a flowing straight drive off Shastri. An exquisite caress off Marshall followed, the ball going like a rocket past cover. John Emburey, who replaced Marshall at the pavilion end, was taken for two lofted boundaries in one over. The capacity crowd went into raptures.

Border essayed an aggressive cameo of 26 that ended with Rice taking another good catch, this time in the covers, off Shastri. The left-arm spinner all but struck one more time in the closing moments of the second day. He hit Sunil on the back foot, and made an unsuccessful appeal, even as the ball got stuck between Sunil's feet. It then trickled towards the middle-stump and made contact, but the bails did not budge!

World XI were 169-3 at stumps, with Sunil twenty short of his first hundred at Headquarters. With luck having smiled at him not once but twice, a hundred seemed inevitable.

That evening, the media finally heard what sections of it had wanted to hear for two years. At the Mecca of the sport, in the capital of the country that had taught his compatriots the sport, Sunil announced his abdication from Test cricket.

The man had brought the curtains down on his remarkable career on 21 August 1987 – on his own terms.

Despite the five-and-a-half-hour time difference between England and India, the news reached India well in time for the newspapers to get in touch with Sunil's seniors.

The *TOI* carried their tributes the next day:

> 'It is an end of an era. Now we will realise his importance as an opening batsman. – Nari Contractor

> 'No man can go on forever, but Gavaskar almost proved that theory wrong by playing a sheet-anchor role for seventeen years.' – Polly Umrigar

> 'Gavaskar is the greatest talent I have ever seen. The man had an inborn talent and no one could touch his dedication, particularly when the chips were down. . . .' – Bapu Nadkarni

Sunil had barely finished making the announcement when he was reminded by some journalists that he was yet to score a First-class hundred at Lord's. He asked them to 'wait for the next day's play'.

He and his fans had to wait a while before the battle resumed on day three, thanks to a shower that delayed play by thirty minutes. Jeffrey Dujon, who had come in at number five instead of the indisposed Miandad, got his and Sunil's feet moving with a quick single. Sunil got three runs from another caress off Marshall through the covers. The paceman persisted with his around-the-wicket approach and induced Dujon to hit one, which was clasped by Gooch at gully. Imran came in and nicked his first ball, but the cherry fell just short of Rice in the slips.

Meanwhile, Sunil had entered the 90s. He may have adhered to the principle of not looking at the scoreboard for the better part of his career, but here, as at Ahmedabad, there was no chance of his doing likewise. For all his misgivings about Lord's, he left no one in any doubt as to what he wanted above everything else. Although he never owned it up at the conscious level, it was evident that at a sub-conscious level, Lord's mattered. He had made it obvious a year previously, by breaking down after India's first Test win at the Mecca of cricket. That he had chosen Lord's of all venues to announce his abdication was not lost on all those who had been nonplussed with his aversion to the venue. Hours after he had made that announcement, he was fidgety, when within touching distance of his first hundred at the ground.

A gasp went up when he tucked Hadlee to fine-leg for a comfortable one, called his partner for a second, and then sent him back. Imran managed to get home in the nick of time, and received an apology. There was more than a hint of a sheepish grin on Sunil's face.

He set off for another non-existent run when on 99, driving Shastri straight to the cover fielder and dashing down. This time, Imran sent him back. Sunil made a backward return to the crease and permitted himself another smile.

The wait ended when Shastri pitched one on the leg-stump. Sunil turned it around the corner, Imran responded, and the single was duly completed. Shastri was the first to extend his congratulations.

A fascinating partnership ensued, with Imran at his imperial best against the pacemen and spinners. At lunch, he was 43 and Sunil 128. The resumption witnessed a bout between Test cricket's highest scorer and second-highest wicket-taker. Richard Hadlee, who was tied with Dennis Lillee at 355 Test wickets with only Botham in front, bowled two slower deliveries to Sunil. The first was pitched on a length and aimed at getting the batsman to mistime it to mid-off. Sunil played it quite magnificently, reducing his bat-speed just before the moment of impact and loosening his grip on the bat. The ball fell well short of Gatting at mid-off. Not to be outdone, Hadlee served another slow gem, and this time, Sunil all but fell for it. He square-drove it uppishly through the vacant gully area for four. The spectators, marvelling as they were at Sunil's mastery, could not get enough of two strokes off Rice. The first, a flick that sped to the mid-wicket fence, brought up his 150. The second was a majestic drive that breached the covers and fetched him four more.

Just when a double hundred seemed imminent, Sunil gave Shastri a return catch on 188. He had batted for 408 minutes and 351 deliveries, and hit twenty-three boundaries.

The ground rose to applaud the departure of the greatest opening batsman in Test history. His wasn't the first or last hundred in the Bi-Centenary Test, but by far the most memorable, as much for its quality as for its significance. Bombay had been no more than a cluster of seven islands in 1787, when the MCC was instituted; two hundred years later, a resident of what was now a throbbing metropolis had provided cricket's originators a masterclass in their own sport. It had been a swansong to savour.

'It was made with such touch and assurance, indeed such mastery, as to make his retirement at thirty-eight seem altogether premature.' – John Woodcock, *The Times*

There were many who subsequently advised Sunil to carry on. His former DU captain Vasu Paranjpe was among those who suggested that he at least play the four-Test series against the West Indies after the World Cup and thus complete a cycle, having made his debut against the same team. But Sunil, having made up his mind, wasn't going to renege.

Sunil was of course aware that he could have easily continued, but he never spoke about it. The first time he did so, although in a roundabout manner, was during India's tour of England in 1990, when Tony Lewis, the former England captain, interviewed Boycott and him on batsmanship. Boycott, a proud and vain individual, commented that he would have been the first to score 10,000 Test runs had he not been on self-imposed exile from 1974 to 1977. Sunil did not react immediately. He let the discussion proceed, and delivered a telling rejoinder just when the interviewer, his fellow interviewee and the listeners would have been on the verge of forgetting Boycott's claim; 'Had Geoffrey played from

1974 to 1977,' he said, 'I would have played Test cricket for two more years!'

Both sides went out of their way to ensure an absorbing finish to the Bi-Centenary Test. The third consecutive declaration of the game left the World XI needing 353 to win in six overs on the fourth day, and the whole of the fifth. Sunil was greeted warmly when he took strike to Marshall, for what would be his final First-class innings on English soil. He was keen to set up another chase, but Marshall played spoilsport with one that went through the gate and smashed into his off-stump. As Sunil cast a look at the heavens and made his exit, his fans were disappointed, and the statisticians thrilled. The fans were hoping for another big score, while the statisticians were happy that Sunil had emulated the Don by not troubling the scorers in his final first-class innings on English soil.

The World XI were 13-1 at stumps and an eventful last day was anticipated, but rain, which had only put in a fleeting appearance on the first four days, took centrestage on the fifth. It ruined what might well have been a cracker of a climax.

On his return to India, Sunil admitted to fielding becoming a chore in an interview with *Mid-Day*. 'I find myelf looking at the clock and thinking of the time when I can go off,' he said.

It was the right time to go.

Cricket's first World Cup outside the United Kingdom got underway in the first week of October 1987. While India's 1983 triumph was the event that had emboldened the administrators in both nations to make a successful bid, the impact of the achievements of Sunil, Imran and Kapil Dev, to name just three individuals, on the international stage, had played no less important a role.

Not that the establishment of the time, which comprised Australia and England, was taking things lying down. Aspersions had been cast on the organisational abilities of India and Pakistan, and every single opportunity to slam the event was being grabbed with both hands. This wasn't the exclusive preserve of the administrators either; the likes of David Gower, Ian Botham and Richard Hadlee stayed away from the event. Joining them were Malcolm Marshall and Gordon Greenidge. Different reasons were cited, from injury to exhaustion, but only a lunatic would have believed that the players in question would have cited similar reasons had the event been held in England as originally scheduled.

India and Pakistan ended up laughing last, and loudest—but not before the cricket lovers in both countries cried.

The tournament commenced with an opening ceremony at Delhi's Jawaharlal Nehru stadium. It was followed by an exhibition match between the co-hosts, which India won.

The defending champions were in 'A,' the easier of the two groups, alongside Australia, New Zealand and Zimbabwe. With Zimbabwe far from experienced and New Zealand expected to struggle in Hadlee's absence, it was a given that Australia and India would make it to the semis, unless something remarkable happened. 'B' was the group of 'death,' with Pakistan, West Indies and England vying for two semi-final spots. The Sri Lankans were also there, but in 1987, nobody was inclined to take them seriously.

Whether the organising committee did it intentionally or unintentionally, one does not know, but India were slated to begin their defence of the title against Australia at the same venue where the two sides had produced Test cricket's second tie a year previously. Australia batted first and scored 268-8 from the allotted fifty overs. They gained two runs at the interval, when it transpired that Dean Jones had hit Maninder for a six instead of a boundary.

Not many teams had successfully chased a target of over 250 in the mid-1980s. The Indians had fared poorly in their previous two One Day series, but this was a new season, it was the World Cup, and they were the holders. The players were raring to go after strenuous conditioning camps at Udaipur and Delhi, and seemed to be enjoying the 'favourites' tag for a change. Theirs was a well-balanced side, the only surprise being the omission of the 1983 hero Mohinder Amarnath.

The capacity crowd at the Chidambaram stadium found its voice when Sunil dispatched Craig McDermott off the back foot for four in the very first over. The assault had only just begun, and at its forefront was Srikkanth's partner. Border was forced to introduce off-spinner Peter Taylor into the attack a lot earlier than he would have liked, and Sunil's response was a stinging cover-drive off his first ball.

But Taylor persisted, and was rewarded when Sunil drove him to Reid at mid-off. It was the twelfth over of the innings, and India were

69-1. Sunil's 37 comprised six fours and one six. Navjot Sidhu, who was representing India for the first time since 1983, maintained the momentum with Srikkanth. The start ensured that India needed only 64 from the last thirteen overs, with seven wickets in hand.

The Australians then found a saviour in McDermott. He bowled quick and straight, and was aided by some horrendous batting. The wickets tumbled as they had in the same city a year previously, with the Australians tightening the screws. Maninder found himself on strike with six needed from the final six balls. He did rather well to take two twos off Steve Waugh. With two needed from the final three balls, all of India egged Maninder on to keep a cool head, but the tailender in him came to the fore. He played a typical tailender's slog, missed and was bowled. Australia won by one run.

The Indians came back strongly, with consecutive wins over New Zealand and Zimbabwe. They also had the better of Australia in the first return encounter. Sunil failed against the Kiwis, scoring only 2, but hit the Zimbabweans for 43, in which his first ten scoring strokes were boundaries. He then took 61 off the Australians at Delhi, setting up a 56-run win.

That win enabled India to catch up with Australia in terms of points, although the latter were ahead on the run rate. One did not have to be a genius to deduce that the Indians would prefer to top their Group, and thus play England, the number two side from Group 'B,' in the second semi-final at Bombay, instead of finishing second in their group and travelling to Lahore to play Pakistan, the Group 'B' toppers, in the first semi-final.

A dash to increase the run rate was therefore expected against the Zimbabweans at Ahmedabad, after the tourists scored 191-7. However, the Indian batsmen opted to crawl rather than cruise. Sunil scored 50, but took too many deliveries to do so. Kapil Dev did a Sydney by promoting himself to get a move on. At the post-match press conference, the Indian skipper declared that he had twice sent messages to accelerate, but to no avail. 'I am disappointed with Gavaskar,' he was reported to have said.

India's last chance of pipping the Aussies was in their final league game against the Kiwis at Nagpur. Sunil was running a temperature, and wanted to pull out, but Bapu Nadkarni, the chairman of selectors, prevailed upon him to play.

Nadkarni did not know it then, but in exhorting Sunil to play, he did the batsman and his fans a monumental favour.

New Zealand scored 221-9 from the allotted overs, the highlight of the innings being Chetan Sharma's all-bowled hattrick. He packed off Ken Rutherford's middle-stump, Ian Smith's off-stump and then, Ewen Chatfield's leg-stump. In the dressing room, the Indians learnt that they needed to achieve the target in 42.3 overs to go past Australia.

The first thirty minutes of the Indian innings prompted Allan Border and his colleagues, who were watching the game on TV, to start packing their bags for Lahore.

Sunil, far from one hundred percent fit, announced his intent by thumping Chatfield to the square-leg fence. He kept it simple, plonking his front foot ahead, and then swinging! He wasn't finished with Chatfield. When two consecutive deliveries by the bowler demanded to be hit, Sunil obliged with two mighty drives that cleared the boundary. He then joined the crowd in the applause, and made another straight hit, this time for four.

His acknowledgement of his own strokes suggested that he was out to make a point. His captain's words after the Ahmedabad game may well have been at the back of his mind. It seemed that he was out to make a point, just as Kapil Dev himself had done at Bombay in 1979-80. The world was well and truly round!

A twirl of the wrists gave him another boundary, and the excuse to share a joke with Srikkanth. The fifty came up in 7.1 overs, and if the Kiwis had hoped for some respite, they did not get it.

The Nagpur spectators watched in disbelief as the epitome of technical perfection outscored the model of unconventional batsmanship. But Srikkanth, not one to accept defeat, caught up pretty soon. When the 100 was completed in the fourteenth over, Sunil was on 51 and Srikkanth on 49. Sunil had by then patented a sequence of movements. After every booming stroke, he would squat in the crease and let his fever assert itself for a while. He would forget about it the moment the bowler returned to the top of his run-up. He would then essay another booming stroke, after which he would meet his partner mid-pitch, have a laugh, and then turn to look at the New Zealand keeper Ian Smith and shrug his shoulders, as if to say, 'I can't help it'. He would then squat, and rise to give the next ball the treatment. This sequence was repeated time and again.

Srikkanth drove, glanced, hoisted, flayed, and even essayed a left-hander's orthodox sweep by altering his grip on the bat twenty years before Kevin Pietersen gained worldwide acclaim for the same deed. At the other end, Sunil adopted a slightly more classical approach, although the effects of both approaches were very much the same.

> 'I remember thinking to myself that there was no need to watch the post-match highlights on television, as they were unfolding in front of our eyes.' – John Wright

Only the formalities remained when Srikkanth was brilliantly caught by Rutherford at mid-wicket. He had scored 75 off only fifty-eight balls, and India were 135-1, at more than a run-a-ball. Azharuddin surprisingly came in ahead of Sidhu, who had scored four fifties in four outings in the tournament. However, watchers ignored the move when they sensed the imminence of a special moment.

A flurry of strokes off the off-spinner Dipak Patel took Sunil close to what would be his maiden hundred in the shorter variety of the sport. Fours off seamers Danny Morrison and Willie Watson took him into the 90s. He had moved to 99 when Morrison served him a half-volley on middle-and-leg. Sunil on-drove, watched the cherry pierce the gap between mid-wicket and mid-on, and took off. Two runs were completed, and the crowd rose. In his 107th One Day international, Sunil had done it.

The match was won in 32.1 overs, and the capacity crowd stayed on to watch Sharma and Sunil share the Man of the Match award.

The Indians were a confident lot on the morning of 6 November 1987, the day they were to play England in the second semi-final. Pakistan's loss to Australia in the first semi-final the day before had boosted their spirits further. The bogey team had gone, or so it seemed, and nothing could come in the way of an encore of 1983.

Imran Khan's dream of ending his career on a high had come a cropper, but for Sunil, there was still hope. There were those who wondered whether he would lift his embargo on Calcutta, the venue of the final. It was of course ridiculous to even assume that he would refuse to play a game as important as the World Cup final.

However, the critical thing was to get there first. England, India's semi-final opponents, had played well in the tournament, leaving the West Indies behind, and Graham Gooch was in tremendous nick.

At the Wankhede, he swept just about everything Shastri and Maninder hurled at him, in an innings of 115. However, the Indian bowlers pulled things back in the final overs, and England's total of 254-6 was by no means adequate.

Sunil and Srikkanth opened the innings in front of a capacity crowd and two teenagers who were to rewrite the record books three months later.

'Vinod (Kambli) and I were among the ballboys. It was during this particular game that I first met Mr Gavaskar. I distinctly remember entering the Indian dressing room and walking towards him.' – Sachin Tendulkar

Had a scriptwriter dictated the course of events, India would have won handsomely, with Sunil making a substantial contribution in his last international game at his home-ground. Unfortunately for the hosts, Philip DeFreitas knew nothing about scriptwriting.

The Middlesex all-rounder landed one on a length. The seam hit the deck and came on to Sunil a little quicker than he expected. The cherry kissed his front pad before sending the off-stump for a walk. India were 7-1, and the spectators shellshocked.

The silence soon gave way to murmurs, and the murmurs to curses.

The law of averages caught up with Sidhu, who fell twenty-eight short of what would have been his fifth fifty of the competition. Srikkanth fell for 31, but Azharuddin batted splendidly. Pandit, who had replaced the ill Vengsarkar, got 24. Kapil Dev came in at 121-4 with the match in the balance. He went for his strokes, at one stage slog-sweeping off-spinner Eddie Hemmings for six. With Azharuddin going strong at the other end and Shastri still to come, the Indians were in charge. But then came the moment that changed everything.

Hemmings requested Gatting, his skipper, to push himself back to the mid-wicket boundary. He then tossed the ball up to Kapil Dev, a brave thing to do considering the Indian captain's mood. Kapil Dev's eyes lit up, and he swung hard. As he made off for a run, he glimpsed Gatting taking a couple of backward steps from his new fielding position. Like Richards in the 1983 World Cup final, the Indian captain gathered more height than distance. Unlike that game, wherein Kapil Dev had to run yards to catch Richards, Gatting did not have to do anything as drastic. He kept his hands together and clasped the ball comfortably. For the England captain, his colleagues Lamb and Downton, and the whole of India, it was a replay of Delhi 1984-85. Was there any need to go for another six when he had just hit one? But then, that was the way Kapil Dev played.

With 56 required from the final ten overs and five wickets in hand, India were by no means out of it. But England, taking a cue from Australia's performances in Madras on two famous occasions, produced tight cricket. Hemmings struck another blow, when Azhar attempted to essay his trademark paddle-sweep, and missed. He could have been forgiven for walking without waiting for the umpire to raise his index finger.

The innings went downhill thereafter. The final wicket epitomised the recklessness of the Indian batting, as Shastri, who rarely allowed himself to get ruffled, rushed down the wicket to Hemmings, found that he was not quite there, and lunged forward to make an ungainly slog that Downton ran and pouched.

The champions of 1983 packed their gear and left the ground, leaving behind an incredulous nation. The crowds trooped out of the Wankhede stadium, silent, inconsolable and angry. They pondered over Kapil Dev's dismissal, and shed tears over the absence of Vengsarkar, who had suffered from food-poisoning prior to the game. But all their anger was reserved for Sunil. His character was doubted, and integrity questioned.

Therein lay the irony. The fury of the masses spoke volumes about their perception of the man. To them, he was an extraordinary individual who was capable of doing not only the expected, but also the unexpected. They weren't used to him failing in a big game, and could not accept that he had had one of his rare failures. The fact was that even allowing for Sunil's early dismissal, India would have won had Vengsarkar played the game, Kapil Dev targeted another area of the field, and Azhar got bat onto ball. However, the public did not deem such thoughts worthwhile. As far as they were concerned, Sunil had cost them the match, and that was that.

When Sunil made his debut in 1971, most Indian cricket lovers were content even if their side stretched the premier cricketing nations, leave alone beat them. By the end of his first decade in international cricket, more and more people had begun to view a hard-earned draw as a victory. By the time he played his last international game in 1987, the same people were incensed with their team's absence from the final of the sport's premier tournament.

In 1971, India were part of cricket's second rung, alongside Pakistan and New Zealand. In 1987, they were jostling for the titles of the best limited-overs team in the world, and the second-best in Tests (after the West Indies).

Indeed, a lot had changed since 1971, a year that signalled the start of an age. That age ended at the Wankhede stadium on the afternoon of 6 November 1987.

Fifth
All-Rounder

23

BEYOND THE BOUNDARY

The Indian cricket team under Sunny's captaincy travels to the country of Bandookstan for a series. The Test match at the Golibar stadium is about to start, when Raj Singh, the Indian manager, receives a phone call. The caller informs him that a bomb has been planted in the stadium, which will explode at 4.00 pm sharp. The objective of the terrorists is to force the Indian government to release all Bandookstani prisoners. Raj Singh informs the captain, who asks him to keep mum and assures him that he will sort things out. The match commences, and Sunny makes his way to a half century. Incensed at the designs of the terrorists, he takes it out on Rehman, the bowler, and hits him for a six. The bowler retaliates with a bouncer, and Sunny allows himself to be struck on the cheek. He retires hurt, but the doctor does not detect even a scratch. Instead of returning to the middle, Sunny decides to sort things out. He dons his trademark tracksuit and head-band, and slips out of the stadium. He activates his special boots, and flies towards one of the light towers around the ground, even as a bird exclaims, 'Is that a bird? Is it Superman? No, it's Sunny!'

From the light tower, Sunny scans the faces of the spectators with his super-binoculars. He spots some distinctly unfriendly faces, and sets into motion a chain of events that culminate with the hoodlums being enticed out of the stadium, and a fist-fight in which Sunny obviously prevails. The hoodlums are rounded up, and Sunny tracks down the bomb with his locater and defuses it. He then resumes his innings and completes his thirty-fifth Test hundred. At the end of the game, the president of Bandookstan felicitates him for his batting and bravery. . . .

. . . The England team led by Bob Bower arrives in India for a Test series. At the press conference, the English skipper announces that his trumpcard is Jack Gotham. As the photographers go bananas, Gotham flexes his muscles. A pre-match party follows, where Gotham exchanges pleasantries with Sunny, the Indian captain, before being accosted by a pesky journalist. This individual offers to show Gotham the nightspots of Mumbai. Gotham accepts the invitation, and he and the journalist jump into a taxi. The vehicle stops at a petrol pump, and the journalist steps out to make a call. Suddenly, thugs arrive from nowhere and get into the cab. Gotham is overpowered and gagged. It's a kidnap! The manager of the England team is handed over a letter the following morning. It informs him about the kidnap, and mentions the ransom that would be needed to rescue Gotham. The manager confides in Sunny. They keep the scoop to themselves and Sunny goes about gathering clues. The Test is about to begin, and he exhorts his boys to hold the fort till he returns. The public is informed that Gotham is 'indisposed'. Sunny then follows the instructions of the kidnappers, stacks two suitcases with the Rs 50 lakhs that they want, and deposits them at the 'lost-and-found' department of the Borivli National Park, as indicated. The suitcases are duly collected by a group that calls itself the Piranha, and Sunny trails them in his Marzuki car. The kidnappers have hardly sensed what is happening, when Sunny changes gears, and gets the Marzuki to fly over their car and block the road. A fist-fight follows, and Sunny, the victor, liberates Jack Gotham.

Both Gotham and he proceed to take their respective places in the Test that has already begun....

... India and England are engaged in a day-night match at Delhi's Jawaharlal Nehru stadium when strange things start happening. The cricket ball turns blue, the lights go off and a message threatening Sunny appears on the electronic scoreboard. It is a challenge issued by Rangraj, the Colour-King, who loves to bathe in light in his abode somewhere in the Himalayas. Sunny accepts the challenge, and leaves the field to attend to it. He jumps into his Marzuki and takes the aerial route to the Himalayas. Alongside him is Noon Noon Zen, a female actor who has a score to settle with the Colour King. Sunny and Noon Noon invade the Colour-King's-home, and get the better of him and his henchmen Alpha and Beta. Sunny traps Rangraj in the latter's spaceship and packs him off into outer space. He and Noon Noon then return to Delhi, where he resumes his innings and hits a gigantic six off the final ball....

These tales are very much the products of a creative thinker's imagination. They appeared in comic form in a series titled *Sunny the Supersleuth*, which hit the stands in 1984-85. The brainchild of Bharat Shavur, who had been SMG's classmate at St. Xavier's College, and his wife Shalan; the series generated a fair deal of enthusiasm among children, but the critics panned it for reinforcing superhuman qualities to ordinary humans. In this sense, the series found itself in the same boat as the one it was modelled on. The previous year had seen the advent of a *Supremo* series of comics, which sought to make a superhero out of Amitabh Bachchan. Successive editions showcased Amitabh shuttling between the dual roles of the Bollywood megastar and Supremo, the nemesis of evil-doers everywhere.

Sunny the Supersleuth may have taken a leaf out of Supremo's book, but nevertheless, SMG earned the distinction of being the first Indian sports personality to have a comic book series dedicated to him.

It wasn't his first tryst with magazines. SMG edited the Calcutta-based *Indian Cricketer* for a number of years. After his retirement, he had a stint as editor of the popular *Sportsweek* magazine, for which he had contributed columns in his playing days. His tenure witnessed a transformation in the look and feel of the publication, with the name being changed to *Sportsweek and Lifestyle*. One of its most successful issues was the one that had Viv Richards dressed as an Indian Maharaja on its cover.

SMG didn't just inspire future generations by his exploits on the cricket field, his achievements off the field were as stirring.

He wasn't the first Indian cricketer to write an autobiography, although he was, by a fair margin, the most successful of the lot. *Sunny Days* attained cult status in the subcontinent. Published in 1976, it has run into several editions, and has never been out of print. Javed Miandad and Rahul Dravid are two of many individuals who have hailed its inspirational value.

His next literary venture was *Idols,* a compilation of monographs on his thirty-one favourite cricketers. It sold more than 50,000 copies in six weeks, a lot more than what *Sunny Days* had sold in seven years. *Runs N' Ruins,* his take on the see-saw events of the 1983-84 season, wasn't as successful, but its successor *One Day Wonders,* a captain's log of the World Championship of Cricket, was a blockbuster.

He was the first superstar among cricketer-models, as could be judged by the number of products he endorsed, and continues to endorse. From TV sets to shaving equipment to tea to suitings to soft-drinks to airlines to banks, SMG 'did' them all over the years.

He was one of the first Indian middle-class cricketers to realise the significance of investing, planning and stacking up for the future. He had seen many a star of yore fall by the wayside after his playing days were over, and had promised himself that he would never suffer the same fate. By doing what he did, he acted as torchbearer for the cricketing generations to come.

An individual with whom he formed a fruitful off-the-field partnership was Jairaj 'Raju' Mehta. They had become friends by the time Rajubhai arranged a net for SMG in Pune in the 1981-82 season, so that Kamal Bhandarkar could take a close look at him.

> 'Bhandarkar Sir's advice helped, as Sunil returned to form with an innings of 172 in the second Test of that 1981-82 series against

England. It was during that series that I decided to start a book shop in partnership with Theo Braganza of Marine Sports. We named it 'Sunny's Book Treat'. Sunil permitted us to use his photographs on T-shirts. He then visited Pune as the chief guest to release an appeal for Mr Bhandarkar. For this, I had to fetch him from Solapur, where he was playing a benefit game for Baba Sidhaye. He stayed with us that night, and said that he wanted to talk about a business venture. He had been offered the agency for Raymonds Legwear trousers. He told me that we could start a shop together, since there was space at my place. Sunny's Sports Boutique was thus born on 11 November 1982. It was Diwali. We began with an investment of Rs 10,000, and the first cheque was Sunil's. Shubhangi Kulkarni, who captained India in women's cricket, was the third partner. Sunil designed the logo. We started by selling leg-wear.' – Raju Mehta

The partnership quickly gained momentum, with SMG playing a pivotal role.

'India toured Pakistan in 1982-83. Sunil wrote from there and asked me to inquire whether *Smash* T-shirts would be willing to give us their dealership. In the week wherein he delayed his departure for the subsequent tour of the Caribbean, we acquired the agency for *Smash* T-shirts. *Proline* started operations soon after that, and whilst the team was in the West Indies, we got together with a company called *Polyurethane Footwear* that had promised to make shoes with polyurethane soles for the first time in India. This marked the fulfilment of a desire of Sunil's, which was to get top quality cricket shoes made in India, as there was an acute need of the same. We had already thought of the name of the first model. Sunil had crossed the 7,000-run mark in Tests, and our first model was appropriately named the SG7000. It was launched during the Ahmedabad Test against the West Indies in 1983. Ironically, it was the Test in which he passed 8,000 runs! The formal launch took place before the Baroda ODI that preceded the Ahmedabad Test. Vijay Hazare was the guest of honour. Sunil wore the shoes when he scored 236 against the

West Indies at Madras. They were a success, and thereafter we joined hands with a company called *Life Shoes*, and introduced spike shoes with soles imported from England. We then added the Sunny helmet, as also the skullcap that Sunil made so famous. Before the 1987 World Cup, we introduced personalised kitbags and unique wrist and head-bands, which Viv Richards and the West Indian fast bowlers became synonymous with. In fact, they were used by all the sides that participated in the World Cup. We started our clothing factories in Tirupur and Delhi in 1988, and were the official suppliers to the BCCI from then on till 2002. Sunil always had the ideas and we worked as a team. We pioneered the concept of franchise shops. His constant guidance and encouragement helped us achieve whatever we did.' – Raju Mehta

The skullcap was withdrawn from the market, when a shocking fact came to light after SMG retired and then donated his headgear to the MCC museum at Lord's. It caught the eye of an expert, who expressed his wish to examine it. One look at it, and the man was agitated. He asked SMG whether the latter had ever been hit on the head when he had the skullcap on. SMG's negative reply did not surprise him. The expert then revealed that the make of the skullcap was such that it would not have absorbed the shock of a head injury. On the contrary, it would have accentuated the intensity of the blow. Simply put, had SMG been hit on the head while wearing the skullcap, he would have died on the spot!

His partnership with Raju Mehta apart, there was another pioneering effort that SMG was part of—one that this writer had the fortune to be associated with.

'Trikaya, the agency of which I was a part, produced the highlights capsules for DD during the India-West Indies series in 1983-84. It was the first time an agency had done so for the national channel. We did a reasonable job given the times and limitations, getting the likes of Raj Singh Dungarpur and Farookh Engineer to anchor the capsules. Engineer didn't figure in our plans initially, but then I got a call from Sunil, quite out of the blue. He requested me to consider Engineer for the capsules, for

the latter's benefit match was scheduled to be played later that season, and his presence on national TV would have earned him some pre-match publicity. Sunil was doing his bit to ensure that his old team-mate's benefit game got the prominence it deserved.'
– Sumedh Shah

An individual with over twenty years' experience in the field of advertising, Sumedh Shah had been a cricket lover since his boyhood in the 1940s. Like most Indians of the time, he had followed SMG's career with interest, and even penned a complimentary review of *Sunny Days* for *Debonair*, a popular monthly periodical. Vinod Mehta, the editor of the periodical, had taken particular care to ensure that the issue comprising the review landed in SMG's hands during the India-England Test series in 1976-77. SMG did not revert, nor did he ever bring up the review during their conversations almost a decade later, but Shah believes it was always at the back of his mind.

In May 1985, Shah sought an appointment with SMG in his Nirlons office. He wanted him to host a TV series of curtain-raisers for India's forthcoming tour of Australia.

'I realised that he had [a] good TV presence, and was keen that he accept my offer. I remember him sitting in solitary splendour in his office. It was just him and a peon there. I told him what I had in mind, and he liked the idea. When I brought up the subject of the fees, he told me to talk to Pammi. We were waiting for the coffee, when I asked him whether he had read Mark McCormack's *What They Don't Teach You at Harvard*. Sunil hadn't. But he had heard about McCormack's International Management Group (IMG), the world's largest Sports Management Company. "Why don't you start something like that?" I asked him. He said that he did not know anything about starting companies, but would appreciate if I sent him a note on the same. I agreed, but forgot all about it as I was part of a chaotic advertising agency. He called to ask for it a few days later. I told him that I would send it to him the following week. He then informed me that he was leaving for the US the next day, and would be away for two months. So could the note be delivered the next day?

I then worked out a document, outlining the financial structure and the various options – Pvt. Ltd, proprietorship, etc. He went through the note and said that it should be a Pvt. Ltd company. "Why don't we go ahead with it?" he asked. I was flabbergasted, to say the least. I made some noises, telling him that he and his wife were to be away for a long time. "Do whatever is necessary," he said. That was how Professional Management Group was born.' – Sumedh Shah

Shah got into the nitty-gritties after SMG left for the US. To his annoyance, he encountered resistance from Doordarshan. He had no option but to continue chasing the mandarins who occupied Mandi House, the base of the DD bigwigs in Delhi. It was a time when the sponsored programme craze was at its peak, and getting a letter from DD was equivalent to printing your own currency. As it turned out, the Mandi House mandarins inadvertently did Professional Management Group and the Indian Sports Media a huge favour, for it led to an unprecedented development.

With no progress on the TV front, Shah started thinking of other revenue-generating methods.

An outcome was the Syndicated Column. Shah came up with the idea to start a fortnightly column, penned by SMG, which would be written in English, but offered to newspapers all over the land, giving them the option of translating it into regional languages. SMG, whom he tracked down in the US, was amenable to the idea. The first 'Sunil Gavaskar Fortnightly' appeared in the *Hindustan Times*, *The Sunday Observer*, and regional publications across the country, within a month. Each publication was obviously granted exclusivity in a certain region. The fees they paid to carry the fortnightly were decided keeping in mind their reach and circulation. *The Sunday Observer* paid Rs 1,000 per article, a substantial amount in 1985.

The 'Sunil Gavaskar Fortnightly' has appeared in prominent Indian publications since 1985. It continues to feature its writer in prime form. Through the fortnightly, SMG expresses himself on cricketing and sports-related issues, and showcases his penchant for reading between the lines. His columns have been a source of enlightenment for cricket lovers, especially those from the subcontinent, and embarrassment for the denizens of the western world who believe that words and meaningless jargon speak louder than actions.

The sponsored Syndicated Column was another brainwave. It was a time when the Hyderabad-based Vazir Sultan Tobacco (VST) Industry was sponsoring virtually all Indian sport and sporting activities. In cricket for instance, they were backing Tests, One Day Internationals and domestic cricket.

> 'Being gentlemen sponsors, they had allocated all their money to different sporting associations and boards, thinking that these entities would publicise the events. However, no such thing happened. They signed us as consultants. While marketing the fortnightly, we had realised that newspapers did not have the budget to buy editorial content. That led to the advent of the sponsored Syndicated column. The deal was that eminent personalities like Sunil, Imran Khan, Allan Border or Viv Richards would write on a day's cricket. PMG would give the article to newspapers with a 5"x1" VST advertisement, to be placed in an island position within the article. This barter deal was a big hit with the Indian media, for most newspapers, except the *TOI*, had lots of advertising space. Since they were getting top quality editorial matter free of cost, it was a win-win situation for them.' – Sumedh Shah

Initially, each writer got paid around Rs 10,000 per article. VST would pay PMG Rs 20,000 per piece, which accounted for the writer's fees and PMG's administrative expenses.

Within a few years, the sponsored column had become a common feature in newspapers, and other agencies had entered the fray.

> 'If only PMG had registered the idea! We would have been billionaires today.' – Sumedh Shah

Even as PMG was in the process of creating watersheds, the DD dam remained unbreachable. India's tour of Australia was followed by a tour of England and a busy home season in 1986-87. By then, Mr Shah had revised his plan of making curtain-raisers. What he had in mind was a weekly series that would showcase memorable cricket matches played all over the world.

'Frustrated with DD's intransigence, I wrote a letter to Mr Harish Khanna, who was then the director-general of the channel. It was one of the better letters I have written . . .

Dear Mr Khanna,

I have been meeting yourself and your various colleagues for one year, and have been promised that 'Sunil Gavaskar Presents . . .' would be telecast by DD. So far, there is no action. I have four options:

1. Forget about the whole thing.
2. Approach the Consultative Committee of Parliament (Ministry of Information and Broadcasting) and present my case.
3. Get Sunil Gavaskar to address a press conference to explain the facts.
4. A combination of 2 and 3.

Please let me know what course I should take.' – Sumedh Shah

Shah learnt that his friend Kundan Shah, director of the celebrated black comedy *Jaane Bhi Do Yaaron* and popular TV serials like *Yeh Jo Hain Zindagi* and *Nukkad*, was to visit Mandi House. He asked him to deliver the letter.

'Kundan read it and refused outright. He said, "If I deliver it, not only will you be banned from entering Mandi House for life, but I will also be handed out the same sentence!" However, I insisted. DD responded with an 'Urgent' telegram, apologising for the distress, approving the programme, and asking me to meet the concerned officials at the earliest.' – Sumedh Shah

The result was *Sunil Gavaskar Presents* . . . As the name suggested, SMG was the host. The series featured footage from memorable Test matches played by India in England, Australia and Pakistan in the 1970s and early '80s. A lasting regret of the producers was that they could not showcase India's victories at Port of Spain in 1971 and 1976. The TV footage of both games did not exist.

Not that the cricket lovers in India were complaining. Having only read or listened to the matches in question, *SGP* (*Sunil Gavaskar Presents*...) was a godsend for them. The inaugural episode featured Indian cricket's showpiece – the victory at the Oval in 1971, the footage of which PMG acquired from the BBC. An added attraction was SMG's tete-a-tete with two individuals who had figured prominently in the game in question – Ajit Wadekar and B.S. Chandrasekhar.

The next two episodes spotlighted the second and third Tests of the 1980-81 series in Australia, which comprised Sandeep Patil's stirring hundred at Adelaide (plus footage of his injury at Sydney), and Kapil Dev's death-or-glory spell at Melbourne respectively. The subsequent episodes featured two Tests played by India in Australia in 1977-78, the 1979 Oval Test wherein SMG scored 221, and Pakistan's sensational win at Karachi in 1978-79, among others.

While the series focussed primarily on India matches, there were exceptions. Two full episodes were dedicated to the 1977 Centenary Test between Australia and England. Another episode was devoted to the Leeds Test of the 1981 Ashes series, which Botham and Willis won for England.

It will be safe to say that like *Sunny Days, SGP* impacted many cricket-crazy Indians. The match footage apart, what endeared the series to the cricket-loving community was the insights of the celebrity guests. When Sandeep Patil recalled his injury at Sydney in 1980-81 and then his 174 in the next Test against the same bowling attack, and Kapil Dev reminisced about taking pain-killing injections through the night to be able to bowl on the crucial last day of the 1981 Melbourne Test, the audience was exposed to the attributes that distinguished the achievers from the others – temperament and resilience. It was one thing for the youngsters and wannabe cricketers among the viewers to read about the exploits of their heroes, and another to see and hear them talk about the same.

SGP proved that Sunil was as adept a TV personality as he was a batsman and writer. He wrote his own scripts, and expressed himself superbly. Aziz and Saeed Mirza, the directors, handled him superbly, bringing out his knowledge of the sport and sense of humour.

SGP was telecast at prime time – 10.00 am on Sunday mornings. It was preceded by Ramanand Sagar's *Ramayan*, which had viewers across the land worshipping TV screens, shedding tears and jumping with joy, depending on the events unfolding on screen. However, there was a minority that found this national obsession technically shoddy, its pace worse than that of a Boycott innings, and the special effects downright hilarious. The members of this fraternity would roll on the floor whenever the bow-and-arrow duels would begin, and place bets on which colour would pop out of every arrow. The cricket lovers among them would brave the proceedings stoically and wait for *SGP* to begin.

> 'The serial was like many of Gavaskar's masterly batting displays: meticulously conceived and beautifully executed. The appeal of the stars and the use of clippings from famous matches conveyed a lot about the game . . . *SGP* is how TV can be utilised to spread sport. Those involved with other disciplines, notably football, hockey and athletics, would do well to follow suit.' – Sunder Rajan, *TOI*, 19 August 1987

The final line was proof that Mr Rajan was an optimist. It was left to PMG to take up the cause of other sports, through a series of curtain-raisers for the 1988 Olympics titled *The Quest for Gold*. The highlights of this series, from an Indian viewpoint, were the clippings of legendary Olympians like Jesse Owens, Al Oerter, Mark Spitz, Nadia Commaneci, Edwin Moses, Daley Thompson and Carl Lewis.

The year 1988 also witnessed the second instalment of *Sunil Gavaskar Presents*. *SGP – II* spotlighted twelve unforgettable One-dayers, with one whole episode devoted to an exhaustive interview with Dennis Lillee. The other episodes featured interactions with the likes of Mohinder Amarnath, K. Srikkanth, Gordon Greenidge, Ravi Shastri, Mohsin Khan, and Viv Richards. The series showcased classic encounters like the 1975 World Cup final, the low-scoring thriller between India and Pakistan at Sharjah in 1985, the first-ever limited-overs 'tie' between Australia and the Windies in 1983-84, and New Zealand's successful chase of England's 296 in 1982-83. The series also gave Indian viewers their first look of a Packer game between Australia and West Indies in the first reason of WSC.

PMG went on to produce many more TV programmes for DD and other channels after the start of the satellite age in 1991. Curtain-raisers on the 1987 World Cup and 1989 Nehru Cup were followed by a three-part preview of India's tour of Australia in 1991-92. One of its highlights was the eighteen-year-old Sachin Tendulkar's admission that he had watched cassettes of matches in Australia, and was looking forward to bat on tracks conducive to strokeplay. He proceeded to walk the talk with exceptional hundreds at Sydney and Perth, even as his seasoned team-mates floundered.

One of PMG's prominent TV productions of the 1990s was *Beyond the Boundary*, a weekly on ESPN-STAR, which featured Sunil discussing topics ranging from 'killer instinct' to 'hero worship', with guests ranging from Sachin Tendulkar to billiards maestro Geet Sethi. It was telecast in 1996-97, one year after the same channel telecast *SGP-III*. The third instalment featured a combination of Tests and One-dayers. Two episodes were dedicated to the second Test of the 1990 series between India and England, in which Sachin Tendulkar scored his maiden Test hundred at the age of seventeen. The second of the two episodes is remembered to this day because of Sunil's threat to throttle Tendulkar, his studio-guest, if he was to finish his career with less than 15,000 Test runs and forty Test hundreds.

PMG was also involved in the institution of the first international and Indian cricket ratings to actually reward the toppers at the end of a designated twelve-month period, as opposed to merely recognising them. The Ceat Cricket Rating for International cricket, endorsed by the trinity of Sunil Gavaskar, Ian Chappell and Clive Lloyd, was instituted in 1995. The Castrol Awards for Excellence in Indian cricket were initiated in 1997.

At least three big names in Indian television—Harsha Bhogle, Charu Sharma and Cyrus Broacha—have a lot to thank PMG for.

Mr Shah retired in June 2007 after offloading his stake to SMG, Sam Balsara, chairman and managing director of Madison World, one of India's largest independent communication agencies, and Noomi Mehta, chairman, Selvel Outdoor Advertising.

This writer's seven-year stint in PMG, which commenced in August 2000, primarily concerned content creation, management and execution.

Executives of diverse talents have served the company with distinction down the years. They were, and are, being complemented by unsung heroes and heroines.

There is Juliana, who ought to be awarded by Ceat and Castrol for maintaining and updating both ratings with unerring accuracy for over a decade. That is the least both companies can do, given their propensity to institute additional awards every year. Raghu, who went from being secretary to Mr Shah and SMG to senior manager and master-seller of newspaper columns, is another luminary. Then there is Ravi, the no-nonsense accountant. The company's Man Friday is Anil, an epitome of resourcefulness. He has for company, the ever-smiling Srikant. There is Jaswanth, PMG's production-manager since the late 1990s, and lastly, Vasanthan, who is driver to Mr Shah, and probably the only PMG staffer who could speak to the latter in a cranked-up volume and get away with it.

With Mr Shah and SMG at the helm, PMG conceived and staged some innovative ventures over the years. The Tied Test Rematch, staged in Chennai in March 2001, was an unprecedented event. Played at the Guru Nanak College ground a day prior to the third Test of the epic 2001 series between the two countries, the rematch featured the players who had shaped the tie in September 1986. Dara Dotiwala and Vikram Raju, the umpires, replayed their roles, as did TV commentator Kishore Bhimani. Australia won the forty-overs-a-side game with lots of deliveries to spare, thanks to David Boon's blistering hundred.

A similar event was the silver jubilee of the 1983 World Cup win, which was held at Lord's on 25 June 2008. It was during his commentary assignment on India's tour of England in 2007 that SMG remembered the imminent twenty-fifth anniversary, and booked the Long Room.

The dinner at Lord's followed the World Cup Silver Jubilee celebrations organised by the BCCI in Delhi on 22 June 2008, which this writer was privileged to emcee.

Commentary has been another pioneering area for SMG, at least from the Indian perspective. The likes of Tiger Pataudi and Lala Amarnath, to name just two prominent ex-cricketers, had had their stints on television before he did, but after his retirement, SMG was the first choice as the voice and face of Indian cricket all over the world. He was part of the BBC commentary team during India's tour of England in 1990. One year later, Channel Nine invited him to join Richie Benaud, Bill Lawry, Tony Greig, and the Chappell brothers in the commentary box on India's tour of Australia.

SMG treated his foray into commentating as an innings: he took his time to get used to it, kept working on it, and eventually prevailed, thanks to his fluency in English, knowledge of the game, and innate professionalism. He learnt a lot from the abrasive Geoff Boycott, the amiable Tony Lewis, the sagely Richie Benaud, the forthright Ian Chappell, and the voluble Tony Greig. An on-air experience that he viewed as a great teacher came about during the Australia tour in 1991-92. Even as something significant happened on the field and the spectators applauded, SMG's first inclination was to describe it. However, he was silenced by his co-commentator Benaud, who raised his right hand, to indicate to him that the applause was doing all the talking; words were superfluous.

There were times early in his commentating career, when the slightest hint of a casual approach on the field would infuriate him. The writer remembers a One-Day International between India and England at Gwalior in March 1993, wherein the Indians got off to a flying start in pursuit of a stiff target of over 260, and then suffered a mid-innings collapse, largely of their own making. As batsman after batsman perished to cavalier strokes, SMG found the goings-on too much to take. He cooled down only after Anil Kumble helped Navjot Sidhu take the side past the target.

His patience and comfort levels grew as the years went by, leading to some insightful and at the same time, entertaining stints alongside Boycott, Shastri, Greig and Holding. There was a gem of a moment during the 1996 World Cup, when he had Ian Chappell of all people struggling for words. 'Tell me Ian, why do wicketkeepers make good lovers?' he asked while on air. When Chappell expressed his ignorance, Sunil replied, 'Because they go up at the slightest opportunity!'

It was a while before Chappell uttered another word.

> 'In the commentary box, he has retained that shrewdness you would expect. He remains a good judge of a cricketer and has that twinkle in the eye, that little mischievous humour that adds to the experience and makes him easy to work alongside.'
> – David Gower

In 1995, the government of Maharashtra nominated SMG as the Sheriff of Mumbai. It was a ceremonial designation, but the cricketing fraternity and his fans were delighted. Over the years, the sheriff's post had been graced by luminaries in the fields of politics, medicine, architecture, business, entertainment and sports. SMG, who was forty-five at the time, was one of the youngest sheriffs the city ever had.

He had the unique distinction of leading India in a cricket tournament during his one-year tenure. The competition in question was the World Masters, a limited-overs competition for over-35s featuring teams from Australia, the West Indies, England, South Africa, Sri Lanka and India. All the matches were played at the Cricket Club of India in the first half of March 1995. Some quality cricket was played.

England were the pre-tournament favourites, for they comprised several individuals who were still playing County cricket. The same could not be said about the other sides, which comprised players who had either retired from First-class cricket, or had coached the sport a lot more than played it, in the recent past.

But flair had the final say, and India and the West Indies made it to the final. SMG, who had batted well, led intelligently, fielded and even bowled with zest in the previous games, missed the summit clash due to an injured hamstring. However, he made his presence felt. India batted first, and Dilip Vengsarkar scored a glorious hundred. Like the other veterans who had played long innings earlier in the tournament, the knock took a lot out of him. He elected not to take the field, but the umpires refused to allow a substitute. India fielded with ten men for a couple of overs before Sunil utilised one of the tournament's innovations to splendid effect.

A microphone had been attached to one member of the fielding side in every game, to facilitate a dialogue between him and the TV commentators. SMG had done the needful for India in the earlier games, often interjecting a response to a commentator's question with a shout to one of his team-mates to move slightly forward, backward or sideways. TV viewers loved these exchanges, for it was almost as if they were out there, in the thick of things.

Sunil was wired up in the final as well, although he wasn't playing. The umpires' stubbornness prompted him to stride out, the microphone on, to explain the Indian point of view. Not only did the officials hear him out, but so did the television audience! His contention was accepted and a substitute allowed.

With both sides comprising a fair number of players who had figured in the 1983 World Cup final, it was hardly surprising that memories of the 1983 World Cup final were relived on the eve of the summit clash. The Indians thrilled the nostalgia-lovers by nominating Kapil Dev as captain in Sunil's absence. However, the West Indians were not inclined to live in the past. They cruised to the target, and that man Viv Richards finished it off with a six off Madan Lal, who had dismissed him on 25 June 1983. The proficiency of cricket's dominators of the 1970s and '80s in this Masters event was ironic, in that the numero uno position they had helped their islands reach in world cricket, was about to be usurped by the Australians. Mark Taylor's team beat Richie Richardson's West Indians in a Test series in the Caribbean in May 1995.

At the turn of the century, SMG joined hands with Nana Chudasama, another former Sheriff of Mumbai, and Khalid Ansari, the man behind *Mid-Day*, the city's most successful tabloid, to fulfil a long-cherished dream. The objective of the CHAMPS (Caring, Helping, Assisting, Motivating and Promoting Sportspersons) Foundation was to provide monthly financial aid to sportspersons who had brought glory to the country at the international level, but had since fallen on bad days. It was launched in Mumbai in January 1999 with a double-wicket tournament, wherein India's biggest CEOs and magnates were invited to team up with members of the 1983 World Cup winning team. A corpus was raised through generous donations. Now in its tenth year, the foundation is providing a monthly honorarium to seven sportspersons – Ms M.C. Mary Kom (boxing), Mr Bir Bahadur (football), Mr Keshav Datt (hockey), Mr Gajanan Hemmady (badminton), Mr Gopal Bhengra (hockey), Mr Salim Durani (cricket) and Mr Premjit Lal (tennis).

Although he didn't do it for publicity, ventures like the CHAMPS Foundation have endeared him even to those who could not quite come to terms with him during his playing days.

> 'We once travelled to Jamshedpur by train for a Ranji game in the late '70s. Invariably, we were woken up at every station by crowds, who would bang on the doors and windows of our compartment. We were somewhere near Ranchi, when

a mob virtually laid siege to the train and tried to enter our compartment. We did our best to keep them out, and in the process, I lost my temper and landed a few punches on one of the mobsters. That offended them, and they blocked the train. It was left to Sunil to placate them. Had it not been for him, I might have been lynched.' – Dilip Vengsarkar

It wasn't the last time SMG had taken on a mob. He had saved a Muslim family from being torched alive during the communal riots that rocked Bombay in 1992-93. He was standing on the balcony of his sea-facing flat in Worli when he noticed that something was amiss on the road in front of him. He ran downstairs to confront the mob, which chose to turn back.

Two decades after his retirement as a cricketer, SMG's schedule remains as hectic as ever. His stature in world cricket twenty years after his retirement was underscored during the ICC Cricket World Cup in 2007. He was writing as many as four different columns during the tournament – one syndicated by PMG, the second for a prominent website, the third for a weekly periodical, and the fourth for a newspaper based in South-East Asia. His memorable innings continue to be screened by various sports-based TV channels.

A few years after their marriage, SMG and Mrs Gavaskar shifted from their joint family set-up in Dadar to an apartment in Worli in south-central Mumbai. The senior Gavaskars later moved to Pune, where they recently celebrated their sixtieth wedding anniversary.

In the late 1980s, the junior Gavaskars moved to another apartment in a building, appropriately named 'Sportsfield'. Situated on Worli Seaface, one of the quieter stretches in the metropolis, this edifice is home to other sporting icons. Some of them—cricketers Polly Umrigar, Gulabrai Ramchand, Ashok Mankad, Eknath Solkar, Ramakant Desai and Sharad Diwadkar, and billiards wizard Wilson Jones—have passed away since. SMG presently has for neighbours Ajit Wadekar, Bapu Nadkarni, Dilip Vengsarkar, Ravi Shastri, Yajurvindra Singh, tennis ace (and Ashok Mankad's wife) Nirupama Mankad, former hockey captain M.M. Somaya, and badminton star Pradeep Gandhe.

> 'I was at the other end when he scored his first Test run, and I was in the commentary box when he scored his 10,000th Test run. Providentially, we became neighbours. He lives one storey above me. As a cricketer of course, he was several storeys above me.' – Late Ashok Mankad

Whenever he finds the time to be in Mumbai, SMG divides his day between PMG and the badminton courts of the Bombay Gymkhana. The evenings are generally devoted to Miss Raeya, who was born to Rohan and his wife Swati in 2001. The boy who broke his mother's nose with a fierce straight-drive in the early 1950s is now a grandfather.

> 'He is an icon, an inspiration, a celebrity. But he hasn't changed one bit as a human being. He is still the same person. That, to me, is his greatest achievement.' – Ashok Ambaye

> 'Sunil has remained the same person. The only difference is that I do not get the opportunity nowadays to open his bags after a tour and take whatever I want!' – Dr Vishwas Raut

24

THE LEGEND AND HIS LEGACY

'I will never be able to repay what cricket has given me even in 25-30 lifetimes... I bleed everytime the Indian team doesn't do well ... the boys have potential, talent... I didn't have the natural ability like all these guys. My greatest strength was my mental strength... I used to get over periods of uncertainty by letting the opponent waste his energy... When I don't see mental strength, I get upset. ...' – Sunil Gavaskar, *The Boy from Chikalwadi* (PMG, 1999)

In early 1993, when the Indian team was struggling on its inaugural tour of South Africa, and there were suggestions that the captaincy would change hands from Mohammad Azharuddin to Kapil Dev, Rajan Bala came up with an out-of-the-box suggestion in his column in the *Sunday Observer*.

He devoted the piece to explain how it made perfect sense to hand the sceptre back to SMG. His contention was that the Indian cricketers needed a father figure to get their focus and wits back on track, and no one fitted the bill as perfectly as SMG. He could bat in the middle order, Bala suggested. He had kept himself fit enough by playing badminton on a regular basis, and there was no reason to believe that he would have problems against the England bowling on Indian wickets.

Had the selectors and forty-three-year-old SMG himself taken Bala seriously, it would have been the equivalent of the Australians requisitioning the services of the forty-two-year-old Bob Simpson after the outbreak of the Packer crisis in 1977. However, the Indian team that was to host England in early 1993 wasn't as badly placed as the Australians back then. The selectors instead took cognisance of the fact that sixteen of Azharuddin's seventeen Tests as captain had been played overseas. His lone Test at home, India had won by an innings. They decided to give him another chance on Indian soil. The rest is history.

Bala's piece emphasised the reverence that cricketers, cricket writers and cricket lovers in India had for the man. In an era that became synonymous with first Sachin Tendulkar and Anil Kumble, and subsequently the class of '96—Ganguly, Dravid and Laxman—SMG came to be regarded as Indian cricket's Emeritus. Nothing has changed in the new millennium.

> 'Sunil is the most intelligent cricketer India has ever produced. He is a systematic thinker, who can visualise the future far better than most people that I have known. He is a person of habit and is very meticulous and neat. He would make a very good politician and maybe a likely candidate as our President in the future.' – Yajurvindra Singh

SMG's standing is unprecedented in the annals of Indian cricket. He has continued to battle for Indian and subcontinental cricket with the same fervour that he displayed during his playing days. At no point has he caught on to the 'In-my-day' disease, which has afflicted some of the most accomplished practitioners of the sport in India and overseas. One cannot remember him talking and behaving like some other ex-cricketers, who talk and behave as if they scored a double hundred and took ten wickets in an innings everytime they set foot on a cricket field.

Regular readers of SMG's columns will recall his strong reaction to a childish comment made by a contemporary of his that even Stevie Wonder, the visually challenged American performer of the 1970s, would have scored runs against the bowlers of the new millennium. The gist of what SMG wrote that it was unfair to deride the capabilities of the likes of Shane Warne, Shaun Pollock, Anil Kumble and Glenn McGrath, among others; a champion in one era would have almost certainly been a champion in another.

His own experiences of being at the receiving end of mob-fury made him touchy whenever his successors found themselves in similar situations.

> The spectator must be made to understand that when he pays for a ticket to the match, he pays to watch the game, and if he does not like what he is watching, then he is free to leave and go home . . . Just as he does not show his pleasure by throwing expensive gifts or items at the players, he is simply not entitled to show his displeasure by throwing rubbish at the players whose performance he finds disappointing. Tell me, how any other professional—whether he is a banker, engineer, journalist, businessman, chemist, doctor or even a student—would feel if people came up and threw rubbish at them just because they did not do their job well. Also tell me how many professionals would be able to do their jobs watched by 30,000-50,000 noisy spectators. Would a surgeon be able to perform an operation, a journalist write his piece, a student do his studies if he had 50,000 people watching and screaming at him? Perhaps the next time a spectator picks up an object to throw at the players, maybe he should think about this. – Sunil Gavaskar, *The Sportstar*, 3 April 1993

It is not as if he has seen eye-to-eye with the modern generation of Indian Cricketers on everything.

> Every schoolboy who is playing cricket dreams of receiving his cap – be it that of his school team, his club team or later as he progresses through the various grades of cricket, that of his national team. It is the ultimate fulfilment of ambition to be able to wear the country's cap. To get it in one's hand and then to wear it for the first time is a thrill beyond words. Even getting the team shirts or sweaters or blazers doesn't give the same tingle as wearing the cap for the first time does . . . We have

made a mockery of the India cap by having it made by all and sundry. Since the caps are so freely available there is no feeling or importance attached to them and players look upon them as just another article to put in their kit bags. The players also think little of the shirts given to them and are seen distributing them to all and sundry at the end of the tour so as to lessen the weight in their kit bags. It's one of the saddest sights to see some young members of the Indian team standing on the balcony and throwing their India shirts to the crowd below. This is to enable them to accommodate the things they have bought on tour in their kit bags. One can understand the shirts or caps being given away as memorabilia to a collector who will give them the respect they deserve or to a person who has been helpful to the particular player or to the team, but to throw them away as discarded, unwanted stuff is a painful sight. – Sunil Gavaskar, *Sportstar*, 1 December 2001

He is probably as revered on the other side of the Radcliffe Line as he is in India. His prediction that Imran Khan's cornered tigers would go the distance in the 1992 World Cup, at a time when they were hanging on for dear life, took the subcontinent by surprise. When his words came true, he was invited to Pakistan to participate in the victory celebrations, and inundated with gifts. His old friend Javed Miandad wasn't amused. 'I win the World Cup, but you get all the goodies,' he said to Sunil, embellishing the statement with a couple of colourful Hindustani expletives.

In the years following his retirement, the little master of the 1970s and '80s formed a close bond with a cricketer who valued his country's cap as much as Miandad and he did theirs.

Sachin Tendulkar hit the headlines with his 664-run stand with Vinod Kambli in February 1988, three months after SMG's retirement. The comparisons between the duo, both short-statured and Mumbaikars to boot, were inevitable.

> 'Sachin was felicitated at Sahitya Sahawas, where he resided, after being picked for Mumbai. Sunil was the chief guest. On our way to the function, Sunil revealed to me that he hadn't seen the boy bat. I told him, "Sunil, you are now a father figure in cricket. But

I am telling you, this boy will end up being your grandfather!"'
– Hemant Waingankar

The senior statesman made his way to the Wankhede a few days later, when the Mumbai team was at practice. He did his best to keep his presence a secret, lest it affect the boy's composure. One stroke that Tendulkar essayed—a forcing stroke between what would have been mid-wicket and mid-on—was more than enough to convince him that the country and city were blessed.

He went on to proclaim to the media that Sachin Tendulkar was the best batsman in Mumbai after Dilip Vengsarkar. Some members of the fourth estate were initially dumbfounded, and subsequently amused. The reason was simple—the boy was yet to play a First-class match. Members of their fraternity would react in pretty much the same manner when Imran Khan waxed eloquent about Inzamam-ul-Haq in the early 1990s.

Tendulkar then scored a hundred on his First-class debut. He was only fifteen. When SMG gifted his featherweight leg-guards to the youngster, many viewed it as a symbolic gesture.

A year after his First-class debut, the teenager was picked in the Indian team for the tour of Pakistan. He scored two fifties in the four-Test series. The second of those knocks marked his coming of age. He went in with the scoreboard reading 38-4, and was almost immediately struck on the nose by a Waqar Younis snorter. Offered the option of retiring for repairs, he did not take it. Waqar's first delivery after the resumption, he drove to the cover boundary.

> 'He was very happy when I scored my maiden Test hundred at Manchester in 1990. I had spoken to him during the earlier Test at Lord's about batting in English conditions. We have had discussions and shared thoughts on several occasions thereafter.'
> – Sachin Tendulkar

In 1992, SMG helped the wonder boy negotiate a deal with the Yorkshire County Cricket Club. The club initially offered him 20,000 Pounds, which was 10,000 Pounds less than what Craig McDermott, the club's original choice, was to get. SMG played a key role in ensuring that Tendulkar was paid the same amount as the Australian speedster.

He was accused in later years of being soft on Tendulkar. However, that wasn't quite the case.

'... Over the years, he has hardly said anything of importance about certain aspects of the game, preferring to stay out of controversy rather than offer an opinion. But it is crucial for the development and growth of the game that players of his stature and following speak on aspects that are damaging to the game and harmful to its progress. When he was captain of the team to Australia (1999-2000) he had the media there looking for a comment or two about how to give the game a new direction. Owing to his phenomenal batting in the home series (1997-98), the Australian media was waiting to lap up every word of his, but he disappointed them by hardly saying anything of consequence. There were plenty of topics that were making news then, like the throwing issue, the sledging or mental disintegration subject, use of technology for TV, to name just a few, but he did not venture an opinion and as one India-loving Australian veteran mediaperson said, "It was as if 'no comment' was two words too many for him." Perhaps Tendulkar was taking shelter under the ICC Code of Conduct regarding comments, but there comes a time when the good of cricket counts before anything else and one has to stick one's neck out for the betterment of the game. For, when Tendulkar speaks, the world will stop and listen. – Sunil Gavaskar, *The Sportstar*, 12 January 2002

Tendulkar and Kumble, two of the greatest match-winners of all time, were joined in 1996 by three outstanding batsmen.

The quintet of Tendulkar, Kumble, Ganguly, Dravid and Laxman initiated the third phase in India's cricketing history. Phase I, which featured many a defeat, disaster and humiliation, lasted from 1932 to 1970. Phase II commenced in March 1971, when Dilip Sardesai steered the team out of choppy waters at Kingston, Jamaica. Sunil took the process initiated by his Bombay colleague to the next level. As the 1970s progressed and then gave way to the '80s, his efforts were complemented by those of Viswanath and the great spinners. Kapil Dev emerged at the end of the 1970s, and Vengsarkar came into his own as a batsman at around the same time. This was the phase wherein the team realised that it was good enough not to lose on a regular basis, and was in fact capable of turning the tables on the most fancied of opponents. If Phase I's silver lining had been outstanding individual feats interspersed within clusters of collective disasters, Phase II witnessed a greater degree of consistency in team performances, and outstanding individual achievements. Both Sunil and Kapil Dev held the individual world records for batting and bowling for a number of years, and inspired those who followed them.

Phase III commenced exactly thirty years after the start of Phase II. It was on 14 March 2001, to be precise, that V.V.S. Laxman and Rahul Dravid batted for a whole day to take India to a winning position against an Australian team that had won sixteen Tests on the trot.

> 'Mr Gavaskar, Navjot Sidhu and I were part of a TV cricket quiz show in the late 1990s. SMG was talking to Sidhu and at one point, he expressed his regret that his 236 remained the highest individual score by an Indian in Tests. India was the only Test-playing country not to have posted a single individual score of over 250. Coincidentally, I went past him in the Kolkata Test of the 2000-01 series against Australia.' – V.V.S. Laxman

The batsmanship of the two men, and the bowling of Harbhajan Singh, made it only the third instance in Test history of a team winning after being asked to follow-on.

From 1932 to 1999, India won only thirteen Tests on foreign soil. It was a fact that deserved the derision it got. The team of the new millennium sorted things out. What Sourav Ganguly initiated as captain, Rahul Dravid and Anil Kumble, and now, Mahendra Singh Dhoni, built upon.

With the impact he had on Indian cricket, SMG became the bridge between a generation that was unsure and underperforming, and one that was proud, assured, and backed itself every inch of the way.

He represented the pinnacle of one of the three schools of Indian batsmanship. This was the Vijay Merchant school of orthodoxy. His contemporary G.R. Viswanath on the other hand epitomised all the attributes imparted by the Ranji school of wristy wizardry. The proficiency of the brothers-in-law in their respective streams gave their juniors the confidence to innovate, improvise and incorporate the methods taught by all the three schools.

Dilip Vengsarkar, who combined Merchant's run-hunger with the belligerence preached by the C.K. Nayudu school, was a forebearer to Tendulkar, whose paddle sweeps suggest that there is a bit of Ranji in him as well. Rahul Dravid is a keen practitioner of Merchant's methods as well as Ranji's wristwork, but some of his innings in limited-overs cricket have borne the Nayudu stamp. V.V.S. Laxman of course carries forward the legacy of Ranji, with a bit of Merchant thrown in. Virender Sehwag is mostly Nayudu and partly Ranji. Then there are the southpaws, who constitute a category of their own.

SMG has done his bit to advise and encourage his successors through his various incarnations – former player, commentator, columnist, chairman of India's National Cricket Academy, and someone who has been through it all.

When Sachin Tendulkar fell for the sixth time in the 90s in One Day Internationals in the calendar year of 2007, SMG excelled himself in his column:

> While there is understandable anxiety to get to the three-figure mark, which is more to do with temperament, the little champion will also have noticed that he has got out when he is playing off the back foot and that too on the back half of his body. If one takes the nose as the centre part of the body and draws an imaginary line straight down, there would be two halves of the body and any batsman who plays in the back half, which in a right-hander's case would be the right side of the nose, is not going to be in full control of the shot. The hands will be cramped for room and the eyes will not be on top of the ball and there won't be the control that is required to play the ball in the direction it is intended to, and so more likely, there will be an inside edge onto the stumps or an outside nick to the wicketkeeper. Rahul Dravid too, when he is in trouble, is out when he is playing in the wrong half of his body. The little champion's game is based on the front foot, and when he is hitting it off the middle of the bat, he is playing it with his eyes on top of the ball as it is on

the front half of his body. Even when he hits off the back foot, the contact with the ball is made more in the front half of the body, and that's how the power comes through as well.

While he was always available for the cricketers whenever they approached him for advice during series, SMG also got to spend some time in the Indian dressing room, during his stint as batting consultant of the side in the 2004-05 season.

> 'His analyses were straightforward. What struck me during our conversations was that he would keep things simple.' – V.V.S. Laxman

SMG also had had a stint as cricket manager of the Indian team when the incumbent Ajit Wadekar suffered a heart attack during the Austral-Asia Cup, played in Sharjah in 1994. His stint as chairman of the National Cricket Academy from 2001 to 2005 witnessed the advent of Mahendra Singh Dhoni, Suresh Raina, V.R.V. Singh, R.P. Singh, Piyush Chawla, Dinesh Kartik and Parthiv Patel, among others.

He was appointed chairman of ICC's Cricket Committee in 2000. This twelve-man committee, comprising as it did eminent former cricketers, umpires and even representatives of contemporary cricketers, made quite a few recommendations in the first half of the new millennium, all of which were aimed at enhancing the sport, especially its fifty-over version. The idea of a 'Supersub' did not sustain, but that of 'Powerplays' did. By SMG's own admission, the recommendation closest to his heart was the one advocating the lifting of restrictions on bouncers in limited-overs cricket. He and the others believed that allowing bowlers to deliver one bouncer per over in the limited-overs format would help redress the balance between bat and ball.

> The annual Captains-Coaches Conclave that we have at the end of the season was his idea. He suggested that the captains and coaches of all the Ranji sides get a common platform to express themselves, and thereby provide us with inputs. Everybody in the BCCI respects his views on cricketing matters and advice. He was the one who suggested Gary Kirsten's name as a prospective Coach of the national side in 2007-08. As chairman of the Board's

Technical Committee, he has recommended improvements in the quality of pitches and umpiring standards over the years, all of which have been taken seriously.' – Prof Ratnakar Shetty, Chief Administrative Officer, BCCI

There is a lot that SMG has in common with the Board of Control for Cricket in India. The BCCI is probably the only Indian sporting institution that has been villified more than SMG. Other sporting bodies in India have, for reasons best known to themselves, elected to treat the BCCI as a punching bag rather than a yardstick, just as SMG has been castigated at every step by the usual suspects. Both institutions are reaping the rewards of keeping things simple. In ther words, they did not, and do not 'muck around'. What SMG and the BCCI have done is devote themselves to the fulfilment of their respective objectives. Not surprisingly, their singleminded approach yielded results. The abuses heaped upon them are powered by a deep-rooted inferiority complex and a sour grapes mentality. It is after all a lot easier to pass the buck onto others, than to accept your shortcomings and work towards getting your own house in order.

Considering this state of affairs, the use of cricket in general and SMG in particular by the Indian Olympic Association (IOA) to win the bid for the Commonwealth Games in 2010 was ironic. SMG accepted the IOA's request to be part of the Indian contingent that participated in the bidding process in Jamaica in 2003. His presence was a masterstroke, given his stature in that part of the world. There, he was his usual professional self, going out of his way to talk to the delegates, especially those representing the Caribbean nations, and convincing them to vote for a land that like theirs, that had been branded as 'third world', instead of Canada, the other prominent contender.

Five years after India won the bid, the IOA president was quoted as saying that he had signed a proposal to include cricket in the Commonwealth Games only to win the bid, having lost on two earlier occasions.

This was bizarre.

In the new millennium, SMG was among those who promoted the 'Jayadevan' method for computing revised targets in truncated limited-overs matches. His efforts bore fruit when the BCCI adopted the system in its domestic competitions in the 2006-07 seasons. It was a huge moment for M. Jayadevan, who had been running from pillar to post for nearly a decade, in an attempt to prove that his method was sounder and fairer than the one devised by Messrs Duckworth and Lewis.

The 1990s witnessed many an outcry over the hopelessly one-sided and batting-friendly nature of the Ranji Trophy. Nothing of note changed in the new millennium, and that prompted the Board to ask its Technical Committee to suggest ways and means to stem the rot.

It was during this period that SMG discussed one of his ideas with this writer and another PMG executive. It entailed splitting the 450 overs of a five-day game between the two teams. We brainstormed, and the consensus was that the first innings could be restricted to 120 overs, and the second to 105. These many overs were more than enough, SMG reckoned, to amass significant scores in first-class cricket. After all, 120 overs amounted to four full sessions of play.

We then checked out the Ranji scorecards of the previous few seasons, and discovered that most sides had indeed finished their respective first innings in less than 120 overs. SMG was of the view that every match ought to have a result. Hence, if a team finished the final innings at 300-5, when it had been set 350 for a win, it would count as a defeat for the former, and not a draw.

These intra-office discussions were of course at an elementary level, and hence did not take into account the fallout of an interruption for rain or bad light. In the event, a less radical, and lot more effective modification was mooted at the Technical Committee meeting that year.

> 'He suggested that the top two teams from each of the five zones ought to be classified into one group. The Board accepted the proposal, with one alteration. The top three teams from each zone were accommodated in the Elite Group, instead of two. That is how you have fifteen teams in the "Elite" Group, and twelve in the "Plate" Group. The idea of these two groups has proved to be very successful. I remember coaches like Bishan Bedi, Lalchand Rajput and Chandrakant Pandit saying that it

> was the best thing to happen to domestic cricket, as one would not be sure which teams would qualify for the knockout stage, till the very end.' – Prof Shetty, Mumbai Cricket Association

Considering all this, it becomes difficult, if not impossible, to figure out where the individuals who recently branded him as a 'destructive influence' on Indian cricket, were coming from. An Indian member of the anti-SMG brigade recently went on record to say that the game was better run at a time when countries like Australia and England enjoyed the veto power.

All one can say in response is that the Indian contention that the England players had applied vaseline to the ball in 1976-77 would have been taken a lot more seriously, had India been as influential a cricketing force then as it is now.

> 'If I slam Sunil in an article or interview, I stand to gain, as people will start talking about me overnight! Those who criticise him do so only to gain publicity.' – Hemant Waingankar

The problem with his detractors is their credibility. There is nothing that needs to be said, when SMG, who scored thirteen Test hundreds against the West Indies without wearing a helmet, is criticised by someone who reportedly justified his penchant for skipping matches on a Caribbean tour in the 1980s, by saying that it was better to be a king in the Ranji Trophy than face the West Indies fast bowlers.

The usual suspects have accused him of back-seat driving – wanting to dominate Indian cricket without assuming additional responsibility. However, what they have conveniently failed to take into account is that SMG has been as invaluable as anybody else in championing the cause of his country and continent on the international stage. When he talks and writes, the cricketing world does listen.

> 'The greatest quality that Sunil has is that he still is a student of the game. He is still willing to learn, and even we, who were not fit to tie his shoelaces as cricketers, could point out his mistakes and he would always listen, even after scoring 10,000 Test runs!' – Raju Mehta

It is hardly a secret that sections of the cricketing fraternity in countries like England and Australia do not think highly of him. These sections comprise those who are still struggling to reconcile to the fact that the India of the 2000s is a far cry from the India of 1947.

His description of the English cricketers as the game's champion whingers in 2001 infuriated Duncan Fletcher, the coach of the England team, among others. It was just one of the many instances wherein SMG had attacked what he and many others perceived as England's patronising attitude towards the subcontinent. The English have traditionally attributed their travails in Asia to the pollution, food, umpires, climate, and even 'unfavourable planetary alignment', never to their ineptitude on the field.[1]

SMG has been consistent in this regard, pointing out things that most people miss. When the South African batsmen had problems picking the ball due to a reflection over the sightscreen in the Oval Test of the 2008 series against England, he had this to say:

> The sad part was that the ground authorities did nothing to ensure that the batsmen were not inconvenienced. . . . So was there any adverse word in the Brit papers about the inadequacy at the ground? Nope. Just imagine the hullabaloo if it had happened on a ground in the subcontinent and the England batsmen were the victims. – Sunil Gavaskar, *Mid-Day*, 10 August 2008

When he was offered Life Membership of the MCC in 1990, he declined it, ostensibly because of his run-ins with the rude stewards at the ground. His refusal triggered off reactions that ranged from the rational to the ridiculous. He was accused of virtually everything, from being petty, to having let down the Indian community in Britain. The MCC approached him again a few years later, and this time, he acquiesced, having made his point earlier.

The club invited him to deliver the annual Sir Colin Cowdrey 'Spirit of Cricket' Lecture in 2003. He spoke on the scourge of sledging, and

---

[1] Kevin Peterson's England cricket team endeared itself to India by returning for a two-Test series in December 2008, days after the horrors of 26/11. In doing so, they effectively erased memories of their predecessors' pletulance.

ended up incensing many a cricketer from the land that has patented the art.

A war of words with Ricky Ponting on this issue four years later resulted in an indiscretion on his part. After he flayed the world champions' on-field behaviour in an article during the 2007 World Cup, the Australian skipper likened his outburst to throwing stones from a glass house. Ponting cited the walkout at Melbourne in 1981.

SMG then delivered the following riposte on a sports channel:

> Some day, some other hot-headed guy might actually get down and, you know, whack somebody who abuses him. There's the example of the late David Hookes. Would the Australians, who use that kind of language on the field, and, not all of them do, in a bar, get away with it? Would they have a fist coming at their face or not? – SMG on *ESPN-STAR*, as reported by *Cricinfo* on 12 March 2007

His reference to the late Hookes, a folk-hero of sorts in Australia, angered a lot of people, including his old friend Allan Border.

> 'Sadly, the reaction of many here was, "Oh, that's just Sunny, here he goes again." Certainly there is a perception that while he admires Australian cricketers, he doesn't like the way they play the game. Of course, he is entitled to that opinion, but one senses he harps on it so much that his outbursts lack credibility. Too often, it looks like a vendetta. Just why he is so combative when talking about Australia and Australian cricket, I don't know. Clearly, he has clashed heavily with some of the Australians down the line, and remains uneasy about it. His Hookes comments were really out of line and tarnished his image here. While Australians generally have grown weary of his carping, his greatness as a batsman is always recognised and acknowledged, especially his courage and resourcefulness against great fast bowling.' – Mike Coward

The Hookes controversy drew to an end when SMG apologised.

On the other hand, not many people were apologetic when the Sydney Test of the 2007-08 series between India and Australia drew to an acrimonious close.

Shortly after the Australians had celebrated their sixteenth consecutive Test win, SMG questioned how the umpires had chosen to trust players who were anything but paragons of virtue. Michael Clarke, who while batting, had stood his ground after giving a knee-high catch to slip, claimed a catch on the fateful last day, which did not come across as a clean 'take' on the TV cameras. However, Ricky Ponting, his captain, then 'declared' Sourav Ganguly, the batsman, out, and Mark Benson, the umpire, 'seconded' the verdict. Ponting then claimed a catch a little later, when the TV replays again suggested that the cherry had made contact with the turf.

Even as Anil Kumble, the Indian skipper, did a William Woodfull by declaring at the post-match conference that 'only one team had been playing in the spirit of the game, the Match Referee Mike Procter chose to believe the claim of the Australians that Harbhajan Singh had racially abused Andrew Symonds earlier in the game. The version of Sachin Tendulkar, who was batting along with Harbhajan at the time, was ignored.

> By accepting the word of the Australian players and not the Indian players, the match referee has exposed himself to the charge of taking a decision based not on facts, but on emotion. Worse still, his decision has incensed millions of Indians, who are quite understandably asking why his decision shouldn't be considered a racist one considering the charges that were levied on Harbhajan were of a racist remark.

> Millions of Indians want to know if it was a white man taking the white man's word against that of the brown man. Quite simply, if there was no audio evidence, nor did the officials hear anything then the charge did not stand. This is what has incensed the millions of Indians who are flabbergasted that the word of one of the greatest players in the history of the game, Sachin Tendulkar was not accepted. In effect, Tendulkar has been branded a liar by the Match referee. At the hearing the Indians were represented by the Manger Chetan Chauhan, the media manager Dr M. V. Sridhar, the skipper Anil Kumble and the two men at the crease when the incident was said to have happened, Sachin Tendulkar and Harbhajan Singh. The Australians were represented by Ricky

> Ponting, who lodged the complaint against Harbhajan Singh, Andrew Symonds against whom the remark was supposed to have been made, Matthew Hayden, Michael Clarke and Adam Gilchrist. Ponting claimed he didn't hear anything nor did Gilchrist, so it all boiled down to the word of Hayden and Clarke, and don't forget, Clarke had stood his ground after being caught at first slip and claiming that debatable catch of Ganguly. – Sunil Gavaskar, *Mid-Day*, 13 January 2008

As it turned out, Harbhajan was exonerated for lack of audio evidence. But SMG wasn't. His reference to white men and brown men prompted some people to cry foul. There was talk of his being asked to choose between his professional commitments, and those that he discharged in an honorary capacity at the ICC.

He did what most professionals would have done.

> I love the way he zeroes in on double standards, especially when they affect India. Obviously, he is an important and influential voice in the game. He can be called upon to preside over important agendas, but at the end of the day, his media work is his main occupation, and that's what the establishment should respect. You can't have Gavaskar heading a high level committee and take offence to what he writes. – Clayton Murzello

> 'He did a fine job during his eight-year tenure as chairman of the ICC Cricket Committee. I hope to continue the good work.'
> – Clive Lloyd (his successor)

India fought back splendidly to win the next Test at Perth. The Emeritus of Indian cricket tagged it as the country's best Test win ever, and widened the smiles on the faces of his compatriots with his post-match comments on Andrew Symonds, for whom, life had come full circle. At Sydney, he had outside-edged Ishant Sharma into Dhoni's gloves, but the umpire hadn't heard the snick. Symonds had then gone on to score a big hundred. At Perth, he inside-edged a Kumble delivery onto his pads, but was declared out leg-before wicket.

> I don't think you should blame the umpiring at all. You should blame that bat of his. It is a silent bat, so it does not tell you when you have got an edge. It did not tell Symonds that he had got an edge at Sydney, and it did not tell him at Perth. It's the bat, it has got nothing to do with the umpiring. – SMG on *ESPN-STAR*, 19 January 2008

His appearances on TV have made SMG one of the more recognisable faces in the cricketing world. It is unlikely that like Richie Benaud, he will find himself being asked by a youngster whether he had ever played cricket. But what a recent cricket convert might want to know is the rank he holds in the pantheon of the all-time greats.

Benaud earmarked SMG to open the batting in his dream team, which he selected in 2004. His playing XI comprised SMG, Sir Jack Hobbs, Sir Donald Bradman (captain), Sir Viv Richards, Sachin Tendulkar, Adam Gilchrist (wk), Imran Khan, Dennis Lillee, Shane Warne and Sydney Barnes.

SMG missed out on the dream team purported to have been picked by Sir Don Bradman. Announced after the latter's death, the team created a bit of a stir. A prominent bone of contention was the inclusion of Barry Richards as opening partner to Bradman's fellow Invincible Arthur Morris. Richards, who played only four Tests, may well have played many more had South Africa, his country, not been banned in 1970. But then, there was no place for ifs and buts in cricket. Quite simply, his presence in the squad was incongruous with Bradman's reputation as a realist. For the record, Richards scored 508 runs at 72.57 in his first (and only) four Tests, while SMG scored 774 at 154.80 in his first four!

There cannot be any doubt that SMG is the greatest opening batsman of all time. His runs and records against the premier purveyors of cricket's pace age cannot be ignored. Neither can his technique and resilience. In the first half of his career, he batted without a helmet, for the simple reason that they didn't exist; in the second, he acquired a skullcap, but it never came into the equation for the simple reason that he did not let himself get hit. In any case, as the expert claimed years later, he would not have lived had he been hit!

Regrettably, some of his own compatriots have sought to devalue his achievements. The backbone of their stance is his record in the Packer years. The scorebooks state that he scored seven hundreds against Packer-hit teams that had supposedly weak attacks—three against Australia in 1977-78, and four against the Windies in 1978-79. Hence, they contend, his achievements are far from extraordinary.

The response to this contention is four-pronged:

A. If SMG's performances against supposedly weak teams are to be devalued or derecognised, then every single century, double century and triple century scored against India from 1979 to 1992, when their bowling attack essentially began and ended with Kapil Dev Nikhanj, ought to be expunged from the record books.
B. One is not sure how Jeff Thomson, off whom SMG took three hundreds in the 1977-78 series on Australian pitches, would react to being described as a weak bowler. Unfortunately, one will never know how Sylvester Clarke and Malcolm Marshall, who conceded four hundreds to SMG in 1978-79, would have reacted to a similar accusation, for they are no more. It would be safe to say that they would not have been very happy.
C. At no point did SMG have a say in the selection of the opposing teams. A cricketer can only play against the team that has been chosen to play against his.
D. Had he faced the Indian bowling of his time in Tests, he might well have scored close to 15,000 Test runs.

Cricinfo.com on 27 July 2007 made the point that SMG averaged an astounding 56.60 in the fourth innings, whenever India had to battle to either win or save the match.

As he approaches the diamond jubilee of what has been a remarkable life, his admirers may well be thinking of two areas that he has been associated with only cursorily – cricket administration and coaching.

'When Ramakant Desai passed away during his tenure as vice-president of the Mumbai Cricket Association, Ajit Wadekar suggested that we propose SMG as his replacement. He accepted, but made it clear that he would not like to be referred to as belonging to a certain group. He did not want to get involved in politics of any sort. He served as vice-president for six months. He attended all the meetings, participated in the deliberations. He would invariably come prepared, after having studied the items on the agenda. The elections then came up, and we wanted him to contest. But politics played spoilsport. The MCA thus lost out on the opportunity to have someone of his stature. His presence in the administration would have made a huge impact, and Mumbai cricket would have benefited immensely. But that was not to be.' – Prof Ratnakar Shetty

'He opted not to contest the elections against his senior cricketing stalwarts as a mark of respect for them. Mumbai thus lost out on his services off the field. It was unfortunate that someone who was chairman of ICC's Cricket Committee for several years has had no role to play in the affairs of his parent association.' – Milind Rege

The possibility of his venturing into the other area is greater.

'He has achieved just about everything. The only thing left is his indoor cricket school, which he has wanted to start since his retirement. I would like to see him fulfil his dream of setting up a state-of-the-art academy, which will surely produce batsmen like Sachin Tendulkar, Dilip Vengsarkar, Sanjay Manjrekar, and Sunil himself.' – Hemant Waingankar

For Sunil and his fans, the wait for the academy has been long and exasperating. But when it does materialise on the plot of land allotted to him in the western Mumbai region of Bandra, the majority might just get convinced that the wait was worth it. The man has plans and aims up his sleeve, all of which he is determined to achieve.

When he got the opportunity to play First-class and later Test cricket, he decided that he would make it count. When he cemented his place in the national team, he set high goals and standards for himself, and strove to maintain them. When he hung up his cricket boots, he continued to serve the sport, championing the cause of Indian cricket by becoming its voice and face.

'His impact on Indian cricket has been phenomenal. He inspired a whole generation of cricketers with his feats on the field, and his fearlessness to voice his opinion on different issues off it. He possesses the ability to express himself lucidly, and it is no secret that his views are valued. You may or may not agree with everything he says, but there is no doubt that he has enhanced the profile of the game in general, and that of Indian cricket in particular.' – Rahul Dravid

Sunil Gavaskar's impact on Indian cricket can be compared to the Mahatma's on India's struggle for independence. Both men evoked, and continue to evoke, extreme reactions. Some people swore by them, while others swore at them. While the Mahatma took the freedom movement to the common man, SMG took the initiative in showing the world that Indian cricketers could be as consistently good, if not better, than the others.

Of course, it wasn't as if the two individuals waged a lone battle. They were preceded by illustrious personalities, supported by equally committed compatriots, and even opposed by seasoned rivals. Not all their decisions and moves were correct either. It was just that they were extraordinary beings, who made fewer mistakes than others.

Both fell short of their ultimate objective. The 1947 vivisection destroyed the Mahatma's dream of a united subcontinent, while SMG could not convince the world that the Indian cricket *team* was the best in the world. But they laid the foundation for their respective successors to build upon.

During the course of the past thirty years and more, SMG has played the lead role in changing the cricketing world's perception of the planet's most populous cricket-playing nation. He has been emulated splendidly by his successors on the field, and by the BCCI off it.

The man defied and destroyed old traditions, and instituted new ones. Like all good middle-class Indians, he achieved his objectives by doing the basics right and making optimal use of his brains. While this approach was by no means unprecedented, the fact is that SMG elevated it to a hitherto inconceivable level.

Simply put, he made Indian cricket, and in the process, more than one generation of Indians, believe in itself.

If his track record is anything to go by, then one can rest assured that Sunil Manohar Gavaskar's desire to nurture a whole new generation of cricketers will also be a success.

SUNIL GAVASKAR FACT FILE

Full name
Sunil Manohar Gavaskar

Date of birth
10 July 1949

Place of birth
Bombay, India

Education
BA (Economics), Bombay University

School
St. Xavier's High School, Bombay

College
St. Xavier's College, Bombay

Major teams represented in First-class cricket
India, West Zone, Bombay, Rest of India, Somerset, World XI

Right-handed batsman, Right-arm bowler

Major awards and distinctions

Arjuna Award	– 1975
Padma Bhushan	– 1980
Maharashtra Bhushan	– 1999
Castrol Lifetime Achievement in Cricket Award	– 2003

- Inducted into the ICC's inaugural Hall of Fame with fifty-four other all-time greats in January 2009.)
- Chairman, Technical Committee, BCCI.
- Was chairman of The ICC's Cricket Committee From 2000 to 2008.
- Was chairman of The BCCI's National Cricket Academy From 2001 to 2005.
- Had a one-year term as Sheriff of Mumbai in 1995.

I. SUNIL GAVASKAR IN FIRST-CLASS CRICKET

by Sudhir Vaidya

SMG is the first and only Indian till date to score over 25,000 runs in First-class cricket.

Debut

For Vazir Sultan Tobacco XI v/s Dungarpur XI at Hyderabad in the Moin-ud-Dowla Trophy in 1966-67. The match was played from 11-13 October 1966. He scored 9 and 6.

Last Game

For the World XI v/s MCC in the Bi-Centenary Test at Lord's, London, in 1987. The match was played from 20-25 August 1987. He scored 188 and 0.

SMG IN FIRST-CLASS CRICKET – A SYNOPSIS

Tournament	M	I	No	Runs	Higest Scores	AVE	100s	50s	8s
TESTS (debut v W I at Port of Spain, 1970-71)	125	214	16	10,122	236* v W I at Chennai, 1983-84	51.12	34	45	12

Tournament	M	I	No	Runs	Higest Scores	AVE	100s	50s	8s
UNOFFICIAL TEST - debut v Sri Lanka in India, 1975-76	3	6	0	344	203 v S L at Hyderabad, 1975-76	57.33	1	1	0
RANJI TROPHY - debut for Mumbai v Mysore at Mumbai, 1969-70	66	93	17	5,335	340 v Bengal at Mumbai, 1981-82	70.20	20	14	7
DULEEP TROPHY - debut for West Zone v East Zone at Jamshedpur, 1971-72	22	33	3	1,859	228 for West Zone v South Zone at Vadodara, 1976-77	61.97	6	7	0
IRANI CUP - debut for Bombay v Rest of India at Mumbai (CCI), 1967-68	12	22	4	733	156* for Rest of India v Karnataka at Ahmedabad, 1974-75	40.72	3	1	3
Moin-Ud-Dowla Gold Cup at Hyderabad - 1966-67 to 1973-74 - debut for VST Colts v/s Dungarpur XI in 1966-67 - his maiden first-class game.	9	13	0	476	94 for Associated Cement Co v Hyderabad XI at Hyderabad, 1971-72	36.62	0	4	1
FOR THE REST OF THE WORLD IN AUSTRALIA, 1971-72	11	20	2	559	95 for Rest of the World XI v New South Wales at Sydney, 1971-72	31.06	0	4	0
FOR THE REST OF THE WORLD IN ENGLAND, 1987	1	2	0	188	188 v M C C at Lord's, 1987	94.00	1	0	1
For SOMERSET in the County Cricket Championship in England, 1980	15	23	3	686	155* for Somerset v Yorkshire at Weston Super-Mare, 1980	34.30	2	2	1

Tournament	M	I	No	Runs	Higest Scores	AVE	100s	50s	8s
OTHER FIRST-CLASS MATCHES	85	136	15	5,483	194 for Indians v Worcestershire at Worcester, 1971	45.31	14	25	6
TOTAL	349	562	60	25,785	340 v Bengal at Mumbai, 1981-82 (In the RANJI TROPHY)	51.36	81	103	31

Note: '*' and 'NO' denote 'not out'.

II. SUNIL GAVASKAR IN TEST CRICKET

Debut

Against West Indies at the Queen's Park Oval, Port of Spain, 1970-71. He scored 65 and 67*. The match was played from 6-10 March 1971.

Last game

Against Pakistan at the KSCA Stadium, Bangalore, 1986-87. He scored 21 and 96. The match was played from 13-17 March 1987.

PROMINENT FEATS AND FIRSTS

SMG held the following Test records at the time of his retirement in 1987:

Highest scorer -	- 10, 122
Highest number of appearances	- 125
Highest number of consecutive appearances	- 106
Highest number of centuries	- 34
Highest number of fifties	- 45

- He was the first batsman to score 9,000 and 10,000 runs in Test history, and the first Indian to score 4,000–10,000 runs in Tests.
- He was the first cricketer to play a hundred consecutive Tests. He figured in all of India's 106 Tests, from the Bombay Test of the 1974-75 series against the West Indies, to the Madras Test of the 1986-87 series against Pakistan.
- He was the first batsman to score over 1,000 Test runs in a calendar year, on four occasions:

Year	Runs	Tests
1976	1,024	11
1978	1,044	9
1979	1,555	18
1983	1,310	18

- He scored over 1,014 runs in a seventy-eight-day period, from 16 October 1978 to 2 January 1979.
- He was the first batsman in Test history to score twin hundreds in a single Test on three occasions:

124 and 220 v/s West Indies at Port of Spain, 1970-71.
111 and 137 v/s Pakistan at Karachi, 1978-79.
107 and 182* v/s West Indies at Kolkata, 1978-79.

Ricky Ponting is the only other batsman to have done so thrice.

- He holds the world record for the highest aggregate by a batsman in his debut series. SMG scored 774 runs in his maiden Test series in 1970-71.
- SMG is the only Indian to score four hundreds in successive Tests on two separate occasions.
- 1970-71 – 116, 117*, 124 and 220 in consecutive Tests against the West Indies (the last three in successive innings).
- 1976-78 – 108 v/s England at Bombay in 1976-77, and 113, 127 and 118 in the first three Tests of India's next Test series against Australia in 1977-78).
- SMG was the first Indian to carry his bat through a completed Test innings. He achieved this feat in the second innings of the Faisalabad Test against Pakistan in 1982-83. He contributed an unbeaten 127 to his team's total of 286.
Virender Sehwag emulated him in 2008.

- SMG was the first batsman in Test history to score over 2,000 runs against three teams.

PERFORMANCES IN TESTS (team-wise):

Opponent	Tests	Innings	Runs	NO	Average	100s	50s	0s
West Indies	27	48	2,749	6	65.45	13	7	5
England	38	67	2,483	2	38.20	4	16	3
New Zealand	9	16	651	1	43.40	2	3	-
Australia	20	31	1,550	1	51.66	8	4	2
Pakistan	24	41	2,089	4	56.45	5	12	1
Sri Lanka	7	11	600	2	66.66	2	3	1
HOME	65	108	5,067	7	50.16	16	23	6
AWAY	60	106	5,055	9	52.11	18	22	6
TOTAL	125	214	10,122	16	51.12	34	45	12

Highest score: 236* v/s West Indies at the M.A. Chidambaram Stadium, Madras, in 1983-84.

FROM FOUR FIGURES TO FIVE:

Milestone	Date	Opponent	Test number	His score at that point	His final score in that innings	Venue
1,000 runs	25 January 1973	England	11	25	69	Green Park, Kanpur
2,000 runs	11 April 1976	West Indies	23	47	102	Queen's Park Oval, Port of Spain

Sunil Gavaskar Fact File — 505

Milestone	Date	Opponent	Test number	His score at that point	His final score in that innings	Venue
3,000 runs	20 December 1977	Australia	34	104	127	WACA Ground, Perth
4,000 runs	29 December 1978	West Indies	43	49	107	Eden Gardens, Kolkata
5,000 runs	20 September 1979	Australia	52	3	10	KSCA Stadium, Bangalore
6,000 runs	24 January 1981	Australia	65	16	23	Adelaide Oval, Adelaide
7,000 runs	14 December 1982	Pakistan	80	49	83	Gaddafi Stadium, Lahore
8,000 runs	29 October 1983	West Indies	95	104	121	Ferozeshah Kotla Ground, New Delhi
9,000 runs	17 December 1985	Australia	110	160	166	Adelaide Oval, Adelaide
10,000 runs	7 March 1987	Pakistan	124	58	63	Gujarat Stadium, Ahmedabad

TEST CENTURIES – 34

Number	Innings of the match	Score	Opponent	Venue	Season
1	1st	116 #	West Indies	Bourda Oval, Georgetown	1970-71

Number	Innings of the match	Score	Opponent	Venue	Season
2	2nd	117* #	West Indies	Kensington Oval, Bridgetown	1970-71
3	1st	124 + #	West Indies	Queen's Park Oval, Port of Spain	1970-71
4	2nd	220 + #	West Indies	Queen's Park Oval, Port of Spain	1970-71
5	1st	101	England	Old Trafford, Manchester	1974
6	1st	116	New Zealand	Eden Park, Auckland	1975-76
7	1st	156	West Indies	Queen's Park Oval, Port of Spain	1975-76
8	2nd	102	West Indies	Queen's Park Oval, Port of Spain	1975-76
9	1st	119	New Zealand	Wankhede Stadium, Mumbai	1976-77
10	1st	108 #	England	Wankhede Stadium, Mumbai	1976-77
11	2nd	113 #	Australia	Woolongabba, Brisbane	1977-78
12	2nd	127 #	Australia	WACA Ground, Perth	1977-78

Number	Innings of the match	Score	Opponent	Venue	Season
13	2nd	118 #	Australia	Melbourne Cricket Ground, Melbourne	1977-78
14	1st	111 +	Pakistan	National Stadium, Karachi	1978-79
15	2nd	137 +	Pakistan	National Stadium, Karachi	1978-79
16	1st	205	West Indies	Wankhede Stadium, Mumbai	1978-79
17	1st	107 +	West Indies	Eden Gardens, Kolkata	1978-79
18	2nd	182* +	West Indies	Eden Gardens, Kolkata	1978-79
19	1st	120	West Indies	Ferozeshah Kotla Ground, New Delhi	1978-79
20	2nd	221	England	The Oval, London	1979
21	1st	115	Australia	Ferozeshah Kotla Ground, New Delhi	1979-80

Number	Innings of the match	Score	Opponent	Venue	Season
22	1st	123	Australia	Wankhede Stadium, Mumbai	1979-80
23	1st	166	Pakistan	M.A. Chidambaram Stadium, Chennai	1979-80
24	1st	172	England	KSCA Stadium, Bangalore	1981-82
25	1st	155	Sri Lanka	M.A. Chidambaram Stadium, Chennai	1982-83
26	2nd	127*	Pakistan	Iqbal Stadium, Faisalabad	1982-83
27	1st	147*	West Indies	Bourda Oval, Georgetown	1982-83
28	2nd	103*	Pakistan	KSCA Stadium, Bangalore	1983-84
29	1st	121	West Indies	Ferozeshah Kotla Ground, New Delhi	1983-84
30	1st	236*	West Indies	M.A. Chidambaram Stadium, Chennai	1983-84
31	1st	166*	Australia	Adelaide Oval, Adelaide	1985-86

Number	Innings of the match	Score	Opponent	Venue	Season
32	1st	172	Australia	Sydney Cricket Ground, Sydney	1985-86
33	1st	103	Australia	Wankhede Stadium, Mumbai	1986-87
34	1st	176	Sri Lanka	Green Park, Kanpur	1986-87

Note:

* denotes 'not out.'
+ denotes the same Test.
# denotes his four hundreds scored in consecutive Tests.

- SMG scored 33 of his 34 hundreds as an opening batsman. Interestingly, he posted his highest Test score the only time he did not cross the three-figure mark as an opener! Batting at number four, he scored an unbeaten 236 against the West Indies at Madras in 1983-84.
- SMG has scored a century on debut against three countries. This is an Indian record.
  116 v/s New Zealand at Auckland, 1975-76.
  113 v/s Australia at Brisbane, 1977-78.
  155 v/s Sri Lanka at Chennai, 1982-83.

Positions Held In The Batting Order (Innings-wise):

Opening (No. 1 or No. 2)	203
No. 4	1
No. 5	4
No. 6	3
No. 7	1
No. 8	1
No. 9	1
Total	**214**

Modes Of Dismissal (Innings-wise):

Caught in the field	82
Caught by the wicketkeeper	54
Bowled	33
Leg-before wicket	17
Stumped	5
Caught-and-bowled	5
TOTAL	214

Scoring Pattern – (Innings-wise):

Not Out On Zero	– 1
Ducks	– 12
Score Between 1 and 9	– 45
Score Between 10 and 49	– 77
Score Between 50 and 89	– 40
Score Between 90 and 99	– 5
Score Between 100 and 149	– 22
Score Between 150 and 199	– 8
Score Over 200	– 4
Total	214

Batting Doubles:

A century in both innings of a Test	– 3
A century and fifty in a Test	– 3
A century and a duck in a Test	– 1
A fifty and a duck	– 1
A fifty in both innings	– 3
A 'pair'	– 0

III. SUNIL GAVASKAR IN ONE-DAY CRICKET
by Sudhir Vaidya

List 'A' Matches (One-Day Internationals, plus official limited-overs competitions like the Deodhar and Wills Trophies in India, the Benson and Hedges Cup and Natwest Trophy for Somerset, etc):

Matches	Innings	Runs	NO	Average	100s	50s
151	144	4,594	17	36.17	5	37

Highest score: 123 for Somerset v/s Middlesex in the Benson and Hedges Cup quarter-final, 1980.

One-day Internationals:

Debut: v/s England at Leeds on 13 July 1974. He scored 28.
Last game: v/s England at Mumbai on 5 November 1987. He scored 4.

Matches	Innings	Runs	NO	Average	100s	50s
108	102	3,092	14	35.13	1	27

Highest score: 103* v/s New Zealand at Nagpur in 1987-88 (1987 World Cup).

Rohan Jaivishwa Gavaskar played eleven One-Day Internationals in 2004. His debut made SMG and him the second father-son combination to represent India in ODIs, after Yograj Singh and Yuvraj Singh.

He was named after three of his father's heroes – Rohan Kanhai, M.L. Jaisimha and G.R. Viswanath.

IV. SUNIL GAVASKAR THE FIELDER

- He was declared the 'Best Fielder' in the series between Australia and the World side in 1971-72.
- He was the first Indian 'non-wicketkeeper' to take a hundred catches in Test cricket. He finished with a tally of 108 catches.
- He was emulated in later years by Mohammad Azharuddin, Rahul Dravid, V.V.S. Laxman and Sachin Tendulkar.
- He contributed to three of India's most memorable limited-overs wins as a fielder; he held two catches in the 1983 World Cup final, and ran the dangerous Imran Khan out in the 1985 World Championship of Cricket final. A few days later, he held a record four catches in the Rothmans Cup semi-final against Pakistan at Sharjah.

Catches held:

First-class cricket	- 291
Tests	- 108
List 'A' matches	- 37
One-Day Internationals	- 22

V. SUNIL GAVASKAR THE BOWLER
by Sudhir Vaidya

First-class cricket

20 wickets @ 61.35 with a personal best of 3-43 in the Ranji Centenary match at Bhuj, 1971-72.

Test cricket

1 wicket @ 216 with a personal best of 1-34 against Pakistan at Faisalabad in 1978-79.

List 'A' matches

2 wickets @ 40.50 with a personal best of 1-10 against Pakistan at Sialkot in 1978-79.

One-Day Internationals

1 wicket @ 25 with a personal best of 1-10 against Pakistan at Sialkot in 1978-79.

Zaheer Abbas holds the dubious distinction of being SMG's only victim in Tests as well as One-Day Internationals.

VI. SUNIL GAVASKAR THE CAPTAIN

First-class cricket

Won	Lost	Drawn	Total
37	15	72	124

Captain of India

Won	Lost	Drawn	Total
9	8	30	47

His debut as captain of India, against New Zealand at Auckland in 1975-76, was memorable.

He became only the second Indian after Polly Umrigar, to win his first Test as captain.

Ravi Shastri, Sachin Tendulkar, Sourav Ganguly, Virender Sehwag, Anil Kumble and Mahendra Singh Dhoni have all done so since.

He also became the second Indian after Vijay Hazare to score a century on his debut as skipper. Dilip Vengsarkar is the only other Indian to have done so.

Ranji Trophy

Overall:

Won	Lost	Drawn	Total
19	1	19	39

He captained Bombay to victory in the Ranji Trophy final on three occasions:
    1976-77 – Beat Delhi by 129 runs.
    1983-84 – Beat Delhi on first-innings lead.
    1984-85 – Beat Delhi by 90 runs*.

Note: *Although SMG was the Bombay captain, he did not take the field on the last two days due to illness. Sandeep Patil deputised and received the trophy on behalf of the team.

Duleep Trophy

Overall:

Won	Lost	Drawn	Total
3	1	6	10

He captained West Zone to victory in the Duleep Trophy final thrice:
  1976-77 – Beat North Zone by nine wickets.
  1977-78 – Beat North Zone on first-innings lead.
  1981-82 – Beat East Zone on first-innings lead.

Irani Cup

Overall:

Won	Lost	Drawn	Total
2	1	3	6

He captained Bombay to an outright win over the Rest of India in 1976-77. Mumbai won by ten wickets.

He captained the Rest of India to an outright win over Delhi in 1982-83. The Rest won by five wickets.

One-Day Internationals

Overall:

Won	Lost	Drawn	Total
14	21	2	37

He led India to victory in the World Championship of Cricket, played in Australia in early 1985.

OTHER LIMITED-OVERS TOURNAMENTS:

Deodhar Trophy

He led West Zone to victory in 1982-83. They beat North Zone in the final by 13 runs.

Wills Trophy

He led Mumbai to victory in 1981-82. Mumbai beat the Board President's XI in the final by 15 runs.

VII. SUNIL GAVASKAR THE ICC REFEREE

He had a stint as the ICC Match Referee during the 1993-94 series between England and the West Indies in the Caribbean. He occupied the 'hot seat' for one Test and five One-Day Internationals.

VIII. SUNIL GAVASKAR THE AUTHOR

Sunny Days	(1976)
Idols	(1983)
Runs n' Ruins	(1984)
One-Day Wonders	(1985)

One of the world's most popular cricket columnists, SMG had penned 605 'fortnightly' pieces for newspapers by the end of the calendar year of 2008. In addition to this, he has written scores of match and series previews and reviews, players' profiles, etc.

IX. SUNIL GAVASKAR THE COMMENTATOR

He has commentated in matches and series played in all the cricket-playing countries, plus 'outposts' like the UAE, Singapore and Canada.

X. SUNIL GAVASKAR THE BRAND AMBASSADOR

Prominent brands / products endorsed by him over the years:

Dinesh Suitings
Sanspareils Greenlands (SG)
Lipton Tea
Thums Up
Coca Cola
Chiclets Chewing Gum
Yahoo
Deutsche Bank

BIBLIOGRAPHY AND REFERENCES

ALMANACS
Wisden Cricketers' Almanack – 1969 to 1989

BOOKS
Amarnath Mohinder: *Grit and Grace* (Vakils, Feffer and Simons, 1996)
Amarnath Mohinder: *Learn To Play Good Cricket* (UBSPD, 1996)
Ansari Khalid (editor): *Champions of One-day Cricket – Wills Tribute To Excellence* (Orient Longman, 1985)
Abbas Zaheer: *Zed* (Rupa, 1983)
Bala Rajan: *All the Beautiful Boys* (Rupa, 1990)
Bala Rajan: *Glances at Perfection* (Dronequill, 2002)
Bala Rajan: *The Covers Are Off* (Rupa, 2004)
Bamzai Sandeep: *Gavaskar and Tendulkar – Shaping Indian Cricket's Destiny* (Jaico, 1999)
Bamzai Sandeep: *Guts and Glory – The Bombay Cricket Story* (Rupa, 2002)
Bhogle Harsha: *Azhar – The Authorized Biography of Mohammad Azharuddin* (Viking, Penguin India, 1994)
Border Allan: *Allan Border, An Autobiography* (Methuen, Australia, 1986)
Border Allan: *Beyond Ten Thousand – My Life Story*
Bose Mihir: *A History Of Indian Cricket* (Rupa, 1990)
Brearley Mike: *The Art of Captaincy* (Channel 4 Books, 2001)
Coward Mike: *Cricket Beyond the Bazaar* (Allen and Unwin – Australia, 1990)
Cricket World Cup '83 (Unwin Paperbacks, Great Britain, 1983).
Director's Special Book Of Cricketing Controversies (Ritam, Shaw Wallace, 1992)

Doshi Dilip: *Spin Punch* (Rupa, 1991)
Gatting Mike: *Leading From The Front* (Queen Anne Press, 1988)
Gavaskar Sunil: *Idols* (Rupa, 1983)
Gavaskar Sunil: *Runs 'n Ruins* (Rupa, 1984)
Gavaskar Sunil: *One Day Wonders* (Rupa, 1986)
Gower David: *Gower, An Autobiography* (Indus, HarperCollins, India, 1992)
Guha Ramchandra: *Wickets In The East* (Oxford University Press, 1992)
Guha Ramchandra: *Spin And Other Turns* (Penguin, India, 1994)
Guha Ramchandra (Editor): *The Picador Book of Cricket* (Picador, 2001)
Guha Ramchandra: *A Corner of a Foreign Field* (2002)
Jaishankar Vedam: *Casting A Spell – The Story of Karnataka Cricket* (UBSPD, 2005)
Johnson Martin and Blofeld Henry: *The Independent – World Cup Cricket '87* (Kingswood Press, London 1987)
Kapil Dev Nikhanj: *Cricket My Style* (Allied, 1987)
Kapil Dev Nikhanj and Vinay Kumar Verma: *By God's Decree* (Harper and Row, 1985)
Kapil Dev and Romi Dev: *The World of Kapil Dev* (UBSPD, 1992)
Kapil Dev Nikhanj: *Straight From the Heart, an Autobiography* (Macmillan, 2004)
Khan Imran: *Imran – The Autobiography Of Imran Khan* (Pelham, 1983)
Khan Imran: *All Round View* (Chatto and Windus, 1988)
Marshall Malcolm: *Marshall Arts* (Queen Anne Press, Great Britain, 1987)
McDonald Trevor: *Viv Richards – The Authorised Biography* (Sphere, 1985)
Miandad Javed: *Cutting Edge – My Autobiography* (Oxford, 2003)
Moraes Dom: *Sunil Gavaskar – An Illustrated Biography* (Macmillan, India, 1987)
Mukherjee Raju: *Cricket In India – Origin and Heroes* (UBSPD, 2005)
Mukherjee Sujit: *Matched Winners* (Disha, Orient Longman, 1996)
Mukherjee Sujit: *Playing For India* (Orient Longman, 1988)
Mukherjee Sujit: *An Indian Cricket Century – Selected Writings* (Orient Longman, 2002)
Narinesingh Clifford: *Gavaskar – Portrait of a Hero* (Royards, 1995)
Patherya Mudar: *Wills Book of Excellence – Cricket* (Orient Longman, 1987)
Patil Sandeep: *Sandy Storm* (Rupa, 1984)
Prasanna E.A.S.: *One More Over* (Rupa, 1977)
Ramchand Partap: *Indian Cricket; The Captains – Nayudu to Tendulkar* (Marine Sports, 1997)
Richards I.V.A.: *Sir Vivian – The Definitive Autobiography* (Penguin, 2000)

Salve N.K.P.: *The Story Of The Reliance Cup* (Vikas, 1987)
Tarafdar Amiya: *The Hidden Treasure Gavaskar* (Loyal Art Press, 1987)
Tendulkar Ajit: *The Making of a Cricketer – Formative Years of Sachin Tendulkar in Cricket* (Ajit Tendulkar, 1996)
Wadhwaney K.R: *Gavaskar – India's Cricket God* (Siddharth Publications, 1996)
Wadhwaney K.R: *India-Pakistan Ashes* (Har-Anand Publications, 2000)
Wadhwaney K.R: *Indian Cricket Controversies* (Diamond Pocket Books, 2000)

ANNUALS
Benson And Hedges Cricket Year, 2nd edition (Pelham, 1983)
Benson And Hedges Cricket Year, 3rd edition (Pelham, 1984)
Benson And Hedges Cricket Year, 4th edition (Pelham, 1985)
Benson And Hedges Cricket Year, 5th edition (Pelham, 1986)

PERIODICALS
Cricinfo magazine
Sportsweek
Sportsweek World of Cricket
Sportstar
The Week
Wisden Asia Cricket

NEWSPAPERS
Daily Mirror
Fress Press Journal
Mid-Day
The Afternoon Despatch And Courier
The Hindu
The Indian Express
The Times
The Times of India

VIDEOS
Madras Magic (ABC, 2006)
Richie Benaud's Greatest XI (Fremantle Media, 2004)
The Art of Batting – Sunil Gavaskar (Marine Sports, 1984)

TELEVISION CHANNELS
BBC
Channel Nine's Wide World of Sports
Doordarshan
ESPN - STAR
Pak TV
Sony Entertainment Television
Ten Sports

WEBSITES
Cricinfo.com
Cricketnext.com
Rediff.com
Youtube.com

Index

Abbas, Zaheer, 84, 176, 179, 181, 217, 284-285, 288, 324, 326, 351, 354, 356
Adelaide Oval, 173, 403
Adoring home-crowd, 84
Aggressive
    batsman, 28
    captain, 27
    players, 261
Ahmed, Tauseef, 392, 433, 440
Ahmed, Younis, 439
Akhtar, Javed, 124
Akram, Wasim, 413, 435
Albion sports complex, 306
Alexander, P.C., 419
Ali, Abid, 50, 52, 55, 61-63, 66, 76, 82, 91, 101, 104-105
Ali, Ashraf, 354, 392
Ali, Inshan, 61
Ali, Syed Mushtaq, 182, 205
Alkazi, Faisal, 332
All India Radio, 136, 144, 163, 180, 254
All The Beautiful Boys, 116, 209, 342

Allott, Paul, 316, 320
Altaf, Salim, 181, 186
Amarnath, Lala, 6, 89, 127, 288, 291, 293, 472
Amarnath, Mohinder, 127-128, 130, 151, 169, 175, 215, 274-275, 283-284, 287, 302, 309, 319, 330, 341, 349, 355, 357, 398, 449, 470
Amarnath, Surender, 129, 160, 183, 274
Ambaye, Ashok, 11, 14-15, 18, 29, 48, 82, 477
Ambedkar, B.R., 5
Ambidextrous
    captain, 271
    display, 272
Ambulkar, Navin, 24, 31-32, 35, 68, 98
Amin High School, 21
'Amitabh Bachchan of Indian cricket', 211, 216, 236
Amritraj, Vijay, 197
Anand, Dev, 117, 238

Anglo-Australian experience, 69
Anglo-Indian Test cricketer, 218
Anjuman-e-Islam, 18
Anti-Gavaskar banners, 368
Anti-SMG brigade, 489
Apte, Bhausaheb, 25
Apte, Madhav, 25, 32
Arnold, Geoff, 107, 118
Art of Captaincy, 204
Ashes, 39, 73, 90, 95, 146, 195, 212-213, 253, 260-261, 263, 376, 402-403, 416, 439, 469
    -winning innings, 253
Asia Cup, 350, 353-354
Asian Games, Delhi, 285
Associated Cement Companies (ACC), 15, 70, 90, 188
Audi 100, 387-388, 391
Austral-Asia Cup, 90, 412, 415, 422, 486
Australian Academy, 193
Australian Broadcasting Corporation (ABC), 166
Australian
Cricket Board, 83, 85, 166, 200, 245
media, 245, 483
umpires, 242
wickets, 249
Awami League, 59
Azad maidan, 15, 19, 27
Azad, Kirti, 244, 263, 312, 327, 336, 393
Azad, Maulana, 110
Azharuddin, 364-367, 369-370, 374-375, 377, 381, 383, 388, 391, 398-400, 409-410, 416-418, 420, 422, 432-433, 452-453

Bachchan, Amitabh, 124, 211, 236, 461
Bachchan, Harivanshrai, 124
Baig, Abbas Ali, 72, 286, 340
Bakht, Sikander, 185
Bala, Rajan, 44, 115-116, 141, 151, 198-199, 209, 222, 341-342, 353, 361, 478
Ballboys, 453
Bandit Queen, 9
Bandookstani prisoners, 459
Baptiste, Eldine, 329
Bari, Wasim, 186
Barrett, Arthur, 55
Barrington, Ken, 191
Batting
capabilities, 169
failures, 84
schools, 142
skills, 267
BBC commentary team, 473
Bedi, Bishan, 40, 67, 84, 112, 127, 139, 192, 213, 258, 284, 312, 363, 489
Benaud, Richie, 201, 251, 317, 384, 407, 473, 494
Best Fielder Award, 84
Best Junior Cricketer Award, 442
Best Schoolboy Cricketer of the Year, 21
Bhagirathi team, 17
Bhandarkar, Kamal, 182, 249, 267, 462
Bhat, Raghuram, 271-272
Bhogle, Harsha, 471
Bhosle, Vijay, 30

Bhuta, Jitendra, 71
Bhutto, Zulfiqar Ali, 180
Bi-Centenary test, 442-443, 447
Big-innings players, 49
Bindra, I.S., 320
Binny, Roger, 218, 312, 326, 398, 417
Bird, Harold, 105, 318, 402, 443
'Black Magic' – box of chocolates, 360
Board of Control for Cricket in India (BCCI), 5-6, 37, 56, 65, 67, 72, 89, 99, 118-119, 127, 159-160, 166, 177, 187, 193, 197-200, 202, 241, 274, 302, 316, 319-320, 325, 352, 363, 373, 389, 420, 425-426, 434, 439, 464, 472, 476, 487-488, 498
  Golden Jubilee celebrations of the, 226
Bombay Cricket Association, 46, 67, 89, 156, 191, 431
Bombay film industry, 124, 193
Bombay Gymkhana, 6, 19, 477
Bombay Racecourse, 82
Boon, David, 403-404, 409, 426-427, 472
Borde, Chandrakant, 41, 89, 312, 395
Borde, Messrs Chandu, 363
Border, Allan, 213, 253, 380, 402, 406-407, 426, 429, 442, 451, 467, 491
Borivli National Park, 460
Bose, Gopal, 100-101
Bose, Mihir, 17, 162, 223, 236
Bose, Subhash Chandra, 110
Botham, Ian, 202, 217, 229, 260, 277, 282, 421, 442, 448

Bouncer, 61, 74, 76, 79, 98, 101, 140, 146-147, 149, 170, 175, 178-179, 181, 189-190, 243-244, 252, 281, 285, 296, 306, 309, 322-323, 327, 347-348, 404, 459, 487
Bouncy wickets, 91, 242, 255, 269
Bowling captains, 157
Boycott, Geoffrey, 73, 201, 260, 334, 354
Brabourne stadium, 36, 49, 89, 220
Bradman, Sir Donald, 65, 73, 85, 146, 152, 173, 230, 251, 268, 323, 332, 335, 337, 348, 411, 494
Brearley, Mike, 201
Brisbane test, 261
British paparazzi, 217
Broacha, Cyrus, 471
Broken finger, 113
Burge, Peter, 40
Burki, Javed, 286

C.K. Nayudu school of belligerence, 142
Cairns, Lance, 132, 155, 382
Camacho, Steve, 53
Campbell, Forbes, 11, 15
Captains-Coaches Conclave, 487
Carbine Club of New Zealand, 255
Cardboard cricket game, 13
Carew, Joey, 62
Caribbean tour, 44, 60, 72, 82, 91, 223-225, 241, 302, 325, 367, 489
Caribbean trip, 85

Castrol Awards for Excellence in Indian cricket, 471
Cavalier batsmanship, 107
Ceat Cricket Rating, 471
Central Lancashire league, 419
Chachad, Phanindranath, 14
Champion of Champions, 388
CHAMPS Foundation, 475-476
Chand, Dhyan, 170
Chandavarkar, Leena, 237
Chandgadkar, Prof, 65, 72, 82, 117
Chandrasekhar, B.S., 40, 469
Chandrasekhar, Bhagwat, 72
Channel Nine, 166, 196, 381-382, 410, 473
Chappell brothers, 84, 197, 212, 422, 473
Chappell, Greg, 161, 242, 245, 303, 402
Chappell, Ian, 84, 95, 174, 245, 376, 389, 471, 473
Charity game, 259
Chauhan, Chetan, 92, 167, 171, 182, 193, 252, 261, 360, 393, 493
Chawla, Piyush, 486
Chepauk wicket, 115
Chest-guard, 168
Chidambaram stadium, 212, 224, 282, 347, 449
Chikalwadi, 10-11, 28, 64, 373
Chinnaswamy stadium, 439
Chinnaswamy, M., 166, 198
Chopra, Yash, 124
Chupke Chupke, 124
Clarke, C.D., 52, 119, 204
Clarke, Michael, 492-493
Clarke, Sylvester, 189-190, 495
Collinge, Richard, 34, 129
Commonwealth Games, 487-488
cricket in the, 488
Contractor, Behram, 197, 331
Contractor, Dolly, 132
Contractor, Nari, 40, 43, 445
Contracts with the manufacturers of sports equipment, 236
Cooch Behar Trophy, 25
Corporate sponsorship of sport, 56
County championship, 39, 240
Cowans, Norman, 359, 361, 367
Cowdrey, Colin, 66, 354, 421-422, 491
Crafter, Tony, 386
Crash helmet-like cap, 155
Cricket Association of Bengal, 341, 434
Cricket Club of India, 6, 177, 474
Cricket My Style, 315, 337, 363, 390, 399
Cricketing
achievements, 3-4
career, 18, 313
fraternity, 474, 490
Crowe, Martin, 442
Curator, 322

D'Oliveira, Basil, 100
Dadar Union, 24-27, 29-30, 32, 37, 68, 70-71, 91, 125-126, 131, 142, 165, 191, 203, 229, 239, 290, 323
Dalmiya, Jagmohan, 434
Dalpat, Anil, 377, 386

Damp wickets, 76
Dani, H.T., 93
Daniel, Wayne, 145, 230, 334
Davis Cup, 197
Davis, Charlie, 54
Davis, Winston, 323, 329
De Mel, Asantha, 397
Dead wickets, 439
'death-or-glory' pyrotechnics, 277
Debutant
captain, 128
wicketkeeper, 416
Deewar, 124
Defensive
batsmanship, 268
captaincy, 327
Denness, Mike, 101
Deodhar Trophy, 101, 117, 177, 200, 259-260
Deodhar, D.B., 6
Desai, Manmohan, 10
Desai, Ramakant, 37, 179, 189, 477, 496
Dev, Kapil, 67, 176, 179, 181, 183-184, 186, 189, 193, 203, 207-208, 210, 214-215, 218-220, 222-223, 225, 227, 243, 246, 249, 252-254, 256-257, 263-265, 269, 274, 277, 280, 282-285, 288-289, 291-292, 294, 296-297, 299-301, 304-307, 312-319, 322, 325, 328, 330-331, 333, 336-338, 340-343, 347-348, 350-351, 355, 357-358, 360-363, 365-366, 368-369, 374, 376, 378-380, 382-385, 387-392, 395-399, 401, 403-404, 406-407, 409-412, 414-416, 418-421, 423-424, 426-428, 430, 432, 439-441, 443, 448, 450-451, 453-454, 469, 475, 478, 484, 495
autobiography of, 414
Dexter, Ted, 75
Dhobi Talao, 14
Dhoni, Mahendra Singh, 486
Dilley, Graham, 415
Diwadkar, Sharad, 125, 229, 477
Doshi, Dilip, 86, 213, 249, 264-265, 280, 289, 389
Dotiwala, Dara, 430, 472
Double hundred, 8, 50, 64-65, 107, 110, 190-191, 206-207, 209, 228, 278, 285, 327, 348, 366, 369, 447, 479
Dravid, Rahul, 409, 438, 462, 484-486, 497
Duckworth and Lewis, 488
Dujon, Jeffrey, 306, 445
Duleep Trophy, 42-43, 45-46, 86, 96, 110, 164, 284, 399-401
Duleepsinhji, K.S., 55, 202
Dungarpur, Raj Singh, 40, 355, 413, 421, 464
Durani, Salim, 40, 45, 54-56, 412, 475
Dyson, John, 252

Eden Gardens, 158, 191, 434
Edmonds, Phil, 202, 204, 208, 361
Edrich, John, 80, 105
Elahi, Manzoor, 392, 432
Electronic scoreboard, 461
Elizabeth II, Queen, 337

Elizabeth, 9
Ellison, Richard, 367, 417
Elphinstone College, 11
Emburey, John, 275, 444
Emergency in August 1975, 123
Engineer, Farookh, 44, 72, 80, 238, 464
English County Championship, 95, 213, 261
ESPN-STAR, 471, 491, 494
Essex, 261
Everton Weekes, 64, 69
Extra padding in the gloves, 115, 155

Faqih, Ijaz, 436, 439
Fateh Maidan, 117
Fearnley, Duncan, 126, 202, 267
Felicitation of the players, 320
Ferozeshah Kotla, 154, 322, 355
First Indian millionaire through cricket, 236
First One Day International on Indian soil, 263
First-ball duck, 191
First-class cricket, 26, 32, 110, 142, 354, 366, 474, 488
Fletcher, Duncan, 490
Fletcher, Keith, 77, 80, 260, 264, 269
'flying sikh' *see* Singh, Milkha
Fokker Friendship aircraft, 352
Forjett Hill, 13
Four-nation tournament, 391, 432
Fowler, Graeme, 366
Fraser, Malcolm, 174-175
Fredericks, Roy, 53

Front-foot players, 380
Fun-bottles, 333

Gaddafi stadium, 181, 288, 354, 356
Gaddafi, Col Muammar, 180
Gaekwad, Anshuman, 116, 135, 147, 184, 228, 266, 283, 307, 323, 326
Gaekwad, Fatehsinghrao, 177, 284
Galvankar, Dilip, 32
Gamesmanship, question of, 271
Gandhi, Indira, 59, 68, 82, 91, 123, 144, 281, 320, 358
Gandhi, Rajiv, 391, 426
Ganguly, Sourav, 229, 485, 492
Gannon, Sam, 171, 215
Gattani, Kailash, 25, 189
Gatting, Mike, 179, 366, 420, 422
Gauze strip, 159-160
Gavaskar Fund, 70
Gavaskar, Meenal, 10, 23
Gentleman cricketer, 221
Georgetown games, 307
Georgetown Test, 59, 311
Ghanshyamsinhji, Prince, 5
Ghavri, Karsan, 70, 90, 114, 116-117, 126, 164, 169-170, 187, 197, 217, 250
Gibbs, Lance, 52
Gifford, Norman, 75-76, 100
Gilchrist, Adam, 493-494
Giles Shield inter-school, 20
Gilligan, Arthur, 5
Gokhale, Vikram, 237
Golibar stadium, 459
Gomes, Larry, 309

Gooch, Graham, 204, 263, 275, 416, 452
Googly, 378, 386
Gopinath, C.D., 161, 199
Gosein, Ralph, 136, 148
Govindraj, K., 46
Gower, David, 154, 201, 209, 226, 264, 358, 360, 362, 364, 369, 416, 448, 474
Grace, W.G., 79
Grand cricket career, 191, 194
Green Park, 328
Greenidge, Gordon, 111, 307, 310, 338, 443, 448, 470
Greig, Anthony William, 156
Greig, Tony, 84, 90, 94, 159-160, 167, 276, 318, 473
Gritty batsmanship, 136
Guaracara Park, 51
Guard, Ghulam, 189
Guha, Subroto, 189
Gupte, Subhash, 74, 170

Hadlee, Dayle, 34, 129, 131
Hadlee, Richard, 131-133, 215, 255, 402, 444, 446, 448
Hafiz, Azeem, 354, 357, 386
Haji Ali mosque, 14
Halt, 57, 136, 309, 357, 377
Hammond, Walter, 191, 422
Hampshire, 111
Hamstring injury, 474
Hardikar, Manohar, 15
Harper, Roger, 443
Harris, Lord, 4
Hattea, Saeed Ahmed, 83

Hayat, Khizer, 355
Haynes, Desmond, 443
Hazare, Capt Vijay, 89, 202
Hazare, Vijay, 142, 170, 463
Headley, George, 65, 73
Headley, Ron, 100
Hendren, Patsy, 64
Higgs, Jim, 248
Hindu Gymkhana, 25, 32-34, 179
History of Indian Cricket, 9, 17, 223
Hitler, Adolf, 59
Hobbs, Sir Jack, 142, 494
Hockey World Cup, 170
Hogg, Rodney, 212-213, 381
Holder, Roland, 60
Holder, Vanburn, 53, 63, 100, 145, 189
Holding, Michael, 133, 139, 146, 197, 215, 225, 310
Holford, David, 63
Holland, Robert, 408
Home Guards Association, 16
Hookes, David, 196, 404, 491
Horizontal-bat strokes, 310
Horrendous batting, 450
Hughes, Kimberley, 212, 312
Hutton, Richard, 84

Ibrahim Rahimtoola Cup, 34
ICC, 39, 95, 99, 198, 245, 351, 476, 483, 486, 493-494, 496
  annual meet, 200
  code of conduct, 483
Idols, 273, 340, 462
Illingworth, Ray, 90
Index finger injury, 115, 155
Indian Cricket controversies, 120

Indian High Commission in Guyana, 136
Indian National Congress, 4
Indian Olympic Association (IOA), 487
India-Pakistan rivalry, 188
In-dippers, 291, 296
In-swingers, 296
Inter-club cricket tournament, 8
Inter-collegiate games, 25
Inter-locality games, 17
International Cricket Conference, 39
International Management Group (IMG), 465
Inter-university Rohinton Baria tournament, 32
Inter-university tournament, 33, 43, 436
Iqbal, Asif, 176, 183, 186, 197, 217, 219, 223, 225, 289, 300, 402
Irani Cup, 31, 112, 274, 400
Irani Trophy, 91, 96, 126, 150, 154, 240-241, 283-284, 351
Isherwood, Ray, 385, 406
Ismail, Abdul, 97, 126

J.C. Mukherjee Trophy, 21
Jaisimha, M.L., 31, 40, 42, 65, 187
Jameson, John, 39, 79
Jardine, Douglas, 6, 45, 73, 146, 156, 253, 276
Jarman, Barry, 40
Jayadevan, M., 488
Jayantilal, 46, 48-50, 53, 56, 61, 80
Jaywant, Sanjay, 29, 44
John Player League, 239

Johnston, Brian, 74
Jones, Dean, 141, 427, 449
Jones, Sam, 79
Jones, Wilson, 170, 477
Jubilee Test, 223-225, 227, 241, 260
Jumadeen, Rafique, 134, 138
Justice Tendolkar trophy, 67

K.S. Ranjitsinhji school, 142
Kallicharran, 134, 139, 150, 190-192
Kambli, Vinod, 453, 482
Kanga game, 239
Kanga League, 8, 24, 29, 239
Kanhai, Rohan, 31, 53, 56, 66, 77, 84, 213
Kanmadikar, 302, 374
Kapur, Shekhar, 9
Karhade, Sanjay, 308-309
Kartik, Dinesh, 486
Kenny, Ramnath, 15, 27
Kensington Oval, 309-310
Kent, Clark, 80
Kerr, Robbie, 380
Khan, Imran, 106, 176, 184, 197, 215, 217, 284, 286, 291, 293, 298, 301, 311, 321, 324, 354, 376, 391, 401, 406, 431, 439, 452, 467, 481-482, 494
Khan, Majid, 176, 183, 186, 220
Khan, Mansoor Ali, 26, 40, 92
Khan, Mohsin, 288, 354, 385, 470
Khan, Salim, 124
Khanna, Rajesh, 124
Khanna, Surender, 350
Kingston, 49, 51, 54, 60, 144, 146, 152, 160, 224, 304, 484

Kirmani, Syed, 72, 96, 98, 128, 131, 135, 151, 169, 172, 174-175, 180, 183, 185-187, 193, 197, 199, 214-215, 218, 220, 222, 227, 246, 247-250, 252-254, 256, 263, 269, 273, 281, 310, 312, 314, 316, 318, 327, 336, 338, 348, 350, 359, 366, 375, 399, 406, 416
Kishen, Swaroop, 345
Knott, Alan, 74, 118
Krishnamurthy, Pochiah, 46, 49, 128
Krishnan, Ramanathan, 170
Kukreja, Arun, 332
Kulkarni, Raju, 304, 349, 360, 393, 400, 437
Kumar, V.V., 95
Kumar, Vijay, 96
Kumble, Anil, 473, 479, 480, 485, 492-493
Kutty, P. Karunakaran, 342

Lagoo, Dr Shriram, 237
Laker, Jim, 75
Lal, Madan, 98, 104, 114, 127-131, 134, 136, 151, 160, 165, 173-174, 262, 264, 281, 283, 285, 289, 291, 294, 296, 312, 314-318, 326-327, 329, 332, 350, 374-376, 378-380, 382, 385, 391-393, 420-421, 475
Lamba, Raman, 432
Lancashire team, 229
Larkins, Wayne, 201
Lawry, Bill, 42
Lawson, Geoffrey, 381

Laxman, Shankar, 170
Laxman, V.V.S., 323, 484-486
Leeds, 90, 144, 203, 419-420, 469
Leg-guards, 220, 303, 310, 325, 482
Leg-theory, 146
Lewis, Tony, 90, 94, 141, 447
Liberty ground, 16
Life Shoes, 464
Lillee, Dennis, 84-85, 145, 151, 197, 212, 241, 244, 250, 255, 290, 321, 402, 446, 470, 494
Limited-overs cricket, advent of, 7
Lindwall, Ray, 13
Little Bombay Bradman, 73
Lloyd, Clive, 53, 64, 84, 110, 115, 133, 144, 150, 155-156, 197, 304, 316, 323, 328, 348, 354, 389, 441, 471, 494
Luckhurst, Brian, 76, 78

Maalamaal, 238
Madgaonkar, Ajay, 22, 24, 34
Madhya Pradesh Cricket Association, 163
Mahendra, Ranbir Singh, 351, 373
Malhotra, Ashok, 283, 338, 375
Malik, Salim, 292, 354, 386, 392, 435
Man of the Series award, 209, 413
Manchester Test, 103
Mangeshkar, Lata, 298, 320
Manjrekar, Vijay, 87, 142, 203
Mankad, Ashok, 25-26, 31, 35, 46, 59, 64, 98, 100, 112, 117, 125-126, 165, 167, 188, 227, 272, 279, 303, 369, 437, 477

Mankad, Rahul, 270
Mankad, Vinoo, 38, 92, 94, 170, 223, 238, 277, 348
Mann, Tony, 169, 171
Mansingh, P.R., 259, 314
Mantri, Madhav, 11, 15, 19-21, 25, 29, 35, 43, 70, 119, 125, 143-144
Marginal decisions, 210
Marsh, Geoffrey, 409
Marsh, Rodney, 212, 402
Marshall, Malcolm, 189, 192, 225, 306, 310, 322, 328, 443, 448, 495
Marylebone Cricket Club, *see* MCC
Masurekar, Narayan, 10
Match-winning knocks, 223
Match-winning score, 74
MCC, 5, 66, 89, 146, 159, 162, 201, 319, 422, 441-443, 447, 464, 491
   life membership, 491
McDermott, Craig, 403, 428-429, 449, 483
McEwan, Paul, 383
McGrath, Glenn, 480
Mecca of Cricket, 73
Mecca of the sport, 316, 445
Meherhomji, Kersi, 19, 95
Mehra, Prakash, 81, 124
Mehra, R.P., 127
Mehra, Vijay, 187
Mehrotra, Marshneil, 86, 110
Mehta, Noomi, 471
Mehta, Raju, 463-464, 490
Melbourne Cricket Ground, (MCG), 166, 242, 248, 254, 263, 375-376, 385, 388, 398
Melbourne Test, 257, 265, 410, 469
Merchant, Vijay, 39, 70, 87, 111, 117, 142, 182, 191, 194, 205, 485
Miandad, Javed, 176, 185-186, 217, 284, 295, 326, 355, 398, 413, 430, 462, 481
Middlesex, 73, 230, 453
Miniature ball, 333
Mini-World Cup, 388, 402
Mody, Urmikant, 28, 71
Mohammed, Hanif, 28, 179
Mohammed, Mushtaq, 175
Moin-ud-Dowla tournament, 26, 259-260
Morrison, Danny, 452
Mukherjee, Raju, 3
Mumbai Cricket Association, 411-442, 489, 496
Mumbaikar, 7-8,, 88
Murray, Dereyck, 149

Nadkarni, Bapu, 40, 70, 87-88, 243, 247, 365, 445, 450, 477
Nagabhushan, K., 43
Nagdev, Ramesh, 21, 25, 33-34
Naik, Sudhir, 36, 89, 101
   shoplifting charges 108
Namak Haraam, 124
Nandy, Ashis, 3
Naqqash, Tahir, 297, 326, 386
Narayanan, K.R., 281
Narvekar, Bharat, 98
National Cricket Academy, 485-486

National Defence Fund game, 109, 213
National Selection Committee, 37, 39
Nawaz, Sarfraz, 176, 217, 285-286, 298, 324
Nayak, Suru, 71, 172, 188, 272-274
Nayudu, Col C.K., 5, 89
Nazar, Mudassar, 183-184, 186, 222-223, 281, 295-298, 326, 384, 441
Negative batting, 272
Nehru, B.K., 108, 419
Nehru, Jawaharlal, 6, 110, 449, 461
'Never Again in Calcutta', 364
Nevill Ground, 314
New-ball
 attack, 40, 243
 bowler, 5-6, 25, 35, 38, 40, 46, 52-53, 83, 96, 98, 106, 126, 128, 139, 184, 243, 380-381, 385, 397
 combinations, 262
 duties, 138, 174
Nichols, Gray, 22
Nightwatchman, 60, 102, 171, 185, 215, 254, 345, 403
Ninth-wicket pair, 248
Nirlons, 188, 211, 259, 270, 272-273, 425, 465
Nirlons and Mafatlals, rivalry between, 188
Nissar, Mohammed, 5, 277
Non-cooperation movement, 110
Non-cricketing tactics, 104
Non-violent struggle, 5
North West Frontier Province, 294

Northamptonshire, 176, 416
Nottinghamshire, 78, 109, 213, 215
NSCI Ground, 14

O'Donnell, Simon, 381
O'Neill, Norman, 73
Old, Chris, 93, 103, 107, 239
'old-mindsets-die-hard', 170
Omar, Qasim, 357, 376, 385
One Day Wonders, 462
One-innings-one-day tournament, 33
Operation Vengeance, 328, 348
Orient Cricket Club, 6
Orthodox batsmanship, 142, 356
Oval, 26, 52, 55, 61, 78-79, 81, 91, 101, 135, 138-139, 144, 203-204, 209-210, 212, 218, 227, 265, 278-279, 295, 313-314, 415, 429, 469, 490
Oxbridge, 106

P. Saravanamutthu stadium, 396
P.J. Hindu Gymkhana, 50, 141, 412
Pace Age, 152
Packer, Kerry, 166, 195-196
Packer's World Series Cricket, 174, 197
Paddle-sweep, 454
Padmakar Talim Shield, 33
Padmore, Albert, 138
Pakistan Cricket Board, 439
Pakistan's dictatorial regime, protest against, 297
Pal, Rajinder, 189
Palekar, Amol, 237
Palwankar, Baloo, 5
Pandit, Chandrakant, 228, 416, 489

532 • Index

Paranjape, Vasu, 27-29, 33, 447
Parkar, Ghulam, 271-273, 348, 350
Parkar, Ramnath, 28, 91
Parker, John, 100, 129
Parle Gluco biscuits, lifelong fan of, 30
Parochialism, 256
Parris, Stanton, 133
Pataudi, Iftikar Ali Khan, 45
Pataudi, Mansoor Ali Khan, 26, 92
Patel, Brijesh, 96, 144, 149
Patel, Dipak, 452
Patel, Jasu, 213
Patel, Jitu, 326
Patel, Parthiv, 486
Patel, Vallabhbhai, 110
Patil, Sandeep, 156, 188, 211, 221, 242-244, 279, 299, 302, 316, 321, 327, 355, 361, 400, 425, 469
Pearl Harbour, devastation of, 26
Perfume ball, 346
Phadkar, Dattu, 99, 187
Philip, Norbert, 189
Pietersen, Kevin, 452
Pocock, Pat, 361
Pollock, Shaun, 480
Polyurethane Footwear, 463
Pongal Test, 366
Ponting, Ricky, 400, 491-493
Port of Spain, 52, 54, 56-57, 137-139, 145-146, 148, 151, 158, 174, 205, 208, 257, 307, 429, 468
Post-1991 liberalisation phase, 3
Post-match press briefings, 380
Post-war National Defence Fund, 86
Prabhakar, Manoj, 350, 375, 419

Prabhu, K.N., 42, 51, 59, 61, 65, 76, 86, 98, 136, 148-149, 152-153, 155, 158, 188, 195-197, 216, 236, 245, 259, 263, 305, 330, 340, 345, 347
Prasanna, E.A.S., 49, 66, 97, 115, 374, 379, 383
Presidency match, 4
Principle of batsmanship, 140
Pringle, Derek, 277, 420
Privy-purse, 91
Procter, Mike, 197, 492
Professional Management Group, 466
Protagonist, 124, 238
Puri, Dr Narottam, 333, 346
Purshottam Shield competition, 32

Qadir, Abdul, 285, 358, 413
Qasim, Iqbal, 219, 221, 436, 439-441
Queen's Park Oval, 52, 55, 61, 135, 139, 144
Qureshi, Anwar, 21

R.A. Podar College of Commerce and Economics, 27
R.N. Ruia College for Arts and Science, 27
Racist, 492
Rahimtoola Cup, 35
Rahman, Sheikh Mujibur, 59
Raina, Suresh, 486
Raja, Wasim, 220, 327, 356, 385-387
Rajan, Sunder, 30, 44, 68, 71, 258, 260, 326-327, 401, 403, 410, 440, 470
Rajasthan Cricket Club, 11, 25-26

Rajput, Ghulam Parkar Lalchand, 348
Rajput, Lalchand, 396, 398, 489
Raju, Vikram, 430, 472
Ramaswami, K.B., 213
Ramchand, Gulabrai, 41, 89, 118-119, 477
Rana, Shakoor, 178, 292, 355
Randall, Derek, 203, 277
Ranji Trophy, 6, 28, 30, 32, 36-37, 42, 44, 67, 88-89, 95-96, 112, 125-127, 241, 266, 273, 311, 348-349, 393, 426, 488-489
   golden jubilee of, 352
Ranjitsinhji, K.S., 4, 6, 55, 143
Rao, Hanumantha, 335
Rao, Sudhakar, 96
Ratnayake, Rumesh, 396
Rawson, Peter, 314
Reckless batting, 409
Rege, Milind, 12-16, 20-21, 23, 28, 35, 86-87, 235, 496
Regional considerations, 273
Reid, Bruce, 403, 428
Reshamwalla, 19
Reverse swing, 291
Richards, Barry, 197, 408, 494
Richards, Viv, 111, 114, 134, 149, 152, 197, 201, 204, 222, 229, 256, 305, 337-338, 380, 442, 462, 464, 467, 470, 475, 494
Richardson, Richie, 475
Ritchie, Greg, 403
Rixon, Steve, 169
Roberts, Andy, 111, 134, 197, 215, 225, 290, 304, 320, 329, 339, 347

Robinson, Ray, 71
Robinson, Tim, 366, 416
Rohinton Baria Trophy, 34
Rothmans Cup, 393
Round-robin game, 351, 379
Roy, Ambar, 363
Roy, Pankaj, 18, 38, 312
Ruchika Theatre Group, 332
Ruia-Podar ground, 26-27, 30
Rungta, Kishan, 187
Rungta, P.M., 118
Run-hunger, 64, 321, 485
Runs n' Ruins, 183, 325, 341, 462
Rutnagur, Dicky, 39, 44, 54, 94, 169, 171, 244, 308

S.V. Rajadhyaksha Trophy, 95
Saavli Premachi, 236
Sagar, Ramanand, 469
Sagar, Virenchee, 188
Salgaonkar, Pandurang, 98, 113, 189, 284
Salve, N.K.P., 302, 316, 319
Sandhu, Balwinder Singh, 188
Sandy Storm, 425
Sardar Patel stadium, 333
Sardesai, Dilip, 46, 58, 60, 64, 70, 80, 87, 330, 484
Sarwate, Chandrakant, 312
Scindia, Madhavrao, 426
Selvel Outdoor Advertising, 471
Selvey, Mike, 21
Shah, Kundan, 468
Shah, Naseeruddin, 238
Shah, Sumedh, 465-468
Shameless performance, 289
Sharjah Cricket Ground, 349, 413

Sharjah, Limited-overs tournament in, 412
Sharma, Charu, 471
Sharma, Chetan, 208, 328, 350, 354, 358, 369, 374, 385, 389, 398, 403, 417, 419, 422, 428, 450
Sharma, Ishant, 494
Sharma, Parthasarathy, 134
Sharma, Yashpal, 176, 208, 214, 222, 243, 246, 269, 277, 283, 299, 307, 313, 360
Shastri bowling capabilities, 256
Shastri, Ravi, 188, 229, 256, 279, 296-297, 312, 345, 359, 376, 387-388, 390-391, 422, 430, 441, 470, 477
Shepherd, David, 402
Shillingford, Grayson, 50
Shirdi, 82
Shivaji Park Gymkhana, 27, 37, 239
Shivalkar, Padmakar, 126, 238, 270
Sholay, 9
Sidhu, Navjot, 328, 334, 449, 473, 484
Simla Accord, 180
Simpson, Bob, 23, 167, 394, 422, 428, 479
Singh, Amar, 5-6, 142, 277
Singh, Amrik, 43
Singh, Balbir, 170
Singh, Giani Zail, 320
Singh, Hanumant, 24, 311-312, 363, 434
Singh, Harbhajan, 484, 492-493
Singh, Jasdev, 358
Singh, Kripal, 363

Singh, Maninder, 284, 288, 293, 396-397, 417, 424, 430, 440
Singh, Milkha, 170
Singh, R.P., 486
Singh, Ranbir, 351, 373, 434
Singh, V.R.V., 486
Singh, Yajurvindra, 114, 160-161, 163, 165, 177, 182, 207-208, 240-241, 266, 393, 477, 479
Single-wicket tournament, 360
Sitaram special, 322
Sivaramakrishnan, L., 284, 359, 366, 374, 376, 380, 386, 391, 397-400, 417, 424
Six-day Test, 173
Skullcap, 325, 327, 403, 433, 464, 495
Sledgehammer batsmanship, 306
Slow pitch, 255, 393
Sobers, Sir Garry, 44, 84, 260, 265, 295, 334, 422
Solkar, Eknath, 17, 21, 46, 50, 80, 105, 115, 160, 477
Somerset County Cricket Club, 229
Spin Punch, 249, 265, 280, 289
Spofforth, Frederick, 79
Sponsored cricket tournament, 230
Sports and Pastime, 13
Srikkanth, K., 208, 262, 282, 292, 299, 387, 412, 470
St. Xavier's College, 24-25, 461
Stump-microphones, 381
Sunday Club, 172
Sunil Gavaskar, India's Cricket God, 238
Sunny Days, 107, 157, 244, 266, 304, 462, 465, 469

criticism in, 224
Sunny the Supersleuth, 461
Surplus players, 439
Surti, Rusi, 40, 44
Sussex, 117, 299
Sydney Cricket Ground, 196
Symonds, Andrew, 384, 492-494

Tagore, Sharmila, 31
Tamil Nadu Cricket Association, 92
Tarapore, Keki, 49, 63, 177
Taylor, Bob, 227
Taylor, Lynton, 197-198
10,000th Test run, 437, 477
Tendulkar, Sachin, 36, 103, 222, 251, 411, 442, 453, 471, 479, 482-483, 485, 492-494, 496
Tennis-ball cricket, 13, 17
Test and County Cricket Board (TCCB), 275
Test career beginning, 53
Test debut, 94
Test defeat, 213
Texaco Trophy, 416
The Boy from Chikalwadi, 10, 478
The Covers are Off, 151, 198
The Decline of Indian Cricket, 236
The History of Indian Cricket, 162
The Record-breaking Sunil Gavaskar, 52, 119
The Spirit and Technique of Cricket, 39
Thirtieth hundred, 346
Thomson, Jeff, 151, 168, 242, 250, 255, 290, 495
Three-day games, 34, 52, 61, 73, 106, 134, 163, 201, 215, 249, 263, 288, 305
Thums Up, 239, 333
Tied Test Rematch, 472
Time-killing tactics, 207
Time-tested technique, 329
Tokyo Olympics, 39
Toohey, Peter, 173
Trans-Harbour tussle, 113
Trans-Tasman tussle, 37
Trinidad Cricket Council, 67
Turner, Glenn, 100, 128-129, 239
Tyson, Frank, 194

Umrigar, Polly, 36, 70, 87, 89, 125, 131, 149, 168, 185, 259, 445, 477
Unconventional batsmanship, 451
Under-16 Harris Shield competition, 21
Underwood, Derek, 81, 90, 92, 260, 367
Untouchables, 5

Vaidya, Sudhir, 163, 180, 358
Vazir Sultan Tobacco (VST), 26, 467
Vengsarkar, Dilip, 117, 126, 150, 191, 203, 228-229, 269-270, 275, 277, 318, 323, 350, 417, 444, 474, 476-477, 482, 485-496
Venkat Sunderam, 164
Venkataraghvan, 42, 45, 50-51, 55, 63, 66, 72, 74, 80, 91, 94-95, 98-99, 101-102, 107-108, 113-114, 117-119, 125, 128-129, 135,

151, 164, 190, 192, 198-200, 207-210, 213-214, 227, 304-305, 410
Vidanagamage, P.W., 397
Vishwanath, Sadanand, 359, 375, 379, 388, 399
Viswanath, Gundappa, 42, 56, 142-143, 248, 257, 291, 302
Vizzy Trophy, 31-32

Wadekar, Ajit, 24, 36, 38, 43, 51, 66, 88, 469, 477, 486, 496
Wadsworth, Ken, 129
Wagah border, 181, 300
Waingankar, Hemant, 35, 411, 442, 482, 489, 496
Walcott, Clyde, 64
Walters, Doug, 65
Wankhede stadium, 115, 155-156, 200, 215, 226, 320, 337, 454-455
Wankhede, S.K., 127, 241, 274
War of Independence in 1857, 4
War of the Willows, 341
Warnapura, Bandula, 282
Warne, Shane, 480, 494
Waugh, Stephen Rodger, 406
Waugh, Steve, 428, 450
Wessels, Kepler, 380
West Indies Cricket Board, 133
Western Australian Cricket Association (WACA), 84, 171
'Whispering Death', 139, 225
White ball, 196, 381
Whitehead, Rex, 248, 251
'whites-are-superior' perception, 58

WICB, 133, 225
Wicketkeeper-batsman, 11, 44, 46, 83, 96, 359
Wicket-taking bowlers, 289
Willey, Peter, 204
Williams, Dr Eric, 54
Wills Trophy, 177, 200
Woodfull, William, 146, 492
Woolmer, Bob, 158
Worcestershire, 239
World Championship, 54, 375, 388, 390, 423, 462
  in Australia, 54
  test cricket, 133, 145
World Cup, 110, 116-117, 125, 145, 200, 281, 312-313, 315-316, 319-320, 324, 328, 331, 333, 336, 341-342, 348, 350-351, 356, 362, 375-376, 380, 388, 392, 419, 423, 441, 447-449, 452, 464, 472-473, 475, 481, 491
  hattrick of, 317
  of 1975, 185, 236, 410, 470
  of 1979, 198, 282, 315
  of 1983, 67, 319, 351-352, 362, 381-382, 384, 389, 416, 424, 440, 453, 464, 470, 472, 475-476
  of 1992, 279, 481
  of limited overs matches, 110
  silver jubilee celebrations, 472
  winning squad, 350
World Series Cricket, 167, 174, 197, 199, 290
World-class players, 315
Worrell, Frank, 394

Wright, John, 127, 175, 256, 382, 452
Wrist-band, 168
WWF mania, 14

Xavier's captain, 18
Xavier's college team, 25

Yadav, Arunlal, 282
Yadav, Shivlal, 244, 256, 337, 369, 405, 428, 430

Yardley, Bruce, 247, 254
Yorker, 104, 147-148, 248, 385
Yorker, Gilbert, 407
Yorkshire County Cricket Club, 483
Yorkshireman, 265

Zakhol, 237
Zanjeer, 124
Zia-ul-Haq, 181, 296, 299, 354, 435

Devendra,

There are some things you know about me which I didn't know myself. Just goes to show how much effort you put in this compilation.

Thanks v. much for it shows sentiments which are truly appreciated.

with every good wish,

7th Nov 2002